THE NEW ANNOTATED

Dracula

The Life and Times of Mr. Sherlock Holmes,
John H. Watson, M.D., Sir Arthur Conan Doyle,
and Other Notable Personages

"The Date Being?"—A Compendium of Chronological Data
(with Andrew Jay Peck)

The Adventure of the Wooden Box

Baker Street Rambles

Conan Doyle, Sherlock Holmes, and
The Bookman: *Pastiches, Parodies, Letters, Columns,*
and Commentary (1895–1933)
(with S. E. Dahlinger)

Leslie S. Klinger is also the editor of the
Sherlock Holmes Reference Library, a nine-volume
scholarly edition of the Sherlock Holmes stories published by
Gasogene Press. The *Reference Library* quotes extensively
from published Sherlockian criticism and provides detailed
reviews of the scholarly literature.

W. W. NORTON & COMPANY
New York   London

THE NEW ANNOTATED

Dracula

BRAM STOKER

EDITED WITH A FOREWORD AND NOTES BY
LESLIE S. KLINGER

ADDITIONAL RESEARCH BY JANET BYRNE

INTRODUCTION BY NEIL GAIMAN

Copyright © 2008 by Leslie S. Klinger
Introduction copyright © 2008 by Neil Gaiman

For information about permission to reproduce selections from this book,
write to Permissions, W. W. Norton & Company, Inc.,
500 Fifth Avenue, New York, NY 10110

For information about special discounts for bulk purchases, please contact
W. W. Norton Special Sales at specialsales@wwnorton.com or 800-233-4830

Manufacturing by RR Donnelley Willard
Book design by JAMdesign
Production manager: Julia Druskin

Library of Congress Cataloging-in-Publication Data

Stoker, Bram, 1847–1912.
[Dracula]
The new annotated Dracula / Bram Stoker ; edited with a foreword and notes by Leslie S. Klinger ;
additional research by Janet Byrne ; introduction by Neil Gaiman.—1st ed.
p. cm.
Includes bibliographical references.
ISBN 978-0-393-06450-6 (hardcover)
1. Dracula, Count (Fictitious character)—Fiction. 2. Stoker, Bram, 1847–1912. Dracula. 3. Transylvania
(Romania)—Fiction. 4. Whitby (England)—Fiction. 5. Vampires—Fiction. I. Klinger, Leslie S.
II. Title.
PR6037.T617D7 2008b
823'.8—dc22
2008025919

W. W. Norton & Company, Inc.
500 Fifth Avenue, New York, N.Y. 10110
www.wwnorton.com

W. W. Norton & Company Ltd.
Castle House, 75/76 Wells Street, London W1T 3QT

1 2 3 4 5 6 7 8 9 0

TO BRAM STOKER

"We want no proofs; we ask none to believe us!"

CONTENTS

EDITOR'S PREFACE

WHEN I COMPLETED work on *The New Annotated Sherlock Holmes* for W. W. Norton, I found myself so immersed in the Victorian world that I hated the thought of leaving its study behind. In considering what to do with my newfound spare time, I cast my thoughts over the other compelling books of that era. One stood out: *Dracula*, one of the most influential books of the nineteenth century. I remembered reading it for the first time, sitting on the floor in the hall of my college dormitory in order not to disturb my roommate. I was alone in the semidarkened space, it was late at night, and to my great surprise, I was genuinely frightened by the book. How could a work then almost seventy years old (yes, my college days were a long time ago) have such power? I've reread it many times since, but only recently did I see how I might bring a fresh perspective to this timeless work.

I crossed paths with Leonard Wolf's *The Annotated Dracula* shortly after its appearance in 1975. It shared a prime virtue, in my eyes, with William S. Baring-Gould's *The Annotated Sherlock Holmes* (1967)—"endlessly delicious minutiae," in Christopher Morley's apt phrase. Its scope and erudition were broad, and its production values beautiful. Wolf took *Dracula* seriously, and I wanted to as well. Other annotated editions have followed Wolf's, including the groundbreaking *The Essential Dracula* by Raymond McNally and Radu Florescu in 1979, which made extensive use of Bram Stoker's then newly discovered notes for the book (termed the "Notes" in my own notes) but leaned heavily on the erroneous theory that Vlad the Impaler and Dracula were the same person. Wolf's updated 1993 volume, also titled *The Essential Dracula*, did not, however, include references to the Notes.

There is also a Norton Critical Edition with notes by Nina Auerbach and David J. Skal published in 1997. John Paul Riquelme did an edition with notes in 2002, and Clive Leatherdale's 1998 *Bram Stoker's Dracula Unearthed* is the most heavily annotated of any edition. However, this is the first annotated version of *Dracula* to make use of the manuscript of the book (termed the "Manuscript" in my notes). Prior to 2005, only a few pages of the Manuscript—owned by a private collector—had been examined by scholars. I arranged to examine the entire Manuscript for two days, and the startling results are included in my notes to this book. For a complete discussion of the textual sources and the nature of the Notes and the Manuscript, see "Textual Sources" at the back of this book.

In recent years, *Dracula* has become a cottage industry for esteemed academics and serious scholars, who see the text as proof of virtually every wrong that may be blamed on the Victorians. I generally avoid a discussion of the subtexts of the work. These themes—sexual politics, cultural bias, the clash of the modern and the mystical—have been widely written on, and I survey such studies in Part II of this volume. Also included in Part II are considerations of *Dracula* on stage and screen and the ancestors and descendants of *Dracula* in literature. I also provide information regarding the fan clubs and groups of readers and scholars that *Dracula* has attracted, including website references.

My principal aim, however, has been to restore a sense of wonder, excitement, and sheer fun to this great work. To that end, perhaps for the first time, I examine Stoker's published compilation of letters, journals, and recordings as Stoker wished: I employ a gentle fiction here, as I did in *The New Annotated Sherlock Holmes*, that the events described in *Dracula* "really took place" and that the work presents the recollections of real persons, whom Stoker has renamed and whose papers (termed the "Harker Papers" in my notes) he has recast, ostensibly to conceal their identities. In looking at the materials from this historical perspective, I point out the "cover-ups," inconsistencies, and errors in the names, dates, locations, and descriptions of people and events. I also provide background information on the times, using contemporary Victorian sources, to understand the history, culture, technology, and vocabulary of those remarkable individuals. I compare the knowledge gleaned about vampires from these records with other accounts, including those of Anne Rice, Chelsea Quinn Yarbro, and the creators of *Buffy the Vampire Slayer.*

In examining *Dracula*, I must admit that I have found many more questions than answers. In some cases, I suggest theories that may be controversial; I hope they lead to further exploration. In the words of Bernard Davies, a lifelong student of *Dracula*, in his provocative "Unearthing *Dracula*—Burying Stoker," "We shall fit in all the pieces of the puzzle as neatly as we can, then throw the odd one or two left back in the box. With *Dracula* you've always got some pieces left over." I hope that I can help encourage a new generation of *Dracula* students to enjoy solving the puzzle.

LESLIE S. KLINGER
Los Angeles, California
September 2007

INTRODUCTION
by Neil Gaiman

A FEW DAYS AGO there was an article in the English newspapers that purported to show how badly history was being taught these days, or perhaps display the state of ignorance of history in Britain. In it we learned that many British teenagers believe that Winston Churchill and Richard the Lionheart were mythical or fictional, while over half of them are sure that Sherlock Holmes was a real person, just as they believe King Arthur was. Nothing was said in the article about Dracula, however—perhaps because he was not British, although the adventure that brought him to public consciousness was certainly British, even though the chronicler was an Irishman.

I wonder what people would have said if they had been asked, how many of them would have believed that there really was a Dracula. (Not the historical Dracula, mind, Vlad Dracula, the son of the Dragon, the impaler. He existed all right, although whether he shares anything more than a name with the real, as opposed to the historical, Dracula is debatable.)

I think they would have believed in him.

I do.

I first read Bram Stoker's *Dracula* when I was about seven, having found it on a friend's father's bookshelf, although my encounter with it at that point consisted of reading the first part of the story, Jonathan Harker's unfortunate visit to Castle Dracula, and then immediately turning to the end of the book, where I read enough to be certain that Dracula died and could not get out of the book to harm me. Having established this, I put it back on the shelf and did not pick up another copy of the book until I was a teenager, impelled by Stephen King's vampire novel *Salem's Lot* and by *Danse Macabre*, King's examination of the horror genre.

(I watched the film *Son of Dracula* as an eight-year-old, though, wondering whether young Quincy Harker had, as I expected, grown up to be a vampire, and was disappointed to discover that the son was only Dracula himself, in the bayou, calling himself "Count Alucard," a name that seemed fairly transparent even then. But I digress.)

Every so often, other books would send me back to reread *Dracula:* Fred Saberhagen's *The Dracula Tape*, Kim Newman's *Anno Dracula*. Books which would, by reimagining the events or the results of the novel, cast enough light on it to make me want to revisit the castle, the madhouse, the graveyard for myself, to lose myself in the letters and the newspaper clippings, the diary entries, and to wonder once more about Dracula's actions and his motives. To wonder about the things in the book that are, ultimately, unknowable. The characters do not know them, so neither do we.

Dracula the novel spawned Dracula the cultural meme—all the various Nosferati, the movie Draculas, Bela Lugosi and the fanged throngs who followed him. Over 160 films, according to Wikipedia, feature Dracula in a major role ("second only to Sherlock Holmes"), while the number of novels that feature Dracula himself, or Dracula-inspired characters, is impossible to guess at. And then there are novels that lead into or lead out of Dracula. Even poor, mad, bug-devouring Renfield has two prose novels named after him, by two different authors, not to mention a graphic novel, all telling the story from his point of view.

In the twenty-first century any encounter with vampire literature or vampire tales is like hearing a million variations on a musical theme, and the theme began, not with *Varney the Vampire*, or even with *Carmilla*, but with Bram Stoker and with *Dracula*.

Even so, I suspect that the reasons why *Dracula* lives on, why it succeeds as art, why it lends itself to annotation and to elaboration, are paradoxically because of its weaknesses as a novel.

Dracula is a Victorian high-tech thriller, at the cutting edge of science, filled with concepts like dictation to phonographic cylinders, blood transfusions, shorthand, and trepanning. It features a cast of stout heroes and beautiful, doomed women. And it is told entirely in letters, telegrams, press cuttings, and the like. None of the people who are telling us the story knows the entirety of what is actually going on. This means that *Dracula* is a book that forces the reader to fill in the blanks, to hypothesize, to imagine, to presume. We know only what the characters know, and the characters neither write down all they know, nor know the significance of what they do tell.

So it's up to the reader to decide what's happening in Whitby; to connect Renfield's rants and behaviour in the asylum with the events that happen in the house next door; to decide what Dracula's true motives are. It's also up to the reader to decide whether Van Helsing knows anything about medicine, whether Dracula crumbles to dust at the end, or even, given the combination of kukri knife and bowie knife that, unconvincingly, finishes the vampire off, whether he simply transmutes into fog and vanishes.

The story is built up in broad strokes, allowing us to build up our picture of what's happening. The story spiderwebs, and we begin to wonder what occurs in the interstices. Personally, I have my doubts about Quincy Morris's motives. (The possibility that he is Dracula's stooge—or even Dracula himself—cannot, I am convinced, entirely be discounted. I would write a novel to prove it, but that way lies madness.)

Dracula is a book that cries out for annotation. The world it describes is no longer our world. The geography it describes is often not of our world. It is a book that is good to traverse with someone informed and informative by your side.

Les Klinger is both of those things. I first met Les Klinger, who is, in his daily life, a lawyer, at the annual dinner of the Baker Street Irregulars, a group of people who, like 58 percent of British teenagers, are pleased to believe that Sherlock Holmes was indeed a real person. Mr. Klinger is best known for his work annotating the Sherlock Holmes stories: his knowledge of Victoriana, of crime, of travel, is remarkable. His enthusiasm is delightful and contagious; his convictions and discoveries are, of course, uniquely his own.

One of the remarkable things about Mr. Klinger's annotations is that they are illuminating whether or not you subscribe to the theories you will encounter here, of whether or not Dracula actually exists or existed, of whether or not Bram Stoker compiled and edited this book or whether he wrote it. Whatever you choose to believe, you will learn about Carpathian geography and Victorian medical theories. You will learn about the differences between the hardback and paperback editions of *Dracula*. You will be alerted to the wandering location of Shooter's Hill.

One of the drawbacks to reading editions of *Dracula* is they come, like this one, with introductions, and the introductions tell you how *Dracula* should be read. They tell you what it is about. Or rather, what it is "about." It is "about" Victorian sexuality. It is "about" Stoker's presumed repressed homosexuality, or his relationship with Henry Irving, or his rivalry with Oscar Wilde for the hand of

Florence Balcombe. Such introductions will comment ironically on Stoker's writing against pornographic books when there is so much that is sexual seething in *Dracula*, barely under the surface, text not subtext.

This introduction does not presume to tell you what *Dracula* is about. (It is about Dracula, of course, but we see so little of him, less than we would like. He does not wear out his welcome. It is not about Van Helsing, and we would happily see so much less of him. It might be about lust or desire or fear or death. It might be about a lot of things.)

Instead of telling you what the book you are holding is about, this introduction merely cautions you: *Beware. Dracula* can be a flypaper trap. First you read it, casually, and then, once you've put it away, you might find yourself, almost against your will, wondering about things in the crevices of the novel, things hinted at, things implied. And once you begin to wonder, it is only a matter of time before you will find yourself waking in the moonlight to find yourself writing novels or stories about the minor characters and offstage events—or worse, like mad Renfield forever classifying and sorting his spiders and his flies, before, finally, consuming them, you might even find yourself annotating it.

NEIL GAIMAN
February 2008
In the Moonlight

THE CONTEXT OF *DRACULA*
Leslie S. Klinger

. . . did you see with my eyes and know with my knowledge,
you would perhaps better understand.

—COUNT DRACULA

BOOKMAN VINCENT STARRETT spoke of Sherlock Holmes as one "who never lived and so can never die."[1] Yet there cannot be a more apt description of Dracula, the vampire-king whose name was first made public in 1897 in Bram Stoker's eponymous book. Although vampires had been in the public eye for hundreds of years, it was Dracula who caught the imagination of the world and led "the triumphal march of the un-dead Transylvanian vampire," in the words of one critic, "through the newspapers, books, cinema screens and stages of the Anglo-Saxon world."[2] Ironically, publication of the book did not significantly change the life of Stoker (1847–1912), who reportedly made little money from it and returned to writing minor romances and managing Sir Henry Irving's Lyceum Theatre.

THE VICTORIAN WORLD

AT LEAST a rudimentary understanding of Victorian history is necessary to appreciate the contemporary readership for *Dracula*. By the beginning of Victoria's reign in 1837, Britain was in the process of not only creating the Industrial

---

[1] Vincent Starrett, "221B," in "Two Sonnets" (Ysleta, TX: Edwin B. Hill, 1942).
[2] Gabriel Ronay, *The Truth about Dracula* (New York: Stein and Day, 1972), 164.

Benjamin Disraeli.

"NEW CROWNS FOR OLD ONES!"

(ALADDIN *adapted.*)

Victoria is offered the crown of India by Disraeli.
John Tenniel, *Punch*, 1876

Revolution but becoming the greatest industrialised nation in Europe. Spurred on by the acquisition of overseas territories, England witnessed an exponential burst of industrial growth. New, surprisingly complex forms of commerce arose, much of it as a response to the masses who suddenly swelled cities like Manchester, Birmingham, and London, creating sprawling urban centres where crime and poverty abounded.

By 1868, when Benjamin Disraeli became prime minister, Britain had unequivocally become the world's most powerful nation, and Disraeli loudly and frequently advocated this expansion, epitomised by the coronation of Victoria, at his instigation, as Empress of India in 1876. Disraeli's "imperialist" foreign policies were further justified by invoking generalisations partly derived from Darwin's theory of evolution. The argument was that imperialism was a manifestation of what Kipling would refer to in the title of an 1899 poem as "The White Man's Burden." The Empire existed, argued its supporters, not for the benefit—economic, strategic, or otherwise—of Britain, but in order that "primitive" peoples, incapable of self-government, could, with British guidance, eventually become Christian and civilised. This mentality served to legitimise Britain's acquisition of portions of central Africa and her domination, in concert with other European powers, of China and other parts of Asia.

In the Victorian age, the study of "natural philosophy" and "natural history" became "science," and students who in an earlier time had been exclusively gentlemen and clerical naturalists became, after their course of study, professional scientists. In the general population, belief in natural laws and continuous progress began to grow, and there was frequent interaction among science, government, and industry. As science education was expanded and formalised, a fundamental transformation occurred in beliefs about nature and the place of humans in the universe. A revival of religious activity, largely unmatched since the days of the Puritans, swept England. This religious revival shaped that code of moral behaviour which became known as Victorianism. Above all, religion occupied a place in the public conscious- ness that it had not had a century before and did not retain in the twentieth century.

The end of the Victorian age brought a variety of literature to the public. Robert Louis Stevenson's *The Master of Ballant- rae* (1889), several novels of J. M. Barrie (who later wrote *Peter Pan*), Hall Caine's *The Bondman* (1890), Oscar Wilde's *The Picture of Dorian Gray* (1890) and several of Wilde's plays, Arthur Conan Doyle's *The Adventures of Sher- lock Holmes* (1891) and *The Memoirs of Sherlock Holmes* (1893), many works of Rudyard Kipling, and H. G. Wells's *The Time Machine* (1895) and *The Invisible Man* (1897) all caught the public's eye, to greater or lesser degrees. American works such as Mark Twain's *A Connecticut Yan- kee in King Arthur's Court* (1889) also drew attention.

Trilby hypnotized by Svengali.
George du Maurier, *Trilby* (1894)

A runaway best seller of the decade was George du Maurier's *Trilby* (1894), a novel that, with its striking central image of a swooning young woman, bears some similarities to Stoker's narrative.[3] Although little read today, the book tells of a young artist and his model, Trilby, who are lovers but separated by social class. When the artist leaves her, Trilby falls under the influence of Svengali, a psychically vampiric impresario and hypnotist, who moulds her into a great singer, "La Svengali." How- ever, she is only able to—and is compelled to—sing in his trances. When Svengali himself dies, Trilby appears to be freed, but a picture of him causes her to mechan- ically sing again, and she dies.

Upon publication, the novel caused a sensation in Britain and the United States. In its first year of publication, it sold two hundred thousand copies in the

---

[3] Professor of English literature Nina Auerbach suggests that *Trilby* influenced Stoker's narrative (*Woman and the Demon: The Life of a Victorian Myth* [Cambridge, MA: Harvard University Press, 1982], 15–34). As is evident from the Notes, however, *Dracula* was far along by the time *Trilby* was published.

Scene from the first performance of Puccini's opera
La Bohème in 1896 (based on Murger's novel).

United States alone, and the term "Svengali" came to be applied to any hypnotist. The book was turned into a popular play, revivified the allure of *la vie bohème*, last glorified in Henri Murger's *Scènes de la vie de bohème* (1848), and probably sparked interest in Puccini's 1896 opera *La Bohème*.

DRACULA APPEARS

WHEN *DRACULA* APPEARED in 1897, popular and critical reception of it (it was regarded as fiction) was mixed. Certainly in its early years, the book did not sell particularly well. The first print run was reportedly a mere three thousand copies, although a second print run occurred within a few months, and some reviewers praised the book. The *Daily News* (London, 27 May 1897) called it "a long story with an earnestness, a directness, and a simple good faith which ought to go far to induce readers of fiction to surrender their imaginations into the novelist's hands" and described it as "rich in sensations." The *Daily Mail* (London, 1 June 1897) characterised the book as "powerful, and horrorful. . . . The recollection of this weird and ghostly tale will doubtless haunt us for some time to come." "[H]orrid and creepy to the last degree," said the *Pall Mall Gazette* (London, 1 June 1897). "It is also excellent and one of the best things in the supernatural line that we have been lucky enough to hit upon."

Not all of the initial reviews were positive, however. For example, the *Athenaeum* (London, 26 June 1897) described the work as "highly sensational," complaining that "it is wanting in the constructive art as well as in the higher literary sense." *Punch* (26 June 1897) cautioned, "It is a pity that Mr. BRAM STOKER was not content to employ such supernatural anti-vampire receipts as his wildest imagination might have invented without rashly venturing on a domain where angels fear to tread. But for this, [this reviewer] could have unreservedly recommended so ingenious a romance to all who enjoy the very weirdest of weird tales." *The Spectator* (31 July 1897) called *Dracula* "decidedly mawkish. . . . The up-to-dateness of the book—the phonograph diaries, typewriters, and so on—hardly fits in with the medieval methods which ultimately secure the victory for Count Dracula's foes." *The Bookman* (London, August 1897) perhaps summed up the balance of English reaction: "A summary of the book would shock and disgust; but we must own that, though here and there in the course of the tale we hurried over things with repulsion, we read nearly the whole thing with rapt attention." The *Times* (London, 23 August 1897) counseled: "We would not . . . recommend it to nervous persons for evening reading."

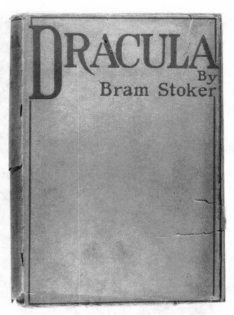

Dracula first-edition cover.

When *Dracula* was first published in the United States in 1899, the American press was mixed in its reaction. The *Wave* (San Francisco, 9 December 1899) called it "a literary failure," suffering from "a lack of artistic restraint. . . . If you have the bad taste, after this warning, to attempt the book, you will read on to the finish, as I did,—and go to bed, as I did, feeling furtively of your throat." The *San Francisco Chronicle* (17 December 1899) termed it "one of the most powerful novels of the day . . . a superb tour de force which stamps itself on the memory."

Initially, Stoker claimed full credit for the narrative. An extended interview with him in the *British Weekly* reported that "the plot of the story had been a long time in his mind." Asked about the historical basis for the tale, he mentioned reports of encounters with vampires in "Styria . . . China, Iceland, Germany, Saxony, Turkey, the Chersonese, Russia, Poland, Italy, France, and England, besides all the Tartar communities. Stoker admitted that Van Helsing was "founded on a real character" but said no more about the histories of the people of *Dracula*.[4]

---

[4] Jane Stoddard, "Mr. Bram Stoker. A Chat with the Author of *Dracula*," *British Weekly*, 1 July 1897.

Count von Count of *Sesame Street*.

Only one reviewer—apparently familiar with Stoker's gregarious and genial nature, his burdensome job as the manager of the Irving theatrical company, and the poor reception his earlier literary work had received—apprehended that Stoker's claim of creating the book was a hoax: "It is almost inconceivable that Bram Stoker wrote 'Dracula.' Still, he must have done it. There is his name on the title page. . . . [I]t is hard enough to imagine Bram Stoker a business man, to say nothing of his possessing an imagination capable of projecting Dracula upon paper" (*Detroit Free Press*, 18 November 1899).

The book eventually achieved enormous commercial success (although claims of outselling the Bible are exaggerated), with sales in the millions of copies. Since its first English publication in 1897 by Constable & Co., it has remained in print, with the first American publication by Doubleday & McClure and a second publication in England in 1912 by William Rider & Son. Stoker's copyrights expired in 1962. The work has appeared in over a hundred English editions and numerous translations.

Dracula's presence in the world, of course, has never been confined to books. He stalked the stage as early as 1897. Drawings of the Count appeared in numerous magazines and newspapers. Film—an unlikely medium for the not-to-be-photographed vampire—captured tales of Dracula (or thinly disguised versions of him) as early as the 1920s; today, the Internet Movie Database lists over 150 films (including adult, animated, and television films) containing "Dracula" in the title and over 200 actors portraying Dracula in one form or another.[5] Children as well as adults have been exposed to Dracula: there are dozens of children's books dealing with Dracula and his offspring,[6] as well as toys, dolls, games, puppets (including *Sesame Street*'s Count von Count), and even a breakfast cereal (Count Chocula). The country of Roumania, where many of the events of the narrative occur, has for practical purposes adopted Dracula as

[5] Those who count these sorts of things have crowned Sherlock Holmes as the most filmed person of all time, followed by Dracula and then Tarzan. However, Dracula-related films seem to appear regularly, whereas Tarzan may be lost in the jungles.

[6] For a partial list, see J. Gordon Melton and Robert Eighteen-Bisang, "Vampire Fiction for Children and Youth, 1960–Present," *Transylvanian Journal* 2 (1996): 24–30.

Roumanian postcard.
From the collection of Leslie S. Klinger

Sign outside Casa Vlad Dracul, Sighisoara, Roumania.
Photograph by Leslie S. Klinger, May 2007

its national symbol and conflated the histories of a national hero, Vlad Ţepeş (known as Vlad Dracula or Vlad the Impaler), and Count Dracula into a major industry.

VAMPIRE LITERATURE BEFORE *DRACULA*

TO UNDERSTAND the initial appeal of the Count and his hunters, we must consider the prior popularisation of vampires. *Dracula* was the culmination of a Victorian interest in vampires that had been growing since the beginning of the nineteenth century, and which had its roots in scientific accounts dating from as early as the sixteenth century.

According to the *Encyclopædia Britannica* (9th ed., 1888), the vampire was supposed to be the soul of a decedent that had quit the buried body by night to suck the blood of living persons.

Bust of Vlad the Impaler as a vampire, sold at Castle Bran, Roumania.
From the collection of Leslie S. Klinger

Hence, when the vampire's grave is opened, his corpse is found to be fresh and rosy from the blood which he has thus absorbed. To put a stop to his ravages, a stake is driven through the corpse, or the head cut off, or the heart torn out and the body burned, or boiling water and vinegar are poured on the grave. . . . The belief in vampires chiefly prevails in Slavonic lands, as in Russia (especially White Russia and the Ukraine), Poland and Servia and among the Czechs of Bohemia and the other Slavonic races of Austria. It became especially prevalent in Hungary between the years 1730 and 1735, whence all Europe was filled with reports of the exploits of vampires. Several treatises were written on the subject, among which may be mentioned Ranft's *De masticatione mortuorum in tumulis*[7] (1734) and Calmet's *Dissertation on the Vampires of Hungary* [1751].

The first popular account of vampirism published in England was the physician John William Polidori's "The Vampyre," which appeared in 1819.[8] In 1816, Dr.

---

[7] In the vernacular, "Concerning chewed-up corpses."

[8] John William Polidori, "The Vampyre," *New Monthly Magazine*, April 1819.

The Nightmare.
Henry Fuseli, 1781

John Polidori.

Polidori accompanied his friend and patient Lord Byron on a trip to Italy and Switzerland. That summer, they stayed at the Villa Diodati near Lake Geneva, where they were visited by poet Percy Bysshe Shelley, his wife, Mary, and her stepsister, Jane "Claire" Claremont. When incessant rain kept the five friends indoors, they began reading aloud a book of ghost tales. According to Mary Shelley, Byron suggested they each write a ghost story to rival those in the book.[9] Mary Shelley's effort became *Frankenstein*, published two years later. Her husband wrote nothing in response to the challenge; Byron started on a story but reportedly abandoned it.[10] Polidori produced "The Vampyre." Originally heralded as a work of Byron—and then seen as a satire of Byron—the story recounts some of the activities of the vampire Lord Ruthven, a nobleman marked by his aloof manner and the "deadly hue of his face, which never gained a warmer tint." In the early part of the nineteenth century, the enigmatic yet strangely compelling Ruthven befriends a gentle-

[9] The events are depicted in Ken Russell's controversial 1986 film *Gothic*, starring Gabriel Byrne as Byron and Natasha Richardson as Mary Shelley. A central image of the film, reproduced here, is the haunting painting *The Nightmare* by Fuseli (1781), which may well show a vampire.

[10] The completed but lost novel is brilliantly imagined in John Crowley's *Lord Byron's Novel: The Evening Land* (New York: William Morrow, 2005).

6 Handbill for James Planchés' theatrical version of *The Vampyre*, performed at the height of the Lord Ruthven craze in autumn 1820. Note the kilt worn by Mr T. P. Cooke in the role of Lord Ruthven.

The Vampyre handbill.

man named Aubrey, who finds that even Ruthven's death does not rid him of his deadly companion. When Ruthven returns from death, he rejoins Aubrey, to the latter's horror, and soon attacks and kills Ianthe, the object of Aubrey's affections. Plunged into a breakdown, Aubrey recovers only to find that his beloved sister has also become the victim of the creature, who then vanishes.

Polidori was no great writer, as is evident from the concluding lines of the book: "Lord Ruthven had disappeared, and Aubrey's sister had glutted the thirst of a VAMPYRE!" Polidori's work is credited as the first of the great vampire tales, however, primarily for its revelation of a *gentleman* vampire—a far remove from the disgusting, blood-sucking corpses detailed in the accounts of Calmet and other historians. It was immensely successful; within Polidori's lifetime (he died two years after publication), the work was translated into French, German, Spanish, and Swedish and adapted into several stage plays, which played to horror-struck audiences until the early 1850s.

Also extremely popular was *Varney, the Vampyre*, written by James Malcolm Rymer[11] and serialised in 109 weekly installments from 1845 to 1847. It is the first novel-length account of a vampire in English, and the prose is sensational: "Her bosom heaves, and her limbs tremble, yet she cannot withdraw her eyes from that marble-looking face. . . . With a plunge he seizes her neck in his fang-like teeth—a gush of blood, and a hideous sucking noise follows. The girl has swooned, and the vampire is at his hideous repast!" Despite its artistic shortcomings, *Varney* delivers a vivid, monstrous portrait of the undead. The vampire is Sir Francis Varney, born in the seventeenth century, frequently reborn

[11] There remains some controversy over whether Rymer wrote *Varney* or whether it was the product of Thomas Peckett Prest (1810–1859?), author of numerous "penny dreadfuls" and creator of the demon barber Sweeney Todd. Prest claimed that *Varney* was based on true events occurring in the early eighteenth century, but he also claimed that Sweeney Todd was truthful.

The quotes that follow come from *Varney, the Vampyre; or, The Feast of Blood* (1847; reprint, New York: Dover Books, 1972).

from the dead—a "tall gaunt figure" whose face, similar to Ruthven's, is "perfectly white—perfectly bloodless," with eyes like "polished tin" and "fearful-looking teeth—projecting like those of some wild animal, hideously, glaringly white, and fang-like." It is possible that Polidori and Rymer (or Prest) were writing about the same figure, whose description bears a marked resemblance to that of Dracula.[12]

The most influential record of vampires published before *Dracula*, which Bram Stoker specifically acknowledged reading, is the Irish fantasy writer Joseph Sheridan Le Fanu's 1872 story "Carmilla."[13] The tale records the history of a female vampire. After a carriage accident, the charming and beautiful Carmilla is taken in by Laura, the narrator, a lonely young lady. Laura experiences terrifying dreams in which a mysterious woman visits her in bed and kisses her neck. She recalls that in the daytime the doting Carmilla occasionally "would press me more closely in her trembling embrace, and her lips in soft kisses gently glow upon

Title page, *Varney, the Vampyre; or, The Feast of Blood* by James Malcolm Rymer (1847).

my cheek. . . . In these mysterious moods I did not like her. I experienced a strange tumultuous excitement that was pleasurable, ever and anon, mingled with a vague sense of fear and disgust. . . . I was conscious of a love growing into adoration, and also of abhorrence."[14]

Laura discovers that Carmilla is the double of Carmilla's ancestor, the Countess Mircalla Karnstein (of Styria), dead for more than a century. With the help

---

[12] According to Polidori, Ruthven vanishes after killing Aubrey's sister. Sir Francis Varney reportedly cast himself into Mount Vesuvius, but (as will be seen in *Dracula*) rumours of a vampire's death are oft exaggerated.

[13] "Carmilla" was first published in the magazine *The Dark Blue* in the January, February, and March 1872 issues; it was subsequently included in Le Fanu's 1872 collection of short stories *In a Glass Darkly*.

[14] Joseph Sheridan Le Fanu, "Carmilla," in *A Clutch of Vampires*, ed. Raymond T. McNally (Greenwich, CT: New York Graphic Society, 1974).

From "Carmilla."
D. M. Friston, *The Dark Blue*, 1872

of her father's friend General Spielsdorf, Laura travels to the village of Karnstein in Styria, where she learns from the general that Carmilla (who also calls herself Millarca) *is* the Countess Mircalla, a vampire. Laura and a band of men exhume Countess Mircalla's body and destroy her by driving a stake through her heart.[15]

The public consciousness of vampires is perhaps best illustrated by "The Sussex Vampire," a Sherlock Holmes adventure set in 1896 (inexplicably, not published until 1924). Called in on a case by a firm of solicitors by means of a dry letter headed "Re Vampires," Holmes asks Watson to look up in their commonplace book what they know about vampires (of course, he might as well have con-

---

[15] The events of "Carmilla" are dramatised in several films. Danish director Carl Dreyer loosely adapted the story for his 1932 film *Vampyr*. French director Roger Vadim's *Et mourir de plaisir* ("And to die of pleasure"), released in England as *Blood and Roses* (1960; starring Annette Vadim as Carmilla and with cinematography by Claude Renoir), is based on "Carmilla" and is considered one of the greatest of the vampire genre. Hammer Film Productions also produced loose adaptations of "Carmilla," with its trilogy *The Vampire Lovers* (1970), *Lust for a Vampire* (1971), and *Twins of Evil* (1971). Ingrid Pitt appeared in the first of these films as Carmilla and Peter Cushing as General Spielsdorf, and the film featured plentiful bosoms and blood in traditional Hammer style. Although Cushing—also known for his numerous portrayals of Van Helsing and Sherlock Holmes—may be regarded as essential to any Hammer vampire film, he is curiously absent from *Lust for a Vampire*.

Ingrid Pitt as Mircalla Karnstein.
The Vampire Lovers (Hammer Film Productions, 1970)

The alleged Sussex vampire, from "The Adventure of the Sussex Vampire."
W. T. Benda, *Hearst's International*, 1924

sulted the *Britannica*). After reading summaries of legends and superstitions in Hungary and Transylvania, Holmes explodes, "Rubbish, Watson, rubbish! What have we to do with walking corpses who can only be held in their grave by stakes driven through their hearts? It's pure lunacy. . . . This Agency stands flat-footed upon the ground, and there it must remain. The world is big enough for us. No ghosts need apply."[16]

Holmes nevertheless accepts the case and soon learns that Robert Ferguson, a former football-player pal of Watson's, believes that his foreign-born wife may be a vampire. Ferguson is no fool—he has caught his wife sucking puncture marks on the neck of their baby, and she refuses to give him any explanation. Holmes quickly determines that no undead are involved here. Instead, the wife is making a desperate attempt to remove poison from the child without disclosing the poisoner. For Holmes the rationalist, no conclusion of vampirism is even remotely possible—but for Dr. Watson and big Bob Ferguson, it takes Sherlock Holmes to eliminate the possibility.[17]

THE LIFE OF BRAM STOKER

ABRAHAM "BRAM" STOKER, theatre manager and prolific author of sentimental and sensational fiction, would have struck few of his acquaintances as likely to be involved with the best-known narrative of horror ever published. Born on 8 November 1847, at Clontarf, a seaside suburb of Dublin, Stoker was the son of Abraham Stoker (1799–1876), a lifelong civil servant, and Charlotte Mathilda Blake Thornley Stoker (1818–1901), a dynamic woman of many social causes. Stoker was the third of seven children, four of whom became professionals. Three of his brothers studied medicine; the fourth took a post in the Indian Civil Service. A sickly child (suffering from an unknown disease), Stoker was bed-confined until the age of seven, when a near-miraculous recovery returned him to a normal youth. It is tempting to speculate that the memory of his reviv-

[16] "The Adventure of the Sussex Vampire," in Arthur Conan Doyle, *The New Annotated Sherlock Holmes*, vol. 2, ed. with notes by Leslie S. Klinger (New York: W. W. Norton, 2005), 1556–58.

[17] Sir Arthur Conan Doyle, a longtime colleague of Dr. Watson, wrote to Bram Stoker on 20 August 1897, "I write to tell you how very much I have enjoyed reading *Dracula*. I think it is the very best story of diablerie which I have read for many years" (original letter in Harry Ransom Humanities Research Center, University of Texas at Austin; quoted in Elizabeth Miller, ed., *Bram Stoker's Dracula: A Documentary Volume* [Detroit, MI: Thomson Gale, 2005]).

Abraham "Bram" Stoker.

Stoker at age thirty-seven.

Sir Henry Irving.

ification remained with him forever and put its stamp on the narrative he fashioned from the Harker Papers.

Stoker attended the University of Dublin from the mid-1860s to 1870 and read history, literature, mathematics, and physics at Trinity College. At university, he quickly became a popular athlete. Although he did not shine in academics, he served as president of the University Philosophical Society, a prominent debating club. His first paper for the society, "Sensationalism in Fiction and Society," won him some acclaim in the college. Later, he actively defended the poetry of Walt Whitman against harsh campus criticism. After completing his education, at his father's behest Stoker took up a post as a civil servant in Dublin Castle. This left him far from satisfied, however, and in 1871 he began writing theatre criticism without pay for the *Dublin Evening Mail*, at about the time Joseph Sheridan Le Fanu was disposing of his interest in the paper. Le Fanu, the author of "Carmilla," may have shared an enthusiasm for vampires with the young critic, but there is no evidence that they met. Stoker also published his first short story, "The Crystal Cup," in 1872 in *London Society* magazine. This was followed by three short novels, *The Primrose Path*, *Buried Treasures*, and *The Chain of Destiny*, all of which appeared in 1875 in *The Shamrock*, a Dublin magazine, to little notice.

Stoker was tireless in his promotion of theatre in Dublin, and in 1876 his penetrating review of a Dublin production of *Hamlet*, which featured the rising star Henry Irving, won him an introduction to the actor, with fateful results. The two were by all accounts greatly taken with one another and maintained a correspondence for several years. Stoker continued writing while he pursued his civil service career. His chief product—unpublished

The Lyceum Theatre.

until 1879—was *The Duties of Clerks of Petty Sessions in Ireland*, said to be the definitive handbook for officials like Stoker, although he later called it "dry as dust."[18] Sadly, Abraham Stoker died in 1876 before seeing his son promoted to the office of inspector of petty sessions.

In 1878, Irving approached Stoker with a proposition—become the business manager of Irving's new venture, the Lyceum Theatre in London. Stoker accepted, gave up his civil service position—not, however, without completing his book—and married his childhood sweetheart, Florence Balcombe, a noted beauty who had been courted by another Dublin acquaintance, Oscar Wilde. The

[18] Bram Stoker, *Personal Reminiscences of Henry Irving*, vol. 1 (New York: Macmillan & Co., 1906).

Florence Anne Lemon Balcombe.
Drawing by Oscar Wilde (?)

Bram Stoker and his family.
George du Maurier, *Punch*, 11 September 1886

newlyweds moved to London. There Stoker began the career as Irving's secretary, confidant, accountant, public spokesperson, business associate, tireless companion, and friend that was to last until Irving's death in 1905. Sir Hall Caine, Stoker's close friend, was to write of their relationship in Stoker's obituary: "Much has been said of [Stoker's] relation to Henry Irving, but I wonder how many were really

Irving and Stoker leaving the Lyceum Theatre.
The Tattler, 9 October 1901

MR. IRVING IS PACKING UP.

Irving and Stoker go on tour.
Entr'Acte, 6 October 1883

Mark Twain.
Library of Congress, 1907

Walt Whitman.

aware of the whole depth and significance of that association. Bram seemed to give up his life to it. . . . I say without any hesitation that never have I seen, never do I expect to see, such absorption of one man's life in the life of another."[19]

Stoker's position at the Lyceum Theatre was challenging, for this was a heady and highly politicised world. Irving, the leading actor of the day, movemd in circles of celebrity, power, and prestige. Stoker plunged into the demands of the job, and although he and Florence had a child in 1879, Irving Noel Stoker, Stoker's long hours at the theatre and many months on tour made him frequently absent from home. For most of his twenty-seven years with Irving, he arranged every provincial tour of the company, planned the financial aspects of all its productions, and handled the business aspects of Irving's ensemble of players. In 1883, Stoker arranged the first of several North American tours for the Lyceum Theatre Company, giving him the opportunity to meet his idol Walt Whitman as well as Mark Twain.

[19] Hall Caine, "Bram Stoker: The Story of a Great Friendship," [London] *Daily Telegraph*, 24 April 1912.

Stoker's restless energy had already led him to try his hand at writing fiction. After his move to London, however, his writing was necessarily part-time, fit in around the demands of the theatre, and he concentrated mainly on short stories. A collection of eight children's tales of fantasy and wonder, *Under the Sunset*, was published in 1881, the same year in which he received a medal for heroism in an unsuccessful attempt to rescue a suicide who had plunged into the Thames. In 1886, he produced *A Glimpse of America*, recounting the Irving theatre company's tour, and did not try his hand at fiction again until 1890, when he published an Irish romantic adventure of novel length titled *The Snake's Pass*.

In March 1890, Stoker also began assembling the many disparate pieces of material that would become the narrative of *Dracula*. He spent his summer in Whitby, Yorkshire, where he encountered the name "Dracula" in a library book. When and where he met the "Harkers" is unknown, although in 1890 Stoker also completed his legal studies and was called to the bar in London. It is possible he may have met the young solicitor through one or another bar. He may have undertaken to work with the Harker Papers at this time, but his duties apparently kept him from devoting much concentrated effort to *Dracula*, although the Notes indicate constant though sporadic effort over the next seven years. Two other books were to arrive before *Dracula* appeared in print: *The Watter's Mou'* (1895), a tale inspired by summers spent in Cruden Bay, Scotland, and *The Shoulder of Shasta* (1895), another romantic adventure, this time set in the United States.

Although *Dracula* was indeed published to some critical acclaim, commercial success eluded Stoker. He continued his writing, producing eight more books of fiction before his death: *Miss Betty* (1898), a romance; *The Mystery of the Sea* (1902), set in Cruden Bay; *The Jewel of Seven Stars* (1903), a strange tale based on Stoker's interest in Egyptology; *The Man* (1905; also published as *The Gates of Life*), a novel about an outspoken woman; *Lady Athlyne* (1908), a romantic novel; *Snowbound: The Record of a Theatrical Touring Party* (1909), a collection of fictional tales; *The Lady of the Shroud* (1909), the story of a woman falsely accused of vampirism; and *Lair of the White Worm* (1911), a virtually indescribable supernatural tale of a giant worm in Yorkshire. In 1910, Stoker also published *Famous Imposters*, a nonfiction book about some great historical frauds, including the Tichborne claimant (a celebrated Victorian imposter whose claim to be the long-lost heir to the Tichborne fortunes electrified London in the 1860s) and the questionable tale of the "false" Elizabeth I. However, Stoker's best-received book was his two-volume *Personal Reminiscences of Henry Irving*, published shortly after the actor's death in 1905. Although criticised for failing to discuss the less-than-admirable side of the egotistical Irving, the book disclosed much about Stoker and the life he spent happily in Irving's shadow.

" *They could follow the tall white shaft.*"

[FACING PAGE 222.

Illustration from *Lair of the White Worm.*
Pamela Coleman Smith (London: William
Rider and Son, Ltd., 1911)

Photograph of Bram Stoker at work, used to publicise his 1906 memoir of Henry Irving.

Dracula's Guest and Other Weird Stories.
(London: Routledge, 1914)

Stoker's fiction has been little examined and generally poorly regarded by critics and academics. Not until Skidmore College professor Phyllis A. Roth published *Bram Stoker* in 1982 did a Stoker biographer pay any serious attention to his writing. Roth considers each of Stoker's novels and concludes they are all romances, depicting the traditional rituals of mating, the common conflicts, and the happy outcomes prevalent in eighteenth-century novels of sentiment. On the whole, the heroines are beautiful but in need of rescue; the heroes are broad shouldered, noble of countenance, and strong but lacking in their understanding of women, a deficiency usually rectified in the tale. Even Stoker's tales of horror, although they include mystery, the supernatural, and traditional Gothic components of horror and the outré, follow this formula. Roth, observing that Stoker's fictions idealised fraternal and filial relationships and vastly simplified heterosexual relations, suggests that perhaps Stoker "longed for a simpler age, that depicted in the novel of sentiment or, even earlier, in the prose or metrical romance."[20] In any event, Stoker's fiction, with the possible exception of *Lair of the White Worm*, is largely lost in obscurity.

Soon after Irving's death, Stoker suffered a stroke and began a prolonged convalescence. As can be seen from the above list of his works, this was in fact the most prolific phase of his writing career. However, it seems that Stoker's fortunes were in decline, and except for the modest success of *Personal Reminiscences*, the books and business ventures brought him small financial reward. He died in 1912 in his bed. The death certificate stated the cause of death to be "exhaustion," although one biographer claimed it was tertiary syphillis. In 1914 Florence published a posthumous collection

[20] Phyllis A. Roth, *Bram Stoker* (Boston: Twayne Publishers, 1982), 137.

of some of Stoker's previously unpublished horror/fantasy stories, including "Dracula's Guest" and "The Judge's House."[21]

THE PEOPLE OF *DRACULA*

LITTLE IS KNOWN of the life of Count, or Voivode, Dracula, as he is named in Bram Stoker's *Dracula*. It is, of course, unlikely that "Dracula" is his real name,[22] and although some scholars insist that the vampire depicted in Stoker's narrative is Vlad Ţepeş or Vlad Dracula, also known as Vlad the Impaler, an historical leader of Wallachia, there is, bluntly stated, no evidence that Vlad had any vampiric characteristics. Elizabeth Miller, one of the most astute *Dracula* scholars, declares, "The case for Count Dracula and Vlad is wafer thin."[23] The Stoker narrative contains no references to "Vlad" or "the Impaler" and no discussion of the grisly history of Vlad except in the vaguest, most general remarks about "iron nerve" and "subtle brain."

The few facts of family history are based on the conversations recorded by Jonathan Harker, a solicitor in the employ of Dracula who visits him in Transylvania. According to Harker's recollection of the Count's account, Dracula is a Szekely, descended from an "old family," and he terms himself a "Transylvanian noble," or *boyar*. He apparently was a military leader, who led his troops "again, and again, and again" against the Turks, often retreating alone to his homeland, abandoning the field. There is no evidence that any others

Bela Lugosi as Dracula.
U.S. Postal Service stamp, 1997

Vlad the Impaler.
Dracole Wayda Barth (Ghotan Edition, Lübeck, 1485)

---

[21] *Dracula's Guest and Other Weird Stories* (London: Routledge, 1914).

[22] Stoker found the name in William Wilkinson's 1820 partial account of the history of Transylvania and adopted it for the creature he originally styled "Count Wampyr."

[23] Elizabeth Miller, *Dracula: Sense & Nonsense* (Southend-on-Sea, England: Desert Island Books, 2006), 160.

Christopher Lee as Dracula.
El Conde Dracula (Corona Filmproduktion, 1970)

of his family remain, although some suggest that the three women who occupy Castle Dracula with him are sisters, daughters, or former wives.

Records of his physical appearance are consistent. Jonathan Harker describes Dracula as a tall old man, prodigiously strong, clean shaven except for a long white moustache.[24] His eyebrows are bushy, virtually a single brow, and he has "peculiarly sharp" teeth and notably red lips. Dracula is thin cheeked but with a broad, strong chin, and the tops of his ears are extremely pointed. Harker's overall impression of Dracula's face is one of extraordinary pallor. He describes Dracula's hands as coarse and broad, with squat fingers, hairy palms, and long, fine nails cut to sharp points. He also observes that Dracula has foul breath—surprising in a presumably non-breathing dead being! Mina Harker supplements this description with her own observations of the Count, calling him a "tall, thin man, with a beaky nose," a hard, cruel, and sensual face, big white teeth, and extremely red lips.

There are scant traces of his personal history. In life, he made a reputation as clever, cunning, and brave. He studied diabolical secrets at the Scholomance at Lake Hermannstadt, and it appears that he became a vampire there. Before his mortal death, he sired great men and good women. How long he lived in Castle Dracula, and whether he had other homes, is unknown. It appears that he was poorly travelled outside eastern Europe, but despite never having been to England, he is recorded as speaking only English, learned from his extensive reading of English newspapers, magazines, and books. It is highly likely that he spoke fluent German, Hungarian, Slovak, Serbian, Wallachian, and Romany.

According to the narrative published by Bram Stoker, Dracula perished at the hands of Quincey Morris and Jonathan Harker. As discussed in the notes to chapter 27, there is substantial reason to doubt this claim. There are numerous accounts of Dracula's life after the events of the narrative, including Kim Newman's fine *Anno Dracula* (1992), Marv Wolfman's *The Tomb of Dracula* and *Dracula Lives!* (1972–

---

[24] However, Mina Harker observes him later with a "black moustache and pointed beard." See text accompanying chapter 13, note 38.

Laurence Olivier as Professor Van Helsing.
Dracula (Universal Pictures, 1979)

1979), and Fred Saberhagen's *The Dracula Tape* (1975). However, these accounts are contradictory, and there is no reason to believe one over another.

Dracula's principal opponent—according to Stoker's narrative—was the Dutch physician, philosopher, man of letters, lawyer, folklorist, and teacher Abraham Van Helsing. A man of medium weight, he is strongly built, with a broad, deep chest; his head is described as "noble, well-sized, broad, and large behind the ears." Although he is clean shaven, he has big bushy eyebrows beneath a broad forehead, over wide-set blue eyes. Van Helsing is old, grey, and lonely. His wife (like Mr. Rochester's in *Jane Eyre*) is insane and probably confined; his son, possibly the same age as Dracula-hunter Arthur Holmwood, is dead.

Little is known of his career. Van Helsing studied in London, and although he reportedly speaks many languages, English is not one of his more successful attainments. Apparently occupying a chair at a European school of medicine at the time of Stoker's narrative—probably in Amsterdam, to which he frequently travels—he has taught more than one generation of doctors, including Dracula-hunter John Seward and Dr. Vincent. A devout Catholic, he is a specialist in obscure diseases, termed "one of the most advanced scientists of his day." As

Keanu Reeves as Jonathan Harker and Gary Oldman as Dracula.
Bram Stoker's Dracula (American Zoetrope, 1992)

Dracula scholar and publisher Clive Leatherdale points out, Van Helsing is "principally a medical man: he is not a trained vampire hunter."[25] Casting aside science, he quotes folklore as if it were a fixed body of knowledge and appears more magician or faith healer than doctor. It also appears that his medical skills are more theoretical than practical: in the course of Stoker's narrative, his treatment of his patients falls short of the standard of care of the contemporary medical community.[26] Van Helsing's circle of friends includes one Vanderpool, a grower of garlic; Arminius, a student of eastern European folklore; and Palmieri, a leading seismologist of the day (who was deleted from Stoker's narrative). He may have

[25] Clive Leatherdale, *Dracula: The Novel & The Legend: A Study of Bram Stoker's Gothic Masterpiece* (rev. ed., Westcliff-on-Sea, England: Desert Island Books, 2001), 125.

[26] Dr. John Seward's medical behaviour—and especially his medical ethics—were not significantly better, perhaps as a direct result of Van Helsing's influence. See, for example, chapter 10, note 27, and chapter 21, notes 1 and 7.

been acquainted with the great French neurologist Jean-Martin Charcot as well.

Jonathan Harker must be counted high on the list of Dracula's enemies. A recently qualified solicitor in his twenties, practising in Exeter, he is assigned to fill in for his ailing employer, bringing him into contact with Dracula. Harker is a member of the Church of England, a sweet and simple man with a clever, strong, youthful face and brown hair. Although interested in foreign customs, he is prudish, lacking in intellectual curiosity, and fixed in his habits, with a rigid sense of class and propriety. Like many tightly wound individuals, however, Harker has a violent, perhaps perverse side. He readily succumbs to the seduction of the three women in Castle Dracula, physically attacks the Count in his coffin, attacks him again later with a decidedly out-of-character kukri knife, and becomes a whirlwind of action in the final confrontation with the Count and his armed guards.

Harker's sweetheart since childhood, whom he marries during the course of events described in Stoker's narrative, is Mina Murray Harker. Mina, probably about the same age as Harker, is an assistant schoolmistress, at a school that she likely attended. While a schoolgirl there, she was part of a circle of friends including Lucy Westenra (although Lucy was younger than Mina), Kate Reed (deleted from mention in the narrative), and several other unnamed girls. Mina has studied shorthand and typing in order to assist Jonathan Harker with his law career, and she is well read in psychology and sociology. She is logical and orderly in thought, sensitive to the feelings of others and the impressions she and her friends create on those around them. A "man's brain" is the unfortunate description applied by Van Helsing to her intellect, but Mina has little patience with the "New Woman." Even though she is comfortable handling a carriage or a pistol, she clings to homely values and is willing to allow the men around her to place her on a pedestal.

John (Jack) Seward, another of Dracula's hunters, is a physician, the proprietor of a private insane asylum. A former student and close friend of Van Helsing, Seward is twenty-nine, young for his position. He is of good birth, handsome,

Edith Craig, who portrayed Mina in *Dracula, or The Un-Dead* in Stoker's production at the Lyceum Theatre, 1895.

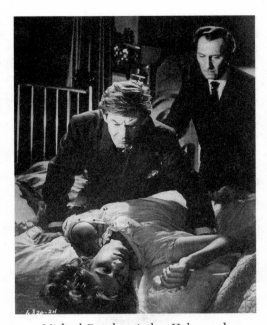

Michael Gough as Arthur Holmwood,
Melissa Stribling as Mina, and Peter Cushing
as Van Helsing.
Horror of Dracula (Hammer Film Productions, 1958)

Frank Langella as Dracula
and Kate Nelligan as Lucy.
Dracula (Universal Pictures, 1979)

and strong jawed; and although he has travelled the world seeking adventure, he is shy and awkward in the company of women. Devoted to his work and a compulsive diarist, Seward yearns to make a name for himself in his field, although he displays little compassion for his patients and little regard for medical ethics or law. He is credulous, sycophantic—at least with respect to Van Helsing, whose life he once saved—slow-witted, materialistic, and clings to rationalism.

Little is known about Arthur Holmwood, later Lord Godalming, or Quincey Morris, who round out the list of Dracula's hunters. Holmwood is tall, handsome, and curly haired (or straight haired, depending on the account), the heir of "Ring," the family home. He apparently possesses substantial inherited wealth. Although he, Morris, and Seward travelled together to places of high adventure, he has little practical sense (other than an ability to repair boilers) and relies on his privileged upbringing and title to obtain anything he desires. Although he must have been educated in traditional schools, he knows little and says less. He woos Mina's friend Lucy Westenra over the course of Stoker's narrative, only to lose her to Dracula, but apparently marries someone else within seven years of her death.

Quincey Morris is a man of some mystery. An American from Texas, he may have been an inventor and may have been wealthy, but in either case, what little is revealed of his life consists of vague allusions to adventures in remote places in the company of Seward and Holmwood. Regardless of this life of travel, he speaks no foreign languages, appears uncomfortable in social settings, and seems devoid of intellectual curiosity or attainments. Although Morris is a poor shot—probably even with his beloved Winchester rifle—he is reasonably adept with a bowie knife, although he is the only one of the troupe to perish in the final assault on Dracula.

Dwight Frye as Renfield.
Dracula (Universal Pictures, 1931)

Two others of the circle around Dracula are worthy of mention. Lucy Westenra, longtime friend of Mina, is Dracula's first English victim. Lucy, nineteen at the time of the events described in Stoker's narrative, is the pampered child of an upper-middle-class family. *Dracula* scholar Leonard Wolf describes her as "silly, transparent, gushy, giggly, beautiful, and good."[27] Her education is (as might be expected) limited to some years spent at the same institution attended by Mina and Kate Reed, and her life revolves around walking, picture galleries, riding, rowing, tennis, and fishing. Perhaps the key to her doom is her tendency to sleepwalk, inherited from her father. There is little else to explain why Dracula, while still in Transylvania, chooses her as his first English victim.[28] Lucy is courted by Holmwood, Seward, and Morris, all of whom propose to her, and Van Helsing is clearly smitten by her as well. However, she appears unremittingly unaware. She is near comatose during every encounter with Dracula and goes to her grave with apparently no knowledge whatsoever of what befell her.

The last figure of significance in the narrative is R. M. Renfield, a fifty-nine- (or forty-nine-)year-old patient in Seward's asylum, probably self-admitted. Renfield (privately referred to rudely as the "fly-man" by Seward for his zoöphagous habits) is a man of great physical strength and strong intellectual character, highly educated and articulate. He is also selfish, secretive, obsessive, morbidly excitable, and prone to violent acts. Although his physician, John Seward, is the last to see it, Renfield's mania connects him to Dracula, and he seeks to rationalise vampirism on psychic or spiritual grounds. Little is known of Renfield's life before the asylum, and he is never visited by any friends or family. Renfield is the only person whose death can be directly attributed to Dracula.[29]

---

[27] Leonard Wolf, *A Dream of Dracula: In Search of the Living Dead* (Boston: Little, Brown and Co., 1972), 208–09.

[28] This is one of the most troubling aspects of the Harker Papers—why did Dracula select Whitby as his first destination in England? Could it be that he made long-distance telepathic contact with Lucy Westenra before Harker's journey to Castle Dracula and planned his voyage to land at Whitby because he knew Lucy would be there? Two films, Francis Ford Coppola's *Bram Stoker's Dracula* (1992), written by James V. Hart, and Dan Curtis's made-for-television *Dracula* (1973), written by the eminent science-fiction author Richard Matheson and starring Jack Palance as Dracula, both posit that Dracula was drawn to England by his discovery of the reincarnation of his first wife as Mina (Coppola's film) or Lucy (Curtis's film) and planned to be reunited eternally with her. However, there is no suggestion in the Harker Papers that Dracula had any foreknowledge of Lucy (or Mina for that matter), and although romantically satisfying, the notion must be rejected.

[29] There is no definite evidence that Dracula was the cause of the deaths of the captain or crew of the *Demeter*. Lucy likely died from the hazards of medical science. Morris was killed by the Szgany.

HOW *DRACULA* CAME TO BE WRITTEN

WHAT CONNECTION CAN be drawn between theatre-manager/author Bram Stoker and this group of people? To understand how the Stoker narrative came to be, one must begin with the hidden truth: Dracula did not die at the hands of his hunters.

Bram Stoker, who was called to the bar himself in April 1890, may well have met the young lawyer Jonathan Harker in the course of his legal studies, probably in early 1890, when Stoker's first notes on Dracula are dated. Harker, anxious to publish the Harker Papers to alert the public to the danger of the vampire's presence in England, sought the help of his acquaintance Stoker—little published, but nonetheless a more "literary" man than Harker or any other of his circle of friends. Stoker undertook to help the Harkers, but the press of work kept him from devoting his undivided energy to the task. Then the unexpected occurred—Dracula himself approached Stoker. Realising that it was too late to suppress the Harker Papers entirely, Dracula pressured Stoker—presumably with threats against his person and his family—into distorting the papers, hiding the facts essential to permit (or induce) readers to track the vampire. This required changing not only the names of the people involved but also the location of Castle Dracula and—most important—putting out the story that Dracula had perished and Castle Dracula had been destroyed.[30]

---

[30] Stoker worked through this process in camera with Dracula, without consulting the Harkers or anyone else. Dracula, in editing and approving the final version, perhaps understandably emphasised the worst and weakest aspects of the characters of his opponents. Only after the narrative was published did the survivors contact Stoker and persuade him to soften their harsh portraits, which he did in a text published in 1901. The 1901 paperback edition of *Dracula* (hereafter referred to as the "Abridged Text") was abridged and revised, reducing the text by approximately 15 percent. In the 1994 reprint of it (titled *Dracula: The Rare Text of 1901*), *Dracula* scholar Raymond T. McNally asserts in his introduction that the abridgement was made by Stoker, as does editor Robert Eighteen-Bisang in his foreword, although neither has any evidence. Similarly, Richard Dalby and William Hughes, editors of *Bram Stoker: A Bibliography*, state definitively that the 1901 edition "was skilfully revised and abridged by Stoker himself." (Dalby reportedly owns a copy of *Dracula* that contains pencilled notes in a hand that is likely Stoker's, apparently in preparation for an abridgement.) The possibility that the abridgement was the work of an editor is suggested by Elizabeth Miller in "Shape-Shifting Text: Editions and Versions of Dracula."

Although many of the changes to the Abridged Text may have been made to meet the requirements of the publisher for fewer words (and a less sophisticated readership), many more appear to have been made to improve the "image" of some of the principals and players of the narrative, who undoubtedly had no opportunity to approve Stoker's original version in advance. Stoker's preface to the Icelandic edition of the narrative (see p. 5) makes clear that he was personally acquainted with the principals, and it seems quite likely that, with the unexpected popularity of the publication, he made changes to the narrative to please them and others affected. Other changes, however, are of more obscure origin and may be corrections

The result was the narrative in its present form. Full of transparent plagiarisms, inconsistencies, made-up names, places, and dates, the narrative can hardly be relied upon as a source of definite knowledge about virtually anything associated with Dracula—not the name or history of the vampire-count, not the true characteristics of vampires, not the reasons for the inexplicable behaviour of so many people on so many occasions. Instead, the published version must be regarded as largely a work of fiction, created by Bram Stoker from the Harker Papers under the iron control of the master vampire. Too many people had already heard the Harkers' wild tale, and perhaps too many had already seen the Harker Papers, for the essential facts to be completely obfuscated, but only the most diligent cryptographer will be able to decode the secrets of *Dracula*.

As Dracula enters his third century in the spotlight, interest in the vampire continues to swell. Whether this is spurred by nostalgia for an era when a woman could utter "thank God for good brave men!" or when the sexual themes of a work about a vampire could pass virtually uncommented upon; fascination with the supernatural; a secret desire for immortality, however obtained; or fear of the vampires among us, Dracula and his descendants seem omnipresent in Western culture. Here, then, is the text of Stoker's powerful narrative with its secrets revealed—a look beneath the shroud so carefully placed by Stoker (or perhaps by Dracula himself) over the true history of the vampire-king and his hunters.

---

resulting from a reexamination of the Harker Papers by Stoker or someone else. Some also evidence additional editing by Dracula himself, further encrypting his secrets. Although the text presented in this volume follows the text of the first edition, noteworthy differences between it and the Abridged Text are indicated in situ.

Part I

THE TEXT OF *DRACULA*

I do not suppose there will be much of

interest to other people . . .

—MINA MURRAY HARKER
letter to Lucy Westenra

Dracula.
(London: Archibald Constable & Co., 1901)

1 The original title of the novel, as it appeared on the hand-lettered title page for the Manuscript, was *The Un-Dead*. Stoker's notes also indicate that he was considering "The Dead Un-Dead." The printed program for the prepublication theatrical reading (given to secure dramatic copyright at the Lyceum Theatre on 18 May 1897) billed the work as *Dracula, or the Un-Dead*. Stoker's contract with Constable & Co., signed on 20 May 1897, specified the title as *The Un-Dead*. However, no published English-language edition carried any title other than *Dracula*.

2 First published in 1897 by Constable & Co. in an edition of three thousand copies. A Colonial edition was published in 1897 by Hutchinson & Co. The first American edition did not appear until 1899. The first "paperback" edition appeared in 1901; it was published by Constable & Co. and contained (on the cover) the first illustration of the tale. The 1901 text, which was substantially abridged (see note 30 on p. xlix) was reprinted in 1994 as *Dracula: The Rare Text of 1901*. The first foreign translation was a 1901 Icelandic edition, under the title *Makt Myrkranna* [Powers of Darkness], abridged (by Stoker?) and translated by Valdimar Asmundsson. Stoker wrote a preface for the Icelandic edition, reproduced on pages 5–7.

DRACULA[1]

by

Bram Stoker[2]

To My Dear Friend Hommy-Beg[3]

Hall Caine.

3 Scholars agree that Stoker's dedication refers to writer Sir Thomas Henry Hall Caine (1853–1931), who dedicated to Stoker a collection of three novellas (*Cap'n Davy's Honeymoon*, *The Last Confession*, and *The Blind Mother*, in the 1893 *Cap'n Davy's Honeymoon*). Caine was a best-selling writer of his era, yet none of his works remain in print. He and Stoker were firm friends, and when Stoker died in 1912, Caine wrote an obituary titled "Bram Stoker: The Story of a Great Friendship." Caine's biographer, Vivien Allen, recounts that Stoker asked Caine for a loan in 1896, with the expectation that he would repay Caine from sales of a forthcoming book (*Dracula*). Caine's Manx grandmother reportedly called Caine "little Tommy," or in Manx, "an Thommy Beag" (pronounced "Hommy Beg").

4 This text appears in the English first edition and subsequent editions of *Dracula*.

HOW THESE PAPERS have been placed in sequence will be made manifest in the reading of them. All needless matters have been eliminated, so that a history almost at variance with the possibilities of later-day belief may stand forth as simple fact. There is throughout no statement of past things wherein memory may err, for all the records chosen are exactly contemporary, given from the standpoints and within the range of knowledge of those who made them.[4]

AUTHOR'S PREFACE [5]

THE READER OF this story will very soon understand how the events outlined in these pages have been gradually drawn together to make a logical whole. Apart from excising minor details which I considered unnecessary, I have let the people involved relate their experiences in their own way; but, for obvious reasons, I have changed the names of the people [6] and places concerned. In all other respects I leave the manuscript unaltered, in deference to the wishes of those who have considered it their duty to present it before the eyes of the public. [7]

I am quite convinced that there is no doubt whatever that the events here described really took place, however unbelievable and incomprehensible they might appear at first sight. And I am further convinced that they must always remain to some extent incomprehensible, although continuing research in psychology and natural sciences may, in years to come, give logical explanations of such strange happenings which, at present, neither scientists nor the secret police can understand. I state again that this mysterious tragedy which is here described is completely true in all its external respects, though naturally I have reached a different conclusion on certain points than those involved in the story. [8] But the events are incontrovertible, and so many people know of them that they cannot be denied. This series of crimes has not yet passed

5 This preface was written by Bram Stoker for the Icelandic edition of *Dracula*. As noted, the edition was published in 1901, but the preface was likely written as early as 1898. An English version of this preface first appeared in the 1986 *Bram Stoker Omnibus*, with an introduction and preface by the major *Dracula* collector Richard Dalby.

6 For convenience of reference, and in light of the difficulty in fixing any definite identification on the persons described in *Dracula*, they will be referred to in these notes by the names assigned by Stoker.

7 Stoker implies that he has been provided with the materials reproduced under the title *Dracula* and that he did no editing. If the Notes are understood—as they must be—to be Stoker's notes on the actual papers presented to him by his friends (referred to in these notes as the Harker Papers), then this statement must be rejected. It is clear from a careful examination of the Notes that in fact Stoker did alter many details by combining individuals, changing dates (and perhaps places), and inserting material that, by its nature, could not have been part of the Harker Papers. Why Stoker made these alterations will be considered in later notes.

There are also significant questions about the

authenticity of the Harker Papers themselves, the chief question being whether the papers accurately record the events that occurred. As will be seen, for the benefit of her colleagues, and not for purposes of publication, Mina Harker undertook to copy over by typewriter the various original source materials, which she identified as handwritten diary entries, phonographic recordings, and newspaper clippings. It is quite possible that in creating the typewritten transcript, Mina altered the journal and phonographic records. Her reasons for doing so will be considered in later notes. Furthermore, it may be that she or another member of the group altered the typewritten material before it was delivered to Stoker. Jonathan Harker himself admits—in his final "Note" on page 499—that "in all the mass of material of which the record is composed, there is hardly one authentic document; nothing but a mass of type-writing, except the later note-books of Mina and Seward and myself, and Van Helsing's memorandum."

8 Stoker never disclosed to the public what "different conclusions" he reached.

9 The name Jack the Ripper was given to a serial killer active in the East End of London in 1888 and was drawn from a letter sent to the Central News Agency purportedly written by the killer. Notwithstanding his enduring notoriety, more than a hundred years after the killer's gruesome career, there remains no agreement among scholars about the number of his victims. Generally attributed to his knife are: (1) Mary Ann (Polly) Nichols, died Friday, 31 August 1888; (2) Annie Chapman, murdered Saturday, 8 September 1888; (3) Elizabeth Stride, killed Sunday, 30 September 1888; (4) Catharine Eddowes, murdered that same date; and (5) Mary Jane (Marie Jeanette) Kelly, horribly slaughtered and disemboweled on Friday, 9 November 1888.

Although Stoker's sentence is somewhat convoluted, he does not mean to say that the Ripper murders were committed by Dracula,

from the memory—a series of crimes which appear to have originated from the same source, and which at the same time created as much repugnance in people everywhere as the murders of Jack the Ripper,[9] which came into the story a little later.[10] Various people's minds will go back to the remarkable group of foreigners who for many seasons together played a dazzling part in the life of the aristocracy here in London; and some will remember that one of them disappeared suddenly without apparent reason, leaving no trace. All the people who have willingly—or unwillingly—played a part in this remarkable story are known generally and well respected.[11] Both Jonathan Harker[12] and his wife (who is a woman of character) and Dr. Seward[13] are my friends and have been so for many years, and I have never doubted that they were telling the truth; and the highly respected scientist, who appears here under a pseudonym,[14] will also be too famous all over the educated world for his real name, which I have not desired to specify, to be hidden from people—least of all those who have from experience learnt to value and respect his genius and accomplishments, though they adhere to his views on life no more than I. But in our times it ought to be clear to all serious-thinking men that "there are more things in heaven and earth / than are dreamt of in your philosophy."[15]

London,
August 1898
B.S.

Mary Kelly, fifth victim of Jack the Ripper.
Photographer unknown, 1888

only that the public outcry was as loud. Others, however, do suggest an intersection of Dracula and the Ripper; see, for example, Rickey Shanklin and Mark Wheatley's brilliant series of comic books *Blood of the Innocent*, in which Dracula himself confronts the Ripper. In fact, no scholars have found any contemporary news accounts of any of the events recounted in *Dracula*, and the reports attributed to the *Pall Mall Gazette* (see text accompanying chapter 11, note 14) have been falsified.

The connection between the Ripper and vampires is not new, however. In the 6 October 1888 *East London Advertiser*, an anonymous article titled "A Thirst for Blood" declaimed: "It is so impossible to account, on any ordinary hypothesis, for these revolting acts of blood that the mind turns as it were instinctively to some theory of occult force, and myths of the Dark Ages arise before the imagination. Ghouls, vampires, blood-suckers . . . take form and seize control of the excited fancy. . . . [W]hat can be more appalling than the thought that there is a being in human shape stealthily moving about

a great city, burning with the thirst for human blood?" (quoted in Robert Eighteen-Bisang, "Dracula, Jack the Ripper, and A Thirst for Blood," *Ripperologist* 60 [Jul. 2005]: 3–12).

10 It is difficult to parse this sentence. Does Stoker mean that "This series of crimes . . . came into the story a little later" or that the Ripper murders of 1888 "came into the story a little later"? The latter seems unlikely, because the Ripper murders do not explicitly come into the story at all. However, there are tantalising hints of Dracula-Ripper connections, and Stoker may here be pointing the reader to the coincidental(?) location of at least one of Dracula's hideouts. (See chapter 20, note 3.)

11 Stoker went to great lengths to conceal the involvement of several people in the events. Among those mentioned in the Notes but eventually suppressed in the narrative are a painter named Francis Aytown or Aytonn, an undertaker, an undertaker's man, a maid engaged to the undertaker's man, and a "crank."

12 It is probable that Stoker concealed the identity of the lawyer under a name drawn from Joseph Harker, a scenic designer who worked at the Lyceum Theatre. Harker's 1924 memoir, *Studio and Stage*, reports Stoker as saying so. However, local historian Colin Waters, in *Whitby and the Dracula Connection*, suggests that the name Harker was borrowed from Fanny Harker, Stoker's landlady in Whitby. Interestingly, there is another lawyer mentioned in the Notes, with the last name of Young, although what rôle Young and his sister, another deleted person described in the Notes only as "shrewd" and "skeptical," played in the affair is unknown.

13 The identity of John (Jack) Seward remains unknown. In the Notes he is initially described as the "madhouse doctor." Kim Newman, in *Anno Dracula*, proposes that Seward is the man later known to the public as Jack the Ripper.

14 The "pseudonym" is Abraham Van Helsing. The Notes indicate that there were three figures involved in the hunt for Dracula who appear to have been combined in "Van Helsing": a detective inspector named Cotford; a psychic research agent, Alfred Singleton; and a "German professor," also described as a "German professor of history" and a "philosophic historian." In the Notes, this professor is tentatively identified as Max Windeshoeffel, a fictitious name apparently considered by Stoker but later dropped. Cotford and Singleton soon disappear from the Notes as well.

The most likely candidate for the real Van Helsing is Friedrich Max Müller (1823–1900), professor of modern European languages and comparative philology at Oxford. Professor of German language and literature Clemens Ruthner, in "Bloodsuckers with Teutonic Tongues," points out that Müller was also a specialist in religion and mythology and apparently was familiar with an article by Wilhelm Mannhardt on vampirism. McNally and Florescu (*The Essential* Dracula) erroneously identify Müller as the author of *"Magyarland,"* references to which appear throughout the Notes (see chapter 1, note 18). However, *"Magyarland"* does refer to Müller's seminal essay "The Science of Language."

Sir Christopher Frayling, editor of the 1991 book *Vampyres: Lord Byron to Count Dracula*, believes that Stoker and Müller had corresponded in the 1880s but cites no evidence. A letter from Müller to Henry Irving is extant (cited by Ruthner), requesting tickets for a performance of *Faust* on 14 April 1886, but though the letter was undoubtedly seen by Stoker in his capacity as Irving's secretary, this is hardly conclusive proof of correspondence between Stoker and Müller.

David B. Dickens, in "The German Matrix of Stoker's *Dracula*," makes the fascinating argument that "Van Helsing" was in fact an expatriate German professor teaching in Amsterdam. He points out the Professor's frequent use of German expressions, grammar, and sentence construction and notes that the only identifications of him as Dutch are by Quincey Morris (who speaks no foreign languages) and the madman Renfield. Dickens also notes that like the Professor, whose son died young, Müller suffered the loss of a sixteen-year-old daughter.

15 Stoker here slightly misquotes the Prince of Denmark in *Hamlet*, act 1, scene 5, omitting "Horatio" at the end of the first line. It should be recalled that Henry Irving repeatedly performed the rôle of Hamlet as well as other Shakespearean parts. Stoker's first meeting with Irving was on the occasion of Irving's performance as Hamlet (11 December 1876) in Dublin, a performance Stoker reviewed favourably.

Professor Friedrich Max Müller.
Strand Magazine, July 1893

Henry Irving as Hamlet.
From the statue by E. Onslow Ford
(Guildhall, City of London)

Chapter 1[1]

Jonathan Harker's Journal
—(kept in shorthand.)[2]

3 May. Bistritz.[3]—Left Munich[4] at 8:35 P.M., on 1st May, arriving at Vienna[5] early next morning; should have arrived at 6:46, but train was an hour late.[6] Buda-Pesth seems a wonderful place, from the glimpse which I got of it from the train and the little I could walk through the streets.[7] I feared to go very far from the station, as we arrived late and would start as near the correct time as possible. The impression I had was that we were leaving the West and entering the East; the most Western of splendid bridges over the Danube,[8] which is here of noble width and depth, took us among the traditions of Turkish rule.[9]

We left in pretty good time, and came after nightfall to Klausenburgh.[10] Here I stopped for the night at the Hotel Royale. I had for dinner, or rather supper, a chicken done up some way with red pepper, which was very good but thirsty. (*Mem.*, get recipe for Mina.)[11] I asked the waiter, and he said it was called "paprika hendl,"[12] and that, as it was a national dish, I should be able to get it anywhere along the Carpathians.[13] I found my smattering of German very useful here; indeed, I don't know how I should be able to get on without it.[14]

Having had some time at my disposal when in London,[15] I had visited the British Museum,[16] and made search among the books and maps in the library regarding Transylvania;[17] it had struck me that some foreknowledge of the country could hardly fail to have some importance in dealing with a

1 It appears from the Notes that Stoker originally intended the work to begin with a chapter consisting of correspondence, including a letter from Sir Robert Parton, president of the Law Society, referring a new client, Count Dracula, to Peter Hawkins; a letter from Kate Reed to Lucy Westenra, telling her of a visit by Jonathan Harker to the school to visit Mina Murray; and correspondence between Mr. Hawkins (later revealed to be Harker's employer) and Count Dracula concerning the purchase of residential property in London. This chapter has never been published, and little is known about it, except that Harker would, at its end, "start for Munich." In the Manuscript, the present chapter is plainly headed "ii" (changed to "I") and the second page is numbered "103."

A succeeding chapter, also discarded, is outlined in the Notes as set in Munich, describing Harker's arrival, his stay at the Mar[indecipherable] Hoff (later disguised in the Notes as the Quatre Saisons hotel), and visits to a museum and a "Dead House" (a morgue). The Notes place "adventure snowstorm and wolf" on 27 April. This event has been identified by some scholars as the material published by Stoker's widow in 1914 as a short story titled "Dracula's Guest," in *Dracula's Guest and Other Weird Stories.* Clive Leatherdale argues in "Stoker's Banana Skins" that the chapter may have been intended for publication as a short story in 1890. It is unknown who ultimately excised the chapter from *Dracula*. "Dracula's Guest" is included in this volume as appendix 1, with notes demonstrating the few ties between that story and *Dracula* as well as numerous inconsistencies between them.

The material following was therefore likely initially intended to be the third chapter of the work.

2 Modern shorthand was invented in England by the educator Isaac Pitman (1813–1897) in 1837. Breaking new ground, his Stenographic Soundhand used phonetics, rather than normal spelling, to represent full words. Different degrees of shading indicated the various phonetic sounds. Although it is considered perhaps the most rapid shorthand system—making it a preferred choice among many court reporters today—and it predominates in England, the Pitman method has been largely supplanted in the United States by Gregg Shorthand, a system that uses curves instead of Pitman's shading to indicate sounds. The Irish-born John Robert Gregg (1867–1948) introduced his system in *Light-Line Phonography* (1888). Although Harker likely used Pitman's method, many alternative systems did flourish. In 1888, The *Encyclopædia Britannica* (9th ed.) estimated that no fewer than 483 distinct systems of English shorthand had been published ("and doubtless many more of them have been invented for private use").

It is evident from Jonathan's expectation, expressed later (see text accompanying chapter 3, note 50), that communications written in shorthand would be intelligible by Mina Harker (neé Wilhelmina Murray), either because the two of them employed the same "private" shorthand or because they knew a common, standardised shorthand method.

3 Capital of the county of Bistriz-Naszod, on the Bistritz River (the Hungarian name is Besztercze). It had a population in 1896 of only 10,300 (Karl Baedeker, *Austria, Including Hungary, Transylvania, Dalmatia, and Bosnia*; hereafter referred to as "1896 Austria 'Baedeker'").

4 München in German, the fourth largest town in the German empire, was the capital of the kingdom of Bavaria. Its notable buildings lined the Ludwigstrasse and Maximilianstrasse, and the *Encyclopædia Britannica* (9th ed.) called it "almost unrivalled for architectural magnificence among the smaller capitals of Europe." By the late nineteenth century, it was also becoming one of the great industrial centres of Europe, especially renowned for its beer production. If Harker truly spent five days there, as the Notes indicate, he may have had business unrelated to Dracula; the tourist attractions of Munich can hardly have held his attention on such an important trip.

In the Notes, the agent of the English solicitor travels to Munich, visits a Munich "dead house" (where he first catches sight of Dracula), has an "adventure snowstorm and wolf" (see appendix 1, "Dracula's Guest"), and visits the Old Pinakothek Museum (a picture gallery and treasure-house of ancient and modern art) and the Opera (the latter to see Wagner's *Flying Dutchman*) before travelling by train to Styria, where he is met by Dracula in the guise of a coachman.

The Munich dead house appears in several works of Victorian literature. The law in Munich required all who died to be laid out in a dead house for three days before interment. Each adult corpse had a ring affixed to the thumb, and a string was tied to the ring and went through a pulley above and communicated with a bell in the attendant's room. The purpose was to alert the attendant if one of the "corpses" moved. Charles Dudley Warner, in his 1872 travelogue *Saunterings*, remarks, "How frightened he would be if the bell should ever sound, and he should go into that hall of the dead to see who rang! And yet it is a most wise and humane provision; and many years ago, there is a tradition, an entombment alive was prevented by it." In *Life on the Mississippi* (1883), Mark Twain recounts his own visit to a Munich dead house and a subsequent conversation with a retired night-watchman.

5 Wien in German, the capital and largest city of the Austro-Hungarian empire, had by the late nineteenth century established its reputation as the intellectual and material capital of Austria and possessed large and handsome modern buildings on a par with any European capital. The *Encyclopædia Britannica* (9th ed.) termed the Ring-Strasse "one of the most imposing achievements of recent street architecture."

In the Abridged Text, Harker's journal entry has been considerably shortened to omit mention of any stops between Munich and Klausenburg, and the recipe he records for his fiancée Mina is also omitted.

6 We will learn that Harker departed from the offices of his employer, Peter Hawkins, in Exeter and apparently has travelled to Munich, Vienna, Buda-Pesth, and hence to Bistritz. The Notes indicate that Hawkins received a telegram from Dracula on Monday, 24 April. Harker departed the following day for Paris, arriving there early on the morning of 26 April; he left for Munich that night. In fact, the Notes are quite specific about the trains, recording an 8:35 P.M. departure from Munich (on 1 May), a 6:45 A.M. arrival in Salzburg (2 May), an 8:25 A.M. departure from Vienna (2 May), a 1:30 P.M. arrival in Buda-Pesth (2 May), a 2:00 P.M. departure from Buda-Pesth to Klausenburg, arriving at 10:34 P.M. (2 May), an 8:00 A.M. arrival in Klausenburg (3 May), and an arrival in Bistritz at 8:00 P.M. (3 May). This ties to the date of the journal entry, which must have been made late that evening at Harker's hotel.

There is no apparent reason for Harker's trip to Munich, and it would have been far more expedient to have travelled directly to Vienna. In 1910, the trip from London to Vienna could be made in about thirty-seven hours, via Dover, Calais, Brussels, Cologne, Mayence, Darmstadt, Würzburg, Nuremberg, Ratisbon, Passau, and Linz; from Paris, the direct journey could have been made in as few as twenty-six hours by special sleeping-car service or thirty-three hours by regular express, via Strasbourg and Munich (W. J. Rolfe, *Satchel Guide to Europe*). Instead, Harker took from 25 April to 2 May to travel to Vienna, consuming eight days.

We may conclude that Harker had been to Paris previously, for otherwise he surely would have commented on the City of Light, a much more impressive sight than Buda-Pesth. He apparently spent five days (27 April–1 May) in Munich, but nothing is known definitely of his activities there. Although some scholars assert that "Dracula's Guest," appendix 1 to this volume, is a partial record of Harker's stay in Munich, there is substantial reason to doubt that the individual described there is Harker. See the notes to appendix 1.

7 In fact, Harker must have run rapidly through the streets if the arrival and departure times in the Notes are correct. The train from Vienna arrived at either the West Station of the Hungarian State Railways, at the north end of the Waitzner-Ring, or the East Station at the end of Kerepeser-Strasse, depending on whether the train traveled via Marchegg or Bruck. Both lines offered express trains, which made the journey in approximately five hours, matching the schedule of the Notes.

However, it is possible that Harker was confused about the local time. Standardisation of time was a new phenomenon. Although the modern system of time zones based on Greenwich was adopted at the International Meridian Conference in Washington, D.C., in 1884, only twenty-seven countries attended the conference (including Austria-Hungary), and many countries were slow to adopt the system. Central Europe was far from uniform; as late as 1910, Belgium and Holland used Greenwich time, whereas Switzerland, Italy, and central Germany used the time of fifteen degrees east of Greenwich, and France had still not converted from Paris time. The 1896 Austria "Baedeker" advises that Vienna local time is five minutes in advance of central Europe time, which is observed by the railways.

In 1873, the cities of Buda (Ofen in German), Ó Buda (Alt-Ofen), Köbánya (Steinbruch), and Pest or Pesth, across the Danube from each other, were joined to become the official capital of Hungary. Buda-Pesth (usually termed

Pest.
John Paget, *Hungary and Transylvania* (1850)

Buda-Pesth, ca. 1900.

The Széchenyi Chain Bridge.

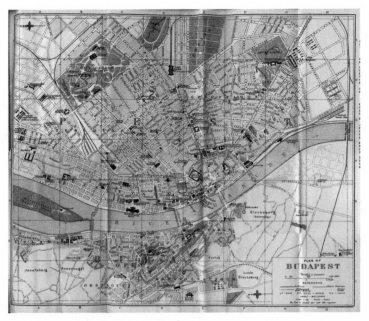

Budapest.
Bradshaw's Continental Railway, Steam Transit, and General Guide.
(London: Henry Blacklock & Co., Ltd., 1903)

Budapest in English publications) was the second residence of the Austrian emperor, the seat of the Hungarian ministry, diet (parliament), and supreme courts, and the headquarters of the Houvéds, or Hungarian Landwehr. In 1880, the population of Budapest was 370,767, including a garrison of 10,000 troops of the Austro-Hungarian monarchy; by 1896, the population was 506,000, with a garrison of 11,000 troops and over 100,000 Jews (1896 Austria "Baedeker").

8 Harker presumably refers to the Széchenyi Chain Bridge, a suspension bridge over the Danube connecting Buda and Pesth, built at the behest of Count István Széchenyi (1791–1860), the great Hungarian reformer popularly known as "The Greatest Hungarian." Constructed by the British engineers William Tierney Clark and Adam Clark in 1842–1849, the bridge was one of the largest in Europe: 1,278 feet long and 42 feet above the mean water level. Unlike modern suspension bridges, it uses a great chain rather than cables. At the ends are four colossal stone lions. In 1897, construction of another suspension bridge across the Danube, known as the Elisabeth Bridge, commenced in Buda-Pesth; when completed in 1903, it was the longest in the world, spanning 951 feet. Both bridges were destroyed in 1945 and reconstructed.

9 Buda was captured by Sultan Süleyman in 1541, who garrisoned the town and established a vizier's seat there. It remained under Turkish control for nearly 150 years, until the allied Germans (under Charles of Lorraine and Lewis of Baden) expelled the Turks in 1686.

10 Spelled "Klausenburg" later in the text (Kolozsvár in Hungarian, modern-day Cluj, with a population over 200,000). According to the 1896 Austria "Baedeker," this was a town of 33,000 inhabitants, "very animated in winter" and "the headquarters of the numerous noblesse of Transylvania." The Hotel Royale is fictional; however, the "Baedeker" recommends the Kónigen von England (Queen of England) hotel, and the name likely appealed to Harker (and suggested the alias). McNally and Florescu (*The Essential Dracula*) identify the hotel as the Royal Mathias Hotel, a venue not listed by the "Baedeker" and so unlikely to have been chosen by the Englishman. In the Manuscript, the hotel is identified as the Kron, and the phrase "which the Count had advised in his letter" has been deleted.

11 "Mina" will be identified later as Wilhelmina Murray, to whom Harker is apparently engaged. (Mina later refers in her correspondence to Harker's proposal, and Lucy Westenra calls Mina "engaged." This must have predated Harker's departure.)

12 John Paget's 1850 *Hungary and Transylvania* recounts: "I do not think I have yet enlightened the reader as to the mystery of a *paprika hendel*; to forget it, would be a depth of ingratitude of which, I trust, I shall never be guilty. Well, then, reader, if ever you travel in Hungary, and want a dinner or supper quickly, never mind the variety of dishes your host names, but fix at once on

paprika hendel. Two minutes afterwards, you will hear signs of a revolution in the *basse cour*; the cocks and hens are in alarm; one or two of the largest, and probably oldest members of their unfortunate little community, are seized, their necks wrung, and, while yet fluttering, immersed in boiling water. Their coats and skins come off at once; a few unmentionable preparatory operations are rapidly despatched—probably under the traveller's immediate observation—the wretches are cut into pieces, thrown into a pot, with water, butter, flour, cream, and an inordinate quantity of red pepper, or paprika, and very shortly after, a number of bits of fowl are seen swimming in a dish of hot greasy gravy, quite delightful to think of."

A more modern version of the recipe is as follows.

1 chicken, cut up, 8 to 10 pieces
2 Tbs oil
1 onion, grated
1 Tbs Hungarian paprika
Salt
2 to 3 Tbs tomato paste

Wash and dry the chicken pieces. Heat the oil in a pan, add the grated onion, and brown. Add the paprika, and when the mixture bubbles, put in the chicken pieces, turning to coat. Salt the chicken and cover. Braise over a low heat, turning the chicken from time to time, for 45 minutes to 1 hour. Add tomato paste to thicken if desired. (This is a lower-cholesterol version of Paget's recipe, which was thickened with butter, cream, and flour.)

Harker's interest in this rural "comfort food" is a reminder of how foreign Hungarian cuisine was to the English palate. Although Isabella Beeton's *Book of Household Management* (1861) and other popular English cookbooks of the day included curried and other Indian dishes, these tastes were a novelty.

13 Second only to the Alps as the greatest mountain range of central Europe, the Carpathians extend in a semicircle from Presburg on the Danube to Orsova on the same

Map of Carpathians, showing contemporary place names.
Encarta

river, over a distance of 880 miles. At the time of the events of *Dracula*, they lay almost entirely within the borders of the Austro-Hungarian empire, with one great mass in Hungary and the other in Transylvania.

14 The 1896 Austria "Baedeker" notes that the official language of Transylvania is Hungarian. "German, however, will carry the traveller through in most places. . . . Travellers among the mountains will find the knowledge of a few Roumanian phrases convenient." Harker's linguistic skills apparently extend only to English and German. Later, en route to Bukovina, he notes that he is unable to understand "the languages" his fellow passengers are speaking. Harker may have intended to conceal his knowledge of German from Dracula, for Dracula apparently insisted in his original commission to Harker's employer that any agent to Dracula not speak German. There is no direct evidence as to whether Harker's employer himself spoke German, but he must not have or else Dracula would not have consented to his visit. See chapter 2, note 16.

15 In fact, Harker had only one day to do his research. According to the Notes, Dracula telegraphed Peter Hawkins on 24 April. Harker departed London at 8:05 P.M. on 25 April. The material beginning with this sentence has been cut and pasted from elsewhere in the Manuscript, suggesting it may have been part of the earlier discarded chapters. The phrase "when in London" is inserted in the Manuscript in what appears to be Stoker's hand.

16 The core of the British Museum's original holdings consisted of the vast collection—a museum in its own right—of Sir Hans Sloane, who sold it to the nation for far less than its real value upon his death in 1753. Sloane's collection, comprising valuable prints, drawings, and manuscripts as well as fossils, precious stones, dried plants, and human and animal skeletons, was housed along with the Harleian Library (a collection of legal documents compiled by Robert Harley, the first Earl of Oxford and Mortimer) and Sir Robert Cotton's library of Greek and Hebrew manuscripts and Anglo-Saxon charters in a house once belonging to the Dukes of Montague. The museum was opened to the public in 1759. In its early years, the British Museum was, in historian Roy Porter's words, "ill-managed and inaccessible" (*London: A Social History*); in fact, the ninth edition of the *Encyclopædia Britannica* notes that the fields behind the museum were once "so solitary, that they were usually selected as the place for deciding what were called affairs of honour." Throughout the nineteenth century, however, the museum went through several crucial expansions and made many important acquisitions, including the Rosetta Stone, sculptures from the Parthenon, and the books of George III's library. By 1883, the natural history exhibits were moved off-site to a location in South Kensington, ultimately becoming the separate Natural History Museum in 1963; the British Library was split off as a distinct organization in 1973.

The Reading Room of the British Museum opened in 1857 and was accessible only to those visitors with a "reader's ticket." Every reader was provided with a chair, a folding desk, a small hinged shelf for books, pens, and ink, a blotting pad, and a peg for one's hat. On a visit to the Reading Room in the mid-1970s, this editor obtained a brochure listing famous readers, including Karl Marx but not including Jonathan Harker or another famous user, Sherlock Holmes. When a guard who appeared quite ancient was questioned about this omission, he curtly stated that he had "never seen them here." After being opened to the public in 2000, the Reading Room closed for restoration. Today it is again in its 1857 splendour and houses public-access computer touch screens for the museum's extensive databases. The reading materials, however, now reside in the new, separately housed British Library, near St. Pancras station.

17 The Notes make clear that Stoker originally planned to recount a trip to Styria rather than Transylvania.

It is tantalising to note that Countess Mircalla Karnstein, whose vampiric activities were reported to the public in Joseph Sheridan Le Fanu's "Carmilla" (1872), was of a "very ancient and noble family" of Styria. Could Mircalla/ Carmilla and Dracula have been related? See "Dracula's Family Tree" in Part II. That Stoker considered siting Harker's adventures in Styria suggests that his first instinct may have been to conceal the true location of Dracula's castle in a region already associated with vampires. Whether Transylvania is in fact the true location or merely a more plausible "cover story" will be considered further later. Bernard Davies, in "Bram Stoker's Transylvania—A Critical Reassessment," speculates that the Hungarian orientalist and traveller Arminius Vambéry may have suggested to Stoker that Transylvania would be a suitable setting for the events described in the narrative. See chapter 18, note 41.

"A strange little country is this Transylvania!" remarks John Paget, writing in 1850 (*Hungary and Transylvania*). "Very likely the reader never heard its name before, and yet some hundred years ago it was in close alliance with England; and, long before religious liberty, annual parliaments, payment of members, and the election of magistrates were dreamed of, amongst us, they were granted to Transylvania, by a solemn charter of their Prince, the Emperor of Austria. Here is this country on the very limits of European civilization, yet possessing institutions and rights, for which the most civilized have not been thought sufficiently advanced." Transylvania belonged to the Roman province of Dacia until the eleventh century, when it became part of Hungary. Conquered by the Turks in the fifteenth century, it was a semiautonomous principality until annexed to Austria in 1713.

18 It is not possible to know exactly what books Harker consulted, but the Notes suggest that they included the following:

Charles Boner, *Transylvania: Its Products and Its People* (1865).

Andrew F. Crosse, *Round About the Carpathians* (1878).

A Fellow of the Carpathian Society, *"Magyarland": Being the Narrative of our Travels Through the Highlands and Lowlands of Hungary* (1881).

Major E. C. Johnson, *On the Track of the Crescent: Erratic Notes from the Piræus to Pesth* (1885).

Rev. W. Henry Jones, and Lewis L. Kropf, *The Folk-Tales of the Magyars* (1889).

William Wilkinson, *An Account of the Principalities of Wallachia and Moldavia: with various Political Observations Relating to Them* (1820).

It will be seen that many of Harker's observations parallel closely the descriptions provided by these earlier travellers and writers. There are many possible explanations:

1. The similarity is coincidental and is a testament to Harker's observational skills. As will be seen from various inconsistencies later in Harker's observations, this is not likely.

2. Harker was a lazy journalist and copied the descriptions into his journal later. This also seems unlikely, inasmuch as the descriptions add little to the vital information about Dracula which Harker aimed (later) to preserve. It is possible that Harker was encouraged to add the material by Stoker to expand the Harker Papers beyond a bare outline of "my encounters with Dracula."

3. In preparing the Harker Papers, Mina Harker added the descriptions, to enhance the public image of her husband.

4. In preparing the manuscript of *Dracula* from the Harker Papers, Stoker himself added the descriptions, to "pad out" the work for commercial purposes or out of some sense of "artistry."

nobleman of that country.[18] I find that the district he[19] named is in the extreme east of the country, just on the borders of three states, Transylvania,[20] Moldavia,[21] and Bukovina,[22] in the midst of the Carpathian mountains; one of the wildest and least known portions of Europe. I was not able to light on any map or work giving the exact locality of the Castle Dracula, as there are no maps of this country as yet to compare with our own Ordnance Survey maps;[23] but I found that Bistritz, the post town[24] named by Count Dracula, is a fairly well-known place. I shall enter here some of my notes, as they may refresh my memory when I talk over my travels with Mina.[25]

In the population of Transylvania there are four distinct nationalities: Saxons in the south, and mixed with them the Wallachs, who are descendants of the Dacians; Magyars in the west, and Szekelys in the east and north.[26] I am going among the latter, who claim to be descended from Attila and the Huns.[27] This may be so, for when the Magyars conquered the country in the eleventh century they found the Huns settled in it. I read that every known superstition in the world is gathered into the horseshoe of the Carpathians, as if it were the centre of some sort of imaginative whirlpool; if so my stay may be very interesting. (*Mem.*, I must ask the Count all about them.)[28]

I did not sleep well, though my bed was comfortable enough, for I had all sorts of queer dreams.[29] There was a dog howling all night under my window, which may have had something to do with it; or it may have been the paprika, for I had to drink up all the water in my carafe, and was still thirsty. Towards morning I slept and was wakened by the continuous knocking at my door, so I guess I must have been sleeping soundly then. I had for breakfast more paprika, and a sort of porridge of maize flour which they said was "mamaliga,"[30] and egg-plant stuffed with forcemeat, a very excellent dish, which they call "impletata." (*Mem.*, get recipe for this also.)[31] I had to hurry breakfast, for the train started a little before eight, or rather it ought to have done so, for after rushing to the station at 7:30 I had to sit in the carriage for more than an hour before we began to move. It seems to me that the further East you go the more unpunctual are the trains.[32] What ought they to be in China?[33]

All day long we seemed to dawdle[34] through a country

However, there is another explanation that cannot be discarded: Harker never went to Transylvania. If Harker (or Stoker) determined to conceal the true location of Dracula's castle (for reasons considered in the introductory essay "The Context of *Dracula*"), a "cover story" was needed, to provide a plausible place of origin for Dracula. Where better than the legend-shrouded land of Transylvania? If one were constructing such a lie, then a careful liar would import accurate descriptions of the imagined locale into the narrative. This realisation goes a long way towards explaining the errors and plagiarisms in the geographical descriptions appearing in the published version of *Dracula*.

Note that this is the first mention of the purpose of the trip recorded by Harker.

19 The "nobleman" remains nameless. This oddity could be the result of the deletion of introductory material.

20 Its German name is Siebenbürgen, the source of which name is most likely Cibinburc, "the fortress on the Cibin." Or the name may refer to seven fortified towns in the Saxon region of Transylvania (the name means "seven castles" or "seven towns" in German). It is called Erdély by the Magyars, and Ardealu by the Roumanians, both meaning "forest-land." It lies between Hungary on the west and Roumania on the east.

21 Harker errs here in describing Moldavia as a "state." A former principality, Moldavia, together with Wallachia, was part of the kingdom of Roumania, which gained its independence in 1878, after publication of the Boner and Crosse books on which Harker apparently relied for his information (see note 18 above). Its chief town was Jassy, not far from the Pruth River. Moldavia is situated between the Carpathians to the west, the Dniester River to the east, and Wallachia to the south.

22 The Bukowina, as the 1896 Austria "Baedeker" calls it, was severed from Moldavia and annexed to Austria in 1786. A hilly, wooded region, it had a population at the time of *Dracula* of about 600,000, consisting of Ruthenians, Roumanians, Germans, Poles, and Armenians. Gernauti (Czernowitz) was its capital, from which it was administered by an Austrian governor, and German was its principal language.

23 The Board of Ordnance—Britain's defence ministry—began surveying southern Britain in 1791, in part to prepare for impending war with France. Its first map, a one-inch to one-mile map of Kent, was published in 1801. By the Victorian era, the Ordnance Survey was producing detailed maps of varying scales for Ireland as well as the whole of Great Britain.

24 A "post town" is a town (or collection of villages) with a head post office, today generally the focus of a postal code. Historically, a town was also called a "post town" to denote that post-horses were stabled there, for the use of post-riders or for hire by travellers.

25 This sentence is added to the Manuscript in Stoker's handwriting. It probably appeared in earlier excised material.

26 The source of Harker's information here appears to be Major E. C. Johnson's 1885 *On the Track of the Crescent*. Johnson writes: "This strange country, which was originally a part of Dacia, is inhabited by Magyars, Saxons, Wallachs, and Székelys. The Magyars inhabit the west, the Székelys the north and east, and the Saxons the south, with them the Wallachs—the descendants of the Dacians—being mixed in great numbers. The Székelys—who claim to be descended from Attila and the Huns—were found settled on the eastern frontier when the country was conquered by the Magyars, and the two races at once fraternised. This was in the eleventh century. . . . To replace the waste of inhabitants in the constant wars of which Transylvania was the theatre, colonists were brought from Germany, and these colonists were the ancestors of the present Saxons of that country."

Emily Gerard.

The 1896 Austria "Baedeker" gives a different description of the inhabitants. The governing or "privileged" races were the Magyars, including the Szekelys, about 698,000, and the Saxons, who numbered about 217,000. However, the largest population was the Roumanians or Wallachians, which the "Baedeker" puts at 1,270,000. Smaller groups included the Armenians (8,800), Gypsies (88,000), Jews (26,000), Slovaks, Ruthenians, Bulgarians, Servians, and Greeks. The "Baedeker" estimates the total population at 2,251,000. These statistics are close to those given by Emily Gerard in *The Land Beyond the Forest* (1888). While Harker surely must have possessed a "Baedeker"—it is hard to imagine a European traveller without a copy—it does not appear that he read Gerard's book; otherwise, he would have had more information about Transylvanian customs respecting vampires. However, he may have read the chapters previously printed as Gerard's 1885 article "Transylvanian Supersititions," for Stoker lists that article in the Notes.

27 The Huns were a nomadic Tartar tribe. Attila (ca. 406–453), known as the "Scourge of God," was the son of the king of the Huns. In 434, he succeeded to the rule of an array of tribes and led them to conquer a region stretching from the Rhine to the frontiers of China. In 451, he marched his hordes westward but was defeated in the valley of the Marne by Theodoric, king of the Visigoths, and Ætius, the Roman leader, in one of the bloodiest battles ever waged, with over 250,000 dead left on the fields. Many regarded this event as the "saving" of Western civilisation from the "inferior" races of the East. Legend recounts that upon Attila's death (some believe he was murdered by his wife on their wedding day, others attribute his death to drunkenness and ruptured esophageal varices; see Michael A. Babcock's *The Night Attila Died*), he was buried in three coffins, of gold, silver, and iron, respectively, and his grave diggers were executed to conceal his burial place.

Edward Gibbon, who in his eighteenth-century *History of the Decline and Fall of the Roman Empire* reports that "modern" Hungarians trace Attila's ancestry to Ham, son of Noah, provides the following description of Attila: "His features, according to the observation of a Gothic historian, bore the stamp of his national origin . . . a large head, a swarthy complexion, small, deep-seated eyes, a flat nose, a few hairs in the place of a beard, broad shoulders, and a short square body, of a nervous strength, though of a disproportioned form. The haughty step and demeanour of the king of the Huns expressed the consciousness of his superiority above the rest of mankind; and he had a custom of fiercely rolling his eyes, as if he wished to enjoy the terror which he inspired. . . . He delighted in war; but, after he had ascended the throne in a mature age, his head, rather than his hand, achieved the conquest of the North; and the fame of an adventurous soldier was usefully exchanged for that of a prudent and successful general."

Johnson (*On the Track of the Crescent*) also asserts that the Szekelys claim to be descended from Attila.

28 At least the "nobleman" now has a title, "Count." This is likely fictional. The title is meaningless among Roumanian aristocracy, and the long line of Gothic villains styled "Count"—including Count Morano in Ann Radcliffe's *The*

Mysteries of Udolpho (1794), Count de Bruno in her *The Italian, or the Confessional of the Black Penitents* (1797), Lord Byron's Count Manfred, in his poem "Manfred" (1817), and Count Fosco in Wilkie Collins's *The Moonstone* (1868)—may have suggested this honorific.

29 The following phrase, which appears in the Manuscript, is deleted from the published narrative: "of the Deadhouse at Munich which gets more strange and terrible to me whenever I think of it. It all seems so strange and mysterious."

30 A dish like the Italian polenta, simple boiled cornmeal.

31 The simplest version of impletata is a scooped-out eggplant stuffed with the pulped eggplant, ground meat, breadcrumbs, and butter, and baked. Dozens of recipes are widely available in English, under "stuffed eggplant."

The details of Harker's meals and his remarks that follow about Eastern trains do not appear in the Abridged Text.

32 On 7 September 1827, the first section of Austrian rail opened for transport; it was opened systemwide in 1832. This was the first narrow-gauge steam-operated railway in any of the Germanic states. In 1857 the undertaking passed to the Kaiserin Elizabeth Railway Company, which operated the Vienna-Salzburg line, and in 1869 that company rebuilt the railway to standard gauge, converted it to locomotive working, and made several improvements. By the late nineteenth century, the system was well developed, although the 1896 Austria "Baedeker" cautions that in Transylvania, imperfect connections and a scarcity of trains on the branch railways "render deviations from the main lines very inconvenient." The trains provided at least three classes of service (and in some cases, four—the last without seats). The "Baedeker" characterises the second-class carriages as "sometimes nearly as good of those of the first class in England" and describes the typical third-class passengers as "generally quiet and respectable."

Johnson (*On the Track of the Crescent*) describes his departure from Buda-Pesth for Transylvania: "I was at the Theiss Railway Station. ... All was hubbub and bustle.... Representatives of every nation under the sun seemed to be jostling together in the motley crew. Slovachs from the Eastern Carpathians, Wallachs, Saxon colonists from South Transylvania, Dalmatians, Bulgarians, Serbs, Croats, Poles, Lithuanians, Turks, Jews, infidels and heretics, all in one confused mass, struggling and squeezing to get to the ticket-office, if I can dignify the small hole through which the official put his head by such a name. At last ... I was 'ticketed,' luggage and all ... and deposited in a gorgeous, velvet-lined, first-class carriage. From this safe retreat I watched the surging, struggling crowd, which besieged the third-class carriages, and disputed possession of the station with mountains of milk-cans and sacks of flour."

The notion that the trains were "unpunctual" may be drawn from Emily Gerard's *The Land Beyond the Forest*, in which she comments, "The railway communications are very badly managed."

33 Clive Leatherdale, in *Bram Stoker's Dracula Unearthed* (hereafter referred to as *Dracula Unearthed*), observes that the joke is misplaced: Chinese railways of the time were well managed. The limited Chinese railroad lines that were constructed in the nineteenth century (the first was not built until 1876) were largely financed and built by foreign concessionaires; the two main Manchurian lines, the Chinese Eastern Railway and the South Manchurian Railway, were Russian ventures with little Chinese participation, and the Shantung railway from Kiaochow to Tsinan was a German-financed and -operated line.

34 The 1896 Austria "Baedeker" indicates that the journey from Klausenburg to Bistritz is only 74 miles and should take 4¾ hours by rail. Although the guidebook warns that trains in Austria do not generally travel faster than 25 miles per hour, the length of this journey seems excessive. This is the first of many geographical lacunae that suggest the region has been fictionalised rather than actually observed.

35 Leatherdale (*Dracula Unearthed*) warns that hilltop towns are not generally found in snowy climes like the Carpathians. Gerald Walker and Lorraine Wright, in "Locating *Dracula*: Contextualising the Geography of Transylvania," disagree: "The block and step structure of the Carpathians allowed cultivation in the midst of the mountains. There were actually farms and villages in the zone [identified by the narrators] as nearly empty." The grade approaching the Borgo Pass is gentle, and the hillsides rolling. This and many of the remaining "tourist" descriptions in these paragraphs do not appear in the Abridged Text.

36 Compare Johnson's description in *On the Track of the Crescent*: "The women wore a loose-sleeved white under-garment or chemisette, and over this a coloured apron called a Catrintsa, which descended both before and behind, and fitted so tightly as to show the figure. They also wore necklaces and large earrings, white cloths on the head which descended on the back of the neck, coloured stockings and ankle-boots. Some of the women wore that which I constantly saw afterwards in Transylvania—a broad belt or girdle, called an Obreska, tightly round the

The Borgo Pass, looking west.
Photograph by Leslie S. Klinger, May 2007

which was full of beauty of every kind. Sometimes we saw little towns or castles on the top of steep hills such as we see in old missals;[35] sometimes we ran by rivers and streams which seemed from the wide stony margin on each side of them to be subject to great floods. It takes a lot of water, and running strong, to sweep the outside edge of a river clear. At every station there were groups of people, sometimes crowds, and in all sorts of attire. Some of them were just like the peasants at home or those I saw coming through France and Germany, with short jackets and round hats and home-made trousers; but others were very picturesque. The women looked pretty, except when you got near them, but they were very clumsy about the waist. They had all full white sleeves of some kind or other, and the most of them had big belts with a lot of strips of something fluttering from them like the dresses in a ballet, but of course there were petticoats under them.[36] The strangest figures we saw were the Slovaks, who are more barbarian than the rest, with their big cowboy hats, great baggy dirty-white trousers, white linen shirts, and enormous heavy leather belts, nearly a foot wide, all studded over with brass nails.[37] They wore high boots, with their trousers tucked into them, and had long black hair and heavy black moustaches. They are very picturesque, but do not look prepossessing. On the stage they would be set down at once as some old Oriental band of brigands. They are, however, I am told, very harmless and rather wanting in natural self-assertion.

It was on the dark side of twilight when we got to Bistritz, which is a very interesting old place.[38] Being practically on the frontier—for the Borgo Pass[39] leads from it into Bukovina—it has had a very stormy existence, and it certainly shows marks of it. Fifty years ago a series of great fires took place, which made terrible havoc on five separate occasions.[40] At the very beginning of the seventeenth century it underwent a siege of three weeks and lost 13,000 people, the casualties of war proper being assisted by famine and disease.

Count Dracula[41] had directed me to go to the Golden Krone Hotel,[42] which I found, to my great delight, to be thoroughly old-fashioned, for of course I wanted to see all I could of the ways of the country. I was evidently expected, for when I got waist. It was handsomely embroidered in various colours, and had a thick fringe of black and red pendent from it to the bottom of the skirt, as if the other apron had been cut into strips; the wearers of this costume having coloured handkerchiefs instead of the white head-cloths. Among all the women, however, I saw nothing like a pretty face."

37 Harker may have copied this description from *"Magyarland"* (see note 18 above): "Their garments consist of a loose jacket and large trousers, and are made of a coarse woollen material the colour of which is originally white, while their waists are encircled by enormous leather belts, more than half an inch thick and from twelve to sixteen broad, studded with brass-headed nails so arranged as to form a variety of patterns. In these belts they keep their knives, scissors, tobacco-pouch, a primitive arrangement for striking light and a number of other small useful articles."

Although Harker refers frequently to Slovaks (and "Cszeks") on the journey to the Borgo Pass and in the employ of the Count, census data from the late nineteenth century show that Slovaks were a tiny fraction of the Transylvanian population. Geography professor Duncan Light reports that in the 1880 census, only 25,196 Slovaks were recorded in the entire country of Transylvania, with over 90 percent in the western portion ("The People of Bram Stoker's Transylvania"). Harker seems to rely on Johnson's somewhat distorted account (in *On the Track of the Crescent*) rather than his own observations. Although Harker might have asked Dracula for information about the locals, he does not record doing so.

38 The Bistrita Nord train station is no longer a Victorian structure, and the rail line has now been extended through the Pass to Bukovina.

39 The Borgo Pass is shown on a map in Charles Boner's 1865 *Transylvania: Its Products and Its People*. His description is "Pass into Moldavia, scenery increases in picturesqueness—good

Bistrita Nord train station.
Photograph by Leslie S. Klinger, May 2007

Trains in Bistrita.
Photograph by Leslie S. Klinger, May 2007

road. Near Prund is a territory continuously fought for by Wallachians and Saxons." The 1896 Austria "Baedeker" shows the road from Bistritz, through Borgó-Prund, Tihucza, and through the Borgo Pass to Pajana Stampi. The Pass itself stretches from Borgó-Prund, 14 miles outside Bistritz, for a distance of 33 miles.

40 Charles Boner's *Transylvania: Its Products and Its People* reports that from 1836 to 1850 "there were five conflagrations by which three hundred and twenty-five houses were destroyed." The 1896 Austria "Baedeker" notes the Gothic Protestant church, finished in 1563, and "much injured by repeated fires."

41 At last the nobleman is named. The Notes repeatedly refer to the central figure of the

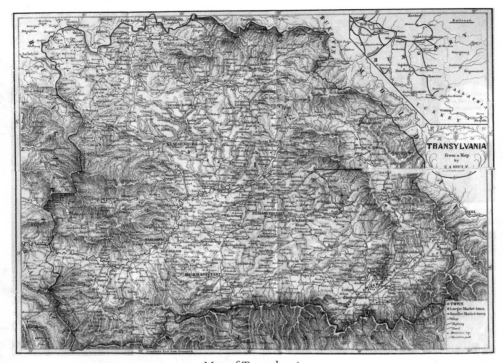

Map of Transylvania.
Charles Boner, *Transylvania: Its Products and Its People* (1865)

book as "Count Wampyr," changed at some point to "Count Dracula." See chapter 2, note 47, for a discussion of the source of the name "Dracula." It appears likely that both names are pseudonyms.

42 A fictitious hotel, added by an editor to the Manuscript (the former name has been deleted and is illegible). There was a Golden Krone in Salzburg, which the Notes suggest may have

been on Harker's actual itinerary as he travelled from Munich to Vienna via Salzburg and Linz. Sir Christopher Frayling, in *Vampyres: Lord Byron to Count Dracula*, points out that Andrew

Castle Dracula Hotel.
Photograph by Leslie S. Klinger, May 2007

Welcome to the Castle Dracula Hotel!
Photograph by Leslie S. Klinger, May 2007

near the door I faced a cheery-looking elderly woman in the usual peasant dress—white undergarment with long double apron, front, and back, of coloured stuff fitting almost too tight for modesty.[43] When I came close she bowed and said, "The Herr Englishman?" "Yes," I said, "Jonathan Harker." She smiled, and gave some message to an elderly man in white shirt-sleeves, who had followed her to the door. He went, but immediately returned with a letter:—

"My Friend,[44]—Welcome to the Carpathians. I am anxiously expecting you. Sleep well to-night.[45] At three to-morrow the diligence will start for Bukovina;[46] a place on it is kept for you. At the Borgo Pass my carriage will await you and will bring you to me. I trust that your journey from London has been a happy one, and that you will enjoy your stay in my beautiful land.[47]

"Your friend,
"Dracula."

4 May.—I found that my landlord had got a letter from the Count, directing him to secure the best place on the coach for me; but on making inquiries as to details he seemed somewhat reticent, and pretended that he could not understand my German. This could not be true, because up to then he had understood it perfectly; at least, he answered my questions exactly as if he did. He and his wife, the old lady who had received me, looked at each other in a frightened sort of way. He mumbled out that the money had been sent in a letter, and that was all he knew. When I asked him if he knew Count Dracula, and could tell me anything of his castle, both he and his wife crossed themselves, and, saying that they knew nothing at all, simply refused to speak further. It was so near the time of starting that I had no time to ask any one else, for it was all very mysterious and not by any means comforting.

Just before I was leaving, the old lady came up to my room and said in a very hysterical way:

"Must you go? Oh! young Herr, must you go?" She was in such an excited state that she seemed to have lost her grip of what German she knew, and mixed it all up with some other

F. Crosse (see note 18 above) also records a Krone Hotel in Oravicza, Transylvania, and it is possible that Harker stayed there. Today there is a Golden Krone Hotel in Bistritz, built by entrepreneur Alexandru Misiuga, that offers a replica of Harker's luncheon, complete with Mediasch wine and "robber steak." Misiuga also built the Castle Dracula Hotel in the Borgo Pass, outside which stands a statue of Stoker.

The only hotels listed for Bistritz in the 1896 Austria "Baedeker" are Sahling's and König von Ungarn. Subsequently, the National Tourist Association of Roumania built a "Golden Crown Hotel" (Hotel Coroana de Auri) to profit from the association with *Dracula*.

Presumably Dracula's telegram of 24 April "directed" whomever Hawkins sent. Did Dracula himself travel to Bistritz to send the telegram? Or did one of the Szgany?

43 This comment may unconsciously reflect Harker's state of mind. He seems here to be attempting to repress any possibility that he might find another woman attractive and—distant from Mina—might do anything about that attraction. John Paget, writing in 1850, describes an old Wallachian woman wearing a shift "open as low as the waist," exposing "pendulous breasts" (*Hungary and Transylvania*). Perhaps this more closely reflects what Harker observed, only to be suppressed with a Victorian expression of a sense of impropriety.

44 Dracula expects Peter Hawkins himself to come.

45 The Manuscript contains the following, which does not appear in the published narrative: "and in the morning see something of the beautiful bastioned town, Bistritz." Stoker evidently deleted this unexpected tour-guide advice from Dracula as inconsistent with the dark picture he intended to paint in the narrative.

46 A diligence, called an *Eilwagen* or *malle-poste* in Austria, was a public stagecoach.

Vorspann (carriages).
John Paget, *Hungary and Transylvania* (1850)

The 1896 Austria "Baedeker" describes the Austrian version as generally carrying only three passengers, two inside and one up top with the driver, although the diligence that carried Harker evidently had many more passengers. The 79-mile trip by diligence from Bistritz to Kimpolung (see the map on p. 22) in the Bukovina was scheduled to take seventeen hours; see note 81 below.

47 John Paget, in *Hungary and Transylvania*, quotes the words of a German writer, which Dracula echoes: " 'There is perhaps no country which has not some beauties to exhibit, but I never saw any which, like Transylvania, is all beauty,'—*welches so wie Siebenbürgen ganz Schönheit wäre.*" The letter continues in the Manuscript: " . . . so that at some future time we may together investigate the many interesting places still remaining . . ."

A diligence.

language which I did not know at all. I was just able to follow her by asking many questions. When I told her that I must go at once, and that I was engaged on important business, she asked again:

"Do you know what day it is?" I answered that it was the fourth of May. She shook her head as she said again:

"Oh, yes! I know that, I know that! but do you know what day it is?" On my saying that I did not understand, she went on:

"It is the eve of St. George's Day.[48] Do you not know that to-night, when the clock strikes midnight, all the evil things in the world will have full sway? Do you know where you are going, and what you are going to?"[49] She was in such evident distress that I tried to comfort her, but without effect. Finally she went down on her knees and implored me not to go; at least to wait a day or two before starting.[50] It was all very ridiculous, but I did not feel comfortable. However, there was business to be done, and I could allow nothing to interfere with it. I therefore tried to raise her up, and said, as gravely as I could, that I thanked her, but my duty was imperative, and that I must go. She then rose and dried her eyes, and taking a crucifix from her neck offered it to me.[51] I did not know what to do, for, as an English Churchman,[52] I have been taught to regard such things as in some measure idolatrous, and yet it seemed so ungracious to refuse an old lady meaning so well and in such a state of mind.[53] She saw, I suppose, the doubt in my face, for she put the rosary round my neck, and said, "For your mother's sake," and went out of the room. I am writing up this part of the diary whilst I am waiting for the coach, which is, of course, late;[54] and the crucifix is still round my neck. Whether it is the old lady's fear, or the many ghostly traditions of this place, or the crucifix itself, I do not know, but I am not feeling nearly as easy in my mind as usual. If this book should ever reach Mina before I do, let it bring my good-bye. Here comes the coach!

5 May. The Castle.—The grey of the morning has passed, and the sun is high over the distant horizon, which seems jagged, whether with trees or hills I know not, for it is so far off that big things and little are mixed.[55] I am not sleepy, and, as I am

St. George Fighting the Dragon.
Raphaël, 1505

48 *The Golden Legend, or Lives of the Saints*, compiled by Jacobus de Voragine, Archbishop of Genoa, in 1275 and first published in 1470 (first English edition 1485), recounts the legend of the knight known as Saint George, who lived ca. 250–300. In his journeys, he came to the city of Silene, where a dragon ravaged the countryside. The populace soon tired of appeasing the dragon, especially when their children became the sacrifices. Eventually even the king's daughter was required to be offered to the dragon. George, passing by, learned of her plight and conquered the dragon with his sword and spear. According to *The Golden Legend*, George then said to the maid: "Deliver to me your girdle, and bind it about the neck of the dragon and be not afeard." When she had done so, "the dragon followed her as it had been a meek beast and debonair." The couple led the dragon into town, where George admonished the townspeople to believe in God; he then slew the dragon. The king and fifteen thousand men were reportedly baptised following this great victory, and a church with a miraculous fountain was established.

George went on to become the patron saint of England. The famous Order of the Garter, the highest chivalric rank in England, venerates St. George and (among numerous other orders) refers to its members as Knights of St. George. St. George's Day was established in 1222 by the Council of Oxford as 23 April. The date Harker reckoned as 4 May (presumably using an English, Gregorian calendar) would have been denoted as 22 April on the Julian calendar, still in use in Transylvania at that time. Thus it may have slipped Harker's mind—focussed on English dates—that it was the eve of St. George's Day.

But of what significance was the date? The English clergyman Montague Summers explains in *The Vampire in Europe* (1929) that throughout eastern Europe, it is believed that vampires are most active on the eve of St. Andrew's Day and on the eve of St. George's Day. "In Roumania upon these particular days when the vampire is most malicious the country folk anoint the windows with garlic, they tie bundles of garlic on the door and in the cow sheds. All lights throughout the house must be extinguished and it is well that every utensil should be turned topsy-turvy. Pious people will pass the whole night in prayer, and even those who have not this devotion do their best to keep awake."

49 Leatherdale (*Dracula Unearthed*) wonders, in light of the woman's highly protective attitude, why Dracula insisted that Harker stay at this inn. One would have expected the innkeepers to be Dracula's puppets.

50 Why would waiting improve Harker's chances of survival? Dracula certainly is not a creature of the forces of the eve of St. George's Day.

51 The woman's slight knowledge of German and her gift of a cross suggest that she (and her husband) were Hungarian Catholics. In fact, the area of Bistritz was heavily Saxon (German); even Boner (*Transylvania: Its Products and Its People*), whose geographical knowledge was of mixed reliability, reports that over 75 percent of the population of the Bistritz area were German.

52 This commonly used phrase means that he is an Anglican, a member of the Church of England, not that he is a member of the clergy. In the Manuscript, the word is "Englishman."

53 The Church of England went through several major changes in the nineteenth century. Early in the century, Newman, Pusey, Keble, and others had reshaped the doctrine of the church, under the banner of the Oxford Movement, or high church, revival. The next generation of high churchmen, however, changed the performance of the church services, adopting customs termed "Ritualist." In particular, these required standing at the east end of the Communion table, rather than north, to symbolise that the Eucharist was Christ's banquet to be celebrated in the New Jerusalem; the lighting of candles on the Holy Table and the use of incense; and the wearing of Eucharistic vestments.

Victoria herself was upset with the Ritualists. Once, when staying at Balmoral, she had taken her Communion with the local Presbyterians rather than at the Anglican church. In response to outrage among certain Anglicans, she wrote to Dean Stanley, "She [meaning herself, in Victoria's Imperial style] thinks a *complete Reformation* is what we want. But if *that* is *impossible*, the archbishop should have the *power* given him, by *Parliament*, to *stop* all these ritualistic practices, dressings, bowings, etc. and everything of that kind" (in A. N. Wilson, *The Victorians*).

In 1874, Parliament—under the leadership of Prime Minister Benjamin Disraeli—passed the Public Worship Regulation Act, forbidding certain Ritualist practises that seemed to emphasise the Catholic nature of the Church of England. However, as A. N. Wilson demonstrates, what he terms "pleasing evidence of human counter-suggestibility" shows that following adoption of the Act, the use of incense and vestments increased dramatically and quickly became the normal practise of Anglicans. Harker's reaction to the crucifix, then, is the response of the conservative to ritualism, not the popular response.

not to be called till I awake,[56] naturally I write till sleep comes. There are many odd things to put down, and, lest who reads them may fancy that I dined too well before I left Bistritz, let me put down my dinner exactly. I dined on what they called "robber steak"—bits of bacon, onion, and beef, seasoned with red pepper, and strung on sticks and roasted over the fire, in the simple style of the London cat's-meat![57] The wine was Golden Mediasch, which produces a queer sting on the tongue, which is, however, not disagreeable.[58] I had only a couple of glasses of this, and nothing else.[59]

When I got on the coach the driver had not taken his seat, and I saw him talking with the landlady. They were evidently talking of me, for every now and then they looked at me, and some of the people who were sitting on the bench outside the door—which they call by a name meaning "word-bearer"[60]—came and listened, and then looked at me, most of them pityingly. I could hear a lot of words often repeated, queer words, for there were many nationalities in the crowd; so I quietly got my polyglot dictionary[61] from my bag and looked them out. I must say they were not cheering to me, for amongst them were "Ordog"—Satan,[62] "pokol"—hell, "stregoica"—witch,[63] "vrolok" and "vlkoslak"—both of which mean the same thing one being Slovak and the other Servian[64] for something that is either were-wolf or vampire.[65] (*Mem.*, I must ask the Count about these superstitions.)[66]

When we started, the crowd round the inn door, which had by this time swelled to a considerable size,[67] all made the sign of the cross and pointed two fingers towards me. With some difficulty I got a fellow-passenger to tell me what they meant; he would not answer at first, but on learning that I was English he explained that it was a charm or guard against the evil eye.[68] This was not very pleasant for me, just starting for an unknown place to meet an unknown man; but every one seemed so kind-hearted, and so sorrowful, and so sympathetic that I could not but be touched. I shall never forget the last glimpse which I had of the inn-yard and its crowd of picturesque figures, all crossing themselves, as they stood round the wide archway, with its background of rich foliage of oleander and orange trees in green tubs clustered in the centre of the yard. Then our

54 It is not clear whether the coach did in fact leave "late." Although the Notes indicate that it departed at 2:00 P.M., Dracula's note to his "friend" puts the departure time at 3:00 P.M. (presumably central Europe time). Bernard Davies, reviewing and correcting Leatherdale's *Dracula Unearthed* in "Unearthing *Dracula*— Burying Stoker," points out that local time in Bistritz was approximately 3:37 P.M., and Harker may have gauged the timeliness of the departure by local hotel time, not railway time.

55 Note that Harker's room faces east, and the horizon is "distant." Therefore the mountains are behind the castle, which must be on either a southern or eastern face of the mountains. (Because this is the southern end of the Carpathians, a northern face would have mountains to the east.)

56 Leonard Wolf (*The Annotated Dracula*) ponders: Who will do the calling, and how will they know when Harker awakes? This is a misunderstanding. There is, in fact, no "calling," and Harker makes this remark because he is under the misconception that there are servants in the castle.

57 A tradition in London was the "cat's-meat man," a vendor who sold little bits of meat on skewers for consumption by cats. As recently as 1929, *Time* magazine reported on a London entrepreneur who had plied the trade for over thirty years. "Robber steak" in Harker's account sounds a lot like shish kebab, a traditional Armenian or Turkish dish. Andrew F. Crosse reports an identical dish in his 1878 travelogue *Round About the Carpathians*, which appears among the sources listed in the Notes. There are also references to "robbers steak" in gourmet cuisine: legend has it that chateaubriand, the prime filet of beef, was originally cooked between two cheap cuts of steak which were then discarded. This was done to prevent overcooking the filet. The discarded steaks were termed "robber steaks."

Again, the Abridged Text does not contain

STREET IN HERMANNSTADT.

Hermannstadt.
Charles Boner, *Transylvania: Its Products and Its People* (1865)

the recipe and the oenological comments that follow.

58 The wine is mentioned by name (but styled "golden Mediasch") by Andrew Crosse (*Round About the Carpathians*), who calls it "one of the best wines grown in Transylvania." Crosse also mentions the "agreeable prickling on the tongue," called *tschirpsen* in German. It is impossible at this remove to definitely identify the wine Harker calls "Golden Mediasch." Mediasch, or Medgyes in Hungarian, was a village near Hermannstadt, its name derived from the Hungarian word *meggy*, or "sour cherry." About halfway between Klausenburg and Hermannstadt, or about 50 miles from Bistritz, it is described in the 1896 Austria "Baedeker" as "the centre of the wine-trade of Transylvania." According to André L. Simon's *Wines of the World*, local names for grape varietals are common, and the name likely described a particular varietal grown in the village. From the description given by the unsophisticated Harker, it is possible that this was a sparkling or fortified (high-alcohol) wine: either might produce a "sting" on the tongue.

While some scholars have derided the wine as fictional, the only possible motive for either Harker or Stoker to change the name of the wine consumed by Harker (or to insert a wholly fictional episode of imbibing) would be to make the (false) identification of Bistritz more convincing. That is, if one believes that the name Golden Mediasch is fictitious, then one must also doubt whether Harker really travelled to Bistritz and the Borgo Pass. (See the discussion of possible reasons for concealing the location in the introductory essay "The Context of *Dracula.*")

59 The Manuscript contains the following remark, which has been omitted from the published narrative, perhaps because it made Harker appear insufficiently English: "until supper with which I had two glasses of old Tokay—the nicest wine I ever tasted; but I did not take as much as I should have liked for I feared it might be too strong and the Count might want to talk business at once. A roast chicken was my supper."

60 This strange term—*szohordok* in Hungarian—is, according to *Magyarland* (see note 18 above), for benches outside peasants' homes, perhaps meaning a place for conversation.

61 A dictionary with text in several languages.

62 "Armlog" in the Manuscript. Errors such as these (and the blanks for place names and historical data) give credence to the idea that Stoker changed the location of the events described in the Harker Papers, at a relatively late stage in his preparation of the narrative.

63 The translator has misspelt the word, which should read *strigoaica*, the female undead vampire; *strigoi* is the male undead vampire.

COACHMAN IN SHEEPSKIN.   WALLACH.   SAXON WOMAN.

Examples of native dress.
Major E. C. Johnson, *On the Track of the Crescent* (1885)

driver, whose wide linen drawers covered the whole front of the box-seat—"gotza" they call them[69]—cracked his big whip over his four small horses, which ran abreast,[70] and we set off on our journey.

I soon lost sight and recollection of ghostly fears in the beauty of the scene as we drove along, although had I known the language, or rather languages, which my fellow-passengers were speaking, I might not have been able to throw them off so easily.[71] Before us lay a green sloping land full of forests and woods, with here and there steep hills, crowned with clumps of trees or with farmhouses, the blank gable end to the road. There was everywhere a bewildering mass of fruit blossom—apple, plum, pear, cherry; and as we drove by I could see the green grass under the trees spangled with the fallen petals. In and out amongst these green hills of what they call here the "Mittel Land"[72] ran the road, losing itself as it swept round the grassy curve, or was shut out by the straggling ends of pine woods, which here and there ran down the hillsides like tongues of flame. The road was rugged, but still we seemed to fly over it with a feverish haste. I could not understand then what the haste meant, but the driver was evidently bent on losing no time in reaching Borgo Prund. I was told that this road is in summer-time excellent, but that it had not yet been put in order after the winter snows. In this respect it is different from the general run of roads in the Carpathians, for it is an old tradition that they are not to be kept in too good order. Of

64 Serbian, that is, the language of Serbia, a Balkan state between Roumania and Bosnia.

65 Montague Summers (see note 48 above) identifies the *vârcolac* as a mythical being, but he cites Agnes Murgoçi ("The Vampire in Roumania") as the source of the information that the name also applies to "dead" vampires, distinct from "live" vampires closely associated with witches.

66 Harker never does so, and the reminder does not appear in the Abridged Text.

67 There is no note of the crowd size in the Abridged Text.

68 Frederick Thomas Elworthy, in his classic study *The Evil Eye* (1895), considers wards in common use: "If in past ages the hand has been looked upon as an instrument of evil when used by the malignant, much more has it been regarded as an instrument of good— the powerful protector against that special form of evil which was supposed to be flashed from

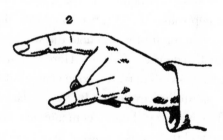

Mano cornuta.
Frederick Thomas Elworthy, *The Evil Eye* (1895)

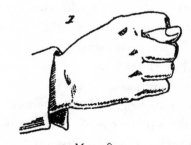

Mano fica.
Frederick Thomas Elworthy, *The Evil Eye* (1895)

one person to another, whether through the eye or the touch of malice." The *mano cornuta*, or "horned hand," is a gesture found depicted in many cultures and religions (including ancient Hindu statuary and Christian icons) as a means to ward off the "evil eye" or other bad fortune. Why horns would ward against evil is unknown. Elworthy advises: "When, however, it is desired to use the sign specially against a particular individual, the hand so posed is thrust out towards him, and if there is no fear of his person, towards his very eyes, from which so much is dreaded. That is, of course, if he be present, but if absent, the sign is made in the direction of his supposed whereabouts." A similar sign, but which could not be described by Harker as "two fingers" pointing, is the *mano fica* or *manus obscœna*, a gesture recorded throughout history as one of contempt or defiance and also used to avert witchery or other evil. Harker is apparently mistaken in thinking that the gesture was directed at him—surely the locals sensed no evil in him. McNally and Florescu (*The Essential Dracula*) state that Roumanian folklore records few hand signs used to ward off evil, except the sign of the cross, made using three fingers.

Leatherdale, in *Dracula Unearthed*, suggests that Harker's "Englishness" accounts for his ignorance and makes him particularly vulnerable. However, Elworthy quotes a reminiscence of Dean Ramsay, who remembered how in Yorkshire he and his schoolfellows, from 1800 to 1810, "used to put our thumb between the first and second finger, pointing it downwards as the infallible protection against the evil influences of one particularly malevolent and powerful witch" (from John Christopher Atkinson, *Forty Years in a Moorland Parish*). Perhaps the locals were aware of Dracula's plans for England (see text accompanying chapter 4, note 53).

69 Johnson (*On the Track of the Crescent*) describes the men as wearing a "loose, embroidered shirt, and immense linen drawers, called 'gatya.' So large are these that when a magnate's coachman is seated on his box,

HUNGARIAN PEASANT DANDY.
Gatya.
Major E. C. Johnson, *On the Track
of the Crescent* (1885)

they cover the whole front of the carriage." This is another suspicious example of Harker's descriptions matching those of other travellers. This observation does not appear in the Abridged Text.

70 Although this sounds unusual (and Wolf, in *The Essential Dracula*, dismisses it as never having been recorded in any film of the novel), Crosse (*Round About the Carpathians*) also reports carts hauled by four horses abreast. This apparently is a function of the size of the diligence. Francis Ford Coppola includes this nice touch in his *Bram Stoker's Dracula* (1992), which otherwise bears few resemblances to the narrative.

71 In the Abridged Text, Harker's comment about the incomprehensibility of the passengers' remarks is omitted.

72 Described by Boner (see note 18 above) as "a ridge of low hills rising in the vale between

old the Hospadars would not repair them, lest the Turk should think that they were preparing to bring in foreign troops, and so hasten the war which was always really at loading point.[73]

Beyond the green swelling hills of the Mittel Land rose mighty slopes of forest up to the lofty steeps of the Carpathians themselves.[74] Right and left of us they towered, with the afternoon sun falling full upon them and bringing out all the glorious colours of this beautiful range, deep blue and purple in the shadows of the peaks, green and brown where grass and rock mingled, and an endless perspective of jagged rock and pointed crags, till these were themselves lost in the distance, where the snowy peaks rose grandly. Here and there seemed mighty rifts in the mountains, through which, as the sun began to sink, we saw now and again the white gleam of falling water. One of my companions touched my arm as we swept round the base of a hill and opened up the lofty, snow-covered peak of a mountain, which seemed, as we wound on our serpentine way, to be right before us:—

"Look! Isten szek!"—"God's seat!"—and he crossed himself reverently.[75] As we wound on our endless way, and the sun sank lower and lower behind us, the shadows of the evening began to creep round us. This was emphasized by the fact that the snowy mountain-top still held the sunset, and seemed to glow out with a delicate cool pink. Here and there we passed Cszeks and Slovaks, all in picturesque attire, but I noticed that goitre was painfully prevalent.[76] By the roadside were many crosses, and as we swept by, my companions all crossed themselves. Here and there was a peasant man or woman kneeling before a shrine, who did not even turn round as we approached, but seemed in the self-surrender of devotion to have neither eyes nor ears for the outer world. There were many things new to me: for instance, hay-ricks in the trees, and here and there very beautiful masses of weeping birch, their white stems shining like silver through the delicate green of the leaves. Now and again we passed a leiter-wagon—the ordinary peasant's cart, with its long, snake-like vertebra, calculated to suit the inequalities of the road.[77] On this were sure to be seated quite a group of home-coming peasants, the Cszeks with their white, and the Slovaks with their coloured, sheepskins, the latter

Lemnitzer Head, the highest of the Carpathians.
G. F. Hering, in John Paget, *Hungary and Transylvania* (1850)

the high mountains," near Borgó-Prund, east of Bistritz.

73 In his 1820 *Account of the Principalities of Wallachia and Moldavia*, Wilkinson writes, "The Hospodars purposely neglect to repair these roads; the fear of creating suspicions at the Porte that they wish to facilitate the passage of foreign troops into the principalities, induces them to abstain from an undertaking, which in other respects has become so imperiously necessary." "Hospodar" or "Hospadar," as Harker would have it, is a corruption of *gospodar*, a common Roumanian word meaning "landholder" or "lord"; here it connotes the aristocracy. That Harker makes the same mistake as Wilkinson is suspicious. Note that this comment on the politics of the area predates Harker's briefing by Dracula in chapter 3.

Walker and Wright ("Locating *Dracula*") point out that Harker (and subsequently Van Helsing, Seward, and Mina Harker) seem to have failed to observe any of the changes "accompanying the industrialisation of the European world. The railways into Transylvania functioned as military links with the great Habsburg fortresses of Vienna and Budapest, but also led to the reorganisation of the textile industry. At the same time, redefinition of private property in agriculture brought about the dissolution of the peasantry and the creation of an industrial working class." Harker and the vampire hunters record only what Walker and Wright term "a frozen bit of the antediluvian world surviving in the impenetrable mountain interior."

74 Most of the "local colour" has been pruned from the following paragraphs in the Abridged Text.

75 Again, Harker seems to have lifted his picturesque description from another source: Johnson, in his 1885 *On the Track of the Crescent*, writes: "In front of us, as far as the eye could reach, was an interminable stretch of forest, right up to the base of the mountain range, brilliant in numberless shades of green, blue, and brown, and melting into a dusky purple as it became more stunted, and was lost in the haze surrounding the rocky crags. These towered range above range till they were

Bikasu (Bicaz) Gorge.
Photograph by Leslie S. Klinger,
May 2007

The actual site of Castle Dracula?
Photograph by Leslie S. Klinger, May 2007

crowned by the mighty 'Isten-Szék' (God's Seat), the abode of eternal snow."

Leatherdale (*Dracula Unearthed*) notes a serious problem with Harker's descriptive passages: he maintains that they do not describe the Borgo Pass. Leatherdale writes: "An actual journey through the Borgo Pass does little to merit [this] atmospheric description. Rocky crags do not tower range upon range. The actual ascent is gradual and nowhere rises above the tree-line. The top of the Pass is open and exposed, offering expansive views of distant hills and pine forests. To find examples of jagged landscape, such as around the Bicaz Gorge, one needs to travel some distance from the Borgo Pass."

Johnson's descriptions, from which Harker's are evidently copied, do not claim to be of the Borgo Pass. Instead, they describe an area near the town of Sächsich-Regen, or Szász Régen, then a town of six thousand, now called Regihn, 50 miles south of Bistritz. It is possible that Harker in fact travelled here by train and not to Bistritz. The 1896 Austria "Baedeker" reports the train journey from Klausenburg as 58 miles, in four hours, through the "fertile valley of the Maros" (that is, about forty-five minutes shorter than the train trip to Bistritz). From Sächsich-Regen, Harker could have taken a coach to the Pékas

Pass, near Bikasu (now known as the Bicaz Gorge or Canyon, Cheile Bicazului in Roumanian, Békás-szoros in Hungarian, near the town of Bicaz). This region, filled with Szeklers (as Dracula later describes himself), bears a close resemblance to Harker's description, and it is easy to imagine Castle Dracula atop one of the spectacular cliffs of the gorge.

76 A goitre (or goiter; Latin *struma*) is a swelling in the neck caused by an enlarged thyroid gland. It is most commonly caused by a hormonal imbalance or a diet deficient in iodine. If many of the locals suffered from goitres, the latter is a likely diagnosis. Iodine is generally consumed in adequate quantities in the form of naturally iodized salt. However, in some regions, insufficient iodine accumulates in either natural salt or plants. In addition, consumption of vegetables such as cabbage, Brussel sprouts, broccoli, and cauliflower increases the requirements for iodine, especially if consumed raw. Soy beans, raw flaxseed, sweet potatoes, lima beans, maize, and millet also increase the requirements for iodine. Wilkinson (*Account of the Principalities of Wallachia and Moldovia*) noted the high prevalence of goitre among Transylvanians, and carrying lance-fashion their long staves, with axe at end. As the evening fell[78] it began to get very cold, and the growing twilight seemed to merge into one dark mistiness the gloom of the trees, oak, beech, and pine, though in the valleys which ran deep between the spurs of the hills, as we ascended through the Pass, the dark firs stood out here and there against the background of late-lying snow. Sometimes, as the road was cut through the pine woods that seemed in the darkness to be closing down upon us, great masses of greyness which here and there bestrewed the trees, produced a peculiarly weird and solemn effect, which carried on the thoughts and grim fancies engendered earlier in the evening, when the falling sunset threw into strange relief the ghost-like clouds which amongst the Carpathians seem to wind ceaselessly through the valleys.[79] Sometimes the hills were so steep that, despite our driver's haste, the horses could only go slowly.[80] I wished to get down and walk up them, as we do at home, but the driver would not hear of it. "No, no," he said; "you must not walk here; the dogs are too fierce;" and then he added, with what he evidently meant for grim pleasantry—for he looked round to catch the approving smile of the rest—"and you may have enough of such matters before you go to sleep." The only stop he would make was a moment's pause to light his lamps.

When it grew dark there seemed to be some excitement amongst the passengers, and they kept speaking to him, one after the other, as though urging him to further speed.[81] He lashed the horses unmercifully with his long whip, and with wild cries of encouragement urged them on to further exertions. Then through the darkness I could see a sort of patch of grey light ahead of us, as though there were a cleft in the hills. The excitement of the passengers grew greater; the crazy coach rocked on its great leather springs, and swayed like a boat tossed on a stormy sea. I had to hold on. The road grew more level, and we appeared to fly along. Then the mountains seemed to come nearer to us on each side and to frown down upon us; we were entering on the Borgo Pass.[82] One by one several of the passengers offered me gifts, which they pressed upon me with an earnestness which would take no denial; these were certainly of an odd and varied kind, but each was given in

the condition has persisted, with data from the 1960s and 1970s showing over 60 percent of the adult population of the Carpathians suffering from the disease.

Harker completely misidentifies the population. The region of the Mittel-land was primarily occupied by Roumanians (Wallachians), with a small number of Germans, the latter diminishing in the mountainous regions; see note 26 above. Yet the Roumanian population is virtually invisible throughout the narrative, both in Harker's journal and in the accounts of the vampire hunters. See Walker and Wright's "Locating *Dracula*" for a discussion of the transformation of the landscape.

77 Harker apparently borrowed this from Andrew Crosse, who writes that the leiter-waggon is "a vehicle which has no counterpart in England, and the literal rendering of a ladder-waggon hardly conveys the proper notion of the thing itself. This long cart, it is needless to say, is without springs; but it has the faculty of accommodating itself to the inequalities of the road in a marvellous manner. It has, moreover, a snake-like vertebrae, and even twists itself when necessary" (*Round About the Carpathians*).

78 Sunset occurred at 7:36 P.M. local time.

79 Compare Crosse: "It is curious to notice sometimes in the higher Carpathians how the clouds march continuously through the winding valleys" (*Round About the Carpathians*).

80 There are few, if any, such steep grades in the Borgo Pass. However, snowcapped peaks are visible in the distance.

81 As noted earlier (note 46 above), the 1896 Austria "Baedeker" gives the expected travel time from Bistritz to Kimpolung, a distance of 79 miles, as seventeen hours. The Borgo Pass is less than half that distance from Bistritz. The average speed of the diligence noted in the "Baedeker" is 4 to 5 miles per hour; therefore, travelling about 30 miles to the Pass would be

Snow-covered peaks in the Borgo Pass.
Photograph by Leslie S. Klinger, May 2007

expected to take six to eight hours. If Harker left Bistritz after "dinner" (say, 1:30 or 2:00 P.M.), then he probably arrived at the Pass between 8:00 and 10:00 P.M. However, if the trip were to the Bicaz Gorge (also known as the Pékas Pass), the distance more closely matches his reported arrival time of midnight. (See map on p. 475.)

82 Today known as the Tihuta Pass, 3,937 feet above sea level.

83 The Notes indicate that it was 9:00 P.M., "an hour early."

84 "Bukovina" is inserted into a blank in the Manuscript in an editor's hand. This suggests that the destination originally reported was not the Bukovina but more likely the town of Piatra (today Piatra-Neamt) in the Moldau, across the Pékas Pass.

85 The Notes reveal that the smell of blood on Dracula has frightened the horses.

86 Leatherdale (*Dracula Unearthed*) points out that it is unlikely that travellers who could afford the diligence are "peasants," who would have little reason to travel anywhere, especially on this night.

87 Also termed a calash or barouche, a horse-drawn carriage having four wheels, with an

simple good faith, with a kindly word, and a blessing, and that same strange mixture of fear-meaning movements which I had seen outside the hotel at Bistritz—the sign of the cross and the guard against the evil eye. Then, as we flew along, the driver leaned forward, and on each side the passengers, craning over the edge of the coach, peered eagerly into the darkness. It was evident that something very exciting was either happening or expected, but though I asked each passenger, no one would give me the slightest explanation. This state of excitement kept on for some little time; and at last we saw before us the Pass opening out on the eastern side. There were dark, rolling clouds overhead, and in the air the heavy, oppressive sense of thunder. It seemed as though the mountain range had separated two atmospheres, and that now we had got into the thunderous one. I was now myself looking out for the conveyance which was to take me to the Count. Each moment I expected to see the glare of lamps through the blackness; but all was dark. The only light was the flickering rays of our own lamps, in which the steam from our hard-driven horses rose in a white cloud. We could see now the sandy road lying white before us, but there was on it no sign of a vehicle. The passengers drew back with a sigh of gladness, which seemed to mock my own disappointment. I was already thinking what I had best do, when the driver, looking at his watch, said to the others something which I could hardly hear, it was spoken so quietly and in so low a tone; I thought it was "An hour less than the time."[83] Then turning to me, he said in German worse than my own:—

"There is no carriage here. The Herr is not expected after all. He will now come on to Bukovina,[84] and return to-morrow or the next day; better the next day." Whilst he was speaking the horses began to neigh and snort and plunge wildly, so that the driver had to hold them up.[85] Then, amongst a chorus of screams from the peasants[86] and a universal crossing of themselves, a calèche,[87] with four horses, drove up behind us, overtook us, and drew up beside the coach. I could see from the flash of our lamps, as the rays fell on them, that the horses were coal-black and splendid animals. They were driven by a tall man, with a long brown beard and a great black hat, which seemed to hide his face from us.[88] I could only see the gleam of a pair of very bright eyes, which seemed red in the lamplight, as he turned to us. He said to the driver:—

"You are early to-night, my friend." The man stammered in reply:—

"The English Herr was in a hurry," to which the stranger replied:—

"That is why, I suppose, you wished him to go on to Bukovina. You cannot deceive me, my friend; I know too much, and my horses are swift."[89] As he spoke he smiled, and the lamplight fell on a hard-looking mouth, with very red lips and sharp-looking teeth, as white as ivory. One of my companions whispered to another the line from Burger's "Lenore":—

"Denn die Todten reiten schnell"—*("For the dead travel fast.")*[90]

The strange driver evidently heard the words, for he looked up with a gleaming smile. The passenger turned his face away, at the same time putting out his two fingers and crossing

"Is this the coach from Count Dracula?"
Bela Lugosi as the coachman and Dwight Frye as Renfield.
(Note: In this film, Renfield, not Harker, travels to the castle.)
Dracula (Universal Pictures, 1931)

A caleche.

outside seat for the driver, facing inside seats for four passengers, and a folding top.

88 The commentators are in agreement that this is Dracula in disguise. The purpose of the disguise is obscure, for the coachman and all of the passengers seem perfectly able to identify the "tall man."

89 Either Dracula read the mind of the coachman or he has extraordinarily sharp hearing. Leatherdale (*Dracula Unearthed*) observes that neither the driver nor the passengers seem afraid of Dracula, having armed themselves with crucifixes and other homely protections, and that this is precisely why Dracula now seeks the "greener pastures" of England.

90 Gottfried August Burger (1748–1794) wrote the ballad "Lenore," a dark tale of a young woman waiting for her William to return from the wars. When he finally arrives, he is an animated corpse, who proposes to take her with him by horseback to their "nuptial bed." On arrival at the graveyard, after a wild ride, she is drawn down by the ghosts of the graveyard into his coffin. The line, or a version of it, acts as a kind of chorus.

First printed in 1773, "Lenore" suffered, in the words of Montague Summers (*The Vampire: His Kith and Kin*), "legions of hostile comments and parodies, [but] long remained a household word." In 1796, an English translation was published; Sir Walter Scott rendered another translation, privately circulated. Shelley was reportedly enchanted by the poem as well. Dante Gabriel Rossetti, a neighbour of Bram Stoker and close friend of Stoker's friend Sir Hall Caine (see note 3 on p. 3), made his own translation in 1844, at age sixteen, under the signature "Gabriel Charles Rossetti." (Rossetti was, perhaps coincidentally, the nephew of John Polidori, author of "The Vampyre.") "Lenore" is credited as one of the first vampire poems, preceded only by Heinrich August Ossenfelder's *Der Vampir* (1748), although there is no mention of blood drinking in "Lenore."

Interestingly, the Abridged Text omits the line—one of the most memorable in Harker's journal—and the driver's reaction to it.

91 Slivovitz is a Slavic Balkan plum brandy. The Roumanian variety is known as țuică and is made by both private and commercial distillers; traditionally, every meal begins with a shot of it. In order to research its efficacy, this editor consumed a great deal of țuică on a recent trip to Transylvania and can report that it staves off chills, even on hot May nights.

92 Harker has been in the caleche for almost three hours. Why Dracula delays Harker's arrival at the castle is unclear. Midnight is regarded as the most important hour on the eve of St. George's Day, Harker has been told, when the power of evil spirits is at its height. But Dracula makes nothing of this opportunity. He also uselessly obscures the location of the castle. First, the coach travels back into the Pass (that is, to the west); then it makes a "complete turn," presumably heading east. *Dracula* scholar Roger Johnson suggests, in private correspondence with this editor, that the delay was all part of Dracula's plan to hide the location of the treasures (see text accompanying chapter 2, note 45), but it is equally unclear why the seemingly wealthy Dracula would bother to protect these small hordes.

The sentence does not appear in the Abridged Text.

himself. "Give me the Herr's luggage," said the driver; and with exceeding alacrity my bags were handed out and put in the calèche. Then I descended from the side of the coach, as the calèche was close alongside, the driver helping me with a hand which caught my arm in a grip of steel; his strength must have been prodigious. Without a word he shook his reins, the horses turned, and we swept into the darkness of the Pass. As I looked back I saw the steam from the horses of the coach by the light of the lamps, and projected against it the figures of my late companions crossing themselves. Then the driver cracked his whip and called to his horses, and off they swept on their way to Bukovina.

As they sank into the darkness I felt a strange chill, and a lonely feeling came over me; but a cloak was thrown over my shoulders, and a rug across my knees, and the driver said in excellent German:—

"The night is chill, mein Herr, and my master the Count bade me take all care of you. There is a flask of slivovitz (the plum brandy of the country)[91] underneath the seat, if you should require it." I did not take any, but it was a comfort to know it was there all the same. I felt a little strangely, and not a little frightened. I think had there been any alternative I should have taken it, instead of prosecuting that unknown night journey. The carriage went at a hard pace straight along, then we made a complete turn and went along another straight road. It seemed to me that we were simply going over and over the same ground again; and so I took note of some salient point, and found that this was so. I would have liked to have asked the driver what this all meant, but I really feared to do so, for I thought that, placed as I was, any protest would have had no effect in case there had been an intention to delay.[92] By-and-by, however, as I was curious to know how time was passing, I struck a match, and by its flame looked at my watch; it was within a few minutes of midnight. This gave me a sort of shock, for I suppose the general superstition about midnight was increased by my recent experiences. I waited with a sick feeling of suspense.

Then a dog began to howl somewhere in a farmhouse far down the road—a long, agonised wailing, as if from fear.

The sound was taken up by another dog, and then another and another, till, borne on the wind which now sighed softly through the Pass, a wild howling began, which seemed to come from all over the country, as far as the imagination could grasp it through the gloom of the night. At the first howl the horses began to strain and rear, but the driver spoke to them soothingly, and they quieted down, but shivered and sweated as though after a run-away from sudden fright. Then, far off in the distance, from the mountains on each side of us began a louder and a sharper howling—that of wolves—which affected both the horses and myself in the same way—for I was minded to jump from the calèche and run, whilst they reared again and plunged madly, so that the driver had to use all his great strength to keep them from bolting. In a few minutes, however, my own ears got accustomed to the sound, and the horses so far became quiet that the driver was able to descend and to stand before them. He petted and soothed them, and whispered something in their ears, as I have heard of horse-tamers doing, and with extraordinary effect, for under his caresses they became quite manageable again, though they still trembled. The driver again took his seat, and shaking his reins, started off at a great pace. This time, after going to the far side of the Pass, he suddenly turned down a narrow roadway which ran sharply to the right.[93]

Soon we were hemmed in with trees, which in places arched right over the roadway till we passed as through a tunnel; and again great frowning rocks guarded us boldly on either side. Though we were in shelter, we could hear the rising wind, for it moaned and whistled through the rocks, and the branches of the trees crashed together as we swept along. It grew colder and colder still, and fine, powdery snow began to fall, so that soon we and all around us were covered with a white blanket. The keen wind still carried the howling of the dogs, though this grew fainter as we went on our way. The baying of the wolves sounded nearer and nearer, as though they were closing round on us from every side. I grew dreadfully afraid, and the horses shared my fear; but the driver was not in the least disturbed. He kept turning his head to left and right, but I could not see anything through the darkness.

93 Presumably to the south, if the "far side" of the Pass means the eastern boundary. This fits with the notion that the castle is on an eastern or southern face of the mountains.

94 Boner, in his 1865 *Transylvania: Its Products and Its People*, recounts an incident in his travels, when his driver pointed out a spot where he had seen a "gold fire": " 'And what is that?' I asked. ' 'Tis a light which hovers over the spot where gold is buried.' " Emily Gerard, in "Transylvanian Superstitions," an article listed in Stoker's Notes, makes a similar observation: "In the night of St. George's Day (so say the legends) [treasures of gold] begin to burn, or, to speak in mystic language, to 'bloom' in the bosom of the earth, and the light they give forth, described as a bluish flame resembling the colour of lighted spirits of wine, serves to guide favoured mortals to their place of concealment." She also notes that lights seen before midnight mark treasures kept by benevolent spirits, whereas those that appear later are those of pernicious spirits. This may explain Dracula's delay—he wished to hunt treasures not accessible to those less powerful than he.

95 This and the two succeeding sentences do not appear in the Abridged Text.

96 See chapter 2, note 68, for a discussion of vampiric transparency.

97 An entire page apparently is cut from the Manuscript here (made evident by cutting and pasting), and the only surviving fragment at the top of what appears to be the succeeding page of the Manuscript is "on our way faster than before, and the wolves seemed to yelp close around me."

98 Harker's notes of the appearance of the moon imply that it had some significant aspect and had risen. On 4 May 1893, a date ascribed to these events by many scholars, the moon rose at approximately 11:30 P.M. and was 90 percent illuminated. Thus, unusually, Harker's record of the moon is accurate. Compare chapter 3, note 56. (But see appendix 2, "The Dating of *Dracula*," for a complete discussion of the moon data.)

Suddenly, away on our left, I saw a faint flickering blue flame.[94] The driver saw it at the same moment; he at once checked the horses and, jumping to the ground, disappeared into the darkness. I did not know what to do, the less as the howling of the wolves grew closer; but while I wondered the driver suddenly appeared again, and without a word took his seat, and we resumed our journey. I think I must have fallen asleep and kept dreaming of the incident, for it seemed to be repeated endlessly, and now looking back, it is like a sort of awful nightmare. Once the flame appeared so near the road, that even in the darkness around us I could watch the driver's motions. He went rapidly to where the blue flame arose—it must have been very faint, for it did not seem to illumine the place around it at all—and gathering a few stones, formed them into some device. Once there appeared a strange optical effect:[95] when he stood between me and the flame he did not obstruct it, for I could see its ghostly flicker all the same.[96] This startled me, but as the effect was only momentary, I took it that my eyes deceived me straining through the darkness. Then for a time there were no blue flames, and we sped onwards through the gloom, with the howling of the wolves around us, as though they were following in a moving circle.[97]

At last there came a time when the driver went further afield than he had yet gone, and during his absence the horses began to tremble worse than ever and to snort and scream with fright. I could not see any cause for it, for the howling of the wolves had ceased altogether; but just then the moon, sailing through the black clouds, appeared behind the jagged crest of a beetling, pine-clad rock, and by its light I saw around us a ring of wolves, with white teeth and lolling red tongues, with long, sinewy limbs and shaggy hair.[98] They were a hundred times more terrible in the grim silence which held them than even when they howled. For myself, I felt a sort of paralysis of fear. It is only when a man feels himself face to face with such horrors that he can understand their true import.[99]

All at once the wolves began to howl as though the moonlight had had some peculiar effect on them. The horses jumped about and reared, and looked helplessly round with eyes that rolled in a way painful to see; but the living ring of terror encompassed them on every side, and they had perforce to remain within it. I called to the coachman to come, for it seemed to me that our only chance was to try to break out through the ring and to aid his approach. I shouted and beat the side of the calèche, hoping by the noise to scare the wolves from that side, so as to give him a chance of reaching the trap.[100] How he came there, I know not, but I heard his voice raised in a tone of imperious command, and looking towards the sound, saw him stand in the roadway. As he swept his long arms, as though brushing aside some impalpable obstacle, the wolves fell back and back further still.[101] Just then a heavy cloud passed across the face of the moon, so that we were again in darkness.

When I could see again the driver was climbing into the calèche, and the wolves had disappeared. This was all so strange and uncanny that a dreadful fear came upon me, and I was afraid to speak or move. The time seemed interminable as we swept on our way, now in almost complete darkness, for the rolling clouds obscured the moon. We kept on ascending, with occasional periods of quick descent, but in the main always ascending.[102] Suddenly, I became conscious of the fact that the driver was in the act of pulling up the horses in the courtyard of a vast ruined castle, from whose tall black windows came no ray of light, and whose broken battlements showed a jagged line against the moonlit sky.

99 This somewhat puzzling sentence does not appear in the Abridged Text. There is material deleted here that gives a clue about "Dracula's Guest" (see appendix 1). Although some is illegible, one deleted sentence reads: "As I looked at them I unconsciously put my hand to my throat which was still sore from the licking of the gray wolf's file-like tongue."

100 Another term for a horse-drawn carriage. This refers to the caleche.

101 McNally and Florescu (*The Essential Dracula*) credit Emily Gerard's "Transylvanian Superstitions" as the source of the idea that vampires command the wolves, but it is not stated there.

102 The Manuscript reads "till waking up from a sort of reverie the sleep into which I must have fallen I found the driver in the act . . . ," differing from the published narrative.

Chapter 2[1]

1 Numbered chapter "iii" in type in the Manuscript, changed by hand to "II."

2 A colloquial word meaning personal effects or belongings—here, Harker's baggage.

JONATHAN HARKER'S JOURNAL
—continued.

5 May.—I must have been asleep, for certainly if I had been fully awake I must have noticed the approach to such a remarkable place. In the gloom the courtyard looked of considerable size, and as several dark ways led from it under great round arches it perhaps seemed bigger than it really is. I have not yet been able to see it by daylight.

When the calèche stopped the driver jumped down, and held out his hand to assist me to alight. Again I could not but notice his prodigious strength. His hand actually seemed like a steel vice that could have crushed mine if he had chosen. Then he took out my traps,[2] and placed them on the ground beside me as I stood close to a great door, old and studded with large iron nails, and set in a projecting doorway of massive stone. I could see even in the dim light that the stone was massively carved, but that the carving had been much worn by time and weather. As I stood, the driver jumped again into his seat and shook the reins; the horses started forward, and trap and all disappeared down one of the dark openings.

I stood in silence where I was, for I did not know what to do. Of bell or knocker there was no sign; through these frowning walls and dark window openings it was not likely that my voice could penetrate. The time I waited seemed endless, and I felt doubts and fears crowding upon me. What sort of place had I come to, and among what kind of people? What

Cover of the French translation of *Dracula, L'homme de la nuit.*
(Paris: L'Edition Française Illustrée, 1920)

3 The material following, up to "I began to rub…" is added in Stoker's hand in the Manuscript.

4 English solicitors are attorneys qualified to conduct legal proceedings for their clients. (Outside the courtroom, for other than on a limited basis, the courts were the domain of the barristers—see chapter 3, note 40). At this time, the requirements were a period of apprenticeship (as a clerk) with a practising attorney (the length dependent on the clerk's education) and the passing of an examination. We learn nothing of Harker's formal education, and his clerkship may have been as long as ten years (or as short as three years). The examination was held in the Incorporated Law Society hall at 103–113 Chancery Lane, known as the Institute. Sir Joseph Porter, in Gilbert and Sullivan's *H.M.S. Pinafore* (1878), sings of his career at an attorney's firm: "In serving writs I made such a name / That an articled clerk I soon became; / I wore clean collars and a brand-new suit / For the pass examination at the Institute, / And that pass examination did so well for me, / That now I am the Ruler of the Queen's Navee!"

5 The Manuscript contains the following, which does not appear in the published text: "and as far as I knew miles and miles away from any human being except the man who had brought me here." At this point, Harker had no reason to believe that he was alone, and Stoker must have recognised that Harker's comment here was a matter of hindsight.

6 The Manuscript continues with this sentence, omitted from the published narrative: "I do not think I was ever so glad to see anything in my life for the sense of loneliness and fear was becoming intolerable." Harker himself (or his supportive wife) may have requested that this display of his weakness be omitted.

7 Curiously, there are very few physical descriptions of Dracula. Unlike in most cinematic representations, he is an "old man,"

sort of grim adventure was it on which I had embarked?[3] Was this a customary incident in the life of a solicitor's clerk sent out to explain the purchase of a London estate to a foreigner? Solicitor's clerk! Mina would not like that. Solicitor,—for just before leaving London I got word that my examination was successful; and I am now a full-blown solicitor![4] I began to rub my eyes and pinch myself to see if I were awake. It all seemed like a horrible nightmare to me, and I expected that I should suddenly awake, and find myself at home, with the dawn struggling in through the windows, as I had now and again felt in the morning after a day of overwork. But my flesh answered the pinching test, and my eyes were not to be deceived. I was indeed awake and among the Carpathians.[5] All I could do now was to be patient, and to wait the coming of the morning.

Just as I had come to this conclusion I heard a heavy step approaching behind the great door, and saw through the chinks the gleam of a coming light.[6] Then there was the sound of rattling chains and the clanking of massive bolts drawn back. A key was turned with the loud grating noise of long disuse, and the great door swung back.

Within, stood a tall old man, clean shaven save for a long white moustache, and clad in black from head to foot, without a single speck of colour about him anywhere.[7] He held in his hand an antique silver lamp, in which the flame burned without chimney or globe of any kind, throwing long quivering shadows as it flickered in the draught of the open door.[8] The old man motioned me in with his right hand with a courtly gesture, saying in excellent English, but with a strange intonation:—

"Welcome to my house! Enter freely and of your own will!"[9] He made no motion of stepping to meet me, but stood like a statue, as though his gesture of welcome had fixed him into stone. The instant, however, that I had stepped over the threshold, he moved impulsively forward, and holding out his hand grasped mine with a strength which made me wince, an effect which was not lessened by the fact that it seemed as cold as ice—more like the hand of a dead than a living man. Again he said:—

"Welcome to my house. Come freely. Go safely; and leave something of the happiness you bring!" The strength of the handshake was so much akin to that which I had noticed in the driver, whose face I had not seen, that for a moment I doubted if it were not the same person to whom I was speaking; so to make sure, I said interrogatively:—

"Count Dracula?" He bowed in a courtly way as he replied:—

"I am Dracula; and I bid you welcome, Mr. Harker, to my house.[10] Come in; the night air is chill, and you must need to eat and rest."[11] As he was speaking, he put the lamp on a bracket on the wall, and stepping out, took my luggage; he had carried it in before I could forestall him. I protested but he insisted:—

"Nay, sir, you are my guest. It is late, and my people are not available. Let me see to your comfort myself." He insisted on carrying my traps along the passage, and then up a great winding stair, and along another great passage, on whose stone floor our steps rang heavily. At the end of this he threw open a heavy door, and I rejoiced to see within a well-lit room in which a table was spread for supper, and on whose mighty hearth a great fire of logs, flamed and flared.

The Count halted, putting down my bags, closed the door, and crossing the room, opened another door, which led into a small octagonal room lit by a single lamp, and seemingly without a window of any sort.[12] Passing through this, he opened another door, and motioned me to enter. It was a welcome sight; for here was a great bedroom well lighted and war med with another log fire, which sent a hollow roar up the wide chimney. The Count himself left my luggage inside and withdrew, saying, before he closed the door:—

"You will need, after your journey, to refresh yourself by making your toilet. I trust you will find all you wish.[13] When you are ready come into the other room, where you will find your supper prepared."

The light and warmth and the Count's courteous welcome seemed to have dissipated all my doubts and fears. Having then reached my normal state, I discovered that I was half famished with hunger; so making a hasty toilet, I went into the other room.

I found supper already laid out.[14] My host, who stood on one with a "white moustache." There are also no servants in the castle.

8 Leatherdale (*Dracula Unearthed*) points out that Dracula appears unafraid of fire, even though Van Helsing later advises that in order to kill him, the hunters should cut off his head "and burn his heart."

9 Wolf comments, in *The Essential Dracula*, that this reflects the tradition that the Devil can transact only with willing "customers." This is evidenced as early as the curious vampire tale of an anonymous author, "The Mysterious Stranger" (translated into English in 1860), in which the following dialogue between Azzo (the vampire) and Franziska (his female victim) is recorded:

"'You wish it?—You press the invitation?' asked the stranger [Azzo] earnestly and decidedly. 'To be sure, for otherwise you will not come,' replied the young lady shortly. 'Well, then, come I will!' said the other, again fixing his gaze on her. 'If my company does not please you at any time, you will have yourself to blame for an acquaintance with one who seldom forces himself, but is difficult to shake off.'"

This consensual element is part of the nineteenth-century image of the "seductive" vampire but sounds a lot like the archaic view that female rape victims always consent to or invite the rape. See "Dracula's Family Tree" in Part II for a discussion of the shared traits of reports of vampires. Whether Harker or Stoker had read "The Mysterious Stranger" is unknown, but there are numerous incidents in the story that are echoed in Harker's account, including, for example, the nocturnal habits of the knight Azzo and the dreamy quality of the meetings between Azzo and Franziska.

In the Abridged Text, the phrase reads: "Come freely," not "Enter freely."

10 How did Dracula know Harker's name? Dracula has not yet received the letter from Peter Hawkins carried by Harker, nor does the excerpt incorporated in Harker's journal identify the "young man." Perhaps the owner of the Golden Krone Hotel in Bistritz passed along the information, by means unknown. The identification of "Mr. Harker" does not appear in the Abridged Text—either Harker or Stoker must have noticed this error.

11 This sentence does not appear in the Abridged Text.

12 Wolf (*The Essential Dracula*) finds it significant that some Victorian coffins (although not Dracula's—see chapter 4, note 18) were octagonal in shape. Leatherdale (*Dracula Unearthed*), however, makes the reasonable observation that the room was likely the base of a turret of the castle.

13 This sentence is not in the Abridged Text.

14 There is no supper and no supping in the Abridged Text.

15 In the era of Jane Austen's novels (that is, the early nineteenth century), "dinner" was a large meal following breakfast, usually at 3:00 or 4:00 P.M., followed by a lighter evening meal, termed "supper." By the late nineteenth century, "lunch" was well established, and the upper classes (and the middle classes following their lead) had moved dinner to 5:00 or 6:00 P.M. *Cassell's Household Guide* for the 1880s advised: "Supper parties are simply late dinners, shorn of fish, soup, and dessert as separate courses. At suppers most of the viands are placed on the table at the same time, and servants attend throughout the repast." As noted above, Dracula has dispensed with servants. Harker would have taken Dracula's "I do not sup" simply to mean that he had had dinner recently.

This conversation has none of the drama or subtext given the scene in the Tod Browning film adaption of *Dracula* (1931), in which Bela Lugosi archly intones, "I never drink—wine."

side of the great fireplace, leaning against the stonework, made a graceful wave of his hand to the table, and said:—

"I pray you, be seated and sup how you please. You will, I trust, excuse me that I do not join you; but I have dined already, and I do not sup."[15]

I handed to him the sealed letter which Mr. Hawkins had entrusted to me.[16] He opened it and read it gravely; then, with a charming smile, he handed it to me to read. One passage of it, at least, gave me a thrill of pleasure:[17]

"I must regret that an attack of gout,[18] from which malady I am a constant sufferer, forbids absolutely any travelling on my part for some time to come; but I am happy to say I can send a sufficient substitute, one in whom I have every possible confidence. He is a young man, full of energy and talent in his own way, and of a very faithful disposition. He is discreet and silent, and has grown into manhood in my service. He shall be ready to attend on you when you will during his stay, and shall take your instructions in all matters."

The Count himself came forward and took off the cover of a dish, and I fell to at once on an excellent roast chicken.[19] This, with some cheese and a salad and a bottle of old Tokay,[20] of which I had two glasses, was my supper. During the time I was eating it the Count asked me many questions as to my journey, and I told him by degrees all I had experienced.[21]

By this time I had finished my supper, and by my host's desire had drawn up a chair by the fire and begun to smoke a cigar which he offered me, at the same time excusing himself that he did not smoke. I had now an opportunity of observing him, and found him of a very marked physiognomy.[22]

His face was a strong—a very strong—aquiline, with high bridge of the thin nose and peculiarly arched nostrils; with lofty domed forehead, and hair growing scantily round the temples, but profusely elsewhere. His eyebrows were very massive, almost meeting over the nose,[23] and with bushy hair that seemed to curl in its own profusion. The mouth, so far as I could see it under the heavy moustache, was fixed and rather cruel-looking, with peculiarly sharp white teeth; these protruded over the lips, whose remarkable ruddiness showed astonishing vitality in a man of his years.[24] For the rest, his

16 Jonathan (or Mina) seems to have forgotten that the reader has no idea who Mr. Hawkins is. Peter Hawkins is later revealed to be Dracula's Exeter solicitor. In the Notes, Stoker first gives the name as Nathan Abbott and later as Abraham Aaronson, then as John Hawkins, and finally as Peter Hawkins. Dracula, writing from Styria (a predominantly German-speaking province), asks Aaronson to come in person or send a trustworthy agent who, he stipulates, must not be able to speak German. As we have already seen, Harker speaks a "smattering" of German. See text accompanying chapter 1, note 14. Christopher Frayling (*Vampyres*) suggests that by this precaution, Dracula intended to protect himself from gossiping peasants. Harker's German does little to inform him of his peril.

The letter seems surprisingly unbusinesslike, making no mention of Harker's professional credentials and containing the ominous phrase "full of energy and talent in his own way," implying that Harker's ways may be very different from those of the solicitor Dracula engaged. Indeed, Hawkins's note makes Harker sound like little more than a messenger boy of whom Hawkins is fond. As will be seen, there is little evidence of what Harker's "way" may be, for he reports virtually no professional acts performed by him while staying with Dracula. It is quite a surprise when, in chapter 12, we are informed that Harker has become a partner in the firm.

17 This entire paragraph is added in Stoker's hand in the Manuscript.

18 Gout is a disorder that strikes predominantly men, usually over the age of thirty, and is characterised by chronic inflammation of the joints. A buildup of urate deposits in the tissue surrounding the joints can cause deformity and extreme stiffness, particularly in the feet and hands. Although extremely painful, gout is not fatal in itself, though it is often associated with high blood pressure.

19 Harker serves himself in the Abridged Text.

20 This sweet, white wine is produced in the area around the town of Tokay (or Tokaj, in Hungarian), in the foothills of the Carpathians. It is made from three grapes: Furmint, Hárslevelü, and occasionally Muscat or Muskotály, with the Furmint contributing approximately 50 percent. The bottle's label would have read Tokaji (the possessive) followed by Aszu, Szamorodui, or Essencia, indicating the *terroir*. In 1865, Dr. Robert Druitt published a popular pamphlet titled "Report on the Cheap Wines from France, Italy, Austria, Greece, and Hungary; their quality, wholesomeness, and price, etc.," in which he advocated Tokay as possessed of remarkable medicinal qualities. He described the taste as "a flavour of green tea, but an amalgam of the scents of meadowsweet, acacia blossom, and the lime tree flower." Harker apparently had some familiarity with the wine, for he makes no comment on its unusual taste (compare his amateurish wine notes on "Golden Mediasch," chapter 1, note 58).

21 The Manuscript adds: "He seemed very interested especially at my adventures in Munich. When I told him of the coming of the soldiers he appeared quite excited and exclaimed:" This material, omitted from the published narrative, clearly refers to "Dracula's Guest" (see appendix 1). Leatherdale (*Dracula Unearthed*) points out that Harker apparently omitted any discussion of the strange gifts he received from his fellow travellers, for the crucifix later takes Dracula by surprise.

22 The "science" of physiognomy was both a mode of discriminating character by outward appearances and a method of divination from form and feature. Its second aspect was outlawed in England, but the idea that character was determinable from one's appearance lasted for centuries and is espoused by several of the principals in the narrative.

Its greatest proponent was Johann Kaspar Lavater (1741–1801), whose *Physiognomische Fragmente zur Beförderung der Menschenkenntniss und Menschenliebe* (1775–1778) won considerable adherents. In 1888, the *Encyclopædia Britannica* (9th ed.) commented: "The popular style, good illustrations, and pious spirit pervading the writings of Lavater have given to them a popularity they little deserved, as there is really no system in his work, which largely consists of rhapsodical comments upon the several portraits. Having a happy knack of estimating character, especially when acquainted with the histories of the persons in question, the good pastor contrived to write a graphic and readable book, but one much inferior to Porta's or Aristotle's as a systematic treatise. With him the descriptive school of physiognomists may be said to have ended. . . . The few straggling works which have since appeared are scarcely deserving of notice, the rising attraction of phrenology [the determination of character from the shape of the skull] having given to pure physiognomy the *coup de grâce* by taking into itself whatever was likely to live of the older science."

Physiognomy, though discarded in its broadest precepts, is bound up in the ideas of Victorian criminologist Cesare Lombroso (see chapter 25, note 46) and eventually the ideas of Sigmund Freud relating to the connection of outward manifestations—habits, gestures, facial tics, and the like—and interior neuroses and conditions. The remnants of the "science" persist in modern psychology's categories of "body types."

23 "Massive" eyebrows, especially those that met in the middle, known colloquially as "unibrows," were viewed with suspicion by Lombroso (see chapter 25, note 46) and were often associated with werewolves. Dracula shared this trait with Ambrosio, the central figure of Matthew Gregory Lewis's *The Monk* (1796), who is described as having "dark brows almost joined together."

24 Dracula exhibits the classical dentition of the werewolf, described in Sabine Baring-Gould's 1865 *Book of Were-Wolves*: "the teeth were strong and white, and the canine teeth protruded over the lower lip when the mouth was closed."

ears were pale and at the tops extremely pointed; the chin was broad and strong, and the cheeks firm though thin. The general effect was one of extraordinary pallor.[25]

Hitherto I had noticed the backs of his hands as they lay on his knees in the firelight, and they had seemed rather white and fine; but seeing them now close to me, I could not but notice that they were rather coarse—broad, with squat fingers. Strange to say, there were hairs in the centre of the palm. The nails were long and fine, and cut to a sharp point.[26] As the Count leaned over me and his hands touched me, I could not repress a shudder. It may have been that[27] his breath was rank, but a horrible feeling of nausea came over me, which, do what I would, I could not conceal.[28] The Count, evidently noticing it, drew back; and with a grim sort of smile, which showed more than he had yet done his protuberant teeth, sat himself down again on his own side of the fireplace. We were both silent for a while; and as I looked towards the window I saw the first dim streak of the coming dawn. There seemed a strange stillness over everything; but as I listened I heard as if from down below in the valley the howling of many wolves. The Count's eyes gleamed, and he said:—

"Listen to them—the children of the night. What music they make!" Seeing, I suppose, some expression in my face strange to him, he added:—

"Ah, sir, you dwellers in the city cannot enter into the feelings of the hunter." Then he rose and said:—

"But you must be tired. Your bedroom is all ready, and to-morrow you shall sleep as late as you will. I have to be away till the afternoon; so sleep well and dream well!" and, with a courteous bow, he opened for me himself the door to the octagonal room, and I entered my bedroom. . . .

I am all in a sea of wonders. I doubt; I fear; I think strange things, which I dare not confess to my own soul. God keep me, if only for the sake of those dear to me!

7 May.[29]—It is again early morning, but I have rested and enjoyed the last twenty-four hours. I slept till late in the day, and awoke of my own accord. When I had dressed myself I went into the room where we had supped, and found a cold

25 The Manuscript continues: "When I told him of the wolf which lay on my chest saving my life in the cold and whose howling seemed to direct the soldiers to where . . . [balance illegible]." This is another reference to the episode described in "Dracula's Guest" (see appendix 1), probably removed from the published text when that episode was deleted.

26 Baring-Gould's description of the werewolf continues: "The . . . hands were large and powerful, the nails black and pointed like bird's talons" (*Book of Were-Wolves*).

27 The Manuscript reads: "there is a morbid susceptibility about a wound and that we fear any approach to touching it—or it may have been that as the Count leaned over me." This remark was likely deleted from the published narrative when the "Dracula's Guest" material (see appendix 1) was excised.

28 Halitosis is a common symptom ascribed by folklore to vampires. In the *Buffy* universe, the undead are described more literally—because they are dead, they have no respiration. (In a comical scene from the television series *Angel*, the vampire Darla is about to give birth; a mortal companion exhorts her to use the Lamaze "panting" techniques to master the pain, only to be forcefully reminded that Darla does not breathe!)

29 This evidently should be 6 May. Harker speaks of resting for twenty-four, not forty-eight, hours, and later asks about events of the "preceding night."

30 Each of the "Abraham" tapestries commissioned by Henry VIII (ca. 1540) that hang in Hampton Court Palace reportedly cost the same as one of Henry's battleships ([London] *Times*, 26 October 2005). Hampton Court Palace, the largest royal palace in Great Britain, was commenced in 1515 (on an older base) by Cardinal Wolsey, a crony of Henry VIII. Occupied subsequently by numerous monarchs, it ceased to be a royal residence after George II, and at the end of the nineteenth century, over eight hundred of its one thousand rooms were occupied by aristocratic pensioners of the Crown. The 1896 London "Baedeker" estimated over 250,000 visitors annually; the palace was open to the public six days a week. The earliest surviving works at Hampton Court were collected by Henry VIII, and significant portions of his tapestry collection—which numbered over two thousand pieces—were on public display in Harker's youth (and remain so today). Harker's characterisation of these treasures as "worn and frayed and moth-eaten" displays an appalling lack of appreciation of the

breakfast laid out, with coffee kept hot by the pot being placed on the hearth. There was a card on the table, on which was written:—

"I have to be absent for a while. Do not wait for me.—D."

So I set to and enjoyed a hearty meal. When I had done, I looked for a bell, so that I might let the servants know I had finished; but I could not find one. There are certainly odd deficiencies in the house, considering the extraordinary evidences of wealth which are round me. The table service is of gold, and so beautifully wrought that it must be of immense value. The curtains and upholstery of the chairs and sofas and the hangings of my bed are of the costliest and most beautiful fabrics, and must have been of fabulous value when they were made, for they are centuries old, though in excellent order. I saw something like them in Hampton Court, but there they were worn and frayed and moth-eaten.[30] But still in none of the rooms is there a mirror. There is not even a toilet glass on my table, and I had to get the little shaving glass from my bag before I could either shave or brush my hair. I have not yet seen a servant anywhere, or heard a sound near the

One of the tapestries in the Great Hall at Hampton Court.

castle except the howling of wolves. When I had finished my meal—I do not know whether to call it breakfast or dinner, for it was between five and six o'clock when I had it[31]—I looked about for something to read, for I did not like to go about the castle until I had asked the Count's permission. There was absolutely nothing in the room, book, newspaper, or even writing materials; so I opened another door in the room and found a sort of library. The door opposite mine I tried, but found it locked.

In the library I found, to my great delight, a vast number of English books,[32] whole shelves full of them, and bound volumes of magazines and newspapers. A table in the centre was littered with English magazines and newspapers, though none of them were of very recent date. The books were of the most varied kind—history, geography, politics, political economy, botany,[33] geology,[34] law—all relating to England and English life and customs and manners. There were even such books of reference as the London Directory,[35] the "Red" and "Blue" books,[36] Whitaker's Almanack,[37] the Army and Navy Lists,[38] and—it somehow gladdened my heart to see it—the Law List.[39]

Whilst I was looking at the books, the door opened, and the Count entered. He saluted me in a hearty way, and hoped that I had had a good night's rest. Then he went on:—

"I am glad you found your way in here, for I am sure there is much that will interest you. These friends"—and he laid his hand on some of the books—"have been good friends to me, and for some years past, ever since I had the idea of going to London, have given me many, many hours of pleasure. Through them I have come to know your great England; and to know her is to love her. I long to go through the crowded streets of your mighty London, to be in the midst of the whirl and rush of humanity, to share its life, its change, its death, and all that makes it what it is.[40] But alas! as yet I only know your tongue through books. To you, my friend, I look that I know it to speak."

"But, Count," I said, "you know and speak English thoroughly!" He bowed gravely.

"I thank you, my friend, for your all too-flattering estimate,

age and importance of the pieces, some of which were already over three hundred years old at the time of his visit to the palace.

31 Wolf (*The Essential Dracula*) says "A.M.," but it is plainly late afternoon; in the previous paragraph Harker states that he slept "till late in the day" and then got up to find the meal awaiting him. If it were morning, why would he call the meal dinner?

32 Harker does not say that there are only English books in the library, and it may well be that Dracula had contingent plans for other countries and studied those literatures as well. Scholars ponder why Dracula chose England as his target. Professor John Sutherland, in *The Literary Detective: 100 Puzzles in Classic Fiction*, expresses the view that Dracula selected England as the most "civilized"—meaning technologically advanced—country in the world and therefore the best school in which to pursue his study of the impending twentieth century.

33 Why botany? Was Dracula concerned about growths of wolfbane, wild roses, or mountain ash?

34 What possible interest could Dracula have in geology? The only soil he cared about was his native soil, which he intended to bring with him. However, see Van Helsing's comments about strange geological formations in Transylvania in the text accompanying chapter 24, note 21. Perhaps Dracula was seeking similar sources of vampires.

35 The first known London directory appeared in 1677. However, in 1765 a new law requiring streets to be named and houses to be numbered gave birth to a new industry. The first post office directory of London was published in 1799, by the post office itself. Commercial versions soon sprang up. In 1837, Frederick Kelly published an edition that included a "Trades" section; in 1841, the volume gained a street directory. By

1855, the Kelly directory had taken over its last significant rival, *Watkins's Commercial and General London Directory and Court Guide,* and became the standard of choice: the *Kelly's Post Office London Directory,* which ceased publication only in 1991. By the end of the nineteenth century, the directory included listings of government, banking, law courts, police, alphabetical and classified listing of trades, and court officials (that is to say, a "map to the stars' homes") as well as a list of occupants of every metropolitan address.

36 Wolf (*The Essential Dracula*) identifies the "Red Book" as the official list of all persons serving or pensioned by the state; a "Blue Book" is an official British government publication. There are numerous editions of the former, as for example, *A List of the Principal Places, Pensions, and Sinecures, held under the British Government, extracted from the Extraordinary Red Book. With an Appendix; containing an*

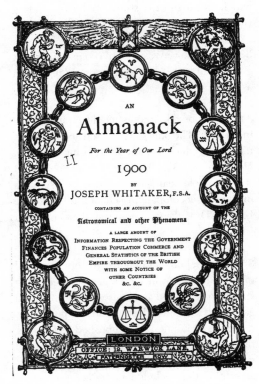

Title page of *Whitaker's Almanack* (1900).

Account of the Income and Expenditure of the Civil List, published by J. Marshall at Newcastle-upon-Tyne in 1817. As to the latter, there are countless examples; in this editor's collection, for example, is a ten-page pamphlet on the Gold Coast, subtitled "Report on the Blue Book for 1888," printed by Her Majesty's Stationery Office in London in 1889.

But it is unclear why Dracula would bother with copies of these reference works. The title "Red Book" has been appropriated by numerous publishers. For example, Charles Dickens Jr., in his 1888 *Dictionary of London,* recommends Webster's *Royal Red Book* as an excellent directory to the West End of London, and such a work would seem much more useful to Dracula than information about pensioners. Similarly, "Blue Book" became a generic term, and Gardiner's *Royal Blue Book* and Kelly's *Royal Blue Book* were other popular London directories. Even if Harker means a government publication, *which* "Blue Book" Dracula owned is open to speculation.

37 Britain's best-known almanac, first published in 1868. A copy of the 1878 edition—along with a *Bradshaw's* railway guide (see note 51 below) and twelve pictures of Britain's most attractive women—is buried in a time capsule under Cleopatra's Needle, the Egyptian granite obelisk erected on Victoria Embankment in 1878. Famously, Sherlock Holmes used the *Almanack* to decipher a cryptic message in *The Valley of Fear* (1914). The *Almanack* continues to be published annually, but the Whitaker family company was purchased in 1987 by The Stationery Office, the privatised successor to Her Majesty's Stationery Office, the official government printer, and subsequently sold to A&C Black, the publisher of *Who's Who* in the United Kingdom.

38 The "Army Lists" were published quarterly or semiannually by the government and listed all officers by grade. The "Navy Lists" were separate publications, one listing officers by grade and the other listing ships. Each list might

Cleopatra's Needle.
Queen's London (1897)

run to dozens of volumes for a single quarter. It seems very unlikely that Dracula would have acquired these works.

39 A directory of attorneys, judges, and related legal personnel, privately published. For many years, the series was known as "Clarke's *Law List.*" An 1842 edition is titled "Cockell, Teesdale. *The Law List; Being a list of the Judges and Officers of the different Courts of Justice: Counsel, with the dates of their call and Inns of Court; special pleaders, conveyancers; and a complete and accurate list of Certificated Attornies, Notaries, & c. in England and Wales, with the London Agents to the Country Attornies. . . .* London: V. and R. Stevens and G. S. Norton (1842)."

Dracula's collection of books is a curious one. It is tempting to view these motley volumes as the product of a decorator's desire for a library

filled with nicely bound tomes. What purpose could be served by these endless lists of names and addresses? Was Dracula planning to build a portfolio of false identities for himself? Was he planning to recruit highly placed protégés (Kim Newman's *Anno Dracula* and its sequels posit an England in which vampirism has become the pedigree of social respectability)? Or were these perhaps a . . . menu?

40 In other words, in the view of most scholars, to find a hunting ground where the prey is more plentiful and less wary. Francis Ford Coppola, in his 1992 film *Bram Stoker's Dracula*, gave Dracula a more specific motive: Coppola imagined that Mina Harker was the reincarnation of the wife of the mortal Dracula. (Compare with Dan Curtis's 1973 *Dracula*, in which Lucy Westenra is the reincarnation of the wife.)

41 "I don't want to talk grammar. I want to talk like a lady." Attributed to Eliza Doolittle, in George Bernard Shaw's *Pygmalion*, act 2 (1916). Leatherdale (*Dracula Unearthed*) makes the amusing point that Dracula, unsophisticated as he is, would not know that he was acquiring a Devon accent rather than a London one: Harker has spent his entire life in Exeter. However, Roger Johnson, in private correspondence with this editor, suggests that as a professional man, Harker was likely to have attended a minor public school, where he would have learned "received pronunciation" and spoken without a regional accent.

42 The highest rank of Roumanian aristocracy, second only to the ruling princes. Transylvanian peasants rose in revolt in 1848, and the power of the boyars was diluted through a land-reform committee of boyars and peasants created by the government. The assemblies of boyars in Moldavia and Wallachia were suppressed by the invading Russians and Austrians, and the terms of the princes elected by them were sharply limited.

43 Exod. 2:22—Moses gave his son by Zipporah the Hebrew name Gershom, from *Ger Sham*, meaning "a stranger there," for, as Moses said, "I have been a stranger in a strange land." Dracula's scriptural knowledge is displayed several times to Harker and his colleagues.

but yet I fear that I am but a little way on the road I would travel. True, I know the grammar and the words, but yet I know not how to speak them."[41]

"Indeed," I said, "you speak excellently."

"Not so," he answered. "Well, I know that, did I move and speak in your London, none there are who would not know me for a stranger. That is not enough for me. Here I am noble; I am *boyar*;[42] the common people know me, and I am master. But a stranger in a strange land,[43] he is no one; men know him not—and to know not is to care not for. I am content if I am like the rest, so that no man stops if he sees me, or pause in his speaking if he hear my words, to say, 'Ha, ha! a stranger!' I have been so long master that I would be master still—or at least that none other should be master of me. You come to me not alone as agent of my friend Peter Hawkins, of Exeter, to tell me all about my new estate in London. You shall, I trust, rest here with me a while, so that by our talking I may learn the English intonation; and I would that you tell me when I make error, even of the smallest, in my speaking. I am sorry that I had to be away so long to-day; but you will, I know, forgive one who has so many important affairs in hand."

Of course I said all I could about being willing, and asked if I might come into that room when I chose. He answered: "Yes, certainly," and added:—

"You may go anywhere you wish in the castle, except where the doors are locked, where of course you will not wish to go. There is reason that all things are as they are, and did you see with my eyes and know with my knowledge, you would perhaps better understand." I said I was sure of this, and then he went on:—

"We are in Transylvania; and Transylvania is not England. Our ways are not your ways, and there shall be to you many strange things. Nay, from what you have told me of your experiences already, you know something of what strange things here may be."

This led to much conversation; and as it was evident that he wanted to talk, if only for talking's sake, I asked him many questions regarding things that had already happened to me or come within my notice. Sometimes he sheered off the subject, or turned the conversation by pretending not to understand; but generally he answered all I asked most frankly. Then[44] as time went on, and I had got somewhat bolder, I asked him of some of the strange things of the preceding night, as, for instance, why the coachman went to the places where we had seen the blue flames. Was it indeed true that they showed where gold was hidden? He then explained to me that it was commonly believed that on a certain night of the year—last night, in fact, when all evil spirits are supposed to have unchecked sway—a blue flame is seen over any place where treasure has been concealed.[45] "That treasure has been hidden," he went on, "in the region through which you came last night, there can be but little doubt; for it was the ground fought over for centuries by the Wallachian, the Saxon, and the Turk.[46] Why, there is hardly a foot of soil in all this region that has not been enriched by the blood of men, patriots or invaders. In old days there were stirring times, when the Austrian and the Hungarian came up in hordes, and the patriots went out to meet them—men and women, the aged and the children too—and waited their coming on the rocks above the passes, that they might sweep destruction on them with their artificial avalanches.[47] When the invader was triumphant he found but little, for whatever there was had been sheltered in the friendly soil."

"But how," said I, "can it have remained so long undiscovered, when there is a sure index to it if men will but take the trouble to look?" The Count smiled, and as his lips ran back over his gum, the long, sharp, canine teeth showed out strangely; he answered:—

"Because your peasant is at heart a coward and a fool! Those flames only appear on one night; and on that night no man of this land will, if he can help it, stir without his doors.[48] And, dear sir, even if he did he would not know what to do. Why, even the peasant that you tell me of who marked the place of the flame would not know where to look in daylight even for his own work.[49] You would not, I dare be sworn, be able to find these places again?"

"There you are right," I said. "I know no more than the dead where even to look for them."[50] Then we drifted into other matters.

44 The Abridged Text omits the material beginning with this sentence and ending three paragraphs later with a drift into "other matters."

45 See chapter 1, note 94.

46 These names are inserted in the Manuscript in the editor's hand, possibly demonstrating the timing of the change in the narrative from a Styria location to Transylvania.

47 The "avalanches" were recorded as a feature of the defeat of Charles Robert of Anjou, king of Hungary, who invaded Roumania in November 1330. Caught in the pass of Posada by the armies of Prince Basarab of Wallachia, the invaders were crushed by boulders hurled down on them.

In 1462, after major battles against the Turks, including guerrilla warfare such as that recounted by Dracula, Vlad Ţepeş (ca. 1431–1476), Voivode (a Roumanian term for "prince") of Wallachia, fled into Transylvania and was held as a prisoner by the Hungarian king Matthias Corvinus. He recovered the throne in 1476 but died shortly thereafter. While he is best known today for the numerous atrocities he committed (or is alleged to have committed), earning him the nickname "Vlad the Impaler," Vlad has been resurrected as a national hero of Roumania, who put his country's needs first. He would be little noted today outside Roumania except for the family name: Dracul. His father, also named Vlad, was initiated in 1431 by the Holy Roman Emperor into the Order of the Dragon. Vlad père apparently took on the nickname "Dracul," meaning "dragon" in Hungarian. Vlad Ţepeş adopted the diminutive "Dracula," "son of Dracul" or "son of the Dragon." The Notes reference William Wilkinson's 1820 account of the martial history of Wallachia and in particular quote that the Voivode was "also named Dracula." Wilkinson notes: "Dracula in the Wallachian language means Devil. The Wallachians were, at that time, as they are at present, used to give this as a surname to any person who rendered himself conspicuous either by courage, cruel actions, or cunning" (*An Account of the Principalities of Wallachia and Moldavia*). This suggests that "Dracula" was not the vampire-king's real name but only an epithet applied by the locals. However, the name may also be an invention to disguise the real vampire-king; see chapter 1, note 41.

48 So why, wonders Leatherdale (*Dracula Unearthed*), were there locals on the diligence?

49 Of course the "peasant" was Dracula himself, dressed as the coachman.

50 The Manuscript continues: "but then it struck me as an odd thing that he should know of the episode for I was sure I had not told him of it." Harker later reaches the conclusion that Dracula and the driver were the same man, but perhaps Stoker felt that deduction should be more of a surprise to his readers and omitted this astute observation from the published text.

51 That is, *Bradshaw's General Railway and Steam Navigation Guide for Great Britain and Ireland.* David St. John Thomas, in his introduction to a modern facsimile of the 1887 guide, calls it "a British national institution. Its contents—advertisement as well as 'editorial'— reflected the prosperity of the times. . . . The man who regularly subscribed to *Bradshaw* had an honoured place in his community; parsons took an especial pride in displaying it on their shelves and understood its intricacies so that they could proffer advice on the best routes. Indeed, plotting the quickest cross-country journey between a West country resort and a Scottish fishing port, or between a Welsh coal-mining valley and the Constable Country, was a frequently-played parlour game in the days that every one and everything going more than a dozen or so miles did so behind a steam engine running on rails to a schedule published in *Bradshaw*." The guide ceased publication

"Come," he said at last, "tell me of London and of the house which you have procured for me." With an apology for my amissness, I went into my own room to get the papers from my bag. Whilst I was placing them in order I heard a rattling of china and silver in the next room, and as I passed through, noticed that the table had been cleared and the lamp lit, for it was by this time deep into the dark. The lamps were also lit in the study or library, and I found the Count lying on the sofa, reading, of all things in the world, an English Bradshaw's Guide.[51] When I came in he cleared the books and papers from the table; and with him I went into plans and deeds and figures of all sorts. He was interested in everything, and asked me a myriad questions about the place and its surroundings. He clearly had studied beforehand all he could get on the subject of the neighbourhood, for he evidently at the end knew very much more than I did.[52] When I remarked this, he answered:—

"Well, but, my friend, is it not needful that I should? When I go there I shall be all alone, and my friend Harker Jonathan— nay, pardon me, I fall into my country's habit of putting your patronymic first[53]—my friend Jonathan Harker will not be by my side to correct and aid me. He will be in Exeter, miles away, probably working at papers of the law with my other friend, Peter Hawkins. So!"[54]

We went thoroughly into the business of the purchase of the estate at Purfleet.[55] When I had told him the facts and got his signature to the necessary papers, and had written a letter with them ready to post to Mr. Hawkins, he began to ask me how I had come across so suitable a place. I read to him the notes which I had made at the time, and which I inscribe here:—

"At Purfleet, on a by-road, I came across just such a place as seemed to be required, and where was displayed a dilapidated notice that the place was for sale. It is surrounded by a high wall, of ancient structure, built of heavy stones, and has not been repaired for a large number of years. The closed gates are of heavy old oak and iron, all eaten with rust.

"The estate is called Carfax, no doubt a corruption of the old *Quatre Face*,[56] as the house is four-sided, agreeing with the cardinal points of the compass. It contains in all some

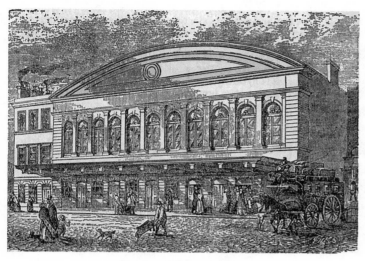

Fenchurch Street station.
T. Gilks, *Illustrated London News*, 10 December 1853

in 2006, citing the advent of Internet railway timetables as the cause of its obsolescence.

Dracula was presumably familiarising himself with the methodology of *Bradshaw's* rather than researching any particular trains. If he were studying the trains to Purfleet, he would have noted that the London, Tilbury, and Southend Railway trains (LT&SR) departed from Fenchurch Street station, located on Railway Place, a small side street in the City of London. While twelve trains a day ran to Purfleet (according to the 1887 *Bradshaw's*), none were expresses, and the trip from London took about forty-five minutes.

Fenchurch Street station, in the neighbourhood of the Corn Exchange, the Leadenhall Market, and various workers' halls, was the first built in the City of London, opening in 1841 to serve the London & Blackwall Railway. It grew slowly, and initially trains ran every fifteen minutes on the same line, alternating up and down. In an effort to increase traffic, bookings were offered on the London & Blackwall to the Woolwich and Gravesend steamers. The LT&SR trains began operating in 1854. As suburbs of London grew up along the Loughton branch line, city merchants began purchasing first-class

season tickets, and by 1900, when the station had five platforms, the clientele of the station had moved "upscale" significantly. However, as traffic from the city dwindled with the advent of the telephone and the decline of steamer passengers, the station's usage diminished, though it remains open today.

52 If by "neighbourhood" Harker means Purfleet, Dracula must have had access to some extraordinary material to provide information about so small a locale. Without this information, Dracula would surely have been deeply disappointed to learn that his new home could hardly be described as located in London.

53 Noted in Crosse (*Round About the Carpathians*) as a common usage.

54 The following paragraph has been added to the Mansucript in Stoker's hand.

55 The 1894 Great Britain "Baedeker" describes Purfleet, located on the left bank of the Thames, in Essex, about 18½ miles below London Bridge, as the seat of large government powder magazines, capable of holding 60,000 barrels of powder. Opposite is the mouth of the small river Darent. The training ship *Cornwall* was moored in the Thames at Purfleet. Charles Dickens Jr., in his 1894 *Dictionary of the Thames*, gives the population as 150, exclusive of the garrison and crew of the *Cornwall*. It was accessible by the London, Tilbury, and Southend Railway. Dickens describes the principal attraction of Purfleet, a "pretty village with some picturesque chalk hills pleasantly wooded, and with a fine view," as the Royal Hotel, widely known for fish dinners. Purfleet received three daily mail deliveries from London, at 7:00 and 8:30 A.M. and 7:00 P.M.; outgoing mail deliveries to London were at 12:35 P.M. and 9:50 P.M.

56 Harker has the concept right but the etymology wrong: The name "Carfax" comes from the Latin word *quadrifucus*, "four-forked"—in other words, a crossroad. For example, Carfax is the centre of the town of Oxford, where the four ancient routes into Oxford meet.

According to folk tradition, criminals (including suicides, guilty of "self-murder" and accordingly denied consecrated burial) were buried at crossroads. This practise may have arisen from a belief that the roads would confuse the ghost of the deceased, preventing it returning to haunt its home. As late as 1784, *The Gentleman's Magazine* reported the case of Thomas Williams of Aberystwyth, who had been poisoned by a woman who shared his house. The poisoner then took poison herself. Reportedly to prevent the murderer-suicide from joining a band of ghosts who had terrorised a nearby village, the coroner proposed that she be buried at a crossroads with a stake through her heart.

Roumanian tradition (as well as the folklore of many other countries, recorded by Montague Summers) expects that suicides will return as vampires. Of course, Harker knew nothing of these connections when he located "Carfax," and there is no indication in the material included in *Dracula* that Dracula provided any directions that would have induced Harker to select it. The Notes indicate that the Harker Papers included a letter from Sir Robert Parton, president of the Law Society, to Peter Hawkins of Cathedral Place, Exeter, referring the matter of purchase of an estate by one "Count Wampyr." This and subsequent letters, evidently suppressed, may have expressed the Count's instructions. Purfleet is an unlikely place for a solicitor to choose as the principal residence of a "nobleman."

57 Vampires, as we will learn later, cannot cross running water; therefore, Dracula must have used extreme caution in flying in and out of his residence.

58 In 1888, the Eastman Dry Plate and Film Company, headquartered in Rochester, New York, introduced its first camera, known simply as "the Kodak camera." (Kodak, despite its Slavic echoes, was a trade name invented by George

twenty acres, quite surrounded by the solid stone wall above mentioned. There are many trees on it, which make it in places gloomy, and there is a deep, dark-looking pond or small lake, evidently fed by some springs, as the water is clear and flows away in a fair-sized stream.**57** The house is very large and of all periods back, I should say, to mediæval times, for one part is of stone immensely thick, with only a few windows high up and heavily barred with iron. It looks like part of a keep, and is close to an old chapel or church. I could not enter it, as I had not the key of the door leading to it from the house, but I have taken with my kodak**58** views of it from various points. The house had been added to but in a very straggling way, and I can only guess at the amount of ground it covers, which must be very great. There are but few houses close at hand, one being a very large house only recently added to and formed into a private lunatic asylum.**59** It is not, however, visible from the grounds."**60**

When I had finished, he said:—

"I am glad that it is old and big. I myself am of an old family, and to live in a new house would kill me. A house cannot be made habitable in a day; and, after all, how few days go to make up a century. I rejoice also that there is a chapel of old times. We Transylvanian nobles love not to think that our bones may lie amongst the common dead. I seek not gaiety nor mirth, not the bright voluptuousness of much sunshine and sparkling waters which please the young and gay. I am no longer young; and my heart, through weary years of mourning over the dead, is not attuned to mirth. Moreover, the walls of my castle are broken; the shadows are many, and the wind breathes cold through the broken battlements and casements. I love the shade and the shadow, and would be alone with my thoughts when I may."

Somehow his words and his look did not seem to accord, or else it was that his cast of face made his smile look malignant and saturnine.**61**

Presently, with an excuse, he left me, asking me to put all my papers together. He was some little time away, and I began to look at some of the books around me. One was an atlas, which I found opened naturally at England, as if that map had been

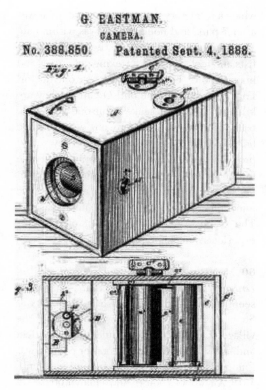

Kodak camera, from George Eastman's 1888
patent application.

Eastman.) Its marketing slogan was "You press
the button—we do the rest." To make good this
boast, the camera was preloaded with enough
film for a hundred exposures. When the film was
exposed, the entire camera had to be sent back
to the manufacturer, which then developed the
pictures and reloaded the camera.

The price of the first camera was US$25 (£5)
and the cost to develop the film was $10 (£2).
In modern purchasing power, this was over
£382 for the camera and £153 for developing.
(The computation is based on the retail price
index. See "Five Ways to Compute the Relative
Value of a UK Pound Amount, 1830–2006," at
www.measuringworth.com/ukcompare/.) However, by 1891, Eastman had introduced less
expensive models (as little as US$6), and with
the introduction of a pocket model in 1895 for
US$5, the cameras began to be affordable for the
masses.

As reported in the influential journal
Amateur Photographer, "the Kodak reached
Britain towards the end of 1888, and was
immediately acclaimed." One reviewer hailed
it as "without exception, the most beautiful
instrument that has ever been offered for the
public in connection with photography" (www
.rieggat.com/photohistory/history/kodak.htm).

The Notes explain that Dracula cannot be
photographed; the pictures either come out
totally overexposed or display a skeleton. (Nor
can he be painted, for the artist's portrait ends
up looking like someone else.) This trait is not
exhibited by vampires in the *Buffy* or Anne Rice
universes.

59 England in the nineteenth century
expended enormous effort to ensure that there
were proper prisons for criminals, appropriate
hospitals for the sick, and the Poor Law system
for paupers. An outgrowth of this custodial
urge was the construction of numerous publicly
supported asylums, motivated by notions of
"work therapy" and an unsupported hope that
lunacy could be cured. The Lunacy Act and the
County Asylums Act, both of 1845, required
all counties and boroughs to erect institutions
for their pauper insane, and the numbers of
insane resident in licensed asylums, hospitals,
or private homes rose dramatically. According

The Warneford Hospital, Oxford, founded
in 1826 as a private asylum (shown as
expanded in 1877).

to one report, between 1859 and 1909 the population of asylum inmates doubled, from 1.6 to 3.7 per 1,000 persons. Figures for 1827 show that the average asylum had 116 patients; by 1910, the number had reached 1,072. (See Kathleen Jones's 1993 *Asylums and After.*)

By 1913, the government was largely convinced that insanity was incurable, and its strategy changed to confinement of the insane in large institutions, to protect them from exploitation and to protect the public from them. The Mental Deficiency Act of 1913 legislated "colonies" to separate the "mad, feeble-minded, or idiotic" (in Francis Galton's phrase in the 1909 report *The Problem of the Feeble-minded*, which estimated that 1 of every 118 persons fit into these categories) from the remainder of the populace. In 1910, Winston Churchill was advocating sterilisation of these "moral degenerates," and as late as 1934 the Brock Commission recommended voluntary sterilisation of mental defectives.

The result of this enormous pressure on institutions was the relegation of physicians to the rôle of caretaker, rather than healer, and to some it seemed that these doctors lead lives resembling those of gentlemen farmers. "Life was not quite so pleasant for the patients," writes Elliot Slater in "Psychiatry in the Thirties." "Confined to locked wards with an enclosed court for exercise, patients whose stormy illness had blown itself out leaving only residual symptoms would remain year after year, unoccupied, deprived of incentive or responsibility of self-determination, getting more and more fixed in the straitjacket of an unchanging daily routine."

English asylums took pride in the abolition of mechanical restraints for disturbed patients. Instead, the system relied on isolation cells that humiliated the patients even more than physical restraint. In his 1921 *Experiences of an Asylum Doctor*, British physician Montagu Lomax recalled an episode in which a paralytic patient had fallen out of bed and broken his leg. "As I went through one of the wards on my way to the hospital I passed a single room in which a refractory patient was 'secluded.' It was after 7 p.m., and no attendant was within call. The patient was beating on the door with his fists and feet, and was shrieking out curses and imprecations. 'For God's sake let me out, doctor! For God's sake let me out! O Christ, they are killing me! For God's sake let me out!' As I came back, after setting the broken leg, the same horrible sounds greeted my ears. They would probably continue for hours, keeping everyone in the vicinity awake, and ultimately might necessitate my giving the man a hypodermic injection. My reflections were not pleasant." The scene is eerily reminiscent of Seward's experiences in chapter 21.

60 McNally and Florescu (*The Essential Dracula*) confidently state that "[i]t would seem almost certain that Lesnes Abbey was Stoker's Carfax." The abbey, located in the village of Erith, about 25 miles from Purfleet and across the Thames in another county, was founded in 1178; construction continued until 1513. An "abbot's house" and a manor house are recorded, with the latter in existence as late as the seventeenth century, succeeded by some sort of farmhouse, as well as several chapels; a barn on the site survived until 1900. However, it is plainly impossible that Lesnes Abbey was Dracula's residence, for by the time of Dracula's presence in England, no habitable structure had been on the property for over a hundred years. Roger Johnson, in private correspondence with this editor, points out that McNally and Florescu seem to have fallen into the common mistake of identifying "Carfax" as an abbey—a label first used in the 1920s in the Hamilton Deane/John L. Balderston play *Dracula* and continued in the 1931 Tod Browning film but with no basis in the Harker Papers.

61 Bitter, sardonic.

much used. On looking at it I found in certain places little rings marked, and on examining these I noticed that one was near London on the east side, manifestly where his new estate was situated;[62] the other two were Exeter, and Whitby on the Yorkshire coast.[63]

It was the better part of an hour when the Count returned. "Aha!" he said; "still at your books? Good! But you must not work always. Come; I am informed that your supper is ready." He took my arm, and we went into the next room, where I found an excellent supper ready on the table. The Count again excused himself, as he had dined out on his being away from home. But he sat as on the previous night, and chatted whilst I ate. After supper I smoked, as on the last evening, and the Count stayed with me, chatting and asking questions on every conceivable subject, hour after hour. I felt that it was getting very late indeed, but I did not say anything, for I felt under obligation to meet my host's wishes in every way. I was not sleepy, as the long sleep yesterday had fortified me; but I could not help experiencing that chill which comes over one at the coming of the dawn, which is like, in its way, the turn of the tide. They say that people who are near death die generally at the change to dawn or at the turn of the tide; any one who has when tired, and tied as it were to his post, experienced this change in the atmosphere can well believe it. All at once we heard the crow of a cock coming up with preternatural shrillness through the clear morning air; Count Dracula, jumping to his feet, said:—

"Why, there is the morning again! How remiss I am to let you stay up so long. You must make your conversation regarding my dear new country of England[64] less interesting, so that I may not forget how time flies by us," and, with a courtly bow, he quickly left me.

I went into my own room and drew the curtains, but there was little to notice; my window opened into the courtyard, all I could see was the warm grey of quickening sky. So I pulled the curtains again, and have written of this day.

8 May.[65]—I began to fear as I wrote in this book that I was getting too diffuse; but now I am glad that I went into detail

62 See the map of the area near Purfleet, reproduced on page 60.

63 The following appears in the Manuscript but is omitted from the published narrative: "There seemed some little ground for surmise here—of London and Exeter I knew but why Whitby? Mem. Try to reason this out, a good study." Exeter is of course where Hawkins practised. Dracula's express reason for seeking a solicitor in this corner of England, remote from his intended destination, appears far-fetched; see text accompanying chapter 3, note 43. Whitby, we shall see, is the Count's intended port of arrival in England, again for reasons uncertain. Dracula intended to ship a large quantity of goods, and it surely would have made more sense to have them disembarked at a location nearer to Purfleet. It may be that Dracula deliberately chose unlikely places to conduct his business in order to maximise his concealment. However, just as there is reason to doubt whether Harker ever travelled to "Transylvania," the location of "Carfax" may be wholly invented by Stoker to conceal the true location of Dracula's English base. See chapter 27, note 8, for a suggestion that the true location might be in Plaistow.

64 This is the first indication that Dracula intends his move to England to be permanent.

65 The Notes identify this as a Monday, which occurs in the years 1882 and 1893. Other dates are also identified by day, consistent with 1893; however, as will be seen, there are inconsistent identifications as well. See appendix 2, "The Dating of *Dracula*."

66 The Manuscript reads "some day it may be of interest to me or to others"; "from the first" has been inserted in Stoker's hand. It is unlikely that Harker actually had the thought expressed in the Manuscript, for he had no reason at this stage to expect anyone but Mina to read his journal, but hindsight—perhaps in the course of Mina's typing of the journal—caused the insertion of a mention of "others" who might be interested.

67 It is perfectly clear from this remark and Harker's recollection of magnificent vistas at the end of this chapter that it is broad daylight, probably late morning. Dracula shows no signs of diminished capacity from the time of day. See "Dracula's Family Tree" in Part II for a further discussion of the myth of the vampire's disability in daylight.

68 Note that this is consistent with Harker's previous observation of the semi-transparency of the Count (see text accompanying chapter 1, note 96), when he can see the blue flames through the body of the coachman. Wolf (*The*

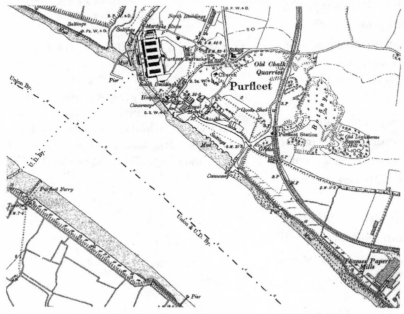

The neighbourhood of Purfleet, Essex, on the Thames.
Ordnance survey map, 1895

from the first, for[66] there is something so strange about this place and all in it that I cannot but feel uneasy. I wish I were safe out of it, or that I had never come. It may be that this strange night-existence is telling on me; but would that that were all! If there were any one to talk to I could bear it, but there is no one. I have only the Count to speak with, and he!—I fear I am myself the only living soul within the place. Let me be prosaic so far as facts can be; it will help me to bear up, and imagination must not run riot with me. If it does I am lost. Let me say at once how I stand—or seem to.

I only slept a few hours when I went to bed, and feeling that I could not sleep any more, got up. I had hung my shaving glass by the window, and was just beginning to shave. Suddenly I felt a hand on my shoulder, and heard the Count's voice saying to me, "Good-morning."[67] I started, for it amazed me that I had not seen him, since the reflection of the glass covered the whole room behind me. In starting I had cut myself slightly, but did not notice it at the moment. Having answered the Count's salutation, I turned to the glass again to see how I had been mistaken. This time there could be no error, for the man was close to me, and I could see him over my shoulder. But there was no reflection of him in the mirror! The whole room behind me was displayed; but there was no sign of a man in it, except myself.[68] This was startling, and, coming on the top of so many strange things, was beginning to increase that vague feeling of uneasiness which I always had when the Count is near; but at the instant I saw that the cut had bled a little, and the blood was trickling over my chin. I laid down the razor, turning as I did so half round to look for some sticking plaster.[69] When the Count saw my face, his eyes blazed with a sort of demoniac fury, and he suddenly made a grab at my throat. I drew away, and his hand touched the string of beads

"I saw that the cut had bled a little . . ." Bela Lugosi as
Dracula and Dwight Frye as Renfield.
Dracula (Universal Pictures, 1931)

Essential Dracula) and others connect this characteristic of vampires with the folkloric belief that mirrors reflect the soul; vampires, being soulless, cannot cast a reflection. As we have already seen, the Notes also indicate that Dracula cannot be photographed. There is no evidence, however, that Harker brought along his Kodak or that any other person tried to photograph Dracula.

69 An invention of long standing, referred to in literature as early as the 1600s. In the nineteenth century, this was fabric (commonly linen or silk) covered with an adhesive, used to bandage superficial wounds; the precursor of the Band-Aid.

which held the crucifix. It made an instant change in him, for the fury passed so quickly that I could hardly believe that it was ever there.

"Take care," he said, "take care how you cut yourself. It is more dangerous that you think in this country." Then seizing the shaving glass, he went on: "And this is the wretched thing that has done the mischief. It is a foul bauble of man's vanity. Away with it!" and opening the heavy window with one wrench of his terrible hand, he flung out the glass, which was shattered into a thousand pieces on the stones of the courtyard far below. Then he withdrew without a word. It is very annoying, for I do not see how I am to shave, unless in my watch-case or the bottom of the shaving-pot, which is fortunately of metal.

When I went into the dining-room, breakfast was prepared; but I could not find the Count anywhere. So I breakfasted alone. It is strange that as yet I have not seen the Count eat or drink. He must be a very peculiar man! After breakfast I did a

70 Therefore, notes Leatherdale (*Dracula Unearthed*), the approach to the castle could not have been from the south.

little exploring in the castle. I went out on the stairs, and found a room looking towards the south. The view was magnificent, and from where I stood there was every opportunity of seeing it. The castle is on the very edge of a terrible precipice.[70] A stone falling from the window would fall a thousand feet without touching anything! As far as the eye can reach is a sea of green tree-tops, with occasionally a deep rift where there is a chasm. Here and there are silver threads where the rivers wind in deep gorges through the forests.

But I am not in heart to describe beauty, for when I had seen the view I explored further; doors, doors, doors everywhere, and all locked and bolted. In no place save from the windows in the castle walls is there an available exit.

The castle is a veritable prison, and I am a prisoner!

Chapter 3

JONATHAN HARKER'S JOURNAL
—continued.

WHEN I FOUND that I was a prisoner a sort of wild feeling came over me. I rushed up and down the stairs, trying every door and peering out of every window I could find; but after a little the conviction of my helplessness overpowered all other feelings. When I look back after a few hours I think I must have been mad for the time, for I behaved much as a rat does in a trap. When, however, the conviction had come to me that I was helpless I sat down quietly—as quietly as I have ever done anything in my life—and began to think over what was best to be done. I am thinking still, and as yet have come to no definite conclusion. Of one thing only am I certain; that it is no use making my ideas known to the Count. He knows well that I am imprisoned; and as he has done it himself, and has doubtless his own motives for it, he would only deceive me if I trusted him fully with the facts. So far as I can see, my only plan will be to keep my knowledge and my fears to myself, and my eyes open. I am, I know, either being deceived, like a baby, by my own fears, or else I am in desperate straits; and if the latter be

Dust jacket of Gaelic translation of *Dracula*.
(Baile Átha Cliath: Oifig Díolta Foillseacháin Rialtais, 1933)

63

1 Leatherdale (*Dracula Unearthed*) wonders, if Dracula regularly uses the front door, why did Harker describe it earlier as grating with "long disuse"?

2 Fred Saberhagen's novel *The Dracula Tape* consists of an extended narration by Dracula himself in which he explains his complete innocence in the slaughter of Lucy Westenra and other crimes ascribed to him. Regardless of whether the reader believes Saberhagen's premise, the book makes several interesting points about Stoker's narrative. Here, for example, Saberhagen suggests that there were some Gypsy servants—an uneducated and unsophisticated lot with no experience in entertaining guests—but that they were occupied with other tasks and that Dracula, hoping to impress Harker, undertook the service himself to avoid embarrassing interactions between Harker and the servants. Contrastingly, in the film *Shadow of the Vampire* (2000), a retelling of the filming of F. W. Murnau's *Nosferatu, eine Symphonie des Grauens* (1922), the genuine vampire who poses as the actor Max Schreck comments that the sight of Dracula setting the dining table is the saddest scene in the entire narrative. To the English Victorian reader, for whom servants were ubiquitous, the absence of servants would suggest that Dracula was ignoble and likely destitute.

Interestingly, the Notes suggest that when Dracula arrives in London, he impresses a deaf-mute woman and a "silent man" into his service by terrorising them.

3 In 1645, the theologian Leo Allatius (1586–1669) published an influential book, *De Graecorum hodie quirundam opionationibus* [On certain modern opinions among the Greeks], in which he laid the foundation for the perception of the vampire as a creature of the Devil, rather than a pagan or natural phenomenon. As real to the Inquisition as witches were (and products of communion with the Devil), so vampires, he contended, were present among the populations of Europe. Allatius

so, I need, and shall need, all my brains to get through. I had hardly come to this conclusion when I heard the great door below shut, and knew that the Count had returned.[1] He did not come at once into the library, so I went cautiously to my own room and found him making the bed. This was odd, but only confirmed what I had all along thought—that there were no servants in the house. When later I saw him through the chink of the hinges of the door laying the table in the dining-room, I was assured of it; for if he does himself all these menial offices, surely it is proof that there is no one else to do them.[2] This gave me a fright, for if there is no one else in the castle, it must have been the Count himself who was the driver of the coach that brought me here. This is a terrible thought; for if so, what does it mean that he could control the wolves, as he did, by only holding up his hand in silence? How was it that all the people at Bistritz and on the coach had some terrible fear for me? What meant the giving of the crucifix,[3] of the garlic,[4] of the wild rose,[5] of the mountain ash?[6] Bless that good, good woman who hung the crucifix round my neck! for it is a comfort and a strength to me whenever I touch it. It is odd that a thing which I have been taught to regard with disfavour and as idolatrous should in a time of loneliness and trouble be of help. Is it that there is something in the essence of the thing itself, or that it is a medium, a tangible help, in conveying memories of sympathy and comfort? Some time, if it may be, I must examine this matter and try to make up my mind about it.[7] In the meantime I must find out all I can about Count Dracula, as it may help me to understand. To-night he may talk of himself, if I turn the conversation that way. I must be very careful, however, not to awake his suspicion.

Midnight.—I have had a long talk with the Count.[8] I asked him a few questions on Transylvania history, and he warmed up to the subject wonderfully. In his speaking of things and people, and especially of battles, he spoke as if he had been present at them all. This he afterwards explained by saying that to a *boyar* the pride of his house and name is his own pride, that their glory is his glory, that their fate is his fate. Whenever he spoke of his house he always said, "we," and spoke almost reasoned that just as witchcraft (according to its codex *Malleus Maleficarum* [The Hammer of Witches—that is, how to destroy witches]) required the Devil, a witch, and the permission of God, vampirism required the Devil, a dead body, and the permission of God. Therefore, alienated from God and sacred things, vampires could be repelled by holy symbols, such as a crucifix, holy water, or the Eucharist.

4 Homer (in the *Odyssey*, ca. 650 BC) credited Ulysses' escape from the sorceress Circe, who turned his men into pigs, to his eating of an herb. The lily leek or yellow garlic (*Allium moly*) has been identified as the herb of Homer's tale, but it does not fit Homer's description: "The root was black, while the flower was as white as milk; the gods call it Moly, and mortal men cannot uproot it, but the gods can do whatever they like" (Samuel Butler translation, 1900). John Gerard's *Herball or General Historie of Plants* (1597) described a garlic he called *Moly homericum*, Homer's moly, and he wrote optimistically, "I doubt not but in time some excellent man or other will find out as many good virtues of them,

3 *Moly Homericum,*
Homers Moly.

Moly homericum.
From John Gerard's *Herball or General Historie of Plants* (1597)

as their stately and comely proportion should seem to be possessed with."

Curiously, although garlic has been praised since ancient times for its strengthening and medicinal qualities, persons who ate garlic were banned from the temples of Cybele. A legend attributed to Mohammedans is: "When Satan stepped out from the Garden of Eden after the fall of man, Garlick sprang up from the spot where he placed his left foot, and Onion from that where his right foot touched."

Agnes Murgoçi, in "The Vampire in Roumania," reports: "Garlic keeps off vampires, wolves, and evil spirits, and millet has a similar action. On St. Andrew's Eve and St. George's Eve, and before Easter and the New Year, windows should be anointed with garlic in the form of a cross, garlic put on the door and everything in the house, and all the cows in the cowshed should be rubbed with garlic. When vampires do enter, they enter by the chimney or by the keyhole, so these orifices call for special attention when garlic is being rubbed in. Even though the window is anointed with garlic, it is wisest to keep it shut."

Similarly, Emily Gerard, in "Transylvanian Superstitions," notes that rubbing the body with garlic preserved one against witchcraft "and the pest."

In the well-known 1931 film of *Dracula*, the first interior scene shows Transylvanian peasants affixing garlands of herbs to the windows of the inn. The herb is not identified in the English-language version (directed, as noted earlier, by Tod Browning); however, in the Spanish-language version (directed by George Melford), the herb is identified as wolfbane (monkshood, or *Aconitum napellus*). Wolfbane is a poisonous plant, the name of which was derived from the idea that arrows tipped with the juice, or baits anointed with it, would kill wolves (were- or normal). In the 1941 film *The Wolf Man*, the blooming of wolfbane is said to mark the time when the lycanthropic change occurs. See "Dracula's Family Tree" in Part II for some suggestions that vampires may be the offspring of werewolves.

5 The references to the "wild rose" and "mountain ash" were blanks in the Manuscript filled in in Stoker's hand. This supports the theory that the actual events did not take place in Transylvania, where these had cultural significance, but were added later as part of the cover-up of the true location.

In Greco-Roman culture, the rose represented beauty, the season of spring, and love. According to Greek mythology, Chloe, the goddess of flowers, resurrected and transformed the body of a nymph into the flower. Eros, the god of love, received a rose from Aphrodite. The blossom's short life also epitomised the swift passage of time and therefore was connected with death and the afterlife. Christianity eventually embraced the rose as a symbol of Christ, although the flower is not mentioned in the Bible, and it became closely associated with the cult of the Virgin Mary, "cult" in this case referring to devotional practises. It should be noted that its five petals and pentagonal shape have pagan significance as well. Roses are part of the same botanical family (*Rosaceae*) as the mountain ash or rowan and the hawthorn (the latter closely associated with Jesus, supposed to be the wood from which his crown of thorns was made).

6 The mountain ash (also known as the rowan tree or witchwood) is associated with the Greek myth of Hebe, the goddess of youth. When she carelessly lost her cup of rejuvenation to demons, the gods sent an eagle to recover it. The feathers and drops of blood that the eagle shed in the ensuing fight with the demons fell to earth and turned into rowan trees, which have feather-shaped leaves and blood-red berries.

Norse mythology credits the rowan as the prime material from which the first woman was made (Woden, also named Odin or Wodin, the father of the gods, and the first man were both made from Yggdrasil, the world tree, an ash). A mountain ash saved Thor's life when he seized its overhanging branches as he was swept away in an underworld river.

Certainly part of the mountain ash's reputation as a potent shield from witchcraft and enchantment is the pentagram that appears on each berry, opposite its stalk (the pentagram being an ancient protective symbol). Its berries' blood-red hue was thought to be the most protective colour, and its white flowers proclaimed the tree to be favoured by faeries.

As a result of these traditions, the mountain ash was believed to afford protection to nearby homes. Pieces of the tree were used as totems to protect one's person and one's livestock from witchcraft.

7 This revealingly philosophical note of Harker's to himself does not appear in the Abridged Text.

8 Scholars who vigorously deny that Dracula could have been the alias for the historical Vlad Țepeș frequently point to the Count's "talk" with Harker—a recitation of Dracula's family history—as full of inaccuracies and therefore definitive proof that Dracula could not be the Impaler. Bernard Davies, in "Grinding Slowly . . . but Exceeding Small"—a review of the first edition of Elizabeth Miller's *Dracula: Sense & Nonsense*—urges that the talk be read giving "due weight to the limitations placed upon Count Dracula, if he was not to do the unthinkable and immediately give himself away." In this light, suggests Davies, the talk can be evaluated not as inaccurate history "but as a string of half-truths, misdirection and evasions designed to impress Harker but leave him none the wiser."

in the plural, like a king speaking. I wish I could put down all he said exactly as he said it, for to me it was most fascinating. It seemed to have in it a whole history of the country. He grew excited as he spoke, and walked about the room pulling his great white moustache and grasping anything on which he laid his hands as though he would crush it by main strength. One thing he said which I shall put down as nearly as I can; for it tells in its way the story of his race:—

"We Szekelys[9] have a right to be proud, for in our veins flows the blood of many brave races who fought as the lion fights, for lordship. Here, in the whirlpool of European races, the Ugric[10] tribe bore down from Iceland the fighting spirit which Thor[11] and Wodin gave them, which their Berserkers displayed to such fell intent on the seaboards of Europe, ay, and of Asia and Africa too, till the peoples thought that the were-wolves themselves had come.[12] Here, too, when they came, they found the Huns, whose warlike fury had swept the earth like a living flame, till the dying peoples held that in their veins ran the blood of those old witches, who, expelled from Scythia[13] had mated with the devils in the desert. Fools, fools! What devil or what witch was ever so great as Attila, whose blood is in these veins?"[14] He held up his arms. "Is it a wonder that we were a conquering race; that we were proud; that when the Magyar,[15] the Lombard,[16] the Avar,[17] the Bulgar,[18] or the Turk[19] poured his thousands on our frontiers, we drove them back? Is it strange that when Arpad and his legions swept through the Hungarian fatherland he found us here when he reached the frontier; that the Honfoglalas[20] was completed there? And when the Hungarian flood swept eastward, the Szekelys were claimed as kindred by the victorious Magyars, and to us for centuries was trusted the guarding of the frontier of Turkey-land; ay, and more than that, endless duty of the frontier guard, for, as the Turks say, 'water sleeps, and enemy is sleepless.'[21] Who more gladly than we throughout the Four Nations[22] received the 'bloody sword,' or at its warlike call flocked quicker to the standard of the King?[23] When was redeemed that great shame of my nation, the shame of Cassova,[24] when the flags of the Wallach and the Magyar went down beneath the Crescent, who was it but one of my own race who at Voivode[25] crossed the Danube and beat the Turk

9 The Szekelys (or Szeklers, as they were also termed) were Magyars who settled in eastern Transylvania at an unknown date in order to act as "széklers," or guardians of the frontier.

10 The Finno-Ugric languages are a subfamily of the Uralic languages. Hungarian, Estonian, and Finnish are the prominent modern languages in the grouping, with the first being part of the Ugric branch. According to some scholars, there are indications that Quenya, the language of the high elves recorded by J. R. R. Tolkien in various works, may be part of the same linguistic family.

11 Thunor, in Anglo-Saxon, the thunder god, armed with a magical hammer. Lord Godalming is later compared to him (see text accompanying chapter 16, note 28).

12 Sabine Baring-Gould, in his 1865 *Book of Were-Wolves* (referenced in the Notes), speaks of the berserkir (the plural of the term "berserkr" as used by Baring-Gould) as described in the Vatnsdæla Saga: "In like manner the word *berserkr*, used of a man possessed of superhuman powers, and subject to accesses of diabolical fury, was originally applied to one of those doughty champions who went about in bear-sarks, or habits made of bear-skin over their armour." In later works, the berserkir were those "who wore the skins of savage animals and went about the country as freebooters; but that popular superstition soon invested them with supernatural powers, and they were supposed to assume the forms of the beasts in whose skins they were disguised." To call someone a berserkr soon meant that the person had become a werewolf and had the ability to change shape. "It did not stop there," states Baring-Gould, "but went through another change of meaning, and was finally applied to those who were afflicted with paroxysms of madness or demonical possession."

13 A Eurasian region of indeterminate location, varying over time but generally situated north of the Black Sea, near Bulgaria and the lower Danube. Priscus of Panium, who visited the court of Attila, repeatedly described his followers as "Scythians." There is no historical record of the meeting of devils and witches described by Dracula.

14 See chapter 1, note 27.

15 In AD 896, Arpad, a chieftain of the Magyars, led an invasion from eastern Europe into the Carpathian Basin, where they remained. Their expansion westward was checked at the battle of Lechfeld in 955. With the crowning of Stephen I, the Magyars (Hungarians) became the official government of the region, and the official Christianization of the region was accomplished.

16 The people of Lombardy, an area of northern Italy. In AD 568, the Teutonic tribe, known as the Longobardi, invaded Italy and established a kingdom there that lasted over two hundred years. They became known as the most formidable of the Teutonic tribes of the Danube and contended constantly with the Franks to the west and the Slavs or Huns to the east. Cooperating with the Avar (see the next note), they also invaded the region of modern Hungary.

17 An ancient tribe of Scythia. The Avar lived in the region of Dacia (incorporating Transylvania) from the sixth to the early ninth century, surrounded by hostile tribes, including the Franks, Lombards, Bulgars, and Slavs. In the late eighth century, the Franks, under Charlemagne, destroyed their capital city of Khunzakh (the "City of the Huns"), and by the early ninth century the Avar Khanate was overthrown by a confederation of various tribes, the people Christianized and largely assimilated. Today the remaining Avar (one source estimates them at 600,000) live in the Caucasus Mountains region, primarily in Dagestan and Azerbaijan.

18 There were numerous tribes of Bulgars, and many were carried along with the Hunnish invasions of western and central Europe. Although "Great Bulgaria" was formed in the early seventh century, it did not last out the century, and the tribes dispersed, often joining with others in territorial wars. At the beginning of the ninth century, the Bulgars, aided by other tribes, crushed the Avar Khanate which had ruled Dacia and incorporated Transylvania into the First Bulgarian Empire. They retained at least nominal control of the region until AD 1000, when the area passed into the control of King Stephen I of Hungary.

19 See note 24 below.

20 The name given to the settlement of the Magyar people in the region. Wolf (*The Essential Dracula*) gives its translation as "conquest of the homeland." Its millennium celebration occurred shortly before publication of *Dracula*.

21 The Turkish proverb is recorded in Wilkinson's 1820 *Account of the Principalities of Wallachia and Moldavia*, and Harker may have heard it there first. However, it does not appear in the Abridged Text.

22 Dracula probably means the Magyars, Wallachs, Saxons (Germans), and Szekelys (the last not truly a nation). The Unio Trium Nationum (Union of the Three Nations) was formed by pact in 1437, comprising of the aristocracy of Hungary (largely the Magyars), the burghers (the Saxons), and the Szekelers.

23 Johnson's 1885 *On the Track of the Crescent* recounts that the nobles of Hungary formerly "were obliged to assemble their retainers, and flock to the king's standard, on receipt of the 'bloody sword,' as a signal of national emergency."

24 Cassova (modern Kosovo, a region in Serbia) was the scene in 1389 of a battle with the Turks, led by their emperor Murad I (who died there). The Turks' victory established their presence in on his own ground?[26] This was a Dracula indeed![27] Woe was it that his own unworthy brother,[28] when he had fallen, sold his people to the Turk and brought the shame of slavery on them! Was it not this Dracula, indeed, who inspired that other of his race[29] who in a later age again and again brought his forces over the great river into Turkey-land; who, when he was beaten back, came again, and again, and again, though he had to come alone from the bloody field where his troops were being slaughtered, since he knew that he alone could ultimately triumph! They said that he thought only of himself.[30] Bah! what good are peasants without a leader? Where ends the war without a brain and heart to conduct it? Again, when, after the battle of Mohács,[31] we threw off the Hungarian yoke,[32] we of the Dracula blood were amongst their leaders, for our spirit would not brook that we were not free. Ah, young sir, the Szekelys—and the Dracula as their heart's blood, their brains, and their swords—can boast a record that mushroom growths like the Hapsburgs[33] and the Romanoffs[34] can never reach. The warlike days are over.[35] Blood is too precious a thing in these days of dishonourable peace; and the glories of the great races are as a tale that is told."[36]

It was by this time close on morning, and we went to bed. (*Mem.*, this diary seems horribly like the beginning of the "Arabian Nights,"[37] for everything has to break off at cockcrow—or like the ghost of Hamlet's father.)[38]

12 May.—Let me begin with facts—bare, meagre facts, verified by books and figures, and of which there can be no doubt. I must not confuse them with experiences which will have to rest on my own observation, or my memory of them. Last evening when the Count came from his room he began by asking me questions on legal matters and on the doing of certain kinds of business.[39] I had spent the day wearily over books, and, simply to keep my mind occupied, went over some of the matters I had been examined in at Lincoln's Inn.[40] There was a certain method in the Count's inquiries, so I shall try to put them down in sequence; the knowledge may somehow or some time be useful to me.[41]

First, he asked if a man in England might have two solicitors, or more. I told him he might have a dozen if he wished, but that

eastern Europe, and the Turks ruled the region of Kosovo until 1913.

25 This is an evident typographical error in the first edition of the narrative (or in Mina Harker's transcription) and should read "as Voivode."

26 Dracula probably refers here to János Hunyadi (1385–1456). In 1441, he became Voivode of Transylvania under King Ladislaus III of Poland and won numerous victories over the Ottomans. In 1444, Ladislaus was slain in a battle at Varna, and in 1446 Hunyadi became regent. When Ladislaus V took the throne in 1453, Hunyadi resumed his crusade (aided by Pope Calixtus III) against the Turks, and in 1456, with St. John Capistran, he achieved a victory at Belgrade that was to defer the Ottoman conquest until the next century. Hunyadi's son became king as Matthias Corvinus, likely the "King" to whom Dracula refers. See text accompanying note 23 above.

János Hunyadi.

Matthias Corvinus.

27 Dracula's meaning here is somewhat unclear. Does he claim a familial relationship with Hunyadi, a national hero? Or, as is more likely, is he using the term "Dracula" in its literal sense: a dragon, a devil, a person of cunning and courage? (See chapter 2, note 47.)

28 Dracula appears to refer here to Radu Ţepeş, the brother of Vlad Ţepeş (see chapter 2, note 47), who assumed the throne after Vlad Ţepeş and proved a weak and ineffectual leader. However, this contradicts the identification of the Voivode who "crossed the Danube" as Hunyadi and confirms that the "history" given here is a hodgepodge of misremembered "facts"—that is, misremembered by Harker.

29 Gabriel Ronay, in *The Truth about Dracula*, identifies the "other" as Vlad III of Wallachia, Dracul, father of Vlad Ţepeş, who ruled from 1436 to 1456. Of course, this makes nonsense of Dracula's "later age" remark, and Mina Harker later concludes that the "other" is Dracula himself.

30 Dracula conflates several national leaders in these remarks, and it is not possible to translate them into accurate history. It is likely that Harker, not Dracula, confused matters and inaccurately recorded Dracula's very confusing speech, relying instead on Wilkinson's 1820 *Account of the Principalities of Wallachia and Moldavia*, which presents an incomplete and distorted chronicle of the succession of rulers and battles. Note that later, Van Helsing and Mina both interpret this particular comment to refer to Dracula himself. See text accompanying chapter 25, note 47.

31 After accession to the throne of the vast Ottoman Turkish empire in 1520, Süleyman, its sultan, set out in earnest to conquer Hungary, probably with the intention of making it a vassal state. In the battle of Mohács in 1526, the Turks slaughtered thousands of Hungarians, including the king, and the government of Hungary was destroyed. However, Hungary did not become immediately part of the Turkish empire, for Süleyman had gone too far. With the throne vacant, the Austrians claimed the right to govern the region (Charles V, the Hapsburg emperor, was related by marriage to King Louis II of Hungary). John Zapolya, Voivode of Transylvania, took advantage of his military strength and put himself at the head of the nationalist Hungarian party, which opposed the succession of the Hapsburg Ferdinand of Austria (later Emperor Ferdinand I) to the Hungarian throne. In the struggle between the two nominal rulers of Hungary, Zapolya was supported by Süleyman I. When Zapolya died in 1540, the Turks, on the pretext of protecting Zapolya's successor, his son, took over central Turkey. This left the country divided among three governments: western Hungary, ruled by the Hapsburgs; Turkish-controlled central Hungary; and Transylvania, where the Austrians and Turks vied for supremacy for almost two centuries.

32 The Manuscript refers to an "Austrian yoke," altered in the published text to "Hungarian"—

again suggestive of research by Stoker rather than reportage by Harker.

33 The Austrian dynasty that produced emperors, dukes, and other notables from the fifteenth through the twentieth century. In Victorian times, the old Holy Roman Empire had been reorganised into the Austro-Hungarian empire, still ruled by Hapsburgs. The assassination of Hapsburg Archduke Ferdinand precipitated World War I in 1914, and in 1918 the Austro-Hungarian empire was dissolved.

34 The Russian imperial dynasty, which began with Michael I in 1613 and continued until the Russian Revolution in 1917. The last of the direct Romanoff line, Prince Alexander Romanoff, grandson of Tzar Alexander III and grandnephew of Tzar Nicholas II, died in 2002.

35 This and the following sentence do not appear in the Abridged Text.

36 Many like to believe that Dracula is only an alias for Vlad the Impaler (see chapter 2, note 47). Elizabeth Kostova's best seller *The Historian* (2005) has this as its premise, and the conclusion is taken as proven by McNally and Florescu (*The Essential Dracula*). However, the most recent scholarship, exemplified by the extensive writings of Elizabeth Miller and Clive Leatherdale, concludes that the only point of coincidence between Count Dracula and Vlad the Impaler is their name. The Notes refer to William Wilkinson's observation on the name "Dracula" (see chapter 2, note 47) and to no other information respecting Vlad. Notwithstanding the later inferences drawn by Van Helsing and Mina Harker from Jonathan Harker's journal entry, as Leatherdale (*Dracula Unearthed*) observes, "[This portrait] is so vague and contradictory as to be worthless as an historical portrait."

37 *The Thousand and One Nights*, a new translation of *The Arabian Nights*, was published in 1885 by Stoker's friend Sir Richard Francis Burton. It is dawn, not cock-crow, that ends each tale of Scheherazade.

38 In *Hamlet*, Hamlet's father's ghost is spotted on the ramparts of Elsinore by guards, who remark that "when the cock crew. / . . . it started like a guilty thing / Upon a fearful summons. . . . / It faded on the crowing of the cock" (act 1, scene 1). The ghost of Hamlet's father is referred to by Stoker in his introduction to the Icelandic edition of *Dracula* (see note 15 on p. 8).

39 Only this sentence remains of this paragraph in the Abridged Text. Also, the entire line of questions about multiple solicitors in the next paragraph does not appear.

40 The Inns of Court (Lincoln's Inn, the Inner Temple, the Middle Temple, and Gray's

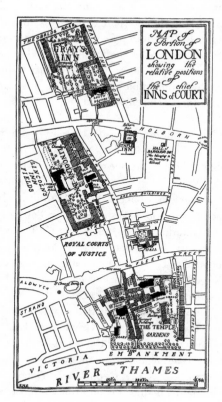

Map of the Inns of Court.
Cecil Headlam, *Inns of Court*
(London: Adam and Charles Black, 1909)

Exeter Cathedral.

Inn) are the unincorporated bodies of English lawyers. For over five hundred years, barristers (lawyers authorized to conduct matters in court) have been drawn from their ranks. Today, they function primarily as educational organisations, and there is little difference among them. As we have seen, Jonathan Harker was successfully examined to become a solicitor (see chapter 2, note 4). His reference here to being "examined" at Lincoln's Inn must refer to the preliminary or entrance examination uniformly imposed by the Inns prior to admission of a candidate, rather than the examinations required to be passed on completion of the curriculum.

41 The Manuscript reads "hereafter—or to others." The phrase does not appear in the published narrative. See chapter 2, note 66.

42 Exeter *is* far from London, 171½ miles, to be exact, by the South Western Railway departing from Waterloo station, according to the 1894 Great Britain "Baedeker." Continuously inhabited since Roman times, it was repeatedly besieged during the various civil disputes that took place on the English stage.

The ancient cathedral first used in 1050, when the see was moved from Crediton to Exeter, has been destroyed, and the oldest parts of the present building date from the twelfth century. Constructed in the Geometrical Decorated style, the cathedral was built (or altered from Norman style) between 1280 and 1370. On 3 May 1942, the cathedral suffered a direct hit with German bombs, and two chapels, two bays,

it would not be wise to have more than one solicitor engaged in one transaction, as only one could act at a time, and that to change would be certain to militate against his interest. He seemed thoroughly to understand, and went on to ask if there would be any practical difficulty in having one man to attend, say, to banking, and another to look after shipping, in case local help were needed in a place far from the home of the banking solicitor. I asked him to explain more fully, so that I might not by any chance mislead him, so he said:—

"I shall illustrate. Your friend and mine, Mr. Peter Hawkins, from under the shadow of your beautiful cathedral at Exeter, which is far from London, buys for me through your good self my place at London.[42] Good! Now here let me say frankly, lest you should think it strange that I have sought the services of one so far off from London instead of some one resident there, that my motive was that no local interest might be served save my wish only; and as one of London residence might, perhaps, have some purpose of himself or friend to serve, I went thus afield to seek my agent, whose labours should be only to my interest.[43] Now, suppose I, who have much of affairs, wish to ship goods, say, to Newcastle,[44] or Durham,[45] or Harwich,[46] or Dover,[47] might it not be that it could with more ease be done by consigning to one in these ports?" I answered that certainly it would be most easy, but that we solicitors had a system of agency one for the other, so that local work could be done locally on instruction from any solicitor, so that the client, simply placing himself in the hands of one man, could have his wishes carried out by him without further trouble.

"But," said he, "I could be at liberty to direct myself. Is it not so?"

"Of course," I replied; and "such is often done by men of business, who do not like the whole of their affairs to be known by any one person."

"Good!" he said, and then went on to ask about the means of making consignments and the forms to be gone through, and of all sorts of difficulties which might arise, but by forethought could be guarded against. I explained all these things to him to the best of my ability, and he certainly left me under the impression that he would have made a wonderful solicitor, for there was nothing that he did not think of or foresee.[48] For a man who was never in the country, and who did not evidently do much in the way of business, his knowledge and acumen were wonderful.[49] When he had satisfied himself on these points of which he had spoken, and I had verified all as well as I could by the books available, he suddenly stood up and said:—

"Have you written since your first letter to our friend Mr. Peter Hawkins, or to any other?" It was with some bitterness in my heart that I answered that I had not, that as yet I had not seen any opportunity of sending letters to anybody.

"Then write now, my young friend," he said, laying a heavy hand on my shoulder; "write to our friend and to any other, and say, if it will please you, that you shall stay with me until a month from now."

"Do you wish me to stay so long?" I asked, for my heart grew cold at the thought.

"I desire it much; nay, I will take no refusal. When your master, employer, what you will, engaged that someone should come on his behalf, it was understood that my needs only were to be consulted. I have not stinted. Is it not so?"

What could I do but bow acceptance? It was Mr. Hawkins's interest, not mine, and I had to think of him, not myself; and besides, while Count Dracula was speaking, there was that in his eyes and in his bearing which made me remember that I was a prisoner, and that if I wished it I could have no choice. The Count saw his victory in my bow, and his mastery in the trouble of my face, for he began at once to use them, but in his own smooth, resistless way:—

"I pray you, my good young friend, that you will not discourse of things other than business in your letters. It will doubtless please your friends to know that you are well, and that you look forward to getting home to them. Is it not so?" As he spoke he handed me three sheets of note-paper and three envelopes. They were all of the thinnest foreign post, and looking at them, then at him, and noticing his quiet smile, with the sharp, canine teeth lying over the red under-lip, I understood as well as if he had spoken that I should be careful what I wrote, for he would be able to read it. So I determined to write only

and most of the glass were destroyed. However, no evidence of the damage remains today.

43 Cautious but far-fetched—Dracula appears to be unacquainted with the ethical responsibilities of lawyers to avoid even the appearance of representing conflicting interests. Perhaps he had bitter experience on which to base his caution.

44 Formally Newcastle-on-Tyne, a river port and chief town of the newly created county of Tyne and Wear, on the river Tyne. Its quay is described as one of the longest and most commodious in England, and it possesses large shipbuilding yards and a substantial coal-exporting business.

45 Chief town of the county of Durham, about 15 miles south of Newcastle-on-Tyne and 175 miles from London on the Great Northern Railway. It is not clear why Durham is on Dracula's list of ports; although situated on the river Wear, it has no port. Wolf (*The Essential Dracula*) points out that it has an ancient castle (reportedly built in AD 995) and thus would interest Dracula.

46 On the German Ocean (the North Sea), the town possesses one of the best harbours on the east coast of England. Harwich is the starting point for Great Eastern Railway steamers to Holland and Belgium.

47 A major seaport, about 88 miles east-southeast of London, Dover is the principal place of embarkation for France and has a thriving business of Continental imports.

48 Harker's praise of Dracula must be contrasted with his later "horror" when faced with an apparent homoerotic display. See note 80, below, and accompanying text.

49 Harker's conclusion about Dracula's abilities does not appear in the Abridged Text.

50 See chapter 1, note 2.

51 A solicitor to whom, it will be seen, Dracula has consigned cargo, making it clear that his question to Harker about "consigning to one in these ports" was rhetorical. Like Peter Hawkins, Billington is not to be found among the names listed in the applicable Kelly's directory. Billington reappears after the wreck of the *Demeter* to recover cargo. See text accompanying chapter 7, note 34.

52 Leutner may be another local "solicitor," but he is not mentioned again. It will be seen that Dracula has made other arrangements in Varna.

53 A prominent English private bank, founded in 1692. In 1739, it took up residence at 59 Strand, where it remained until 1904. The "face" of the bank in the nineteenth century was Baroness Angela Burdett-Coutts, daughter of Sir Francis Burdett and granddaughter of Thomas Coutts. She was known as the richest woman in England, with a fortune in excess of £2 million

Mr. Burdett-Coutts
and the Baroness Burdett-Coutts.
Strand Magazine, March 1894

formal notes now, but to write fully to Mr. Hawkins in secret, and also to Mina, for to her I could write in shorthand,[50] which would puzzle the Count, if he did see it. When I had written my two letters I sat quiet, reading a book whilst the Count wrote several notes, referring as he wrote them to some books on his table. Then he took up my two and placed them with his own, and put by his writing materials, after which, the instant the door had closed behind him, I leaned over and looked at the letters, which were face down on the table. I felt no compunction in doing so, for under the circumstances I felt that I should protect myself in every way I could.

One of the letters was directed to Samuel F. Billington, No. 7, the Crescent, Whitby,[51] another to Herr Leutner, Varna;[52] the third was to Coutts & Co., London,[53] and the fourth to Herren Klopstock & Billreuth, bankers, Buda-Pesth.[54] The second and fourth were unsealed. I was just about to look at them when I saw the door-handle move. I sank back in my seat, having just had time to replace the letters as they had been and to resume my book before the Count, holding still another letter in his hand, entered the room. He took up the letters on the table and stamped them carefully, and then turning to me, said:—

"I trust you will forgive me, but I have much work to do in private this evening. You will, I hope, find all things as you wish." At the door he turned, and after a moment's pause said:—

"Let me advise you, my dear young friend—nay, let me warn you with all seriousness, that should you leave these rooms you will not by any chance go to sleep in any other part of the castle. It is old, and has many memories, and there are bad dreams for those who sleep unwisely. Be warned! Should sleep now or ever overcome you, or be like to do, then haste to your own chamber or to these rooms, for your rest will then be safe. But if you be not careful in this respect, then"—He finished his speech in a gruesome way, for he motioned with his hands as if he were washing them. I quite understood; my only doubt was as to whether any dream could be more terrible than the unnatural, horrible net of gloom and mystery which seemed closing around me.

Later.—I endorse the last words written, but this time there is no doubt in question. I shall not fear to sleep in any place where he is not. I have placed the crucifix over the head of my bed—I imagine that my rest is thus freer from dreams; and there it shall remain.[55]

When he left me I went to my room. After a little while, not hearing any sound, I came out and went up the stone stair to where I could look out towards the south. There was some sense of freedom in the vast expanse, inaccessible though it was to me, as compared with the narrow darkness of the courtyard. Looking out on this, I felt that I was indeed in prison, and I seemed to want a breath of fresh air, though it were of the night. I am beginning to feel this nocturnal existence tell on me. It is destroying my nerve. I start at my own shadow, and am full of all sorts of horrible imaginings. God knows that there is ground for my terrible fear in this accursed place! I looked out over the beautiful expanse, bathed in soft yellow moonlight[56] till it was almost as light as day. In the soft light the distant hills became melted, and the shadows in the valleys and gorges of velvety blackness.[57] The mere beauty seemed to cheer me; there was peace and comfort in every breath I drew. As I leaned from the window my eye was caught by something moving a storey below me, and somewhat to my left, where I imagined, from the order of the rooms, that the windows of the Count's own room would look out. The window at which I stood was tall and deep, stone-mullioned,[58] and though weather-worn, was still complete; but it was evidently many a day since the case[59] had been there. I drew back behind the stonework, and looked carefully out.

What I saw was the Count's head coming out from the window. I did not see the face, but I knew the man by the neck and the movement of his back and arms. In any case I could not mistake the hands which I had had so many opportunities of studying. I was at first interested and somewhat amused, for it is wonderful how small a matter will interest and amuse a man when he is a prisoner. But my very feelings changed to repulsion and terror when I saw the whole man slowly emerge from the window and begin to crawl down the castle wall over that dreadful abyss, *face down*, with his cloak spreading out around him like great wings.[60] At first I could not believe

(the modern equivalent of £125 million), and though her party-giving was on a grand scale, she spent the majority of her inherited wealth on scholarships, endowments, and a wide range of philanthropic interests. Stoker was a friend of the baroness, and therefore the appearance of the bank's name here may be a fictionalisation of the Harker Papers done as a gesture of friendship. See Harker's reference to Ellen Terry, discussed in chapter 13, note 57, and chapter 15, note 9, regarding the proximity of the Westenra vault to the Burdett-Coutts country home.

54 Herren Klopstock & Billreuth appears to be fictional, suggesting that the reference to Coutts & Co. is also false.

55 This sentence is added to the Manuscript in Stoker's hand. The crucifix is, as will be seen, of absolutely no use to Harker, for he is never attacked in his bed, and it seems unlikely that Harker—who saw the crucifix to be efficacious against Dracula earlier—would remove it from his neck. This sentence must be viewed, then, as the exercise of Stoker's artistic license.

56 "Soft yellow moonlight" implies that the moon was more than a quarter full and that it had risen. On Friday, 12 May 1893, a date proposed by many scholars for the events recounted here, the moon rose at 3:15 A.M. and set at about 3:30 P.M. Only 17 percent was illuminated. Therefore, either Harker imagined the "soft yellow moonlight" or he seriously misrecorded the date. (But see appendix 2, "The Dating of *Dracula*," for a discussion of the moon data.)

57 The Abridged Text omits this lovely sentence and the succeeding.

58 That is, with the panes divided by a vertical bar.

59 Harker means the window frame.

60 The scene is reproduced on the cover of the first paperback edition of *Dracula*, issued in 1901 by Constable & Co. (see p. 2). Why climb down this way? Why not change to the form of a bat and simply fly? And why does Dracula's cloak—evidently not held tightly around his body—not fall downward, towards the ground, covering him and impeding his vision?

61 Why, we may ask, does Dracula engage in this odd behaviour? He has removed his shoes and stockings, Harker's description makes clear. Is there no other entrance to the room to which Harker eventually follows him?

my eyes. I thought it was some trick of the moonlight, some weird effect of shadow; but I kept looking, and it could be no delusion. I saw the fingers and toes grasp the corners of the stones, worn clear of the mortar by the stress of years, and by thus using every projection and inequality move downwards with considerable speed, just as a lizard moves along a wall.[61]

What manner of man is this, or what manner of creature is it in the semblance of man? I feel the dread of this horrible place overpowering me; I am in fear—in awful fear—and there is no escape for me; I am encompassed about with terrors that I dare not think of. . . .

15 May.—Once more have I seen the Count go out in his lizard fashion. He moved downwards in a sidelong way, some hundred feet down, and a good deal to the left. He vanished into some hole or window. When his head had disappeared, I leaned out to try and see more, but without avail—the distance was too great to allow a proper angle of sight. I knew he had left the castle now, and thought to use the opportunity to explore more than I had dared to do as yet. I went back to the room, and taking a lamp, tried all the doors. They were all locked, as I had expected, and the locks were comparatively new; but I went down the stone stairs to the hall where I had entered originally. I found I could pull back the bolts easily enough and unhook the great chains; but the door was locked, and the key was gone! That key must be in the Count's room; I must watch should his door be unlocked, so that I may get it and escape. I went on to make a thorough examination of the various stairs and passages, and to try the doors that opened from them. One or two small rooms near the hall were open, but there was nothing to see in them except old furniture, dusty with age and moth-eaten. At last, however, I found one door at the top of the stairway which, though it seemed to be locked, gave a little under pressure. I tried it harder, and found that it was not really locked, but that the resistance came from the fact that the hinges had fallen somewhat, and the heavy door rested on the floor. Here was an opportunity which I might not have again, so I exerted myself, and with many efforts forced it back so that I could enter. I was now in a wing of the castle further to the right than the rooms I knew and a storey lower down. From the windows I could see that the suite of rooms lay along to the south of the castle, the windows of the end room looking out both west and south. On the latter side, as well as to the former, there was a great precipice. The castle was built on the corner of a great rock, so that on three sides it was quite impregnable, and great windows were placed here where sling, bow, or culverin[62] could not reach, and consequently light and comfort, impossible to a position which had to be guarded, were secured. To the west was a great valley, and then, rising far away, great jagged mountain fastnesses, rising peak on peak,[63] the sheer rock studded with mountain ash and thorn, whose roots clung in cracks and crevices and crannies of the stone.[64] This was evidently the portion of the castle occupied by the ladies in bygone days, for the furniture had more air of comfort than any I had seen. The windows were curtainless, and the yellow moonlight, flooding in through the diamond panes, enabled one to see even colours, whilst it softened the wealth of dust which lay over all and disguised in some measure the ravages of time and the moth. My lamp seemed to be of little effect in the brilliant moonlight, but I was glad to have it with me, for there was a dread loneliness in the place which chilled my heart and made my nerves tremble. Still, it was better than living alone in the rooms which I had come to hate from the presence of the Count, and after trying a little to school my nerves, I found a soft quietude come over me. Here I am, sitting at a little oak table where in old times possibly some fair lady sat to pen, with much thought and many blushes, her ill-spelt love-letter, and writing in my diary in shorthand all that has happened since I closed it last. It is nineteenth century up-to-date with a vengeance. And yet, unless my senses deceive me, the old centuries had, and have, powers of their own which mere "modernity" cannot kill.

62 Originally a term for a handgun, by the seventeenth century "culverin" referred to any number of different-sized cannon, called "demi-culverin," "ordinary culverin," "double culverin," and the like, depending on the size of the barrel and calibre of the shot.

63 Leatherdale (*Dracula Unearthed*) comments: "Insofar as any part of the Carpathians merits such a description, it would not be the environs of Bistritz." See chapter 1, note 75.

64 This sentence does not appear in the Abridged Text. Note that this places Castle Dracula to the east of the mountains, which makes textual sense—Harker goes through the Pass and travels to the castle, which must be in the eastern foothills. This is contradicted by the description of their route given by Mina and Van Helsing later; see text accompanying chapter 27, note 15.

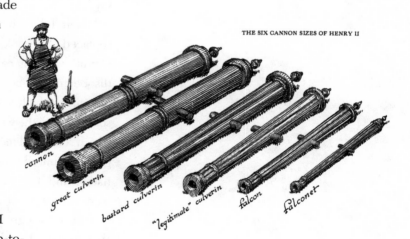

Culverin and other cannon of Henry II.
Edwin Tunis, *Weapons: A Pictorial History* (New York: Thomas Y. Cromwell, 1954)

65 Harker here paraphrases King Lear: "O, that way madness lies" (*King Lear*, act 3, scene 4).

66 This and the remainder of the paragraph do not appear in the Abridged Text.

67 Hamlet actually says: "My tables,—meet it is I set it down / That one may smile, and smile, and be a villain" (*Hamlet*, act I, scene 5). Who is Harker trying to impress with two quick Shakespearean references—Mina?

68 Leatherdale (*Dracula Unearthed*) observes that Harker was fortunate to find ink in the room. Fountain pens were not popularised until the 1920s, and though writers often carried a favourite pen, they required inking from an inkstand. It is difficult to imagine that the female vampires regularly indulged in letter writing and kept a supply of ink at hand.

Later: the morning of 16 May.—God preserve my sanity, for to this I am reduced. Safety and the assurance of safety are things of the past. Whilst I live on here there is but one thing to hope for, that I may not go mad, if, indeed, I be not mad already. If I be sane, then surely it is maddening to think that of all the foul things that lurk in this hateful place the Count is the least dreadful to me; that to him alone I can look for safety, even though this be only whilst I can serve his purpose. Great God! merciful God! Let me be calm, for out of that way lies madness indeed.[65] I begin to get new lights on certain things which have puzzled me.[66] Up to now I never quite knew what Shakespeare meant when he made Hamlet say:—

> "My tablets! quick, my tablets!
> 'Tis meet that I put it down," etc.,

for now, feeling as though my own brain were unhinged or as if the shock had come which must end in its undoing, I turn to my diary for repose.[67] The habit of entering accurately must help to soothe me.

The Count's mysterious warning frightened me at the time; it frightens me more now when I think of it, for in future he has a fearful hold upon me. I shall fear to doubt what he may say!

When I had written in my diary[68] and had fortunately replaced the book and pen in my pocket I felt sleepy. The Count's warning came into my mind, but I took a pleasure in disobeying it. The sense of sleep was upon me, and with it the obstinacy which sleep brings as outrider. The soft moonlight soothed, and the wide expanse without gave a sense of freedom which refreshed me. I determined not to return to-night to the gloom-haunted rooms, but to sleep here, where, of old, ladies had sat and sung and lived sweet lives whilst their gentle breasts were sad for their menfolk away in the midst of remorseless wars. I drew a great couch out of its place near the corner, so that, as I lay, I could look at the lovely view to east and south, and unthinking of and uncaring for the dust, composed myself for sleep.

I suppose I must have fallen asleep; I hope so, but I fear, for all that followed was startlingly real—so real that now, sitting here in the broad, full sunlight of the morning, I cannot in the least believe that it was all sleep.

I was not alone. The room was the same, unchanged in any way since I came into it; I could see along the floor, in the brilliant moonlight, my own footsteps marked where I had disturbed the long accumulation of dust. In the moonlight opposite me were three young women, ladies by their dress and manner.[69] I thought at the time that I must be dreaming when I saw them, for, though the moonlight was behind them, they threw no shadow on the floor. They came close to me, and looked at me for some time, and then whispered together. Two were dark, and had high aquiline noses, like the Count, and great dark, piercing eyes, that seemed to be almost red when contrasted with the pale yellow moon. The other was fair, as fair as can be, with great wavy masses of golden hair and eyes like pale sapphires. I seemed somehow to know her face, and to know it in connection with some dreamy fear, but I could not recollect at the moment how or where.[70] All three had brilliant white teeth that shone like pearls against the ruby of their voluptuous lips. There was something about them that made me uneasy, some longing and at the same time some deadly fear. I felt in my heart a wicked, burning desire that they would kiss me with those red lips. It is not good to note this down; lest some day it should meet Mina's eyes and cause her pain; but it is the truth.[71] They whispered together, and then they all three laughed—such a silvery, musical laugh, but as hard as though the sound never could have come through the softness of human lips. It was like the intolerable, tingling sweetness of water-glasses when played on by a cunning hand.[72] The fair girl shook her head coquettishly, and the other two urged her on. One said:—

"Go on! You are first, and we shall follow; yours is the right to begin."[73] The other added:—

"He is young and strong; there are kisses for us all."[74] I lay quiet, looking out under my eyelashes in an agony of delightful anticipation. The fair girl advanced and bent over me till I could feel the movement of her breath upon me. Sweet it was in one sense, honey-sweet, and sent the same tingling through the

69 Even in the midst of danger, Harker remains solidly middle-class, conscious of the women's dress. Who are these women? Leatherdale (*Dracula Unearthed*) suggests they are "sequential wives" who have "progressed" from being blood supplies to vampires. Wolf (*The Essential Dracula*) proposes that the two dark women may be Dracula's sisters. However, neither author has an explanation for why the women have not aged after death, as Dracula has. It may be that they were "turned" at much younger ages than Dracula, but even if this is so, they do not seem to show ill effects from being between feedings as Dracula does.

70 In the Manuscript, Harker shortly recalls where he has seen the fair vampire; see note 78. When Stoker excised the "Dracula's Guest" material from the narrative, he should have deleted this sentence as well. It does not appear in the Abridged Text.

Note that this is the only vampire described in the narrative who does not have blazing red eyes.

71 Stoker took mercy on Harker's marital relations by eliminating this sentence in the Abridged Text.

72 Wolf writes (*The Essential Dracula*) that Harker refers here to the music made by filling several glasses to varying levels with water, then striking them with a knife or spoon. But Harker may have heard a more sophisticated instrument than this child's parlour trick: the glass armonica, renowned for its eerie sounds. Ironically, its music has been called "the voices of the angels."

The armonica (after the Italian word for "harmony") was invented in 1761 by Benjamin Franklin, who, impressed by the efforts of others to play serious music on glasses partially filled with water (though by running a finger around the rim, not by striking the glass), turned his fertile mind to this pleasing diversion. His design eliminated the problematic water tuning (evaporation made it necessary to constantly

Franklin's armonica.

refill the glasses to the correct levels) through the simple use of glasses with varying size and thickness. He also made the instrument smaller and more playable: The glasses were compacted by nesting inside each other. They were mounted on a spindle which was turned by a foot treadle. As Franklin himself described his armonica, "The advantages of this instrument are that its tones are incomparably sweet beyond those of any other; that they may be swelled and softened at pleasure by stronger or weaker pressures of the finger, and continued at any length; and that the instrument, being once well tuned, never again wants tuning" (quoted in Carl Van Doren, *Benjamin Franklin*).

The instrument virtually disappeared after the beginning of the nineteenth century. E. Power Biggs failed in his attempt to revive interest in it in the 1950s, and it was not until 1982 that a rebirth was achieved through the efforts of the late master glassblower Gerhard Finkenbeiner. Mitch Cullin's *A Slight Trick of*

the Mind (2005) recounts a hitherto unknown adventure of Sherlock Holmes involving a beautiful glass armonicist.

Van Helsing's memorandum for 5 November acknowledges the accuracy of Harker's metaphor for the sound of the women's voices (see text accompanying chapter 27, note 22).

73 No reason appears for the primacy of the blonde vampire, although it is further evidenced by the size of her tomb (see text accompanying chapter 27, note 30). Based solely on Van Helsing's later assertion that her tomb is "as if made to one much beloved," Wolf (*The Essential Dracula*) describes her as apparently the "favored mistress" of Dracula. Of course, it is equally possible that in life she was a high-ranking aristocrat, and her tomb reflected that social status, not any particular fondness of Dracula. Certainly, the women's remarks about Dracula's unloving nature, his denial of that nature (and failure to assert that he loved *them*), and his rough treatment of the fair vampire (see text preceding note 77 below) belie any special relationship between Dracula and her.

Wolf wonders whether we are to understand that these creatures speak English or whether Harker's German was adequate to the task of understanding them.

74 Wolf (*The Essential Dracula*) calls this Harker's "Victorian euphemism for the sexual fantasy he is having." It is clearly not "kisses" that the women contemplate, as Harker feels the first one's teeth denting his throat. However, while Harker may be fantasising about sex, he receives no indication of exactly what the women have in mind. Dracula's earlier reaction to Harker's shaving cut is ambiguous and leaves Harker with no reason to expect blood sucking from these women.

nerves as her voice, but with a bitter underlying the sweet, a bitter offensiveness, as one smells in blood.[75]

I was afraid to raise my eyelids, but looked out and saw perfectly under the lashes. The girl went on her knees, and bent over me, simply gloating.[76] There was a deliberate voluptuousness which was both thrilling and repulsive, and as she arched her neck she actually licked her lips like an animal, till I could see in the moonlight the moisture shining on the scarlet lips and on the red tongue as it lapped the white sharp teeth. Lower and lower went her head as the lips went below the range of my mouth and chin and seemed about to fasten on my throat. Then she paused, and I could hear the churning sound of her tongue as it licked her teeth and lips, and could feel the hot breath on my neck. Then the skin of my throat began to tingle as one's flesh does when the hand that is to tickle it approaches nearer—nearer. I could feel the soft, shivering touch of the lips on the super-sensitive skin of my throat, and the hard dents of two sharp teeth, just touching and pausing there. I closed my eyes in a languorous ecstasy and waited—waited with beating heart.

But at that instant, another sensation swept through me as quick as lightning. I was conscious of the presence of the Count, and of his being as if lapped in a storm of fury. As my eyes opened involuntarily I saw his strong hand grasp the slender neck of the fair woman and with giant's power draw it back, the blue eyes transformed with fury, the white teeth champing with rage, and the fair cheeks blazing red with passion. But the Count! Never did I imagine such wrath and fury, even to the demons of the pit. His eyes were positively blazing. The red light in them was lurid, as if the flames of hell-fire blazed behind them. His face was deathly pale, and the lines of it were hard like drawn wires; the thick eyebrows that met over the nose now seemed like a heaving bar of white-hot

Unknown actress, Jeraldine Dvorak, and Dorothy Tree as the three female vampires.
Dracula (Universal Pictures, 1931)

75 The following, which appears in the Manuscript, is omitted from the published narrative: "She started back and pointed to my throat where the rubbing of the wolf's tongue still left it red. Her eyes flashed angrily with bitter dis-." This is plainly another reference to the "Dracula's Guest" episode (see appendix 1). Note that this vampire's breath is quite different from the unalloyed halitosis of Dracula (see chapter 2, note 28). Leatherdale (*Dracula Unearthed*) wonders at the smell of blood—this is clearly not Harker's, nor is it the smell of recently drunk blood, for the vampire women have not fed for some time. Perhaps it is merely the residue of a steady diet of blood.

76 In the Abridged Text, this is the "fair" girl and she is "fairly," not "simply," gloating.

77 Although literary critics have minutely examined this scene from the perspective of sexual fantasies (and see homoerotic elements in Dracula's claiming Harker for his own), there seems little reason—in light of later developments—to see the scene as other than the establishment of a pecking order with respect to a food source. Of course, Harker has no idea that he is viewed as a "winepress," and so, putting the scene in the only perspective he can understand, he recounts accusations about "love" and "kisses." It is an interesting comment on Harker's character (and perhaps his prior experiences) that despite the warnings of the Transylvanian natives, he appears to be readier to imagine homosexual relations with Dracula than vampiric relations.

78 The Manuscript continues with another reference to the "Dracula's Guest" episode (appendix 1), which is omitted from the published narrative: "As he spoke I was looking at the fair woman and it suddenly dawned on me that she was the woman—or her image—that I had seen in the tomb on Walpurgis night." However, it is likely that Harker was mistaken in identifying this as the same woman—see appendix 1, note 14.

It is unclear what "work" Dracula means, unless it is the three letters he requires Harker to write. As will be seen, there seems to be no purpose to the letters. See chapter 4, note 5, and accompanying text.

79 The balance of the sentence is added to the Manuscript in Stoker's hand. Leatherdale (*Dracula Unearthed*) sees this scene—Dracula the hunter, returning with a baby as his prey—as exemplifying the reasons for Dracula's move to England. He is reduced to stealing children to provide for his "family," for the local peasantry are all wise to the vampires' ways. However, others, including Fred Saberhagen in his novel *The Dracula Tape*, point out that there is no positive identification of the bag's contents as a baby; Saberhagen posits a small pig and contends that Dracula and his women are not

metal. With a fierce sweep of his arm, he hurled the woman from him, and then motioned to the others, as though he were beating them back; it was the same imperious gesture that I had seen used to the wolves. In a voice which, though low and almost in a whisper, seemed to cut through the air and then ring round the room he said:—

"How dare you touch him, any of you? How dare you cast eyes on him when I had forbidden it? Back, I tell you all! This man belongs to me! Beware how you meddle with him, or you'll have to deal with me." The fair girl, with a laugh of ribald coquetry, turned to answer him:—

"You yourself never loved; you never love!" On this the other women joined, and such a mirthless, hard, soulless laughter rang through the room that it almost made me faint to hear; it seemed like the pleasure of fiends. Then the Count turned, after looking at my face attentively, and said in a soft whisper:—

"Yes, I too can love; you yourselves can tell it from the past. Is it not so? Well, now I promise you that when I am done with him you shall kiss him at your will.[77] Now go! go! I must awaken him, for there is work to be done."[78]

"Are we to have nothing to-night?" said one of them, with a low laugh, as she pointed to the bag which he had thrown upon the floor,[79] and which moved as though there were some living thing within it. For answer he nodded his head. One of the women jumped forward and opened it. If my ears did not deceive me there was a gasp and a low wail, as of a half-smothered child. The women closed round, whilst I was aghast with horror; but as I looked they disappeared, and with them the dreadful bag. There was no door near them, and they could not have passed me without my noticing. They simply seemed to fade into the rays of the moonlight and pass out through the window, for I could see outside the dim, shadowy forms for a moment before they entirely faded away.

Then the horror overcame me, and I sank down unconscious.[80]

in the habit of preying on humans. See also chapter 26, note 45.

80 To what "horror" is Harker referring? He perceives that the women seek to "kiss" him, and he finds that highly pleasurable. The only "horror" he experiences is Dracula's demonic rage that the women are going to have first bite. That is, he appears "horrified" that a heterosexual encounter (at least, Harker interprets it as "sexual") is forcibly replaced with the prospect of a homosexual encounter.

The official Victorian attitude towards homosexuality was hostile. Although anti-buggery laws were of long standing, they had fallen into disuse by the late nineteenth century. In 1885, however, Parliament adopted the Criminal Law Amendment Act, making all male homosexual activities—public or private—illegal. Historian K. Theodore Hoppen (*The Mid-Victorian Generation*) suggests that the amendment was enacted in a misguided attempt to make the prohibition ridiculous. However, the result was that until 1967, when the law was repealed by the Sexual Offences Act, England had a draconian prohibition of homosexuality. As a practical matter, candour, rather than homosexuality, seemed to be the crime most prosecuted. In 1889, according to historian Jeffrey Weeks ("Inverts, Perverts, and Mary-Annes"), the public prosecutor adopted an expedient of not giving "unnecessary publicity" to cases of "gross indecency." Rather, the prosecutor believed, "private persons—being full-grown men—[should be permitted] to indulge their unnatural tastes in private." This candour was, many believe, the real crime of Oscar Wilde, who was convicted for violations of the 1885 law. A. N. Wilson writes in *The Victorians* that "though for a modern reader of [Wilde's trial] transcripts Wilde might seem like a gay martyr, to the Victorians his real crime was appalling frankness."

Although Harker expresses admiration for Dracula, then, and appears to find him attractive (see, for example, the text accompanying note 48 above), his public "horror" is certainly in keeping with a proper Victorian rejection of homoerotic appeal.

Chapter 41

JONATHAN HARKER'S JOURNAL
—continued.

1 Formerly "viii," then VI.

2 In the Abridged Text, this and the preceding sentence read as follows: "But these things are no proof, for they may have been evidences that my mind was not as usual, and, from some cause or another."

3 There is no recorded basis for Harker's anticipation of blood sucking. This suggests that large sections of the diary were composed by Harker long after the events and may be fiction. See note 13 below.

I AWOKE IN MY OWN BED. If it be that I had not dreamt, the Count must have carried me here. I tried to satisfy myself on the subject, but could not arrive at any unquestionable result. To be sure, there were certain small evidences, such as that my clothes were folded and laid by in a manner which was not my habit. My watch was still unwound, and I am rigorously accustomed to wind it the last thing before going to bed, and many such details. But these things are no proof, for they may have been evidences that my mind was not as usual, and, from some cause or another, I had certainly been much upset. I must watch for proof.[2] Of one thing I am glad: if it was that the Count carried me here and undressed me, he must have been hurried in his task, for my pockets are intact. I am sure this diary would have been a mystery to him which he would not have brooked. He would have taken or destroyed it. As I look round this room, although it has been to me so full of fear, it is now a sort of sanctuary, for nothing can be more dreadful than those awful women, who were—who *are*—waiting to suck my blood.[3]

18 May.—I have been down to look at that room again in daylight, for I *must* know the truth. When I got to the doorway at the top of the stairs I found it closed. It had been so forcibly driven against the jamb that part of the woodwork was

Cover of 1916 edition of *Dracula*.
(London: William Rider and Son, Ltd.)

4 Nets into which a quarry is driven.

5 It is unclear why Dracula requires these letters. Wolf (*The Essential Dracula*) points out that no one in England (Wolfe omits Peter Hawkins) knows Harker's whereabouts, and Dracula could have killed him at any time. Wolf concludes that the purpose of the letters was to torture Harker subtly and sadistically.

6 The two sentences following are added to the Manuscript in Stoker's hand. Harker is unlikely to have reached these conclusions himself, except with hindsight, and they must be viewed as counterfeit—that is, not part of the Harker Papers.

7 These dates, like many others, are inserted in blanks in the Manuscript in various hands or changed, strongly suggesting fictionalisation.

8 Jonathan later fails to recall these dates. See note 30 below.

9 Usually spelled Tzigane, meaning Hungarian Gypsies. The 1896 Austria "Baedeker" gives the Transylvanian Gypsy population as 88,000 (see chapter 1, note 26). The *Encyclopædia Britannica* (9th ed., 1888) estimates the population much lower, at 46,460. The author of *"Magyarland"* (see chapter 1, note 18) describes an encounter with a Gypsy servant and makes the following telling observations: "It is in truth not until one sees the *Czigánok* translated to an entirely new form of existence, and under circumstances inconsistent with their ordinary lives, that one realises how completely different they are from the rest of mankind in form or feature. . . . They are, indeed, a people so entirely separate and distinct that in whatever clime or quarter of the globe they may be met with, they are instantly recognised, for with them nearly forty centuries of association with civilised races have not succeeded in obliterating one single sign."

The name "Gypsy" stems from a fancied origin in Egypt, but the nomadic peoples probably began migrating to Europe from northern

splintered. I could see that the bolt of the lock had not been shot, but the door is fastened from the inside. I fear it was no dream, and must act on this surmise.

19 May.—I am surely in the toils.[4] Last night the Count asked me in the suavest tones to write three letters, one saying that my work here was nearly done, and that I should start for home within a few days, another that I was starting on the next morning from the time of the letter, and the third that I had left the castle and arrived at Bistritz.[5] I would fain have rebelled, but felt that in the present state of things it would be madness to quarrel openly with the Count whilst I am so absolutely in his power; and to refuse would be to excite his suspicion and to arouse his anger.[6] He knows that I know too much, and that I must not live, lest I be dangerous to him; my only chance is to prolong my opportunities. Something may occur which will give me a chance to escape. I saw in his eyes something of that gathering wrath which was manifest when he hurled that fair woman from him. He explained to me that posts were few and uncertain, and that my writing now would ensure ease of mind to my friends; and he assured me with so much impressiveness that he would countermand the later letters, which would be held over at Bistritz until due time in case chance would admit of my prolonging my stay, that to oppose him would have been to create new suspicion. I therefore pretended to fall in with his views, and asked him what dates I should put on the letters. He calculated a minute, and then said:—

"The first should be June 12,[7] the second June 19, and the third June 29."[8]

I know now the span of my life. God help me!

28 May.—There is a chance of escape, or at any rate of being able to send word home. A band of Szgany[9] have come to the castle, and are encamped in the courtyard. These Szgany are gipsies;[10] I have notes of them in my book. They are peculiar to this part of the world, though allied to the ordinary gipsies all the world over. There are thousands of them in Hungary and Transylvania, who are almost outside all law. They attach

Gypsy group, Transylvania.
Charles Boner, *Transylvania: Its Products and Its People* (1865)

India in the fourteenth century—a good deal later than the *"Magyarland"* author's estimate of a history of forty centuries. Their various ethnicities and languages melded together with outside influences to form a common language—Romany, which shows many traces of Hindi—and an ethnic group: their preferred description is "Roma." The stereotype of the Gypsy was that of a free-spirited, criminally minded wanderer—Gypsies were often accused of stealing babies and even spreading disease—and though there certainly were nomadic Gypsies, such characterisations are more fiction than fact, products of the prevailing ethnocentrism and racism.

The prevailing nineteenth-century view of the European Gypsy (which exemplifies the nineteenth-century stereotypical view of non-English races) is summed up in the *Britannica* (9th ed.): "The Gipsy character, strange medley of evil and of good, presents itself as black and hateful to the outside world, whilst to the Romani race it is all that is fair and lovable. . . . Their principal faults are childish vanity, professional cunning, indolence (caused by the absence of ambition) and a hot passionate temper. But they are as ready to forgive as they are quick to resent a wrong; and before implicit confidence their cunning gives place to inviolate honour. . . . Outwardly as within Gipsies present strong contrasts, some being strangely hideous, others very beautiful, though not with a regular, conventional beauty."

Several nineteenth-century novels, including Emily Brontë's 1847 *Wuthering Heights* (Lockwood describes Heathcliff as a "dark-skinned gipsy in aspect") and George Eliot's 1868 *The Spanish Gypsy*, used Gypsy characters to convey a certain unconventionality and otherness, both racial and cultural.

The Gypsies seem to have a special affinity for Dracula, perhaps recognising in him a fellow outsider.

10 All of the following comments on Gypsies do not appear in the Abridged Text.

11 Harker is mistaken in this respect. The *Encyclopædia Britannica* (9th ed.) notes: "Quick and versatile, all Gipsies readily adapt themselves to any state of life; they have so wonderful a gift of tongues that formerly it was reckoned against them for proof of sorcery." Stoker apparently initially leaves an important locational clue in the Manuscript, which does not appear in the published text: "The band that is here is from the _____. I can tell it by the . . ."

themselves as a rule to some great noble or *boyar*, and call themselves by his name. They are fearless and without religion, save superstition, and they talk only their own varieties of the Romany tongue.[11]

I shall write some letters home, and shall try to get them to have them posted. I have already spoken to them through my window to begin an acquaintanceship. They took their hats off and made obeisance and many signs, which, however, I could not understand any more than I could their spoken language. . . .

I have written the letters. Mina's is in shorthand, and I simply ask Mr. Hawkins to communicate with her. To her I have explained my situation, but without the horrors which I may only surmise. It would shock and frighten her to death were I to expose my heart to her. Should the letters not carry, then the Count shall not yet know my secret or the extent of my knowledge. . . .

I have given the letters; I threw them through the bars of my window with a gold piece, and made what signs I could to

Graf Orlok (Max Schreck) checks the sun.
Nosferatu (Jofa-Atelier Berlin-Johannisthal, 1922)

have them posted. The man who took them pressed them to his heart and bowed, and then put them in his cap. I could do no more. I stole back to the study, and began to read. As the Count did not come in, I have written here. . . .

The Count has come. He sat down beside me, and said in his smoothest voice as he opened two letters:—

"The Szgany has given me these, of which, though I know not whence they come, I shall, of course, take care. See!"—he must have looked at it—"one is from you, and to my friend Peter Hawkins; the other"—here he caught sight of the strange symbols as he opened the envelope, and the dark look came into his face, and his eyes blazed wickedly—"the other is a vile thing, an outrage upon friendship and hospitality! It is not signed. Well! so it cannot matter to us." And he calmly held letter and envelope in the flame of the lamp till they were consumed. Then he went on:—

"The letter to Hawkins—that I shall, of course send on, since it is yours. Your letters are sacred to me. Your pardon, my friend, that unknowingly I did break the seal. Will you not cover it again?" He held out the letter to me, and with a courteous bow handed me a clean envelope. I could only redirect it and hand it to him in silence. When he went out of the room I could hear the key turn softly. A minute later I went over and tried it, and the door was locked.

When, an hour or two after, the Count came quietly into the room; his coming awakened me, for I had gone to sleep on the sofa. He was very courteous and very cheery in his manner, and seeing that I had been sleeping, he said:—

"So, my friend, you are tired? Get to bed. There is the surest rest. I may not have the pleasure of talk to-night, since there are many labours to me; but you will sleep, I pray." I passed to my room and went to bed, and, strange to say, slept without dreaming. Despair has its own calms.

31 May.—This morning when I woke[12] I thought I would provide myself with some paper and envelopes from my bag and keep them in my pocket, so that I might write in case I should get an opportunity, but again a surprise, again a shock!

Every scrap of paper was gone, and with it all my notes, my

12 Leatherdale (*Dracula Unearthed*) believes this to be a mistake: All of Harker's meals to date have been served by Dracula, during the hours of darkness, and Harker has switched over to a nocturnal schedule. Therefore, as before, his awakening was likely at dusk.

13 Why is it that Dracula did not take Harker's diary? In his entry for 16 May, Harker said Dracula must have missed it because he was "hurried" in his search. However, there is no excuse given here, and it seems inconceivable that Dracula would intentionally remove notes and memoranda but leave behind an obviously encrypted journal. One is led to the inescapable conclusion that the diary did not exist, at least not at the time, but was composed after Harker's escape. It may even have been created by Stoker based on his interviews with Harker. This would also explain the strange lapses between entries as well as the erroneous descriptions of the appearances of the moon.

14 Another mistake, by the reckoning of Leatherdale (*Dracula Unearthed*).

15 See chapter 1, note 37.

16 This sentence does not appear in the Abridged Text.

17 A Polish word, meaning "head man" or "captain."

18 Wolf (*The Essential Dracula*) wonders at the inconvenient shape of the square boxes. Although a square is the most efficient shape for packing the boxes into a cargo hold, it is hard to imagine Dracula's body "lying" in one of the boxes unless the box were at least 6 by 6 feet. Roger Johnson, in private correspondence with this editor, suggests that the reference means "squared" at the corners, rather than an irregular, semi-octagonal shape like a coffin.

19 According to Frederick Thomas Elworthy's 1895 *The Evil Eye*. it was customary in many markets for the dealer to return a silver coin ("luck money") to the buyer on conclusion of a transaction and for the receiver to spit on it "for luck." "The same habit of spitting on a coin is very common also by the receiver when won in a bet, or when it is the first money received for the day," Elworthy recounts. "[N]ot only is [spitting]

memoranda, relating to railways and travel, my letter of credit, in fact all that might be useful to me were I once outside the castle.[13] I sat and pondered a while, and then some thought occurred to me, and I made search of my portmanteau and in the wardrobe where I had placed my clothes.

The suit in which I had travelled was gone, and also my overcoat and rug; I could find no trace of them anywhere. This looked like some new scheme of villainy. . . .

17 June.—This morning,[14] as I was sitting on the edge of my bed cudgelling my brains, I heard without a cracking of whips and pounding and scraping of horses' feet up the rocky path beyond the courtyard. With joy I hurried to the window, and saw drive into the yard two great leiter-wagons, each drawn by eight sturdy horses, and at the head of each pair a Slovak, with his wide hat, great nail-studded belt, dirty sheepskin, and high boots.[15] They had also their long staves in hand.[16] I ran to the door, intending to descend and try and join them through the main hall, as I thought that way might be opened for them. Again a shock: my door was fastened on the outside.

Then I ran to the window and cried to them. They looked up at me stupidly and pointed, but just then the "hetman"[17] of the Szgany came out, and seeing them pointing to my window, said something, at which they laughed. Henceforth no effort of mine, no piteous cry or agonised entreaty, would make them even look at me. They resolutely turned away. The leiter-wagons contained great, square boxes,[18] with handles of thick rope; these were evidently empty by the ease with which the Slovaks handled them, and by their resonance as they were roughly moved. When they were all unloaded and packed in a great heap in one corner of the yard, the Slovaks were given some money by the Szgany, and spitting on it for luck,[19] lazily went each to his horse's head. Shortly afterwards, I heard the cracking of their whips die away in the distance.

24 June, before morning.—Last night[20] the Count left me early, and locked himself into his own room. As soon as I dared I ran up the winding stair, and looked out of the window, which opened south.[21] I thought I would watch for the Count, for there is something going on. The Szgany are quartered somewhere in the castle and are doing work of some kind. I know it, for now and then I hear a far-away, muffled sound as of mattock and spade, and, whatever it is, it must be the end of some ruthless villainy.

I had been at the window somewhat less than half an hour, when I saw something coming out of the Count's window. I drew back and watched carefully, and saw the whole man emerge. It was a new shock to me to find that he had on the suit of clothes which I had worn whilst travelling here, and slung over his shoulder the terrible bag which I had seen the women take away. There could be no doubt as to his quest, and in my garb, too! This, then is his new scheme of evil: that he will allow others to see me, as they think, so that he may both leave evidence that I have been seen in the towns or villages posting my own letters, and that any wickedness which he may do shall by the local people be attributed to me.[22]

It makes me rage to think that this can go on, and whilst I am shut up here, a veritable prisoner, but without that protection of the law which is even a criminal's right and consolation.

I thought I would watch for the Count's return, and for a long time sat doggedly at the window. Then I began to notice that there were some quaint little specks[23] floating in the rays of the moonlight. They were like the tiniest grains of dust, and they whirled round and gathered in clusters in a nebulous sort of way. I watched them with a sense of soothing, and a sort of calm stole over me. I leaned back in the embrasure in a more comfortable position, so that I could enjoy more fully the aërial gamboling.

Something made me start up, a low, piteous howling of dogs somewhere far below in the valley, which was hidden from my sight. Louder it seemed to ring in my ears, and the floating moats of dust to take new shapes to the sound as they danced in the moonlight. I felt myself struggling to awake to some call of my instincts; nay, my very soul was struggling, and my half-remembered sensibilities were striving to answer the call. I was becoming hypnotised! Quicker and quicker danced the dust; the moonbeams seemed to quiver as they went by me into the mass of gloom beyond. More and more they gathered till they

practised in the hope of obtaining good fortune, but in all ages, and almost among all peoples, it has ever been considered as an act to safeguard the spitter, whether against fascination or other evils." He notes numerous examples among the ancient Greeks and Romans and reports that the custom as present in a wide variety of cultures.

20 This would have been Midsummer's Eve, the night before St. John's Day and the traditional date for the summer solstice. Although not as important a date as St. George's Day (see chapter 1, note 48) or Walpurgis-Nacht (see appendix 1, note 4), it was nonetheless thought to mark a gathering of witches, demons, and the like.

21 Wolf (*The Essential Dracula*) notes that this is the window from which Dracula crawled.

22 This seems to be utter nonsense. Are we to believe that, after centuries of feasting on the locals, Dracula now seizes the opportunity to have the English visitor blamed? And that the villagers will believe that the Englishman (if they had noted his presence) has somehow gained in height, aged considerably, and acquired white hair and a moustache? See also note 27. This must have been invented by Harker, perhaps to excuse his own behaviour after he escaped from the castle! (Saberhagen, in *The Dracula Tape*, suggests that Dracula borrowed Harker's clothing to have it copied, to provide a wardrobe appropriate for the London scene.)

23 See text accompanying chapter 11, note 52, for an incident of Lucy observing "specks."

24 Omitted from the published text is the following, which appears in the Manuscript: "holding the crucifix before me." This supports the idea that Harker did not leave his crucifix on the head of his bed, as Stoker wrote. See chapter 3, note 55.

25 Evidently a typographical error for "there."

26 Curiously, in the Manuscript the word appears to be "Hungarian" instead of "Monster."

27 Wolf (*The Essential Dracula*) notes that the accusation is directed against Harker, not Dracula, and concludes that the villagers have been duped into believing that Harker is the vampire. However, as Wolf himself observes, the fact that the woman presents herself at Dracula's castle makes it clear that Dracula's depredations in the area—which must have gone on for centuries, if Dracula's own account is to be believed—are well known to the peasants. Therefore, it is hard to see how the woman could have believed that Harker (and not Dracula) was responsible for the disappearance of her child. More likely, she was simply speaking to the only person visible. Saberhagen, in *The Dracula Tape*, points out that the woman was very unlikely to have been speaking German, and therefore Harker—separated from his "polyglot dictionary"—could not possibly have accurately recorded what she said. Saberhagen speculates that she was requesting Dracula's help, not excoriating him, and that the wolves that appear are sent to aid, not devour, her.

28 Leatherdale (*Dracula Unearthed*) finds this scene telling, for there is no mention of Dracula making any use of the woman as a blood supply. Indeed, only the women vampires seem to have indulged in any blood sucking, and that only from the babies supplied by Dracula.

seemed to take dim phantom shapes. And then I started, broad awake and in full possession of my senses, and ran screaming from the place. The phantom shapes, which were becoming gradually materialised from the moonbeams, were those of the three ghostly women to whom I was doomed. I fled,[24] and felt somewhat safer in my own room, where there was no moonlight and where the lamp was burning brightly.

When a couple of hours had passed I heard something stirring in the Count's room, something like a sharp wail quickly suppressed; and then them[25] was silence, deep, awful silence, which chilled me. With a beating heart, I tried the door; but I was locked in my prison, and could do nothing. I sat down and simply cried.

As I sat I heard a sound in the courtyard without—the agonised cry of a woman. I rushed to the window, and throwing it up, peered between the bars. There, indeed, was a woman with dishevelled hair, holding her hands over her heart as one distressed with running. She was leaning against the corner of the gateway. When she saw my face at the window she threw herself forward, and shouted in a voice laden with menace:—

"Monster,[26] give me my child!"[27]

She threw herself on her knees, and raising up her hands, cried the same words in tones which wrung my heart. Then she tore her hair and beat her breast, and abandoned herself to all the violences of extravagant emotion. Finally, she threw herself forward, and, though I could not see her, I could hear the beating of her naked hands against the door.

Somewhere high overhead, probably on the tower, I heard the voice of the Count calling in his harsh, metallic whisper. His call seemed to be answered from far and wide by the howling of wolves. Before many minutes had passed a pack of them poured, like a pent-up dam when liberated, through the wide entrance into the courtyard.

There was no cry from the woman, and the howling of the wolves was but short. Before long they streamed away singly, licking their lips.[28]

I could not pity her, for I knew now what had become of her child, and she was better dead.

What shall I do? what can I do? How can I escape from this dreadful thrall of night and gloom and fear?

25 June, morning.—No man knows till he has suffered from the night how sweet and dear to his heart and eye the morning can be. When the sun grew so high this morning that it struck the top of the great gateway opposite my window, the high spot which it touched seemed to me as if the dove from the ark had lighted there.[29] My fear fell from me as if it had been a vaporous garment which dissolved in the warmth. I must take action of some sort whilst the courage of the day is upon me. Last night one of my post-dated letters went to post, the first of that fatal series which is to blot out the very traces of my existence from the earth.[30]

Let me not think of it. Action!

It has always been at night-time that I have been molested or threatened, or in some way in danger or in fear. I have not yet seen the Count in the daylight.[31] Can it be that he sleeps when others wake, that he may be awake whilst they sleep? If I could only get into his room! But there is no possible way. The door is always locked, no way for me.

Yes, there is a way, if one dares to take it. Where his body has gone why may not another body go? I have seen him myself crawl from his window; why should not I imitate him, and go in by his window? The chances are desperate, but my need is more desperate still. I shall risk it. At the worst it can only be death; and a man's death is not a calf's, and the dreaded Hereafter may still be open to me. God help me in my task! Good-bye, Mina, if I fail; good-bye, my faithful friend and second father;[32] good-bye, all, and last of all Mina!

Same day, later.—I have made the effort, and God helping me, have come safely back to this room. I must put down every detail in order. I went whilst my courage was fresh straight to the window on the south side, and at once got outside on the narrow ledge of stone which runs round the building on this side. The stones are big and roughly cut, and the mortar has by process of time been washed away between them. I took off my boots, and ventured out on the desperate way. I

29 Harker here refers to Noah's release of a dove from the biblical ark to determine whether the flood had ended (Gen. 8:8–12).

30 Harker is in error; the first letter is dated 12 June (see text accompanying note 8 above).

31 This is not so. The shaving incident (see text accompanying chapter 2, note 67) is plainly during the day.

32 Harker here evidently means his employer, Peter Hawkins. We will learn more of their relationship later.

33 A typographical error—should be "trying."

34 Wolf (*The Essential Dracula*) notes Harker's remarkable coolness in examining the dates of the coin. Roger Johnson, however, in private correspondence with this editor, argues that fixation on small details is a classic symptom of extreme agitation. Nonetheless, Harker's observation seems so unlikely that it further buttresses the suggestion that Harker's record of events at the castle is either fiction or a re-creation of his recollections.

The Notes indicate that eventually the Harkers are able to trace Dracula's gold to a Salzburg banking house, perhaps explaining why Harker may have travelled there. (See chapter 1, note 42.)

35 Note that despite his excitement and agitation (his own description), Harker will take the time to count the number of boxes (see text accompanying note 38 below). Although this enumeration will be important later to the hunters, there is no way that Harker could have realised that at this stage, and it is hard to believe that the counting actually occurred.

Why is Dracula lying in one of the boxes now? Is he trying it on for size?

Coins issued by Stephan Bocksay, Prince of Transylvania, Istvan, between 1505 and 1506.

looked down once, so as to make sure that a sudden glimpse of the awful depth would not overcome me, but after that kept my eyes away from it. I knew pretty well the direction and distance of the Count's window, and made for it as well as I could, having regard to the opportunities available. I did not feel dizzy—I suppose I was too excited—and the time seemed ridiculously short till I found myself standing on the window-sill and tying[33] to raise up the sash. I was filled with agitation, however, when I bent down and slid feet foremost in through the window. Then I looked around for the Count, but, with surprise and gladness, made a discovery. The room was empty! It was barely furnished with odd things, which seemed to have never been used; the furniture was something the same style as that in the south rooms, and was covered with dust. I looked for the key, but it was not in the lock, and I could not find it anywhere. The only thing I found was a great heap of gold in one corner—gold of all kinds, Roman, and British, and Austrian, and Hungarian, and Greek and Turkish money, covered with a film of dust, as though it had lain long in the ground. None of it that I noticed was less than three hundred years old.[34] There were also chains and ornaments, some jewelled, but all of them old and stained.

At one corner of the room was a heavy door. I tried it, for, since I could not find the key of the room or the key of the outer door, which was the main object of my search, I must make further examination, or all my efforts would be in vain. It was open, and led through a stone passage to a circular stairway, which went steeply down. I descended, minding carefully where I went, for the stairs were dark, being only lit by loopholes in the heavy masonry. At the bottom there was a dark, tunnel-like passage, through which came a deathly, sickly odour, the odour of old earth newly turned. As I went through the passage the smell grew closer and heavier. At last I pulled open a heavy door which stood ajar, and found myself in an old, ruined chapel, which had evidently been used as a graveyard. The roof was broken, and in two places were steps leading to vaults, but the ground had recently been dug over, and the earth placed in great wooden boxes, manifestly those which had been brought by the Slovaks.[35] There was nobody about, and I made a search for any further outlet, but there was none.[36] Then I went over every inch of the ground, so as not to lose a chance. I went down even into the vaults, where the dim light struggled, although to do so was a dread to my very soul.[37] Into two of these I went, but saw nothing except fragments of old coffins and piles of dust; in the third, however, I made a discovery.

There, in one of the great boxes, of which there were fifty in all, on a pile of newly dug earth, lay the Count![38] He was either dead or asleep, I could not say which—for the eyes were open and stony, but without the glassiness of death—and the cheeks had the warmth of life through all their pallor, and the lips were as red as ever. But there was no sign of movement, no pulse, no breath, no beating of the heart. I bent over him, and tried to find any sign of life, but in vain. He could not have lain there long, for the earthy smell would have passed away in a few hours. By the side of the box was its cover, pierced with holes here and there.[39] I thought he might have the keys on him, but when I went to search I saw the dead eyes, and in them, dead though they were, such a look of hate though unconscious of me or my presence, that I fled from the place, and leaving the Count's room by the window, crawled again up the castle wall.[40] Regaining my room, I threw myself panting upon the bed and tried to think. . . .

29 June.[41]—To-day is the date of my last letter,[42] and the Count has taken steps to prove that it was genuine, for again I saw him leave the castle by the same window, and in my clothes. As he went down the wall, lizard fashion, I wished I had a gun or some lethal weapon, that I might destroy him; but I fear that no weapon wrought alone by man's hand would have any effect on him.[43] I dared not wait to see him return, for I feared to see those weird sisters.[44] I came back to the library, and read there till I fell asleep.

I was awakened by the Count, who looked at me as grimly as a man could look as he said:—

"To-morrow, my friend, we must part. You return to your beautiful England, I to some work which may have such an end that we may never meet. Your letter home has been

36 Evidently Harker missed the "outlet," for how else would the boxes have gotten into the vault? The Slovaks were in the courtyard, and Harker did not remark them entering the castle. Later, in chapter 27, Van Helsing passes through broken doors directly to the "old chapel," without mention of any stairway or funnel-like passage.

37 These cannot be the "vaults" Van Helsing later enters, for there are no tombs here.

38 One wonders where Dracula slept before the Slovaks arrived with the boxes—perhaps in his tomb?

39 What is the purpose of the holes? They cannot be "breathing" holes (as Leatherdale proposes, in *Dracula Unearthed*), for Harker has just made clear that Dracula—at least in repose—does not breathe. No holes are mentioned again by other observers. Harker may have misrecalled this detail (if there is any truth to the scene).

40 Leatherdale (*Dracula Unearthed*) asserts that, contrary to Harker's confident conclusion, Dracula was well aware of Harker's presence and wonders why Dracula makes no mention of the confrontation in the underground chamber. This vampiric state of unconsciousness is contradicted by Mina's later observation—presumably based on telepathy—that Dracula in repose is well aware of his surroundings.

41 The Notes indicate that these events occur on 26 June.

42 This corresponds to the date noted in the text accompanying note 8 above.

43 This remark is difficult to reconcile with Harker's subsequent attacks on Dracula with his kukri blade. Here he expresses the same lesson as that taught by Van Helsing later; yet in the final moment, he uses a "weapon wrought alone by man's hand."

44 The Manuscript contains the following, which is omitted from the published narrative: "—how right was Shakespeare, no one would believe that after three hundred years one should see in this fastness of Europe the counterpart of the witches of Macbeth." Harker has previously demonstrated his familiarity with Shakespeare, and the remark appears wholly in character. This may have been the victim of the publisher's order to shorten the text.

45 In Alexander Pope's 1726 translation of Homer's *Odyssey*, King Menelaus says to Telemachus: "If with desire so strong thy bosom glows, / Ill (said the king) should I thy wish oppose; / For oft in others freely I reprove / The ill-timed efforts of officious love; / Who love too much, hate in the like extreme, / And both the golden mean alike condemn. / Alike he thwarts the hospitable end, / Who drives the free, or stays the hasty friend: / True friendship's laws are by this rule express'd, / Welcome the coming, speed the parting guest."

Dracula's knowledge of English literature is impressive—or Harker fictionalised the scene.

despatched; to-morrow I shall not be here, but all shall be ready for your journey. In the morning come the Szgany, who have some labours of their own here, and also come some Slovaks. When they have gone, my carriage shall come for you, and shall bear you to the Borgo Pass to meet the diligence from Bukovina to Bistritz. But I am in hopes that I shall see more of you at Castle Dracula." I suspected him, and determined to test his sincerity. Sincerity! It seems like a profanation of the word to write it in connection with such a monster, so asked him point-blank:—

"Why may I not go to-night?"

"Because, dear sir, my coachman and horses are away on a mission."

"But I would walk with pleasure. I want to get away at once." He smiled, such a soft, smooth, diabolical smile that I knew there was some trick behind his smoothness. He said:—

"And your baggage?"

"I do not care about. I can send for it some other time."

The Count stood up, and said, with a sweet courtesy which made me rub my eyes, it seemed so real:—

"You English have a saying which is close to my heart, for its spirit is that which rules our *boyars*: 'Welcome the coming, speed the parting guest.'[45] Come with me, my dear young friend. Not an hour shall you wait in my house against your will, though sad am I at your going, and that you so suddenly desire it. Come!" With a stately gravity, he, with the lamp, preceded me down the stairs and along the hall. Suddenly he stopped.

"Hark!"

Close at hand came the howling of many wolves. It was almost as if the sound sprang up at the rising of his hand, just as the music of a great orchestra seems to leap under the bâton of the conductor. After a pause of a moment, he proceeded, in his stately way, to the door, drew back the ponderous bolts, unhooked the heavy chains, and began to draw it open.

To my intense astonishment I saw that it was unlocked. Suspiciously, I looked all round, but could see no key of any kind.

As the door began to open, the howling of the wolves without grew louder and angrier; their red jaws, with champing teeth, and their blunt-clawed feet as they leaped, came in through the opening door. I knew then that to struggle at the moment against the Count was useless. With such allies as these at his command, I could do nothing. But still the door continued slowly to open, and only the Count's body stood in the gap. Suddenly it struck me that this might be the moment and means of my doom; I was to be given to the wolves, and at my own instigation. There was a diabolical wickedness in the idea great enough for the Count, and as a last chance I cried out:—

"Shut the door; I shall wait till morning!" and covered my face with my hands to hide my tears of bitter disappointment. With one sweep of his powerful arm, the Count threw the door shut, and the great bolts clanged and echoed through the hall as they shot back into their places.

In silence we returned to the library, and after a minute or two I went to my own room. The last I saw of Count Dracula was his kissing his hand to me;[46] with a red light of triumph in his eyes, and with a smile that Judas in hell might be proud of.

When I was in my room and about to lie down, I thought I heard a whispering at my door. I went to it softly and listened. Unless my ears deceived me, I heard the voice of the Count:—

"Back, back, to your own place! Your time is not yet come. Wait. Have patience. To-morrow night, to-morrow night is yours!"[47] There was a low, sweet ripple of laughter, and in a rage I threw open the door, and saw without the three terrible women licking their lips. As I appeared they all joined in a horrible laugh, and ran away.

I came back to my room and threw myself on my knees. It is then so near the end? To-morrow! to-morrow! Lord, help me, and those to whom I am dear!

30 June, morning.[48]—These may be the last words I ever write in this diary. I slept till just before the dawn, and when I woke threw myself on my knees, for I determined that if Death came he should find me ready.

46 Wolf (*The Essential Dracula*) calls this "another ambiguous moment," comparing it to the homoerotic scene at the end of chapter 3.

47 The homoerotic element is even more explicit in the first American edition of the narrative (1899), in which the line reads "To-night is mine. Tomorrow night is yours!"

48 The Notes suggest that Jonathan's escape may have occurred on 10 June, not 30 June; an entry indicating that the escape occurred on the earlier date has been erased. The erasures and changes in the calendar set forth in the Notes make its reliability highly suspect. The calendar itself bears no year (other than "189_" in print), and the dates have been inserted by hand against days of the week. It has the appearance, then, not of an effort by Stoker to make sense of the Harker Papers but rather of an effort to work out a plausible fictional narrative based on the papers. See appendix 2, "The Dating of *Dracula.*"

49 Is it credible that Dracula has forgotten to lock Harker in his room, so that the women vampires may enjoy him in the evening?

50 We must again ask why the Count is in this box. He has a perfectly good "lordly" tomb under the castle (presumably complete with a coffin), and it must have been uncomfortable to sleep on dirt in a "square" box. Perhaps he is training himself to endure the hardships of his upcoming sea voyage.

51 Wolf (*The Essential Dracula*) points out that this is the first evidence of blood sucking having occurred. Whose blood is this? Did Dracula dine on another stolen child, or did he at last find an adult victim? The description of postprandial Dracula is at odds with later observations of him after attacking Lucy or Mina, and again, Harker's reaction seems to be one imported to this scene based on his later knowledge.

52 This is hardly the romantic image of filmic vampires.

At last I felt that subtle change in the air, and knew that the morning had come. Then came the welcome cock-crow, and I felt that I was safe. With a glad heart, I opened my door and ran down the hall. I had seen that the door was unlocked, and now escape was before me.**49** With hands that trembled with eagerness, I unhooked the chains and drew back the massive bolts.

But the door would not move. Despair seized me. I pulled, and pulled, at the door, and shook it till, massive as it was, it rattled in its casement. I could see the bolt shot. It had been locked after I left the Count.

Then a wild desire took me to obtain that key at any risk, and I determined then and there to scale the wall again and gain the Count's room. He might kill me, but death now seemed the happier choice of evils. Without a pause I rushed up to the east window, and scrambled down the wall, as before, into the Count's room. It was empty, but that was as I expected. I could not see a key anywhere, but the heap of gold remained. I went through the door in the corner and down the winding stair and along the dark passage to the old chapel. I knew now well enough where to find the monster I sought.

The great box was in the same place, close against the wall, but the lid was laid on it, not fastened down, but with the nails ready in their places to be hammered home. I knew I must search the body for the key, so I raised the lid, and laid it back against the wall; and then I saw something which filled my very soul with horror. There lay the Count,**50** but looking as if his youth had been half renewed, for the white hair and moustache were changed to dark iron-grey; the cheeks were fuller, and the white skin seemed ruby-red underneath; the mouth was redder than ever, for on the lips were gouts of fresh blood, which trickled from the corners of the mouth and ran down over the chin and neck.**51** Even the deep, burning eyes seemed set amongst swollen flesh, for the lids and pouches underneath were bloated. It seemed as if the whole awful creature were simply gorged with blood; he lay like a filthy leech, exhausted with his repletion.**52** I shuddered as I bent over to touch him, and every sense in me revolted at the contact; but I had to search, or I was lost. The coming night might see my own body a banquet in a similar way to those horrid three. I felt all over the body, but no sign could I find of the key. Then I stopped and looked at the Count. There was a mocking smile on the bloated face which seemed to drive me mad. This was the being I was helping to transfer to London, where, perhaps, for centuries to come he might, amongst its teeming millions, satiate his lust for blood, and create a new and ever-widening circle of semi-demons to batten on the helpless.[53] The very thought drove me mad. A terrible desire came upon me to rid the world of such a monster. There was no lethal weapon at hand, but I seized a shovel which the workmen had been using to fill the cases, and lifting it high struck, with the edge downward, at the hateful face. But as I did so the head turned, and the eyes fell full upon me, with all their blaze of basilisk[54] horror. The sight seemed to paralyse me, and the shovel turned in my hand and glanced from the face, merely making a deep gash above the forehead. The shovel fell from my hand across the box, and as I pulled it away the flange of the blade caught the edge of the lid, which fell over again, and hid the horrid thing from my sight. The last glimpse I had was of the bloated face, blood-stained and fixed with a grin of malice which would have held its own in the nethermost hell.

I thought and thought what should be my next move, but my brain seemed on fire, and I waited with a despairing feeling growing over me. As I waited I heard in the distance a gipsy song sung by merry voices coming closer, and through their song the rolling of heavy wheels and the cracking of whips; the Szgany and the Slovaks of whom the Count had spoken were coming. With a last look around and at the box which contained the vile body, I ran from the place and gained the Count's room, determined to rush out at the moment the door should be opened. With strained ears, I listened, and heard downstairs the grinding of the key in the great lock and the falling back of the heavy door. There must have been some other means of entry, or some one had a key for one of the locked doors. Then there came the sound of many feet tramping and dying away in some passage which sent up a clanging echo.[55] I turned to run down again towards the vault, where I might find the new entrance; but at the moment there seemed to come a violent

53 The word "batten" here has nothing to do with bats, vampire or regular; it means to eat gluttonously or to nourish, to fatten, probably derived from an Old Norse or Gothic word meaning "to improve."

Where does Harker get this idea? Surely at this point, he knows (at best) of only four vampires, Dracula and the three women, and he has no information about the propagation of vampires. Once again, Harker's recollections of these events seem to be heavily based on information he obtained much later.

54 According to E. Cobham Brewer's 1894 *Dictionary of Phrase and Fable*, "the king of serpents . . . , supposed to have the power of 'looking any one dead on whom it fixed its eyes.'" Also known as a cockatrice.

55 This must be the outlet Harker fails to discover. See note 36 above.

56 Wolf (*The Essential Dracula*) and Leatherdale (*Dracula Unearthed*) credit this convenient gust to Dracula, who is not as helpless as he appears.

57 At least, Harker assumes so. He did not examine the remainder of the fifty boxes, and it is certainly possible that the women occupied three of them. Could it be that Harker hoped that the women remained behind and that he looked forward to their "kisses"?

58 Again, Harker seems to borrow from his later knowledge that vampires are "created" by other vampires, although Leatherdale (*Dracula Unearthed*) sees this statement as an expression of Harker's fear of emasculation—castration—by the vampire women.

puff of wind, and the door to the winding stair blew to with a shock that set the dust from the lintels flying.[56] When I ran to push it open, I found that it was hopelessly fast. I was again a prisoner, and the net of doom was closing round me more closely.

As I write there is in the passage below a sound of many tramping feet and the crash of weights being set down heavily, doubtless the boxes, with their freight of earth. There was a sound of hammering; it is the box being nailed down. Now I can hear the heavy feet tramping again along the hall, with many other idle feet coming behind them.

The door is shut, and the chains rattle; there is a grinding of the key in the lock; I can hear the key withdrawn: then another door opens and shuts; I hear the creaking of lock and bolt.

Hark! in the courtyard and down the rocky way the roll of heavy wheels, the crack of whips, and the chorus of the Szgany as they pass into the distance.

I am alone in the castle with those awful women.[57] Faugh! Mina is a woman, and there is nought in common. They are devils of the Pit!

I shall not remain alone with them; I shall try to scale the castle wall farther than I have yet attempted. I shall take some of the gold with me, lest I want it later. I may find a way from this dreadful place.

And then away for home! away to the quickest and nearest train! away from this cursed spot, from this cursed land, where the devil and his children still walk with earthly feet!

At least God's mercy is better than that of those monsters, and the precipice is steep and high. At its foot a man may sleep—as a man.[58] Good-bye, all! Mina!

Chapter 5[1]

LETTER FROM MISS MINA MURRAY TO MISS LUCY WESTENRA.[2]

"9 May.

"My dearest Lucy,—

"Forgive my long delay in writing, but I have been simply overwhelmed with work. The life of an assistant schoolmistress is sometimes trying.[3] I am longing to be with you,[4] and by the sea, where we can talk together freely and build our castles in the air. I have been working very hard lately, because I want to keep up with Jonathan's studies, and I have been practising shorthand very assiduously. When we are married I shall be able to be useful to Jonathan,[5] and if I can stenograph well enough I can take down what he wants to say in this way and write it out for him on the typewriter, at which also I am practising very hard.[6] He and I sometimes write letters in shorthand, and he is keeping a stenographic journal of his travels abroad. When I am with you I shall keep a diary in the same way. I don't mean one of those two-pages-to-the-week-with-Sunday-squeezed-in-a-corner diaries, but a sort of journal which I can write in whenever I feel inclined. I do not suppose there will be much of interest to other people; but it is not intended for them. I may show it to Jonathan some day if there is in it anything worth sharing, but it is really an exercise book. I shall try to do what I see lady journalists do: interviewing and writing descriptions and trying to remember conversations. I am told that, with

1 Formerly ix, then VII.

2 Peter Haining and Peter Tremayne, in *The Un-Dead: The Legend of Bram Stoker and Dracula*, assert that the "real" Lucy and Mina were a pair of girls who shared lodgings at 7 The Crescent, Whitby, and whom Stoker met on a holiday trip there. Although it is possible that Stoker's involvement in the Dracula affair began with a chance meeting in Whitby in 1890 (at which time he might also have met "Dr. Seward," who the Notes indicate was called there by Mina), Stoker's preface to the Icelandic edition of *Dracula* (see p. 5) indicates that the "Harkers" and "Dr. Seward" were his friends "for many years." Stoker conspicuously omits the "Westenras" from this list of friends, suggesting that he in fact never met them and belying the speculation of Haining and Tremayne. The year 1890, though a possible date for the events described in *Dracula*, is not a leading candidate—see appendix 2, "The Dating of *Dracula*."

3 This material is added in Stoker's hand to the Manuscript, and the following is crossed out: "I do not know how to say how glad I am that you are so happy. Every blessing, my dear, on you both. I shall try to tell you when we meet how I feel." This clearly relates to the earlier outline of

events, set forth in the Notes, indicating that the Harkers were married in London. See chapter 9, note 10.

Employment as an "assistant schoolmistress" in late-nineteenth-century England was harder to obtain than a position as a governess or tutor; the latter jobs were largely unregulated. Most "schoolmistresses" earned a certificate or diploma after several years of specialised training at a private or government college.

4 Wolf (*The Essential Dracula*) points out that the Trinity term (the third term of the academic school year, the other two being Michaelmas and Hilary) ends in mid- to late June; therefore, Mina had four to seven weeks of school left before the "long vacation," or summer break.

5 Despite Mina's later protestations about the "New Woman," her attitude displayed here put her in a distinct minority. As late as 1891, only 5 percent of clerical employees in England were women. See Lee Holcombe's 1973 *Victorian Ladies at Work.*

6 In 1873, the first commercial typewriter was produced by Philo Remington from the designs of Christopher Latham Sholes and Carlos Glidden. When typewriters were first introduced, shorthand was in common use, but there were few trained operators of the new machines. In 1881, the American YWCA foresaw the advantages of training women to use the typewriter and began classes. By 1886, it was estimated that there were some 60,000 young women typewriting in offices in the United States. Rudyard Kipling, in letters from America (*From Sea to Sea and Other Sketches*), referred at this time to the "typewriter-maiden" who earned her living rather than remain dependent on her parents. It was not uncommon for manufacturers to train women to type and then to "sell" the trained typists to businesses along with their machines. Before he died in 1890, Sholes was quoted as saying "I do feel I have done something for the women who have always had to work so hard. This

Cover of 1902 edition of *Dracula.*
(New York: Doubleday, Page)

a little practice, one can remember all that goes on or that one hears said during a day.[7] However, we shall see. I shall tell you of my little plans when we meet. I have just had a few hurried lines from Jonathan from Transylvania.[8] He is well, and will be returning in about a week. I am longing to hear all his news. It must be nice to see strange countries. I wonder if we—I mean Jonathan and I—shall ever see them together. There is the ten o'clock bell ringing. Good-bye.

"Your loving

"Mina.

"Tell me all the news when you write. You have not told me anything for a long time. I hear rumours,[9] and especially of a tall, handsome, curly-haired man???"

LETTER, LUCY WESTENRA TO MINA MURRAY.[10]

"17, Chatham Street,[11]
"Wednesday.[12]

"My dearest Mina,—

"I must say you tax me *very* unfairly with being a bad correspondent. I wrote to you *twice* since we parted,[13] and your last letter was only your *second*. Besides, I have nothing to tell you. There is really nothing to interest you. Town is very pleasant just now, and we go a good deal to picture-galleries[14] and for walks and rides in the park.[15] As to the tall, curly-haired man, I suppose it was the one who was with me at the last Pop.[16] Some one has evidently been telling tales.[17] That was Mr. Holmwood. He often comes to see us, and he and mamma get on very well together; they have so many things to talk about in common.[18] We met some time ago a man that would just *do for you*, if you were not already engaged to Jonathan. He is an excellent *parti*,[19] being handsome, well off, and of good birth. He is a doctor and really clever.[20] Just fancy! He is only nine-and-twenty, and he has an immense lunatic asylum all under his own care.[21] Mr. Holmwood introduced him to me,[22] and he called here to see us, and often comes now. I think he is one of the most resolute men I ever saw, and yet the most calm. He seems absolutely imperturbable. I can fancy what a wonderful power he must have over his patients. He has a curious habit of looking one straight in the face, as if trying to read one's thoughts. He tries this on very much with me, but I flatter myself he has got a tough nut to crack. I know that from my glass. Do you ever try to read your own face? *I do*, and I can tell you it is not a bad study, and gives you more trouble than you can well fancy if you have never tried it. He says that I afford

will enable them more easily to earn a living" (quoted in Frederic Heath, "The Typewriter in Wisconsin").

7 Another sign of "New Woman"-ish tendencies in Mina. Contrast the comments of Katie Cowper, writing in 1890 in *The Nineteenth Century*: "How many women till lately, however talented and well-educated they were, ever dreamt of openly writing in reviews and newspapers? . . . These and other like innovations, which in so short a time have assumed such immense proportions, 'give one to think;' and we must be excused who do not appreciate and care not to give way to this clamour for absolute equality with men. In this respect the good old times were better, far better than the new."

8 This is not one of the letters written under Dracula's direction later, but must have been posted from Klausenburg or Bistritz on 3 or 4 May.

9 Leatherdale (*Dracula Unearthed*) wonders who could communicate these rumours to Mina, for she is in Exeter and Lucy in London. In fact, it is likely to have been Kate Reed, a mutual friend described in the Notes who has been excised from the narrative. See note 17 below.

10 Lucy's letter has been shortened considerably for the Abridged Text, and in particular her recommendation of Dr. Seward as "*parti*" is omitted.

11 There were two Chatham Streets in London, one in Newington, between the Rodney Road and Darwin Street, in London, S.E., and one in Battersea (London, S.W.), just south of Battersea Park Road, between Culvert Road and Parkside Sreet. The former was not far from Bethlem ("Bedlam") Hospital; the latter was a suburb south of the Thames well known for its park and cycling paths but also near the Middlesex County Lunatic Asylum in Streatham. Thus either location might be in the vicinity of Dr. John Seward.

The significance of the address is unknown, for Lucy's home, Hillingham, is plainly located in north London. (See chapter 9, note 31, and chapter 11, note 28.) Stoker may have erroneously allowed the real address of the real Lucy Westenra to appear here. It is never mentioned again in the narrative.

12 Although Lucy's letter is undated, it could have been written on 10 May (a Wednesday in 1893), the day after Mina's. (See appendix 2, "The Dating of *Dracula*," for a discussion of the year.) The British postal system, then over 250 years old, was a reliable and rapid means of communication, the advent of the railway and the steamship having brought about increasingly speedy and more regular service as the nineteenth century passed. According to the 1900 edition of *Whitaker's Almanack*, in the city district of London there were twelve deliveries daily, and in other London districts there were six to eleven collections and deliveries. Letters were normally delivered within two to four hours of posting. More urgent messages could be designated for "express delivery" at a small additional cost, or the "district messenger service," a private carrier, could be used for 3 pennies per half-mile. Overnight delivery was the standard for mail outside London.

13 Leatherdale (*Dracula Unearthed*) points out that there is no explanation for their "parting," which he believes suggests that Lucy was a student in the school where Mina works. They apparently attended school together as well. See text accompanying note 24 below.

14 Visiting the "picture-galleries" was a popular pastime and afforded the enthusiast an opportunity to see the works of contemporary artists not yet in museums. For example, in *The Hound of the Baskervilles* (1902), Sherlock Holmes, who fancied the "modern Belgian masters" (in particular, the XX Group, James Ensor and his friends, whose work was too avant-garde for more traditional venues), fills in some time by dropping in to "one of the Bond Street picture-galleries," of which there were more than a half-dozen.

15 This could be a reference to Battersea Park, near the Chatham Street address heading this letter, or to the heath near Hillingham, but most likely Lucy means Hyde Park, "one of the most frequented and lively scenes in London," according to the 1896 London "Baedeker." Dickens's 1888 *Dictionary of London* calls it "the great fashionable promenade of London." Rotten Row is a road set aside for equestrians, extending originally from Hyde Park Corner to Queen's-gate. There is also a carriage drive alongside, passing the site of the original Great Exhibition of 1851. According to Dickens, "for two or three hours every afternoon in the season, except Sunday, the particular section of the drive which happens that year to be 'the fashion' is densely thronged with carriages moving round and round at little more than a walking pace, and every now and then coming to a dead-lock." Only the road from Queen's-gate to Victoria-gate was open to cabs; the remainder of the park was open to private carriages only.

The Drive and Rotten Row, Hyde Park.
Queen's London (1897)

16 Charles Dickens Jr., in his 1888 *Dictionary of London*, remarks that the "pops," or "Popular Concerts," held at St. James's Hall on Saturday afternoons and Monday evenings during the winter season are "of the highest musical importance." "These justly celebrated entertainments of chamber classical music have reached their twenty-fifth year, and the manner in which the quartetts [*sic*], trios, &c., are rendered by the first living artists, affords a theme for eulogistic comment throughout the world of art."

17 Who could the tale-teller be? From the Notes, it appears likely to have been Kate or Katie Reed, a schoolfellow and friend of Mina's whose correspondence with Mina is mentioned several times but eventually suppressed. Kate Reed plays an active rôle in Kim Newman's *Anno Dracula* and its sequels, which record events occurring after the narrative of *Dracula*. Apparently Stoker noted that he had inadvertently included more of the Notes than he wished, for the "tale-telling" is not criticised in the Abridged Text. The Manuscript identifies this "some one" as "Kate Lee," never mentioned in the Notes but perhaps merely hastily inserted by Stoker without referring to them. The Manuscript contains the following which is omitted from the published narrative, suggesting that the "some one" is a close friend, perhaps a former schoolmate: "I shall have my eye on that young lynx for the future so tell her to be very discreet and give her a kiss for me."

18 The Manuscript (likely quoting the Harker Papers accurately) makes clear that the real "Lucy" was more than just the empty-headed beauty depicted in the narrative. The following Manuscript material is omitted from the published narrative: "I almost envy mother sometimes for her knowledge when she can talk to people whilst I have to sit by like a dumb animal and smile a stereotyped smile till I find myself blushing at being an incarnate *lie*. And it is so silly and *childish* to *blush* and *without reason* too." For artistic reasons, Stoker apparently chose to distort her character, and unlike the others, who survived to cavil at his artistic choices, no one complained about the published portrayal of "Lucy."

19 French, match. A marriageable person,

viewed from the prospect of suitability. Lord Byron wrote in a letter in 1814, "It is likely she will prove a considerable *parti*" (*Letters and Journals of Lord Byron*).

20 If Seward was twenty-nine, he probably was born between 1857 and 1864. (See appendix 2, "The Dating of *Dracula*.") Another prominent physician of his generation was Arthur Conan Doyle, born in 1859, and Conan Doyle's education is a reasonable estimate of Seward's. Between 1859 and 1866, the General Medical Council of the United Kingdom urged education in general knowledge as a prerequisite for medical school. Conan Doyle studied at Stonyhurst, a Jesuit school in Edinburgh, and in 1876 was admitted to the medical school of the University of Edinburgh (at the age of seventeen, a common age), where he studied for five years. While a student was permitted to graduate in four years, as early as age twenty-one, Conan Doyle took an extra year to earn money to pay for his schooling.

Conan Doyle's studies included basic science as well as clinical medicine. Human dissections were routine, and there was constant exposure to patients. Examinations were a combination of written and oral tests. Years later, Conan Doyle recalled that his medical training was "one long weary grind of botany, chemistry, anatomy, physiology, and a whole list of compulsory subjects, many of which have a very indirect bearing upon the art of curing." (In fact, they were French, German, Moral Philosophy, Natural History, and Medical Jurisprudence.)

Upon graduation, a doctor required licensure. A license would be granted to a member of the Society of Apothecaries, a fellow of the Royal College of Physicians, a member of the Royal College of Surgeons, or a university graduate. Conan Doyle obtained his license on the basis of his education; James Mortimer, friend of Sir Henry Baskerville (*The Hound of the Baskervilles* [1902]), however, although referred to as a doctor, insisted on the title "Mister," a "humble M.R.C.S." In Mortimer's day, the M.R.C.S. was the surgical half of the standard qualification to practise, not an advanced degree, and surgeons in fact occupied a lower position in the medical hierarchy than physicians, who diagnosed patients and prescribed medication. Surgeons' duties included the treatment of wounds and performance of then-standard surgical procedures, the range of which was smaller than today. Mortimer apparently did not possess the medical half of the qualification to practise medicine, usually a license from the Society of Apothecaries, which conferred the letters L.S.A. (originally for Licentiate of the Society of Apothecaries; the title was changed in 1907 to L.M.S.S.A., indicating that the examination included surgery).

It should also be remembered that a medical license in the late nineteenth century was by no means a guarantee of prestige or wealth. Because the practise of medicine was identified as a "technical" craft, and because many students came from the lower middle class, there was no great social standing attached to membership in the profession.

Note that a Continental medical education was not uncommon among English physicians. Seward apparently studied with Van Helsing in Amsterdam; Conan Doyle studied ophthalmology in Vienna, after trying a general practise for several years.

21 Harker previously advised Dracula that Carfax, which Harker purchased for him, was "close at hand" to a private asylum, which we learn later is Seward's. Lucy's description of the asylum as "all under [Dr. Seward's] own care" is consistent with Harker's statement that it was a "private" asylum. The inaccurate use of the word "asylum" should not be taken as an indication that Lucy's letter was written before enactment of the 1890 Lunacy Act; in

Advertisement for private asylum.
The Medical Annual (1896)

him a curious psychological study, and I humbly think I do.[23] I do not, as you know, take sufficient interest in dress to be able to describe the new fashions. Dress is a bore. That is slang again, but never mind; Arthur says that every day. There, it is all out. Mina, we have told all our secrets to each other since we were *children*; we have slept together and eaten together, and laughed and cried together;[24] and now, though I have spoken, I would like to speak more. Oh, Mina, couldn't you guess? I love him. I am blushing as I write, for although I *think* he loves me, he has not told me so in words. But oh, Mina, I love him; I love him; I love him! There, that does me good. I wish I were with you, dear, sitting by the fire undressing, as we used to sit; and I would try to tell you what I feel.[25] I do not know how I am writing this even to you. I am afraid to stop, or I should tear up the letter, and I don't want to stop, for I *do so* want to tell you all. Let me hear from you *at once*, and tell me all that you think about it.[26] Mina, I must stop. Good-night. Bless me in your prayers; and, Mina, pray for my happiness.

"Lucy.

"P.S.—I need not tell you this is a secret. Good-night again.

"L."

Letter from Lucy Westenra to Mina Murray

"24 May.

"My dearest Mina,—

"Thanks, and thanks, and thanks again for your sweet letter! It was so nice to be able to tell you and to have your sympathy.

"My dear, it never rains but it pours. How true the old proverbs are. Here am I, who shall be twenty in September, and yet I never had a proposal till to-day, not a real proposal, and to-day I have had three. Just fancy! THREE proposals in one day! Isn't it awful! I feel sorry, really and truly sorry,

common usage, the "madhouse" or "asylum" encompassed public and private institutions, and many "licensed houses" after 1890 were publicly owned asylums, and there was public involvement in others. See chapter 2, note 59.

22 McNally and Florescu (*The Essential Dracula*) ignore this statement and assert that Lucy likely met Seward on the street near her home. This seems insupportable. See also chapter 18, note 2.

23 The following phrase appears in the Manuscript but is omitted from the published text: "I enclose a circular for Madame as you wish." "Madame" suggests an employer of Mina, perhaps the mistress of Mina's school, and the sentence provides a transition to what otherwise appears to be Lucy's flighty change of topic to fashion. In "dumbing down" Lucy (see note 18 above), Stoker chose to eliminate the reason why she was talking about fashion.

24 This suggests that Mina and Lucy were schoolmates. See note 13 above.

25 Again, the Manuscript contains the following intelligent remarks by Lucy, omitted from the published text: *"That is not love at all*—no, nor the least like it. *Love is a holy thing.* We used to be ashamed of those things then—as we well might be. I glory in my love now." See note 18 above.

26 The Manuscript reads: "I wish you knew the tall straight-haired man—he is so noble and brave and good and tender and true—How the girls would laugh in school if they saw this letter. I must stop. I feel so happy that I could go on writing for ever—telling you my secret is just like telling Arthur that I love him—only of course not quite the same. Mina if a time should come when,—after he had told me that he loved me, of course—I should be able to whisper to him 'Arthur, I love you!'" While the changed version appearing in the published text may be the result of editorial compression of the narrative, the revision raises a question about whether "Arthur Holmwood" was "curly-haired," as noted earlier by Mina and Lucy, or "straight-haired." The revision suggests that in editing the Harker Papers, Stoker changed Holmwood's physical appearance as well as his name.

27 Perhaps another reference to Kate Reed or to other unnamed mutual friends, one of whom may have been the rumourmonger. Again, this suggests that Lucy attended the school in which Mina is employed, where Mina might have contact with "the girls" to whom Lucy refers.

28 Wolf (*The Essential Dracula*) asks why Seward, a psychiatrist, is carrying a lancet, a surgical instrument.

29 This sentence does not appear in the Abridged Text.

30 Leatherdale (*Dracula Unearthed*) wonders that Seward—introduced to Lucy by Holmwood—could have been so insensitive as to have missed their relationship.

31 Evidently a typographical error in the first-edition text.

for two of the poor fellows. Oh, Mina, I am so happy that I don't know what to do with myself. And three proposals! But, for goodness' sake, don't tell any of the girls,[27] or they would be getting all sorts of extravagant ideas and imagining themselves injured and slighted if in their very first day at home they did not get six at least. Some girls are so vain. You and I, Mina dear, who are engaged and are going to settle down soon soberly into old married women, can despise vanity. Well, I must tell you about the three, but you must keep it a secret, dear, from *every one*, except, of course, Jonathan. You will tell him, because I would, if I were in your place, certainly tell Arthur. A woman ought to tell her husband everything—don't you think so, dear?—and I must be fair. Men like women, certainly their wives, to be quite as fair as they are; and women, I am afraid, are not always quite as fair as they should be. Well, my dear, number One came just before lunch. I told you of him, Dr. John Seward, the lunatic-asylum man, with the strong jaw and the good forehead. He was very cool outwardly, but was nervous all the same. He had evidently been schooling himself as to all sorts of little things, and remembered them; but he almost managed to sit down on his silk hat, which men don't generally do when they are cool, and then when he wanted to appear at ease he kept playing with a lancet in a way that made me nearly scream.[28] He spoke to me, Mina, very straightforwardly. He told me how dear I was to him, though he had known me so little, and what his life would be with me to help and cheer him. He was going to tell me how unhappy he would be if I did not care for him, but when he saw me cry he said that he was a brute and would not add to my present trouble.[29] Then he broke off and asked if I could love him in time; and when I shook my head his hands trembled, and then with some hesitation he asked me if I cared already for any one else.[30] He put it very nicely, saying that he did not want to wring my confidence from me, but only to know, because if a woman's heart was free a man might have hope. And then, Nina,[31] I felt a sort of duty to tell him that there was some one. I only told him that much, and then he stood up, and he looked very strong and very grave as he took both my hands in his and said he hoped I would be happy, and that if I ever wanted a friend I must count him one of my best.[32] Oh, Mina dear, I can't help crying; and you must excuse this letter being all blotted. Being proposed to is all very nice and all that sort of thing, but it isn't at all a happy thing when you have to see a poor fellow, whom you know loves you honestly, going away and looking all broken-hearted, and to know that, no matter what he may say at the moment, you are passing quite out of his life. My dear, I must stop here at present, I feel so miserable, though I am so happy.

"Evening.

"Arthur has just gone, and I feel in better spirits than when I left off, so I can go on telling you about the day. Well, my dear, number Two came after lunch. He is such a nice fellow, an American from Texas, and he looks so young and so fresh that it seems almost impossible that he has been to so many places and has had such adventures. I sympathize with poor Desdemona when she had such a dangerous stream poured in her ear, even by a black man.[33] I suppose that we women are such cowards that we think a man will save us from fears, and we marry him. I know now what I would do if I were a man and wanted to make a girl love me. No, I don't, for there was Mr. Morris telling us his stories, and Arthur never told any, and yet—My dear, I am somewhat previous. Mr. Quincy P. Morris found me alone. It seems that a man always does find a girl alone. No, he doesn't, for Arthur tried twice to *make* a chance, and I helping him all I could; I am not ashamed to say it now. I must tell you beforehand that Mr. Morris doesn't always speak slang—that is to say, he never does so to strangers or before them, for he is really well educated and has exquisite manners—but he found out that it amused me to hear him talk American slang, and whenever I was present, and there was no one to be shocked, he said such funny things. I am afraid, my dear, he has to invent it all, for it fits exactly into whatever else he has to say. But this is a way slang has. I do not know myself if I shall ever speak slang; I do not know

32 Tellingly, the Manuscript adds the following, which has been omitted from the published narrative: "and truest who would do for me anything that a man might do." Perhaps this remark struck Stoker as too insightful, or too suggestive!

33 Lucy refers here to Shakespeare's *Othello,* in which the Moorish general Othello finds that his tales of his adventures have captured the heart of Desdemona, the daughter of Brabantio, a Venetian senator. "She loved me for the dangers I had passed, / And I loved her that she did pity them. / This only is the witchcraft I have used" (act 1, scene 3). Lucy's casually racist remark was typical of the period. Victorian racialism, as well as the more aggressive forms of imperialism, drew heavily on allegedly scientific arguments. Both were epitomised by Rudyard Kipling's 1899 poem "The White Man's Burden," which characterised the subject races of the British empire as "Your new-caught, sullen peoples / Half-devil and half-child."

The Shakespearean reference is absent from the Abridged Text.

34 Morris's biblical knowledge is apparently a bit rusty, for there were ten virgins, not seven. He refers here to Matt. 25:1–10: "Then shall the kingdom of heaven be likened unto ten virgins, which took their lamps, and went forth to meet the bridegroom. And five of them were wise, and five were foolish. They that were foolish took their lamps, and took no oil with them: But the wise took oil in their vessels with their lamps. While the bridegroom tarried, they all slumbered and slept. And at midnight there was a cry made, Behold, the bridegroom cometh; go ye out to meet him. Then all those virgins arose, and trimmed their lamps. And the foolish said unto the wise, Give us of your oil; for our lamps are gone out. But the wise answered, saying, Not so; lest there be not enough for us and you: but go ye rather to them that sell, and buy for yourselves. And while they went to buy, the bridegroom came; and they that were ready went in with him to the marriage: and the door was shut."

The point of Quincey's remark is obscure, for the parable relates to the preparedness of the women, not the absence of a suitable bridegroom.

35 American slang for strong character, indomitability. American poet James Russell Lowell (1819–1891) wrote in his 1874 poem "The Courtin' ": "He was six foot o' man, A 1, / Clean grit an' human natur'; / None couldn't quicker pitch a ton / Nor dror a furrer straighter."

36 And here is another ignoramus— undoubtedly also introduced to Lucy by Holmwood, with whom Morris has travelled, together with Seward—wholly unaware that Lucy has been courted by either Holmwood or Seward. The courtship of all three must have been remarkably pallid to have gone unnoticed by the others.

if Arthur likes it, as I have never heard him use any as yet. Well, Mr. Morris sat down beside me and looked as happy and jolly as he could, but I could see all the same that he was very nervous. He took my hand in his, and said ever so sweetly:—

" 'Miss Lucy, I know I ain't good enough to regulate the fixin's of your little shoes, but I guess if you wait till you find a man that is you will go join them seven young women with the lamps when you quit.[34] Won't you just hitch up alongside of me and let us go down the long road together, driving in double harness?'

"Well, he did look so good-humoured and so jolly that it didn't seem half so hard to refuse him as it did poor Dr. Seward, so I said, as lightly as I could, that I did not know anything of hitching, and that I wasn't broken to harness at all yet. Then he said that he had spoken in a light manner, and he hoped that if he had made a mistake in doing so on so grave, so momentous, an occasion for him, I would forgive him. He really did look serious when he was saying it, and I couldn't help feeling a bit serious too—I know, Mina, you will think me a horrid flirt—though I couldn't help feeling a sort of exultation that he was number two in one day. And then, my dear, before I could say a word he began pouring out a perfect torrent of love-making, laying his very heart and soul at my feet. He looked so earnest over it that I shall never again think that a man must be playful always, and never earnest, because he is merry at times. I suppose he saw something in my face which checked him, for he suddenly stopped, and said with a sort of manly fervour that I could have loved him for if I had been free:—

" 'Lucy, you are an honest-hearted girl, I know. I should not be here speaking to you as I am now if I did not believe you clean grit,[35] right through to the very depths of your soul. Tell me, like one good fellow to another, is there any one else that you care for?[36] And if there is I'll never trouble you a hair's breadth again, but will be, if you will let me, a very faithful friend.'

"My dear Mina, why are men so noble when we women are so little worthy of them? Here was I almost making fun of this great-hearted, true gentleman. I burst into tears—I am afraid, my dear, you will think this a very sloppy letter in more ways than one—and I really felt very badly. Why can't they let a girl marry three men, or as many as want her, and save all this trouble?[37] But this is heresy, and I must not say it. I am glad to say that, though I was crying, I was able to look into Mr. Morris's brave eyes, and told him out straight:—

"'Yes, there is some one I love, though he has not told me yet that he even loves me.'[38] I was right to speak to him so frankly, for quite a light came into his face, and he put out both his hands and took mine—I think I put them into his—and said in a hearty way:—

"'That's my brave girl. It's better worth being late for a chance of winning you than being in time for any other girl in the world. Don't cry, my dear. If it's for me, I'm a hard nut to crack; and I take it standing up. If that other fellow doesn't know his happiness, well, he'd better look for it soon, or he'll have to deal with me. Little girl, your honesty and pluck have made me a friend, and that's rarer than a lover; it's more selfish anyhow. My dear, I'm going to have a pretty lonely walk between this and Kingdom Come. Won't you give me one kiss? It'll be something to keep off the darkness now and then. You can, you know, if you like, for that other good fellow—he must be a good fellow, my dear, and a fine fellow, or you could not love him—hasn't spoken yet.' That quite won me, Mina, for it *was* brave and sweet of him, and noble, too, to a rival—wasn't it?—and he so sad; so I leant over and kissed him. He stood up with my two hands in his, and as he looked down into my face—I am afraid I was blushing very much—he said:—

"'Little girl, I hold your hand, and you've kissed me, and if these things don't make us friends nothing ever will.[39] Thank you for your sweet honesty to me, and good-bye.'

37 This provocative sentence and its successor do not appear in the Abridged Text. Perhaps Stoker was criticised by "Lord Godalming" for making Lucy appear so indelicate.

38 Holmwood's reticence may explain the ignorance of her other suitors. The Notes indicate that Lucy may have been engaged to Seward. To confuse matters even further, in the 1931 films of *Dracula* (see p. 559), Mina is Dr. Seward's daughter and Jonathan Harker the only lover, while Lucy has no fiancé at all!

39 The original version of this sentence in the Manuscript is: " 'In my part of the world when one man takes another's hand and calls him friend, he'll die for him if need be. Little girl, I hold your hand, and you've kissed me on the mouth. I call you pard and by the Almighty if ever need be I'll die for your and yours." Stoker's prudishness may have dictated the removal of reference to a kiss on the mouth, but artistically he may have also been concerned by the coincidence of Morris's remarks—for, of course, he did die for Lucy.

40 Thomas Edison invented the phonograph in 1877 but soon abandoned work on the machine. Alexander Graham Bell, Chichester Bell, and Charles Sumner Tainter developed an improved version of the phonograph, naming it the graphophone, patented in 1886. Instead of indenting tinfoil wrapped around a cylinder, the graphophone used a process of engraving a wax cylinder. In a paper read on 7 September 1888 by Henry Edmunds (the English agent for the American Graphophone Company, and the man who later introduced Charles Rolls to Frederick Royce, the founders of Rolls-Royce) to the Bath meeting of the British Association for the Advancement of Science, Edmunds crowed: "The very simplicity of the instrument startles us—but who shall say what its future may be—and what revolutions it may effect. Its introduction into every-day life marks a new era. Truly the unlimited reproduction of the human voice in speech and song is a most wonderful achievement. When we consider its marvelous adaptability to modern life there seems to be no limit to its powers. A child may work it and communicate to those who love it, its childish prattle; or preserving the small cylinder refer in after life to how it spoke. Business men may carry on negotiations, recording each word spoken, preventing misunderstandings as to what was said. Attached to the telephone, even the fleeting words that be recorded for future reference. The stenographer may read his notes to it, leaving it to dictate to others to write them out. And Tennyson's wish for the voice that is still, be realised at last."

The phonograph was not inexpensive. In the 1898 Army & Navy Stores Catalogue, the Edison home phonograph, complete with four selected records and two blanks, was advertised to members of the cooperative for £15 (the modern equivalent of over £1,100, or more than US$2,000).

Wolf (*The Essential Dracula*) notes the first reported use of a phonograph for medical record keeping in a 17 January 1890 letter of A. D. Blodgett, a Massachusetts physician, to *Science*.

He wrung my hand, and taking up his hat, went straight out of the room without looking back, t a tear or a quiver or a pause; and I am crying like a baby. Oh, why must a man like that be made unhappy when there are lots of girls about who would worship the very ground he trod on? I know I would if I were free—only I don't want to be free. My dear, this quite upset me, and I feel I cannot write of happiness just at once, after telling you of it; and I don't wish to tell of the number three until it can be all happy."

"Ever your loving
"Lucy.

"P.S.—Oh, about number Three—I needn't tell you of number three, need I? Besides, it was all so confused; it seemed only a moment from his coming into the room till both his arms were round me, and he was kissing me. I am very, very happy, and I don't know what I have done to deserve it. I must only try in the future to show that I am not ungrateful for all His goodness to me in sending to me such a lover, such a husband, and such a friend.

"Good-bye."

DR. SEWARD'S DIARY—
(Kept in phonograph.)[40]

25 April.[41]—Ebb tide in appetite to-day. Cannot eat, cannot rest, so diary instead. Since my rebuff of yesterday I have a sort of empty feeling; nothing in the world seems of sufficient importance to be worth the doing. . . . As I knew that the only cure for this sort of thing was work, I went down amongst the patients. I picked out one who has afforded me a study of much interest. He is so quaint that I am determined to understand him as well as I can. To-day I seemed to get nearer than ever before to the heart of his mystery.

I questioned him more fully than I had ever done, with a view to making myself master of the facts of his hallucination. In my manner of doing it there was, I now see, something of cruelty. I seemed to wish to keep him to the point of his madness—a thing which I avoid with the patients as I would the mouth of hell. (*Mem.*, under what circumstances would I

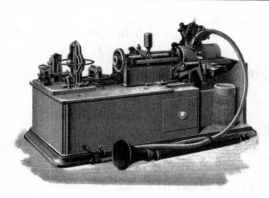

Edison phonograph.
Engineering, 14 September 1878

Any other kind of game not in stock procured to order.
† Can only be obtained through the Society.

THE HOME PHONOGRAPH.

(Sample only kept.)

Records the sound of voice, piano, banjo, cornet, violin, &c. Reproduces all sounds recorded in marvellously clear and distinct tones, loud and resonant, and of sufficient volume to fill a drawing room, parlour or large hall.

A machine specially devised by Mr. Edison for universal use, and brought well within the popular range of prices.

Price for private use only, complete, with recording and reproducing diaphragms, trumpet for recording and repeating sounds, oiler, flexible hearing tube, mounted in polished oak enclosed in case, with carrying handle, and record case with 4 selected records and 2 blanks £15 0 0

Extra records of songs, solos, &c., each, 5/0.

Edison home phonograph.
Army & Navy Stores Catalogue, 1898

Bell-Tainter graphophone.
Engineering, 14 September 1878

41 This has been corrected in subsequent editions to 25 May. The Notes indicate the entry is dated 24 May.

42 Not quite an accurate quotation from the *Bellum Iugurthinum* [Jugurthine Wars] of the Roman historian Sallust (86–34 BC): *Romae omnia venali esse*, "All of Rome is for sale."

43 Slang Latin: *verbum sapienti* means "a word to the wise."

44 In the Manuscript, Renfield's age of forty-nine has been manually changed to fifty-nine.

45 Medical Latin: age.

46 Hippocrates (469–399 BC) saw temperament as stemming from the humours dominant in the body: blood (sanguine), bile from the liver (choleric), phlegm (phlegmatic), and bile from the kidneys (melancholic). The sanguine temperament is generally regarded as happy, buoyant, "up" in modern slang, superficial, optimistic, and extroverted. Certainly Renfield, it will be seen, should be characterised as choleric, ambitious, with a keen intellect, driven, willful, with strong passions and a desire to rule. In either case, it is surprising to find a physician (even though a pre-Freudian) expressing such a superficial diagnosis.

47 Wolf (*The Essential Dracula*) calls this "nineteenth-century psycho-babble." Perhaps, on reflection, Stoker felt the same and spared his friend "Dr. Seward" from criticism, for the two sentences do not appear in the Abridged Text.

48 The Marquesas Islands lie between 400 and 600 miles south of the equator and approximately 1,000 miles northeast of Tahiti and are part of French Polynesia. By 1872, the native population had declined to six thousand; it shrank to a mere two thousand by 1923. Today six of the islands have a population of about seven thousand. Herman Melville's *Typee: A Peep at Polynesian Life* (1846), while criticised as overly romanticised, is a semiautobiographical account of a visit to the Marquesas and depicts the Marquesans as noble savages.

not avoid the pit of hell?) *Omnia Romæ venalia sunt.*[42] Hell has its price! *verb. sap.*[43] If there be anything behind this instinct it will be valuable to trace it afterwards *accurately*, so I had better commence to do so, therefore—

R. M. Renfield,[44] ætat[45] 59.—Sanguine temperament;[46] great physical strength; morbidly excitable; periods of gloom, ending in some fixed idea which I cannot make out. I presume that the sanguine temperament itself and the disturbing influence end in a mentally-accomplished finish; a possibly dangerous man, probably dangerous if unselfish. In selfish men caution is as secure an armour for their foes as for themselves. What I think of on this point is, when self is the fixed point the centripetal force is balanced with the centrifugal; when duty, a cause, etc., is the fixed point, the latter force is paramount, and only accident or a series of accidents can balance it.[47]

LETTER FROM QUINCEY P. MORRIS TO THE HONORABLE ARTHUR HOLMWOOD.

"25 May.

"My dear Art,—

"We've told yarns by the camp-fire in the prairies; and dressed one another's wounds after trying a landing at the Marquesas;[48] and drunk healths on the shore of Titicaca.[49] There are more yarns to be told, and other wounds to be healed, and another health to be drunk. Won't you let this be at my camp-fire to-morrow night? I have no hesitation in asking you, as I know a certain lady is engaged to a certain dinner-party, and that you are free. There will only be one other, our old pal at the Korea,[50] Jack Seward.[51] He's coming, too, and we both want to mingle our weeps over the wine cup, and to drink a health with all our hearts to the happiest man in all the wide world, who has won the noblest heart that God has made and best worth winning. We promise you a hearty welcome, and a loving greeting, and a health as true as your own right hand. We shall both swear to leave you at home if you drink too deep to a certain pair of eyes.[52] Come!

"Yours, as ever and always,

"Quincey P. Morris."

Marquesan native.
Wilhelm Gottlieb Tilesius von Tilenau, 1813

Marquesan village.
Louis Le Breton,
Cases de Naturels a Nouka-Hiva, 1864

The hacienda of Challa and heights of Challa Pata at Lake Titicaca.
Photograph by Adolph F. Bandelier, ca. 1894

49 The second-largest lake in South America, situated at an altitude of 12,500 feet astride the border of Peru and Bolivia. Near the lake's southern shore is the pre-Inca ruin Tiahuanaco.

50 Morris's reference here is obscure. It is possible that this refers to the country of Korea, known more commonly in Victorian times as "Corea." There was a ship out of Liverpool called the *Corea* that sailed Asian routes in the late nineteenth century. Leatherdale (*Dracula Unearthed*) suggests that the reference could be to an unknown tavern or gentlemen's club.

51 This is an odd remark, for surely Holmwood introduced both Seward and Morris to Lucy. Is it possible that Morris did not know of Seward's occasional presence in the Westenra home?

52 Morris makes another malapropic literary reference, this time to Ben Jonson's "The Forest: To Celia" (1616): "Drink to me only with thine eyes, / And I will pledge with mine" (stolen, however, from the love letters of Philostratus [ca. 170–247]). Or perhaps Morris is thinking of a song from Richard Brinsley Sheridan's *School for Scandal* (1777): "Here's to the girl with a pair of blue eyes, / And here's to the nymph with but one, sir" (act 3, scene 3).

53 Corrected to "Holmwood" in subsequent editions.

54 Again, as Leatherdale (*Dracula Unearthed*) points out, the implication is that the three men have not seen each other, although Holmwood introduced Seward to Lucy. Morris's telegram implies that they know all about Holmwood's romance, but Holmwood acts as if he has news for them—the nature of which is unguessable if he is not referring to his engagement.

TELEGRAM FROM ARTHUR HOPWOOD[53] TO QUINCEY P. MORRIS.

26 May.

COUNT ME IN EVERY TIME. I BEAR MESSAGES WHICH WILL MAKE BOTH YOUR EARS TINGLE.[54]

"ART"

Chapter 6

Mina Murray's Journal.

24 July. Whitby.[1]—Lucy met me at the station,[2] looking sweeter and lovelier than ever, and we drove up to the house at the Crescent in which they have rooms.[3] This is a lovely place. The little river, the Esk, runs through a deep valley, which broadens out as it comes near the harbour. A great viaduct runs across, with high piers, through which the view seems somehow further away than it really is. The valley is beautifully green, and it is so steep that when you are on the high land on either side you look right across it, unless you are near enough to see down. The houses of the old town—the side away from us—are all red-roofed, and seem piled up one over the other anyhow, like the pictures we see of Nuremberg. Right over the town is the ruin of Whitby Abbey,[4] which was sacked by the Danes, and which is the scene of part of "Marmion," where the girl was built up in the wall.[5] It is a most noble ruin, of immense size, and full of beautiful and romantic bits; there is a legend that a white lady is seen in one of the windows.[6] Between it and the town there is another church, the parish one,[7] round which is a big graveyard, all full of tombstones. This is to my mind the nicest spot in Whitby, for it lies right over the town, and has a full view of the harbour and all up the bay to where the headland called Kettleness stretches out into the sea.[8] It descends so steeply over the harbour that part of the bank has fallen away, and some of the graves have been

1 Whitby is a small town and watering place on the banks of the Esk, described by the 1894 Great Britain "Baedeker" as "very picturesque, with its crowd of red-tiled houses, clustering on both sides of the river and climbing the sides of the cliff." Reportedly the great mariner-explorer Captain Cook (1728–1779) departed on one of his voyages in a Whitby vessel; the town's tourist trade is derived in part from its Cook memorial museum and the display of a replica of his ship. In 1891, the population was 13,261, and the town was a fishing port, vacation resort, and source of most of the world's jet—coal that is cut, polished, and set in jewellery, and from which the term "jet-black" is derived. The Whitby jet economy was badly hurt in the

Jet workers, Whitby.
F. M. Sutcliffe, 1890

Whitby Harbour.
From a photograph by F. M. Sutcliffe, *Horne's Guide to Whitby* (1891)

late nineteenth century by the importation of plentiful lower-quality, cheaper jet from Spain and France.

If there was any correspondence between Lucy and Mina between 24 May and this date, it may have been omitted as immaterial.

The Abridged Text shortens Mina's description of Whitby, eliminating the references to Nuremberg, "Marmion," and the white lady that follow.

2 Whitby was the terminus of the Whitby branch of the York and Scarborough line of the North Eastern Railway and the North Yorkshire and Cleveland branch of the same railway. The Manuscript reads, "Arrived here at 4.35, ten minutes late." This comment does not appear in the published text. However, there was no 4:25 train. In light of Mina's unfailing accuracy about trains, this suggests that the remark is not

View of Whitby.
F. M. Sutcliffe, ca. 1880

Whitby Abbey.
Horne's Guide to Whitby (1891)

WEST CLIFF BOARDING HOUSE

AND

PRIVATE HOTEL,

ROYAL CRESCENT, WHITBY.

Unrivalled situation; facing the Sea; near the Golf Links; close to the Saloon, Tennis Courts, Sands, and Bathing; and within five minutes' walk of West Cliff Station.

TARIFF ON APPLICATION TO

MRS. NEWBITT, PROPRIETRESS.
(205)

Advertisement for West Cliff Boarding House and Private Hotel.
Horne's Guide to Whitby (1891)

drawn from the Harker Papers but is rather an embellishment tentatively added by Stoker.

3 Although the West Cliff Boarding House and Private Hotel ("Unrivalled situation; uninterrupted Sea View; close to Saloon, Tennis Courts, Sands, and Bathing, and within five minutes' walk of West Cliff Station . . . Mrs. Newbitt, Proprietress") and the Royal Hotel were situated on the Royal Crescent, Mina refers to a "house" (and later to the "people of the house"); it is likely that Lucy and her mother took rooms in a private home. There was no single street named "The Crescent" in Whitby, although several have "Crescent" as part of their names. There are difficulties in ascribing the views depicted by Mina to any of these Crescents.

4 Whitby Abbey—also known as St. Hilda's Abbey, after its British-born, French-educated foundress Hild (her given name, although she was also called Hilda)—was built in the seventh century but dates in its present form from the thirteenth and fourteenth centuries.

5 *Marmion; A Tale of Flodden Field* by Sir Walter Scott (1808), a narrative poem written in tetrameter and set in 1513, concerns (in relevant part) the designs of Lord Marmion, a favourite of Henry VIII, upon a wealthy heiress, Clara de Clare. To eliminate Lady Clare's fiancé, Sir Ralph De Wilton, from the scene, Lord Marmion falsely accuses De Wilton of treason. Marmion is assisted by his mistress, Constance De Beverley, a fallen nun, who seeks to recapture Marmion's affection. Marmion eventually abandons Constance, and she is condemned for breaking her vows and walled up alive in the convent of St. Hilda on the Holy Island at Lindisfarne (that is, in Lindisfarne Abbey, a priory and monastery that Scott turned into a nunnery for the poem). In fact, the abbey at Whitby was home primarily to monks, not nuns, although under Hild it did house both.

West Cliff Estate, Whitby.

ROYAL HOTEL,

For Families and Gentlemen.

OCCUPIES A SITUATION WHICH CANNOT BE EQUALLED
ON THE COAST.

Tariff on Application to the Hotel.

The Royal Hotel.
Horne's Guide to Whitby (1891)

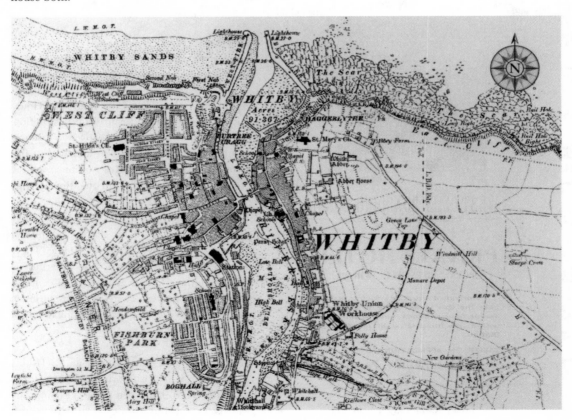

Plan of Whitby.
Ordnance survey map, 1892–1911

St. Mary's Church and graveyard.
Horne's Guide to Whitby (1891)

In 663–664, the Synod of Whitby was held at the abbey, to determine the future of the Northumbrian Church. Wilfrid (later sainted) contended for the Roman Catholic Church, whereas Hild (also sainted later), who had obtained her education in the Frankish monastery at Chelles, strove for the Celtic Church. A majority of the attendees chose Rome, with a by-product of the improvement of England's links to Europe. Lost, however, was the respect for women that was part of the Celtic Church tradition.

6 Lionel Charlton, in his 1779 *History of Whitby*, reports: "At a particular time of the year, viz., in the summer months, at ten or eleven in the forenoon, the sunbeams fall in the inside of the northern part of the choir; and 'tis then that the spectators who stand on the west side of Whitby churchyard, so as just to see the most northerly part of the abbey, past

the north of Whitby Church, imagine that they perceive in one of the highest windows there the resemblance of a woman, arrayed in a shroud. Though we are certain this is only a reflection caused by the splendour of the sun's beams, yet report says, and it is constantly believed among the vulgar, to be an appearance of Lady Hilda, in her shroud, or rather in her glorified state" (quoted in the 1891 *Horne's Guide to Whitby*).

7 St. Mary's Church, reached by a flight of 199 steps at the end of Church Street. *Horne's Guide to Whitby* concurs that "[a] good view of the town is gained from this elevation."

8 About 4 miles by train from the West Cliff, this landmass rises to about 375 feet and held only a few houses. In 1829, the village of Kettleness actually slid into the sea, though no lives were lost. The ruins of an old alum works can be seen from the cliff.

Whitby piers.
From a photograph by F. M. Sutcliffe, *Horne's Guide to Whitby* (1891)

9 The Whitby lighthouses were located on the east and west pier-heads. The western beacon was a fixed green light, visible for 10 miles. It shone from two hours before until two hours after high water; in the daytime, a red flag was used to indicate high water. The eastern beacon was a fixed light as well, but with red and green sectors, visible for 8 miles. Approaches from the south displayed a red light, whereas the light appeared green from the north (*Ainsley's Nautical Almanac and Tide Tables for 1887*).

destroyed. In one place part of the stonework of the graves stretches out over the sandy pathway far below. There are walks, with seats beside them, through the churchyard; and people go and sit there all day long looking at the beautiful view and enjoying the breeze. I shall come and sit here very often myself and work. Indeed, I am writing now, with my book on my knee, and listening to the talk of three old men who are sitting beside me. They seem to do nothing all day but sit up here and talk.

The harbour lies below me, with, on the far side, one long granite wall stretching out into the sea, with a curve outwards at the end of it, in the middle of which is a lighthouse.[9] A heavy sea-wall runs along outside of it. On the near side, the sea-wall makes an elbow crooked inversely, and its end too has a lighthouse. Between the two piers there is a narrow opening into the harbour, which then suddenly widens.

It is nice at high tide; but when the tide is out it shoals away to nothing, and there is merely the stream of the Esk, running between banks of sand, with rocks here and there. Outside the harbour on this side there rises for about half a mile a great reef, the sharp edge of which runs straight out from behind the south lighthouse. At the end of it is a buoy with a bell, which swings in bad weather, and sends in a mournful sound on the wind. They have a legend here that when a ship is lost bells are heard out at sea.[10] I must ask the old man about this; he is coming this way. . . .

He is a funny old man. He must be awfully old, for his face is all gnarled and twisted like the bark of a tree. He tells me that he is nearly a hundred, and that he was a sailor in the Greenland fishing fleet when Waterloo was fought.[11] He is, I am afraid, a very sceptical person, for when I asked him about the bells at sea and the White Lady at the abbey he said very brusquely:—

"I wouldn't fash masel' about them, miss. Them things be all wore out. Mind, I don't say that they never was, but I do say that they wasn't in my time. They be all very well for comers and trippers, an' the like, but not for a nice young lady like you. Them feet-folks from York and Leeds that be always eatin' cured herrin's an' drinkin' tea an' lookin' out to buy cheap jet would creed aught. I wonder masel' who'd be bothered tellin' lies to them—even the newspapers, which is full of fool-talk."[12] I thought he would be a good person to learn interesting things from, so I asked him if he would mind telling me something about the whale-fishing in the old days.[13] He was just settling himself to begin when the clock struck six, whereupon he laboured to get up, and said:—

"I must gang ageeanwards home now, miss. My grand-daughter doesn't like to be kept waitin' when the tea is ready, for it takes me time to crammle aboon the grees, for there be a many of 'em; an', miss, I lack belly-timber sairly by the clock."[14]

He hobbled away, and I could see him hurrying, as well as he could, down the steps. The steps are a great feature on the place.[15] They lead from the town up to the church; there are hundreds of them—I do not know how many[16]—and they wind up in a delicate curve; the slope is so gentle that a horse could easily walk up and down them. I think they must originally have had something to do with the Abbey. I shall go home too. Lucy went out visiting with her mother, and as they were only duty calls, I did not go.[17] They will be home by this.

10 *Horne's Guide to Whitby* (1891) recounts: "A favourite story told in connection with the abbey is one concerning its bells. It runs thus:— The magnificent peal excited the cupidity of some sea-roving freebooter, and, landing with a sufficient force, he extracted the bells from the sacred building and conveyed them onboard his vessel. This desecration was, however, not suffered to go unpunished, for 'ere the vessel had gone many miles she struck and foundered a short distance from the projecting ridge of rock called the 'Black Nab.' As a fitting conclusion to this we are told, that he who dares, on Hallowe'en to spend some time on the rock, and call his sweetheart's name, will hear it echoed by the breeze, accompanied with the ringing of marriage bells from the sunken chime."

11 The Waterloo campaign occurred in the spring of 1815 and resulted in Wellington's defeat of Napoleon, who subsequently abdicated. The old man's presence in the Greenland fishing fleet then does little to fix the date of the narrative, which could have taken place as few as sixty-five (1880) or as many as seventy-five (1890) years later, making the sailor between twenty-three and thirty-three at the time. See appendix 2, "The Dating of *Dracula*."

12 Translations of Mr. Swale's speech are derived from F. K. Robinson's 1876 *A Glossary of Words Used in the Neighbourhood of Whitby*. How Mina managed to decode his often-impenetrable dialect is unknown. For linguists, a partial glossary is included in this volume as appendix 4. Here, Mr. Swales says in sum, "I wouldn't bother myself about those things, miss. They may have been true once but not any more. Those tales are fine for tourists, who would believe anything, but not for you. I wonder who bothers to repeat such stories."

13 According to *Horne's Guide to Whitby* (1891), "[t]he Davis Straits and Greenland whale fishery, which commenced from Whitby in 1753, gave a great impetus to shipping and trade generally. From first to last 53 fine vessels were employed in this trade. In the year 1814, eight ships brought home 172 whales, producing 1390 tons of oil, and 42 tons of fins. The number of whales brought to Whitby in 50 years, from 1767 to 1816, inclusive, amounted to 2761; besides about 25,000 seals, 55 bears, 43 unicorns, and 64 sea-horses."

14 "I must be going home now. My grand-daughter doesn't like to be kept waiting at teatime, and it takes me a while to climb those steps, and I'm awfully hungry."

15 Curiously, the Abridged Text does not contain the description of the famous Whitby steps.

16 See note 7 above.

17 The custom of "duty calls" is explained in *Cassell's Household Guide* (ca. 1880): "On a stranger or a family arriving in a neighbourhood, it is the duty of the elder inhabitants to leave cards. If the acquaintances thus presenting themselves are desirable, it is usual for the visit to be returned personally, or cards left, within one week. . . . In all cases, it is the person who is the new comer that first receives offers of hospitality." The system of visiting cards also allowed for subtle rudeness and social one-upmanship. For example, *Cassell's* advises, "Cards turned down at the corner signify either that they have been sent by a servant, or that the visitor had no intention of paying a personal visit beyond the threshold of the residence."

18 This date is incorrect and should properly be 25 July. Note that Mina's next entry is dated 26 July (see text accompanying note 62 below).

19 Gratiano, in act 1, scene 1 of Shakespeare's *The Merchant of Venice*, describes a pompous fool who declaims, "I am Sir Oracle, / And when I ope my lips let no dog bark!" The sentence does not appear in the Abridged Text.

1 August.[18]—I came up here an hour ago with Lucy, and we had a most interesting talk with my old friend and the two others who always come and join him. He is evidently the Sir Oracle of them,[19] and I should think must have been in his time a most dictatorial person. He will not admit anything, and downfaces everybody. If he can't out-argue them he bullies them, and then takes their silence for agreement with his views. Lucy was looking sweetly pretty in her white lawn frock; she has got a beautiful colour since she has been here. I noticed that the old men did not lose any time in coming and sitting near her when we sat down. She is so sweet with old people; I think they all fell in love with her on the spot. Even my old man succumbed and did not contradict her, but gave me double share instead. I got him on the subject of the legends, and he went off at once into a sort of sermon. I must try to remember it and put it down:—

"It be all fool-talk, lock, stock, and barrel; that's what it be, an' nowt else. These bans an' wafts an' boh-ghosts an' bar-guests an' bogles an' all anent them is only fit to set bairns an' dizzy women a-belderin'. They be nowt but air-blebs! They, an' all grims an' signs an' warnin's, be all invented by parsons an' illsome beuk-bodies an' railway touters to skeer an' scunner hafflin's, an' to get folks to do somethin' that they don't other incline to. It makes me fretful to think o' them. Why, it's them that, not content with printin' lies on paper an' preachin' them out of pulpits, does want to be cuttin' them on the tombsteans. Look here all around you in what airt ye will; all them steans, holdin' up their heads as well as they can out of their pride, is acant—simply tumblin' down with the weight o' the lies wrote on them, 'Here lies the body' or 'Sacred to the memory' wrote on all of them, an' yet in nigh half of them there bean't no bodies at all; an' the memories of them bean't cared a pinch of snuff about, much less sacred. Lies all of them, nothin' but lies of one kind or another! My gog, but it'll be a quare scowderment at the Day of Judgment when they come tumblin' up in their death-sarks, all jouped together an' tryin' to drag their tombsteans with them to prove how good they was; some of them trimmlin' an' ditherin', with their hands that dozzened an' slippy from lyin' in the sea that they can't even keep their gurp o' them."[20]

I could see from the old fellow's self-satisfied air and the way in which he looked round for the approval of his cronies that he was "showing off," so I put in a word to keep him going:—

"Oh, Mr. Swales,[21] you can't be serious. Surely these tombstones are not all wrong?"

"Yabblins! There may be a poorish few not wrong, savin' where they make out the people too good; for there be folk that do think a balm-bowl be like the sea, if only it be their own. The whole thing be only lies. Now look you here; you come here a stranger, an' you see this kirk-garth." I nodded, for I thought it better to assent, though I did not quite understand his dialect. I knew it had something to do with the church. He went on: "And you consate that all these steans be aboon folk that be happed here, snod an' snog?" I assented again. "Then that be just where the lie comes in. Why, there be scores of these lay-beds[22] that be toom[23] as old Dun's 'bacca-box on Friday night." He nudged one of his companions, and they all laughed. "And my gog! how could they be otherwise? Look at that one, the aftest abaft the bier-bank; read it!"[24] I went over and read:—

"Edward Spencelagh, master mariner, murdered by pirates off the coast of Andres, April, 1854, æt. 30."[25] When I came back Mr. Swales went on:—

"Who brought him home, I wonder, to hap him here? Murdered off the coast of Andres! an' you consated his body lay under![26] Why, I could name ye a dozen whose bones lie in the Greenland seas above"—he pointed northwards—"or where the currants may have drifted them. There be the steans around ye. Ye can, with your young eyes, read the small-print of the lies from here. This Braithwaite Lowery—I knew his father, lost in the *Lively* off Greenland in '20; or Andrew Woodhouse, drowned in the same seas in 1777; or John Paxton, drowned off Cape Farewell a year later; or old John Rawlings, whose grandfather sailed with me, drowned in the Gulf of Finland in '50.[27] Do ye think that all these men will have to make a rush to Whitby when the trumpet sounds? I have me antherums aboot it![28] I tell ye that when they got here they'd be jommlin'

20 "It's all nonsense. These ghosts and spirits are fit tales only to make children and foolish women cry. They're nothing but phantoms, invented by preachers and evil-minded scholars and promoters, and used by them to scare people. They're not content with printing or preaching their stories either; they've put them on the tombstones! All these jumbled stones are covered with lies. Half of them cover empty tombs, and no one cares about them. It'll be something to see on Judgement Day when the dead show up in their shrouds, with their hands shrivelled up from being in the sea, trying to carry their tombstones with them as proof of their worth."

21 Wolf (*The Essential Dracula*) points out that the proprietor of the Granby Hotel in Whitby in 1897 was George Swales, perhaps a relative of the old sailor. The Notes record that one Ann Swales died in Whitby on 6 February 1795 at the age of one hundred.

22 Graves.

23 Empty.

24 "Possibly. There may be a few that are true, except those that make out the deceased as really virtuous—some people think a chamber pot is the sea, if it's theirs! Mostly they're lies. You come as a stranger to this churchyard, and you believe that all these stones are for people neatly buried here. And yet many of them are empty! How could it be otherwise? Look at that one over by the path."

25 The Notes record a tombstone inscription in Whitby: "Edward Spencelagh M.M. murdered by pirates, Coast of Andres 12th April 1854. aet [short for the Latin *aetat*, age] 30."

26 "Who brought him home to bury him here? Murdered off the coast of Andres, and you believe that he's buried here?"

27 Similarly, the Notes record: "Braithwaite Lowrey lost in the ship 'Lively' that foundered at Greenland 18th April 1820. aet 29." "Andrew Woodhouse drowned in the Greenland Seas. 16th April. 1777. aet 19." "John Paxton drowned off Cape Farewell 4th April 1778."; "John Rawling drowned Gulf of Finland Novr 1850. aet 61."

28 "I doubt it."

29 Corrected to "lines" in the Abridged Text.

30 A table tomb covering the entire body.

31 Corrected to "is" in the Abridged Text.

32 "That's because you didn't know his mother—a hell-cat who hated him because he was deformed. He hated her too and committed suicide so she wouldn't collect his life insurance."

33 "It brought flies and carrion birds."

and jostlin' one another that way that it 'ud be like a fight up on the ice in the old days, when we'd be at one another from daylight to dark, an' tryin' to tie up our cuts by the light of the aurora borealis." This was evidently local pleasantry, for the old man cackled over it, and his cronies joined in with gusto.

"But," I said, "surely you are not quite correct, for you start on the assumption that all the poor people, or their spirits, will have to take their tombstones with them on the Day of Judgment. Do you think that will be really necessary?"

"Well, what else be they tombsteans for? Answer me that, miss!"

"To please their relatives, I suppose."

"To please their relatives, you suppose!" This he said with intense scorn. "How will it pleasure their relatives to know that lies is wrote over them, and that everybody in the place knows that they be lies?" He pointed to a stone at our feet which had been laid down as a slab, on which the seat was rested, close to the edge of the cliff. "Read the lies[29] on that thruff-stean,"[30] he said. The letters were upside down to me from where I sat, but Lucy was more opposite to them, so she leant over and read:—

"Sacred to the memory of George Canon, who died, in the hope of a glorious resurrection, on July, 29, 1873, falling from the rocks at Kettleness. This tomb was[31] erected by his sorrowing mother to her dearly beloved son. 'He was the only son of his mother, and she was a widow.'—Really, Mr. Swales, I don't see anything very funny in that!" She spoke her comment very gravely and somewhat severely.

"Ye don't see aught funny! Ha! ha! But that's because ye don't gawm the sorrowin' mother was a hell-cat that hated him because he was acrewk'd—a regular lamiter he was—an' he hated her so that he committed suicide in order that she mightn't get an insurance she put on his life.[32] He blew nigh the top of his head off with an old musket that they had for scarin' the crows with. 'Twarn't for crows then, for it brought the clegs and the dowps to him.[33] That's the way he fell off the rocks. And, as to hopes of a glorious resurrection, I've often heard him say masel' that he hoped he'd go to hell, for his mother was so pious that she'd be sure to go to heaven, an he didn't want to addle[34] where she was. Now isn't that stean at any rate"—he hammered it with his stick as he spoke—"a pack of lies? and won't it make Gabriel keckle when Geordie comes pantin' up the grees with the tombstean balanced on his hump, and asks it to be took as evidence!"[35]

I did not know what to say, but Lucy turned the conversation as she said, rising up:—

"Oh, why did you tell us of this? It is my favourite seat, and I cannot leave it; and now I find I must go on sitting over the grave of a suicide."[36]

"That won't harm ye, my pretty; an' it may make poor Geordie gladsome to have so trim a lass sittin' on his lap. That won't hurt ye. Why, I've sat here off an' on for nigh twenty years past,[37] an' it hasn't done me no harm. Don't ye fash about them as lies under ye, or that doesn' lie there either! It'll be time for ye to be gettin scart when ye see the tombsteans all run away with, and the place as bare as a stubble-field. There's the clock, an' I must gang. My service to ye, ladies!" And off he hobbled.

Lucy and I sat awhile, and it was all so beautiful before us that we took hands as we sat; and she told me all over again about Arthur and their coming marriage. That made me just a little heart-sick, for I haven't heard from Jonathan for a whole month.[38]

The same day.—I came up here alone, for I am very sad. There was no letter for me. I hope there cannot be anything the matter with Jonathan.[39] The clock has just struck nine.[40] I see the lights scattered all over the town, sometimes in rows where the streets are, and sometimes singly; they run right up the Esk and die away in the curve of the valley. To my left the view is cut off by a black line of roof of the old house next to the Abbey. The sheep and lambs are bleating in the fields away behind me, and there is a clatter of a donkey's hoofs up the paved road below. The band on the pier is playing a harsh waltz in good time, and further along the quay there is a Salvation Army meeting [41] in a back street. Neither of the bands hears the other, but up here I hear and see them both. I wonder where Jonathan is and if he is thinking of me! I wish he were here.[42]

34 "Addle" means to earn property. Swales means it here in the sense of "settle down."

35 "Won't Gabriel chuckle when Geordie goes upstairs and asks to be let into Heaven on the evidence of his tombstone?"

36 In 1096, a church synod decided that suicides would be excluded from burial in "white" soil. Instead they would be interred outside the churchyard, or even outside the city (Ronald M. Holmes and Stephen T. Holmes, *Suicide: Theory, Practice, and Investigation*). Eventually a custom developed that allowed a suicide's body to be buried nestled by the churchyard wall. If Canon's mother had told the truth about his death, his tomb would have been elsewhere.

37 Leatherdale (*Dracula Unearthed*) sees this as an important confirmation of an 1893 date (twenty years after the 1873 date of George Canon's death). However, Swales says "nigh" twenty years, which could mean any year after 1888. See appendix 2, "The Dating of *Dracula*."

38 Mina must refer to the letter dated 29 June posted by Dracula. See note 42 below.

39 The balance of this picturesque paragraph does not appear in the Abridged Text.

40 American readers should note that British Summer Time (the rough equivalent of Daylight Saving Time) was not introduced until the 1910s. Therefore, it would be quite dark by 9:00 P.M., even in the summer.

41 Charles Booth (no relation to "General" William Booth, founder of the Salvation Army) gave this cold assessment of the organisation in his seminal work *Life and Labour of the People in London* (1902–1903): "The Salvation Army originated in the east of London in 1865, claims (Christmas 1888) to have 7107 officers, 2587 corps, and 653 outposts, established in 33 countries or colonies; and so rapid is its growth,

"General" William Booth.

that 1423 officers and 325 corps have been added in the past 12 months. . . . Of the slum officers it is said that 'they live amongst the people in the darkest and most wretched courts and alleys. They nurse the sick, care for the dying, visit the lodging-houses, hold meetings continually, and by their self-sacrificing lives win hundreds of poor outcasts for Christ.'

"No one who has attended the services, studied the faces, and listened to the spoken words, can doubt the earnest and genuine character of the enthusiasm which finds in them its expression. . . . If the student of these matters turns his eyes from those conducting the service to those for whom it is conducted, he sees for the most part blank indifference. . . . Not by this road (if I am right) will religion be brought to the mass of the English people.

"In rescue work I should suppose that the methods pursued would touch many, but I

DR. SEWARD'S DIARY.

5 June.—The case of Renfield grows more interesting the more I get to understand the man. He has certain qualities very largely developed; selfishness, secrecy, and purpose. I wish I could get at what is the object of the latter. He seems to have some settled scheme of his own, but what it is I do not know. His redeeming quality is a love of animals, though, indeed, he has such curious turns in it that I sometimes imagine he is only abnormally cruel. His pets are of odd sorts. Just now his hobby is catching flies. He has at present such a quantity that I have had myself to expostulate. To my astonishment, he did not break out into a fury, as I expected, but took the matter in simple seriousness. He thought for a moment, and then said: "May I have three days? I shall clear them away." of course, I said that would do. I must watch him.[43]

18 June.—He has turned his mind now to spiders, and has got several very big fellows in a box. He keeps feeding them with his flies, and the number of the latter is becoming sensibly diminished, although he has used half his food in attracting more flies from outside to his room.

1 July.—His spiders are now becoming as great a nuisance as his flies, and to-day I told him that he must get rid of them. He looked very sad at this, so I said that he must clear out some of them, at all events. He cheerfully acquiesced in this, and I gave him the same time as before for reduction. He disgusted me much while with him, for when a horrid blowfly, bloated with some carrion food, buzzed into the room, he caught it, held it exultantly[44] for a few moments between his finger and thumb, and, before I knew what he was going to do, put it in his mouth and ate it. I scolded him for it, but he argued quietly that it was very good and very wholesome; that it was life, strong life, and gave life to him. This gave me an idea, or the rudiment of one. I must watch how he gets rid of his spiders. He has evidently some deep problem in his mind, for he keeps a little notebook in which he is always jotting down something. Whole pages of it are filled with masses of figures, generally single numbers added up in batches, and then the totals added in batches again, as though he were "focussing" some account, as the auditors put it.[45]

8 July.—There is a method in his madness,[46] and the rudimentary idea in my mind is growing. It will be a whole idea soon, and then, oh, unconscious cerebration![47] you will have to give the wall[48] to your conscious brother. I kept away from my friend for a few days, so that I might notice if there were any change. Things remain as they were except that he has parted with some of his pets and got a new one. He has managed to get a sparrow, and has already partially tamed it. His means of taming is simple, for already the spiders have diminished. Those that do remain, however, are well fed, for he still brings in the flies by tempting them with his food.

19 July.—We are progressing. My friend has now a whole colony of sparrows, and his flies and spiders are almost obliterated. When I came in he ran to me and said he wanted to ask me a great favour—a very, very great favour; and as he spoke he fawned on me like a dog. I asked him what it was, and he said, with a sort of rapture in his voice and bearing:—

"A kitten, a nice little, sleek playful kitten, that I can play with, and teach, and feed—and feed—and feed!"[49] I was not unprepared for this request, for I had noticed how his pets went on increasing in size and vivacity, but I did not care that his pretty family of tame sparrows should be wiped out in the same manner as the flies and spiders; so I said I would see about it, and asked him if he would not rather have a cat than a kitten. His eagerness betrayed him as he answered:—

"Oh, yes, I would like a cat! I only asked for a kitten lest you should refuse me a cat. No one would refuse me a kitten, would they?" I shook my head, and said that at present I feared it would not be possible, but that I would see about it. His face fell, and I could see a warning of danger in it, for there was a sudden fierce, sidelong look which meant killing. The man is an undeveloped homicidal maniac.[50] I shall test him with his present craving and see how it will work out; then I shall know more.[51]

should need better evidence than any I have seen to convince me that of those touched many would be permanently affected by the heightened emotions and excitement which are so unsparingly used. On the other hand, something more than their own salvation must result from lives of devotion such as are in truth led by these modern soldiers of the cross."

42 Note that Mina on 9 May expected that Jonathan would be home in about a week. If Dracula posted Jonathan's letters as planned, the letter dated 12 June (almost a month after Jonathan's expected return) stated he would leave in a few days; the letter dated 29 June placed him in Bistritz. Here almost another month has passed since Jonathan's supposed arrival at Bistritz (a destination to which he should have travelled *from* London in four or five days). Yet only now does Mina express "wonder" at Jonathan's whereabouts. This strains belief and provides further corroboration that the events described in Jonathan Harker's journal and the dates placed on them are essentially fictional.

43 Although Renfield will become psychically attuned to Dracula as matters progress, at this time Dracula's influence is absent. Harker's journal is silent about events between 31 May and 17 June, but there is no reason to believe that Dracula was focussing on his neighbours in the vicinity of his yet-to-be-visited new home. In other words, Renfield's mania or zeal for the consumption of life is his own conception, his own particular form of vampirism.

44 Altered to "exultingly" in the Abridged Text.

45 The *Oxford English Dictionary* does not recognise this usage of the word "focus," but in the sense of "convergence" it must mean that the figures "balance," as American accountants would put it.

46 Seward is as tritely proverbial as Polonius (*Hamlet*, act 2, scene 2).

47 The term is derived from the writings of Dr. William Carpenter (1813–1885) on the relationship of the will to the reflex responses of the mind and body. In his *Principles of Mental Physiology* (1874), Carpenter observes that the unconscious mind can produce logical conclusions "below the plane of consciousness, either during profound sleep, or while the attention is wholly engrossed by some entirely different train of thought. . . . When we have been *trying to recollect* some name, phrase, occurrence, &c., it will often occur *spontaneously* a little while afterwards, suddenly flashing (as it were) into our consciousness, either when we are thinking of something altogether different, or on awaking out of profound sleep" (italics in original). The sentence does not appear in the Abridged Text.

48 Seward refers to the custom of gentlemen permitting ladies to walk on the inside of a sidewalk, away from the street, to avoid the mud and dirt flung up from carriages.

49 In the world of *Buffy the Vampire Slayer*, the vampire Spike and his demon cronies play poker using kittens as chips.

There is a remarkable parallel to Renfield's behaviour reported in the 1888 article "A Thirst for Blood," covering the Jack the Ripper murders (see note 9 on p. 6). The anonymous reporter consulted the works of contemporary prominent psychologists for precedents for the murders and recorded that Dr. G. Savage, whose essay "Homicidal Mania" appeared in the *Fortnightly Review* for October 1888, "gives a ghastly instance of a child who commenced his career . . . by pulling off the wings of flies. After a time this amusement palled, and the pleasing child took to baking frogs. He next turned his young intelligence to capturing birds and boring out their eyes. And later on nothing would satisfy him but ill-treating other children."

Renfield's apparent delight in killing insects and animals would likely be viewed by a modern psychiatrist as an early warning sign of a serial

10 p.m.—I have visited him again and found him sitting in a corner brooding. When I came in he threw himself on his knees before me and implored me to let him have a cat; that his salvation depended upon it. I was firm, however, and told him that he could not have it, whereupon he went without a word, and sat down, gnawing his fingers, in the corner where I had found him. I shall see him in the morning early.

20 July.—Visited Renfield very early, before the attendant[52] went his rounds.[53] Found him up and humming a tune. He was spreading out his sugar, which he had saved, in the window, and was manifestly beginning his fly-catching again; and beginning it cheerfully and with a good grace. I looked around for his birds, and not seeing them, asked him where they were. He replied, without turning round, that they had all flown away. There were a few feathers about the room and on his pillow a drop of blood. I said nothing, but went and told the keeper to report to me if there were anything odd about him during the day.

11 a.m.—The attendant has just been to me to say that Renfield has been very sick and has disgorged a whole lot of feathers. "My belief is, doctor," he said, "that he has eaten his birds, and that he just took and ate them raw!"

11 p.m.—I gave Renfield a strong opiate to-night, enough to make even him sleep, and took away his pocket-book to look at it.[54] The thought that has been buzzing about my brain lately is complete, and the theory proved. My homicidal maniac is of a peculiar kind. I shall have to invent a new classification for him, and call him a zoöphagous[55] (life-eating) maniac; what he desires is to absorb as many lives as he can, and he has laid himself out to achieve it in a cumulative way. He gave many flies to one spider and many spiders to one bird, and then wanted a cat to eat the many birds. What would have been his later steps? It would almost be worth while to complete the experiment.[56] It might be done if there were only a sufficient cause. Men sneered at vivisection, and yet look at its results to-day! Why not advance science in its most difficult and vital aspect—the knowledge of the brain? Had I even the secret of one such mind—did I hold the key to the fancy of even one lunatic—I might advance my own branch of science to a pitch compared with which Burdon-Sanderson's physiology[57] or Ferrier's brain-knowledge[58] would be as nothing. If only there were a sufficient cause! I must not think too much of this, or I may be tempted; a good cause might turn the scale with me, for may not I too be of an exceptional brain, congenitally?[59]

How well the man reasoned; lunatics always do within their own scope.[60] I wonder at how many lives he values a man, or if at only one. He has closed the account most accurately, and to-day begun a new record. How many of us begin a new record with each day of our lives?

To me it seems only yesterday that my whole life ended with my new hope, and that truly I began a new record. So it will be until the Great Recorder sums me up and closes my ledger account with a balance to profit or loss. Oh, Lucy, Lucy, I cannot be angry with you, nor can I be angry with my friend whose happiness is yours; but I must only wait on hopeless and work. Work! work!

If I only could have as strong a cause as my poor mad friend there—a good, unselfish cause to make me work—that would be indeed happiness.[61]

MINA MURRAY'S JOURNAL.

26 July.—I am anxious, and it soothes me to express myself here; it is like whispering to one's self and listening at the same time. And there is also something about the shorthand symbols that makes it different from writing.[62] I am unhappy about Lucy and about Jonathan. I had not heard from Jonathan for some time, and was very concerned; but yesterday dear Mr. Hawkins, who is always so kind, sent me a letter from him. I had written asking him if he had heard, and he said the enclosed had just been received. It is only a line dated from Castle Dracula, and says that he is just starting for home.[63] That is not like Jonathan; I do not understand it, and it makes me uneasy. Then, too, Lucy, although she is so well,[64] has lately taken to her old habit of walking in her sleep. Her mother has spoken to me about it, and we have decided that I am to lock

killer. For example, Daniel Goleman, writing in the *New York Times* in 1991 about notorious serial killer Jeffrey Dahmer, noted that as a teenager, Dahmer was fond of impaling animals and keeping their skeletons. "For forensic psychiatrists, such a fascination with death and cruelty to animals is an almost predictable sign in the lives of people accused of being serial killers. . . . 'Murderers like this very often start out by killing and torturing animals as kids,' said Robert K. Ressler, who developed profiles of serial killers while an agent with the Federal Bureau of Investigation's behavioral sciences unit."

50 Seward here displays his familiarity with the literature referred to in the anonymous 1888 article "A Thirst for Blood."

51 Stoker again attempts to show Seward's character in a better light by suppressing this hardly ethical sentiment; the sentence does not appear in the Abridged Text.

52 The word "attendant" has replaced the more vernacular "keeper" in numerous places in the Manuscript, sometimes in Stoker's hand and sometimes in the editor's. It is unlikely that a doctor would use the pejorative term "keeper," and this casts some doubt on the authenticity of Seward's journal. More particularly, in conjunction with other shortcomings of Seward's treatment of his patients, it casts doubt on whether "Dr." Seward was in fact a physician.

53 Some historians of medicine assert that Victorian asylum attendants were generally otherwise unemployable. Many former military men filled these jobs, as would be expected, to fulfill the need for physical restraint of male patients. Women were routinely excluded from dealing with male patients but were amply employed to deal with the burgeoning population of female inmates. Another significant segment of the asylum workforce was male skilled artisans—former carpenters, shoemakers, tailors, basketmakers—who accepted positions as "trades attendants," carrying out Victorian work therapy (which also resulted in a steady income for the asylum from the sale of inmate-crafted goods). Although studies concluded that prior to 1860, few, if any, asylum attendants had previous institutional experience, later studies showed as many as 20 percent of attendants came from other asylum employment. In 1885, the first edition of *Handbook for the instruction of attendants on the insane*, prepared by a subcommittee of the Medico-Psychological Association, appeared in London, teaching the rudiments of nursing both physically and mentally ill patients to the untrained.

54 Leatherdale (*Dracula Unearthed*) points out that no therapeutic reason is given for the adminstration of the opiate, and to use it for the purpose of permitting Seward to spy on Renfield's pocketbook is highly unethical.

55 "Zoöphagous" (derived from the Greek *zoo*, "animals," and *phagos*, "eating") means only the eating of animals (although occasionally used to mean eating live animals) and therefore equates to carnivorous.

56 Meaning . . . permit Renfield to feed cats to higher animals, or perhaps to humans, and then consume the end-product, a human? It is impossible to take Seward's suggestion as anything other than a distasteful private joke.

57 Sir John Scott Burdon-Sanderson (1828–1905), a pioneering physiologist and patho-

Sir John Scott Burdon-Sanderson.
"Spy," *Vanity Fair*, 1894

James Frederick Ferrier.

logist who often found himself in the middle of the vivisection battles of the nineteenth century. In 1895, he was appointed regius professor of medicine at Oxford University. Charles Darwin professed in 1881 to be a "great admirer" of Burdon-Sanderson.

58 James Frederick Ferrier (1808–1864), a Scottish philosopher best known for his *Institutes of Metaphysic* (1854). In that work, he wrote, "Our only safety lies in the consideration—a consideration which is a sound, indeed inevitable logical inference—that our sensitive modes of apprehension are mere contingent elements and conditions of cognition; and that the ego or subject alone enters, of necessity, into the composition of everything which any intelligence can know." Presumably this is the "brain-knowledge" to which Seward refers.

59 The notion that a brain might be congenitally better than others had many adherents among the Victorians, and "better" was generally defined as "bigger." Viennese physician Franz Joseph Gall (founder of the pseudoscience of phrenology—the idea that the shape of the

the door of our room every night. Mrs. Westenra has got an idea that sleep-walkers always go out on roofs of houses and along the edges of cliffs, and then get suddenly wakened and fall over with a despairing cry that echoes all over the place.[65] Poor dear, she is naturally anxious about Lucy, and she tells me that her husband, Lucy's father, had the same habit; that he would get up in the night and dress himself and go out, if he were not stopped. Lucy is to be married in the autumn,[66] and she is already planning out her dresses and how her house is to be arranged. I sympathise with her, for I do the same, only Jonathan and I will start in life in a very simple way, and shall have to try to make both ends meet. Mr. Holmwood—he is the Hon. Arthur Holmwood, only son of Lord Godalming[67]—is coming up here very shortly—as soon as he can leave town, for his father is not very well, and I think dear Lucy is counting the moments till he comes. She wants to take him up to the seat on the churchyard cliff and show him the beauty of Whitby. I daresay it is the waiting which disturbs her; she will be all right when he arrives.

27 July.—No news from Jonathan. I am getting quite uneasy about him, though why I should I do not know; but I *do* wish he would write, if it were only a single line. Lucy walks more than ever, and each night I am awakened by her moving about the room. Fortunately, the weather is so hot that she cannot get cold; but still the anxiety and the perpetually being wakened is beginning to tell on me, and I am getting nervous and wakeful myself. Thank God, Lucy's health keeps up. Mr. Holmwood has been suddenly called to Ring[68] to see his father, who has been taken seriously ill. Lucy frets at the postponement of seeing him, but it does not touch her looks; she is a trifle stouter, and her cheeks are a lovely rose-pink. She has lost the anæmic look which she had.[69] I pray it will all last.

3 August.—Another week gone, and no news from Jonathan, not even to Mr. Hawkins, from whom I have heard. Oh, I do hope he is not ill. He surely would have written. I look at that last letter of his, but somehow it does not satisfy me. It does not read like him, and yet it is his writing. There is no mistake

head indicated personality traits), in a letter of 1 October 1798 to Joseph von Retzer, explained: "A man like you possesses more than double the quantity of brain in a stupid bigot; and at least one-sixth more than the wisest or the most sagacious elephant" (in Paul Eling, *Reader in the History of Aphasia*).

Stoker again softens his portrayal of the egotistical "Dr. Seward" by omitting the preceding three sentences from the Abridged Text.

60 The Manuscript contains the following, which does not appear in the published narrative: "but with the simplicity of lunacy he valued all lives the same. His note book proves it. One fly is a life and the total of its lives goes into one spider's but he only adds one for the spider when the total passes into the bird and the bird in turn counted only one when it passed into him." In short, Seward answers his own succeeding question: Renfield valued a human life neither more nor less than that of a fly. This suggests that the following sentence was invented by Stoker, which is of course far more flattering to Seward (who later is almost victimised by Renfield) than the truth.

61 Seward comes across here as unbalanced and obsessive. Almost two months have elapsed since the refusal of his proposal by Lucy, a woman he had known "so little," yet here he continues to indulge his despondence. Kim Newman, in his brilliant *Anno Dracula*, makes much of this, suggesting that Seward's fixation on Lucy and her ultimate death turned him to a killer of vampire harlots, assuming the working name of "Jack the Ripper"!

62 In the Abridged Text, Mina's musings are shortened through the elimination of the first two sentences of this paragraph.

63 This is the letter dated 19 June written at Dracula's command (see text accompanying chapter 4, note 5). The Manuscript continues: "but will probably stop for a holiday somewhere on the way." This material does not appear in the published narrative. Stoker must have mistakenly deleted the addendum; Mina's " not like Jonathan" remark that follows undoubtedly addressed his cavalier decision to take a holiday.

64 Lucy is apparently chronically ill; Mina makes numerous comments about her health which suggest constant concern. The Notes indicate that it is Mina who first brings Lucy's medical condition to a doctor's attention, arranging for Seward (Lucy's fiancé) to travel to Whitby to examine her.

65 Romantic writers saw the sleepwalker as caught between heaven and earth, suspended between dreams and reality, similar to the perceived effects of mesmeric attraction and animal magnetism. The plots of Charles Brockden Brown's *Edgar Huntly* (1799) and Wilkie Collins's *The Moonstone* (1868) both depend on sleepwalkers who betray their true selves during their nocturnal digressions. Heinrich von Kleist's 1811 play *The Prince of Homburg* depicts a Prussian soldier who sleepwalks on the eve of battle, dreaming of military glory and erotic bliss. Still distracted on the following day, he ignores his orders, winning a dashing victory. For his disobedience, he is court-martialled and sentenced to death. In Vincenzo Bellini's opera *La Sonnambula*, first performed in 1831, a girl in a Swiss village sleepwalks on the eve of her wedding and finds her way into the bedroom of a stranger. Her fiancé surprises her and furiously calls off the marriage. She is forgiven only when, while sleepwalking again, she nearly dies by falling off a roof. Lucy Westenra too, it will be seen, hovers between two different worlds in her somnambulism.

In the modern view of sleepwalking, or somnambulism, the sleepwalker is not truly asleep but is in a dissociated arousal state that occurs during the period of slow wave sleep. It is estimated that about 18 percent of the population has experienced sleepwalking, which is sometimes accompanied by sleep talking or somniloquy. While there is a childhood peak in the prevalence of sleepwalking and the condition appears most frequently at the onset of puberty, the behaviour often continues into adulthood. It is often popularly believed to be associated with an underlying psychological disorder, but studies suggest to the contrary; one of the most important determinants is a family history of the condition (Lucy's father suffered from it as well). Sleep deprivation, anxiety, and alcohol use are the three most common triggers for sleepwalking.

Unless prompted afterward and unless they wake up, sleepwalkers usually remember nothing of their adventures, which, in rare cases, have included driving a car. Sleepwalking is sometimes marked by a stubborn industriousness, with the somnambulist busily moving items from one place to another, usually for no obvious purpose. It may be random and patternless, or the behaviour can be repetitive: a child might wake twice a week for several months and determinedly transport a specific object from one place to another, then abruptly outgrow this pattern and either cease to sleepwalk or adopt a new ritual.

Lucy's sleepwalking episodes commence before Dracula arrives in Whitby, when he is hundreds of miles away in the Bay of Biscay (see appendix 3, "The Chronology of *Dracula*"). We must conclude that Lucy's sleepwalking is not a response to a long-distance telepathic communication from Dracula but rather a natural condition that makes her sensitive to Dracula's presence and of which Dracula avails himself. If Dracula could indeed sense the presence of individuals at a distance, he would not find himself in some of the embarrassing situations that occur later in the narrative.

66 The Manuscript reads "October" instead of "autumn," suggesting that Stoker fictionalised the 28 September date given in chapter 9 to avoid identification of "Lucy."

67 The Notes indicate that Lord Godalming is a viscount, the second lowest rank of the of that.[70] Lucy has not walked much in her sleep the last week, but there is an odd concentration about her which I do not understand; even in her sleep she seems to be watching me. She tries the door, and finding it locked, goes about the room searching for the key.

6 August.—Another three days, and no news. This suspense is getting dreadful. If I only knew where to write to or where to go to, I should feel easier;[71] but no one has heard a word of Jonathan since that last letter. I must only pray to God for patience. Lucy is more excitable than ever, but is otherwise well.[72] Last night was very threatening, and the fishermen say that we are in for a storm. I must try to watch it and learn the weather signs. To-day is a grey day, and the sun as I write is hidden in thick clouds, high over Kettleness. Everything is grey[73]—except the green grass, which seems like emerald amongst it; grey earthy rock; gray clouds, tinged with the sunburst at the far edge, hang over the grey sea, into which the sandpoints stretch like grey figures. The sea is tumbling in over the shallows and the sandy flats with a roar, muffled in the sea-mists drifting inland. The horizon is lost in a grey mist. All is vastness; the clouds are piled up like giant rocks, and there is a "brool"[74] over the sea that sounds like some presage of doom. Dark figures are on the beach here and there, sometimes half shrouded in the mist, and seem "men like trees walking."[75] The fishing-boats are racing for home, and rise and dip in the ground swell as they sweep into the harbour, bending to the scuppers.[76] Here comes old Mr. Swales. He is making straight for me, and I can see, by the way he lifts his hat, that he wants to talk. . . .

I have been quite touched by the change in the poor old man. When he sat down beside me, he said in a very gentle way:—

"I want to say something to you, miss." I could see he was not at ease, so I took his poor old wrinkled hand in mine and asked him to speak fully; so he said, leaving his hand in mine:—

"I'm afraid, my deary, that I must have shocked you by all the wicked things I've been sayin' about the dead, and such-like, for weeks past; but I didn't mean them, and I want ye to

hereditary peerage (above the rank of baron and below the ranks of earl, marquis, and duke).

68 The name of the Holmwood family seat.

69 Leatherdale (*Dracula Unearthed*) observes that Lucy is naturally anaemic, long before she is visited by Dracula—making her a poor choice as a blood supply. Could the attraction of Lucy to Dracula be her anaemia, the "yang" to Dracula's "yin"?

70 Apparently the third letter written by Harker at Dracula's command (see chapter 4, note 5), dated 29 June, has not yet arrived. Mina's patience is amazing.

71 Why, wonders Leatherdale (*Dracula Unearthed*), does Mina not write—or even travel—to Castle Dracula? Surely Peter Hawkins could have supplied the mailing address.

72 Again, note that Lucy's excitation and other odd behaviours occur before Dracula is within physical proximity. This suggests that Dracula somehow "broadcasts" his presence to those sensitive to his "signals." See chapter 8, note 50, for further discussion of this idea.

73 The balance of Mina's evocative description of the fog does not appear in the Abridged Text.

74 A low roar, a murmuring sound. The Beat poet Gregory Corso (1930–2001), in his unpublished poem "Humanity," writes: "What simple profundities / What profound simplicities / To sit down among the trees / and breathe with them / in murmur brool and breeze —"

75 Mina paraphrases Mark 8:22–25, in which Christ heals a blind man. When asked what he sees with his partially restored vision, the man replies, "I see men as trees, walking."

76 Vents in the sides of ships to allow water to run off. While Mina may have overheard this terminology during her two weeks in Whitby, she shows no other interest in matters nautical, and it seems more likely to be an interpolation by Stoker, who spent many holidays at one shore or another.

77 "We weak-minded old folks, with one foot in the grave, are scared of death, and we like to make fun of it to cheer ourselves up."

78 "I can't just stop, though—it's a habit."

79 Grieve and weep.

80 Mist.

81 The Manuscript reads, "She seems to be steered ~~by a dead man~~ mighty strangely . . . " Stoker wisely omits this phrase in the published narrative, recognising it to have been misremembered by Mina based on hindsight.

remember that when I'm gone. We aud folks that be daffled, and with one foot abaft the krok-hooal, don't altogether like to think of it, and we don't want to feel scart of it; an' that's why I've took to makin' light of it, so that I'd cheer up my own heart a bit.[77] But, Lord love ye, miss, I ain't afraid of dyin', not a bit; only I don't want to die if I can help it. My time must be nigh at hand now, for I be aud, and a hundred years is too much for any man to expect; and I'm so nigh it that the Aud Man is already whettin' his scythe. Ye see, I can't get out o' the habit of caffin' about it all at once; the chafts will wag as they be used to.[78] Some day soon the Angel of Death will sound his trumpet for me. But don't ye dooal an' greet,[79] my deary!"—for he saw that I was crying—"if he should come this very night I'd not refuse to answer his call. For life be, after all, only a waitin' for somethin' else than what we're doin'; and death be all that we can rightly depend on. But I'm content, for it's comin' to me, my deary, and comin' quick. It may be comin' while we be lookin' and wonderin'. Maybe it's in that wind out over the sea that's bringin' with it loss and wreck, and sore distress, and sad hearts. Look! look!" he cried suddenly. "There's something in that wind and in the hoast[80] beyont that sounds, and looks, and tastes, and smells like death. It's in the air; I feel it comin'. Lord, make me answer cheerful when my call comes!" He held up his arms devoutly, and raised his hat. His mouth moved as though he were praying. After a few minutes' silence, he got up, shook hands with me, and blessed me, and said good-bye, and hobbled off. It all touched me, and upset me very much.

I was glad when the coastguard came along, with his spyglass under his arm. He stopped to talk with me, as he always does, but all the time kept looking at a strange ship.

"I can't make her out," he said; "she's a Russian, by the look of her; but she's knocking about in the queerest way. She doesn't know her mind a bit; she seems to see the storm coming, but can't decide whether to run up north in the open, or to put in here. Look there again! She is steered mighty strangely,[81] for she doesn't mind the hand on the wheel; changes about with every puff of wind. We'll hear more of her before this time to-morrow."

Chapter 7

CUTTING FROM "THE DAILYGRAPH," 8 AUGUST.[1]

(Pasted in Mina Murray's Journal.)

FROM A CORRESPONDENT.

Whitby.

ONE OF THE GREATEST and suddenest storms on record has just been experienced here, with results both strange and unique. The weather had been somewhat sultry, but not to any degree uncommon in the month of August. Saturday evening was as fine as was ever known,[2] and the great body of holiday-makers laid out yesterday[3] for visits to Mulgrave Woods,[4] Robin Hood's Bay,[5] Rig Mill, Runswick,[6] Staithes,[7] and the various trips in the neighbourhood of Whitby. The steamers *Emma*[8] and *Scarborough* made trips up and down the coast, and there was an unusual amount of "tripping" both to and from Whitby. The day was unusually fine till the afternoon, when some of the gossips who frequent the East Cliff churchyard, and from that commanding eminence watch the wide sweep of sea visible to the north and east, called attention to a sudden show of "mares'-tails"[9] high in the sky to the north-west. The wind was then blowing from the south-west in the mild degree which in barometrical language is ranked "No. 2: light breeze." The coastguard on duty at once made report, and one old fisherman, who for more than half a century has kept watch on weather signs from the East Cliff, foretold in an emphatic manner the coming of a sudden storm. The approach of sunset was so very beautiful, so grand in its masses of splendidly-coloured clouds, that there was quite an

1 Leatherdale (*Dracula Unearthed*) points out that this cannot be a fictional name for one of the Whitby papers, for there were only two—the *Whitby Gazette*, first published in 1854, and the *Whitby Times*, first published in the 1860s—both of which were weeklies. Perhaps this is a disguise for a newspaper published in a nearby town, such as the *Leeds Mercury*, or a regional newspaper, such as the *Yorkshire Post*. Roger Johnson, in private correspondence with this editor, suggests it was a disguise for the London-based, nationally distributed *Daily Telegraph*, which might well have picked up an interesting story like this.

2 There is a great confusion of dates here. Mina's prior journal entry on 6 August refers

Mulgrave Old Castle.
From a photograph by F. M. Sutcliffe,
Horne's Guide to Whitby (1891)

Rig Mill.
Horne's Guide to Whitby (1891)

Dracula," the Notes are at best unreliable with respect to dates.

4 Described in *Horne's Guide to Whitby* (1891) as delightful "both to the antiquarian and to nature's students, in whatever department. To the artist, no lovelier bits of sylvan scenery can anywhere be found . . . whilst to the antiquarian, here are stones, the history of which leads back to myth and legend."

5 A nearby village "of a most romantic description," rhapsodises *Horne's Guide to Whitby*, which "has preserved its ancient and

Robin Hood's Bay.
From a photograph by F. M. Sutcliffe, *Horne's Guide to Whitby* (1891)

to "last night" as "threatening," which would suggest that it was written on Saturday, before what the *Dailygraph* correspondent described as an evening "as fine as was ever known." Yet if, as Mina records, the coastguard spotted the *Demeter*, it must have been written on Sunday, and Mina's description of the "threat" is based on psychological indicia, not meteorological ones.

3 Therefore, this account, dated 8 August, appears to describe the events that took place on Sunday, 7 August, prior to and during the late-evening storm, and the early morning of Monday, 8 August. Annoyingly, the Notes specify that the wreck occurs on Monday, 7 August, and the captain's burial on Thursday, 10 August, but as discussed in appendix 2, "The Dating of

Runswick.
From a photograph by F. M. Sutcliffe, *Horne's Guide to Whitby* (1891)

East Cliff and Tate Hill Sands.
F. M. Sutcliffe, ca. 1880

romantic character in spite of the burning desire of later generations for so-called and oft-times mis-called 'improvements.' "

6 "A favourite resort of the artist," claims *Horne's Guide to Whitby*, "who finds here inexpressible delights."

7 A small fishing village that claims a connection to Captain Cook, who, it is said, served an apprenticeship here.

8 Turnbull & Sons built a screw steamer in 1875 named *Emma Lawson*, and according to Lloyd's Register of British and Foreign Shipping for 1889–1890, her port was Whitby. There is no record of an actual *Scarborough*. This and the preceding sentence regarding excursions do not appear in the Abridged Text.

9 "Mare's tail" is a folk name for a high-level cloud formation that meteorologists call a fallstreak, a fibrous hook-shaped cloud composed of ice. The formation of a mare's tail indicates a shear vector (the differential between wind speeds at different altitudes) and temperature advection (the transfer of heat by horizontal air movement). The physics of the shape is explained by Craig Bohren and Alistair Fraser in "Fall Streaks: Parabolic Trajectories with a Twist" (1992). For navigators, mares' tails forecast strong winds affecting the surface of the water or land within a day or two.

10 Royal Academy of Arts, in London, members of which were characterised as "of the most distinguished rank in the respective lines of their profession" (*Mogg's New Picture of London and Visitor's Guide to Its Sights*). R. I. likely meant the Royal Institute of Painters in Water-Colours, formed in 1831 as an alternative to the Royal Society of Painters in Water-Colours, formed in 1804. The latter organisation, known as the Old Society, was to water-colour art in Great Britain what the Royal Academy was to fine arts in general. When dissension arose among its ranks, the R.I. came into being. The painterly

assemblage on the walk along the cliff in the old churchyard to enjoy the beauty. Before the sun dipped below the black mass of Kettleness, standing boldly athwart the western sky, its downward way was marked by myriad clouds of every sunset-colour—flame, purple, pink, green, violet, and all the tints of gold; with here and there masses not large, but of seemingly absolute blackness, in all sorts of shapes, as well outlined as colossal silhouettes. The experience was not lost on the painters, and doubtless some of the sketches of the "Prelude to the Great Storm" will grace the R. A. and R. I.[10] walls in May next. More than one captain made up his mind then and there that his "cobble" or his "mule," as they term the different classes of boats,[11] would remain in the harbour till the storm had passed. The wind fell away entirely during the evening, and at midnight there was a dead calm, a sultry heat, and that prevailing intensity which, on the approach of thunder, affects persons of a sensitive nature. There were but few lights in sight at sea, for even the coasting steamers, which usually "hug" the shore so closely, kept well to seaward, and but few fishing-boats were in sight. The only sail noticeable was a foreign schooner with all sails set, which was seemingly going westwards. The foolhardiness or ignorance of her

Boats moored at the New Quay.
F. M. Sutcliffe, ca. 1880

description does not appear in the Abridged Text.

11 This phrase, points out Leatherdale (*Dracula Unearthed*), confirms that the newspaper account was not written for a Whitby paper, for the locals would surely not have needed such explanations.

12 The correspondent quotes Samuel Taylor Coleridge's "Rime of the Ancient Mariner" (originally published in 1798 and republished in 1834 in *The Poetical Works of S. T. Coleridge* with modernised text): "Day after day, day after day / We stuck, nor breath nor motion; / As idle as a painted ship / Upon a painted ocean."

13 That is, 10:00 P.M. Sunday, 7 August. It is possible that the writer's earlier comment about the "fine" Saturday evening referred only to the early portion of the evening, but that makes nonsense of the writer's "yesterday" in referring to the afternoon before the storm.

officers was a prolific theme for comment whilst she remained in sight, and efforts were made to signal her to reduce sail in face of her danger. Before the night shut down she was seen with sails idly flapping as she gently rolled on the undulating swell of the sea,

"As idle as a painted ship upon a painted ocean."[12]

Shortly before ten o'clock[13] the stillness of the air grew quite oppressive, and the silence was so marked that the bleating of a sheep inland or the barking of a dog in the town was distinctly heard, and the band on the pier, with its lively French air, was like a discord in the great harmony of nature's silence.[14] A little after midnight came a strange sound from over the sea, and high overhead the air began to carry a strange, faint, hollow booming.

Then without warning the tempest broke. With a rapidity which, at the time, seemed incredible, and even afterwards is impossible to realize, the whole aspect of nature at once became convulsed. The waves rose in growing fury, each overtopping its fellow, till in a very few minutes the lately glassy sea was like a roaring and devouring monster. White-crested waves beat madly on the level sands and rushed up the shelving cliffs; others broke over the piers, and with their spume swept the lanthorns of the lighthouses which rise from the end of either pier of Whitby Harbour. The wind roared like thunder, and blew with such force that it was with difficulty that even strong men kept their feet, or clung with grim clasp to the iron stanchions. It was found necessary to clear the entire piers from the mass of onlookers, or else the fatalities of the night would have been increased manifold. To add to the difficulties and dangers of the time, masses of sea-fog came drifting inland[15]—white, wet clouds, which swept by in ghostly fashion, so dank and damp and cold that it needed but little effort of imagination to think that the spirits of those lost at sea were touching their living brethren with the clammy hands of death, and many a one shuddered as the wreaths of sea-mist swept by.[16] At times the mist cleared, and the sea for some distance could be seen in the glare of the lightning, which now came thick and fast, followed by such sudden peals of thunder that the whole sky overhead seemed trembling under the shock of the footsteps of the storm. Some of the scenes thus revealed were of immeasurable grandeur and of absorbing interest—the sea, running mountains high, threw skyward with each wave mighty masses of white foam, which the tempest seemed to snatch at and whirl away into space; here and there a fishing-boat, with a rag of sail, running madly for shelter before the blast; now and again the white wings of a storm-tossed sea-bird. On the summit of the East Cliff the new searchlight was ready for experiment, but had not yet been tried. The officers in charge of it got it into working order, and in the pauses of the inrushing mist swept with it the surface of the sea. Once or twice its service was most effective, as when a fishing boat, with gunwale[17] under water, rushed into the harbour, able, by the guidance of the sheltering light, to avoid the danger of dashing against the piers. As each boat achieved the safety of the port there was a shout of joy from the mass of people on shore, a shout which for a moment seemed to cleave the gale and was then swept away in its rush. Before long the searchlight discovered some distance away a schooner with all sails set, apparently the same vessel which had been noticed earlier in the evening. The wind had by this time backed to the east,[18] and there was a shudder amongst the watchers on the cliff as they realised the terrible danger in which she now was. Between her and the port lay the great flat reef on which so many good ships have from time to time suffered, and, with the wind blowing from its present quarter, it would be quite impossible that she should fetch the entrance of the harbour. It was now nearly the hour of high tide,[19] but the waves were so great that in their troughs the shallows of the shore were almost visible, and the schooner, with all sails set, was rushing with such speed that, in the words of one old salt, "she must fetch up somewhere, if it was only in hell." Then came another rush of sea-fog, greater than any hitherto—a mass of dank mist, which seemed to close on all things like a grey pall, and left available to men only the organ of hearing, for the roar of the tempest, and the crash of the thunder, and the booming

14 The Abridged Text does not mention the band.

15 This is likely a manifestation of Dracula's power, for if the wind were from the southwest, the fog would not drift inland but rather out to sea.

16 This fine sentence does not appear in the Abridged Text.

17 The top rail of the ship's hull.

18 That is, the wind is blowing east to west, towards the shore.

19 The following table shows the high tides for 8 and 9 August:

Year	8 August	9 August
1885	1:16 A.M.	2:17 A.M.
1886	4:07 A.M.	5:35 A.M.
1887	12:05 A.M.	12:37 A.M.
1888	4:03 A.M.	4:43 A.M.
1889	12:36 A.M.	1:40 A.M.
1890	3:13 A.M.	4:27 A.M.

Computed using Tide Prediction Program 2.42 by Hans Pieper.

Sunrise occurred around 4:30 A.M. Except for a few dates, this confirms the correspondent's description of high tide occurring before the sky begins to redden.

20 This is precisely the wind needed to drive the ship into the harbour, and we must assume that it is under Dracula's command.

21 Latin: marvelous to relate.

22 To shorten the overly long article, the following, which appears in the Manuscript, has been removed from the published narrative: "The method of her arrival is thus graphically given in the words of a bystander—merely reduced into conventional phrase for the benefit of those to whom the Yorkshire dialect is not familiar. 'She ran in as soft as a seal flappin' under an ice floe!' "

23 Properly, top-hamper; the upper masts, riggings, and sails of a ship.

24 Van Helsing later explains that Dracula has the ability to change himself into a wolf, and this is evidently what the witnesses saw.

of the mighty billows came through the damp oblivion even louder than before. The rays of the searchlight were kept fixed on the harbour mouth across the East Pier, where the shock was expected, and men waited breathless. The wind suddenly shifted to the north-east,[20] and the remnant of the sea fog melted in the blast; and then, *mirabile dictu*,[21] between the piers, leaping from wave to wave as it rushed at headlong speed, swept the strange schooner before the blast, with all sail set, and gained the safety of the harbour. The searchlight followed her, and a shudder ran through all who saw her, for lashed to the helm was a corpse, with drooping head, which swung horribly to and fro at each motion of the ship. No other form could be seen on deck at all. A great awe came on all as they realised that the ship, as if by a miracle, had found the harbour, unsteered save by the hand of a dead man! However, all took place more quickly than it takes to write these words. The schooner paused not, but rushing across the harbour, pitched herself on that accumulation of sand and gravel washed by many tides and many storms into the south-east corner of the pier jutting under the East Cliff, known locally as Tate Hill Pier.[22]

There was of course a considerable concussion as the vessel drove up on the sand heap. Every spar, rope, and stay was strained, and some of the "top-hammer"[23] came crashing down. But, strangest of all, the very instant the shore was touched, an immense dog[24] sprang up on deck from below, as if shot up by the concussion, and running forward, jumped from the bow on the sand. Making straight for the steep cliff, where the churchyard hangs over the laneway to the East Pier so steeply that some of the flat tombstones—"thruff-steans" or "through-stones," as they call them in Whitby vernacular—actually project over where the sustaining cliff has fallen away, it disappeared in the darkness, which seemed intensified just beyond the focus of the searchlight.

It so happened that there was no one at the moment on Tate Hill Pier, as all those whose houses are in close proximity were either in bed or were out on the heights above. Thus the coastguard on duty on the eastern side of the harbour, who at once ran down to the little pier, was the first to climb on board. The men working the searchlight, after scouring the entrance of the harbour without seeing anything, then turned the light on the derelict and kept it there. The coastguard ran aft, and when he came beside the wheel, bent over to examine it, and recoiled at once as though under some sudden emotion. This seemed to pique general curiosity, and quite a number of people began to run. It is a good way round from the West Cliff by the Drawbridge to Tate Hill Pier, but your correspondent is a fairly good runner, and came well ahead of the crowd. When I arrived, however, I found already assembled on the pier a crowd, whom the coastguard and police refused to allow to come on board. By the courtesy of the chief boatman, I was, as your correspondent, permitted to climb on deck, and was one of a small group who saw the dead seaman whilst actually lashed to the wheel.

It was no wonder that the coastguard was surprised, or even awed, for not often can such a sight have been seen. The man was simply fastened by his hands, tied one over the other, to a spoke of the wheel. Between the inner hand and the wood was a crucifix, the set of beads on which it was fastened being around both wrists and wheel, and all kept fast by the binding cords. The poor fellow may have been seated at one time, but the flapping and buffeting of the sails had worked through the rudder of the wheel and dragged him to and fro, so that the cords with which he was tied had cut the flesh to the bone. Accurate note was made of the state of things, and a doctor—Surgeon J. M. Caffyn, of 33, East Elliot Place[25]—who came immediately after me, declared, after making examination, that the man must have been dead for quite two days.[26] In his pocket was a bottle, carefully corked, empty save for a little roll of paper, which proved to be the addendum to the log. The coastguard said the man must have tied up his own hands, fastening the knots with his teeth. The fact that a coastguard was the first on board may save some complications, later on, in the Admiralty Court; for coastguards cannot claim the salvage which is the right of the first civilian entering on a derelict. Already, however, the legal tongues are wagging, and one young law student is loudly asserting that the rights of the

25 Curiously, the surgeon's name and address do not appear in the Abridged Text.

26 Written some time on 8 August, this is not inconsistent with the date of the final diary entry (4 August) of the *Demeter*'s captain, who must have lasted a day or two.

27 The mortmain (literally, "dead hand"—a macabre joke in light of the circumstances) statutes were enacted to prevent the inalienable holdings of land, primarily by corporations or ecclesiastical bodies. The student is loudly asserting legal-sounding nonsense. The sentence does not appear in the Abridged Text.

28 The correspondent here refers to the maudlin popular poem of Felicia Hemans (1826), "Casabianca," in which "[t]he boy stood on the burning deck" and would not relinquish his post without his father's command. The battle was fierce "[b]ut the noblest thing which perished there / Was that young faithful heart!"

29 This signals the dawn of 8 August, likely a Monday. The "wolds" are the forest lands. The sentence does not appear in the Abridged Text.

30 The reference to "last night" must be taken to mean the early morning of 8 August, the previous day—in other words, the correspondent meant "yesterday," not "last night."

31 A fortified seaport of Bulgaria, about midway between the delta of the Danube and the Bosphorus. In 1889, its population of about 25,000 was approximately one third Bulgarians, one third Turks, and the balance Greeks, Jews, and Gypsies. With communication through the Pravadi with Lake Devno and ample railway connections, it was the chief outlet for agricultural produce of Bulgaria.

32 Wolf (*The Essential Dracula*) identifies the ship as the *Demetra*, 133 feet, 4 inches long, 29 feet, 4 inches in breadth, and 16 feet, 8 inches in depth, which sailed under the Norwegian flag out of Christiania throughout the 1890s.

However, the Notes contain an extended account of the wreck of a Russian schooner named *Dimitry* (which McNally and Florescu, in *The Essential Dracula*, identify incorrectly as the *Demeter*). Stoker notes, "On 24 Oct. 1885 the Russian schooner 'Dimetry' [?] about 120 tons was sighted off Whitby about 2 pm wind

owner are already completely sacrificed, his property being held in contravention of the statutes of mortmain,[27] since the tiller, as emblemship, if not proof, of delegated possession, is held in a *dead hand.* It is needless to say that the dead steersman has been reverently removed from the place where he held his honourable watch and ward till death—a steadfastness as noble as that of the young Casabianca[28]—and placed in the mortuary to await inquest.

Already the sudden storm is passing, and its fierceness is abating; the crowds are scattering homeward, and the sky is beginning to redden over the Yorkshire wolds.[29] I shall send, in time for your next issue, further details of the derelict ship which found her way so miraculously into harbour in the storm.

Whitby.

9 August.—The sequel to the strange arrival of the derelict in the storm last night[30] is almost more startling than the thing itself. It turns at that the schooner is a Russian from Varna,[31] and is called the *Demeter.*[32] She is almost entirely in ballast of silver sand,[33] with only a small amount of cargo—a number of great wooden boxes filled with mould. This cargo was consigned to a Whitby solicitor, Mr. S. F. Billington, of 7, The Crescent, who this morning went aboard and formally took possession of the goods consigned to him.[34] The Russian consul, too, acting for the charter-party,[35] took formal possession of the ship, and paid all harbour dues, etc. Nothing is talked about here to-day except the strange coincidence; the officials of the Board of Trade have been most exacting in seeing that every compliance has been made with existing regulations.[36] As the matter is to be a "nine days' wonder,"[37] they are evidently determined that there shall be no cause of after complaint. A good deal of interest was abroad concerning the dog which landed when the ship struck, and more than a few of the members of the S.P.C.A.,[38] which is very strong in Whitby, have tried to befriend the animal. To the general disappointment, however, it was not to be found; it seems to have disappeared entirely from the town. It may be that it was frightened and made its way on to the moors, where it is still hiding in terror. There are some who look with dread on such a possibility, lest later on it should in itself become a danger, for it is evidently a fierce brute. Early this morning a large dog, a half-bred mastiff belonging to a coal merchant close to Tate Hill Pier, was found dead in the roadway opposite to its master's yard. It had been fighting, and manifestly had had a savage opponent, for its throat was torn away, and its belly was slit open as if with a savage claw.[39]

Later.—By the kindness of the Board of Trade[40] inspector, I have been permitted to look over the log-book of the *Demeter*,[41] which was in order up to within three days, but contained nothing of special interest except as to facts of missing men. The greatest interest, however, is with regard to the paper found in the bottle, which was to-day produced at the inquest; and a more strange narrative than the two between them unfold it has not been my lot to come across.

northeast force 8 (fresh gale) strong sea on coast (cargo silver sand–from mouth of Danube) ran into harbor by pure chance avoiding rocks." He then went on to type out the following detailed account copied from the log book of the Coast Guard: "At 1.0 p.m. observed vessel apparently in distress and making for harbour called out L.S.A. Company wind N.E. Force 8 & Strong Sea on Coast followed the vessel along coast where most likely to strand. The Life Boat at same time was launched but drove ashore & became of no further use. The Vessel Stranded at about 2.0 p.m. Got communication with 1st Rocket & landed 4 of the crew by whip & buoy fearing the mast would go whip snatch block getting out of order Sent off Hawser & landed safe the remaining 2 of crew being 6 all told. During this service observed a 'Russian' schooner making for harbour & likely to drive back of South

Wreck of the *Dimitry*.
F. M. Sutcliffe, 1885

Pier Called out S Pier L.S.A. Company & both companys watched her progress on each side of harbour the 'Russian' go in but became a wreck during the night Crew landed safe by their own resources The 1st L.S.A. Company were out 5 hours & the 2nd L.S.A. Company 4 hours on these services. 125 fms of Rocket Line & 9 fms. of Hawser was expended on the 1st service having cut the hawser with hawser cutter when the 2nd vessel was observed in distress.

Names of Ships
Mary & Agnes   British
Dimitry   Russian"

The photograph on page 145 was made by Frank Meadow Sutcliffe, best known for his photographs of Whitby and its natives. However, as Roger Johnson points out in "The Bloofer Ladies," Sutcliffe's principal business was as a commercial photographer, and it is "just conceivable that among the numerous surviving negatives and prints in the archives of the Sutcliffe Gallery is a studio portrait of Miss Lucy Westenra."

33 A sharp, fine sand containing no iron oxides and having a silvery appearance, used for grinding lithographic stones and the like; occasionally, a term meaning pure silica.

34 Thus the ship is connected to Dracula, who consigned cargo to solicitor Billington (see chapter 3, note 51). Interestingly, the Notes indicate that the cargo was consigned to Harker—was this an error corrected by Harker himself later?

35 The charter party is the technical term for a written contract by which the owner or master of a ship lets the whole or part of the vessel to a merchant for the transportation of goods on a particular voyage. Here, the correspondent seems to mean the owner; because the ship is denoted as Russian, the Russian consul is acting on behalf of the owner. However, according to Leatherdale (*Dracula Unearthed*), there was no

As there is no motive for concealment, I am permitted to use them, and accordingly send you a rescript,[42] simply omitting technical details of seamanship and supercargo. It almost seems as though the captain had been seized with some kind of mania before he had got well into blue water, and that this had developed persistently throughout the voyage. Of course my statement must be taken *cum grano*,[43] since I am writing from the dictation of a clerk of the Russian consul, who kindly translated for me, time being short.

LOG OF THE "DEMETER."
Varna to Whitby.

Written 18 July, things so strange happening, that I shall keep accurate note henceforth till we land.

On 6 July we finished taking in cargo, silver sand and boxes of earth.[44] At noon set sail. East wind, fresh. Crew, five hands . . . two mates, cook, and myself (captain).

On 11 July at dawn entered Bosphorus.[45] Boarded by Turkish Customs officers. Backsheesh.[46] All correct. Under way at 4 p.m.

On 12 July through Dardanelles.[47] More Customs officers and flagboat of guarding squadron. Backsheesh again. Work of officers thorough, but quick. Want us off soon. At dark passed into Archipelago.

On 13 July passed Cape Matapan. Crew dissatisfied about something. Seemed scared, but would not speak out.

On 14 July was somewhat anxious about crew. Men all steady fellows, who sailed with me before. Mate could not make out what was wrong; they only told him there was *something*, and crossed themselves. Mate lost temper with one of them that day and struck him. Expected fierce quarrel, but all was quiet.

Russian consul; the Baltic trade was controlled by the Russian (Muscovy) Company in London, and the correspondent mistakenly refers to officials of that company as working for the consulate.

36 The Board of Trade was an office of H. M. Government, headquartered in Whitehall Gardens in London. Presumably the wreck fell within the jurisdiction of the Fisheries and Harbour Department, which may have had local representatives. This and the following sentence do not appear in the Abridged Text.

37 A fad or passing sensation. The catchphrase appears in Chaucer's *Troilus and Criseyde* (ca. 1385) and various works of Shakespeare. Actor William Kempe, a popular clown who appeared in several of Shakespeare's early plays and was once a part owner of the Globe Theatre, staged a publicity stunt in which he danced a morris dance from London to Norwich, almost 100 miles north. The account he wrote of the event is titled *Kempe's Nine Days Wonder* (1600). Also used as "ten days' wonder," and in that variant, the phrase appeared as the title of an Ellery Queen mystery novel in 1948.

38 Founded in 1824, the Society for the Prevention of Cruelty to Animals (in 1840, it became the Royal Society) was the first successful national group to address animal protection. Its starting premise was to enforce Martin's Act, existing legislation designed to abolish wanton cruelty to animals. The bill had been pushed through the House of Commons in 1822 by Richard Martin, a highly regarded Irish member of Parliament nicknamed "Humanity Dick" for his efforts by George IV. Martin teamed up with a Devonshire vicar, the Reverend Arthur Broome, whose own life was as storied as the history of the society; although far from a wealthy man, he funded the group largely out of pocket and was once locked up in a debtors' prison. RSPCA chapters were established throughout England and eventually around the world. The society's infamous but much-ridiculed inspectors earned 10 shillings

a week in the early days, plus half the fines paid by owners found to have beaten, inhumanely slaughtered, or otherwise mistreated their animals.

Legislation for the prevention of cruelty to animals predated protection of children in most areas. Until nearly the end of the nineteenth century, English law permitted children eight and nine years old to work longer hours in the coal mines than the pit mules. In 1884, John Colam, secretary of the RSPCA, together with Reverend Benjamin Waugh, helped form the National Society for the Prevention of Cruelty to Children, and in 1889 the Prevention of Cruelty to Children Act was passed, due largely to the lobbying efforts of Waugh and his supporters.

The SPCA chapter for the area covered Scarborough and District (that is, Staithes to Filey), as it continues to do today, and was run from Scarborough.

39 The Manuscript adds the following interesting material, omitted from the published text: "such as a tiger wields. One of our local scientists has photographed its eyes in the hopes that he may be able to reproduce the image of the last thing it saw whilst alive. This dog's death is generally attributed to the newcomer, and a close watch is being kept for the latter lest it should cause further harm to either brute or human." The Notes indicate that Dracula cannot be photographed. It would be fascinating to learn if this trait also applied to the image retained by the dog's eyes.

The Manuscript here refers to the curious scientific concept that the retina of the eye retains an image of the last thing seen at the moment of death. The nineteenth-century German physiologist Willy Kühne, who coined the terms "optogramm" and "optographie" in an 1877 paper, famously promulgated the concept of optography in a demonstration since cited by generations of scientists and others. Kühne's subject was a live rabbit, and his experiment was conducted as follows: the rabbit's eye was covered and absorbed the pigment rhodopsin; it was uncovered and trained for three minutes on an image; the rabbit was killed, the eye removed and placed in an alum solution; finally, on the following day, imprinted on the rabbit's retina was the image the rabbit had gazed upon.

While it is true that early scientific experimentation demonstrated that the retina functions much like a photographic plate and it is theoretically possible that the image would be obtained, the conditions of light necessary to develop a clear image, the long period of exposure required, and the requirement that the retina not be exposed to any light after death all make it extremely unlikely that any recognisable image could ever be obtained from the retina. See Arthur B. Evans's "Optograms and Fiction: Photo in a Dead Man's Eye" for an overview of the later scientific work.

Although now regarded as implausible, Kühne's efforts to "turn a rabbit into a pinhole camera," in the words of Michael Sperlinger, writing in the online film magazine *Mute*, live on and not strictly in the annals of folklore. For example, in the 1902 *Les Frères Kip* [*The Kip Brothers*], the fiftieth novel in Jules Verne's Voyages Extraordinaires series, the eponymous protagonists are cleared of murder through optography.

40 *Horne's Guide to Whitby* (1891) lists no Board of Trade. Presumably the correspondent refers here to the Harbour Board, chaired by Robert Harrowing in 1891.

41 In the Manuscript, the ship is here named the *Demetrius Pupoff*.

42 A handwritten copy.

43 That is, *cum grano salis*, with a grain of salt. The expression figuratively refers to making something palatable—to take a wild idea and accept it sceptically.

44 Dracula departed from his castle on 30 June (see Harker's 30 June journal entry in which he records that he is alone, at the text accompanying chapter 4, note 57). The Slovaks evidently transported the fifty boxes to Varna in

On 16 July mate reported in the morning that one of crew, Petrofsky, was missing. Could not account for it. Took larboard[48] watch eight bells last night; was relieved by Abramoff,[49] but did not go to bunk. Men more downcast than ever. All said they expected something of the kind, but would not say more than there was *something* aboard. Mate getting very impatient with them; feared some trouble ahead.

On 17 July, yesterday, one of the men, Olgaren, came to my cabin, and in an awestruck way confided to me that he thought there was a strange man aboard the ship. He said that in his watch he had been sheltering behind the deckhouse, as there was a rain-storm, when he saw a tall, thin man, who was not like any of the crew, come up the companionway, and go along the deck forward, and disappear. He followed cautiously, but when he got to bows found no one, and the hatchways were all closed. He was in a panic of superstitious fear, and I am afraid the panic may spread. To allay it, I shall to-day search entire ship carefully from stem to stern.

Later in the day I got together the whole crew, and told them, as they evidently thought there was some one in the ship, we would search from stem to stern.[50] First mate angry; said it was folly, and to yield to such foolish ideas would demoralise the men, said he would engage to keep them out of trouble with a handspike. I let him take the helm, while the rest began a thorough search, all keeping abreast, with lanterns: we left no corner unsearched. As there were only the big wooden boxes, there were no odd corners where a man could hide. Men much relieved when search over, and went back to work cheerfully. First mate scowled, but said nothing.

18   22 July.—Rough weather last three days, and all hands busy with sails—no time to be frightened. Men seem to have forgotten their dread. Mate cheerful again, and all on good terms. Praised men for work in bad weather. Passed Gibraltar and out through Straits. All well.

24 July.—There seems some doom over this ship. Already a hand short, and entering on the Bay of Biscay with wild weather

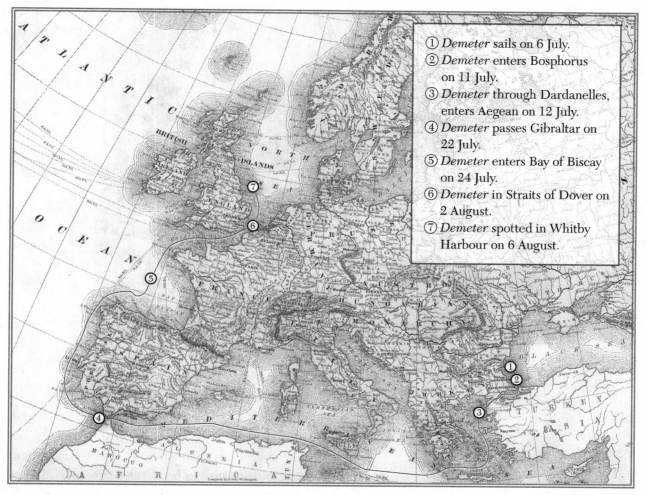

① *Demeter* sails on 6 July.
② *Demeter* enters Bosphorus on 11 July.
③ *Demeter* through Dardanelles, enters Aegean on 12 July.
④ *Demeter* passes Gibraltar on 22 July.
⑤ *Demeter* enters Bay of Biscay on 24 July.
⑥ *Demeter* in Straits of Dover on 2 August.
⑦ *Demeter* spotted in Whitby Harbour on 6 August.

Map of the course of the *Demeter*.

a mere six days, remarkably fast—see chapters 25 and 26 for a description of the much longer reverse journey.

45 Bosphorus, or Bosporus, is the channel that separates Europe from Asia and connects the Black Sea and the Sea of Marmora. The 1901 *Student's Cyclopædia* notes: "The Bosporus has long been under the control of Turkey, and by common consent of the European powers, is closed to all but her own war vessels, though the sultan may open them to his allies in time of war."

46 From the Middle Persian *bakhshishn*, to give presents. A gratuity, tip, or bribe paid to expedite service, especially in Middle and Near Eastern countries.

47 The ancient Hellespont, a narrow channel separating Europe from Asia and uniting the Sea of Marmora with the archipelago. Since 1841, like the Bosporus, the Dardanelles have been under Turkish control.

48 Port, in modern terminology—the left side.

Graf Orlok (Max Schreck) on shipboard.
Nosferatu (Jofa-Atelier Berlin-Johannisthal, 1922)

49 "Abramoff," evidently a late-devised pseudonym, is inserted in Stoker's hand in the Manuscript.

50 Does it seem incredible that no one except the mate considers searching *in* the boxes? Note that the mate is Roumanian, suggesting he may have experience or knowledge of vampires.

51 The Bay of Biscay extends from Brest in France to the northern coast of Spain. The region is well known for rough seas.

52 Changed to "Mate violent" in the Abridged Text.

ahead,[51] and yet last night another man lost—disappeared. Like the first, he came off his watch and was not seen again. Men all in a panic of fear; sent a round robin, asking to have double watch, as they fear to be alone. Mate angry.[52] Fear there will be some trouble, as either he or the men will do some violence.

28 July.—Four days in hell, knocking about in a sort of maelstrom, and the wind a tempest. No sleep for any one. Men all worn out. Hardly know how to set a watch, since no one fit to go on. Second mate volunteered to steer and watch, and let men snatch a few hours' sleep. Wind abating; seas still terrific, but feel them less, as ship is steadier.

29 July.—Another tragedy. Had single watch to-night, as crew too tired to double. When morning watch came on deck could find no one except steersman. Raised outcry, and all came on deck. Thorough search, but no one found. Are now without second mate, and crew in a panic. Mate and I agreed to go armed henceforth and wait for any sign of cause.

30 July.—Last night. Rejoiced we are nearing England. Weather fine, all sails set. Retired worn out; slept soundly; awaked by mate telling me that both man of watch and steersman missing. Only self and mate and two hands left to work ship.

1 August.—Two days of fog and not a sail sighted. Had hoped when in the English Channel to be able to signal for help or get in somewhere. Not having power to work sails, have to run before wind. Dare not lower, as could not raise them again. We seem to be drifting to some terrible doom. Mate now more demoralised than either of men. His stronger nature seems to have worked inwardly against himself. Men are beyond fear, working stolidly and patiently, with minds made up to worst. They are Russian, he Roumanian.

2 August, midnight.—Woke up from few minutes' sleep by hearing a cry, seemingly outside my port. Could see nothing in fog. Rushed on deck, and ran against mate. Tells me heard cry and ran, but no sign of man on watch. One more gone. Lord, help us! Mate says we must be past Straits of Dover, as in a moment of fog lifting he saw North Foreland,[53] just as he heard the man cry out. If so we are now off in the North Sea, and only God can guide us in the fog, which seems to move with us; and God seems to have deserted us.

3 August.—At midnight I went to relieve the man at the wheel, but when I got to it found no one there. The wind was steady, and as we ran before it there was no yawing. I dared not leave it, so shouted for the mate. After a few seconds he rushed up on deck in his flannels. He looked wild-eyed and haggard, and I greatly fear his reason has given way. He came close to me and whispered hoarsely, with his mouth to my ear, as though fearing the very air might hear: "*It* is here; I know it, now. On the watch last night I saw It, like a man, tall and thin, and ghastly pale. It was in the bows, and looking out. I crept behind It, and

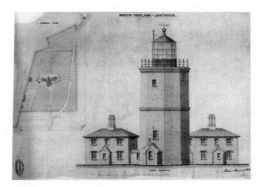

Plans for North Foreland lighthouse, 1860.

53 A lighthouse near the bathing resort of Margate, on a promontory (the Promontorium Acantium of the Romans) almost due east from London, built in 1691 and modernised several times since then. The Dutch fleet was defeated by the English off North Foreland in 1666.

54 Leatherdale (*Dracula Unearthed*) notes that in the nighttime, when this attack occurs, Dracula has the power to become incorporeal at will—as contrasted with Harker's daytime attack resulting in a scar on Dracula's forehead (see text immediately following chapter 4, note 55).

55 Saberhagen, in *The Dracula Tape*, asserts that we cannot understand this to mean that the mate opened a box and found Dracula within, for it is after midnight, and Dracula would no longer be confined to the box. Furthermore, note that there is no indication of damage to any of the boxes on arrival at Whitby. See the next note.

gave It my knife; but the knife went through It, empty as the air." And as he spoke he took his knife and drove it savagely into space.[54] Then he went on: "But It is here, and I'll find It. It is in the hold, perhaps, in one of those boxes. I'll unscrew them one by one and see. You work the helm." And, with a warning look and his finger on his lip, he went below. There was springing up a choppy wind, and I could not leave the helm. I saw him come out on deck again with a tool-chest and a lantern, and go down the forward hatchway. He is mad, stark, raving mad, and it's no use my trying to stop him. He can't hurt those big boxes: they are invoiced as "clay," and to pull them about is as harmless a thing as he can do. So here I stay, and mind the helm, and write these notes. I can only trust in God and wait till the fog clears. Then, if I can't steer to any harbour with the wind that is, I shall cut down sails and lie by, and signal for help. . . .

It is nearly all over now. Just as I was beginning to hope that the mate would come out calmer—for I heard him knocking away at something in the hold, and work is good for him—there came up the hatchway a sudden, startled scream, which made my blood run cold, and up on the deck he came as if shot from a gun—a raging madman, with his eyes rolling and his face convulsed with fear. "Save me! save me!" he cried, and then looked round on the blanket of fog. His horror turned to despair, and in a steady voice he said: "You had better come too, captain, before it is too late. *He* is there! I know the secret now. The sea will save me from Him, and it is all that is left!"[55] Before I could say a word, or move forward to seize him, he sprang on the bulwark and deliberately threw himself into the sea. I suppose I know the secret too, now. It was this madman who had got rid of the men one by one, and now he has followed them himself. God help me! How am I to account for all these horrors when I get to port? *When* I get to port! Will that ever be?

4 August.—Still fog, which the sunrise cannot pierce. I know there is sunrise because I am a sailor, why else I know not. I dared not go below, I dared not leave the helm; so here all night I stayed, and in the dimness of the night I saw It—Him! God forgive me, but the mate was right to jump overboard. It was better to die like a man; to die like a sailor in blue water no man can object. But I am captain, and I must not leave my ship. But I shall baffle this fiend or monster, for I shall tie my hands to the wheel when my strength begins to fail, and along with them I shall tie that which He—It!—dare not touch; and then, come good wind or foul, I shall save my soul, and my honour as a captain. I am growing weaker, and the night is coming on. If He can look me in the face again, I may not have time to act. . . . If we are wrecked, mayhap this bottle may be found, and those who find it may understand; if not, . . . well, then all men shall know that I have been true to my trust. God and the Blessed Virgin and the saints help a poor ignorant soul trying to do his duty. . . .'[56]

Of course the verdict was an open one. There is no evidence to adduce; and whether or not the man himself committed the murders there is now none to say. The folk here hold almost universally that the captain is simply a hero, and he is to be given a public funeral. Already it is arranged that his body is to be taken with a train of boats up the Esk for a piece and then brought back to Tate Hill Pier and up the Abbey steps; for he is to be buried in the churchyard on the cliff.[57] The owners of more than a hundred boats have already given in their names as wishing to follow him to the grave.

No trace has ever been found the great dog; at which there is much mourning, for, with public opinion in its present state, he would, I believe, be adopted by the town. To-morrow[58] will see the funeral; and so will end this one more "mystery of the sea."

MINA MURRAY'S JOURNAL.

8 August.—Lucy was very restless all night,[59] and I, too, could not sleep. The storm was fearful, and as it boomed loudly among the chimney-pots, it made me shudder. When a sharp puff came it seemed to be like a distant gun. Strangely enough, Lucy did not wake, but she got up twice and dressed herself. Fortunately, each time I awoke in time and managed to undress her without waking her, and got her back to bed. It is a very strange thing, this sleep-walking, for as soon as her

56 The captain's account of the voyage is, frankly, baffling, because the behaviour attributed by implication to Dracula is wholly illogical. It surely was in Dracula's best interests to do everything in his not inconsiderable power to assure that the voyage was swift and uneventful. Instead, he conjures up a fog (is he *trying* to ensure that the ship will founder?) and kills off the crew one by one until it is absolutely certain that the ship will be wrecked. Are we to believe that his appetite for human blood was insatiable and that he could not control himself for a period of a month? That the vampire-king who for years existed on the blood of babies (shared, we may conclude, with his vampire-brides) or the occasional sustenance of a peasant or two now is suddenly unable to stop himself from murdering an entire ship's crew? If he wished to enter England secretly and required sustenance, surely it would have been better to have discreetly slipped from his box from time to time, preyed on a victim without killing him (as he demonstrates that he can do), and left the crew intact, albeit somewhat "drained." (Leatherdale, in *Dracula Unearthed*, argues that the "ghastly pale" Dracula, who is normally ruddy after feeding, did not kill the crew but simply scared them to death, one at a time, and that they leapt overboard without his intervention. Leatherdale contends that Dracula does not ever indulge in drinking the blood of males.)

What conclusions can we reach?

1. Dracula's "child-mind" is incapable of strategic planning. This contradicts Van Helsing's later assertion of Dracula's "mighty brain" and furthermore is demonstrably wrong. He manages to flee England and return to Transylvania without slaughtering the crew of the *Czarina Catherine*.

2. Dracula's feeding habits have been described completely incorrectly by Harker in his journal and misunderstood by Van Helsing and the others. This is certainly possible. Harker was privy only to a few scenes of baby hunting and really had no way of knowing what Dracula's private habits were. In fact, Dracula may well

have needed to sustain a peasant-a-day habit and concealed that need from Harker. Once Dracula is in England, the narrative focuses on Lucy and Mina. But as will be seen, Dracula intends to "turn" these victims, to make them into vampires. He may well have attacked numerous other English victims for sustenance. Although Leatherdale, as noted above, makes much of the absence of male victims in the narrative, this may say more about the Harker Papers than about Dracula.

3. Some force other than Dracula is the cause of the disaster that befalls the *Demeter*. This theory has some facts to recommend it. The captain himself concludes that the Roumanian mate has murdered all of the others, and there is no way to prove or disprove this. Saberhagen, in *The Dracula Tape*, posits that this is in fact what occurred. If the Roumanian had earlier concluded that a vampire was present onboard and was feeding nonlethally on the sailors, the mate may have taken it on himself to purge the ship of potential vampires before they could "turn." There is nothing to indicate that the captain was killed by Dracula, and the journal's record of a vision of "He—It!" could have been the captain's fancy or perhaps a genuine observation of a very nervous (and ghastly pale, meaning unfed) Dracula, pacing the deck with worry that his transport was about to founder.

Leatherdale also wonders that Dracula did not pitch the captain's body overboard or at least destroy the log, to reduce suspicion in Whitby.

57 In fact, St. Mary's churchyard accepted no new burials after the early 1870s. A local reporter would not be likely to make this mistake.

58 According to Mina's journal, the funeral was on 10 August; therefore, the correspondent's "to-morrow" is evidence that the 9 August date on this entry is correct.

59 Further confirmation that the storm occurred on the night of Sunday, 7 August, and the early morning of Monday, 8 August.

will is thwarted in any physical way, her intention, if there be any, disappears, and she yields herself almost exactly to the routine of her life.

Early in the morning we both got up and went down to the harbour to see if anything had happened in the night. There were very few people about, and though the sun was bright, and the air clear and fresh, the big, grim-looking waves, that seemed dark themselves because the foam that topped them was like snow, forced themselves in through the narrow mouth of the harbour—like a bullying man going through a crowd. Somehow I felt glad that Jonathan was not on the sea last night, but on land. But, oh, is he on land or sea? Where is he, and how? I am getting fearfully anxious about him. If I only knew what to do, and could do anything![60]

10 August.—The funeral of the poor sea-captain to-day was most touching.[61] Every boat in the harbour seemed to be there, and the coffin was carried by captains all the way from Tate Hill Pier up to the churchyard. Lucy came with me, and we went early to our old seat, whilst the cortège of boats went up the river to the Viaduct and came down again. We had a lovely view, and saw the procession nearly all the way. The poor fellow was laid to rest quite near our seat so that we stood on it when the time came and saw everything. Poor Lucy seemed much upset. She was restless and uneasy all the time, and I cannot but think that her dreaming at night is telling on her. She is quite odd in one thing: she will not admit to me that there is any cause for restlessness; or if there be, she does not understand it herself. There is an additional cause in that poor old Mr. Swales was found dead this morning on our seat, his neck being broken.[62] He had evidently, as the doctor said, fallen back in the seat in some sort of fright, for there was a look of fear and horror on his face that the men said made them shudder. Poor dear old man! Perhaps he had seen Death with his dying eyes! Lucy is so sweet and sensitive that she feels influences more acutely than other people do. Just now she was quite upset by a little thing which I did not much heed, though I am myself very fond of animals. One of the men who came up here often to look for the boats was followed by his dog. The dog is always with him. They are both quiet persons,[63] and I never saw the man angry, nor heard the dog bark. During the service the dog would not come to its master, who was on the seat with us, but kept a few yards off, barking and howling. Its master spoke to it gently, and then harshly, and then angrily; but it would neither come nor cease to make a noise. It was in a sort of fury, with its eyes savage, and all its hairs bristling out like a cat's tail when puss is on the warpath.[64] Finally the man, too, got angry, and jumped down and kicked the dog, and then took it by the scruff of the neck and half dragged and half threw it on the tombstone on which the seat is fixed. The moment it touched the stone the poor thing became quiet and fell all into a tremble. It did not try to get away, but crouched down, quivering and cowering, and was in such a pitiable state of terror that I tried, though without effect, to comfort it. Lucy was full of pity, too, but she did not attempt to touch the dog, but looked at it in an agonised sort of way. I greatly fear that she is too super-sensitive a nature to go through the world without trouble. She will be dreaming of this to-night, I am sure. The whole agglomeration of things— the ship steered into port by a dead man; his attitude, tied to the wheel with a crucifix and beads; the touching funeral; the dog, now furious and now in terror—will all afford material for her dreams.

I think it will be best for her to go to bed tired out physically, so I shall take her for a long walk by the cliffs to Robin Hood's Bay and back. She ought not to have much inclination for sleep-walking then.

60 This entire paragraph does not appear in the Abridged Text.

61 The funeral was on Tuesday, 10 August.

62 Leatherdale (*Dracula Unearthed*) speculates that Mr. Swales was killed by Dracula because he inadvertently blocked Dracula's entry into the suicide's grave, where his presence is revealed by the disturbed dog.

63 Not in the Abridged Text.

64 Wolf (*The Essential Dracula*) takes the dog's behaviour as a clue that Dracula is reposing in the ground beneath the stone on which the master is seated. This is inconsistent with Van Helsing's later assertion that Dracula cannot rest in "soil barren of holy memories" (see chapter 18, note 48). Although the seat is in the churchyard, Mr. Swales has earlier revealed that the placement has been fraudulently obtained: the tombstone marks the grave of a suicide. Therefore, it is unlikely that the soil here contains holy memories. Perhaps, contrary to Van Helsing's understanding, the soil of a *suicide's* grave was still acceptable to vampires—after all, the folkloric tradition is that suicides often become vampires (see chapter 2, note 56).

Chapter 8

1 This odd-sounding phrase is a superlative, recorded by the *Oxford English Dictionary* as first appearing in John C. Atkinson's novel *Stanton Grange, or, at a Private Tutor's . . .* (1864). Coincidentally, Atkinson also wrote *A handbook for Whitby & its ancient abbey* (1882).

2 The "New Woman" represented a rejection of traditional Victorian rôles of women and

DONNA QUIXOTE.
["A world of disorderly notions *picked out of books, crowded into his (her) imagination."—Don Quixote.*]

The "New Woman" satirised as "Donna Quixote."
Punch, 1894

MINA MURRAY'S JOURNAL.

Same day, 11 o'clock p.m.—Oh, but I am tired! If it were not that I had made my diary a duty I should not open it to-night. We had a lovely walk. Lucy, after a while, was in gay spirits, owing, I think, to some dear cows who came nosing towards us in a field close to the lighthouse, and frightened the wits out of us. I believe we forgot everything except, of course, personal fear, and it seemed to wipe the slate clean and give us a fresh start. We had a capital "severe tea"[1] at Robin Hood's Bay in a sweet little old-fashioned inn, with a bow-window right over the seaweed-covered rocks of the strand. I believe we should have shocked the "New Woman" with our appetites.[2] Men are more tolerant, bless them! Then we walked home with some, or rather many, stoppages to rest, and with our hearts full of a constant dread of wild bulls. Lucy was really tired, and we intended to creep off to bed as soon as we could. The young curate came in, however, and Mrs. Westenra asked him to stay for supper. Lucy and I had both a fight for it with the dusty miller;[3] I know it was a hard fight on my part, and I am quite heroic. I think that some day the bishops must get together and see about breeding up a new class of curates, who don't take supper, no matter how they may be pressed to, and who will know when girls are tired. Lucy is asleep and breathing softly. She has more colour in her cheeks than usual, and looks, oh, so sweet. If Mr. Holmwood fell in love with her seeing her only in the drawing-room, I wonder what he would say if he saw her now. Some of the "New Women" writers will some day start an idea that men and women should be allowed to see each other asleep before proposing or accepting. But I suppose the New Woman won't condescend in future to accept; she will do the proposing herself. And a nice job she will make of it, too! There's some consolation in that I am so happy to-night, because dear Lucy seems better. I really believe she has turned the corner, and that we are over her troubles with dreaming. I should be quite happy if I only knew if Jonathan . . . God bless and keep him.

11 August, 3 a.m.—Diary again. No sleep now, so I may as well write. I am too agitated to sleep. We have had such an adventure, such an agonising experience. I fell asleep as soon as I had closed my diary. . . .[4] Suddenly I became broad awake, and sat up, with a horrible sense of fear upon me, and of some feeling of emptiness around me. The room was dark, so I could not see Lucy's bed; I stole across and felt for her. The bed was empty. I lit a match, and found that she was not in the room. The door was shut, but not locked, as I had left it. I feared to wake her mother, who has been more than usually ill lately, so threw on some clothes and got ready to look for her. As I was leaving the room it struck me that the clothes she wore might give me some clue to her dreaming intention. Dressing-gown would mean house; dress, outside. Dressing-gown and dress were both in their places. "Thank God," I said to myself, "she cannot be far, as she is only in her nightdress."[5] I ran downstairs and looked in the sitting-room. Not there! Then I looked in all the other open rooms of the house, with an ever-growing fear chilling my heart. Finally I came to the hall-door and found it open. It was not wide open, but the catch of the lock had not caught. The people of the house are careful to lock the door every night, so I feared that Lucy must have gone out as she was. There was no time to think of what might happen; a vague, overmastering fear obscured all details. I took a big, heavy shawl and ran out. The clock was striking one as I was in the Crescent, and there was not a soul in sight. I ran along the North Terrace, but could see no

was championed by a variety of journalists, pamphleteers, authors, and playwrights, among them George Bernard Shaw, Grant Allen, Henry Arthur Jones, and H. G. Wells. The key principles of New Womanhood were an adequate education, financial independence (and of course the ability to earn money to achieve that independence), meaningful participation in the political process, freedom of choice respecting marriage and childbearing, and general defiance of convention and social norms. Comfortable clothing, beyond being a practicality, was regarded as a visible sign of status. Of course, not all of these principles were embraced by all proponents. For example, while many acknowledged that the Victorian moral code and its double standards were obsolete, only a few advocated the concept of free love.

In 1904, art lecturer and suffragist Winnifred Harper Cooley, in her book *The New Womanhood*, wrote: "The finest achievement of the new woman has been personal liberty. This is the foundation of civilization; and as long as any one class is watched suspiciously, even fondly guarded, and protected, so long will that class not only be weak, and treacherous, individually, but parasitic, and a collective danger to the community. Who has not heard wives commended for wheedling their husbands out of money, or joked because they are hopelessly extravagant? As long as caprice and scheming are considered feminine virtues, as long as man is the only wage-earner, doling out sums of money, or scattering lavishly, so long will women be degraded, even if they are perfectly contented, and men are willing to labor to keep them in idleness! . . . Men have come to see that no advance can be made with one half-humanity set apart merely for the functions of sex; that children are quite liable to inherit from the mother, and should have opportunities to inherit the accumulated ability and culture and character that is produced only by intellectual and civil activity."

Of course, there were dissenting voices. An unidentified woman objected on the pages of the *Illustrated London News* (6 February 1892):

"Home duties she has discarded as degrading to an educated woman, wifely respect she despises as the sign of craven submission to an inferior, children she dislikes as hindrances and nuisances, love is a dream fit only for lunatics and idiots. What she wants is freedom to do as she likes—the key of all the fields of life, not barring one. . . . The two objects of her ambition are—to have plenty of 'oof,' no matter by what means, and to be as much like a man as it is possible for a woman to make herself" (quoted in Wolf, *The Essential Dracula*).

The entire New Woman theme is absent in the Abridged Text.

3 This odd phrase is apparently a colloquial variant on the "dustman," or in American slang, the "sandman," the personification of sleep. Mina means that the young curate was boring and nearly put her and Lucy to sleep.

4 Probably before midnight.

5 Mina's mistaken surmise regarding Lucy's clothing does not appear in the Abridged Text.

6 In fact, on the morning of 11 August 1893, the moon was a waning crescent (only 3 percent illuminated), and moonrise was at 3:11 A.M. However, on the morning of 11 August 1886, the moon was waxing gibbous (83 percent illuminated) and did not set until 1:22 A.M. See appendix 2, "The Dating of *Dracula*."

7 The diorama was an early version of the modern movie theatre, a building for the display of huge paintings (70 by 45 feet) on a translucent medium, with a painting on each side. First established by L. J. M. Daguerre (1787–1851), the inventor of the daguerrotype, and his partner Charles-Marie Bouton in 1821, the Paris diorama exhibited dozens of Daguerre's panoramas and attracted visitors from around the world. Here is a description, from the *Mirror of Literature* (30 June 1827), of *Ruins in a Fog*, shown in Paris in 1826 and in London in 1827: "All is sombre, desolate, and mournful; the long drawn aisles,

sign of the white figure which I expected. At the edge of the West Cliff above the pier I looked across the harbour to the East Cliff, in the hope or fear—I don't know which—of seeing Lucy in our favourite seat. There was a bright full moon,[6] with heavy black, driving clouds, which threw the whole scene into a fleeting diorama[7] of light and shade as they sailed across. For a moment or two I could see nothing, as the shadow of a cloud obscured St. Mary's Church and all around it. Then as the cloud passed I could see the ruins of the abbey coming into view; and as the edge of a narrow band of light as sharp as a sword-cut moved along, the church and the churchyard became gradually visible. Whatever my expectation was, it was not disappointed, for there, on our favourite seat, the silver light of the moon struck a half-reclining figure, snowy white. The coming of the cloud was too quick for me to see much, for shadow shut down on light almost immediately; but it seemed to me as though something dark stood behind the seat where the white figure shone, and bent over it. What it was, whether man or beast, I could not tell; I did not wait to catch another glance, but flew down the steep steps to the pier and along by the fish-market to the bridge, which was the only way to reach the East Cliff. The town seemed as dead, for not a soul did I see; I rejoiced that it was so, for I wanted no witness of poor Lucy's condition. The time and distance seemed endless,[8] and my knees trembled and my breath came laboured as I toiled up the endless steps to the Abbey. I must have gone fast, and yet it seemed to me as if my feet were weighted with lead, and as though every joint in my body were rusty. When I got almost to the top I could see the seat and the white figure, for I was now close enough to distinguish it even through the spells of shadow. There was undoubtedly something, long and black, bending over the half-reclining white figure. I called in fright, "Lucy! Lucy!" and something raised a head, and from where I was I could see a white face and red, gleaming eyes. Lucy did not answer, and I ran on to the entrance of the church-yard.[9] As I entered, the church was between me and the seat, and for a minute or so I lost sight of her. When I came in view again the cloud had passed, and the moonlight struck so brilliantly that I could see Lucy half reclining with her head lying over the back of the seat. She was quite alone, and there was not a sign of any living thing about.[10]

When I bent over her I could see that she was still asleep. Her lips were parted, and she was breathing—not softly as usual with her, but in long, heavy gasps, as though striving to get her lungs full at every breath. As I came close, she put up her hand in her sleep and pulled the collar of her nightdress close around her throat. Whilst she did so there came a little shudder through her, as though she felt the cold.[11] I flung the warm shawl over her, and drew the edges tight around her neck, for I dreaded lest she should get some deadly chill from the night air, unclad as she was. I feared to wake her all at once, so, in order to have my hands free that I might help her, I fastened the shawl at her throat with a big safety-pin;[12] but I must have been clumsy in my anxiety and pinched or pricked her with it, for by-and-by, when her breathing became quieter, she put her hand to her throat again and moaned. When I had her carefully wrapped up I put my shoes on her feet, and then began very gently to wake her. At first she did not respond; but gradually she became more and more uneasy in her sleep, moaning and sighing occasionally. At last, as time was passing fast, and, for many other reasons, I wished to get her home at once, I shook her more forcibly, till finally she opened her eyes and awoke. She did not seem surprised to see me, as, of course, she did not realise all at once where she was. Lucy always wakes prettily, and even at such a time, when her body must have been chilled with cold, and her mind somewhat appalled at waking unclad in a churchyard at night, she did not lose her grace.[13] She trembled a little, and clung to me; when I told her to come at once with me home she rose without a word, with the obedience of a child. As we passed along, the gravel hurt my feet, and Lucy noticed me wince. She stopped and wanted to insist upon my taking my shoes; but I would not. However, when we got to the pathway outside the churchyard, where there was a puddle of water remaining from the storm, I daubed my feet with mud, using each foot in turn on the other, so that as we went home, no one, in case we should meet any one, should notice my bare feet.[14]

Fortune favoured us, and we got home without meeting a

Diorama of *The Temple of Solomon*.
L. J. M. Daguerre, 1836

at first glance, are alone perceived, for a thick fog reigns without, and such is the illusion of the scene that you actually fancy yourself chilled by the cold and damp air. By degrees, however, the fog disperses, and through the vast arches are plainly discovered the forests of pine and larch-trees that cover the valley. The magic of this effect of light is indeed most extraordinary and the illusion is complete and enchanting."

The proprietors opened a London version in 1823, and later exhibitions were mounted in Dublin, Edinburgh, Liverpool, and Manchester. In 1855, long after the London show had closed, John Timbs, in *Curiosities of London*, described it as follows: "The Diorama consisted of two pictures, eighty feet in length and forty feet in height, painted in solid and in transparency, arranged so as to exhibit changes of light and shade, and a variety of natural phenomena; the spectators being kept in comparative darkness, while the picture received a concentrated light from a ground-glass roof." Called "theatres without actors," the dioramas were as much the buildings and the lighting effects as the paintings displayed there. An 1839 fire in the Paris diorama and financial difficulties forced Daguerre to dissolve his partnership with Bouton, and many of Daguerre's paintings were sold to proprietors who opened their own dioramas.

8 Wolf (*The Essential Dracula*) points out that Mina runs over 1 mile to get to Lucy.

9 The Notes indicate that Mina first observes a figure of a man, or perhaps a wolf, which then seems to fly.

10 Dracula has evidently returned to the suicide's grave. Why did he not attack Lucy? He has already killed Mr. Swale.

11 Wolf (*The Essential Dracula*) points out that Lucy here experiences symptoms of her anaemia, gasping for air and feeling cold. In fact, Lucy's reaction is somewhat orgasmic.

12 The Notes indicate that Lucy found a strange brooch on the shore and put it on. Later, she tells Mina, "I must have pricked myself in my sleep putting it on." The "prick-of-the brooch" theory is accepted by Mina and subsequently by Seward after he examines her. There is no further indication of the fate of the brooch, and it is curious that Stoker suppressed mention of it.

13 Mina's loyal comment is omitted in the Abridged Text.

14 The bare feet and their cleaning are not discussed in the Abridged Text.

15 An entry, passageway, or courtyard.

16 The encounter with the man does not appear in the Abridged Text.

17 Of course, Mina is not worried about Lucy's reputation suffering injury because of her sleepwalking—she imagines (and perhaps with good reason) a wholly improper romantic encounter, or worse.

18 Lucy is quite aware of the impropriety of her acts and is apparently concerned that her mother—close to Holmwood—will disclose it.

19 "Reflection" in modern English.

20 A very different response than that of Mina to her first episode with Dracula (see chapter 19,

soul. Once we saw a man, who seemed not quite sober, passing along a street in front of us; but we hid in a door till he had disappeared up an opening such as there are here, steep little closes,[15] or "wynds," as they call them in Scotland.[16] My heart beat so loud all the time that sometimes I thought I should faint. I was filled with anxiety about Lucy, not only for her health, lest she should suffer from the exposure, but for her reputation in case the story should get wind.[17] When we got in, and had washed our feet, and had said a prayer of thankfulness together, I tucked her into bed. Before falling asleep she asked—even implored—me not to say a word to any one, even her mother, about her sleep-walking adventure.[18] I hesitated at first to promise; but on thinking of the state of her mother's health, and how the knowledge of such a thing would fret her, and thinking, too, of how such a story might become distorted—nay, infallibly would—in case it should leak out, I thought it wiser to do so. I hope I did right. I have locked the door, and the key is tied to my wrist, so perhaps I shall not be again disturbed. Lucy is sleeping soundly; the reflex[19] of the dawn is high and far over the sea. . . .

Same day, noon.—All goes well. Lucy slept till I woke her and seemed not to have even changed her side. The adventure of the night does not seem to have harmed her; on the contrary, it has benefited her, for she looks better this morning than she has done for weeks.[20] I was sorry to notice that my clumsiness with the safety-pin hurt her. Indeed, it might have been serious, for the skin of her throat was pierced. I must have pinched up a piece of loose skin and have transfixed it, for there are two little red points like pin-pricks, and on the band of her nightdress was a drop of blood. When I apologised and was concerned about it, she laughed and petted me, and said she did not even feel it. Fortunately it cannot leave a scar, as it is so tiny.

Same day, night.—We passed a happy day.[21] The air was clear, and the sun bright, and there was a cool breeze. We took our lunch to Mulgrave Woods, Mrs. Westenra driving by the road and Lucy and I walking by the cliff-path and joining her at the gate. I felt a little sad myself, for I could not but feel how *absolutely* happy it would have been had Jonathan been with me. But there! I must only be patient. In the evening we strolled in the Casino Terrace,[22] and heard some good music by Spohr[23] and Mackenzie,[24] and went to bed early. Lucy seems more restful than she has been for some time, and fell asleep at once. I shall lock the door and secure the key the same as before, though I do not expect any trouble to-night.

12 August.—My expectations were wrong, for twice during the night I was wakened by Lucy trying to get out. She seemed, even in her sleep, to be a little impatient at finding the door shut, and went back to bed under a sort of protest. I woke with the dawn, and heard the birds chirping outside of the window. Lucy woke, too, and, I was glad to see, was even better than on the previous morning. All her old gaiety of manner seemed to have come back, and she came and snuggled in beside me and told me all about Arthur; I told her how anxious I was about Jonathan, and then she tried to comfort me. Well, she succeeded somewhat, for, though sympathy can't alter facts, it can help to make them more bearable.

13 August.[25]—Another quiet day, and to bed with the key on my wrist as before. Again I awoke in the night, and found Lucy sitting up in bed, still asleep, pointing to the window. I got up quietly, and pulling aside the blind, looked out. It was brilliant moonlight, and the soft effect of the light over the sea and sky—merged together in one great, silent mystery—was beautiful beyond words.[26] Between me and the moonlight flitted a great bat, coming and going in great, whirling circles. Once or twice it came quite close, but was, I suppose, frightened at seeing me, and flitted away across the harbour towards the Abbey.[27] When I came back from the window Lucy had lain down again, and was sleeping peacefully. She did not stir again all night.

14 August.—On the East Cliff, reading and writing all day. Lucy seems to have become as much in love with the spot as I am, and it is hard to get her away from it when it is time to come home for lunch or tea or dinner. This afternoon she

note 34). Here, in the view of Wolf (*The Essential Dracula*), Lucy presents the appearance, at least metaphorically, of a postcoital satisfied woman.

21 The following description of the girls' activities does not appear in the Abridged Text.

22 This does not appear to be a real location. The West Cliff Saloon, built in 1880, had a Floral Pavilion, which may be the place in question.

23 Louis Spohr (1784–1859) was well known during the nineteenth century as a composer, violin virtuoso, conductor, and teacher. Although he wrote the concertos then considered obligatory for a virtuoso (Paganini, among others, set this trend), he also completed nine symphonies, and his compositions included opera, oratorio, cantata, lieder, chamber music, and especially during the time of his first marriage, to the harpist Dorette Scheidler, works for harp and violin, which the couple performed together throughout Europe. Spohr helped pioneer the use of the conductor's baton and the violinist's chin rest, the latter of which

Louis Spohr.

he invented. His four clarinet concertos are in the repertoire today.

24 Sir Alexander Campbell Mackenzie (1847–1935), a violinist and conductor, known as the greatest Scot composer of his day, was educated in Germany and made director of the Royal Academy of Music in 1888. His works included symphonies, operas, and oratorios, as well as several violin compositions written especially for Pablo de Sarasate, one of the greatest violinists of the age and a favourite of Sherlock Holmes. Mackenzie's memoir *A Musician's Narrative* appeared in 1927.

25 The Notes indicate that this took place on 14 August.

Sir Alexander Campbell Mackenzie.
"Spy," *Vanity Fair*, 1904

made a funny remark. We were coming home for dinner, and had come to the top of the steps up from the West Pier and stopped to look at the view, as we generally do. The setting sun, low down in the sky, was just dropping behind Kettleness; the red light was thrown over on the East Cliff and the old Abbey, and seemed to bathe everything in a beautiful rosy glow. We were silent for a while, and suddenly Lucy murmured as if to herself:—

"His red eyes again! They are just the same." It was such an odd expression, coming *apropos* of nothing, that it quite startled me. I slewed round a little, so as to see Lucy well without seeming to stare at her, and saw that she was in a half-dreamy state, with an odd look on her face that I could not quite make out; so I said nothing, but followed her eyes. She appeared to be looking over at our own seat, whereon was a dark figure seated alone.[28] I was a little startled myself, for it seemed for an instant as if the stranger had great eyes like burning flames; but a second look dispelled the illusion.[29] The red sunlight was shining on the windows of St. Mary's Church behind our seat, and as the sun dipped there was just sufficient change in the refraction and reflection to make it appear as if the light moved. I called Lucy's attention to the peculiar effect, and she became herself with a start, but she looked sad all the same; it may have been that she was thinking of that terrible night up there. We never refer to it; so I said nothing, and we went home to dinner. Lucy had a headache and went early to bed. I saw her asleep, and went out for a little stroll myself; I walked along the cliffs to the westward, and was full of sweet sadness, for I was thinking of Jonathan. When coming home—it was then bright moonlight, so bright that, though the front of our part of the Crescent was in shadow, everything could be well seen—I threw a glance up at our window, and saw Lucy's head leaning out.[30] I thought that perhaps she was looking out for me, so I opened my handkerchief and waved it. She did not notice or make any movement whatever. Just then, the moonlight crept round an angle of the building, and the light fell on the window. There distinctly was Lucy with her head lying up against the side of the window-sill and her eyes shut. She was fast asleep, and by her, seated on the window-sill, was something that looked like a good-sized bird. I was afraid she might get a chill, so I ran upstairs, but as I came into the room she was moving back to her bed, fast asleep, and breathing heavily; she was holding her hand to her throat, as though to protect it from cold.

I did not wake her, but tucked her up warmly; I have taken care that the door is locked and the window securely fastened.

She looks so sweet as she sleeps; but she is paler than is her wont, and there is a drawn, haggard look under her eyes which I do not like. I fear she is fretting about something. I wish I could find out what it is.

15 August.—Rose later than usual. Lucy was languid and tired, and slept on after we had been called. We had a happy surprise at breakfast. Arthur's father is better, and wants the marriage to come off soon. Lucy is full of quiet joy, and her mother is glad and sorry at once. Later on in the day she told me the cause. She is grieved to lose Lucy as her very own, but she is rejoiced that she is soon to have some one to protect her. Poor dear, sweet lady! She confided to me that she has got her death-warrant. She has not told Lucy, and made me promise secrecy; her doctor told her that within a few months, at most, she must die, for her heart is weakening. At any time, even now, a sudden shock would be almost sure to kill her. Ah, we were wise to keep from her the affair of the dreadful night of Lucy's sleep-walking.

17 August.—No diary for two whole days. I have not had the heart to write. Some sort of shadowy pall seems to be coming over our happiness. No news from Jonathan, and Lucy seems to be growing weaker, whilst her mother's hours are numbering to a close. I do not understand Lucy's fading away as she is doing. She eats well and sleeps well, and enjoys the fresh air; but all the time the roses in her cheeks are fading, and she gets weaker and more languid day by day; at night I hear her gasping as if for air. I keep the key of our door always fastened to my wrist at night, but she gets up and walks about the room, and sits at the open window. Last night I found her leaning out

26 Only in 1889 (full moon 11 August) and 1886 (full moon 14 August) could the moonlight be described as "brilliant"; in other years, it was either a new moon or less than a half-full moon. Perhaps wisely, the Abridged Text does not contain the sentence.

27 Unfortunately none of the "Crescent" streets have a view of the harbour. However, Mina may have simply noted that the bat flew in the direction of the East Cliff.

28 Wolf (*The Essential Dracula*) points out that Dracula here is active during daylight.

29 Dracula sits in full sunlight. How did he emerge from the grave if, as Van Helsing states, his powers are limited during daylight hours?

30 Another date, another bright moon. The moon was definitely visible on the evening of 14 August 1893, but it set at 8:40 P.M., a bit early for Mina's statement that Lucy had already gone to bed. In addition, the moon on that day was a waxing crescent, with only 8 percent illuminated, hardly consistent with Mina's description of bright moonlight. On 14 August 1886, however, the moon rose at 7:22 P.M. and was full. See appendix 2, "The Dating of *Dracula*," for a more complete discussion of the relevance of moon data.

Modern Carter-Paterson trucks, 1920s.

when I woke up, and when I tried to wake her I could not; she was in a faint. When I managed to restore her she was as weak as water, and cried silently between long, painful struggles for breath. When I asked her how she came to be at the window she shook her head and turned away. I trust her feeling ill may not be from that unlucky prick of the safety pin. I looked at her throat just now as she lay asleep, and the tiny wounds seem not to have healed. They are still open, and, if anything, larger than before, and the edges of them are faintly white. They are like little white dots with red centres. Unless they heal within a day or two, I shall insist on the doctor seeing about them.

31 A well-known cartage firm, founded in 1860 and headquartered in the Goswell Road. W. J. Gordon's *The Horse World of London* (1893) describes its operations, which spanned twenty London depots and employed two thousand horses: "The parcels are collected from the senders on information received at the numerous order stations, which the public know by the show-boards. . . . [As a rule, collection is] by one-horse vans to the nearest depot, where they are transhipped into vans drawn by pairs or teams, and find their way across London to the depot nearest the address of the consignee, from which depot they are sent out to their destination in the local single-horse vans."

32 As early as 1827, a railway between London and York was proposed. It was not until 1848 that a section opened, and the line did not arrive in London until 1852. By 1860, however, it had reached a substantial number of significant towns north of London, including Cambridge, Manchester, Nottingham, Leicester, and Sheffield, and had begun to derive substantial revenues both from the English coalfields and from long-term excursion traffic, such as trips to the Doncaster races. By the 1870s, the Great Northern Railway (GNR) had more express trains than any other major line. The famed London-Edinburgh Flying Scotsman (or as it was officially known, Special Scotch Express) ran, as it still does today, on the East Coast Main Line

LETTER FROM SAMUEL F. BILLINGTON & SON, SOLICITORS, WHITBY, TO MESSRS. CARTER, PATERSON & CO.,[31] LONDON.

"17 August

"Dear Sirs,

"Herewith please receive invoice of goods sent by Great Northern Railway.[32] Same are to be delivered at Carfax, near Purfleet,[33] immediately on receipt at goods station King's Cross.[34] The house is at present empty, but enclosed please find keys, all of which are labelled.

"You will please deposit the boxes, fifty in number, which form the consignment, in the partially ruined building forming part of the house and marked 'A' on rough diagram enclosed. Your agent will easily recognise the locality, as it is the ancient chapel of the mansion. The goods leave by the train at 9:30 to-night, and will be due at King's Cross at 4:30 to-morrow afternoon. As our client wishes the delivery made as soon as possible, we shall be obliged by your having teams ready at King's Cross at the time named and forthwith conveying the goods to destination. In order to obviate any delays possible through any routine requirements as to payment in your departments, we enclose cheque herewith for ten pounds (£10), receipt of which please acknowledge. Should the charge be less than this amount, you can return balance; if greater, we shall at once send cheque for difference on hearing from you. You are to leave the keys on coming away in the main hall of the house, where the proprietor may get them on his entering the house by means of his duplicate key.

"Pray do not take us as exceeding the bounds of business courtesy in pressing you in all ways to use the utmost expedition.

"We are, dear Sirs,
"Faithfully yours,
"Samuel F. Billington & Son."

LETTER FROM MESSRS. CARTER, PATERSON & CO., LONDON, TO MESSRS. SAMUEL F. BILLINGTON & SON, WHITBY.

"*21 August.*

"Dear Sirs,

"We beg to acknowledge £10 received and to return cheque £1 17s. 9d., amount of overplus, as shown in receipted account herewith. Goods are delivered in exact accordance with instructions, and keys left in parcel in main hall, as directed.

"We are, dear Sirs,
"Yours respectfully,
"Pro Carter, Paterson & Co."

MINA MURRAY'S JOURNAL.

18 August.—I am happy to-day, and write sitting on the seat in the churchyard. Lucy is ever so much better. Last night she slept well all night, and did not disturb me once. The roses seem coming back already to her cheeks, though she is still sadly pale and wan-looking. If she were in any way anemic I could understand it, but she is not. She is in gay spirits and full of life and cheerfulness. All the morbid reticence seems to have passed from her, and she has just reminded me, as if I needed any reminding, of *that* night, and that it was here, on this very seat, I found her asleep. As she told me she tapped playfully with the heel of her boot on the stone slab and said:—

"My poor little feet didn't make much noise then! I daresay

King's Cross station.

built by the GNR, the North British Railway, and the North Eastern Railway. The express was operated jointly by the three companies, the 390-mile trip in 1862 taking ten and a half hours, inclusive of a half-hour lunch layover at York. The year 1888 brought a reduction in running time (eight and a half hours) and the near-scandalous admission of third-class travellers. Handsomely designed dining cars (as well as toilets, heat, and interior lights) were added to the Flying Scotsman in 1900, reducing the York stop to a mere fifteen minutes. In 1923, when rails across Britain underwent major consolidations, the line became part of the London & North Eastern Railway.

33 Inserted in Stoker's hand in the Manuscript, as is the name of Billington and the number of boxes.

34 King's Cross station was the first terminus of the Great Northern Railway (GNR) in London. When the permanent terminus was built in 1852, it was the largest station in Britain. Built on the 10-acre site formerly occupied by the Small Pox and Fever Hospitals, it was much admired—so much so that the GNR shareholders complained of extravagance. In 1854, the railway opened the nearby Great Northern Hotel, which continues in use (now a Best Western) and claims to be the oldest purpose-built hotel remaining in London.

35 George Canon, that is, the suicide buried here.

36 The name is inserted twice in Stoker's handwriting in the Manuscript. Was Stoker still using Hawkins's real name? Again, this suggests that the Manuscript is a quiltwork of pieces from different times, some predating a final decision on the alias given to the real "Peter Hawkins."

poor old Mr. Swales would have told me that it was because I didn't want to wake up Geordie."[35] As she was in such a communicative humour, I asked her if she had dreamed at all that night. Before she answered, that sweet, puckered look came into her forehead, which Arthur—I call him Arthur from her habit—says he loves; and, indeed, I don't wonder that he does. Then she went on in a half-dreaming kind of way, as if trying to recall it to herself:—

"I didn't quite dream; but it all seemed to be real. I only wanted to be here in this spot—I don't know why, for I was afraid of something—I don't know what. I remember, though I suppose I was asleep, passing through the streets and over the bridge. A fish leaped as I went by, and I leaned over to look at it, and I heard a lot of dogs howling—the whole town seemed as if it must be full of dogs all howling at once—as I went up the steps. Then I had a vague memory of something long and dark with red eyes, just as we saw in the sunset, and something very sweet and very bitter all around me at once; and then I seemed sinking into deep green water, and there was a singing in my ears, as I have heard there is to drowning men; and then everything seemed passing away from me; my soul seemed to go out from my body and float about the air. I seem to remember that once the West Lighthouse was right under me, and then there was a sort of agonising feeling, as if I were in an earthquake, and I came back and found you shaking my body. I saw you do it before I felt you."

Then she began to laugh. It seemed a little uncanny to me, and I listened to her breathlessly. I did not quite like it, and thought it better not to keep her mind on the subject, so we drifted on to other subjects, and Lucy was like her old self again. When we got home the fresh breeze had braced her up, and her pale cheeks were really more rosy. Her mother rejoiced when she saw her, and we all spent a very happy evening together.

19 August.—Joy, joy, joy! although not all joy. At last, news of Jonathan. The dear fellow has been ill; that is why he did not write. I am not afraid to think it or say it, now that I know. Mr. Hawkins[36] sent me on the letter, and wrote himself, oh, so kindly. I am to leave in the morning and go over to Jonathan, and to help to nurse him if necessary, and to bring him home. Mr. Hawkins says it would not be a bad thing if we were to be married out there. I have cried over the good Sister's letter till I can feel it wet against my bosom, where it lies. It is of Jonathan, and must be next my heart, for he is *in* my heart. My journey is all mapped out, and my luggage ready. I am only taking one change of dress; Lucy will bring my trunk to London and keep it till I send for it, for it may be that . . . I must write no more; I must keep it to say to Jonathan, my husband. The letter that he has seen and touched must comfort me till we meet.

LETTER FROM SISTER AGATHA, HOSPITAL OF ST. JOSEPH AND STE. MARY, BUDA-PESTH, TO MISS WILHELMINA MURRAY.

"12 August.[37]

"Dear Madam,

"I write by desire of Mr. Jonathan Harker, who is himself not strong enough to write, though progressing well, thanks to God and St. Joseph and Ste. Mary. He has been under our care for nearly six weeks,[38] suffering from a violent brain fever. He wishes me to convey his love, and to say that by this post I write for him to Mr. Peter Hawkins, Exeter, to say, with his dutiful respects, that he is sorry for his delay, and that all of his work is completed. He will require some few weeks' rest in our sanatorium in the hills, but will then return. He wishes me to say that he has not sufficient money with him,[39] and that he would like to pay for his staying here, so that others who need shall not be wanting for help.

"Believe me,

"Yours, with sympathy and all blessings,

"Sister Agatha.

"P. S.—My patient being asleep, I open this to let you know something more. He has told me all about you, and that you are shortly to be his wife. All blessings to you both! He has had some fearful shock—so says our doctor—and in

37 The Notes indicate that the letter was received in Exeter on 15 August, but the relevant note is deleted in Stoker's hand and so may be incorrect.

38 This confirms that Harker departed from Castle Dracula on or about 30 June. The Notes indicate that his hospital confinement began on 4 July.

39 Leatherdale (*Dracula Unearthed*) wonders what happened to the gold taken by Harker from Dracula's castle.

40 Wolf (*The Essential Dracula*) puzzles over the mention of poison, which has no apparent reference to any events at Castle Dracula. Professor Kathryn Marocchino, however, in her essay "Structural Complexity in Bram Stoker's *Dracula*," suggests that this is a reference to the effect of the vampire's bite. Dr. Seward uses much the same metaphor in his journal entry of 5 October (see text accompanying chapter 24, note 29).

41 Seward's "dog" simile is apt; see chapter 7, note 64, and note 50 below.

his delirium his ravings have been dreadful; of wolves and poison[40] and blood; of ghosts and demons; and I fear to say of what. Be careful with him always that there may be nothing to excite him of this kind for a long time to come; the traces of such an illness as his do not lightly die away. We should have written long ago, but we knew nothing of his friends, and there was on him nothing that any one could understand. He came in the train from Klausenburg, and the guard was told by the Station-master there that he rushed into the station shouting for a ticket for home. Seeing from his violent demeanour that he was English, they gave him a ticket for the furthest station on the way thither that the train reached.

"Be assured that he is well cared for. He has won all hearts by his sweetness and gentleness. He is truly getting on well, and I have no doubt will in a few weeks be all himself. But be careful of him for safety's sake. There are, I pray God and St. Joseph and Ste. Mary, many, many, happy years for you both."

DR. SEWARD'S DIARY.

19 August.—Strange and sudden change in Renfield last night. About eight o'clock he began to get excited and sniff about as a dog does when setting.[41] The attendant was struck by his manner, and knowing my interest in him, encouraged him to talk. He is usually respectful to the attendant and at times servile; but to-night, the man tells me, he was quite haughty. Would not condescend to talk with him at all. All he would say was:—

"I don't want to talk to you; you don't count now; the Master is at hand."

The attendant thinks it is some sudden form of religious mania which has seized him. If so, we must look out for squalls, for a strong man with homicidal and religious mania at once might be dangerous. The combination is a dreadful one. At nine o'clock I visited him myself. His attitude to me was the same as that to the attendant; in his sublime self-feeling the difference between myself and the attendant seemed to him as nothing. It looks like religious mania, and he will soon think that he himself is God. These infinitesimal distinctions between man and man are too paltry for an Omnipotent Being. How these madmen give themselves away! The real God taketh heed lest a sparrow fall; but the God created from human vanity sees no difference between an eagle and a sparrow.[42] Oh, if men only knew!

For half an hour or more Renfield kept getting excited in greater and greater degree. I did not pretend to be watching him, but I kept strict observation all the same. All at once that shifty look came into his eyes which we always see when a madman has seized an idea, and with it the shifty movement of the head and back which asylum attendants come to know so well. He became quite quiet, and went and sat on the edge of his bed resignedly, and looked into space with lack-lustre eyes. I thought I would find out if his apathy were real or only assumed, and tried to lead him to talk of his pets, a theme which had never failed to excite his attention. At first he made no reply, but at length said testily:—

"Bother them all! I don't care a pin about them."

"What?" I said. "You don't mean to tell me you don't care about spiders?" (Spiders at present are his hobby and the notebook is filling up with columns of small figures.) To this he answered enigmatically:[43]—

"The bride-maidens rejoice the eyes that wait the coming of the bride; but when the bride draweth nigh, then the maidens shine not to the eyes that are filled."

He would not explain himself, but remained obstinately seated on his bed all the time I remained with him.

I am weary to-night and low in spirits. I cannot but think of Lucy, and how different things might have been.[44] If I don't sleep at once, chloral, the modern Morpheus—$CH_2Cl_3O \cdot H_2O$![45] I must be careful not to let it grow into a habit. No, I shall take none to-night! I have thought of Lucy, and I shall not dishonour her by mixing the two. If need be, to-night shall be sleepless. . . .[46]

Glad I made the resolution; gladder that I kept to it. I had lain tossing about, and had heard the clock strike only twice, when the night-watchman came to me, sent up from the ward, to say that Renfield had escaped. I threw on my clothes and

42 Seward here demonstrates his class consciousness, for surely he is the eagle and the attendant a mere sparrow.

43 "Enigmatically" is right. Although what follows sounds vaguely biblical, no source can be traced. In simple English, Renfield says: The bridesmaids (flies, spiders, etc.) are pretty enough while you're waiting for the bride. But when the bride shows up, one look at her makes you forget about the bridesmaids.

44 It is now three months after Seward's rejection, and he is still depressed. See chapter 6, note 61, for a discussion of Seward's obsession.

45 The oldest of the hypnotic (sleep-inducing) depressants, chloral hydrate was first synthesized in 1832. It takes effect in a relatively short time (thirty minutes) and will induce sleep in about an hour. Although historically used for insomnia and nervous patients, it has largely been replaced by other drugs. The 1899 *Merck Manual* gives the common form as loose crystals or flakes, which were to be mixed with water. Standard doses were ten to thirty grains, with a maximum recommended dose of sixty grains.

A solution of chloral hydrate and alcohol probably constituted the infamous "knockout drops," or Mickey Finn Special, a drink reputedly invented in 1896 on Chicago's State Street (known then as Whiskey Row) by its namesake, a saloon owner and former pickpocket. The phrase "slip him a Mickey," said to be derived from Finn's disreputable practise of having his "house girls" stupefy patrons with the cocktail and then go through their pockets, slipped quickly into common parlance. Other sources identify the alien components of the sinister cocktail as Glauber's salt, a sulfate (sodium sulfate decahydrate) used in the making of glass and paper, in solar energy systems, and as an equine laxative, or croton oil, a purgative. In these cases, the Mickey, rather than knocking the saloon patron out cold, would simply drive him to the water closet, straight home, or possibly even to the nearest hospital.

46 The paragraph does not appear in the Abridged Text.

47 The Manuscript reads, "fly-man, as I always think of him—," replaced in the published text with "patient." References to "fly-man" or "the flyman" or even "the Flyman" are found throughout the Manuscript, intermixed with the name "Renfield." This derogatory name, given to a patient with the education and gentlemanly qualities of Renfield, can only reflect poorly on its giver and is a further suggestion that the real "John Seward" was no doctor (or at least quite young and inexperienced).

48 Wolf (*The Essential Dracula*) notes that the fifty-nine-year-old Renfield readily scales the wall, whereas Seward, age twenty-nine, requires a ladder.

49 Now Renfield is a "naked lunatic"; apparently, he threw off the night gear in which he was clothed only a few moments earlier.

50 There is no evidence that there has been any verbal or written communication between Renfield and Dracula. Either Dracula has deliberately communicated telepathically with Renfield (perhaps in the same manner as with the wolves at Castle Dracula) or Renfield's madness has produced in him a telepathic sensitivity to the vampiric life force of Dracula (perhaps through his massive ingestion of lives). Certainly at this point, Dracula has no plans for Renfield (Dracula cannot possibly know of the connection between Lucy and Seward), and there seems to be little reason why Dracula would have intentionally communicated with Renfield. Therefore, this again seems to be confirmation that Dracula in some way transmits his presence to those sensitive enough to detect it. We have seen that Lucy exhibits signs of sensing his approach to Whitby while he is still onboard the *Demeter* (see chapter 6, note 72). Dogs appear to sense Dracula's presence as well (see text accompanying chapter 7, note 64).

ran down at once; my[47] patient is too dangerous a person to be roaming about. Those ideas of his might work out dangerously with strangers. The attendant was waiting for me. He said he had seen him not ten minutes before, seemingly asleep in his bed, when he had looked through the observation-trap in the door. His attention was called by the sound of the window being wrenched out. He ran back and saw his feet disappear through the window, and had at once sent up for me. He was only in his night-gear, and cannot be far off. The attendant thought it would be more useful to watch where he should go than to follow him, as he might lose sight of him whilst getting out of the building by the door. He is a bulky man, and couldn't get through the window. I am thin, so, with his aid, I got out, but feet foremost, and, as we were only a few feet above ground, landed unhurt. The attendant told me the patient had gone to the left, and had taken a straight line, so I ran as quickly as I could. As I got through the belt of trees I saw a white figure scale the high wall which separates our grounds from those of the deserted house.

I ran back at once, told the watchman to get three or four men immediately and follow me into the grounds of Carfax, in case our friend might be dangerous. I got a ladder myself, and crossing the wall, dropped down on the other side.[48] I could see Renfield's figure just disappearing behind the angle of the house, so I ran after him. On the far side of the house I found him pressed close against the old iron-bound oak door of the chapel. He was talking, apparently to some one, but I was afraid to go near enough to hear what he was saying, lest I might frighten him, and he should run off. Chasing an errant swarm of bees is nothing to following a naked lunatic,[49] when the fit of escaping is upon him! After a few minutes, however, I could see that he did not take note of anything around him, and so ventured to draw nearer to him—the more so as my men had now crossed the wall and were closing him in. I heard him say:—

"I am here to do Your bidding, Master. I am Your slave, and You will reward me, for I shall be faithful. I have worshipped You long and afar off.[50] Now that You are near, I await Your commands, and You will not pass me by, will You, dear Master, in Your distribution of good things?"

He is a selfish old beggar anyhow. He thinks of the loaves and fishes even when he believes he is in a Real Presence.[51] His manias make a startling combination. When we closed in on him he fought like a tiger. He is immensely strong, for he was more like a wild beast than a man. I never saw a lunatic in such a paroxysm of rage before; and I hope I shall not again. It is a mercy that we have found out his strength and his danger in good time. With strength and determination like this, he might have done wild work before he was caged. He is safe now at any rate. Jack Sheppard[52] himself couldn't get free from the strait-waistcoat that keeps him restrained, and he's chained to the wall in the padded room.[53] His cries are at times awful, but the silences that follow are more deadly still, for he means murder in every turn and movement.

Just now he spoke coherent words for the first time:—

"I shall be patient, Master. It is coming—coming—coming!"

So I took the hint, and came too.[54] I was too excited to sleep, but this diary has quieted me, and I feel I shall get some sleep to-night.

There is no folkloric reference to the "aura" that at least this master vampire seems to project. Note that Dracula is still in the Bay of Biscay when Renfield's restlessness commences.

51 The miracle of the loaves and fishes is the only miracle (apart from the resurrection of Jesus) common to all of the four Gospels. Seward's point here is that, like the multitudes in the Bible, Renfield is focussed on the bounty of the miracle rather than the miracle maker.

52 Described in Rayner and Crook's *The Complete Newgate Calendar* as "A Daring Housebreaker, who made Ingenious Escapes from Prison and even tried to foil his Executioner at Tyburn on 16th of November, 1724," Sheppard was as proverbial in Victorian England for his escapes as Houdini was in twentieth-century America.

53 Restraint was the primary therapeutic tool of the early-nineteenth-century asylum. By the middle of the century, however, English pioneers—Edward Parker Charlesworth and Robert Gardiner Hill at the Lawn, in

Mentally ill patient restrained.
Undated wood engraving, photographed 1908

Lincoln (known as the Lincoln Asylum) and John Conolly and William Charles Ellis at the Middlesex County Lunatic Asylum at Hanwell, London—had introduced the "nonrestraint system," abolishing the policy of restraining agitated patients and replacing restraint with moral therapy and a busy regimen of crafts. Hill explained the change: "What is the substitute for coercion? The answer may be summed up in a few words, viz,—classification—vigilant and unceasing attendance by day and by night—kindness, occupation, and attention to health, cleanliness, and comfort, and the total absence of every description of other occupation of the attendant. This treatment in a properly constructed and suitable building, with a sufficient number of strong and active attendants always at their post, is best calculated to restore the patient; and all instruments of coercion and torture are rendered absolutely and in every case unnecessary" (quoted in Roy Porter, *Madness*).

54 Students have puzzled over the meaning of this queer phrase, but it likely means nothing more than that, like Renfield, Seward is waiting for developments.

Buffy the Vampire Slayer, starring Kristy Swanson as Buffy Summers. (Twentieth Century-Fox Film Corporation, 1992)

Chapter 9

LETTER FROM MINA HARKER TO LUCY WESTENRA.

"Buda-Pesth, 24 August.[1]

"My dearest Lucy,—

"I know you will be anxious to hear all that has happened since we parted at the railway station at Whitby. Well, my dear, I got to Hull[2] all right, and caught the boat to Hamburg,[3] and then the train on here.[4] I feel that I can hardly recall anything of the journey, except that I knew I was coming to Jonathan, and, that as I should have to do some nursing, I had better get all the sleep I could. . . . I found my dear one, oh, so thin and pale and weak-looking. All the resolution has gone out of his dear eyes, and that quiet dignity which I told you was in his face has vanished. He is only a wreck of himself, and he does not remember anything that has happened to him for a long time past. At least, he wants me to believe so, and I shall never ask. He has had some terrible shock, and I fear it might tax his poor brain if he were to try to recall it. Sister Agatha, who is a good creature and a born nurse, tells me that he raved of dreadful things whilst he was off his head. I wanted her to tell me what they were; but she would only cross herself, and say she would never tell; that the ravings of the sick were the secrets of God, and that if a nurse through her vocation should hear them, she should respect her trust. She is a sweet, good soul, and the next day, when she saw I was troubled, she opened up the subject again,

1 Probably written on 22 August—see note 15 below.

2 Also known as Kingston-on-Hull, this major seaport is about 60 miles from Whitby, at the great inlet of the Humber and the conflux of the river Hull. Mina would likely have travelled here by the North Eastern Railway, a journey of about two and a half hours, changing trains in Scarborough.

3 A distance of 370 miles. Hamburg was then a flourishing port on the "German Ocean," with connections to all of Europe. From Hamburg, Mina would have likely taken the train to Berlin, through Frankfort, and on to Buda-Pesth, a taxing journey. The direct route from London to Buda-Pesth would have been to Paris via Calais or Boulogne and on by the Orient Express, a thirty-seven-hour trip, or on the Ostend-Vienna Express, through Vienna, a thirty-six-hour trip, either way a less arduous journey than the route Mina took.

4 Mina's route does not appear in the Abridged Text.

5 Not appearing in the Abridged Text are Mina's comments about jealousy, including her ingenuous consolation—soon disproved—about "no other woman" being a cause for trouble.

6 Harker's "coat" and "things" are evidently items that he stole after he fled Castle Dracula, for Dracula took all of Harker's possessions.

7 Harker gives up this principle quite soon.

8 "Brain fever" was a popular plot element in fiction. In the sixty tales of Sherlock Holmes, for example, seven cases of brain fever are recorded. Alvin E. Rodin and Jack D. Key write, in *Medical Casebook of Dr. Arthur Conan Doyle*, "we can characterize [the disease] . . . as one which follows quickly on a severe emotional shock, which exhibits weight loss, weakness, pallor, and high fever, and which has a protracted course. Most patients recover, but insanity or death is possible." Although the details of the affliction are vague, it is well reported by many nineteenth-century writers, including, for example, Emily Brontë (Catherine Linton in *Wuthering Heights*), Gustave Flaubert (Emma Bovary in *Madame Bovary*), and George Meredith (Lucy Feverel in *The Ordeal of Richard Feverel*). Such preponderance of brain fever in the literature of the day would seem to validate it as a medical diagnosis; Rodin and Key further cite an 1892 medical textbook that lists "fever" as a manifestation of an hysterical reaction, as well as a modern dictionary that equates brain fever with meningitis.

and after saying that she could never mention what my poor dear raved about, added: 'I can tell you this much, my dear: that it was not about anything which he has done wrong himself; and you, as his wife to be, have no cause to be concerned. He has not forgotten you or what he owes to you. His fear was of great and terrible things, which no mortal can treat of.' I do believe the dear soul thought I might be jealous lest my poor dear should have fallen in love with any other girl. The idea of *my* being jealous about Jonathan! And yet, my dear, let me whisper, I felt a thrill of joy through me when I *knew* that no other woman was a cause of trouble.[5] I am now sitting by his bedside, where I can see his face while he sleeps. He is waking! . . .When he woke he asked me for his coat, as he wanted to get something from the pocket; I asked Sister Agatha, and she brought all his things.[6] I saw amongst them was his note-book, and was going to ask him to let me look at it—for I knew then that I might find some clue to his trouble—but I suppose he must have seen my wish in my eyes, for he sent me over to the window, saying he wanted to be quite alone for a moment. Then he called me back, and when I came he had his hand over the note-book, and he said to me very solemnly:—

"'Wilhelmina'—I knew then that he was in deadly earnest, for he has never called me by that name since he asked me to marry him—'you know, dear, my ideas of the trust between husband and wife: there should be no secret, no concealment.[7] I have had a great shock, and when I try to think of what it is I feel my head spin round, and I do not know if it was all real or the dreaming of a madman. You know I have had brain fever,[8] and that is to be mad. The secret is here, and I do not want to know it. I want to take up my life here, with our marriage.' For, my dear, we had decided to be married as soon as the formalities are complete. 'Are you willing, Wilhelmina, to share my ignorance? Here is the book. Take it and keep it, read it if you will, but never let me know; unless, indeed, some solemn duty should come upon me to go back to the bitter hours, asleep or awake, sane or mad, recorded here.' He fell back exhausted, and I put the book under his pillow, and kissed him. I had asked Sister Agatha to beg the Superior to let our wedding be this afternoon, and I am waiting her reply. . . .

"She has come and told me that the chaplain of the English mission church has been sent for.[9] We are to be married[10] in an hour, or as soon after as Jonathan awakes. . . .

"Lucy, the time has come and gone. I feel very solemn, but very, very happy. Jonathan woke a little after the hour, and all was ready, and he sat up in bed, propped up with pillows. He answered his 'I will' firmly and strongly. I could hardly speak; my heart was so full that even those words seemed to choke me. The dear Sisters were so kind. Please God, I shall never, never forget them, nor the grave and sweet responsibilities I have taken upon me.[11] I must tell you of my wedding present. When the chaplain and the Sisters had left me alone with my husband—oh, Lucy, it is the first time I have written the words 'my husband'[12]—left me alone with my husband, I took the book from under his pillow, and wrapped it up in white paper, and tied it with a little bit of pale blue ribbon which was round my neck, and sealed it over the knot with sealing-wax, and for my seal I used my wedding ring. Then I kissed it and showed it to my husband, and told him that I would keep it so, and then it would be an outward and visible sign for us all our lives that we trusted each other; that I would never open it unless it were for his own dear sake or for the sake of some stern duty. Then he took my hand in his, and oh, Lucy, it was the first time he took *his wife's* hand, and said that it was the dearest thing in all the wide world, and that he would go through all the past again to win it, if need be. The poor dear meant to have said a part of the past, but he cannot think of time yet, and I shall not wonder if at first he mixes up not only the month, but the year.[13]

"Well, my dear, what could I say? I could only tell him

9 Parishes in Europe were not referred to in the late nineteenth century as "missions" but rather chaplaincies. Typically, the head of the chaplaincy was the chaplain to the British embassy or legation, and any church building was an embassy church. There was a Presbyterian Scottish mission in Buda-Pesth at the time, but Mina no doubt means the chaplain of the legation (Buda-Pesth had no British embassy until 1963).

10 Wolf (*The Essential Dracula*) points out that it is unclear whether this is an Anglican or Catholic sacrament.

Curiously, the Notes indicate that Jonathan and Mina are married in London, after his return, and that Lucy attends the wedding. Perhaps Stoker believed that recounting a London wedding might lead to an easier identification of the real identities of the Harkers.

11 This and the preceding sentence do not appear in the Abridged Text.

12 Mina evidently means the first time she has written those words to Lucy, for she wrote them previously in her journal entry of 19 August.

13 It is not only Jonathan Harker who manages to mix up the month and year; see appendix 2, "The Dating of *Dracula*." The sentence does not appear in the Abridged Text.

14 Little is known of the history of the relationship between Lucy and Mina. There are intimations that they have been friends for a long time, and this line, among others, seems to confirm that Mina is older than Lucy. They are evidently from different social classes: Mina works and Lucy does not. In light of Mina's remarks about the "New Woman," it does not appear that her employment is a matter of defiance or social philosophy. Stoker suppressed references to the connection with their mutual friend Kate Reed (see chapter 5, note 17).

15 This date is plainly erroneous, for the communication from Lucy dated 24 August indicates that she has returned to Hillingham, the family home in London, and on 31 August Arthur Holmwood notes that she "looks awful, and is getting worse every day." Wolf (*The Essential Dracula*) believes that Lucy may simply be politely disguising her own problems. The placement of the letter in the papers, before Lucy's diary entry of 24 August, also suggests that the date has been miscopied. Wolf proposes correcting the date to 20 August. A more likely date is 23 August. Mina departed for Buda-Pesth on 20 August and could not have arrived there before 22 August—barely time for her letter to Lucy to arrive in London. However, Lucy's letter cannot have been written on 23 August from Whitby, for she arrived home at Hillingham that day, in time to have nightmares. Admittedly the dates are problematic.

16 Cormorants are web-footed birds, in the same order as pelicans and frigatebirds. Noted as big eaters, they dine exclusively on fish and in China are trained for fishing.

that I was the happiest woman in all the wide world, and that I had nothing to give him except myself, my life, and my trust, and that with these went my love and duty for all the days of my life. And, my dear, when he kissed me, and drew me to him with his poor weak hands, it was like a very solemn pledge between us. . . .

"Lucy dear, do you know why I tell you all this? It is not only because it is all sweet to me, but because you have been, and are, very dear to me. It was my privilege to be your friend and guide when you came from the schoolroom to prepare for the world of life.[14] I want you to see now, and with the eyes of a very happy wife, whither duty has led me; so that in your own married life you too may be all happy as I am. My dear, please Almighty God, your life may be all it promises: a long day of sunshine, with no harsh wind, no forgetting duty, no distrust. I must not wish you no pain, for that can never be; but I do hope you will be *always* as happy as I am *now*. Good-bye, my dear. I shall post this at once, and, perhaps, write you very soon again. I must stop, for Jonathan is waking—I must attend to my husband!

> "Your ever-loving
> "Mina Harker."

LETTER FROM LUCY WESTENRA TO MINA HARKER.

"Whitby, 30 August.[15]

"My dearest Mina,—

"Oceans of love and millions of kisses, and may you soon be in your own home with your husband. I wish you could be coming home soon enough to stay with us here. The strong air would soon restore Jonathan; it has quite restored me. I have an appetite like a cormorant,[16] am full of life, and sleep well. You will be glad to know that I have quite given up walking in my sleep. I think I have not stirred out of my bed for a week, that is when I once got into it at night. Arthur says I am getting fat. By the way, I forgot to tell you that Arthur is here. We have such walks and drives, and rides, and rowing,[17] and tennis,[18] and fishing together; and I love him more than ever. He *tells me* that he loves me more, but I doubt that, for at first he told me that he couldn't love me more than he did then. But this is nonsense. There he is, calling to me. So no more just at present from your loving

"Lucy.

"P. S.—Mother sends her love. She seems better, poor dear.

"P. P. S.—We are to be married on 28 September."[19]

DR. SEWARD'S DIARY.

20 August.—The case of Renfield grows even more interesting. He has now so far quieted that there are spells of cessation from his passion. For the first week after his attack he was perpetually violent.[20] Then one night, just as the moon rose, he grew quiet, and kept murmuring to himself: "Now I can wait; now I can wait." The attendant came to tell me, so I ran down at once to have a look at him. He was still in the strait-waistcoat[21] and in the padded room, but the suffused look had gone from his face, and his eyes had something of their old pleading—I might almost say, "cringing"—softness. I was satisfied with his present condition, and directed him to be relieved. The attendants hesitated, but finally carried out my wishes without protest. It was a strange thing that the patient had humour enough to see their distrust, for, coming close to me, he said in a whisper, all the while looking furtively at them:—

"They think I could hurt you! Fancy *me* hurting *you*! The fools!"

It was soothing, somehow, to the feelings to find myself disassociated even in the mind of this poor madman from the others; but all the same I do not follow his thought. Am I to take it that I have anything in common with him, so that we are, as it were, to stand together; or has he to gain from me some good so stupendous that my well-being is needful to him? I must find out later on.[22] To-night he will not speak. Even the

17 *Horne's Guide to Whitby* (1891) advises: "One of the most popular plans is to hire a pleasure boat from one of the proprietors at the pier side or near the bridge steps, and row up the river to Cockmill Creek, which is a lovely spot about a mile up the river. Care must be taken that there be plenty of water in the river. The best plan is to row up with the tide, that is, as the tide flows. Then, after a short time on land, in which refreshment may be indulged in at Glen Esk, the rowers may then re-embark and glide down the river with the ebbing tide."

18 Court tennis developed before the twelfth century. However, lawn tennis, the outdoor game (and the word "tennis" without "lawn" was an American usage), to which Lucy evidently refers, was developed at a Welsh country estate in 1874, many historians of the sport maintain, by retired cavalry officer Major Walter C. Wingfield, who gave it the unlikely Greek name of "Sphairistikè" and briefly had a stranglehold on its licensing and marketing. Wingfield's claim of proprietorship of the concept is not, however, undisputed: it is said that a Major Harry Gem and Augurio Perera, a Spaniard, played a similar game fifteen years earlier in Birmingham, borrowing from a Basque sport called *pelota*. Women's singles were introduced as an event at the All England Lawn Tennis and Croquet Club, better known as Wimbledon, in 1884 (with an earlier women's championship having been held in 1879 at Oxford and Dublin), and the sport was immensely popular by the end of the nineteenth century. Whitby had ample facilities. In *Horne's Guide to Whitby* (1891), the author writes that "devotees of [lawn tennis] are well provided for on the West Cliff. In addition to the Lawn Tennis Ground attached to the Saloon, there is a commodious and well laid area near the lodging houses. This plot is well looked after, and will be found to be equal, if not superior, to that of any of our rival watering-places."

19 A Thursday in 1893, a Tuesday in 1886.

20 Seward is in error in his reckoning (or Mina Harker in her transcription); this entry is dated only one day following Renfield's attack.

21 Spelled "straight waistcoat" in the Abridged Text.

22 The preceding egotistic sentences do not appear in the Abridged Text.
23 Did Seward seriously intend this offer?

24 Seward is being somewhat dense here. On Renfield's previous escape, he made a beeline for Carfax. Having made no apparent effort to investigate Carfax, Seward still wonders where Renfield will go.

25 The quotation is usually attributed to the playwright Titus Maccius Plautus (254–184 BC), although what Plautus wrote was "Things which you do not hope happen more frequently than things which you do hope" (*Mostellaria*, act 1, scene 3). Benjamin Disraeli (1804–1881), twice prime minister of England, perhaps cribbing from Plautus, wrote in *Henrietta Temple: A Love Story* (1837), "What we anticipate seldom occurs; what we least expected generally happens." Many refer to this now-common proverb (which has reached bumper-sticker status as "SH*T HAPPENS") as "Thatcher's principle," because former prime minister Margaret Thatcher (1925–) was fond of using it.

The aphorism has been cut in the Abridged Text.

26 This and the preceding three sentences do not appear in the Abridged Text. As noted, Seward is very slow to note the periodicity of Renfield's behaviour, and Stoker kindly minimises this obtuseness.

27 The Manuscript reads, "I took my pistol and sent words for the keepers to take their nets and follow." Stoker seems to have realised that no physician would have sought to retrieve an escaped patient under these circumstances and omits this sentence from the published narrative.

offer of a kitten or even a full-grown cat will not tempt him.[23] He will only say: "I don't take any stock in cats. I have more to think of now, and I can wait; I can wait."

After a while I left him. The attendant tells me that he was quiet until just before dawn, and that then he began to get uneasy, and at length violent, until at last he fell into a paroxysm which exhausted him so that he swooned into a sort of coma.

. . . Three nights has the same thing happened—violent all day then quiet from moonrise to sunrise. I wish I could get some clue to the cause. It would almost seem as if there was some influence which came and went. Happy thought! We shall to-night play sane wits against mad ones. He escaped before without our help; to-night he shall escape with it. We shall give him a chance, and have the men ready to follow in case they are required. . . .[24]

23 August.—"The unexpected always happens." How well Disraeli knew life.[25] Our bird when he found the cage open would not fly, so all our subtle arrangements were for nought. At any rate, we have proved one thing; that the spells of quietness last a reasonable time. We shall in future be able to ease his bonds for a few hours each day. I have given orders to the night attendant merely to shut him in the padded room, when once he is quiet, until an hour before sunrise. The poor soul's body will enjoy the relief even if his mind cannot appreciate it.[26] Hark! The unexpected again! I am called; the patient has once more escaped.

Later.—Another night adventure. Renfield artfully waited until the attendant was entering the room to inspect. Then he dashed out past him and flew down the passage. I sent word for the attendants to follow.[27] Again he went into the grounds of the deserted house,[28] and we found him in the same place, pressed against the old chapel door. When he saw me he became furious, and had not the attendants seized him in time, he would have[29] tried to kill me. As we were holding him a strange thing happened. He suddenly redoubled his efforts, and then as suddenly grew calm. I looked round instinctively, but could see nothing. Then I caught the patient's eye and followed it, but could trace nothing as it looked into the moonlit sky except a big bat, which was flapping its silent and ghostly way to the west.[30] Bats usually wheel and flit about, but this one seemed to go straight on, as if it knew where it was bound for or had some intention of its own. The patient grew calmer every instant, and presently said:—

"You needn't tie me; I shall go quietly!" Without trouble we came back to the house. I feel there is something ominous in his calm, and shall not forget this night. . . .

LUCY WESTENRA'S DIARY.

Hillingham,[31] *24 August.*—I must imitate Mina, and keep writing things down. Then we can have long talks when we do meet. I wonder when it will be. I wish she were with me again, for I feel so unhappy.[32] Last night I seemed to be dreaming again just as I was at Whitby. Perhaps it is the change of air, or getting home again. It is all dark and horrid to me, for I can remember nothing; but I am full of vague fear, and I feel so weak and worn out. When Arthur came to lunch he looked quite grieved when he saw me, and I hadn't the spirit to try to be cheerful. I wonder if I could sleep in mother's room to-night. I shall make an excuse and try.[33]

25 August.—Another bad night. Mother did not seem to take to my proposal. She seems not too well herself, and doubtless she fears to worry me. I tried to keep awake, and succeeded for a while; but when the clock struck twelve it waked me from a doze, so I must have been falling asleep. There was a sort of scratching or flapping at the window, but I did not mind it, and as I remember no more, I suppose I must then have fallen asleep. More bad dreams. I wish I could remember them. This morning I am horribly weak. My face is ghastly pale, and my throat pains me. It must be something wrong with my lungs, for I don't seem ever to get air enough.[34] I shall try to cheer up when Arthur comes, or else I know he will be miserable to see me so.

Renfield has as yet demonstrated no tendencies of violence against humans, and notwithstanding Seward's earlier diagnosis that Renfield was a latent homicidal maniac, no physician would be likely to shoot a patient (especially a private patient), even in self-defence. Therefore, leaving in a reference to this unprofessional conduct would surely reveal that Seward was no doctor.

28 Of course by 23 August the house was no longer "deserted"; Carter, Paterson & Co. had made its delivery.

29 The Manuscript reads, "killed me or I should have had to shoot him in self-defence." See note 27 above.

30 That is, in the direction of London and Hillingham.

31 The reference to Hillingham does not appear in the Manuscript, which names no place for this entry. The exact location of the Westenra home is not given. As will be seen, however, it appears to be in Hampstead, a residential borough (now part of Camden) popular with the artistic and literary crowd. Hampstead was the home of George Du Maurier, John Keats, Karl Marx, and briefly, D. H. Lawrence and Frieda von Richthofen, among others. Hampstead's Highgate Cemetery contains the graves of several luminaries, including Marx, George

Hampstead Heath from the flagstaff, looking west.
Queen's London (1897)

Eliot, Michael Faraday, Elizabeth Siddall (the wife of Dante Gabriel Rossetti), Christina Rossetti, and Herbert Spencer.

Hampstead Heath, arguably London's most beautiful open space, with its three famous outdoor bathing ponds (Ladies, Men's, and Mixed—open year-round for those who enjoy frigid as well as temperate water) is of course also situated there. Dickens's *Dictionary of London* (1888) describes it as "a stretch of real country within easy walk of the heart of London, the only spot within reach as yet unspoiled by improvement." The heath was enjoyed by throngs of people, especially on summer weekends, and its plentiful pony- and donkey-rides were popular with young children and their parents as well as swains and their maids.

32 Lucy's longing for Mina does not appear in the Abridged Text.

33 The Manuscript adds in Stoker's hand, "Her room is higher up and as mine looks out on the verandah I seem to hear every sound that goes on round the house!" This is the only evidence that Hillingham is three stories high. Stoker may have decided that it might lead to identification of the house, and the sentence is omitted from the published text.

Leatherdale (*Dracula Unearthed*) notes a marked change in Lucy's attitude. In Whitby, she made every effort to go to Dracula; here, back in London, she is afraid to be alone. Apparently she has come to her senses about the impropriety of her Whitby "romance."

34 Based on Lucy's symptoms, we must believe that she has this night (if not the previous night) suffered an attack by Dracula. We must also deduce that the attack took place in her bedroom; there is no mention of sleepwalking outside the house. How did Dracula enter? If Van Helsing's "rules" of vampirism (expressed in the text accompanying chapter 18, note 36) are correct, the vampire can only enter when invited by a member of the household. Lucy

LETTER, ARTHUR HOLMWOOD TO DR. SEWARD.

"Albemarle Hotel,[35] 31 August.

"My dear Jack,—

"I want you to do me a favour. Lucy is ill; that is, she has no special disease, but she looks awful, and is getting worse every day. I have asked her if there is any cause; I do not dare to ask her mother, for to disturb the poor lady's mind about her daughter in her present state of health would be fatal. Mrs. Westenra has confided to me that her doom is spoken—disease of the heart—though poor Lucy does not know it yet.[36] I am sure that there is something preying on my dear girl's mind. I am almost distracted when I think of her; to look at her gives me a pang. I told her I should ask you to see her, and though she demurred at first—I know why, old fellow—she finally consented. It will be a painful task for you, I know, old friend, but it is for *her* sake, and I must not hesitate to ask, or you to act. You are to come to lunch at Hillingham[37] to-morrow, two o'clock, so as not to arouse any suspicion in Mrs. Westenra, and after lunch Lucy will take an opportunity of being alone with you. I shall come in for tea, and we can go away together; I am filled with anxiety, and want to consult with you alone as soon as I can after you have seen her. Do not fail!

"Arthur."

TELEGRAM, ARTHUR HOLMWOOD TO SEWARD.

"*1 September.*

"AM SUMMONED TO SEE MY FATHER, WHO IS WORSE. AM WRITING. WRITE ME FULLY BY TO-NIGHT'S POST TO RING. WIRE ME IF NECESSARY."

LETTER FROM DR. SEWARD TO ARTHUR HOLMWOOD.

"2 September.

"My dear old fellow,—

"With regard to Miss Westenra's health, I hasten to let you know at once that in my opinion there is not any functional disturbance or any malady that I know of. At the same time, I am not by any means satisfied with her appearance; she is woefully different from what she was when I saw her last. Of course you must bear in mind that I did not have full opportunity of examination such as I should wish;[38] our very friendship makes a little difficulty which not even medical science or custom can bridge over. I had better tell you exactly what happened, leaving you to draw, in a measure, your own conclusions. I shall then say what I have done and propose doing.

"I found Miss Westenra in seemingly gay spirits. Her mother was present, and in a few seconds I made up my mind that she was trying all she knew to mislead her mother and prevent her from being anxious. I have no doubt she guesses, if she does not know, what need of caution there is.[39] We lunched alone, and as we all exerted ourselves to be cheerful, we got, as some kind of reward for our labours, some real cheerfulness amongst us. Then Mrs. Westenra went to lie down, and Lucy was left with me. We went into her boudoir, and till we got there her gaiety remained, for the servants were coming and going. As soon as the door was closed, however, the mask fell from her face, and she sank down into a chair with a great sigh, and hid her eyes with her hand. When I saw that her high spirits had failed, I at once took advantage of her reaction to make a diagnosis. She said to me very sweetly:—

"'I cannot tell you how I loathe talking about myself.' I reminded her that a doctor's confidence was sacred, but that you were grievously anxious about her. She caught on to my meaning at once, and settled that matter in a word. 'Tell Arthur everything you choose. I do not care for myself, but all for him!' So I am quite free.

Albemarle Hotel.
Photograph by Leslie S. Klinger, February 2006

must have arisen in her hypnotic trance, opened the window, and invited Dracula in.

35 At the corner of Albemarle Street, in Piccadilly. The 1896 London "Baedeker" characterises it as "largely patronized by royalty, the diplomatic corps, and the nobility: excellent wine and cuisine." Oscar Wilde reportedly dined there frequently—perhaps once too often, for Edward Shelley testified in Wilde's libel trial about a dinner there that was a prelude to an invitation to Wilde's bedroom. Curiously, that dinner occu rred on the opening night of Wilde's play *Lady Windermere's Fan* (20 February 1892), a performance attended by Wilde's old flame Florence Balcombe, by then married to Bram Stoker. Wilde again stayed at the hotel from 1 to 17 January 1893, with frequent visits from young men; according to his biographer Richard Ellmann, "[Wilde's] behavior was sufficiently dubious for the proprietor to welcome his departure" (*Oscar Wilde*).

36 Arthur thus becomes the second person to whom Mrs. Westenra confides this secret (Mina being the first).

A gynecological exam.
Jean-Pierre Mayguier, 1822

37 Inserted in Stoker's hand into a blank in the Manuscript (as is "Ring" in the telegram below)—again, a late emendation of the names used to conceal the real locations.

38 Visual examination of a female patient was customarily avoided by a male mid-Victorian physician as inappropriate. Instead, the patient was typically examined tactilely while fully clothed. Arthur Conan Doyle wrote in an 1881 letter (to Reginald Hoare, M.D., or perhaps to his mother; in the Berg Collection, New York Public Library, Sir Arthur Conan Doyle Papers, no. 1, folio 2) of a patient he encountered in the course of his employment on the African Steam Navigation Company's *Mayumba*: "Then there is a frightful horror (Mrs. McSomething) going to Madeira for her health. . . . She won't let me examine her chest. 'Young doctors take such liberties, you know, my dear'—so I have washed my hands of her." Suspected prostitutes, however, were compelled by law to submit to an internal examination; refusal was in itself a crime under the Contagious Diseases Act.

"I could easily see that she is somewhat bloodless, but I could not see the usual anæmic signs, and by a chance I was actually able to test the quality of her blood, for in opening a window which was stiff a cord gave way, and she cut her hand slightly with broken glass. It was a slight matter in itself, but it gave me an evident chance, and I secured a few drops of the blood and have analysed them. The qualitative analysis give a quite normal condition, and shows, I should infer, in itself a vigorous state of health.[40] In other physical matters I was quite satisfied that there is no need for anxiety; but as there must be a cause somewhere, I have come to the conclusion that it must be something mental.[41] She complains of difficulty in breathing satisfactorily at times, and of heavy, lethargic sleep, with dreams that frighten her, but regarding which she can remember nothing. She says that as a child she used to walk in her sleep, and that when in Whitby the habit came back, and that once she walked out in the night and went to East Cliff, where Miss Murray found her;[42] but she assures me that of late the habit has not returned. I am in doubt, and so have done the best thing I know of; I have written to my old friend and master, Professor Van Helsing, of Amsterdam, who knows as much about obscure diseases as any one in the world. I have asked him to come over, and as you told me that all things were to be at your charge, I have mentioned to him who you are and your relations to Miss Westenra. This, my dear fellow, is in obedience to your wishes, for I am only too proud and happy to do anything I can for her.[43] Van Helsing would, I know, do anything for me for a personal reason,[44] so no matter on what ground he comes, we must accept his wishes. He is a seemingly arbitrary man, but this is because he knows what he is talking about better than any one else. He is a philosopher and a metaphysician, and one of the most advanced scientists of his day; and he has, I believe, an absolutely open mind. This, with an iron nerve, a temper of the ice-brook,[45] and indomitable resolution, self-command, and toleration exalted from virtues to blessings, and the kindliest and truest heart that beats— these form his equipment for the noble work that he is

39 This and the following sentence do not appear in the Abridged Text.

40 Wolf (*The Essential Dracula*) notes repeatedly that Lucy suffers symptoms commonly associated with anæmia and hence that a qualitative analysis could not have confirmed "vigorous" health. According to his source, Dr. Herman Schwartz, "Even qualitatively her blood would have been paler because there would be fewer and smaller red blood cells." This is so, Wolf suggests, because when blood volume is lost, the body first replenishes the plasma and other blood components; the red blood cells regenerate more slowly.

The human body contains about 5 quarts of blood and can regenerate blood naturally at the rate of about 2 quarts per week. The American College of Surgeons classes blood loss (haemorrhage) into four groups: Class I, up to 15 percent of total blood volume (typically causing no change in vital signs); Class II, 15 to 30 percent of total blood volume, usually resulting in a rapid heartbeat, narrowing of the difference between the systolic and diastolic blood pressures, and paleness and coolness of the skin; Class III, 30 to 40 percent of total blood volume, resulting in a marked drop in blood pressure, increase in heart rate, and deterioration of the patient's mental state; and Class IV, more than 40 percent of total blood volume, usually resulting in death. According to the college's Advanced Trauma Life Support guidelines, only Class III and IV haemorrhage victims require blood transfusions. Class II victims benefit from the restoration of fluid volume, by means of transfusion of saline or Lactated Ringer's solution (a mixture of sodium, chloride, lactate, potassium, and calcium that is isotonic with blood), but are not in need of a transfusion of red blood cells.

A vampire's victim would initially suffer depleted blood volume, and depending on the hunger of the vampire, might suffer a loss of more than 30 percent of blood volume (Class III or IV trauma). In such cases, the victim's symptoms would likely resemble anaemia. However, if only small amounts of blood were drawn by the vampire (1 to 2 pints), even if repeatedly, the victim's normal blood regeneration could eliminate serious symptoms, and other than paleness and coolness of the victim's skin, the vampire's depredations would be difficult to detect, and a qualitative analysis of the victim's blood, such as that within the capabilities of Dr. Seward, would likely reveal little.

41 Another example of Seward's slipshod medicine: How could Lucy's "somewhat bloodless" state be the result of "something mental"?

42 Leatherdale (*Dracula Unearthed*) terms this a strange entry, because Seward speaks familiarly of the East Cliff to Holmwood even though the narrative gives no other indication that Seward or Holmwood has been to Whitby. The solution to this strangeness is found in the Notes, which make clear that Seward met Lucy and Mina in Whitby (see chapter 6, note 64), a disclosure suppressed in the narrative.

43 This sentence does not appear in the Abridged Text.

44 The Abridged Text omits the curious qualification that completes this sentence.

45 Seward, who after all is only a physician and not a literary man, seems to have mixed his metaphors here. In *Othello* (act 5, scene 2), Othello exclaims, "I have another weapon in this chamber; / It is a sword of Spain, the ice-brook's temper.—"He plainly means that the metal of the weapon has been "tempered" in the ice-brook. If Seward is referring to Van Helsing's "iron nerve," it may be taken as an expression of the strength of that nerve; however, in light of the balance of his remarks, he is more likely trying to express that Van Helsing is cool tempered (that is, the opposite of hot tempered)—"coolheaded" in today's usage.

46 Wolf (*The Essential Dracula*) and Leatherdale (*Dracula Unearthed*) both identify this as Harrods Stores, Ltd., on Brompton Road, justly renowned as a recognised social rendezvous. However, it more likely refers to the stores of the Army & Navy Co-operative Society Ltd. (known colloquially as "the Stores," according to John Richardson, the son of the founder, in his partially autobiographical work *The Sorcerer's Apprentice*, and historian R. H. Langbridge in *Edwardian Shopping*). The Stores were founded in 1871 as a cooperative by a group of subalterns, the object being to act as general dealers for the supply of food, drink, clothes, and articles of general use to shareholders, subscribers, and friends at the lowest prices obtainable though bulk buying and low profit margins. By 1890, the operation had grown into a chain of department stores with branches at major British military bases around the world, its breadth of merchandise rivalling that of Harrods and Selfridges. The 1897 *Queen's London* described the London headquarters as "where innumerable people do nearly all their shopping; and there are invariably a row of carriages and a crowd of dogs waiting outside the entrance beneath the clock." The chain was acquired by Harrods in 1940 and relegated to being an outlet for military surplus and low-end merchandise.

Army & Navy Store.
Queen's London (1897)

doing for mankind—work both in theory and practice, for his views are as wide as his all-embracing sympathy. I tell you these facts that you may know why I have such confidence in him. I have asked him to come at once. I shall see Miss Westenra to-morrow again. She is to meet me at the Stores,[46] so that I may not alarm her mother by too early a repetition of my call.[47]

> "Yours always,
> "John Seward."

LETTER FROM ABRAHAM VAN HELSING, M.D., D.PH., D. LIT., ETC., ETC.,[48] TO DR. SEWARD.

> "2 September.

"My good Friend,—

"When I have received your letter I am already coming to you.[49] By good fortune I can leave just at once, without wrong to any of those who have trusted me. Were fortune other, then it were bad for those who have trusted, for I come to my friend when he call me to aid those he holds dear.[50] Tell your friend that when that time you suck from my wound so swiftly the poison of the gangrene from that knife that our other friend, too nervous, let slip,[51] you did more for him when he wants my aids and you call for them than all his great fortune could do.[52] But it is pleasure added to do for him, your friend; it is to you that I come. Have then rooms for me at the Great Eastern Hotel,[53] so that I may be near to hand, and please it so arrange that we may see the young lady not too late on to-morrow, for it is likely that I may have to return here that night. But if need be I shall come again in three days, and stay longer if it must. Till then good-bye, my friend John,

> "Van Helsing."

LETTER FROM DR. SEWARD TO ARTHUR HOLMWOOD.

"3 September.

"My dear Art,—

"Van Helsing has come and gone. He came on with me to Hillingham, and found that, by Lucy's discretion, her mother was lunching out,[54] so that we were alone with her. Van Helsing made a very careful examination of the patient. He is to report to me, and I shall advise you, for of course I was not present all the time. He is, I fear, much concerned, but says he must think. When I told him of our friendship and how you trust to me in the matter, he said: 'You must tell him all you think. Tell him what I think, if you can guess it, if you will. Nay, I am not jesting. This is no jest, but life and death, perhaps more.' I asked what he meant by that, for he was very serious. This was when we had come back to town, and he was having a cup of tea before starting on his return to Amsterdam. He would not give me any further clue. You must not be angry with me, Art, because his very reticence means that all his brains are working for her good. He will speak plainly enough when the time comes, be sure. So I told him I would simply write an account of our visit, just as if I were doing a descriptive special article for *The Daily Telegraph*.[55] He seemed not to notice, but remarked that the smuts in London were not quite so bad as they used to be when he was a student here. I am to get his report to-morrow if he can possibly make it. In any case I am to have a letter.

"Well, as to the visit. Lucy was more cheerful than on the day I first saw her, and certainly looked better. She had lost something of the ghastly look that so upset you, and her breathing was normal. She was very sweet to the Professor (as she always is), and tried to make him feel at ease; though I could see that the poor girl was making a hard struggle for it. I believe Van Helsing saw it, too, for I saw the quick look under his bushy brows that I knew of old. Then he began to chat of all things except ourselves and diseases and with such an infinite geniality that I could see poor

47 This plan is not mentioned in the Abridged Text.

48 The Notes reveal that there was no Abraham Van Helsing but rather a conflation of three individuals: a German professor of history, a psychic investigator, and a detective (see note 14 on p. 8). This perhaps explains the coincidence of the same first name as Abraham (Bram) Stoker. Therefore, this impressive collection of degrees may also be taken to be a combination of the credentials of the three actual figures. As will be seen, one of the "etceteras" is a law degree (see chapter 13, note 4). It is pleasant to think that another credential might well have been "consulting detective," and there have been numerous suggestions that Sherlock Holmes himself investigated the Dracula affair, perhaps under the name of "Van Helsing." See "Dracula After Stoker" in Part II.

49 The post from London to Amsterdam took fifteen hours, according to *Ainsley's Nautical Almanac and Tide Tables for 1887*.

50 These convoluted sentences are shortened in the Abridged Text to the succinct "By good fortune I can just leave at once."

51 The source of the gangrene is not mentioned in the Abridged Text.

52 Seward is twenty-nine, and as has been seen, his medical studies must have taken place no longer than ten years earlier (see chapter 5, note 20). Antisepsis (in particular, the use of carbolic acid for the prevention of infection during surgery) was advocated by Joseph Lister (1827–1912) in 1860, and it is surprising to hear that as recently as ten years before the events of the narrative (certainly not earlier than 1875), an eminent physician such as Van Helsing would permit himself to be infected by a germ-laden knife. Then again, he shows no signs of understanding the principles of antisepsis in any of his medical treatments recorded in the Harker Papers.

Great Eastern Hotel.

53 On Liverpool Street in the City of London, the hotel was "largely frequented by Germans and other visitors to the great wool sales" held in the neighbourhood, according to the 1896 London "Baedeker." Adjacent to the Liverpool Street station, the terminus of the Great Eastern Railway, the last major terminus built in London, the hotel was completed in 1884 and continues in operation today. Perhaps the "German professor of history" (see note 48 above) preferred to associate with his fellow countrymen. If Stoker attempted to ensure concealment of the investigator's identity by changing the name of the hotel to the Berkeley (see chapter 11, note 4), he may have missed this reference.

Why did Van Helsing believe that staying in the city would be "near to hand" to Hampstead? Surely a hotel near any of the major stations with connections for Hampstead (Euston, St. Pancras, King's Cross) would have been more convenient. The Berkeley is in Piccadilly, quite near Holmwood's lodgings at the Albemarle Hotel; perhaps Van Helsing was led to believe he would be examining Lucy there. In fact, this is

Lucy's pretense of animation merge into reality.[56] Then, without any seeming change, he brought the conversation gently round to his visit, and suavely said:—

"'My dear young miss, I have the so great pleasure because you are so much beloved. That is much, my dear, even were there that which I do not see. They told me you were down in the spirit, and that you were of a ghastly pale. To them I say: "Pouf!"' And he snapped his fingers at me and went on: 'But you and I shall show them how wrong they are. How can he'—and he pointed at me with the same look and gesture as that with which once he pointed me out to his class, on, or rather after, a particular occasion which he never fails to remind me of[57]—'know anything of a young ladies? He has his madmans to play with, and to bring them back to happiness and to those that love them. It is much to do, and, oh, but there are rewards, in that we can bestow such happiness. But the young ladies! He has no wife nor daughter, and the young do not tell themselves to the young, but to the old, like me, who have known so many sorrows and the causes of them. So, my dear, we will send him away to smoke the cigarette in the garden, whiles you and I have little talk all to ourselves.' I took the hint, and strolled about, and presently the Professor came to the window and called me in. He looked grave, but said: 'I have made careful examination, but there is no functional cause. With you I agree that there has been much blood lost; it has been, but is not. But the conditions of her are in no way anæmic. I have asked her to send me her maid, that I may ask just one or two question, that so I may not chance to miss nothing. I know well what she will say. And yet there is cause;[58] there is always cause for everything. I must go back home and think. You must send to me the telegram every day; and if there be cause I shall come again. The disease—for not to be all well is a disease—interest me, and the sweet young dear, she interest me too. She charm me, and for her, if not for you or disease, I come.'

"As I tell you, he would not say a word more, even when we were alone. And so now, Art, you know all I know. I shall keep stern watch. I trust your poor father is rallying. It must be a terrible thing to you, my dear old fellow, to be placed in such a position between two people who are both so dear to you. I know your idea of duty to your father, and you are right to stick to it; but, if need be, I shall send you word to come at once to Lucy, so do not be over-anxious unless you hear from me."

DR. SEWARD'S DIARY.[59]

4 September.—Zoöphagous patient still keeps up our interest in him. He had only one outburst and that was yesterday at an unusual time. Just before the stroke of noon he began to grow restless. The attendant knew the symptoms, and at once summoned aid. Fortunately the men came at a run, and were just in time, for at the stroke of noon he became so violent that it took all their strength to hold him. In about five minutes, however, he began to get more and more quiet, and finally sank into a sort of melancholy, in which state he has remained up to now. The attendant tells me that his screams whilst in the paroxysm were really appalling; I found my hands full when I got in, attending to some of the other patients who were frightened by him. Indeed, I can quite understand the effect, for the sounds disturbed even me, though I was some distance away.[60] It is now after the dinner-hour of the asylum, and as yet my patient sits in a corner brooding, with a dull, sullen, woe-begone look in his face, which seems rather to indicate than to show something directly. I cannot quite understand it.

Later.—Another change in my patient. At five o'clock I looked in on him, and found him seemingly as happy and contented as he used to be. He was catching flies and eating them, and was keeping note of his capture by making nail-marks on the edge of the door between the ridges of padding. When he saw me, he came over and apologised for his bad conduct, and asked me in a very humble, cringing way to be led back to his own room and to have his note-book again. I thought it well to humour him: so he is back in his room with the window open. He has the sugar of his tea spread out on the window-sill, and is reaping quite a harvest of flies. He is not now eating them,

more consistent with Seward's plan not to upset Mrs. Westenra by meeting Lucy at the Stores. When Lucy learned that her mother planned to have lunch out, it was more convenient to be examined at home. (Of course, Van Helsing never spends the night at the Great Eastern.) From this confusion, the only safe conclusion may be that neither of the hotels is where "Van Helsing" stayed. In fact, if "Van Helsing" is in fact Professor Müller of Oxford (see note 14 on p. 8), he may not have stayed at a hotel at all; more likely, he lodged in town at a club of which he was a member.

No hotel is indicated here in the Abridged Text.

54 The ploy is not mentioned in the Abridged Text.

55 The *Daily Telegraph* was founded by Colonel Sleigh on 29 June 1855, and printed for him by Joseph Moses Levy, owner of the *Sunday Times* (which was deliberately named after the *Times* but not connected to it otherwise). When Sleigh proved unable to pay his bills, Levy took over, lowering the price—the *Daily Telegraph* became the first "penny newspaper" in London—and appointing his son, Edward Levy-Lawson, and Thornton Leigh Hunt to serve as editors. The paper relaunched on 17 September 1855. The reading public early embraced the *Daily Telegraph*'s colourful style, and within less than a year it was outselling not only the *Times* but also every other newspaper in England.

This and the following sentence do not appear in the Abridged Text.

56 This sentence does not appear in the Abridged Text. However, the phrase "without any seeming change" in the following sentence has not been deleted, making no sense.

57 The Abridged Text does not contain the personal reminiscence.

58 In the Abridged Text, Van Helsing fails to question the maid.

59 The Manuscript refers to this originally as "John Seward's Case-book" or "John Seward's private Case-book." Perhaps Stoker balked at this further emphasis on Seward's supposed medical training.

60 Seward's reaction does not appear in the Abridged Text.

61 This patronising comment is eliminated in the Abridged Text.

62 Leatherdale (*Dracula Unearthed*) points out that the timing recorded by Seward is impossible: the previous entry by Seward was made after 5:00 P.M., and Seward here states that in the interim between 5:00 P.M. and sunset (which would have occurred at around 6:30 or 6:45 P.M.), he visited Hillingham and returned. Unless, as McNally and Florescu (*The Essential Dracula*) contend, the asylum was not in Purfleet but rather on Chatham Street (see chapter 5, note 22), this is plainly impossible and must be ascribed as another transcription error by Mina.

63 This self-reflection does not appear in the Abridged Text.

but putting them into a box, as of old, and is already examining the corners of his room to find a spider. I tried to get him to talk about the past few days, for any clue to his thoughts would be of immense help to me; but he would not rise. For a moment or two he looked very sad, and said in a sort of far-away voice, as though saying it rather to himself than to me:—

"All over! all over! He has deserted me. No hope for me now unless I do it for myself!" Then suddenly turning to me in a resolute way, he said: "Doctor, won't you be very good to me and let me have a little more sugar? I think it would be good for me."

"And the flies?" I said.

"Yes! The flies like it, too, and I like the flies; therefore I like it." And there are people who know so little as to think that madmen do not argue.[61] I procured him a double supply, and left him as happy a man as, I suppose, any in the world. I wish I could fathom his mind.

Midnight.—Another change in him. I had been to see Miss Westenra, whom I found much better, and had just returned, and was standing at our own gate looking at the sunset,[62] when once more I heard him yelling. As his room is on this side of the house, I could hear it better than in the morning. It was a shock to me to turn from the wonderful smoky beauty of a sunset over London, with its lurid lights and inky shadows and all the marvellous tints that come on foul clouds even as on foul water, and to realise all the grim sternness of my own cold stone building, with its wealth of breathing misery, and my own desolate heart to endure it all.[63] I reached him just as the sun was going down, and from his window saw the red disc sink. As it sank he became less and less frenzied; and just as it dipped he slid from the hands that held him, an inert mass, on the floor. It is wonderful, however, what intellectual recuperative power lunatics have, for within a few minutes he stood up quite calmly and looked around him. I signalled to the attendants not to hold him, for I was anxious to see what he would do. He went straight over to the window and brushed out the crumbs of sugar; then he took his fly-box and emptied it outside, and threw away the box; then he shut the window, and crossing over, sat down on his bed. All this surprised me, so I asked him: "Are you not going to keep flies any more?"

"No," said he; "I am sick of all that rubbish!" He certainly is a wonderfully interesting study. I wish I could get some glimpse of his mind or of the cause of his sudden passion. Stop; there may be a clue after all, if we can find why to-day his paroxysms came on at high noon and at sunset. Can it be that there is a malign influence of the sun at periods which affects certain natures—as at times the moon does others?[64] We shall see.

TELEGRAM, SEWARD, LONDON, TO VAN HELSING, AMSTERDAM.

"*4 September.*—PATIENT STILL BETTER TO-DAY."

TELEGRAM, SEWARD, LONDON, TO VAN HELSING, AMSTERDAM.

"*5 September.*—PATIENT GREATLY IMPROVED. GOOD APPETITE; SLEEPS NATURALLY; GOOD SPIRITS; COLOUR COMING BACK."

TELEGRAM, SEWARD, LONDON, TO VAN HELSING, AMSTERDAM.

"*6 September.*—TERRIBLE CHANGE FOR THE WORSE. COME AT ONCE; DO NOT LOSE AN HOUR. I HOLD OVER TELEGRAM TO HOLMWOOD TILL HAVE SEEN YOU."

64 The idea that the cycles of the sun and the moon have an influence on human behaviour is old, dating back at least to the Romans, and of course is intimately connected with the pseudoscience of astrology. However, scientists studying animal and plant behaviour now see circadian (that is, twenty-four-hour) biological cycles or rhythms in many behavioural patterns and in some cases (e.g., leaf growth, ovulation) observe much longer cycles. Many of these behaviours are triggered by exposure to or withdrawal from light stimuli and temperature variation. Although much has been learned about behaviours resulting from events occurring at the cellular level, it is too soon to determine whether the sun's or moon's cycles cause the events or are merely synchronous.

Chapter 10

LETTER, DR. SEWARD TO THE HONORABLE ARTHUR HOLMWOOD.

"6 September.

"My dear Art,—

"My news to-day is not so good. Lucy this morning had gone back a bit. There is, however, one good thing which has arisen from it: Mrs. Westenra was naturally anxious concerning Lucy, and has consulted me professionally about her.[1] I took advantage of the opportunity, and told her that my old master, Van Helsing, the great specialist, was coming to stay with me, and that I would put her in his charge conjointly with myself; so now we can come and go without alarming her unduly, for a shock to her would mean sudden death, and this, in Lucy's weak condition, might be disastrous to her. We are hedged in with difficulties, all of us, my poor old fellow; but, please God, we shall come through them all right. If any need I shall write, so that, if you do not hear from me, take it for granted that I am simply waiting for news. In haste,

"Yours ever,
"John Seward."

DR. SEWARD'S DIARY

7 September.—The first thing Van Helsing said to me when we met at Liverpool Street[2] was:—

1 Why would Mrs. Westenra consult Dr. Seward, whom she knows only as a friend of Lucy's, rather than the family physician? In the 1931 film of *Dracula*, Seward is in fact the family physician.

2 That is, outside the Great Eastern Hotel (see chapter 9, note 53).

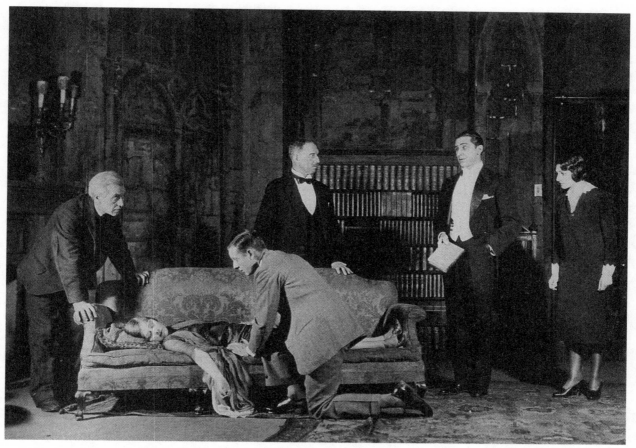

Scene from Broadway production of *Dracula*, starring Edward Van Sloan as Van Helsing,
Dorothy Peterson as Lucy, Terence Neill as Jonathan Harker, Herbert Bunston as Dr. Seward,
Bela Lugosi as Dracula, and Nedda Harrigan as Wells, the maid (1927).

"Have you said anything to our young friend the lover of her?"

"No," I said. "I waited till I had seen you,[3] as I said in my telegram. I wrote him a letter simply telling him that you were coming, as Miss Westenra was not so well, and that I should let him know if need be."

"Right, my friend," he said, "quite right! Better he not know as yet; perhaps he shall never know. I pray so; but if it be needed, then he shall know all. And, my good friend John, let me caution you. You deal with the madmen. All men are mad in some way or the other; and inasmuch as you deal discreetly with your madmen, so deal with God's madmen, too—the rest

3 The balance of the paragraph does not appear in the Abridged Text. Apparently Stoker, on reviewing the Harker Papers, realised that this was not what Seward wrote to Holmwood.

4 An English term for wheat; maize (American, corn) has no chaff.

5 It is hard to believe a professor of medicine whose instructional methods include tugging on his students' ears. In fact, there is much to disbelieve about this "professor," whose English is so fractured on occasion that his orations sometimes resemble those of Donald Duck's comically pedantic, heavily accented uncle, Professor Ludwig von Drake. Here Van Helsing carries on at length with a pseudobiblical parable, the lesson of which is to be patient and observe.

6 Translating Van Helsing's laboured similes, it would seem that he is saying this case may be more significant than many others. If this is his meaning, it is an extraordinary insight, for he has not even seen Lucy's throat wound. The metaphor does not appear in the Abridged Text.

of the world. You tell not your madmen what you do nor why you do it; you tell them not what you think. So you shall keep knowledge in its place, where it may rest—where it may gather its kind around it and breed. You and I shall keep as yet what we know here, and here." He touched me on the heart and on the forehead, and then touched himself the same way. "I have for myself thoughts at the present. Later I shall unfold to you."

"Why not now?" I asked. "It may do some good; we may arrive at some decision." He stopped and looked at me, and said:—

"My friend John, when the corn[4] is grown, even before it has ripened—while the milk of its mother-earth is in him, and the sunshine has not yet begun to paint him with his gold, the husbandman he pull the ear and rub him between his rough hands, and blow away the green chaff, and say to you: 'Look! he's good corn; he will make good crop when the time comes.' " I did not see the application, and told him so. For reply he reached over and took my ear in his hand and pulled it playfully, as he used long ago to do at lectures,[5] and said: "The good husbandman tell you so then because he knows, but not till then. But you do not find the good husbandman dig up his planted corn to see if he grow; that is for the children who play at husbandry, and not for those who take it as of the work of their life. See you now, friend John? I have sown my corn, and Nature has her work to do in making it sprout; if he sprout at all, there's some promise; and I wait till the ear begins to swell." He broke off, for he evidently saw that I understood. Then he went on, and very gravely:—

"You were always a careful student, and your case-book was ever more full than the rest. You were only student then; now you are master, and I trust that good habit have not fail. Remember, my friend, that knowledge is stronger than memory, and we should not trust the weaker. Even if you have not kept the good practice, let me tell you that this case of our dear miss is one that may be—mind, I say *may be*—of such interest to us and others that all the rest may not make him kick the beam; as your peoples say.[6] Take then good note of it. Nothing is too small. I counsel you, put down in record even your doubts and surmises. Hereafter it may be of interest to you to see how true you guess.[7] We learn from failure, not from success!"

When I described Lucy's symptoms—the same as before, but infinitely more marked—he looked very grave, but said nothing. He took with him a bag in which were many instruments and drugs, "the ghastly paraphernalia of our beneficial trade," as he once called, in one of his lectures, the equipment of a professor of the healing craft.[8] When we were shown in, Mrs. Westenra met us. She was alarmed, but not nearly so much as I expected to find her. Nature in one of her beneficent moods has ordained that even death has some antidote to its own terrors. Here, in a case where any shock may prove fatal, matters are so ordered that, from some cause or other, the things not personal—even the terrible change in her daughter to whom she is so attached—do not seem to reach her. It is something like the way Dame Nature gathers round a foreign body an envelope of some insensitive tissue which can protect from evil that which it would otherwise harm by contact. If this be an ordered selfishness, then we should pause before we condemn any one for the vice of egoism, for there may be deeper roots for its cause than we have knowledge of.[9]

I used my knowledge of this phase of spiritual pathology,[10] and laid down a rule that she should not be present with Lucy or think of her illness more than was absolutely required. She assented readily, so readily that I saw again the hand of Nature fighting for life. Van Helsing and I were shown up to Lucy's room. If I was shocked when I saw her yesterday, I was horrified when I saw her to-day. She was ghastly, chalkily pale; the red seemed to have gone even from her lips and gums, and the bones of her face stood out prominently; her breathing was painful to see or hear. Van Helsing's face grew set as marble, and his eyebrows converged till they almost touched over his nose. Lucy lay motionless, and did not seem to have strength to speak, so for a while we were all silent. Then Van Helsing beckoned to me, and we went gently out of the room. The instant we had closed the door he stepped quickly along the passage to the next door, which was open. Then he pulled me quickly in with him and

7 The Abridged Text does not include this sentence. Perhaps Stoker was embarrassed or covering for "Dr. Seward," who never makes a single guess about the matter.

8 By the early 1880s, diagnostic instruments began to appear in the doctor's bag, alongside the ether bottle and laudanum. The stethoscope, invented in 1819, was now commonplace, although in the form of a rigid tube rather than the now familiar flexible tubing. A compact clinical thermometer was available, although the sphygmomanometer (blood pressure cuff) had yet to be developed.

9 In short, Seward concludes that Mrs. Westenra's illness has made her so selfish that she will take no notice of Lucy's medical problems. Seward is correct, but instead of taking this danger into account, he encourages it with, as will be seen, fatal consequences for Lucy.

10 This pompous phrase does not appear in the Abridged Text.

11 The Manuscript quotes another example of Van Helsing's humour: "she is as Bismarck said Germany would be if another war with France." The joke does not appear in the published narrative.

12 Again, Van Helsing displays startling insight, for he has seen no overt signs of blood loss—no wound, no blood on Lucy's clothing or bedclothes. How he makes his mysterious but completely accurate diagnosis of vampirism is unknown.

13 Although historians have doubted the credibility of the tale, the fifteenth-century Roman writer Stefano Infessura, perhaps nursing a grudge against the papacy, recorded that in 1492, when Pope Innocent VIII suffered a stroke, blood transfusions (probably oral consumption of blood) were performed to try to save him. The blood was said to have come from three ten-year-old boys, for whom the procedure proved fatal. The transfusions also failed to help the pope, who died before the year was out.

Experiments continued, but with little understanding and a great rate of failure. In 1665, Samuel Pepys's diary records that Richard Lower, an Oxford physician, experimented with some success with dog-to-dog transfusions. He performed these procedures with rigour and not a little showmanship, in one demonstration strapping two healthy dogs together side by side for the benefit of colleagues, who watched as one dog's life hung in the balance. He proceeded to animal-to-human transfusions, including transfusing a man suffering from nervous agitation with blood from a lamb, the hope being to transfer the small, calm creature's temperament to the man. Transfusions at the time were accomplished with quills and silver pipes. The conviction that, besides the blood itself, attributes could be transferred from one body to another was firmly held not only by the public but by physiologists. This included the concept that a "bad" person could be made into an exemplary one through blood transfusion.

closed the door. "My God!" he said; "this is dreadful.**11** There is no time to be lost. She will die for sheer want of blood to keep the heart's action as it should be.**12** There must be transfusion of blood at once.**13** Is it you or me?"

"I am younger and stronger, Professor. It must be me."

"Then get ready at once. I will bring up my bag. I am prepared."

I went downstairs with him, and as we were going there was a knock at the hall-door. When we reached the hall the maid had just opened the door, and Arthur was stepping quickly in. He rushed up to me, saying in an eager whisper:—

"Jack, I was so anxious. I read between the lines of your letter, and have been in an agony. The dad was better, so I ran down here to see for myself. Is not that gentleman Dr. Van Helsing? I am so thankful to you, sir, for coming." When first the Professor's eye had lit upon him he had been angry at his interruption at such a time; but now, as he took in his stalwart proportions and recognised the strong young manhood which seemed to emanate from him, his eyes gleamed. Without a pause he said to him gravely as he held out his hand:—

"Sir, you have come in time. You are the lover of our dear miss. She is bad, very, very bad. Nay, my child, do not go like that." For he suddenly grew pale and sat down in a chair almost fainting.**14** "You are to help her. You can do more than any that live, and your courage is your best help."

"What can I do?" asked Arthur hoarsely. "Tell me, and I shall do it. My life is hers, and I would give the last drop of blood in my body for her." The Professor has a strongly humorous side, and I could from old knowledge detect a trace of its origin in his answer:—

"My young sir, I do not ask so much as that—not the last!"

"What shall I do?"**15** There was fire in his eyes, and his open nostrils quivered with intent. Van Helsing slapped him on the shoulder. "Come!" he said. "You are a man, and it is a man we want. You are better than me, better than my friend John." Arthur looked bewildered, and the Professor went on by explaining in a kindly way:—

"Young miss is bad, very bad. She wants blood, and blood she must have or die.**16** My friend John and I have consulted;

By 1667, a French experimenter reported successful transfusions from sheep to humans. Many patients died, however, from transfusion (and undoubtedly other causes), and in 1678 the Paris Society of Physicians outlawed the practise.

While others may have quietly used the technique, in 1818 James Blundell, a British obstetrician, performed a successful transfusion of human blood to treat a woman suffering from haemorrhage after childbirth. Extracting blood

James Blundell.

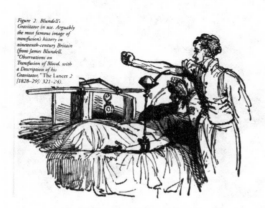

Figure 2. Blundell's Gravitator in use. Arguably the most famous image of transfusion's history in nineteenth-century Britain (from James Blundell, "Observations on Transfusion of Blood, with a Description of his Gravitator," The Lancet 2 [1828-29]: 321-24).

Blundell's Gravitator, an early transfusion instrument.
The Lancet, 1828–1829

from the patient's husband, he used a syringe to successfully transfuse the wife. Blundell was an enormously accomplished researcher and surgeon; outside the science of transfusion, among the dozens of procedures he perfected was the division of the fallopian tubes to prevent further pregnancies, and hysterectomy for cancer of the cervix. Between 1825 and 1830, Blundell performed ten documented transfusions on severely ill patients, four or five of which proved beneficial to his patients. He became wealthy from the sale of various instruments he invented for performing transfusions, including the Impellor (which supplied blood to the recipient) and the Gravitator (which allowed a steady stream of blood from one patient to another without exposing the blood to air). In 1840, Blundell assisted another English physician, Samuel Armstrong Lane, in performing the first successful whole blood transfusion to treat haemophilia.

Notwithstanding Blundell's successes, deaths from transfusions continued to occur from mystifying adverse reactions. In an effort to eliminate the reactions to human blood, American physicians from 1873 to 1880 recorded trials of transfusions of milk (from cows and goats) to humans. Milk itself caused problems, and in 1884 an experimenter tested using a saline infusion in place of milk.

According to N. R. S. Maluf, in his comprehensive "History of Blood Transfusion," "the nineteenth century closed with substantial accomplishment toward safe blood transfusion." By then, experimenters had realised the necessity of transfusing with whole blood rather than with serum when resuscitating from blood loss. The dangers of interspecies transfusion were demonstrated, resulting in the abandonment of animal-to-human transfusion. Detailed studies of the causes of posttransfusion trauma were undertaken. Defibrination of blood to prevent clotting—clearly known to Van Helsing—was advanced, and some researchers began to experiment with calcium as an anticoagulant. Nonetheless, death remained the common result of transfusion.

In 1901, a major breakthrough occurred when Karl Landsteiner (1868–1943), an Austrian physician, observed the first three human blood groups, which he termed A, B, and O. In 1902 a fourth main blood type, AB, was discovered. Landsteiner was awarded the Nobel Prize in Physiology or Medicine in 1930 for his work.

Based on these discoveries, in 1907 Dr. Ludvig Hektoen (1863–1951), a Chicago physician, suggested that transfusion might be improved by cross-matching blood between donors and patients. Based on this suggestion, New York physician Reuben Ottenberg (1882–1959) performed the first blood transfusion using blood typing and cross-matching and reported the compatibility testing in a footnote to a paper. When Ottenberg's methodology was adopted, the frequency of adverse reactions was greatly reduced. In 1932 the world's first "blood bank" (a term actually introduced later, in 1937, by Bernard Fantus) was established, in Stalingrad, Russia. It was not until 1939

and 1940 that the Rh blood group system (so named after the Rhesus monkeys used in the testing) was discovered by Karl Landsteiner, Alex Wiener, Philip Levine, and R. E. Stetson. Mismatching of these groups was soon recognised as the cause of the majority of the remaining transfusion reactions.

Blood transfusion is safest when the donor's and the recipients' blood group and Rh type are compatible. Therefore, modern practise is to test a mixture of the donor blood and the recipient's blood for compatibility before transfusion. However, even this testing can only rule out the so-called hemolytic reaction (the breakdown of red blood cells that usually results in anaemia); other issues that may arise, regardless of compatibility, include the transmission of disease, fever, and allergic reactions.

In addition to endangering the patient with transfused blood, the procedure itself was very painful for donor and recipient, both of whom were wounded to permit insertion of a rather

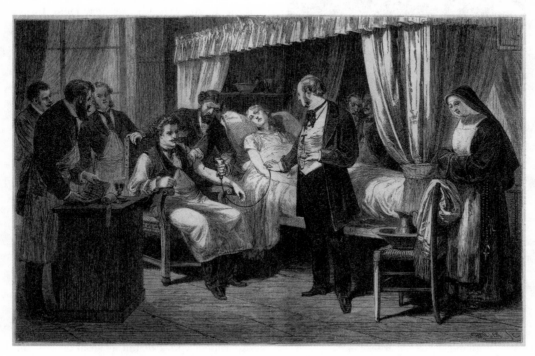

The transfusion of blood—an operation at the Hôpital de la Pitié, Paris.
Harper's Weekly, 4 July 1874

and we are about to perform what we call transfusion of blood—to transfer from full veins of one to the empty veins which pine for him.[17] John was to give his blood, as he is the more young and strong than me"—here Arthur took my hand and wrung it hard in silence—"but, now you are here, you are more good than us, old or young, who toil much in the world of thought. Our nerves are not so calm and our blood so bright than yours!"[18] Arthur turned to him and said:—

"If you only knew how gladly I would die for her you would understand—"

He stopped, with a sort of choke in his voice.

"Good boy!" said Van Helsing. "In the not-so-far-off you will be happy that you have done all for her you love. Come now and be silent.[19] You shall kiss her once before it is done, but then you must go; and you must leave at my sign. Say no word to Madame; you know how it is with her! There must be no shock; any knowledge of this would be one. Come!"

We all went up to Lucy's room. Arthur by direction remained outside. Lucy turned her head and looked at us, but said nothing. She was not asleep, but she was simply too weak to make the effort. Her eyes spoke to us; that was all. Van Helsing took some things from his bag and laid them on a little table out of sight. Then he mixed a narcotic,[20] and coming over to the bed, said cheerily:—

"Now, little miss, here is your medicine. Drink it off, like a good child. See, I lift you so that to swallow is easy. Yes." She had made the effort with success.

It astonished me how long the drug took to act. This, in fact, marked the extent of her weakness. The time seemed endless until sleep began to flicker in her eyelids. At last, however, the narcotic began to manifest its potency; and she fell into a deep sleep. When the Professor was satisfied he called Arthur into the room, and bade him strip off his coat. Then he added: "You may take that one little kiss whiles I bring over the table. Friend John, help to me!" So neither of us looked whilst he bent over her.

Van Helsing turning to me, said:—

"He is so young and strong and of blood so pure that we need not defibrinate it."[21]

large needle. Note that Lucy is given a narcotic before being transfused, and though Holmwood manages to keep silent, Seward must dress his wound. Only in 1892 did a Leipzig internist introduce hollow metal needles for collection of blood from the donor's veins and then its subcutaneous injection.

14 The weakness of "Holmwood" is covered up in the Abridged Text, which omits this and the previous sentence.

15 Here Stoker goes somewhat overboard in making Holmwood appear more manly, and the humorous exchange with Van Helsing in the three preceding sentences, as well as Van Helsing's bracing slap on the shoulder, do not appear in the Abridged Text.

16 Van Helsing is probably making an accurate diagnosis here. See chapter 9, note 40.

17 Of course, Van Helsing speaks metaphorically; veins are never empty.

18 Again, a metaphor: blood's brightness is determined by the number of red blood cells, and anaemic blood—with a reduced number of red blood cells—is brighter than normal blood.

19 The balance of the paragraph does not appear in the Abridged Text.

20 Although in modern usage "narcotics" are used for pain relief and "narcoleptics" are used for sleep, in the late nineteenth century a "narcotic" meant any agent inducing a deep stupor (William Warner, *Warner's Pocket Medical Dictionary*). Opium, for example, was commonly prescribed for insomnia or nervousness and dispensed in many different forms, such as powder, capsules, or mixed with wine or vinegar.

21 Fibrin, a coagulant, could be removed from the blood, usually by means of constant agitation while the blood was collected in a container with glass beads or chips. This should not have been necessary in a donor-to-donor transfusion, regardless of how "pure" the donor's blood was. Van Helsing, not surprisingly, misunderstands the problem, which occurs when blood is collected and stored before transfusion. It was not until 1914 that long-term anticoagulants were discovered, permitting storage of blood. The first stored blood was transfused in 1915, and the technique was successfully used by the British in World War I.

22 Stoker's brother Sir William Thornley Stoker, a well-known physician who apparently read the Manuscript at Stoker's request, has noted in the margin: "As transfusion is performed usually, the blood drawn from one person, and defibrinated before being injected into the other."

23 How much did he give? The customary limit today for donors is 1 pint, although the adult human body contains about 5 quarts. An individual's blood volume depends on body weight, age, and sex. In addition, persons who live at high altitudes may have up to 40 percent more blood volume than low-altitude residents.

24 Again, the sentence does not appear in the Abridged Text.

25 The Abridged Text does not contain this sentence. The Manuscript indicates that Arthur took that kiss.

26 The source of the buckle is not mentioned in the Abridged Text. Perhaps Stoker discovered that the Harker Papers were mistaken in this matter.

27 Why is Van Helsing surprised by this revelation? If, as appears earlier, he is absolutely convinced that Lucy is suffering from vampirism, he should have expected precisely such stigmata.

Then with swiftness, but with absolute method, Van Helsing performed the operation. As the transfusion went on something like life seemed to come back to poor Lucy's cheeks, and through Arthur's growing pallor the joy of his face seemed absolutely to shine.[22] After a bit I began to grow anxious, for the loss of blood was telling on Arthur, strong man as he was.[23] It gave me an idea of what a terrible strain Lucy's system must have undergone that what weakened Arthur only partially restored her. But the Professor's face was set, and he stood watch in hand and with his eyes fixed now on the patient and now on Arthur. I could hear my own heart beat. Presently he said in a soft voice: "Do not stir an instant. It is enough. You attend him; I will look to her." When all was over I could see how much Arthur was weakened.[24] I dressed the wound and took his arm to bring him away, when Van Helsing spoke without turning round—the man seems to have eyes in the back of his head:—

"The brave lover, I think, deserve another kiss, which he shall have presently."[25] And as he had now finished his operation, he adjusted the pillow to the patient's head. As he did so the narrow black velvet band which she seems always to wear round her throat, buckled with an old diamond buckle which her lover had given her,[26] was dragged a little up, and showed a red mark on her throat. Arthur did not notice it, but I could hear the deep hiss of indrawn breath which is one of Van Helsing's ways of betraying emotion.[27] He said nothing at the moment, but turned to me, saying: "Now take down our brave young lover, give him of the port wine, and let him lie down a while. He must then go home and rest, sleep much and eat much, that he may be recruited of what he has so given to his love. He must not stay here.[28] Hold! a moment. I may take it, sir, that you are anxious of result. Then bring it with you that in all ways the operation is successful. You have saved her life this time, and you can go home and rest easy in mind that all that can be is. I shall tell her all when she is well;[29] she shall love you none the less for what you have done. Good-bye."

When Arthur had gone I went back to the room. Lucy was sleeping gently, but her breathing was stronger; I could see the counterpane move as her breast heaved. By the bedside sat Van Helsing, looking at her intently. The velvet band again covered the red mark. I asked the Professor in a whisper:—

"What do you make of that mark on her throat?"

"What do you make of it?"

"I have not seen it yet," I answered, and then and there proceeded to loose the band. Just over the external jugular vein[30] there were two punctures, not large, but not wholesome-looking. There was no sign of disease, but the edges were white and worn-looking, as if by some trituration.[31] It at once occurred to me that this wound, or whatever it was, might be the means of that manifest loss of blood; but I abandoned the idea as soon as formed, for such a thing could not be. The whole bed would have been drenched to a scarlet with the blood which the girl must have lost to leave such a pallor as she had before the transfusion.

"Well?" said Van Helsing.

"Well," said I, "I can make nothing of it." The Professor stood up. "I must go back to Amsterdam to-night," he said.[32] "There are books and things there which I want. You must remain here all the night, and you must not let your sight pass from her."

"Shall I have a nurse?" I asked.

"We are the best nurses, you and I. You keep watch all night; see that she is well fed, and that nothing disturbs her. You must not sleep all the night. Later on we can sleep, you and I. I shall be back as soon as possible. And then we may begin."

"May begin?" I said. "What on earth do you mean?"

"We shall see!" he answered, as he hurried out. He came back a moment later and put his head inside the door and said with warning finger held up:—

"Remember, she is your charge. If you leave her, and harm befall, you shall not sleep easy hereafter!"

DR. SEWARD'S DIARY—*continued.*

8 September.—I sat up all night with Lucy. The opiate worked itself off towards dusk, and she waked naturally; she looked a different being from what she had been before the operation. Her spirits even were good, and she was full of a happy vivacity,

28 Again, Van Helsing's prescription does not appear in the Abridged Text.

29 In fact, Van Helsing never tells Lucy "all," and Stoker cut the line in editing the Abridged Text.

30 The Manuscript changes the description from "the small vein" to the medical jargon which appears in the published text, probably to bolster the disguises of Seward and Van Helsing.

31 Seward's medical jargon is confused here: trituration is a process of grinding or reducing a substance to a powder. Fortunately, we guess, even though he doesn't, what has caused the puncture wounds and why they are "worn-looking."

32 The journey from London to Amsterdam would most likely have been by boat train to Harwich (which departed nightly from Liverpool at 8:30), a sea crossing to Rotterdam (arriving at 6:08 A.M.), and an hour-and-a-half train trip to Amsterdam, arriving about 9:30 A.M. on 8 September.

33 Lucy does not have a conscious awareness of Dracula's depredations, yet she instinctually conceals her throat wounds. Lucy's only clear recollection of an encounter comes to her immediately following Dracula's departure from Whitby on 17 August. Whether this is Dracula's normal technique—using hypnotic powers to cloud his victim's mind—or merely the result of Lucy's heightened sensitivity to the vampire may be considered further in the case of future victims.

34 Surely this is the physician's observation, not the would-be lover's.

but I could see evidences of the absolute prostration which she had undergone. When I told Mrs. Westenra that Dr. Van Helsing had directed that I should sit up with her she almost pooh-poohed the idea, pointing out her daughter's renewed strength and excellent spirits. I was firm, however, and made preparations for my long vigil. When her maid had prepared her for the night I came in, having in the meantime had supper, and took a seat by the bedside. She did not in any way make objection, but looked at me gratefully whenever I caught her eye. After a long spell she seemed sinking off to sleep, but with an effort seemed to pull herself together and shook it off. This was repeated several times, with greater effort and with shorter pauses as the time moved on. It was apparent that she did not want to sleep, so I tackled the subject at once:—

"You do not want to go to sleep?"

"No; I am afraid."

"Afraid to go to sleep! Why so? It is the boon we all crave for."

"Ah, not if you were like me—if sleep was to you a presage of horror!"

"A presage of horror! What on earth do you mean?"

"I don't know; oh, I don't know. And that is what is so terrible. All this weakness comes to me in sleep; until I dread the very thought."[33]

"But, my dear girl, you may sleep to-night. I am here watching you, and I can promise that nothing will happen."

"Ah, I can trust you!" I seized the opportunity, and said: "I promise you that if I see any evidence of bad dreams I will wake you at once."

"You will? Oh, will you really? How good you are to me. Then I will sleep!" And almost at the word she gave a deep sigh of relief, and sank back, asleep.

All night long I watched by her. She never stirred, but slept on and on in a deep, tranquil, life-giving, health-giving sleep. Her lips were slightly parted, and her breast rose and fell with the regularity of a pendulum.[34] There was a smile on her face, and it was evident that no bad dreams had come to disturb her peace of mind.

In the early morning her maid came, and I left her in her

care and took myself back home, for I was anxious about many things. I sent a short wire to Van Helsing and to Arthur, telling them of the excellent result of the operation. My own work, with its manifold arrears, took me all day to clear off; it was dark when I was able to inquire about my zoöphagous patient. The report was good; he had been quiet for the past day and night. A telegram came from Van Helsing at Amsterdam whilst I was at dinner, suggesting that I should be at Hillingham to-night, as it might be well to be at hand, and stating that he was leaving by the night mail and would join me early in the morning.[35]

9 September.—I was pretty tired and worn out when I got to Hillingham. For two nights I had hardly had a wink of sleep, and my brain was beginning to feel that numbness which marks cerebral exhaustion. Lucy was up and in cheerful spirits. When she shook hands with me she looked sharply in my face and said:—

"No sitting up to-night for you. You are worn out. I am quite well again; indeed, I am; and if there is to be any sitting up, it is I who will sit up with you." I would not argue the point, but went and had my supper. Lucy came with me, and, enlivened by her charming presence, I made an excellent meal, and had a couple of glasses of the more than excellent port. Then Lucy took me upstairs, and showed me a room next her own, where a cozy fire was burning. "Now," she said, "you must stay here. I shall leave this door open and my door too. You can lie on the sofa for I know that nothing would induce any of you doctors to go to bed whilst there is a patient above the horizon. If I want anything I shall call out, and you can come to me at once." I could not but acquiesce, for I was "dog-tired," and could not have sat up had I tried. So, on her renewing her promise to call me if she should want anything, I lay on the sofa, and forgot all about everything.

LUCY WESTENRA'S DIARY.

9 September.—I feel so happy to-night. I have been so miserably weak, that to be able to think and move about is

35 The 7:00 P.M. train from Amsterdam arrived in Rotterdam at 8:45 P.M., in ample time for the 10:00 P.M. train/ship that arrived in Liverpool Street at 8:00 A.M. the following morning. However, Van Helsing's plans evidently went awry, or some more urgent matter kept him in Amsterdam. He does not return to London until the morning of 10 September.

36 An east wind is generally regarded in folklore as prolonging bad weather; hence the saying "The west wind brings rain, the east wind blows it back again."

37 Whatever the truth about vampires' sexuality, a subject explored further in "Dracula's Family Tree," in Part II, Stoker's narrative mixes images of blood sucking and sexual intercourse (that is, the exchange of bodily fluids) to the point where it is often difficult to tell what has occurred and what the Victorian editor has substituted. This occurs most notably in Harker's journal record of his confrontation with the three women (see text accompanying chapter 3, note 80) and the different recountings of Mina's conjugation with Dracula (see text accompanying chapter 21, note 23). Here we are surely expected to conclude that Lucy's warm thoughts about her fiancé are the result of transfusion of his blood into her, a notion prevalent as early as the seventeenth century (see note 13).

38 Touching the head of a sleeping man is an uncommon gesture and suggests an intimacy between Seward and Van Helsing.

39 We recall that Van Helsing has "a temper of the ice-brook."

40 Notably a German expression, not Dutch. Again, this is another instance of Stoker's carelessness in erasing traces of the "real" Van Helsing. See note 14 on page 8.

like feeling sunshine after a long spell of east wind out of a steel sky.[36] Somehow Arthur feels very, very close to me. I seem to feel his presence warm about me. I suppose it is that sickness and weakness are selfish things and turn our inner eyes and sympathy on ourselves, whilst health and strength give Love rein, and in thought and feeling he can wander where he wills. I know where my thoughts are. If only Arthur knew! My dear, my dear, your ears must tingle as you sleep, as mine do waking. Oh, the blissful rest of last night! How I slept, with that dear, good Dr. Seward watching me. And to-night I shall not fear to sleep, since he is close at hand and within call. Thank everybody for being so good to me! Thank God! Good-night Arthur.[37]

DR. SEWARD'S DIARY.

10 September.—I was conscious of the Professor's hand on my head,[38] and started awake all in a second. That is one of the things that we learn in an asylum, at any rate.

"And how is our patient?"

"Well, when I left her, or rather when she left me," I answered.

"Come, let us see," he said. And together we went into the room.

The blind was down, and I went over to raise it gently, whilst Van Helsing stepped, with his soft, cat-like tread, over to the bed.

As I raised the blind, and the morning sunlight flooded the room, I heard the Professor's low hiss of inspiration, and knowing its rarity,[39] a deadly fear shot through my heart. As I passed over he moved back, and his exclamation of horror, "Gott in Himmel!"[40] needed no enforcement from his agonised face. He raised his hand and pointed to the bed, and his iron face was drawn and ashen white. I felt my knees begin to tremble.

There on the bed, seemingly in a swoon, lay poor Lucy, more horribly white and wan-looking than ever. Even the lips were white, and the gums seemed to have shrunken back from the teeth, as we sometimes see in a corpse after a prolonged illness.[41] Van Helsing raised his foot to stamp in anger, but the instinct of his life and all the long years of habit stood to him, and he put it down again softly. "Quick!" he said. "Bring the brandy."[42] I flew to the dining-room, and returned with the decanter. He wetted the poor white lips with it, and together we rubbed palm and wrist and heart. He felt her heart, and after a few moments of agonising suspense said:—

"It is not too late. It beats, though but feebly. All our work is undone; we must begin anew. There is no young Arthur here now; I have to call on you yourself this time, friend John." As he spoke, he was dipping into his bag and producing the instruments for transfusion; I had taken off my coat and rolled up my shirt-sleeve.[43] There was no possibility of an opiate just at present, and no need of one;[44] and so, without a moment's delay, we began the operation. After a time—it did not seem a short time either, for the draining away of one's blood, no matter how willingly it be given, is a terrible feeling—Van Helsing held up a warning finger. "Do not stir," he said, "but I fear that with growing strength she may wake; and that would make danger, oh, so much danger. But I shall precaution take. I shall give hypodermic injection of morphia."[45] He proceeded then, swiftly and deftly, to carry out his intent. The effect on Lucy was not bad, for the faint seemed to merge subtly into the narcotic sleep. It was with a feeling of personal pride that I could see a faint tinge of colour steal back into the pallid cheeks and lips. No man knows till he experiences it, what it is to feel his own life-blood drawn away into the veins of the woman he loves.

The Professor watched me critically. "That will do," he said. "Already?" I remonstrated. "You took a great deal more from Art." To which he smiled a sad sort of smile as he replied:—

"He is her lover, her *fiancé*. You have work, much work, to do for her and for others, and the present will suffice."[46]

When we stopped the operation, he attended to Lucy, whilst I applied digital pressure to my own incision. I laid down, whilst I waited his leisure to attend to me, for I felt faint and a little sick. By-and-by he bound up my wound, and sent me down-stairs to get a glass of wine for myself. As I was leaving the room, he came after me, and half whispered:—

41 The medical reasons for this are obscure, but then little is known of the process of "vampirisation."

42 The use of alcohol as a stimulant was widespread at the end of the nineteenth century. In 1907, R. A. Hatcher, in *The Pharmacopeia and the Physician*, could still write: "Alcohol in the form of whisky or brandy is much used in shock or collapse. . . . Its value is strongly asserted by some authorities and disputed by others." Of course, the modern view is that alcohol depresses the central nervous system.

43 Thornley Stoker notes on the Manuscript page: "He would have been put *lying* down."

44 The balance of the sentence and the beginning of the next, up to the word "blood," do not appear in the Abridged Text, making nonsense of the sentences.

45 Unlike the earlier use of a "narcotic," here Van Helsing seems to go beyond the norms of medical practice. Although morphine was often used in place of opium as a sedative, intravenous injection of morphine would be indicated only for severe pain.

46 What "work" Van Helsing expects Seward to be undertaking is unclear. Van Helsing seems to be underlining that blood transfusion = sexual relations, and it would be improper for Seward to be given the same opportunities as a fiancé.

47 Well, yes, definitely "enjealous" in Van Helsing's (or Stoker's) distorted view of blood transfusing.

"Mind, nothing must be said of this. If our young lover should turn up unexpected, as before, no word to him. It would at once frighten him and enjealous him, too.[47] There must be none. So!"

When I came back he looked at me carefully, and then said:—

"You are not much the worse. Go into the room, and lie on your sofa, and rest awhile; then have much breakfast, and come here to me."

I followed out his orders, for I knew how right and wise they were. I had done my part, and now my next duty was to keep up my strength. I felt very weak, and in the weakness lost something of the amazement at what had occurred. I fell asleep on the sofa, however, wondering over and over again how Lucy had made such a retrograde movement, and how she could have been drained of so much blood with no sign anywhere to show for it. I think I must have continued my wonder in my dreams, for, sleeping and waking, my thoughts always came back to the little punctures in her throat and the ragged, exhausted appearance of their edges—tiny though they were.

Lucy slept well into the day, and when she woke she was fairly well and strong, though not nearly so much so as the day before. When Van Helsing had seen her, he went out for a walk, leaving me in charge, with strict injunctions that I was not to leave her for a moment. I could hear his voice in the hall, asking the way to the nearest telegraph office.

Lucy chatted with me freely, and seemed quite unconscious that anything had happened. I tried to keep her amused and interested. When her mother came up to see her, she did not seem to notice any change whatever, but said to me gratefully:—

"We owe you so much, Dr. Seward, for all you have done, but you really must now take care not to overwork yourself. You are looking pale yourself. You want a wife to nurse and look after you a bit; that you do!" As she spoke, Lucy turned crimson, though it was only momentarily, for her poor wasted veins could not stand for long such an unwonted drain to the head. The reaction came in excessive pallor as she turned imploring eyes on me. I smiled and nodded, and laid my finger on my lips; with a sigh, she sank back amid her pillows.

Van Helsing returned in a couple of hours, and presently said to me: "Now you go home, and eat much and drink enough. Make yourself strong. I stay here to-night, and I shall sit up with little miss myself. You and I must watch the case, and we must have none other to know. I have grave reasons. No, do not ask them; think what you will. Do not fear to think even the most not-probable. Good-night."

In the hall two of the maids came to me, and asked if they or either of them might not sit up with Miss Lucy. They implored me to let them; and when I said it was Dr. Van Helsing's wish that either he or I should sit up, they asked me quite piteously to intercede with the "foreign gentleman." I was much touched by their kindness. Perhaps it is because I am weak at present, and perhaps because it was on Lucy's account, that their devotion was manifested; for over and over again have I seen similar instances of woman's kindness. I got back here in time for a late dinner; went my rounds—all well; and set this down whilst waiting for sleep. It is coming.

11 September.[48]—This afternoon I went over to Hillingham. Found Van Helsing in excellent spirits, and Lucy much better. Shortly after I had arrived, a big parcel from abroad came for the Professor. He opened it with much impressment[49]—assumed, of course—and showed a great bundle of white flowers.

"These are for you, Miss Lucy," he said.

"For me? Oh, Dr. Van Helsing!"

"Yes, my dear, but not for you to play with. These are medicines." Here Lucy made a wry face. "Nay, but they are not to take in a decoction[50] or in nauseous form, so you need not snub that so charming nose, or I shall point out to my friend Arthur what woes he may have to endure in seeing so much beauty that he so loves so much distort. Aha, my pretty miss, that bring the so nice nose all straight again. This is medicinal, but you do not know how. I put him in your window, I make pretty wreath, and hang him round your neck, so that you sleep well. Oh yes! they, like the lotus flower, make your

<hr />

48 This must be 12 September, if Lucy's 12 September diary entry and subsequent entries are accurate. Otherwise, there is a missing day between the arrival of the garlic garlands and Lucy's comments on sleeping with them. Seward, whose days and nights have run into one another, can be forgiven for confusing the date of "this afternoon."

49 An archaic term meaning "earnestness" or "ardour."

50 "A solution resulting from boiled vegetable drugs" (William Warner, *Warner's Pocket Medical Dictionary*).

51 The Manuscript adds: " 'No sugar in mine thank you' as Mr. Morris would say." This must be the catchphrase of a popular American joke, now lost in obscurity, and it is omitted from the published text.

52 Garlic is a common herb, grown in England as well as many other places. Did Vanderpool's garlic have special therapeutic or repulsive properties?

trouble forgotten. It smell so like the waters of Lethe, and of that fountain of youth that the Conquistadores sought for in the Floridas, and find him all too late."

Whilst he was speaking, Lucy had been examining the flowers and smelling them. Now she threw them down, saying, with half-laughter, and half-disgust:—

"Oh, Professor, I believe you are only putting up a joke on me. Why, these flowers are only common garlic."[51]

To my surprise, Van Helsing rose up and said with all his sternness, his iron jaw set and his bushy eyebrows meeting:—

"No trifling with me! I never jest! There is grim purpose in all I do; and I warn you that you do not thwart me. Take care, for the sake of others if not for your own." Then seeing poor Lucy scared, as she might well be, he went on more gently: "Oh, little miss, my dear, do not fear me. I only do for your good; but there is much virtue to you in those so common flower. See, I place them myself in your room. I make myself the wreath that you are to wear. But hush! no telling to others that make so inquisitive questions. We must obey, and silence is a part of obedience; and obedience is to bring you strong and well into loving arms that wait for you. Now sit still a while. Come with me, friend John, and you shall help me deck the room with my garlic, which is all the way from Haarlem, where my friend Vanderpool raise herb in his glass-houses all the year.[52] I had to telegraph yesterday, or they would not have been here."

We went into the room, taking the flowers with us. The Professor's actions were certainly odd and not to be found in any pharmacopœia that I ever heard of. First he fastened up the windows and latched them securely; next, taking a handful of the flowers, he rubbed them all over the sashes, as though to ensure that every whiff of air that might get in would be laden with the garlic smell. Then with the wisp he rubbed all over the jamb of the door, above, below, and at each side, and round the fireplace in the same way. It all seemed grotesque to me, and presently I said:—

"Well, Professor, I know you always have a reason for what you do, but this certainly puzzles me. It is well we have no sceptic here, or he would say that you were working some spell to keep out an evil spirit."

"Perhaps I am!" he answered quietly as he began to make the wreath which Lucy was to wear round her neck.

We then waited whilst Lucy made her toilet for the night, and when she was in bed he came and himself fixed the wreath of garlic round her neck. The last words he said to her were:—

"Take care you do not disturb it; and even if the room feel close, do not to-night open the window or the door."

"I promise," said Lucy, "and thank you both a thousand times for all your kindness to me! Oh, what have I done to be blessed with such friends?"

As we left the house in my fly,[53] which was waiting, Van Helsing said:—

"To-night I can sleep in peace, and sleep I want—two nights of travel, much reading in the day between, and much anxiety on the day to follow, and a night to sit up, without to wink.[54] To-morrow in the morning early you call for me, and we come together to see our pretty miss, so much more strong for my 'spell' which I have work. Ho! ho!"

He seemed so confident that I, remembering my own confidence two nights before and with the baneful result, felt awe and vague terror. It must have been my weakness that made me hesitate to tell it to my friend, but I felt it all the more, like unshed tears.

[53] A two-wheeled vehicle, so named in supposed reference to its speed.

[54] However, as seen above, this is not Van Helsing's travel schedule—he spent an unexplained day in Amsterdam.

Chapter 11

LUCY WESTENRA'S DIARY.

12 September.[1]—How good they all are to me. I quite love that dear Dr. Van Helsing. I wonder why he was so anxious about these flowers. He positively frightened me, he was so fierce. And yet he must have been right, for I feel comfort from them already. Somehow, I do not dread being alone to-night, and I can go to sleep without fear. I shall not mind any flapping outside the window. Oh, the terrible struggle that I have had against sleep so often of late; the pain of the sleeplessness, or the pain of the fear of sleep, with such unknown horrors as it has for me! How blessed are some people, whose lives have no fears, no dreads; to whom sleep is a blessing that comes nightly, and brings nothing but sweet dreams. Well, here I am to-night, hoping for sleep, and lying like Ophelia in the play, with "virgin crants and maiden strewments."[2] I never liked garlic before, but to-night it is delightful! There is peace in its smell; I feel sleep coming already. Good-night, everybody.

DR. SEWARD'S DIARY.

13 September.[3]—Called at the Berkeley[4] and found Van Helsing, as usual, up to time. The carriage ordered from the hotel was waiting. The Professor took his bag, which he always brings with him now.

Let all be put down exactly. Van Helsing and I arrived at

1 Possibly a dating error, by either Lucy or the transcriber Mina Harker. From the text of Lucy's entry, this appears to be the same evening as the previous Seward entry, which he dated 11 September (perhaps erroneously).

2 Lucy is recalling the scene of Ophelia's burial in *Hamlet* (act 5, scene 1), when a priest acknowledges that notwithstanding her suicide, "Yet here she is allow'd her virgin crants, / Her maiden strewments, and the bringing home / Of bell and burial." "Crants" are garlands; "strewments" are something strewed, as in flowers on a grave.

3 Again, a questionable date: this appears to succeed Seward's prior entry on 11 September and should be 12 September if Seward's earlier date is correct.

4 Note that there is no mention that Van Helsing has changed hotels; see chapter 9, note 53. The Berkeley, at the corner of Piccadilly Circus and Berkeley Street, was popular with Mayfair debutantes. The structure was white-faced with gilded balconies and was totally remodelled in 1897, including an expansion of its renowned dining room. Purchased by Richard D'Oyly-Carte in 1901, it became part of the Savoy Group; the hotel was eventually closed in the 1960s and reopened in 1972

Hillingham at eight o'clock. It was a lovely morning;[5] the bright sunshine and all the fresh feeling of early autumn seemed like the completion of nature's annual work. The leaves were turning to all kinds of beautiful colours,[6] but had not yet begun to drop from the trees. When we entered we met Mrs. Westenra coming out of the morning room. She is always an early riser. She greeted us warmly and said:—

"You will be glad to know that Lucy is better. The dear child is still asleep. I looked into her room and saw her, but did not go in, lest I should disturb her." The Professor smiled, and looked quite jubilant. He rubbed his hands together and said:—

Smoking Room at the Berkeley Hotel, ca. 1897.

at its present location on Wilton Place in Knightsbridge.

5 This and the following sentence do not appear in the Abridged Text.

6 Leatherdale (*Dracula Unearthed*) notes that this is highly unusual for September, more like October, casting suspicion on the entire series of dates on these journal entries.

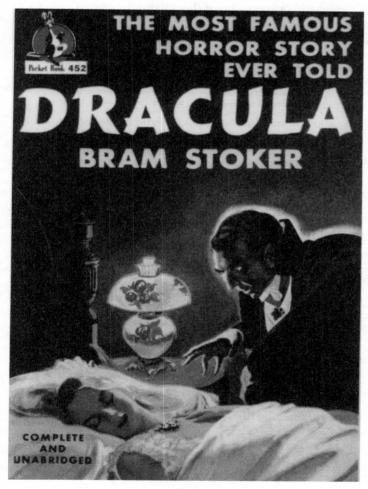

Cover of *Dracula*.
(New York: Pocket Books, 1947)

7 This is the first exhibition of maternal care by Mrs. Westenra, and Leatherdale (*Dracula Unearthed*) surmises that her anxious care was in fact the result of a telepathic command of Dracula.

8 The "temper of the ice-brook" indeed! He would of course have done better to save this exhibition until after he saw his patient.

"Aha! I thought I had diagnosed the case. My treatment is working," to which she answered:—

"You must not take all the credit to yourself, doctor. Lucy's state this morning is due in part to me."

"How do you mean, ma'am?" asked the Professor.

"Well, I was anxious about the dear child in the night, and went into her room.**7** She was sleeping soundly—so soundly that even my coming did not wake her. But the room was awfully stuffy. There were a lot of those horrible, strong-smelling flowers about everywhere, and she had actually a bunch of them round her neck. I feared that the heavy odour would be too much for the dear child in her weak state, so I took them all away and opened a bit of the window to let in a little fresh air. You will be pleased with her, I am sure."

She moved off into her boudoir, where she usually breakfasted early. As she had spoken, I watched the Professor's face, and saw it turn ashen grey. He had been able to retain his self-command whilst the poor lady was present, for he knew her state and how mischievous a shock would be; he actually smiled on her as he held open the door for her to pass into her room. But the instant she had disappeared he pulled me, suddenly and forcibly, into the dining-room and closed the door.

Then, for the first time in my life, I saw Van Helsing break down. He raised his hands over his head in a sort of mute despair, and then beat his palms together in a helpless way; finally he sat down on a chair, and putting his hands before his face, began to sob, with loud, dry sobs that seemed to come from the very racking of his heart.**8** Then he raised his arms again, as though appealing to the whole universe. "God! God! God!" he said. "What have we done, what has this poor thing done, that we are so sore beset? Is there fate amongst us still, sent down from the pagan world of old, that such things must be, and in such way? This poor mother, all unknowing, and all for the best as she think, does such thing as lose her daughter body and soul; and we must not tell her, we must not even warn her, or she die, and then both die. Oh, how we are beset! How are all the powers of the devils against us!" Suddenly he jumped to his feet. "Come," he said, "come, we must see and act. Devils or no devils, or all the devils at once, it matters not;

we fight him all the same." He went to the hall-door for his bag; and together we went up to Lucy's room.

Once again I drew up the blind, whilst Van Helsing went towards the bed. This time he did not start as he looked on the poor face with the same awful, waxen pallor as before. He wore a look of stern sadness and infinite pity.

"As I expected," he murmured, with that hissing inspiration of his which meant so much. Without a word he went and locked the door, and then began to set out on the little table the instruments for yet another operation of transfusion of blood. I had long ago recognised the necessity, and begun to take off my coat, but he stopped me with a warning hand. "No!" he said. "To-day you must operate. I shall provide. You are weakened already." As he spoke he took off his coat and rolled up his shirt-sleeve.[9]

Again the operation; again the narcotic; again some return of colour to the ashy cheeks, and the regular breathing of healthy sleep. This time I watched whilst Van Helsing recruited himself and rested.

Presently he took an opportunity of telling Mrs. Westenra that she must not remove anything from Lucy's room without consulting him; that the flowers were of medicinal value, and that the breathing of their odour was a part of the system of cure. Then he took over the care of the case himself, saying that he would watch this night and the next and would send me word when to come.

After another hour Lucy waked from her sleep, fresh and bright and seemingly not much the worse for her terrible ordeal.[10]

What does it all mean? I am beginning to wonder if my long habit of life amongst the insane is beginning to tell upon my own brain.

LUCY WESTENRA'S DIARY.

17 September.—Four days and nights of peace.[11] I am getting so strong again that I hardly know myself. It is as if I had passed through some long nightmare, and had just awakened to see the beautiful sunshine and feel the fresh air of the morning around

9 Truly remarkable doctoring. Although the science of blood transfusing was still in its infancy, there was some understanding that compatibility of donor and recipient was important. Having transfused Lucy twice successfully (by blind luck), Van Helsing rolls the dice a third time, risking serious problems, rather than fall back on a tested donor.

10 Leatherdale (*Dracula Unearthed*) finds it incredible that one who has been at death's door so recently should emerge looking so healthy. Either Lucy's "turning" is having bipolar effects on her appearance—with swings from a skeletal to a healthful appearance—or Seward is so besotted that the accuracy of his record is questionable.

11 Another questionable date. Lucy's first night of "peace" should have been 12 September, so either this is 16 September or Lucy has miscounted. Resetting this date to 16 September reconciles the problem of Van Helsing's round-trip to Amsterdam, which could not have taken less than twenty-four hours. See the next note.

12 Van Helsing returns on the morning of 18 September, according to Dr. Seward's diary. If Seward's date is correct, then Van Helsing could not have left London for Amsterdam on the evening of 17 September. He must have left on 16 September.

13 Dracula continues to seek entry to the room. One wonders why he did not command Lucy to incapacitate Van Helsing or to again cause Mrs. Westenra to remove the garlic while Van Helsing slept. At this point Dracula has no particular reason to fear Van Helsing any more than the other ineffectual caretakers, Seward and Mina, unless he had prior experiences with Van Helsing.

14 A London evening newspaper, founded in 1865. In 1882, the Liberal *Gazette* reduced its price from twopence to a penny to be more competitive and to appeal to a mass readership rather than strictly to "gentlemen." In 1883, the editorship was assumed by W. T. Stead, one of the greatest Victorian-Edwardian journalists. Born in Northumberland to a Congregationalist minister, Stead founded what Matthew Arnold termed the "New Journalism" and turned the *Gazette* into the forerunner of the hard-hitting tabloids, introducing, among other features, the personal interview. A righteous man who used the paper as his pulpit, Stead attacked slum housing and was largely responsible for enactment of the abandoned Criminal Law Amendment bill, child prostitution legislation that raised the age of consent from thirteen to sixteen. His most influential and inflammatory series was an 1885 exposé in which, borrowing from ancient history and Greek mythology, he graphically described the depraved procurement of underage girls in London (which he likened to Babylon) by well-heeled aristocrats ("Minotaurs"). The series was as popular with the public as it was unpopular with government and the medical profession, the latter for Stead's revelations of payments by brothels to doctors "certifying" the virginity of certain prostitutes. Under intense pressure,

me. I have a dim half-remembrance of long, anxious times of waiting and fearing; darkness in which there was not even the pain of hope to make present distress more poignant; and then long spells of oblivion, and the rising back to life as a diver coming up through a great press of water. Since, however, Dr. Van Helsing has been with me, all this bad dreaming seems to have passed away; the noises that used to frighten me out of my wits—the flapping against the windows, the distant voices which seemed so close to me, the harsh sounds that came from I know not where and commanded me to do I know not what— have all ceased. I go to bed now without any fear of sleep. I do not even try to keep awake. I have grown quite fond of the garlic, and a boxful arrives for me every day from Haarlem. To-night Dr. Van Helsing is going away, as he has to be for a day in Amsterdam.**12** But I need not be watched; I am well enough to be left alone. Thank God for mother's sake, and dear Arthur's, and for all our friends who have been so kind! I shall not even feel the change, for last night Dr. Van Helsing slept in his chair a lot of the time. I found him asleep twice when I awoke; but I did not fear to go to sleep again, although the boughs or bats or something flapped almost angrily against the window-panes.**13**

"THE PALL MALL GAZETTE," **14** *18 SEPTEMBER.*

THE ESCAPED WOLF.
PERILOUS ADVENTURE OF OUR INTERVIEWER.

INTERVIEW WITH THE KEEPER IN THE ZOOLOGICAL GARDENS.

After many inquiries and almost as many refusals, and perpetually using the words, "Pall Mall Gazette" as a sort of talisman, I managed to find the keeper of the section of the Zoölogical Gardens**15** in which the wolf department is included. Thomas Bilder lives in one of the cottages in the enclosure behind the elephant-house, and was just sitting down to his tea when I found him. Thomas and his wife are hospitable folk, elderly, and without children, and if the specimen I enjoyed of their hospitality be of the average kind, their lives must be pretty comfortable.[16] The keeper would not enter on what he called "business" until the supper was over, and we were all satisfied. Then when the table was cleared, and he had lit his pipe, he said:—

"Now, sir, you can go on and arsk me what you want. You'll excoose me refoosin' to talk of perfeshunal subjects afore meals. I gives the wolves and the jackals and the hyenas in all our section their tea afore I begins to arsk them questions."

"How do you mean, ask them questions?" I queried, wishful to get him into a talkative humour.

"'Ittin' of them over the 'ead with a pole is one way; scratchin' of their hears is another, when gents as is flush wants a bit of a show-orf to their gals. I don't so much mind the fust—the 'ittin with a pole afore I chucks in their dinner; but I waits till they've 'ad their sherry and kawffee, so to speak, afore I tries on with the ear-scratchin'. Mind you," he added philosophically, "there's a deal of the same nature in us as in them theer animiles. Here's you a-comin' and arskin' of me questions about my business, and I that grumpy-like that only for your bloomin' 'arf-quid I'd 'a' seen you blowed fust 'fore I'd answer. Not even when you arsked me sarcastic-like if I'd like you to arsk the Superintendent if you might arsk me questions. Without offence did I tell yer to go to 'ell?"

"You did."

"An' when you said you'd report me for usin' of obscene language that was 'ittin' me over the 'ead; but the 'arf-quid made that all right. I weren't a-goin' to fight, so I waited for the food, and did with my 'owl as the wolves, and lions, and tigers does. But, Lor' love yer 'art, now that the old 'ooman has stuck a chunk of her tea-cake in me, an' rinsed me out with her bloomin' old teapot, and I've lit hup, you may scratch my ears for all you're worth, and won't git even a growl out of me. Drive along with your questions. I know what yer a-comin' at, that 'ere escaped wolf."

"Exactly. I want you to give me your view of it. Just tell me how it happened; and when I know the facts I'll get you to say what you consider was the cause of it, and how you think the whole affair will end."

Stead admitted that in researching and writing the first installment of the series, he had improperly failed to secure the consent of the father of Eliza Armstrong, an underprivileged girl Stead featured, and had neglected to deliver a promised advance payment to Eliza's mother. Seizing on these admissions, Stead's enemies procured his conviction for alleged abduction and indecent assault of Armstrong, and he served three month's imprisonment for his crimes.

Nominated for the Nobel Peace Prize several times, Stead left the *Gazette* in 1890, and in 1892 the paper was sold and turned Conservative. Stead had earlier written about disasters involving a mail steamer's lack of lifeboats and a ship's collision with an iceberg, but his prescience failed to save him: en route to a 1912 Carnegie Hall congress on world peace and international arbitration, he died on the *Titanic*.

15　The London Zoological Gardens (the "Zoo") in Regent's Park, with its south entrance about ¾ mile from the Baker Street station of the Metropolitan Railway, was founded as a scientific endeavour in 1828 by the Zoological Society. The initial 430 animals were donated by the Royal Menagerie at the Tower of London. By 1896, the Zoo contained about 2,400 animals. For its first two decades, admission was granted only to members of the Zoological Society and their guests; still, the new attraction was immensely popular, and it became even more so when opened to the general public. Victorian visitors were tickled and awed to witness these exotic animals up close for the first time, and their delight was tinged with the thrill that the Zoo's powerful captives might potentially escape.

The 1896 London "Baedeker" advised that the best time to visit the animals "is at the feeding-hour, when even the lethargic carnivora are to be seen in a state of activity and excitement." Feeding time for the beasts of prey was 4:00 P.M. in September. The "Wolves' and Foxes' Dens" were located opposite the large Lion House and abutted the park. The "house" for the elephants and rhinoceroses, behind which Bilder lived, was about 400 yards from the wolves' enclosure, about as far away as is possible on the Zoo grounds.

16 The sentence does not appear in the Abridged Text.

17 "Berserker" (presumably the wolf's true name) is aptly named. See chapter 3, note 12.

18 Charles Jamrach was an animal dealer and "naturalist" who supplied many menageries from his shop on the Ratcliffe Highway. Jamrach was remembered for an encounter with an escaped tiger in 1857 and as a collector of "Eastern curiosities." Donald Shaw, in his 1908 reminiscence *London in the Sixties*, wrote: "Continuing along St. George's Street will be found Jamrach's menagerie, whence filter most of the rarities that find their way to the Zoological Gardens; and the place is no ordinary bird shop, but a museum of information in more ways than one. Here one large room will be found stuffed with bronzes and curios from all parts of the world, which every American visiting London, who fancies he is a critic, does not fail to inspect; for Mr. Jamrach—like his father—is an authority, and a naturalist in the highest acceptation of the term. Lovers of animals will not regret a pilgrimage to 'the [Ratcliffe] Highway,' a pilgrimage which, by the aid of the District Railway and broad, electric-

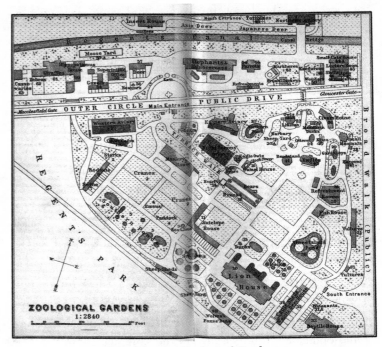

Plan of London Zoological Gardens.
Karl Baedeker, *London and Its Environs: Handbook for Travellers* (1896)

London Zoological Gardens, The Lion House.
Queen's London (1897)

"All right, guv'nor. This 'ere is about the 'ole story. That 'ere wolf what we called Bersicker[17] was one of three grey ones that came from Norway to Jamrach's,[18] which we bought off him four years ago. He was a nice well-behaved wolf, that never gave no trouble to talk of. I'm more surprised at 'im for wantin' to get out nor any other animile in the place.[19] But, there, you can't trust wolves no more nor women."

"Don't you mind him, sir!" broke in Mrs. Tom, with a cheery laugh. "'E's got mindin' the animiles so long that blest if he ain't like a old wolf 'isself! But there ain't no 'arm in 'im."

"Well, sir, it was about two hours after feedin' yesterday when I first hear any disturbance. I was makin' up a litter in the monkey-house for a young puma which is ill;[20] but when I heard the yelpin' and 'owlin' I kem away straight. There was Bersicker a-tearin' like a mad thing at the bars as if he wanted to get out. There wasn't much people about that day, and close at hand was only one man, a tall, thin chap, with a 'ook nose and a pointed beard, with a few white hairs runnin' through it.[21] He had a 'ard, cold look and red eyes, and I took a sort of mislike to him, for it seemed as if it was 'im as they was hirritated at. He 'ad white kid gloves on 'is 'ands,[22] and he pointed out the animiles to me and says: 'Keeper, these wolves seem upset at something.'

" 'Maybe it's you,' says I, for I did not like the airs as he give 'isself. He didn't git angry, as I 'oped he would, but he smiled a kind of insolent smile, with a mouth full of white, sharp teeth. 'Oh no, they wouldn't like me,' 'e says.

" 'Ow yes, they would,' says I, a-imitatin' of him. 'They always like a bone or two to clean their teeth on about tea-time, which you 'as a bagful.'

"Well, it was a odd thing, but when the animiles see us a-talkin' they lay down, and when I went over to Bersicker he let me stroke his ears same as ever. That there man kem over, and blessed but if he didn't put in his hand and stroke the old wolf's ears too!

" 'Tyke care,' says I. 'Bersicker is quick.'

" 'Never mind,' he says. 'I'm used to 'em!'

" 'Are you in the business yourself?' I says, tyking off my 'at, for a man what trades in wolves, anceterer, is a good friend to keepers.

" 'No,' says he, 'not exactly in the business, but I 'ave made pets of several.' And with that he lifts his 'at as perlite as a lord, and walks away. Old Bersicker kep' a-lookin' arter 'im till 'e was out of sight, and then went and lay down in a corner and wouldn't come hout the 'ole hevening. Well, larst night, so soon as the moon was hup, the wolves here all began a-'owling.[23] There warn't nothing for them to 'owl at. There warn't no one near, except some one that was evidently a-callin' a dog somewheres out back of the gardings in the Park road. Once or twice I went out to see that all was right, and it was, and then the 'owling stopped. Just before twelve o'clock I just took a look round afore turnin' in, an', bust me, but when I kem opposite to old Bersicker's cage I see the rails broken and twisted about and the cage empty.[24] And that's all I know for certing."

"Did any one else see anything?"

"One of our gard'ners was a-comin' 'ome about that time from a 'armony,[25] when he sees a big grey dog comin' out through

The Ratcliffe Highway, Stepney, 1896.

lighted streets, is no longer attended with discomfort or danger." As reported by Charles Dickens Jr. (*Dickens's Dictionary of London*), the Ratcliffe Highway had had an extremely unsavoury reputation.

19 The sentence is not in the Abridged Text.

20 Bilder's task is not mentioned in the Abridged Text.

21 Dracula has grown a beard? This may be another disguise, as with the appearance of the "coachman" (see text accompanying chapter 1, note 88), but it is a nice touch to add "a few white hairs" to a costume beard. Wolf (*The Essential Dracula*) again notes that Dracula is active during the daytime.

22 Leatherdale (*Dracula Unearthed*) suggests that these are to conceal his hairy palms and pointed nails, otherwise likely to alarm a zookeeper.

23 The three sentences following do not appear in the Abridged Text.

24 Unless the bars were made of wood (or glass), it is unlikely that Berserker broke them himself. Rather, he was probably aided by some (in)human hand. Leatherdale (*Dracula Unearthed*) suggests that Dracula projected great strength onto Berserker rather than dirty his own hands. However, there is ample evidence elsewhere of Dracula's willingness to do physical labour—the carrying of Harker's luggage and, later, the lifting of large boxes of earth, for example—and without any other hints of Dracula's ability to "project" strength, Leatherdale's suggestion must be viewed as highly speculative.

As we will see, Dracula has a purpose for Berserker.

25 A sing-along. The Cave of Harmony was a vast music hall and popular drinking and singing establishment in London for much of the nineteenth century.

26 The Abridged Text omits Bilder's joke that follows.

27 A half-pound, or 10 shillings. In today's economic purchasing power, this is over £33, or more than US$60, a generous "tip" (or bribe).

28 This is evidence that Hillingham lies north of the Zoo, north of Regents Park, in the vicinity of Hampstead Heath.

the garding 'edges. At least, so he says; but I don't give much for it myself, for if he did 'e never said a word about it to his missis when 'e got 'ome, and it was only after the escape of the wolf was made known, and we had been up all night a-huntin' of the Park for Bersicker, that he remembered seein' anything. My own belief was that the 'armony 'ad got into his 'ead."

"Now, Mr. Bilder, can you account in any way for the escape of the wolf?"[26]

"Well, sir," he said, with a suspicious sort of modesty, "I think I can; but I don't know as 'ow you'd be satisfied with the theory."

"Certainly I shall. If a man like you, who knows the animals from experience, can't hazard a good guess at any rate, who is even to try?"

"Well then, sir, I accounts for it this way; it seems to me that 'ere wolf escaped—simply because he wanted to get out."

From the hearty way that both Thomas and his wife laughed at the joke I could see that it had done service before, and that the whole explanation was simply an elaborate sell. I couldn't cope in badinage with the worthy Thomas, but I thought I knew a surer way to his heart, so I said:—

"Now, Mr. Bilder, we'll consider that first half-sovereign[27] worked off, and this brother of his is waiting to be claimed when you've told me what you think will happen."

"Right y'are, sir," he said briskly. "Ye'll excoose me, I know, for a-chaffin' of ye, but the old woman here winked at me, which was as much as telling me to go on."

"Well, I never!" said the old lady.

"My opinion is this: that 'ere wolf is a-'idin' of, somewheres. The gard'ner wot didn't remember said he was a-gallopin' northward[28] faster than a horse could go; but I don't believe him, for, yer see, sir, wolves don't gallop no more nor dogs does, they not bein' built that way. Wolves is fine things in a story-book, and I dessay when they gets in packs and does be chivyin' somethin' that's more afeared than they is they can make a devil of a noise and chop it up, whatever it is. But, Lor' bless you, in real life a wolf is only a low creature, not half so clever or bold as a good dog; and not half a quarter so much fight in 'im. This one ain't been used to fightin' or even to providin' for hisself, and more like he's somewhere round the Park a-'idin' an' a-shiverin' of, and, if he thinks at all, wonderin' where he is to get his breakfast from; or maybe he's got down some area and is in a coal-cellar.[29] My eye, won't some cook get a rum start when she sees his green eyes a-shinin' at her out of the dark! If he can't get food he's bound to look for it, and mayhap he may chance to light on a butcher's shop in time. If he doesn't, and some nursemaid goes a-walkin' orf with a soldier, leavin' of the hinfant in the perambulator—well then I shouldn't be surprised if the census is one babby the less. That's all."

I was handing him the half-sovereign, when something came bobbing up against the window, and Mr. Bilder's face doubled its natural length with surprise.

"God bless me!" he said. "If there ain't old Bersicker come back by 'isself!"

He went to the door and opened it; a most unnecessary proceeding it seemed to me. I have always thought that a wild animal never looks so well as when some obstacle of pronounced durability is between us; a personal experience has intensified rather than diminished that idea.[30]

After all, however, there is nothing like custom, for neither Bilder nor his wife thought any more of the wolf than I should of a dog. The animal itself was as peaceful and well-behaved as that father of all picture-wolves—Red Riding Hood's quondam friend, whilst moving her confidence in masquerade.

The whole scene was an unutterable mixture of comedy and pathos. The wicked wolf that for a half a day had paralysed London and set all the children in town shivering in their shoes, was there in a sort of penitent mood, and was received and petted like a sort of vulpine prodigal son. Old Bilder examined him all over with most tender solicitude, and when he had finished with his penitent said:—

"There, I knew the poor old chap would get into some kind of trouble; didn't I say it all along? Here's his head all cut and full of broken glass. 'E's been a-gettin' over some bloomin' wall or other. It's a shyme that people are allowed to top their walls with broken bottles.[31] This 'ere's what comes of it. Come along, Bersicker."

29 This and the following sentence do not appear in the Abridged Text.

30 In the Abridged Text, this sentence, evidencing the pomposity of the reporter, does not appear.

31 The custom was apparently prevalent among the owners of walled houses; compare, for example, the experience of Holmes and Watson in scaling a wall in the course of burgling the Hampstead Heath home of the blackmailer Charles Augustus Milverton (in the eponymous "Adventure").

32 No such article appears in the archives of the *Pall Mall Gazette*. The Notes record that an escaped wolf was killed near Lucy's home. The whole affair seems to be a fictionalised account inserted by Stoker to dramatise the events. See note 45 below.

33 In the Abridged Text, "Dr. Seward's" negligence is not mentioned, and the subject of his "engagement" is left undescribed.

34 The "Superintendent" of the typical private asylum was the chief medical/executive officer, reporting to a board of trustees or "committee of visitors," as such a body was often styled.

35 It is surprising that an asylum would allow patients access to sharp dinner knives; the common practise was to use only blunt, dull instruments to avoid self-injury. Seward seems to run a lax institution, with inadequate patient monitoring (resulting in frequent escapes), unnecessarily padded cells, and readily accessible dangerous implements.

36 Renfield, like the Devil, has twisted the Scriptures to his own purpose: the biblical source is a *prohibition* on the consumption of blood: "For the life of the flesh is in the blood. . . . Therefore I said unto the children of Israel, No soul of you shall eat blood, neither shall any stranger that sojourneth among you eat blood" (Lev. 17:11–12).

He took the wolf and locked him up in a cage, with a piece of meat that satisfied, in quantity at any rate, the elementary conditions of the fatted calf, and went off to report.

I came off, too, to report the only exclusive information that is given to-day regarding the strange escapade at the Zoo.[32]

DR. SEWARD'S DIARY.

17 September.—I was engaged after dinner in my study posting up my books, which, through press of other work and the many visits to Lucy, had fallen sadly into arrear.[33] Suddenly the door was burst open, and in rushed my patient, with his face distorted with passion. I was thunderstruck, for such a thing as a patient getting of his own accord into the Superintendent's study is almost unknown.[34] Without an instant's pause he made straight at me. He had a dinner-knife in his hand, and, as I saw he was dangerous, I tried to keep the table between us.[35] He was too quick and too strong for me, however; for before I could get my balance he had struck at me and cut my left wrist rather severely. Before he could strike again, however, I got in my right, and he was sprawling on his back on the floor. My wrist bled freely, and quite a little pool trickled on to the carpet. I saw that my friend was not intent on further effort, and occupied myself binding up my wrist, keeping a wary eye on the prostrate figure all the time. When the attendants rushed in, and we turned our attention to him, his employment positively sickened me. He was lying on his belly on the floor licking up, like a dog, the blood which had fallen from my wounded wrist. He was easily secured, and, to my surprise, went with the attendants quite placidly, simply repeating over and over again: "The blood is the life! the blood is the life!"[36]

I cannot afford to lose blood just at present; I have lost too much of late for my physical good, and then the prolonged strain of Lucy's illness and its horrible phases is telling on me. I am over-excited and weary, and I need rest, rest, rest. Happily Van Helsing has not summoned me, so I need not forego my sleep; to-night I could not well do without it.

TELEGRAM, VAN HELSING, ANTWERP,[37] TO SEWARD, CARFAX.
(Sent to Carfax, Sussex, as no county given; delivered late by twenty-two hours.)[38]

"*17 September.*—DO NOT FAIL TO BE AT HILLINGHAM TO-NIGHT. IF NOT WATCHING ALL THE TIME, FREQUENTLY VISIT AND SEE THAT FLOWERS ARE AS PLACED; VERY IMPORTANT; DO NOT FAIL. SHALL BE WITH YOU AS SOON AS POSSIBLE AFTER ARRIVAL."[39]

DR. SEWARD'S DIARY.

18 September.—Just off for train to London.[40] The arrival of Van Helsing's telegram filled me with dismay.[41] A whole night lost, and I know by bitter experience what may happen in a night. Of course it is possible that all may be well, but what *may* have happened? Surely there is some horrible doom hanging over us that every possible accident should thwart us in all we try to do. I shall take this cylinder with me, and then I can complete my entry on Lucy's phonograph.[42]

MEMORANDUM LEFT BY LUCY WESTENRA.

17 September. Night.—I write this and leave it to be seen, so that no one may by any chance get into trouble through me. This is an exact record of what took place to-night. I feel I am dying of weakness, and have barely strength to write, but it must be done if I die in the doing.

I went to bed as usual, taking care that the flowers were placed as Dr. Van Helsing directed, and soon fell asleep.

I was waked by the flapping at the window, which had begun after that sleep-walking on the cliff at Whitby when Mina saved me, and which now I know so well. I was not afraid, but I did wish that Dr. Seward was in the next room—as Dr. Van Helsing said he would be—so that I might have called him. I tried to go to sleep, but could not. Then there came to me the

37 The main seaport of Belgium, population 180,000 (1873); a stop on the trip from London to Amsterdam.

38 In other words, the telegram was apparently delayed because Van Helsing failed to address it properly. The arrogant doctor makes no apology for his fatal error.

39 The date of this telegram confirms that Van Helsing was travelling on 17 September but of course does not indicate whether he was on his way to or from Amsterdam. If he left London on 16 September, as Seward indicates (see note 12 above), then he could have passed through Antwerp on the morning of 17 September, conducted his business in Amsterdam, and returned to London on 18 September. According to *Bradshaw's* continental guide, the journey from London to Amsterdam via Brussels and Antwerp could be accomplished by the 9:00 P.M. train from Charing Cross, arriving in Brussels at 5:42 A.M. A 6:00 A.M. train (stopping in Antwerp) would arrive in Amsterdam at 12:08 P.M., for total travel time of about fifteen hours by train and steamship. Although this is not the swiftest route (London-Rotterdam-Amsterdam would have been quicker—see chapter 10, note 32), Van Helsing may have had business in Brussels or Antwerp.

40 This is a reminder that Seward's asylum (and its neighbour Carfax) are remote from Hillingham, probably a distance of more than 20 miles. It is a complete and utter coincidence, keep in mind, that Dracula's victim Lucy Westenra and Dracula's neighbour John Seward are acquainted—or is it?

41 Leatherdale (*Dracula Unearthed*) points out that Seward never expected to be summoned to Hillingham and that responsibility for the pending disaster falls completely on Van Helsing, who should have notified Seward of his trip. Did Dracula telepathically learn of Van Helsing's trip and conclude that Lucy would be

unguarded, or did he perhaps arrange for Van Helsing to be called away?

42 It is unclear why Lucy has a phonograph. Although by the end of the nineteenth century the phonograph was sold with musical recordings, at this earlier time its primary use was for home (and business) recordings. There is certainly no evidence of Lucy using it. Perhaps it was a relic of Mr. Westenra's business.

43 Once again, Mrs. Westenra displays unwonted maternal care—probably to check that Lucy was not under anyone's protection.

44 The Manuscript has an insertion, in Stoker's hand, that reads, "and then a pattering of quick paws on the verandah." This does not appear in the published text. The removal of the reference to the verandah relates to concealing the identity of the house (see chapter 9, note 33).

45 The average male grey wolf weighs about 100 pounds and is about 3 feet high and 5 feet long. Although Berserker is described as "great" and "gaunt," it is impossible to imagine such an animal leaping to the height of a second-story (English first-story) window with enough strength to smash through it unless all the devils of hell were on its tail (a possibility, of course). If Dracula could inspire a wolf to such an amazing feat of strength, why not a bat or a more agile neighbourhood dog? Of course, if the house had a verandah outside the window (see note 44 above), the wolf could have leapt to it first and then broken the window.

Wolf (*The Essential Dracula*) contends that the forcible entry of Berserker, followed by Dracula, violates the "rule" enunciated by Van Helsing that vampires can only enter where invited previously (see text accompanying chapter 18, note 36). However, it is clear that Lucy herself must have invited Dracula in on an earlier occasion (see chapter 9, note 34), and the purpose of Berserker's forcible entry was merely to breach the barrier of the window— and presumably in the process knock down the

old fear of sleep, and I determined to keep awake. Perversely sleep would try to come then when I did not want it; so, as I feared to be alone, I opened my door and called out: "Is there anybody there?" There was no answer. I was afraid to wake mother, and so closed my door again. Then outside in the shrubbery I heard a sort of howl like a dog's, but more fierce and deeper. I went to the window and looked out, but could see nothing, except a big bat, which had evidently been buffeting its wings against the window. So I went back to bed again, but determined not to go to sleep. Presently the door opened, and mother looked in;[43] seeing by my moving that I was not asleep, came in, and sat by me. She said to me even more sweetly and softly than her wont:—

"I was uneasy about you, darling, and came in to see that you were all right."

I feared she might catch cold sitting there, and asked her to come in and sleep with me, so she came into bed, and lay down beside me; she did not take off her dressing-gown, for she said she would only stay a while and then go back to her own bed. As she lay there in my arms, and I in hers, the flapping and buffeting came to the window again. She was startled and a little frightened, and cried out: "What is that?" I tried to pacify her, and at last succeeded, and she lay quiet; but I could hear her poor dear heart still beating terribly. After a while there was the low howl again out in the shrubbery,[44] and shortly after there was a crash at the window, and a lot of broken glass was hurled on the floor. The window blind blew back with the wind that rushed in, and in the aperture of the broken panes there was the head of a great, gaunt grey wolf.[45] Mother cried out in a fright, and struggled up into a sitting posture, and clutched wildly at anything that would help her. Amongst other things, she clutched the wreath of flowers that Dr. Van Helsing insisted on my wearing round my neck, and tore it away from me.[46] For a second or two she sat up, pointing at the wolf, and there was a strange and horrible gurgling in her throat; then she fell over—as if struck with lightning, and her head hit my forehead and made me dizzy for a moment or two. The room and all round seemed to spin round. I kept my eyes fixed on the window, but the wolf drew his head back, and a whole myriad of little specks seems to come blowing in through the broken window, and wheeling and circling round like the pillar of dust that travellers describe when there is a simoom in the desert.[47] I tried to stir, but there was some spell upon me, and dear mother's poor body, which seemed to grow cold already—for her dear heart had ceased to beat—weighed me down; and I remembered no more for a while.

The time did not seem long, but very, very awful, till I recovered consciousness again. Somewhere near, a passing bell was tolling; the dogs all round the neighbourhood were howling; and in our shrubbery, seemingly just outside, a nightingale was singing.[48] I was dazed and stupid with pain and terror and weakness, but the sound of the nightingale seemed like the voice of my dead mother come back to comfort me. The sounds seemed to have awakened the maids, too, for I could hear their bare feet pattering outside my door. I called to them, and they came in, and when they saw what had happened, and what it was that lay over me on the bed, they screamed out. The wind rushed in through the broken window, and the door slammed to. They lifted off the body of my dear mother, and laid her, covered up with a sheet, on the bed after I had got up. They were all so frightened and nervous that I directed them to go to the dining-room and have each a glass of wine. The door flew open for an instant and closed again.[49] The maids shrieked, and then went in a body to the dining-room; and I laid what flowers I had on my dear mother's breast. When they were there I remembered what Dr. Van Helsing had told me, but I didn't like to remove them, and, besides, I would have some of the servants to sit up with me now. I was surprised that the maids did not come back. I called them, but got no answer, so I went to the dining-room to look for them.

My heart sank when I saw what had happened. They all four lay helpless on the floor, breathing heavily. The decanter of sherry was on the table half full, but there was a queer, acrid smell about.[50] I was suspicious, and examined the decanter. It smelt of laudanum, and looking on the sideboard, I found that the bottle which mother's doctor uses for her—oh! did use—was empty. What am I to do? what am I to do? I am back in the room with mother. I cannot leave her, and I am alone, save for the sleeping servants, whom some one has drugged.[51] Alone

garlands of garlic that likely surrounded it. The massive presence of garlic in the room must have blocked Dracula's customary hypnotic commands to Lucy to remove it and open the window. See chapter 3, note 4, for an instance in the *Odyssey* in which garlic counteracted the effects of a sorceress's spell.

Leatherdale (*Dracula Unearthed*) wonders, however, why Dracula required Berserker's assistance at all, for Dracula has the ability to "dematerialise" and could easily pass through the window unopened (or through the crack between the windows). This further suggests that the involvement of the wolf was a dramatisation introduced by Stoker in the narrative. See also note 32 above.

46 Evidently at Dracula's telepathic command.

47 A hot, dry, suffocating sand-wind prevalent in the deserts of Africa, especially Egypt. The deserts of Africa had been much in the public's mind after the uproar over the death in 1885 of General Charles "Chinese" Gordon, who served as governor of the Sudan from 1877 to 1879. In 1884 he returned to defend the capital, Khartoum, from the Mahdi (Muhammad Ahmad), who claimed to be the messianic twelfth Imam and who sought to eliminate the Egyptian authority and purify Islam. Khartoum was besieged for ten months, but despite the entreaties of the British public, Prime Minister William Gladstone delayed in sending reinforcements. Shortly before his death (according to Lytton Strachey's 1918 *Eminent Victorians*), a defiant Gordon wrote in his journals: "[I]f any emissary or letter comes up here ordering me to come down, I WILL NOT OBEY IT, BUT WILL STAY HERE, AND FALL WITH TOWN, AND RUN ALL RISKS." On 26 January 1885, two days before the arrival of a British relief expedition, the Mahdists took Khartoum, and General Gordon was killed, his head brought to the Mahdi as a trophy. Gordon was martyred in the popular imagination, and some speculate that the eccentric general might have sought out such adulation in rushing towards certain death.

Lucy's use of the word is therefore a slight hint that the date of the events is closer to 1885, when the newspapers were filled with accounts of the desert, than later. Somehow, one does not imagine Lucy lingering over travel books devoted to the desert climes.

48 Nightingales generally arrive in England in April and sing until late May and early June. They leave again from July to September. Leatherdale (*Dracula Unearthed*) takes the presence of the bird to be part of the dream-nature of the occasion (complete with a wolf miraculously suspended on the sill of a second-[English first-] floor window), but nightingales are not miraculous in September.

49 Dracula passes invisibly through the door.

50 It is a wonder that the doctor instantly notices the distinctive smell but the maids did not. We need not believe that Dracula carried the laudanum with him; laudanum, a tincture of opium, was widely used as a sedative and common in many households. Isabella Beeton's *Book of Household Management* (1861), for example, in its advice regarding childhood diseases, prescribes laudanum as part of an emollient for thrush and part of an emetic for "hooping-cough" and lists powdered opium and laudanum as part of a well-stocked home medical cabinet. In fact, laudanum was much abused by

Laudanum bottle (American).

mothers who did lacework and other piecework—the equivalent of today's sweatshop employment, but performed at home—to tranquilise their infants. Advertisements for laudanum covered the windows of every chemist's shop.

The Victorians had little understanding of the physical or psychological dangers presented by the depressants and opiates commonly found in the

with the dead! I dare not go out, for I can hear the low howl of the wolf through the broken window.

The air seems full of specks, floating and circling in the draught from the window, and the lights burn blue and dim.[52] What am I to do? God shield me from harm this night! I shall hide this paper in my breast, where they shall find it when they come to lay me out. My dear mother gone! It is time that I go too. Good-bye, dear Arthur, if I should not survive this night. God keep you, dear, and God help me!

household, notwithstanding Seward's self-cautionary remark about chloral hydrate (see chapter 8, note 45), and it was widely believed that the use of drugs such as opium, morphine, and cocaine could be beneficial. For example, the 1888 *Encylopædia Britannica* scoffed at any notion that smoking opium might be considered dangerous, comparing the smoking of opium—which enabled smokers "to undergo great fatigue and to go for a considerable time with little or no food"—to moderate alcohol or tobacco consumption. Ultimately, "[w]hen carried to excess it becomes an inveterate habit; but this happens chiefly in individuals of weak will-power, who would just as easily become the victims of intoxicating drinks, and who are practically moral imbeciles, also addicted to other forms of depravity."

The British government took steps to curb opium use in the late 1800s and early 1900s, but by then the genie was well out of the bottle. Although opium was commonly viewed as a symbol of Eastern licentiousness and corruption, the lure of its calming, euphoric properties claimed some famous literary addicts, including poets George Gordon Byron and Percy Bysshe Shelley, both heavy laudanum users (at least during the famous summer of 1816 when John William Polidori's "The Vampyre" and Mary Shelley's *Frankenstein* were conceived), Charles Baudelaire, Elizabeth Barrett Browning, Samuel Coleridge (whose "Kubla Khan" was inspired by an opium-induced dream), and John Keats and novelist Wilkie Collins (*The Moonstone, The Woman in White*). Critics have speculated that Lewis Carroll's fantastic *Alice's Adventures in Wonderland* (1865) was written as a result of (or at least referred to) opium use.

51 Fred Saberhagen (*The Dracula Tape*) does not believe for one moment that Dracula drugged these servants; Dracula's hypnotic powers, later demonstrated on the "stuporous" Jonathan Harker, would have sufficed to remove them from the scene. Saberhagen points out that the only person with means and opportunity was Lucy—whose motive, he posits, was a desire to spend some uninterrupted time with the highly attractive (and, in Saberhagen's view, innocent) Dracula.

52 Jonathan Harker noted "specks" in the apparition of the three women (see text accompanying chapter 4, note 23) and blue flames outside Castle Dracula.

Chapter 12

DR. SEWARD'S DIARY.

1 Harker means he took a hansom cab from the train station. It is puzzling why he keeps the cab driver waiting at the gate for what he clearly expects to be more than a brief stay (he brings his phonograph recording with him, intending to complete it at Hillingham).

2 This is an important identifying characteristic of any candidate for the real "Hillingham": the house is set back from the main road, with a tree-lined avenue leading to the front door. Leatherdale (*Dracula Unearthed*) deduces from Van Helsing's haste that he has realised he did not tell Seward in advance of his departure; however, it is unlikely Van Helsing would have been informed by the telegraph company that delivery was delayed.

3 Van Helsing verifies that he saw the cab waiting.

18 September.—I drove at once to Hillingham and arrived early. Keeping my cab[1] at the gate, I went up the avenue alone. I knocked gently and rang as quietly as possible, for I feared to disturb Lucy or her mother, and hoped to only bring a servant to the door. After a while, finding no response, I knocked and rang again; still no answer. I cursed the laziness of the servants that they should lie abed at such an hour—for it was now ten o'clock—and so rang and knocked again, but more impatiently, but still without response. Hitherto I had blamed only the servants, but now a terrible fear began to assail me. Was this desolation but another link in the chain of doom which seemed drawing tight round us? Was it indeed a house of death to which I had come, too late? I know that minutes, even seconds of delay, might mean hours of danger to Lucy, if she had had again one of those frightful relapses; and I went round the house to try if I could find by chance an entry anywhere.

I could find no means of ingress. Every window and door was fastened and locked, and I returned baffled to the porch. As I did so, I heard the rapid pit-pat of a swiftly driven horse's feet. They stopped at the gate, and a few seconds later I met Van Helsing running up the avenue.[2] When he saw me, he gasped out:—

"Then it was you, and just arrived.[3] How is she? Are we too late? Did you not get my telegram?"

I answered as quickly and coherently as I could that I had

Publicity photo of John Carradine as Dracula.
House of Dracula (Universal Pictures, 1945)

4 Seward does not inform Van Helsing of the reason for the delay, and so Van Helsing sees it as "God's will" rather than his own fault. It is surprising that he allowed publication of the information of his culpability in Lucy's death, but even afterward his ignorance of English practises may have concealed from him his part in the chain of events.

5 The Manuscript reads: "saying: 'You are a surgeon—this is your work,' and . . ." Stoker may have concluded that he was overdoing his insistence that Seward was a physician, and the phrase does not appear in the published narrative. Roger Johnson, in private correspondence to this editor, makes the interesting suggestion that Seward may not have been a surgeon—that is, a member of the Royal College of Surgeons—and that Stoker remembered that after publication; see chapter 5, note 20. This does not mean he was not a "doctor," only that he was perhaps less qualified than his underling Patrick Hennessey, who first appears in these papers on 20 September. However, Seward did carry a lancet (see text accompanying chapter 5, note 28), so perhaps the deletion is not significant.

6 This is a remarkable job of sawing with a surgical tool intended for bone, not iron. Furthermore, it is unlikely that any surgeon would treat his instruments so unkindly, by using them in a manner highly likely to ruin them for their intended purpose.

7 Laboured breathing caused by a partially obstructed upper airway, producing a heavy snorting sound, often associated with snoring, comatose patients, and drug overdose.

8 The phrase "knelt down beside the bed and groaned outwardly as he said an inward prayer. As he bent forward," which appears in the Manuscript, is changed in the published text to "bent over the bed." The version Stoker chose to publish emphasised Van Helsing's professional qualities rather than his religious nature. It seems more likely that "Van Helsing" was in fact a

only got his telegram early in the morning, and had not lost a minute in coming here, and that I could not make any one in the house hear me. He paused and raised his hat as he said solemnly:—

"Then I fear we are too late. God's will be done!"[4] With his usual recuperative energy, he went on: "Come. If there be no way open to get in, we must make one. Time is all in all to us now."

We went round to the back of the house, where there was a kitchen window. The Professor took a small surgical saw from his case, and handing it to me,[5] pointed to the iron bars which guarded the window. I attacked them at once and had very soon cut through three of them.[6] Then with a long, thin knife we pushed back the fastening of the sashes and opened the window. I helped the Professor in, and followed him. There was no one in the kitchen or in the servants' rooms, which were close at hand. We tried all the rooms as we went along, and in the dining-room, dimly lit by rays of light through the shutters, found four servant-women lying on the floor. There was no need to think them dead, for their stertorous breathing[7] and the acrid smell of laudanum in the room left no doubt as to their condition. Van Helsing and I looked at each other, and as we moved away he said: "We can attend to them later." Then we ascended to Lucy's room. For an instant or two we paused at the door to listen, but there was no sound that we could hear. With white faces and trembling hands, we opened the door gently, and entered the room.

How shall I describe what we saw? On the bed lay two women, Lucy and her mother. The latter lay farthest in, and she was covered with a white sheet, the edge of which had been blown back by the draught through the broken window, showing the drawn, white, face, with a look of terror fixed upon it. By her side lay Lucy, with face white and still more drawn. The flowers which had been round her neck we found upon her mother's bosom, and her throat was bare, showing the two little wounds which we had noticed before, but looking horribly white and mangled. Without a word the Professor[8] bent over the bed, his head almost touching poor Lucy's breast; then he gave a quick turn of his head, as of one who listens, and leaping to his feet, he cried out to me:—

"It is not yet too late! Quick! quick! Bring the brandy!"

I flew downstairs and returned with it, taking care to smell and taste it, lest it, too, were drugged like the decanter of sherry which I found on the table. The maids were still breathing, but more restlessly, and I fancied that the narcotic was wearing off. I did not stay to make sure, but returned to Van Helsing. He rubbed the brandy, as on another occasion, on her lips and gums and on her wrists and the palms of her hands. He said to me:

"I can do this, all that can be at the present. You go wake those maids. Flick them in the face with a wet towel, and flick them hard. Make them get heat and fire and a warm bath. This poor soul is nearly as cold as that beside her. She will need be heated before we can do anything more."[9]

I went at once, and found little difficulty in waking three of the women. The fourth was only a young girl, and the drug had evidently affected her more strongly, so I lifted her on the sofa and let her sleep. The others were dazed at first, but as remembrance came back to them they cried and sobbed in a hysterical manner. I was stern with them, however, and would not let them talk. I told them that one life was bad enough to lose, and that if they delayed they would sacrifice Miss Lucy. So, sobbing and crying, they went about their way, half clad as they were, and prepared fire and water.[10] Fortunately, the kitchen and boiler fires were still alive, and there was no lack of hot water. We got a bath, and carried Lucy out as she was and placed her in it. Whilst we were busy chafing her limbs there was a knock at the hall-door. One of the maids ran off, hurried on some more clothes, and opened it. Then she returned and whispered to us that there was a gentleman who had come with a message from Mr. Holmwood. I bade her simply tell him that he must wait, for we could see no one now. She went away with the message, and, engrossed with our work, I clean forgot all about him.

I never saw in all my experience the Professor work in such deadly earnest. I knew—as he knew—that it was a stand-up fight with death, and in a pause told him so. He answered me in a way that I did not understand, but with the sternest look that his face could wear:—

cleric or professor of philosophy rather than a doctor.

9 Wolf (*The Essential Dracula*) and Leatherdale (*Dracula Unearthed*) both note that this is dangerous medical treatment: heat dilates the blood vessels and encourages the flow of blood away from the brain when blood volume is low.

10 This sentence does not appear in the Abridged Text.

11 A chess metaphor.

12 This is testimony to the painful and dangerous nature of blood transfusions. See chapter 10, note 13.

"If that were all, I would stop here where we are now, and let her fade away into peace, for I see no light in life over her horizon." He went on with his work with, if possible, renewed and more frenzied vigour.

Presently we both began to be conscious that the heat was beginning to be of some effect. Lucy's heart beat a trifle more audibly to the stethoscope, and her lungs had a perceptible movement. Van Helsing's face almost beamed, and as we lifted her from the bath and rolled her in a hot sheet to dry her he said to me:—

"The first gain is ours! Check to the King!"[11]

We took Lucy into another room, which had by now been prepared, and laid her in bed and forced a few drops of brandy down her throat. I noticed that Van Helsing tied a soft silk handkerchief round her throat. She was still unconscious, and was quite as bad, if not worse than, we had ever seen her.

Van Helsing called in one of the women, and told her to stay with her and not to take her eyes off her till we returned, and then beckoned me out of the room.

"We must consult as to what is to be done," he said as we descended the stairs. In the hall he opened the dining-room door, and we passed in, he closing the door carefully behind him. The shutters had been opened, but the blinds were already down, with that obedience to the etiquette of death which the British woman of the lower classes always rigidly observes. The room was, therefore, dimly dark. It was, however, light enough for our purposes. Van Helsing's sternness was somewhat relieved by a look of perplexity. He was evidently torturing his mind about something, so I waited for an instant, and he spoke:—

"What are we to do now? Where are we to turn for help? We must have another transfusion of blood, and that soon, or that poor girl's life won't be worth an hour's purchase. You are exhausted already; I am exhausted too. I fear to trust those women, even if they would have courage to submit.[12] What are we to do for some one who will open his veins for her?"

"What's the matter with me, anyhow?"

The voice came from the sofa across the room, and its tones brought relief and joy to my heart, for they were those of

Quincey Morris. Van Helsing started angrily at the first sound, but his face softened and a glad look came into his eyes as I cried out: "Quincey Morris!" and rushed towards him with outstretched hands.

"What brought you here?" I cried as our hands met.

"I guess Art is the cause."

He handed me a telegram:—

"HAVE NOT HEARD FROM SEWARD FOR THREE DAYS, AND AM TERRIBLY ANXIOUS. CANNOT LEAVE. FATHER STILL IN SAME CONDITION. SEND ME WORD HOW LUCY IS. DO NOT DELAY.—HOLMWOOD."

"I think I came just in the nick of time. You know you have only to tell me what to do."

Van Helsing strode forward, and took his hand, looking him straight in the eyes as he said:—

"A brave man's blood is the best thing on this earth when a woman is in trouble.[13] You're a man, and no mistake. Well, the devil may work against us for all he's worth, but God sends us men when we want them."

Once again we went through that ghastly operation.[14] I have not the heart to go through with the details. Lucy had got a terrible shock, and it told on her more than before, for though plenty of blood went into her veins, her body did not respond to the treatment as well as on the other occasions. Her struggle back into life was something frightful to see and hear. However, the action of both heart and lungs improved, and Van Helsing made a subcutaneous injection of morphia, as before, and with good effect. Her faint became a profound slumber. The Professor watched whilst I went downstairs with Quincey Morris, and sent one of the maids to pay off one of the cabmen who were waiting. I left Quincey lying down after having a glass of wine, and told the cook to get ready a good breakfast. Then a thought struck me, and I went back to the room where Lucy now was. When I came softly in, I found Van Helsing with a sheet or two of note-paper in his hand. He had evidently read it, and was thinking it over as he sat with his hand to his brow. There was a look of grim satisfaction in his face, as of one who has had a doubt solved.[15] He handed me

13 Leatherdale (*Dracula Unearthed*) calls this "one of the most bizarre statements" in the entire narrative.

14 That's four different donors. It's a miracle that Lucy isn't dead from a reaction.

15 Leatherdale (*Dracula Unearthed*) chides that Van Helsing's reaction should have been one of shamefaced guilt rather than satisfaction.

16 The doctors are conspiring to conceal a violent death, which would otherwise surely have led to an inquest. Under English law, in such circumstances one of the duties of the coroner was to hold an inquest, that is, enquire into a violent or unexplained death. The coroner supervised a jury of up to twenty-three persons (twelve of whom had to agree on a verdict), took evidence on oath, and directly questioned witnesses. Upon conclusion of the inquest, if a person was found guilty of murder or manslaughter, the person was jailed and held for trial.

the paper saying only: "It dropped from Lucy's breast when we carried her to the bath."

When I had read it, I stood looking at the Professor, and after a pause asked him: "In God's name, what does it all mean? Was she, or is she, mad; or what sort of horrible danger is it?" I was so bewildered that I did not know what to say more. Van Helsing put out his hand and took the paper, saying:—

"Do not trouble about it now. Forget it for the present. You shall know and understand it all in good time; but it will be later. And now what is it that you came to me to say?" This brought me back to fact, and I was all myself again.

"I came to speak about the certificate of death. If we do not act properly and wisely, there may be an inquest, and that paper would have to be produced. I am in hopes that we need have no inquest, for if we had it would surely kill poor Lucy, if nothing else did. I know, and you know, and the other doctor who attended her knows, that Mrs. Westenra had disease of the heart, and we can certify that she died of it. Let us fill up the certificate at once, and I shall take it myself to the registrar and go on to the undertaker."[16]

"Good, oh my friend John! Well thought of! Truly Miss Lucy, if she be sad in the foes that beset her, is at least happy in the friends that love her. One, two, three, all open their veins for her, besides one old man. Ah, yes, I know, friend John; I am not blind! I love you all the more for it! Now go."

In the hall I met Quincey Morris, with a telegram for Arthur telling him that Mrs. Westenra was dead; that Lucy also had been ill, but was now going on better; and that Van Helsing and I were with her. I told him where I was going, and he hurried me out, but as I was going said:—

"When you come back, Jack, may I have two words with you all to ourselves?" I nodded in reply and went out. I found no difficulty about the registration, and arranged with the local undertaker to come up in the evening to measure for the coffin and to make arrangements.

When I got back Quincey was waiting for me. I told him I would see him as soon as I knew about Lucy, and went up to her room. She was still sleeping, and the Professor seemingly had not moved from his seat at her side. From his putting his finger to his lips, I gathered that he expected her to wake before long and was afraid of forestalling nature. So I went down to Quincey and took him into the breakfast-room, where the blinds were not drawn down, and which was a little more cheerful, or rather less cheerless, than the other rooms. When we were alone, he said to me:—

"Jack Seward, I don't want to shove myself in anywhere where I've no right to be; but, this is no ordinary case. You know I loved that girl and wanted to marry her; but, although that's all past and gone, I can't help feeling anxious about her all the same. What is it that's wrong with her? The Dutchman—and a fine old fellow he is; I can see that—said, that time you two came into the room, that you must have *another* transfusion of blood, and that both you and he were exhausted. Now I know well that you medical men speak *in camera*,[17] and that a man must not expect to know what they consult about in private. But this is no common matter, and, whatever it is, I have done my part. Is not that so?"

"That's so," I said, and he went on:—

"I take it that both you and Van Helsing had done already what I did to-day. Is not that so?"

"That's so."

"And I guess Art was in it too. When I saw him four days ago down at his own place he looked queer. I have not seen anything pulled down so quick since I was on the Pampas[18] and had a mare that I was fond of go to grass[19] all in a night. One of those big bats that they call vampires had got at her in the night,[20] and, what with his gorge and the vein left open, there wasn't enough blood in her to let her stand up, and I had to put a bullet through her as she lay.[21] Jack, if you may tell me without betraying confidence, Arthur was the first; is not that so?" As he spoke the poor fellow looked terribly anxious. He was in a torture of suspense regarding the woman he loved, and his utter ignorance of the terrible mystery which seemed to surround her intensified his pain. His very heart was bleeding, and it took all the manhood of him—and there was a royal lot of it, too—to keep him from breaking down. I paused before answering, for I felt that I must not betray anything which the Professor wished kept secret; but already he knew so much,

17 "In chambers," meaning secretly.

18 From the Guarani Indian word for "level plain," the Pampas are the flat, fertile grasslands spanning an area of 300,000 square miles of South America from the Atlantic Ocean to the Andes Mountains, primarily in the nation of Argentina. The Argentinean Pampas, which also feature salt flats and some hills, are the home of the "gaucho," a national symbol of romantic isolation whose centuries-long adaptation to this largely uninhabited space spawned a powerful mythology. Gauchos have traditionally been perceived as heroic vagabonds who reject all authority other than the laws of nature. Primarily cowboys, they herd sheep and beef cattle, provide meat and leather to the general populace, and practise agriculture. The 1872 epic poem *El gaucho Martín Fierro* (not translated into English until 1974, as *The Gaucho Martín Fierro*), by José Hernández, shaped the notion of the persecuted gaucho, clinging to a little-understood way of life. Equally influential is rancher-turned-writer Ricardo Güiraldes's 1926 novel *Don Segundo Sombra* (the 1935 translation was titled *Shadows on the Pampas*), made into an Argentine film in 1969 (nominated for a Golden Palm award at the Cannes Film Festival). Because the world of the gaucho is so intensely insular and the Pampas a rather forbidding environment, it is anyone's guess what Quincey Morris was doing there.

19 That is, the mare died. Leatherdale (*Dracula Unearthed*) concludes that Van Helsing took too much blood if Holmwood still displays weakness four days after his blood donation.

20 Three species of vampire bats are found in Central and South America. The most common is *Desmodus rotundus*, but all three are quite small, with a wingspan of about 8 inches and a body about 2 to 3 inches long. These bats feed on the blood of large birds, cattle, horses, and pigs, their preternaturally strong hind legs allowing them to jump to avoid their preys' hooves and tails; however, contrary to myth, vampire bats

The vampire bat *Desmodus rotundus*.

do not suck their victims' blood but rather lap up blood oozing from a small wound made by the bats' sharp canines and incisors. Scientists are quite interested in the bats' saliva, which numbs the victim's skin and lulls the victim to sleep while preventing the blood from clotting. Considered by many to be pests because of their opportunistic habit of attacking slumbering cattle, vampire bats are routinely destroyed by ranchers. Quincey Morris's experience of the vampire bat is likely quite exaggerated.

21 Morris's "Pampas" comparison does not appear in the Abridged Text.

22 Thus Morris, the unsophisticated American, is the first to articulate the problem of the missing blood. We know that Van Helsing reached his conclusion much earlier, and now Morris puts a label on that conclusion: a vampire (even though Morris incorrectly suggests a vampire bat). Seward's continued profession of ignorance can only be seen as denial, for vampires were certainly well known in popular literature if not medical literature.

and guessed so much, that there could be no reason for not answering, so I answered in the same phrase: "That's so."

"And how long has this been going on?"

"About ten days."

"Ten days! Then I guess, Jack Seward, that that poor pretty creature that we all love has had put into her veins within that time the blood of four strong men. Man alive, her whole body wouldn't hold it." Then, coming close to me, he spoke in a fierce half-whisper: "What took it out?"[22]

I shook my head. "That," I said, "is the crux. Van Helsing is simply frantic about it, and I am at my wits' end. I can't even hazard a guess. There has been a series of little circumstances which have thrown out all our calculations as to Lucy being properly watched. But these shall not occur again. Here we stay until all be well—or ill." Quincey held out his hand. "Count me in," he said. "You and the Dutchman will tell me what to do, and I'll do it."

When she woke late in the afternoon, Lucy's first movement was to feel in her breast, and, to my surprise, produced the paper which Van Helsing had given me to read. The careful Professor had replaced it where it had come from, lest on waking she should be alarmed. Her eye then lit on Van Helsing and on me too, and gladdened. Then she looked around the room, and seeing where she was, shuddered; she gave a loud cry, and put her poor thin hands before her pale face. We both understood what that meant—that she had realised to the full her mother's death; so we tried what we could to comfort her. Doubtless sympathy eased her somewhat, but she was very low in thought and spirit, and wept silently and weakly for a long time. We told her that either or both of us would now remain with her all the time, and that seemed to comfort her. Towards dusk she fell into a doze. Here a very odd thing occurred. Whilst still asleep she took the paper from her breast and tore it in two. Van Helsing stepped over and took the pieces from her. All the same, however, she went on with the action of tearing, as though the material were still in her hands; finally she lifted her hands and opened them as though scattering the fragments. Van Helsing seemed surprised, and his brows gathered as if in thought, but he said nothing.

19 September.[23]—All last night she slept fitfully, being always afraid to sleep, and something weaker when she woke from it. The Professor and I took it in turns to watch, and we never left her for a moment unattended. Quincey Morris said nothing about his intention, but I knew that all night long he patrolled round and round the house.[24]

When the day came, its searching light showed the ravages in poor Lucy's strength. She was hardly able to turn her head, and the little nourishment which she could take seemed to do her no good. At times she slept, and both Van Helsing and I noticed the difference in her, between sleeping and waking. Whilst asleep she looked stronger, although more haggard, and her breathing was softer; her open mouth showed the pale gums drawn back from the teeth, which thus looked positively longer and sharper than usual;[25] when she woke the softness of her eyes evidently changed the expression, for she looked her own self, although a dying one.[26] In the afternoon she asked for Arthur, and we telegraphed for him. Quincey went off to meet him at the station.

When he arrived it was nearly six o'clock, and the sun was setting full and warm, and the red light streamed in through the window and gave more colour to the pale cheeks. When he saw her, Arthur was simply choking with emotion, and none of us could speak. In the hours that had passed, the fits of sleep, or the comatose condition that passed for it, had grown more frequent, so that the pauses when conversation was possible were shortened. Arthur's presence, however, seemed to act as a stimulant; she rallied a little, and spoke to him more brightly than she had done since we arrived. He too pulled himself together, and spoke as cheerily as he could, so that the best was made of everything.

It is now nearly one o'clock, and he and Van Helsing are sitting with her. I am to relieve them in a quarter of an hour, and I am entering this on Lucy's phonograph. Until six o'clock they are to try to rest. I fear that to-morrow will end our watching, for the shock has been too great; the poor child cannot rally. God help us all.

23 This should be 20 September, for it is 1:00 A.M., although such a mistake is easy enough to make. The "last night" mentioned in the next sentence is the night of 18 September, the day on which Seward arrived at Hillingham. The current night is described in this entry commencing at 6:00 P.M. (on 19 September) and ending at 1:00 A.M. (on 20 September). Lucy dies after this diary entry, during the day of 20 September.

24 From what does Quincey believe he is guarding Lucy? Another wolf attack? Unless Van Helsing has privately filled him in on his belief in vampiric attacks, there appears to be little purpose to Quincey's patrolling.

25 Evidently a symptom of changing from dying to dead to undead.

26 Inserted in the Manuscript in Stoker's hand (but not used) is "She breathed heaving as though fighting for air."

27 Mina's lovely descriptions do not appear in the Abridged Text.

28 The Exeter cathedral is described in chapter 3, note 42.

29 Considering that he has been absent from Exeter for over four months and only written once to his employer, Jonathan Harker has had a truly remarkable career. In mid-April, he was a clerk; by September, he has progressed from clerk to solicitor to partner; and in a few days he will be the sole proprietor of the firm. Harker makes the hero of the musical *How to Succeed in Business Without Really Trying*, who rises from window-washer to chairman of the board in a few short months, look like an underachiever; no wonder he "awakes all trembling," as Mina goes on to say.

LETTER FROM MINA HARKER TO LUCY WESTENRA.—

(Unopened by her.)

"17 September.

"My dearest Lucy,—

"It seems *an age* since I heard from you, or indeed since I wrote. You will pardon me, I know, for all my faults when you have read all my budget of news. Well, I got my husband back all right; when we arrived at Exeter there was a carriage waiting for us, and in it, though he had an attack of gout, Mr. Hawkins. He took us to his house, where there were rooms for us all nice and comfortable, and we dined together. After dinner Mr. Hawkins said:—

"'My dears, I want to drink your health and prosperity; and may every blessing attend you both. I know you both from children, and have, with love and pride, seen you grow up. Now I want you to make your home here with me. I have left to me neither chick nor child; all are gone, and in my will I have left you everything.' I cried, Lucy dear, as Jonathan and the old man clasped hands. Our evening was a very, very happy one.

"So here we are, installed in this beautiful old house,[27] and from both my bedroom and the drawing-room I can see the great elms of the cathedral close,[28] with their great black stems standing out against the old yellow stone of the cathedral; and I can hear the rooks overhead cawing and cawing and chattering and gossiping all day, after the manner of rooks—and humans. I am busy, I need not tell you, arranging things and housekeeping. Jonathan and Mr. Hawkins are busy all day; for, now that Jonathan is a partner,[29] Mr. Hawkins wants to tell him all about the clients.

"How is your dear mother getting on? I wish I could run up to town for a day or two to see you, dear, but I dare not go yet, with so much on my shoulders; and Jonathan wants looking after still. He is beginning to put some flesh on his bones again, but he was terribly weakened by the long illness; even now he sometimes starts out of his sleep in a sudden way and awakes all trembling until I can coax him back to his usual placidity. However, thank God, these occasions grow less frequent as the days go on, and they will in time pass away altogether, I trust. And now I have told you my news, let me ask yours. When are you to be married,[30] and where, and who is to perform the ceremony, and what are you to wear, and is it to be a public or private wedding? Tell me all about it, dear; tell me all about everything, for there is nothing which interests you which will not be dear to me. Jonathan asks me to send his 'respectful duty,' but I do not think that is good enough from the junior partner of the important firm Hawkins & Harker; and so, as you love me, and he loves me, and I love you with all the moods and tenses of the verb, I send you simply his 'love' instead. Good-bye, my dearest Lucy, and all blessings on you.

> "Yours,
> "Mina Harker."

REPORT FROM PATRICK HENNESSEY, M.D., M.R.C.S., L.K.Q.C.P.I.,[31] ETC., ETC., TO JOHN SEWARD, M.D.

> "20 September.

"My dear Sir,—

"In accordance with your wishes, I enclose report of the conditions of everything left in my charge. . . . With regard to patient, Renfield, there is more to say. He has had another outbreak, which might have had a dreadful ending, but which, as it fortunately happened, was unattended with any unhappy results. This afternoon a carrier's cart with two men made a call at the empty house whose grounds abut on ours—the house to which, you will remember, the patient twice ran away.[32] The men stopped at our gate to ask the porter their way, as they were strangers.[33] I was myself looking out of the study window, having a smoke after dinner, and saw one of them come up to the house. As he passed the window of Renfield's room, the patient began to rate him from within, and called him all the foul names he could lay his tongue to. The man, who seemed

30 Mina already knows this, having heard from Lucy on 30 August—see text accompanying chapter 9, note 19. The wedding date is only eleven days hence, and Mina has undoubtedly already received an invitation, planned her dress, arranged her travel, and purchased a gift. Either the letter is dated incorrectly, preceding 30 August, or wholly fictional, a narrative device inserted by Stoker to convey the information that Jonathan and Mina have returned home.

31 That is, Doctor of Medicine, Member of the Royal College of Surgeons, Licentiate of the King's and Queen's College of Physicians, Ireland. See chapter 5, note 20, for a discussion of the significance (in truth, the relative insignificance) of these titles. Certainly the impression conveyed is that of a man who is straining to prove his merit. McNally and Florescu (*The Essential Dracula*) point out that the list of degrees was borrowed by Stoker from his brother, physician Sir William Thornley Stoker; the real credentials of "Dr. Hennessey" remain unknown.

32 Hennessey's reminder of Renfield's previous escapes do not appear in the Abridged Text.

33 Hennessey's description of the incident has been shortened in the Abridged Text, but without significant import.

Carrier's cart.
William Frances Freelove, 1873

a decent fellow enough, contented himself by telling him to 'shut up for a foul-mouthed beggar,' whereon our man accused him of robbing him and wanting to murder him and said that he would hinder him if he were to swing for it. I opened the window and signed to the man not to notice, so he contented himself after looking the place over and making up his mind as to what kind of a place he had got to by saying, 'Lor' bless yer, sir, I wouldn't mind what was said to me in a bloomin' madhouse. I pity ye and the guv'nor for havin' to live in the house with a wild beast like that.' Then he asked his way civilly enough, and I told him where the gate of the empty house was; he went away followed by threats and curses and revilings from our man. I went down to see if I could make out any cause for his anger, since he is usually such a well-behaved man, and except his violent fits nothing of the kind had ever occurred. I found him, to my astonishment, quite composed and most genial in his manner. I tried to get him to talk of the incident, but he blandly asked me questions as to what I meant, and led me to believe that he was completely oblivious of the affair. It was, I am sorry to say, however, only another instance of his cunning, for within half an hour I heard of him again. This time he had broken out through the window of his room, and was running down the avenue. I called to the attendants to follow me, and ran after him, for I feared he was intent on some mischief. My fear was justified when I saw the same cart which had passed before coming down the road, having on it some great wooden boxes. The men were wiping their foreheads, and were flushed in the face, as if with violent exercise.[34] Before I could get up to him the patient rushed at them, and pulling one of them off the cart, began to knock his head against the ground. If I had not seized him just at the moment I believe he would have killed the man there and then. The other fellow jumped down and struck him over the head with the butt-end of his heavy whip. It was a terrible blow; but he did not seem to mind it, but seized him also, and struggled with the three of us, pulling us to and fro as if we were kittens. You know I am no light weight, and the others were both burly men. At first he was silent in his fighting; but as we began to master him, and the attendants were putting a strait-waistcoat on him, he began to shout: 'I'll frustrate them! They shan't rob me! they shan't murder me by inches! I'll fight for my Lord and Master!' and all sorts of similar incoherent ravings. It was with very considerable difficulty that they got him back to the house and put him in the padded room. One of the attendants, Hardy, had a finger broken. However, I set it all right; and he is going on well.[35]

"The two carriers were at first loud in their threats of actions for damages, and promised to rain all the penalties of the law on us. Their threats were, however, mingled with some sort of indirect apology for the defeat of the two of them by a feeble madman. They said that if it had not been for the way their strength had been spent in carrying and raising the heavy boxes to the cart they would have made short work of him. They gave as another reason for their defeat the extraordinary state of drouth to which they had been reduced by the dusty nature of their occupation and the reprehensible distance from the scene of their labours of any place of public entertainment.[36] I quite understood their drift, and after a stiff glass of grog, or rather more of the same, and with each a sovereign in hand,[37] they made

34 Violent indeed, to have loaded the extremely heavy boxes in half an hour.

35 Mention of the broken finger and its repair do not appear in the Abridged Text.

36 This is an important locational clue for Carfax—it is some distance from the pubs of Purfleet.

37 Almost US$100 each in today's economic values.

38 Hennessey's behaviour is inexplicable; for what did he imagine the carriers' addresses would be needed?

39 Walworth (there is no record of a "Great Walworth" in recent history) is an area of London about 2 miles southeast of Charing Cross, today located in the London borough of Southwark, between Camberwell and Elephant & Castle. Charlie Chaplin is perhaps its most famous native son. The street name is fictional.

40 Bethnal Green was the site of the infamous London slum known as the Old Nichol, or the Jago, depicted—some say reasonably accurately— in Arthur Morrison's 1896 novel *A Child of the Jago*, which features a young boy whose father is hanged for murder. Eventually a symbol of civic disgrace, the area had once been bucolic, according to the *Illustrated London News* (24 October 1863): "Anybody whose acquaintance with Bethnal-green commenced more than a quarter of a century ago will remember that some of these names of streets and rows which now seem to have such a grimly sarcastic meaning expressed not inaptly the places to which they originally referred, Hollybush-place, Green-street, Pleasant-place." In 1888, Jack the Ripper operated in the west end of Bethnal Green and neighbouring Whitechapel. In one of the earliest slum clearance projects, in the 1890s, the London County Council built housing known as the Boundary Street Estate. Today located in the London borough of Tower Hamlets, Bethnal Green is about 4 miles northeast of Charing Cross.

41 A central district of London. The 1896 London "Baedeker" describes it as containing "a large colony of Italian cooks, couriers, waiters, tailors, restaurant-keepers, servants, teachers, *etc.*" In fact the area was a melting pot of nationalities and by the end of the nineteenth century was well known as a home for writers, musicians, and artists as well as for its cafés and nightlife. Karl Marx lived in the district, and poet William Blake was born there.

light of the attack, and swore that they would encounter a worse madman any day for the pleasure of meeting so 'bloomin' good a bloke' as your correspondent. I took their names and addresses, in case they might be needed.[38] They are as follows:—Jack Smollet, of Dudding's Rents, King George's Road, Great Walworth,[39] and Thomas Snelling, Peter Parley's Row, Guide Court, Bethnal Green.[40] They are both in the employment of Harris & Sons, Moving and Shipment Company, Orange Master's Yard, Soho.[41]

"I shall report to you any matter of interest occurring here, and shall wire you at once if there is anything of importance.

> "Believe me, dear Sir,
> "Yours faithfully,
> "Patrick Hennessey."[42]

LETTER FROM MINA HARKER TO LUCY WESTENRA.

(Unopened by her.)

"18 September.

"My dearest Lucy,—

"Such a sad blow has befallen us. Mr. Hawkins has died very suddenly.[43] Some may not think it so sad for us, but we had both come to so love him that it really seems as though we had lost a father. I never knew either father or mother, so that the dear old man's death is a real blow to me. Jonathan is greatly distressed. It is not only that he feels sorrow, deep sorrow, for the dear, good man who has befriended him all his life, and now at the end has treated him like his own son and left him a fortune which to people of our modest bringing up is wealth beyond the dream of avarice, but Jonathan feels it on another account. He says the amount of responsibility which it puts upon him makes him nervous. He begins to doubt himself. I try to cheer him up, and my belief in *him* helps him to have a belief in himself. But it is here that the grave shock that he experienced tells upon him the most. Oh, it is too hard that a sweet, simple, noble, strong nature such as his—a nature which enabled him by our dear, good friend's aid to rise from clerk to master in a few years[44]—should be so injured that the very essence of its strength is gone.[45] Forgive me, dear, if I worry you with my troubles in the midst of your own happiness; but, Lucy dear, I must tell some one, for the strain of keeping up a brave and cheerful appearance to Jonathan tries me, and I have no one here that I can confide in.[46] I dread coming up to London, as we must do the day after to-morrow;[47] for poor Mr. Hawkins left in his will that he was to be buried in the grave with his father. As there are no relations at all, Jonathan will have to be chief mourner. I shall try to run over to see you, dearest, if only for a few minutes. Forgive me for troubling you. With all blessings,

"Your loving

"Mina Harker."

DR. SEWARD'S DIARY.

20 September.—Only resolution and habit can let me make an entry to-night. I am too miserable, too low-spirited, too sick of the world and all in it, including life itself, that I would not care if I heard this moment the flapping of the wings of the angel of death. And he has been flapping those grim wings to some purpose of late—Lucy's mother and Arthur's father,[48] and now. . . . Let me get on with my work.

I duly relieved Van Helsing in his watch over Lucy. We wanted Arthur to go to rest also, but he refused at first. It was only when I told him that we should want him to help us during the day, and that we must not all break down for want of rest, lest Lucy should suffer, that he agreed to go. Van Helsing was very kind to him. "Come, my child," he said; "come with me. You are sick and weak, and have had much sorrow and much mental pain, as well as that tax on your strength that we know of. You must not be alone; for to be alone is to be full of fears and alarms. Come to the drawing-room, where there is a big fire, and there are two sofas. You shall lie on one, and I on the other, and our sympathy will be comfort to each other, even though we do not speak, and even if we sleep." Arthur

Harris & Sons appears to be a fictional firm. The 1885 United Telephone Company directory for London lists over twenty similar firms.

42 Curiously, the concluding paragraph and signature do not appear in the Abridged Text.

43 Hawkins's death is unexpected and curiously fortuitous for the Harkers, occurring only a day after Hawkins raised Jonathan to partnership and changed his will. While Hawkins suffers from acute gout (see text accompanying chapter 2, note 18), there is no indication that he has other, fatal ailments. It is possible that Dracula eliminated Hawkins to ensure the secrecy of his entry into England. As far as Dracula knows, Harker has succumbed to the "kisses" of the vampire women at Castle Dracula, and with the death of Hawkins, the Whitby solicitor Samuel F. Billington would be the only remaining connection with Dracula. Did Dracula have plans to dispose of him as well?

44 A few months is more accurate.

45 Tellingly, this entire sentence does not appear in the Abridged Text. Perhaps with hindsight, Stoker desired to show Jonathan Harker in a better light.

46 This is an indication that the "girls" earlier referred to by Lucy (see text accompanying chapter 5, note 27), including Kate Reed, are not residents of Exeter.

47 This implies that the date of the funeral is set for 20 September. However, as will be seen, the funeral likely took place on 22 September.

48 This is the first we hear of Lord Godalming's death.

49 Not the grass: "lawn" was a term for fine linen or cambric. Seward refers here to the bedsheets, although Lucy will also be wrapped in lawn presently by the undertakers.

50 Another blow to dating the events in 1893: the only reasonably proximate full moons from 1885 through 1893 occurred on 17 September (1887), 25 September (1889), and 21 September (1892).

51 Seward observes that Lucy seems to alternate between being human (when she clutches the garlic to her) and being a vampire.

52 This is 6:00 A.M. on the morning of 20 September.

went off with him, casting back a longing look on Lucy's face, which lay on her pillow, almost whiter than the lawn.[49] She lay quite still, and I looked round the room to see that all was as it should be. I could see that the Professor had carried out in this room, as in the other, his purpose of using the garlic; the whole of the window-sashes reeked with it, and round Lucy's neck, over the silk handkerchief which Van Helsing made her keep on, was a rough chaplet of the same odorous flowers. Lucy was breathing somewhat stertorously, and her face was at its worst, for the open mouth showed the pale gums. Her teeth, in the dim, uncertain light, seemed longer and sharper than they had been in the morning. In particular, by some trick of the light, the canine teeth looked longer and sharper than the rest. I sat down by her, and presently she moved uneasily. At the same moment there came a sort of dull flapping or buffeting at the window. I went over to it softly, and peeped out by the corner of the blind. There was a full moonlight,[50] and I could see that the noise was made by a great bat, which wheeled round—doubtless attracted by the light, although so dim—and every now and again struck the window with its wings. When I came back to my seat, I found that Lucy had moved slightly, and had torn away the garlic flowers from her throat. I replaced them as well as I could, and sat watching her.

Presently she woke, and I gave her food, as Van Helsing had prescribed. She took but a little, and that languidly. There did not seem to be with her now the unconscious struggle for life and strength that had hitherto so marked her illness. It struck me as curious that the moment she became conscious she pressed the garlic flowers close to her.[51] It was certainly odd that whenever she got into that lethargic state, with the stertorous breathing, she put the flowers from her; but that when she waked she clutched them close. There was no possibility of making any mistake about this, for in the long hours that followed, she had many spells of sleeping and waking and repeated both actions many times.

At six o'clock Van Helsing came to relieve me.[52] Arthur had then fallen into a doze, and he mercifully let him sleep on. When he saw Lucy's face I could hear the hissing indraw of his breath, and he said to me in a sharp whisper: "Draw up the blind; I want light!" Then he bent down, and, with his face almost touching Lucy's, examined her carefully. He removed the flowers and lifted the silk handkerchief from her throat. As he did so he started back, and I could hear his ejaculation, "Mein Gott!" as it was smothered in his throat. I bent over and looked, too, and as I noticed some queer chill came over me.

The wounds on the throat had absolutely disappeared.

For fully five minutes Van Helsing stood looking at her, with his face at its sternest. Then he turned to me and said calmly:—

"She is dying. It will not be long now. It will be much difference, mark me, whether she dies conscious or in her sleep.[53] Wake that poor boy, and let him come and see the last; he trusts us, and we have promised him."

I went to the dining-room and waked him. He was dazed for a moment, but when he saw the sunlight streaming in through the edges of the shutters he thought he was late, and expressed his fear. I assured him that Lucy was still asleep, but told him as gently as I could that both Van Helsing and I feared that the end was near. He covered his face with his hands, and slid down on his knees by the sofa, where he remained, perhaps a minute, with his head buried, praying, whilst his shoulders shook with grief. I took him by the hand and raised him up. "Come," I said, "my dear old fellow, summon all your fortitude: it will be best and easiest for her."

When we came into Lucy's room I could see that Van Helsing had, with his usual forethought, been putting matters straight and making everything look as pleasing as possible. He had even brushed Lucy's hair, so that it lay on the pillow in its usual sunny ripples.[54] When we came into the room she opened her eyes, and seeing him, whispered softly:—

"Arthur! Oh, my love, I am so glad you have come!" He was stooping to kiss her, when Van Helsing motioned him back. "No," he whispered, "not yet! Hold her hand; it will comfort her more."

So Arthur took her hand and knelt beside her, and she looked her best, with all the soft lines matching the angelic beauty of her eyes. Then gradually her eyes closed, and she

53 There is no known folkloric basis for this interesting suggestion, although we cannot know what sources Van Helsing drew upon for his opinions. In the Spanish film version of *Dracula* (1931), Dracula explains that if his victim dies during the night, she will be his, the implication being that if she dies during the day, she will not become undead. Yet it is plainly daylight when Lucy's death occurs. Van Helsing, who thinks nothing of staking the deceased Lucy, apparently scruples to help her by assisting in dying during the daylight.

54 Lucy's hair seems to be blonde in this description. This contradicts the description in the text accompanying chapter 16, note 14. Roger Johnson, however, in private correspondence with this editor, suggests that the description is only meant to convey the gloss of Lucy's hair, and he points out that some editions (although neither the first edition nor the Abridged Text) refer to it as "shiny" rather than "sunny."

55 The Abridged Text adds the phrase "with both hands, dragged him back."

56 In the 1931 film versions of the tale (see p. 559), a similar scene appears between the lovers Jonathan Harker and his fiancée Mina (Eva) Seward, who has become Dracula's victim. Van Helsing intervenes with a cross, and the near-vampiress is shocked into temporary recovery.

57 There are several possible interpretations of this request. Is Lucy asking Van Helsing to guard Holmwood from Dracula or from herself? If the former, then "peace" means only comfort of mind. If the latter, however, then she—alone among the company, with the exception of Van Helsing—understands at last what has happened to her, and her request for "peace" is a plea for Van Helsing to destroy her.

sank to sleep. For a little bit her breasts heaved softly, and her breath came and went like a tired child's.

And then insensibly there came the strange change which I had noticed in the night. Her breathing grew stertorous, the mouth opened, and the pale gums, drawn back, made the teeth look longer and sharper than ever. In a sort of sleep-waking, vague, unconscious way she opened her eyes, which were now dull and hard at once, and said in a soft, voluptuous voice, such as I had never heard from her lips:—

"Arthur! Oh, my love, I am so glad you have come! Kiss me!" Arthur bent eagerly over to kiss her; but at that instant Van Helsing, who, like me, had been startled by her voice, swooped upon him, and catching him by the neck[55] with a fury of strength which I never thought he could have possessed, and actually hurled him almost across the room.[56]

"Not for your life!" he said; "not for your living soul and hers!" And he stood between them like a lion at bay.

Arthur was so taken aback that he did not for a moment know what to do or say; and before any impulse of violence could seize him he realized the place and the occasion, and stood silent, waiting.

I kept my eyes fixed on Lucy, as did Van Helsing, and we saw a spasm as of rage flit like a shadow over her face; the sharp teeth champed together. Then her eyes closed, and she breathed heavily.

Very shortly after she opened her eyes in all their softness, and putting out her poor, pale, thin hand, took Van Helsing's great brown one; drawing it to her, she kissed it. "My true friend," she said, in a faint voice, but with untellable pathos, "My true friend, and his! Oh, guard him, and give me peace!"[57]

"I swear it!" he said solemnly, kneeling beside her and holding up his hand, as one who registers an oath. Then he turned to Arthur, and said to him: "Come, my child, take her hand in yours, and kiss her on the forehead, and only once."

Their eyes met instead of their lips; and so they parted.

Lucy's eyes closed; and Van Helsing, who had been watching closely, took Arthur's arm, and drew him away.

And then Lucy's breathing became stertorous again, and all at once it ceased.

"It is all over," said Van Helsing. "She is dead!"

I took Arthur by the arm, and led him away to the drawing-room, where he sat down, and covered his face with his hands, sobbing in a way that nearly broke me down to see.

I went back to the room, and found Van Helsing looking at poor Lucy, and his face was sterner than ever. Some change had come over her body. Death had given back part of her beauty, for her brow and cheeks had recovered some of their flowing lines; even the lips had lost their deadly pallor. It was as if the blood, no longer needed for the working of the heart, had gone to make the harshness of death as little rude as might be.

> "We thought her dying whilst she slept,
> And sleeping when she died."[58]

I stood beside Van Helsing, and said:—

"Ah, well, poor girl, there is peace for her at last. It is the end!"

He turned to me, and said with grave solemnity:—

"Not so; alas! not so. It is only the beginning!"

When I asked him what he meant, he only shook his head and answered:—

"We can do nothing as yet. Wait and see."

[58] Presumably Seward's observation, not Van Helsing's epitaph. The line is from Thomas Hood's poem "The Death-Bed" (*The Englishman's Magazine*, August 1831) and, curiously, does not appear in the Abridged Text. Perhaps Seward felt that its inclusion made him appear overly sentimental.

Chapter 13

DR. SEWARD'S DIARY
—continued.

1 Seward's diary entry is dated 20 September; presumably it was recorded that morning. Therefore, Lucy's funeral is on 21 September, the day before Peter Hawkins's funeral. See note 42 below. This is confirmed by the Notes.

2 The woman's oddly inappropriate comments do not appear in the Abridged Text.

3 That is, on the same day as Lucy's, 21 September.

4 Another degree of Van Helsing's.

THE FUNERAL WAS ARRANGED for the next succeeding day,[1] so that Lucy and her mother might be buried together. I attended to all the ghastly formalities, and the urbane undertaker proved that his staff were afflicted—or blessed—with something of his own obsequious suavity. Even the woman who performed the last offices for the dead remarked to me, in a confidential, brother-professional way, when she had come out from the death chamber:—

"She makes a very beautiful corpse, sir. It's quite a privilege to attend on her. It's not too much to say that she will do credit to our establishment!"[2]

I noticed that Van Helsing never kept far away. This was possible from the disordered state of things in the household. There were no relatives at hand; and as Arthur had to be back the next day to attend at his father's funeral,[3] we were unable to notify any one who should have been bidden. Under the circumstances, Van Helsing and I took it upon ourselves to examine papers, etc. He insisted upon looking over Lucy's papers himself. I asked him why, for I feared that he, being a foreigner, might not be quite aware of English legal requirements, and so might in ignorance make some unnecessary trouble. He answered me:—

"I know; I know. You forget that I am a lawyer[4] as well as a doctor. But this is not altogether for the law. You knew

I Vampiri, starring Gianna Maria Canale as Giselle du Grand.
(America, 1956)

5 Why?

6 It is unclear why Van Helsing is so anxious that Lucy's letters and journals (presumably those that appear in the Harker Papers) be kept from the authorities. It is understandable that Van Helsing wishes to go through them, to glean information about possible contacts between Lucy and the vampire that Van Helsing suspects, as well as clues to the vampire's identity and location, but there is no reason for Van Helsing to fear that he might be incriminated by Lucy's records. Perhaps he merely believes that if the records were found by the authorities before him, he would not obtain access to the information for some time. This seems excessively paranoid, for although there were strange circumstances during the evening (the smashed window and drugged servants in particular), there is no reason to expect that Lucy's death would be the subject of an official inquest. Nor in fact is it. Furthermore, if an inquest were held, concealment of her letters and journals would constitute a crime.

7 French: literally, a "burning chapel," but used to signify the chapel or room in which the cadaver of a sovereign or other important person lies in state pending the funeral service.

that, when you avoided the coroner.[5] I have more than him to avoid. There may be papers more—such as this."

As he spoke he took from his pocket-book the memorandum which had been in Lucy's breast, and which she had torn in her sleep.

"When you find anything of the solicitor who is for the late Mrs. Westenra, seal all her papers, and write him to-night. For me, I watch here in the room and in Miss Lucy's old room all night, and I myself search for what may be. It is not well that her very thoughts go into the hands of strangers."

I went on with my part of the work, and in another half hour had found the name and address of Mrs. Westenra's solicitor and had written to him. All the poor lady's papers were in order; explicit directions regarding the place of burial were given. I had hardly sealed the letter, when, to my surprise, Van Helsing walked into the room, saying:—

"Can I help you, friend John? I am free, and if I may, my service is to you."

"Have you got what you looked for?" I asked, to which he replied:—

"I did not look for any specific thing. I only hoped to find, and find I have, all that there was—only some letters and a few memoranda, and a diary new begun.[6] But I have them here, and we shall for the present say nothing of them. I shall see that poor lad to-morrow evening, and, with his sanction I shall use some."

When we had finished the work in hand, he said to me:—

"And now, friend John, I think we may to bed. We want sleep, both you and I, and rest to recuperate. To-morrow we shall have much to do, but for the to-night there is no need of us. Alas!"

Before turning in we went to look at poor Lucy. The undertaker had certainly done his work well, for the room was turned into a small *chapelle ardente*.[7] There was a wilderness of beautiful white flowers, and death was made as little repulsive as might be. The end of the winding-sheet was laid over the face; when the Professor bent over and turned it gently back, we both started at the beauty before us, the tall wax candles showing a sufficient light to note it well. All Lucy's loveliness had come back to her in death, and the hours that had passed, instead of leaving traces of "decay's effacing fingers,"[8] had but restored the beauty of life, till positively I could not believe my eyes that I was looking at a corpse.

The Professor looked sternly grave. He had not loved her as I had, and there was no need for tears in his eyes. He said to me: "Remain till I return," and left the room. He came back with a handful of wild garlic from the box waiting in the hall, but which had not been opened, and placed the flowers amongst the others on and around the bed. Then he took from his neck, inside his collar, a little gold crucifix, and placed it over the mouth.[9] He restored the sheet to its place and we came away.

I was undressing in my own room, when, with a premonitory tap at the door, he entered, and at once began to speak:—

"To-morrow I want you to bring me, before night, a set of post-mortem knives."[10]

"Must we make an autopsy?" I asked.

"Yes and no. I want to operate, but not as you think. Let me tell you now, but not a word to another. I want to cut off her head and take out her heart. Ah! you a surgeon, and so shocked!

Post-mortem instruments (knives in lower portion of case).

Lord Byron.
Richard Westall, 1813

8 Seward quotes Lord Byron's *The Giaour, A Fragment of a Turkish Tale* (1813). The main story of the long poem tells of a female slave, Leila, who loves the Giaour (which means foreigner or infidel, in this case a Christian outsider). Leila is bound and thrown in a sack into the sea by her Turkish lord, Hassan. The Giaour avenges her by killing Hassan and curses him: "But first, on earth as Vampire sent, / Thy corse shall from its tomb be rent: / Then ghastly haunt thy native place, / And suck the blood of all thy race; / There from thy daughter, sister, wife, / At midnight drain the stream of life."

9 It is not clear what Van Helsing believes he will achieve by these steps. He can no longer be concerned about keeping Dracula away. As will be seen, Van Helsing is fully familiar with the proper customs for the disposition of the undead and here merely takes some preliminary (and wholly useless) precautions. Perhaps despite his numerous intimations to the contrary, he is simply not yet certain that Lucy has been "turned" to vampirism. Van Helsing also seems to imply later that the theft of the crucifix permits Lucy's turning to be completed. Kathryn Marocchino ("Structural Complexity in Bram Stoker's *Dracula*") suggests that because Lucy's turning was accomplished while she was in a sleepwalking trance, she could not awaken to her vampire existence without Dracula's "summoning," which Van Helsing sought to prevent.

One must also wonder why Van Helsing did not give this crucifix to Lucy earlier, to ward off her attacker—unless his knowledge of its power was acquired on his next trip to Amsterdam.

10 The word "operating" has been changed to "post-mortem." Thornley Stoker notes "Operating knives would not be used for a post-mortem."

11 Perhaps as a gesture to Holmwood, who must not have wished to be continually reminded that Seward loved Lucy, the Abridged Text omits this sentence.

12 Van Helsing's secrecy is not mentioned in the Abridged Text, which reads "you and I shall do our operation . . . "

You, whom I have seen with no tremble of hand or heart, do operations of life and death that make the rest shudder. Oh, but I must not forget, my dear friend John, that you loved her; and I have not forgotten it, for it is I that shall operate, and you must only help.[11] I would like to do it to-night, but for Arthur I must not; he will be free after his father's funeral to-morrow, and he will want to see her—to see *it*. Then, when she is coffined ready for the next day, you and I shall come when all sleep.[12] We shall unscrew the coffin-lid, and shall do our operation; and then replace all, so that none know, save we alone."

"But why do it at all? The girl is dead. Why mutilate her poor body without need? And if there is no necessity for a post-mortem and nothing to gain by it—no good to her, to us, to science, to human knowledge—why do it? Without such it is monstrous."

For answer he put his hand on my shoulder, and said, with infinite tenderness:—

"Friend John, I pity your poor bleeding heart; and I love you the more because it does so bleed. If I could, I would take on myself the burden that you do bear. But there are things that you know not, but that you shall know, and bless me for knowing, though they are not pleasant things. John, my child, you have been my friend now many years, and yet did you ever know me to do any without good cause? I may err—I am but man; but I believe in all I do. Was it not for these causes that you send for me when the great trouble came? Yes! Were you not amazed, nay horrified, when I would not let Arthur kiss his love—though she was dying—and snatched him away by all my strength? Yes! And yet you saw how she thanked me, with her so beautiful dying eyes, her voice, too, so weak, and she kiss my rough old hand and bless me? Yes! And did you not hear me swear promise to her, that so she closed her eyes grateful? Yes!

"Well, I have good reason now for all I want to do. You have for many years trust me; you have believe me weeks past, when there be things so strange that you might have well doubt. Believe me yet a little, friend John. If you trust me not, then I must tell what I think; and that is not perhaps well. And if I work—as work I shall, no matter trust or not trust—without my friend trust in me, I work with heavy heart and feel, oh! so lonely when I want all help and courage that may be!" He paused a moment and went on solemnly: "Friend John, there are strange and terrible days before us. Let us not be two, but one, that so we work to a good end. Will you not have faith in me?"

I took his hand, and promised him. I held my door open as he went away, and watched him go into his room and close the door. As I stood without moving, I saw one of the maids pass silently along the passage—she had her back towards me, so did not see me—and go into the room where Lucy lay. The sight touched me. Devotion is so rare, and we are so grateful to those who show it unasked to those we love. Here was a poor girl putting aside the terrors which she naturally had of death to go watch alone by the bier of the mistress whom she loved, so that the poor clay might not be lonely till laid to eternal rest. . . .[13]

I must have slept long and soundly, for it was broad daylight when Van Helsing waked me by coming into my room. He came over to my bedside and said:—

"You need not trouble about the knives; we shall not do it."

"Why not?" I asked. For his solemnity of the night before had greatly impressed me.

"Because," he said sternly, "it is too late—or too early. See!" Here he held up the little golden crucifix. "This was stolen in the night."

"How, stolen," I asked in wonder, "since you have it now?"

"Because I get it back from the worthless wretch who stole it,[14] from the woman who robbed the dead and the living. Her punishment will surely come, but not through me; she knew not altogether what she did, and thus unknowing, she only stole. Now we must wait."

He went away on the word, leaving me with a new mystery to think of, a new puzzle to grapple with.

The forenoon was a dreary time, but at noon the solicitor came: Mr. Marquand, of Wholeman, Sons, Marquand & Lidderdale.[15] He was very genial and very appreciative of what we had done, and took off our hands all cares as to details. During lunch he told us that Mrs. Westenra had for some time expected sudden death from her heart, and had put her affairs in absolute order;

13 Seward's characterisation of the maid—which we will soon see is mistaken—does not appear in the Abridged Text.

14 The balance of Van Helsing's excoriation of the maid does not appear in the Abridged Text.

15 A fictitious firm.

16 A limit on the right of succession, usually imposed by a testator's will. By this time, however, land in England could no longer be tied up for a greater period than the lives of persons in existence and twenty-one years thereafter. This is the current law of most of the United States as well, called the "rule against perpetuities." In Jane Austen's *Pride and Prejudice* (1813), the Bennet family, consisting of five daughters, must endure the loss of their Hertfordshire estate, Longbourn, to the girls' father's cousin, William Collins, because of the entail. In Arthur Conan Doyle's *The Hound of the Baskervilles* (1902), the Baskerville estate remains entailed and passes to Henry Baskerville with near-disastrous consequences to him.

The details of the entail and the entire recitation of the fruitless efforts of the law firm to protect its client do not appear in the Abridged Text.

17 The haste with which Mrs. Westenra acted is fairly amazing. The solicitor says that "some time" ago, Mrs. Westenra "had put her affairs in absolute order" (perhaps, interpreting these comments generously, as recently as the month previous). Lucy and Holmwood became engaged in mid-May, yet at most only three months later, Mrs. Westenra changes her will to leave everything to him. There is no indication that Lucy and Arthur had a long previous relationship, although that is possible.

A more sensible (and credible) arrangement would have been to leave the estate in trust for Lucy, with Holmwood named as trustee. Indeed, Mrs. Westenra's disposition can only reflect a deep-seated conviction that Lucy was incompetent to handle her own affairs and likely to be litigious if she were even given the rights of a beneficiary of a trust.

In addition, it was improper for the solicitor to be divulging this information to a stranger prior to probate of Mrs. Westenra's will.

The entire episode of the speedy will and its highly unusual plan of disposition sounds wholly fictional, perhaps invented by the solicitor (with the connivance of Holmwood) to cover their

he informed us that, with the exception of a certain entailed property of Lucy's father[16] which now, in default of direct issue, went back to a distant branch of the family, the whole estate, real and personal, was left absolutely to Arthur Holmwood. When he had told us so much he went on:—

"Frankly we did our best to prevent such a testamentary disposition, and pointed out certain contingencies that might leave her daughter either penniless or not so free as she should be to act regarding a matrimonial alliance. Indeed, we pressed the matter so far that we almost came into collision, for she asked us if we were or were not prepared to carry out her wishes. Of course, we had then no alternative but to accept. We were right in principle, and ninety-nine times out of a hundred we should have proved, by the logic of events, the accuracy of our judgment.[17] Frankly, however, I must admit that in this case any other form of disposition would have rendered impossible the carrying out of her wishes. For by her predeceasing her daughter the latter would have come into possession of the property, and, even had she only survived her mother by five minutes, her property would, in case there were no will—and a will was a practical impossibility in such a case—have been treated at her decease as under intestacy.[18] In which case Lord Godalming, though so dear a friend, would have had no claim in the world; and the inheritors, being remote, would not be likely to abandon their just right, for sentimental reasons regarding an entire stranger. I assure you, my dear sirs, I am rejoiced at the result, perfectly rejoiced."

He was a good fellow, but his rejoicing at the one little part—in which he was officially interested—of so great a tragedy, was an object-lesson in the limitations of sympathetic understanding.

He did not remain long, but said he would look in later in the day and see Lord Godalming.[19] His coming, however, had been a certain comfort to us, since it assured us that we should not have to dread hostile criticism as to any of our acts. Arthur was expected at five o'clock, so a little before that time we visited the death-chamber.[20] It was so in very truth, for now both mother and daughter lay in it. The undertaker, true to his craft, had made the best display he could of his goods, and there was a mortuary air about the place that lowered our spirits at once. Van Helsing ordered the former arrangement to be adhered to, explaining that, as Lord Godalming[21] was coming very soon, it would be less harrowing to his feelings to see all that was left of his *fiancée* quite alone. The undertaker seemed shocked at his own stupidity and exerted himself to restore things to the condition in which we left them the night before, so that when Arthur came such shocks to his feelings as we could avoid were saved.

Poor fellow! He looked desperately sad and broken; even his stalwart manhood seemed to have shrunk somewhat under the strain of his much-tried emotions. He had, I knew, been very genuinely and devotedly attached to his father; and to lose him, and at such a time, was a bitter blow to him. With me he was warm as ever, and to Van Helsing he was sweetly courteous; but I could not help seeing that there was some constraint with him. The Professor noticed it, too, and motioned me to bring him upstairs. I did so, and left him at the door of the room, as I felt he would like to be quite alone with her; but he took my arm and led me in, saying huskily:—

"You loved her too, old fellow; she told me all about it, and there was no friend had a closer place in her heart than you.[22] I don't know how to thank you for all you have done for her. I can't think yet. . . ."[23]

Here he suddenly broke down, and threw his arms round my shoulders and laid his head on my breast, crying:—

"Oh, Jack! Jack! What shall I do? The whole of life seems gone from me at once, and there is nothing in the wide world for me to live for."

I comforted him as well as I could. In such cases men do not need much expression. A grip of the hand, the tightening of an arm over the shoulder, a sob in unison, are expressions of sympathy dear to a man's heart. I stood still and silent till his sobs died away, and then I said softly to him:—

"Come and look at her."

Together we moved over to the bed, and I lifted the lawn from her face. God! how beautiful she was. Every hour seemed to be enhancing her loveliness. It frightened and amazed me somewhat; and as for Arthur, he fell a-trembling, and finally

looting of the estate. With Lucy's demise, they may have expected that no representative of a "distant branch of the family" would appear to challenge a forged will. Although Holmwood appears to be wealthy, many English titles were borne by impoverished gentility.

18 That is, the condition of death without a will, in which the laws of inheritance determine the heirs, not the wishes of the decedent. Here, presumably the members of that "distant branch of the family" would have been the intestate heirs. The "practical impossibility" which impeded Lucy was that she was not twenty-one, as required by English law.

19 This now means Arthur Holmwood. However, it seems incredibly class-conscious of Seward (or the solicitor, if Seward's account is accurate) to so refer to him, before his father has even been buried.

20 The balance of the paragraph does not appear in the Abridged Text.

21 This time it is Van Helsing ennobling Holmwood.

22 An ironic comment in light of Seward's blood donation. In fact, Holmwood knows nothing of what Seward has "done for her," and this is likely Seward's own self-congratulatory interpolation.

23 The Abridged Text omits mention of Holmwood's breakdown that follows.

24 Arthur at least has some sensibility about his title.

25 It's hard to fathom Van Helsing's profusion of emotion here, for he has in truth spent very few hours with Arthur. Perhaps the emotion is caused by having shared a near-sexual experience (that is, exchanging bodily fluids) with the same woman.

was shaken with doubt as with an ague. At last, after a long pause, he said to me in a faint whisper:—

"Jack, is she really dead?"

I assured him sadly that it was so, and went on to suggest—for I felt that such a horrible doubt should not have life for a moment longer than I could help—that it often happened that after death faces became softened and even resolved into their youthful beauty; that this was especially so when death had been preceded by any acute or prolonged suffering. It seemed to quite do away with any doubt, and, after kneeling beside the couch for a while and looking at her lovingly and long, he turned aside. I told him that that must be good-bye, as the coffin had to be prepared; so he went back and took her dead hand in his and kissed it, and bent over and kissed her forehead. He came away, fondly looking back over his shoulder at her as he came.

I left him in the drawing-room, and told Van Helsing that he had said good-bye; so the latter went to the kitchen to tell the undertaker's men to proceed with the preparations and to screw up the coffin. When he came out of the room again I told him of Arthur's question, and he replied:—

"I am not surprised. Just now I doubted for a moment myself!"

We all dined together, and I could see that poor Art was trying to make the best of things. Van Helsing had been silent all dinner-time; but when we had lit our cigars he said:—

"Lord—;" but Arthur interrupted him:—

"No, no, not that, for God's sake! not yet at any rate. Forgive me, sir: I did not mean to speak offensively; it is only because my loss is so recent."[24]

The Professor answered very sweetly:—

"I only used that name because I was in doubt. I must not call you 'Mr.,' and I have grown to love you—yes, my dear boy, to love you—as Arthur."[25]

Arthur held out his hand, and took the old man's warmly.

"Call me what you will," he said. "I hope I may always have the title of a friend. And let me say that I am at a loss for words to thank you for your goodness to my poor dear." He paused a moment, and went on: "I know that she understood your goodness even better than I do; and if I was rude or in any way wanting at that time you acted so—you remember"—the Professor nodded—"you must forgive me."

He answered with a grave kindness:—

"I know it was hard for you to quite trust me then, for to trust such violence needs to understand; and I take it that you do not—that you cannot—trust me now, for you do not yet understand. And there may be more times when I shall want you to trust when you cannot—and may not—and must not yet understand. But the time will come when your trust shall be whole and complete in me, and when you shall understand as though the sunlight himself shone through. Then you shall bless me from first to last for your own sake, and for the sake of others, and for her dear sake to whom I swore to protect."

"And, indeed, indeed, sir," said Arthur warmly, "I shall in all ways trust you. I know and believe you have a very noble heart, and you are Jack's friend, and you were hers. You shall do what you like."

The Professor cleared his throat a couple of times, as though about to speak, and finally said:—

"May I ask you something now?"

"Certainly."

"You know that Mrs. Westenra left you all her property?"

"No, poor dear; I never thought of it."[26]

"And as it is all yours, you have a right to deal with it as you will. I want you to give me permission to read all Miss Lucy's papers and letters. Believe me, it is no idle curiosity. I have a motive of which, be sure, she would have approved. I have them all here. I took them before we knew that all was yours, so that no strange hand might touch them—no strange eye look through words into her soul. I shall keep them, if I may; even you may not see them yet, but I shall keep them safe. No word shall be lost; and in the good time I shall give them back to you. It's a hard thing I ask, but you will do it, will you not, for Lucy's sake?"

Arthur spoke out heartily, like his old self:—

"Dr. Van Helsing, you may do what you will. I feel that in saying this I am doing what my dear one would have approved.[27] I shall not trouble you with questions till the time comes."

26 Holmwood seems surprisingly unsurprised by this startling news. See note 17 above.

27 What can Holmwood—who knows nothing of vampirism or even the details of Lucy's demise—imagine that Van Helsing wants with Lucy's papers? To remove letters embarrassing to Seward and Morris? To exculpate himself from malpractise?

28 The Manuscript has a typed date of "21 Septr." This seems to solidify the conclusion that the funeral was in fact on 21 September, but for artistic reasons Stoker chose to split the day. See note 42 below.

29 The Abridged Text does not include this paragraph.

30 The funeral was not held in central London.

31 Hyde Park Corner is the southeast corner of Hyde Park, "one of the most frequented and lively scenes in London," according to the 1896 London "Baedeker." Dickens's *Dictionary of London* (1888) calls it "the great fashionable promenade of London."

The first Hyde Park was enclosed by Henry VIII, and the French ambassador hunted there in 1550. In the time of Charles I, the park was opened to the public, but Cromwell sold it, and the new owners charged a toll of a shilling for coaches and sixpence for a horse. When the Commonwealth was overthrown, the park was reacquired by the nation. In the late nineteenth century, it was much used for radical meetings, and on Sundays numerous open-air congregations near the Marble Arch held revival meetings.

Hyde Park Corner itself has a handsome gateway built in 1828, with reliefs that are copies of the Elgin marbles. The "Baedeker" reports that "*Apsley House* . . . , the residence of the Duke of Wellington, lies directly to the E. of Hyde

Hyde Park Corner.
Queen's London (1897)

The old Professor stood up as he said solemnly:—

"And you are right. There will be pain for us all; but it will not be all pain, nor will this pain be the last. We and you too—you most of all, dear boy—will have to pass through the bitter water before we reach the sweet. But we must be brave of heart and unselfish, and do our duty, and all will be well!"

I slept on a sofa in Arthur's room that night. Van Helsing did not go to bed at all. He went to and fro, as if patrolling the house, and was never out of sight of the room where Lucy lay in her coffin, strewn with the wild garlic flowers, which sent, through the odour of lily and rose, a heavy, overpowering smell into the night.

MINA HARKER'S JOURNAL.

22 September.[28]—In the train to Exeter. Jonathan sleeping. It seems only yesterday that the last entry was made, and yet how much between then, in Whitby and all the world before me, Jonathan away and no news of him; and now, married to Jonathan, Jonathan a solicitor, a partner, rich, master of his business, Mr. Hawkins dead and buried, and Jonathan with another attack that may harm him. Some day he may ask me about it. Down it all goes. I am rusty in my shorthand—see what unexpected prosperity does for us—so it may be as well to freshen it up again with an exercise anyhow. . . .

The service was very simple and very solemn. There were only ourselves and the servants there, one or two old friends of his from Exeter, his London agent, and a gentleman representing Sir John Paxton, the President of the Incorporated Law Society. Jonathan and I stood hand in hand, and we felt that our best and dearest friend was gone from us. . . .[29]

We came back to town quietly,[30] taking a 'bus to Hyde Park Corner.[31] Jonathan thought it would interest me to go into the Row[32] for a while, so we sat down; but there were very few people there, and it was sad-looking and desolate to see so many empty chairs. It made us think of the empty chair at home; so we got up and walked down Piccadilly.[33] Jonathan was holding me by the arm, the way he used to in the old days before I went to school.[34] I felt it very improper, for you can't go

Three-horse omnibus.
William Francis Freelove, 1873

on for some years teaching etiquette and decorum to other girls without the pedantry of it biting into yourself a bit;[35] but it was Jonathan, and he was my husband, and we didn't know anybody who saw us—and we didn't care if they did—so on we walked. I was looking at a very beautiful girl, in a big cart-wheel hat, sitting in a victoria[36] outside Guiliano's,[37] when I felt Jonathan clutch my arm so tight that he hurt me, and he said under his breath: "My God!" I am always anxious about Jonathan, for I fear that some nervous fit may upset him again; so I turned to him quickly, and asked him what it was that disturbed him.

He was very pale, and his eyes seemed bulging out as, half in terror and half in amazement, he gazed at a tall, thin man, with a beaky nose and black moustache and pointed beard, who was also observing the pretty girl.[38] He was looking at her so hard that he did not see either of us, and so I had a good view of him. His face was not a good face; it was hard, and cruel, and sensual, and his big white teeth, that looked all the whiter because his lips were so red, were pointed like an animal's. Jonathan kept staring at him, till I was afraid he would notice. I feared he might take it ill, he looked so fierce and nasty. I asked Jonathan why he was disturbed, and he answered, evidently thinking that I knew as much about it as he did: "Do you see who it is?"

"No, dear," I said; "I don't know him; who is it?" His answer

Park Corner. The house next it is that of *Baron Rothschild*, and that at the W. Corner of Park Lane is occupied by the *Duke of Cambridge*."

The mention of Hyde Park Corner does not appear in the Abridged Text.

32 Rotten Row, that is (see chapter 5, note 15).

33 A street in west-central London running from Piccadilly Circus to Hyde Park Corner, about ¾ mile in length. The eastern portion is one of the chief business streets in the West End; the western half historically contained a number of fashionable residences and clubs, many now turned to offices.

34 Whether Mina is referring here to her professional training or her employment is unclear.

35 If the school were small, as an assistant schoolmistress Mina would have taught a variety of subjects, perhaps including typewriting and shorthand as well as etiquette and deportment. Mina's somewhat prissy remarks do not appear in the Abridged Text.

36 A two-seater carriage with a folding roof and a perch for a driver.

37 McNally and Florescu (*The Essential Dracula*) identify this as "a well known café on Piccadilly." More likely, this is the highly reputed jewellery shop of Carlo Giuliano (1831–1895) at 115 Piccadilly, listed in the 1884 Business

A victoria.

Directory of London and immortalized by Mary Eliza Joy Haweis in her book *The Art of Beauty* (1878). It is a more enticing picture to envision this "very beautiful girl"—obviously an important customer of the store—waiting outside the fine jeweller for a clerk to bring her some trinket than to imagine her hanging around a café. The reference to Guiliano's is missing in the Abridged Text.

38 Wolf (*The Essential Dracula*) points out that Mina's description of Dracula is far less flattering than Jonathan's earlier description in his journal (see text accompanying chapter 2, note 7). Mina had not yet read Jonathan's journal. Perhaps on reading it, she took pleasure in her unfavourable description. Note also that here Dracula has a black moustache and beard—either he has dyed his facial hair in an effort at disguise or, as Jonathan suggests shortly, has actually grown younger, presumably as a result of steady feeding on Lucy (and perhaps others).

A more interesting question is why Dracula is ogling the beautiful girl. As noted earlier, there is no reason to believe that Dracula was on a Lucy-exclusive diet, and in any event his pantry was now either bare or at least badly reduced. Therefore, it is reasonable to conclude that Dracula was shopping for his next meal. The entire "beautiful girl" element of this scene fails to appear in the Abridged Text, and one wonders if things ended badly with her.

39 The Manuscript continues: "It is the man in the Munich Dead House!" As discussed above, this episode—outlined in the Notes (see chapter 1, note 1)—has been excised from the published narrative, and so this reference was also deleted.

40 A 60-acre parcel between Buckingham Palace and Piccadilly. Constitution Hill Road separates the park from the palace gardens and connects Hyde Park Corner to the Mall.

41 The Abridged Text omits this plea.

seemed to shock and thrill me, for it was said as if he did not know that it was to me, Mina, to whom he was speaking:—

"It is the man himself!"**39**

The poor dear was evidently terrified at something—very greatly terrified; I do believe that if he had not had me to lean on and to support him he would have sunk down. He kept staring; a man came out of the shop with a small parcel, and gave it to the lady, who then drove off. The dark man kept his eyes fixed on her, and when the carriage moved up Piccadilly he followed in the same direction, and hailed a hansom. Jonathan kept looking after him, and said, as if to himself:—

"I believe it is the Count, but he has grown young. My God, if this be so! Oh, my God! my God! If I only knew! if I only knew!" He was distressing himself so much that I feared to keep his mind on the subject by asking him any questions, so I remained silent. I drew away quietly, and he, holding my arm, came easily. We walked a little further, and then went in and sat for a while in the Green Park.**40** It was a hot day for autumn, and there was a comfortable seat in a shady place. After a few minutes' staring at nothing, Jonathan's eyes closed, and he went quietly into a sleep, with his head on my shoulder. I thought it was the best thing for him, so did not disturb him. In about twenty minutes he woke up, and said to me quite cheerfully:—

"Why, Mina, have I been asleep! Oh, do forgive me for being so rude. Come, and we'll have a cup of tea somewhere." He had evidently forgotten all about the dark stranger, as in his illness he had forgotten all that this episode had reminded him of. I don't like this lapsing into forgetfulness; it may make or continue some injury to the brain. I must not ask him, for fear I shall do more harm than good; but I must somehow learn the facts of his journey abroad. The time is come, I fear, when I must open that parcel, and know what is written. Oh, Jonathan, you will, I know, forgive me if I do wrong, but it is for your own dear sake.**41**

Later.—A sad home-coming in every way—the house empty of the dear soul who was so good to us; Jonathan still pale and dizzy under a slight relapse of his malady; and now a telegram from Van Helsing, whoever he may be:—

"You will be grieved to hear that Mrs. Westenra died five days ago, and that Lucy died the day before yesterday. They were both buried to-day."[42]

Oh, what a wealth of sorrow in a few words! Poor Mrs. Westenra! poor Lucy! Gone, gone, never to return to us! And poor, poor Arthur, to have lost such sweetness out of his life! God help us all to bear our troubles.

DR. SEWARD'S DIARY.

22 September.—It is all over. Arthur has gone back to Ring, and has taken Quincey Morris with him. What a fine fellow is Quincey! I believe in my heart of hearts that he suffered as much about Lucy's death as any of us; but he bore himself through it like a moral Viking. If America can go on breeding men like that, she will be a power in the world indeed.[43] Van Helsing is lying down, having a rest preparatory to his journey. He goes over to Amsterdam to-night, but says he returns to-morrow night; that he only wants to make some arrangements which can only be made personally.[44] He is to stop with me then, if he can; he says he has work to do in London which may take him some time. Poor old fellow! I fear that the strain of the past week has broken down even his iron strength. All the time of the burial he was, I could see, putting some terrible restraint on himself. When it was all over, we were standing beside Arthur, who, poor fellow, was speaking of his part in the operation where his blood had been transfused to his Lucy's veins; I could see Van Helsing's face grow white and purple by turns. Arthur was saying that he felt since then as if they two had been really married and that she was his wife in the sight of God. None of us said a word of the other operations, and none of us ever shall. Arthur and Quincey went away together to the station, and Van Helsing and I came on here. The moment we were alone in the carriage he gave way to a regular fit of hysterics.[45] He had denied to me since that it was hysterics, and insisted that it was only his sense of humour asserting itself under very terrible conditions. He laughed till he cried, and I had to draw down the blinds lest any one should see us and misjudge;[46] and then he cried, till he laughed again; and laughed and cried together,

42 Van Helsing speaks of Lucy's funeral as "to-day," which, as shown above, was 21 September. The telegram apparently arrived in Exeter late on the 21st, when Mina and Jonathan had already departed for London. Although the Notes indicate that Hawkins's funeral took place on the 21st, the same day as Lucy's, and that the sighting of Dracula occurs on the 21st, Mina's journal entry is ambiguous on the point: her account is consistent with the funeral's having occurred in the morning, a short bus ride to Hyde Park Corner at midday, a few hours' stroll and nap, and a return train to Exeter—the last departed from Waterloo station at 5:00 P.M., arriving at around 9:30 P.M.

43 Seward's praise of Morris and Americans does not appear in the Abridged Text.

44 Again Van Helsing goes to Amsterdam for a brief visit, and again he offers no explanation of what required his presence.

45 The overreaction of the group might well raise suspicions about the nature of the bodily fluids transferred from the men to Lucy. Van Helsing in particular, his scientific training notwithstanding, seems to be reacting as if he had committed adultery or rather as if he wished he had. Certainly these tightly wound Victorians imbue the transfusions with all the moral and religious significance of sexual congress. Nor can the sheer medical novelty of the procedure be forgotten.

Fortunately for the health of the public, early in the twentieth century, as blood typing and techniques for blood storage were developed, blood transfusions became anonymous (or at least were conducted in an indirect manner); otherwise, continued public expressions of sentiments like those evidenced here might have brought about public legislation banning transfusions on moral grounds.

46 How would Van Helsing's very un-Victorian display of emotions be "misjudged"? An observer would likely conclude that Van Helsing was unfit to be Lucy's physician—a conclusion that Seward evades but that is supported by a fair viewing of the evidence. The following passages—known as the "King Laugh" episode—do not appear in the Abridged Text.

47 But Van Helsing is in error: Lucy is not buried in a coffin and is free to wreak her depredations on the children of Hampstead.

48 Van Helsing reveals that he had a son who died.

just as a woman does. I tried to be stern with him, as one is to a woman under the circumstances; but it had no effect. Men and women are so different in manifestations of nervous strength or weakness! Then when his face grew grave and stern again I asked him why his mirth, and why at such a time. His reply was in a way characteristic of him, for it was logical and forceful and mysterious. He said:—

"Ah, you don't comprehend, friend John. Do not think that I am not sad, though I laugh. See, I have cried even when the laugh did choke me. But no more think that I am all sorry when I cry, for the laugh he come just the same. Keep it always with you that laughter who knock at your door and say, 'May I come in?' is not the true laughter. No! he is a king, and he come when and how he like. He ask no person; he choose no time of suitability. He say, 'I am here.' Behold, in example I grieve my heart out for that so sweet young girl; I give my blood for her, though I am old and worn; I give my time, my skill, my sleep; I let my other sufferers want that so she may have all. And yet I can laugh at her very grave—laugh when the clay from the spade of the sexton drop upon her coffin and say, 'Thud! thud!' to my heart, till it send back the blood from my cheek.**47** My heart bleed for that poor boy—that dear boy, so of the age of mine own boy had I been so blessed that he live, and with his hair and eyes the same.**48** There, you know now why I love him so. And yet when he say things that touch my husband-heart to the quick, and make my father-heart yearn to him as to no other man—not even to you, friend John, for we are more level in experiences than father and son—yet even at such moment King Laugh he come to me and shout and bellow in my ear, 'Here I am! here I am!' till the blood come dance back and bring some of the sunshine that he carry with him to my cheek. Oh, friend John, it is a strange world, a sad world, a world full of miseries, and woes, and troubles; and yet when King Laugh come he make them all dance to the tune he play. Bleeding hearts, and dry bones of the churchyard, and tears that burn as they fall—all dance together to the music that he make with that smileless mouth of him. And believe me, friend John, that he is good to come, and kind. Ah, we men and women are like ropes drawn tight with strain that pull us different ways. Then tears come; and, like the rain on the ropes, they brace us up, until perhaps the strain become too great, and we break. But King Laugh he come like the sunshine, and he ease off the strain again; and we bear to go on with our labour, what it may be."

I did not like to wound him by pretending not to see his idea; but, as I did not yet understand the cause of his laughter, I asked him. As he answered me his face grew stern, and he said in quite a different tone:—

"Oh, it was the grim irony of it all—this so lovely lady garlanded with flowers, that looked so fair as life, till one by one we wondered if she were truly dead; she laid in that so fine marble house in that lonely churchyard, where rest so many of her kin, laid there with the mother who loved her, and whom she loved; and that sacred bell going 'Toll! toll! toll!' so sad and slow; and those holy men, with the white garments of the angel, pretending to read books, and yet all the time their eyes never on the page;[49] and all of us with the bowed head. And all for what? She is dead; so! Is it not?"

"Well, for the life of me, Professor," I said, "I can't see anything to laugh at in all that. Why, your explanation makes it a harder puzzle than before. But even if the burial service was comic, what about poor Art and his trouble? Why, his heart was simply breaking."

"Just so. Said he not that the transfusion of his blood to her veins had made her truly his bride?"

"Yes, and it was a sweet and comforting idea for him."

"Quite so. But there was a difficulty, friend John. If so that, then what about the others? Ho, ho! Then this so sweet maid is a polyandrist,[50] and me, with my poor wife dead to me, but alive by Church's law, though no wits, all gone—even I, who am faithful husband to this now-no-wife, am bigamist."[51]

"I don't see where the joke comes in there either!" I said; and I did not feel particularly pleased with him for saying such things. He laid his hand on my arm, and said:—

"Friend John, forgive me if I pain. I showed not my feeling to others when it would wound, but only to you, my old friend, whom I can trust. If you could have looked into my very heart then when I want to laugh; if you could have done so when the

49 Van Helsing states that the clergy were all staring at the beautiful corpse of Lucy.

50 Literally, a woman with several husbands. However, in 1887 the *Pall Mall Gazette* used the term as a euphemism for "prostitute," viz.: reporting on "attempts to make regulation of movements of female polyandrists a police function" (14 July). Similarly, in an article concerning the Whitechapel murders committed by Jack the Ripper, "a *Star* reporter was said to have 'made inquiries among a number of "polyandrous" women in the East End'" (quoted in Judith R. Walkowitz, *City of Dreadful Delight*).

51 And now Van Helsing reveals that like Rochester of *Jane Eyre*, he has an insane wife whom he cannot divorce. No wonder his "adultery"—or his desire to transgress—caused him to become hysterical.

52 Note that the churchyard is not identified, although it is clearly in the Hampstead area. See chapter 15, note 9, for suggestions of identifications of the cemetery.

53 Technically, Parliament Hill, the southeast end of the heath. However, McNally and Florescu (*The Essential Dracula*) suggest that this is a disguise for Highgate Hill, near the Highgate Cemetery, which they contend is Lucy's resting place. However, if Parliament Hill is correct, then the cemetery must lie west of the heath. See chapter 15, note 9.

54 A newspaper known for its thoughtful Liberalism, it commenced publication in 1893 under the aegis of publisher George Newnes, who had achieved great success with *Tit-Bits* magazine and the *Strand Magazine*, the home of the tales of Sherlock Holmes. As will be seen, it is impossible for the events described to have occurred in 1893, and the newspaper account is either fictionalised or misattributed. See appendix 2, "The Dating of *Dracula*."

55 The last is presumably a play on Wilkie Collins's *The Woman in White* (1860), the immensely popular novel (reputedly so popular that it inspired a song, "The Woman in White Waltz"). "Women in black" have appeared in local legends for centuries, often said to be the ghosts of widows of murdered men or murder victims themselves, seeking revenge.

Names such as "The Kensington Horror" or "The Stabbing Woman" often appeared in lurid Victorian newspaper headlines in an era when sensational journalism and fiction often ran side by side. In 1863, *Punch* magazine satirised the trend with an advertisement for an imaginary new magazine, *The Sensation Times: A Chronicle of Excitement*: "No class of sensational record will be neglected, and readers may rely upon receiving the most graphic accounts of all Crimes with Violence, merciless Corporal Punishments (especially in the case of children), Revolting Cruelties to Animals and other interesting matters" (quoted in Deborah

laugh arrived; if you could do so now, when King Laugh have pack up his crown and all that is to him—for he go far, far away from me, and for a long, long time—maybe you would perhaps pity me the most of all."

I was touched by the tenderness of his tone, and asked why. "Because I know!"

And now we are all scattered; and for many a long day loneliness will sit over our roofs with brooding wings. Lucy lies in the tomb of her kin, a lordly deathhouse in a lonely churchyard,[52] away from teeming London; where the air is fresh, and the sun rises over Hampstead Hill,[53] and where wild flowers grow of their own accord.

So I can finish this diary; and God only knows if I shall ever begin another. If I do, or if I even open this again, it will be to deal with different people and different themes; for here at the end, where the romance of my life is told, ere I go back to take up the thread of my lifework, I say sadly and without hope,

"FINIS."

"THE WESTMINSTER GAZETTE,"[54] *25 SEPTEMBER.*

A HAMPSTEAD MYSTERY.

The neighbourhood of Hampstead is just at present exercised with a series of events which seem to run on lines parallel to those of what was known to the writers of headlines as "The Kensington Horror," or "The Stabbing Woman," or "The Woman in Black."[55] During the past two or three days several cases have occurred of young children straying from home or neglecting to return from their playing on the Heath. In all these cases the children were too young to give any properly intelligible account of themselves, but the consensus of their excuses is that they had been with a "bloofer lady."[56] It has always been late in the evening when they have been missed, and on two occasions the children have not been found until early in the following morning. It is generally supposed in the neighbourhood that, as the first child missed gave as his reason for being away that a "bloofer lady" had asked him to come for a walk, the others had picked up the phrase and used it as occasion served. This is the more natural as the favourite game of the little ones at present is luring each other away by wiles. A correspondent writes us that to see some of the tiny tots pretending to be the "bloofer lady" is supremely funny. Some of our caricaturists might, he says, take a lesson in the irony of grotesque by comparing the reality and the picture. It is only in accordance with general principles of human nature that the "bloofer lady" should be the popular rôle at these *al fresco* performances. Our correspondent naïvely says that even Ellen Terry[57] could not be so winningly attractive as some of these grubby-faced little children pretend—and even imagine themselves—to be.

There is, however, possibly a serious side to the question, for some of the children, indeed all who have been missed at night, have been slightly torn or wounded in the throat. The wounds seem such as might be made by a rat or a small dog, and although of not much importance individually, would tend to show that whatever animal inflicts them has a system or method of its own. The police of the division have been instructed to keep a sharp look-out for straying children, especially when very young, in and around Hampstead Heath, and for any stray dog which may be about.

"THE WESTMINSTER GAZETTE," 25 SEPTEMBER.

EXTRA SPECIAL

THE HAMPSTEAD HORROR[58]
ANOTHER CHILD INJURED.
THE "BLOOFER LADY."

We have just received intelligence that another child, missed last night, was only discovered late in the morning under a furze bush at the Shooter's Hill side of Hampstead Heath,[59] which is, perhaps, less frequented than the other parts.[60] It has the same tiny wound in the throat as has been noticed in other cases. It was terribly weak, and looked quite emaciated. It too, when partially restored, had the common story to tell of being lured away by the "bloofer lady."

Ellen Terry as Lady Macbeth.

Wynne, *The Sensation Novel and the Victorian Family Magazine*).

56 Wolf (*The Essential Dracula*) translates this as a small child's possible pronunciation of "beautiful lady."

57 In 1878 Henry Irving entered into a partnership with the actress Ellen Terry and opened the Lyceum under his own management. With Terry portraying Ophelia, he revived *Hamlet*; subsequently, she appeared as Portia in Irving's *The Merchant of Venice* (1879). Bram Stoker was the manager of the theatre company. Stoker and Terry were close;

Terry frequently referred to Stoker as her "Mama" and to herself as his "daughter."

Terry (1847–1928), who first appeared on stage at the age of seven as the Duke of York in *Richard III*, was the leading Shakespearean actress in England and achieved substantial commercial success. In 1903, she split with Irving and created her own theatrical company with her thirty-one-year-old son, the actor Edward Gordon Craig. She and Stoker remained friends until his death, and according to Stoker biographer Harry Ludlam (*A Biography of Bram Stoker*), she sent a wreath to his funeral. Her autobiography, *The Story of My Life*, calls Stoker "one of the most kind and tender-hearted of men," certainly an unusual description of a theatrical business manager by an actress— unless one considers that two of Terry's brothers also had a hand in theatre management!

Terry was never a proverbial beauty as was, for example, Lillie Langtry, the "New Helen," and her name appearing here is probably an emendation by Stoker of the actual newspaper account, made as a gesture to a dear friend. The Abridged Text does not contain the sentence.

Ellen Terry.
Photograph by Julia Margaret Cameron,
probably ca. 1885

58 Because of the dense cover blanketing much of the heath, it is no surprise that several prominent child murders were committed on or near there. The *Hampstead and Highgate Express* for 15 February 1879 reported that a £50 reward had been posted for information as to child murders—"atrocities"—committed in unspecified locations on the heath; one child's corpse was found in the garden of 59 Avenue Road, St. John's Wood, North London. According to McNally and Florescu (*The Essential Dracula*), "the murderer was never apprehended, and the case remains a total mystery." It is highly unlikely that the death of Lucy Westenra occurred as early as 1879 (see appendix 2, "The Dating of *Dracula*"), and the mystery must be viewed as coincidental.

59 The actual location has been concealed here; Shooter's Hill is located on Eltham Common, southeast of central London, more than 2 miles from Hampstead Heath. Leatherdale (*Dracula Unearthed*) notes a Shoot-Up Hill 2 miles southwest of the heath but thinks it an unlikely location. Bernard Davies, in private correspondence with this editor, suggests that Traitor's Hill (also known as Parliament Hill) was meant, rather than Shooter's Hill.

60 This "hidden" nature of Shooter's Hill is not included in the Abridged Text, perhaps because of its fictional nature.

Chapter 14

MINA HARKER'S JOURNAL.

23 September.—Jonathan is better after a bad night. I am so glad that he has plenty of work to do, for that keeps his mind off the terrible things; and oh, I am rejoiced that he is not now weighed down with the responsibility of his new position. I knew he would be true to himself, and now how proud I am to see my Jonathan rising to the height of his advancement and keeping pace in all ways with the duties that come upon him. He will be away all day till late, for he said he could not lunch at home. My household work is done, so I shall take his foreign journal, and lock myself up in my room and read it. . . .

24 September.—I hadn't the heart to write last night; that terrible record of Jonathan's upset me so. Poor dear! How he must have suffered, whether it be true or only imagination. I wonder if there is any truth in it at all.[1] Did he get his brain fever, and then write all those terrible things; or had he some cause for it all? I suppose I shall never know, for I dare not open the subject to him. . . . And yet that man we saw yesterday![2] He seemed quite certain of him. . . . Poor fellow! I suppose it was the funeral upset him and sent his mind back on some train of thought. . . . He believes it all himself. I remember how on our wedding-day he said: "Unless some solemn duty come upon me to go back to the bitter hours, asleep or awake, mad or sane." There seems to be through it all some thread of continuity. . . .

1 An excellent question in light of the numerous inconsistencies and errors noted above. This comment suggests that Mina as well may have been duped by Jonathan and that the version of the Harker Papers presented to her had already been altered. If this is so, then the alteration may have taken place while Jonathan was supposedly under the care of the Sisters in Buda-Pesth.

2 Mina is definitely mistaken about her "yesterday." Jonathan spotted Dracula on 22 September, according to her journal entry for that day.

Andy Warhol's Dracula (UK title: *Blood for Dracula*),
starring Udo Kier as Dracula.
(C. F. S. Kosutnjak, 1974)

3 Appearing in the Manuscript but omitted from the published narrative is: "and truly he saw that other fearful man . . . and he thought now the Man of the Munich Dead House and Count Dracula were one." See chapter 13, note 39.

That fearful Count was coming to London. . . .[3] 'If it should be, and he came to London, with its teeming millions.'. . . There may be solemn duty; and if it come we must not shrink from it. . . . I shall be prepared. I shall get my typewriter this very hour and begin transcribing. Then we shall be ready for other eyes if required. And if it be wanted; then, perhaps, if I am ready, poor Jonathan may not be upset, for I can speak for him and never let him be troubled or worried with it at all. If ever Jonathan quite gets over the nervousness he may want to tell me of it all, and I can ask him questions and find out things, and see how I may comfort him.

LETTER, VAN HELSING TO MRS. HARKER

"24 September.
(Confidence.)

"Dear Madam,—

"I pray you to pardon my writing, in that I am so far friend as that I sent you sad news of Miss Lucy Westenra's death. By the kindness of Lord Godalming, I am empowered to read her letters and papers, for I am deeply concerned about certain matters vitally important. In them I find some letters from you, which show how great friends you were and how you love her. Oh, Madam Mina, by that love, I implore you, help me. It is for others' good that I ask—to redress great wrong, and to lift much and terrible troubles—that may be more great than you can know. May it be that I see you? You can trust me. I am friend of Dr. John Seward and of Lord Godalming (that was Arthur of Miss Lucy). I must keep it private for the present from all. I should come to Exeter to see you at once if you tell me I am privilege to come, and where and when. I implore your pardon, madam. I have read your letters to poor Lucy, and know how good you are and how your husband suffer;[4] so I pray you, if it may be, enlighten him not, lest it may harm. Again your pardon, and forgive me.

"Van Helsing."

TELEGRAM FROM MRS. HARKER TO VAN HELSING.

"*25 September.*—COME TO-DAY BY QUARTER-PAST TEN TRAIN IF YOU CAN CATCH IT.[5] CAN SEE YOU ANY TIME YOU CALL.

"WILHELMINA HARKER."

MINA HARKER'S JOURNAL.

25 September.—I cannot help feeling terribly excited as the time draws near for the visit of Dr. Van Helsing, for somehow I expect that it will throw some light upon Jonathan's sad experience; and as he attended poor dear Lucy in her last illness, he can tell me all about her.[6] That is the reason of his coming; it is concerning Lucy and her sleep-walking, and not about Jonathan. Then I shall never know the real truth now! How silly I am. That awful journal gets hold of my imagination and tinges everything with something of its own colour. Of course it is about Lucy. That habit came back to the poor dear, and that awful night on the cliff must have made her ill. I had almost forgotten in my own affairs how ill she was afterwards. She must have told him of her sleep-walking adventure on the

4 Van Helsing's mention of Jonathan Harker's suffering should not be taken as prescience of the rôle Harker played in the introduction of Dracula into England. Based on Mina's subsequent record of her conversation with Van Helsing, it is clear that Van Helsing's sympathetic expression did not reflect any particular interest in what happened to Harker. There is no hint in any of Mina's letters to Lucy (or in her journal entries) that would lead Van Helsing to connect Jonathan Harker with vampires. There is a brief mention in a journal entry of Jonathan visiting "Castle Dracula," and it is possible that Mina mentioned the name of the castle to Lucy and that Lucy recorded it in her own papers somewhere (not those in the narrative, however), but there is no intimation that Van Helsing knows the name Dracula at this point.

5 According to the 1887 *Bradshaw's,* Van Helsing could have taken the Great Western Railway train from Paddington station— apparently Mina's choice; see text accompanying note 20 below—but the 10:30 A.M. did not arrive in Exeter until 6:35 P.M. weekdays. The Sunday schedule was equally tedious. Alternatively, Van Helsing could have travelled from Waterloo station on the London and South Western (L&SW) Railway. Again, however, there was no 10:15 A.M. on weekdays, only on Sunday, and it would not arrive until 5:23 P.M. Weekday travel was more expeditious: an 11:00 A.M. express reached Exeter at 2:23 P.M. The time of Van Helsing's arrival, recorded in Mina's subsequent journal entry, indicates that Van Helsing must have taken the L&SW weekday express. In 1893, 25 September was a Monday; only 1887 and 1892 are eliminated by this clue. See appendix 2, "The Dating of *Dracula.*"

Appearing in the Manuscript but not in the published narrative is: "Jonathan away Plymouth." Plymouth is about 57 miles from Exeter, and though it has extensive military fortifications and numerous churches, there is no apparent reason connected to the narrative for Jonathan's having travelled there. The trip appears to have been a routine business journey, with Jonathan continuing on to Launceston later that day or early the following day. See text accompanying note 21 below.

6 Leatherdale (*Dracula Unearthed*) expresses some surprise at this sentence: Mina has no information respecting Lucy's death, and according to the Stoker narrative, she never regarded Lucy's condition at Whitby as an illness, especially not a life-threatening one. If the narrative were true, Mina should have guessed at some accidental death. However, the Notes contradict this, recording that as a result of Mina's worrying, Dr. Seward was called in to see Lucy in Whitby (see chapter 6, note 64). When this fact was suppressed by Stoker, he apparently forgot to alter Mina's comments here.

Mina's expectations about enlightenment regarding Jonathan do not appear in the Abridged Text. Perhaps Stoker realised that these must have been added to the journal entry later, not contemporaneously—see note 4 above.

7 Mina's fears about her rôle in Lucy's death are mostly eliminated in the Abridged Text.

8 The Abridged Text also omits Mina's emotional response in the preceding three sentences.

9 This sentence and the balance of the paragraph do not appear in the Abridged Text.

cliff, and that I knew all about it; and now he wants me to tell him about it, so that he may understand. I hope I did right in not saying anything of it to Mrs. Westenra; I should never forgive myself if any act of mine, were it even a negative one, brought harm on poor dear Lucy.[7] I hope, too, Dr. Van Helsing will not blame me; I have had so much trouble and anxiety of late that I feel I cannot bear more just at present.

I suppose a cry does us all good at times—clears the air as other rain does. Perhaps it was reading the journal yesterday that upset me, and then Jonathan went away this morning to stay away from me a whole day and night, the first time we have been parted since our marriage. I do hope the dear fellow will take care of himself, and that nothing will occur to upset him. It is two o'clock, and the doctor will be here soon now.[8] I shall say nothing of Jonathan's journal unless he asks me. I am so glad I have typewritten out my own journal, so that, in case he asks about Lucy, I can hand it to him; it will save much questioning.

Later.—He has come and gone. Oh, what a strange meeting, and how it all makes my head whirl round! I feel like one in a dream. Can it be all possible, or even a part of it? If I had not read Jonathan's journal first, I should never have accepted even a possibility. Poor, poor, dear Jonathan! How he must have suffered. Please the good God, all this may not upset him again. I shall try to save him from it; but it may be even a consolation and a help to him—terrible though it be and awful in its consequences—to know for certain that his eyes and ears and brain did not deceive him, and that it is all true. It may be that it is the doubt which haunts him; that when the doubt is removed, no matter which—waking or dreaming—may prove the truth, he will be more satisfied and better able to bear the shock. Dr. Van Helsing must be a good man as well as a clever one if he is Arthur's friend and Dr. Seward's, and if they brought him all the way from Holland to look after Lucy. I feel from having seen him that he *is* good and kind and of a noble nature. When he comes to-morrow I shall ask him about Jonathan; and then, please God, all this sorrow and anxiety may lead to a good end.[9] I used to think I would like to practice interviewing; Jonathan's friend on "The Exeter News"[10] told him that memory was everything in such work—that you must be able to put down exactly almost every word spoken, even if you had to refine some of it afterwards. Here was a rare interview; I shall try to record it *verbatim*.

It was half-past two o'clock when the knock came. I took my courage *à deux mains*[11] and waited. In a few minutes Mary[12] opened the door, and announced "Dr. Van Helsing."

I rose and bowed, and he came towards me; a man of medium weight, strongly built, with his shoulders set back over a broad, deep chest and a neck well balanced on the trunk as the head is on the neck. The poise of the head strikes one at once as indicative of thought and power; the head is noble, well-sized, broad, and large behind the ears. The face, clean-shaven, shows a hard, square chin, a large, resolute, mobile mouth, a good-sized nose, rather straight, but with quick, sensitive nostrils, that seem to broaden as the big, bushy brows come down and the mouth tightens. The forehead is broad and fine, rising at first almost straight and then sloping back above two bumps on ridges wide apart; such a forehead that the reddish hair cannot possibly tumble over it, but falls naturally back and to the sides. Big, dark blue eyes are set widely apart, and are quick and tender or stern with the man's moods. He said to me:—

"Mrs. Harker, is it not?" I bowed assent.

"That was Miss Mina Murray?" Again I assented.

"It is Mina Murray that I came to see that was friend of that poor dear child Lucy Westenra. Madam Mina, it is on account of the dead that I come."

"Sir," I said, "you could have no better claim on me than that you were a friend and helper of Lucy Westenra." And I held out my hand. He took it and said tenderly:—

"Oh, Madam Mina, I know that the friend of that poor lily[13] girl must be good, but I had yet to learn—" He finished his speech with a courtly bow. I asked him what it was that he wanted to see me about, so he at once began:—

"I have read your letters to Miss Lucy. Forgive me, but I had to begin to inquire somewhere, and there was none to ask. I

10 A fictitious newspaper. Journals serving Exeter included the *Daily Western Times* and the *Devon Weekly Times*. In the Manuscript, the newspaper name is entered in a blank in the editor's hand, strongly suggesting that—unsurprisingly—the Harkers did not live in Exeter.

11 French: into both hands.

12 Indeed the Harkers have come up in the world, now employing a maid (although probably a maid-of-all-work). "Mary" or "Mary Jane" was a common appellation for maids, regardless of their real names.

13 Evidently a typographical error for "little."

14 Mina's "joke" on Van Helsing, following, does not appear in the Abridged Text.

15 Mina's metaphor is a little mixed up here. The fruit of the tree of knowledge of good and evil—proverbially an apple, although not expressly termed as such—*granted* knowledge.

16 At last a shortcoming in the man of many degrees. It is surprising, however, that the student of medicine and law did not adopt shorthand as a useful tool. Of course it may be that, as suggested earlier, Jonathan and Mina used a private shorthand (of which there were many—see chapter 1, note 2), and so Van Helsing's usually mangled English was this time accurate: he knew not *the* shorthand that had been employed.

know that you were with her at Whitby. She sometimes kept a diary—you need not look surprised, Madam Mina; it was begun after you had left, and was in imitation of you—and in that diary she traces by inference certain things to a sleep-walking in which she puts down that you saved her. In great perplexity then I come to you, and ask you out of your so much kindness to tell me all of it that you can remember."

"I can tell you, I think, Dr. Van Helsing, all about it."

"Oh, then you have good memory for facts, for details? It is not always so with young ladies."

"No, doctor, but I wrote it all down at the time. I can show it to you if you like."**14**

"Oh, Madam Mina, I will be grateful; you will do me much favour." I could not resist the temptation of mystifying him a bit—I suppose it is some of the taste of the original apple that remains still in our mouths**15**—so I handed him the shorthand diary. He took it with a grateful bow, and said:

"May I read it?"

"If you wish," I answered as demurely as I could. He opened it, and for an instant his face fell. Then he stood up and bowed.

"Oh, you so clever woman!" he said. "I knew long that Mr. Jonathan was a man of much thankfulness; but see, his wife have all the good things. And will you not so much honour me and so help me as to read it for me? Alas! I know not the shorthand."**16** By this time my little joke was over, and I was almost ashamed; so I took the typewritten copy from my workbasket and handed it to him.

"Forgive me," I said: "I could not help it; but I had been thinking that it was of dear Lucy that you wished to ask, and so that you might not have time to wait—not on my account, but because I know your time must be precious—I have written it out on the typewriter for you."

He took it and his eyes glistened. "You are so good," he said. "And may I read it now? I may want to ask you some things when I have read."

"By all means," I said, "read it over whilst I order lunch; and then you can ask me questions whilst we eat." He bowed and settled himself in a chair with his back to the light, and became absorbed in the papers, whilst I went to see after lunch, chiefly in order that he might not be disturbed. When I came back, I found him walking hurriedly up and down the room, his face all ablaze with excitement. He rushed up to me and took me by both hands.

"Oh, Madam Mina," he said, "how can I say what I owe to you? This paper is as sunshine. It opens the gate to me. I am daze, I am dazzle, with so much light; and yet clouds roll in behind the light every time. But that you do not, cannot, comprehend. Oh, but I am grateful to you, you so clever woman. Madam"—he said this very solemnly—"if ever Abraham Van Helsing can do anything for you or yours, I trust you will let me know. It will be pleasure and delight if I may serve you as a friend; as a friend, but all I have ever learned, all I can ever do, shall be for you and those you love. There are darknesses in life, and there are lights; you are one of the lights. You will have happy life and good life, and your husband will be blessed in you."

"But, doctor, you praise me too much, and—and you do not know me."

"Not know you—I who am old, and who have studied all my life men and women; I, who have made my specialty the brain and all that belongs to him and all that follow from him! And I have read your diary that you have so goodly written for me, and which breathes out truth in every line. I, who have read your so sweet letter to poor Lucy of your marriage and your trust, not know you! Oh, Madam Mina, good women tell all their lives, and by day and by hour and by minute, such things that angels can read; and we men who wish to know have in us something of angels' eyes. Your husband is noble nature, and you are noble too, for you trust, and trust cannot be where there is mean nature. And your husband—tell me of him. Is he quite well? Is all that fever gone, and is he strong and hearty?" I saw here an opening to ask him about Jonathan, so I said:—

"He was almost recovered, but he has been greatly upset by Mr. Hawkins's death." He interrupted:—

"Oh, yes, I know, I know. I have read your last two letters." I went on:—

17 The Harkers were in town on 22 September and possibly on 21 September as well. The 22nd was a Thursday only in 1887 and 1892 in the range of acceptable dates, and Peter Haining (*The Dracula Centenary Book*) seizes on 1887 as the year, claiming privately expressed assent from Leonard Wolf (editor of *The Annotated Dracula*). As discussed in chapter 13, note 42, it is possible that Hawkins's funeral took place on 21 September, which was a Thursday in 1882 and 1893, and that the Harkers returned to Exeter on 22 September. See appendix 2, "The Dating of *Dracula*," for a more detailed discussion of the problem of the year and the unreliability of the textual references to days and dates.

18 The Abridged Text does not include Van Helsing's prescriptions for Mina, following.

"I suppose this upset him, for when we were in town on Thursday last[17] he had a sort of shock."

"A shock, and after brain fever so soon! That is not good. What kind of a shock was it?"

"He thought he saw some one who recalled something terrible, something which led to his brain fever." And here the whole thing seemed to overwhelm me in a rush. The pity for Jonathan, the horror which he experienced, the whole fearful mystery of his diary, and the fear that has been brooding over me ever since, all came in a tumult. I suppose I was hysterical, for I threw myself on my knees and held up my hands to him, and implored him to make my husband well again. He took my hands and raised me up, and made me sit on the sofa, and sat by me; he held my hand in his, and said to me with, oh, such infinite sweetness:—

"My life is a barren and lonely one, and so full of work that I have not had much time for friendships; but since I have been summoned to here by my friend John Seward I have known so many good people and seen such nobility that I feel more than ever—and it has grown with my advancing years—the loneliness of my life. Believe, me, then, that I come here full of respect for you, and you have given me hope—hope, not in what I am seeking of, but that there are good women still left to make life happy—good women, whose lives and whose truths may make good lesson for the children that are to be. I am glad, glad, that I may here be of some use to you; for if your husband suffer, he suffer within the range of my study and experience. I promise you that I will gladly do *all* for him that I can—all to make his life strong and manly, and your life a happy one. Now you must eat.[18] You are overwrought and perhaps over-anxious. Husband Jonathan would not like to see you so pale; and what he like not where he love, is not to his good. Therefore for his sake you must eat and smile. You have told me all about Lucy, and so now we shall not speak of it, lest it distress. I shall stay in Exeter to-night, for I want to think much over what you have told me, and when I have thought I will ask you questions, if I may. And then, too, you will tell me of husband Jonathan's trouble so far as you can, but not yet. You must eat now; afterwards you shall tell me all."

After lunch, when we went back to the drawing-room, he said to me:—

"And now tell me all about him." When it came to speaking to this great, learned man, I began to fear that he would think me a weak fool, and Jonathan a madman—that journal is all so strange—and I hesitated to go on. But he was so sweet and kind, and he had promised to help, and I trusted him, so I said:—

"Dr. Van Helsing, what I have to tell you is so queer that you must not laugh at me or at my husband. I have been since yesterday in a sort of fever of doubt; you must be kind to me, and not think me foolish that I have even half believed some very strange things." He reassured me by his manner as well as his words when he said:—

"Oh, my dear, if you only know how strange is the matter regarding which I am here, it is you who would laugh. I have learned not to think little of any one's belief, no matter how strange it may be. I have tried to keep an open mind; and it is not the ordinary things of life that could close it, but the strange things, the extraordinary things, the things that make one doubt if they be mad or sane."[19]

"Thank you, thank you, a thousand times! You have taken a weight off my mind. If you will let me, I shall give you a paper to read. It is long, but I have typewritten it out. It will tell you my trouble and Jonathan's. It is the copy of his journal when abroad, and all that happened. I dare not say anything of it; you will read for yourself and judge. And then when I see you, perhaps, you will be very kind and tell me what you think."

"I promise," he said as I gave him the papers; "I shall in the morning, so soon as I can, come to see you and your husband, if I may."

"Jonathan will be here at half-past eleven, and you must come to lunch with us and see him then; you could catch the quick 3:34 train, which will leave you at Paddington before eight."[20] He was surprised at my knowledge of the trains offhand, but he does not know that I have made up all the trains to and from Exeter, so that I may help Jonathan in case he is in a hurry.

So he took the papers with him and went away, and I sit here thinking—thinking I don't know what.

Paddington station.
Queen's London (1897)

19 This sentence does not appear in the Abridged Text.

20 There was a 3:55 P.M. train that arrived at Paddington at 8:10 P.M.

Paddington station, the elegant, graceful iron-and-glass London terminus of the Great Western Railway, serving the rural heartlands, the West Country, industrial Bristol, and the South Wales coalfields, was designed in the image of the Crystal Palace by the British-born, French-educated engineer Isambard Kingdom Brunel in 1849, although the site had been used by the railway since 1838. Brunel was chief engineer of the Great Western Railway during the 1830s and was instrumental in designing the lines themselves.

It was at the Paddington terminus—when the station was still an unassuming wooden building—that Queen Victoria arrived on completing her first railway journey in 1842, on the Phlegethon, which travelled from Slough at 44 miles per hour. One of her travelling companions on that twenty-five-minute trip was Brunel. Reportedly, the prince consort asked afterward that future trains carrying the queen travel more slowly. That request notwithstanding, one of Brunel's chief interests when he took the position on the Great Western had been to increase the speed at which trains could travel; the other had been to create the illusion of near-dreamlike passage over a hilly country defined by almost impassable waterways. He achieved the first goal through use of controversial broad-gauge track and the second through ingenious viaducts, embankments, and bridges that in effect hid the fact that the trains were climbing and descending, and at times squeezing through narrow spaces that were practically obstacle courses.

Brunel, who also designed the largest steamship of the time and a 1,000-bed, first-of-its-kind prefabricated field hospital shipped in pieces to Turkey for use during the Crimean War, worked on the permanent terminus with architect Matthew Digby Wyatt. It was placed in service in 1854, the same year the Great Western Hotel was opened adjacent to the station. Since its original construction, the station has been expanded and rebuilt numerous times.

21 A town in Cornwall about 100 miles southwest of London and about 35 miles from Exeter, and a terminus of the Cornwall and South Devon lines of the Great Western Railway. Cornwall's only walled town, and the site of a royal mint in Saxon times, its principal object of interest is an eleventh-century castle built by Brian de Bretagne, the first Norman Earl of Cornwall. The castle ruins prove it to have been an important Celtic fortress. Launceston (pronounced "Lanson" locally) also boasts a rare ancient clapper, or stone slab, bridge. The town can be reached from Plymouth via the South Devon Railway. What business Jonathan Harker had in Launceston is unknown.

22 Mina's schedule approximates the 1887 *Bradshaw's*, which gives the departure time as 6:05 P.M. and arrival at 10:20 P.M.

23 This is approximately accurate.

LETTER (BY HAND), VAN HELSING TO MRS. HARKER.

"25 September, 6 o'clock.

"Dear Madam Mina,—

"I have read your husband's so wonderful diary. You may sleep without doubt. Strange and terrible as it is, it is *true*! I will pledge my life on it. It may be worse for others; but for him and you there is no dread. He is a noble fellow; and let me tell you from experience of men, that one who would do as he did in going down that wall and to that room—ay, and going a second time—is not one to be injured in permanence by a shock. His brain and his heart are all right; this I swear before I have even seen him; so be at rest. I shall have much to ask him of other things. I am blessed that to-day I come to see you, for I have learn all at once so much that again I am dazzle—dazzle more than ever, and I must think.

"Yours the most faithful,
"Abraham Van Helsing."

LETTER, MRS. HARKER TO VAN HELSING.

"25 September, 6.30 p.m.

"My dear Dr. Van Helsing,—

"A thousand thanks for your kind letter, which has taken a great weight off my mind. And yet, if it be true, what terrible things there are in the world, and what an awful thing if that man, that monster, be really in London! I fear to think. I have this moment, whilst writing, had a wire from Jonathan, saying that he leaves by the 6:25 to-night from Launceston[21] and will be here at 10:18,[22] so that I shall have no fear to-night. Will you, therefore, instead of lunching with us, please come to breakfast at eight o'clock, if this be not too early for you? You can get away, if you are in a hurry, by the 10:30 train, which will bring you to Paddington by 2:35.[23] Do not answer this, as I shall take it that, if I do not hear, you will come to breakfast.

> "Believe me,
> "Your faithful and grateful friend,
> "Mina Harker."

JONATHAN HARKER'S JOURNAL.

26 September.—I thought never to write in this diary again, but the time has come. When I got home last night Mina had supper ready, and when we had supped she told me of Van Helsing's visit, and of her having given him the two diaries copied out, and of how anxious she has been about me. She showed me in the doctor's letter that all I wrote down was true. It seems to have made a new man of me. It was the doubt as to the reality of the whole thing that knocked me over. I felt impotent, and in the dark, and distrustful. But now that I *know*, I am not afraid, even of the Count. He has succeeded after all, then, in his design in getting to London, and it was he I saw. He has got younger, and how? Van Helsing is the man to unmask him and hunt him out, if he is anything like what Mina says. We sat late, and talked it over. Mina is dressing, and I shall call at the hotel in a few minutes and bring him over. . . .

He was, I think, surprised to see me. When I came into the room where he was and introduced myself, he took me by the shoulder, and turned my face round to the light, and said, after a sharp scrutiny:—

"But Madam Mina told me you were ill, that you had had a shock." It was so funny to hear my wife called "Madam Mina" by this kindly, strong-faced old man. I smiled, and said:—

"I *was* ill, I *have* had a shock; but you have cured me already."

"And how?"

"By your letter to Mina last night. I was in doubt, and then everything took a hue of unreality, and I did not know what to trust, even the evidence of my own senses. Not knowing what to trust, I did not know what to do; and so had only to

24 We have already seen this about Harker; see text accompanying chapter 2, note 22.

25 These "papers" are described in the Notes but not in the narrative. See note 7 on page 5.

26 It is evident from the Manuscript that a quantity of material is cut after this sentence. All that remains in the Manuscript of the cut material is "tells me all I want except that I may find the Count. I shall soon let you hear." This phrase does not appear in the published narrative.

keep on working in what had hitherto been the groove of my life. The groove ceased to avail me, and I mistrusted myself. Doctor, you don't know what it is to doubt everything, even yourself. No, you don't; you couldn't with eyebrows like yours." He seemed pleased, and laughed as he said:—

"So! You are physiognomist.[24] I learn more here with each hour. I am with so much pleasure coming to you to breakfast; and, oh, sir, you will pardon praise from an old man, but you are blessed in your wife." I would listen to him go on praising Mina for a day, so I simply nodded and stood silent.

"She is one of God's women, fashioned by His own hand to show us men and other women that there is a heaven where we can enter, and that its light can be here on earth. So true, so sweet, so noble, so little an egoist—and that, let me tell you, is much in this age, so sceptical and selfish. And you, sir—I have read all the letters to poor Miss Lucy, and some of them speak of you, so I know you since some days from the knowing of others; but I have seen your true self since last night. You will give me your hand, will you not? And let us be friends for all our lives."

We shook hands, and he was so earnest and so kind that it made me quite choky.

"And now," he said, "may I ask you for some more help? I have a great task to do, and at the beginning it is to know. You can help me here. Can you tell me what went before your going to Transylvania? Later on I may ask more help, and of a different kind; but at first this will do."

"Look here, sir," I said, "does what you have to do concern the Count?"

"It does," he said solemnly.

"Then I am with you heart and soul. As you go by the 10:30 train, you will not have time to read them; but I shall get the bundle of papers.[25] You can take them with you and read them in the train."

After breakfast I saw him to the station. When we were parting, he said:—[26]

"Perhaps you will come to town if I send to you, and take Madam Mina too."

"We shall both come when you will," I said.

I had got him the morning papers and the London papers of

the previous night, and while we were talking at the carriage window, waiting for the train to start, he was turning them over. His eyes suddenly seemed to catch something in one of them, "The Westminster Gazette"—I knew it by the colour[27]—and he grew quite white. He read something intently, groaning to himself: "Mein Gott! Mein Gott![28] So soon! so soon!"[29] I do not think he remembered me at the moment. Just then the whistle blew, and the train moved off. This recalled him to himself, and he leaned out of the window and waved his hand, calling out, "Love to Madam Mina; I shall write so soon as ever I can."

DR. SEWARD'S DIARY.

26 September.—Truly there is no such thing as finality. Not a week since I said "Finis," and yet here I am starting fresh again, or rather going on with the same record. Until this afternoon I had no cause to think of what is done. Renfield had become, to all intents, as sane as he ever was. He was already well ahead with his fly business; and he had just started in the spider line also; so he had not been of any trouble to me. I had a letter from Arthur, written on Sunday,[30] and from it I gather that he is bearing up wonderfully well. Quincey Morris is with him, and that is much of a help, for he himself is a bubbling well of good spirits. Quincey wrote me a line too, and from him I hear that Arthur is beginning to recover something of his old buoyancy; so as to them all my mind is at rest.[31] As for myself, I was settling down to my work with the enthusiasm which I used to have for it, so that I might fairly have said that the wound which poor Lucy left on me was becoming cicatrised.[32] Everything is, however, now reopened; and what is to be the end God only knows. I have an idea that Van Helsing thinks he knows, too, but he will only let out enough at a time to whet curiosity. He went to Exeter yesterday, and stayed there all night. To-day he came back, and almost bounded into the room at about half-past five o'clock, and thrust last night's "Westminster Gazette" into my hand.

"What do you think of that?" he asked as he stood back and folded his arms.

27 The *Westminster Gazette* was printed on green paper.

28 Wolf (*The Essential Dracula*) notes the incongruity of Van Helsing's ejaculation in German—a Dutchman would more likely have exclaimed "Mijn God!" This is another suggestion of the incomplete erasure of Professor Müller (see note 14 on p. 8).

29 The speed of Lucy's turn into a predator is remarkable. The *Westminster Gazette* account was dated 25 September and reported attacks occurring over "the past two or three days"— that is, the 23rd and 24th (and possibly 22nd). Lucy's burial took place on the 21st. Therefore, she "rose" within two days of burial.

Interestingly, the Notes have a cryptic entry in Stoker's difficult handwriting that reads "Van Helsing sees Polliwell"—or perhaps "Pall Mall"? In other words, it may be that researchers seeking the newspaper accounts should examine the *Pall Mall Gazette* and not the *Westminster Gazette*.

30 So 26 September is not a Sunday. This only eliminates 1886 from consideration. See appendix 2, "The Dating of *Dracula*."

31 Leatherdale (*Dracula Unearthed*) observes that this is remarkable only six days after the death of his fiancée.

32 That is, a scar has formed. Although it sounds obsolete, the term appears in William Warner's 1897 *Pocket Medical Dictionary*.

I looked over the paper, for I really did not know what he meant; but he took it from me and pointed out a paragraph about children being decoyed away at Hampstead. It did not convey much to me, until I reached a passage where it described small puncture wounds on their throats. An idea struck me, and I looked up. "Well?" he said.

"It is like poor Lucy's."

"And what do you make of it?"

"Simply that there is some cause in common. Whatever it was that injured her has injured them." I did not quite understand his answer:—

"That is true indirectly, but not directly."

"How do you mean, Professor?" I asked. I was a little inclined to take his seriousness lightly—for, after all, four days of rest and freedom from burning, harrowing anxiety does help to restore one's spirits—but when I saw his face, it sobered me. Never, even in the midst of our despair about poor Lucy, had he looked more stern.

"Tell me!" I said. "I can hazard no opinion. I do not know what to think, and I have no data on which to found a conjecture."

"Do you mean to tell me, friend John, that you have no suspicion as to what poor Lucy died of; not after all the hints given, not only by events, but by me?"

"Of nervous prostration following on great loss or waste of blood."

"And how was the blood lost or waste?" I shook my head. He stepped over and sat down beside me, and went on:—

"You are a clever man, friend John; you reason well, and your wit is bold; but you are too prejudiced. You do not let your eyes see nor your ears hear, and that which is outside your daily life is not of account to you. Do you not think that there are things which you cannot understand, and yet which are; that some people see things that others cannot? But there are things old and new which must not be contemplate by men's eyes, because they know—or think they know—some things which other men have told them. Ah, it is the fault of our science that it wants to explain all; and if it explain not, then it says there is nothing to explain. But yet we see around us every day the growth of new beliefs, which think themselves new; and which are yet but the old, which pretend to be young—like the fine ladies at the opera. I suppose now you do not believe in corporeal transference.[33] No? Nor in materialisation.[34] No? Nor in astral bodies.[35] No? Nor in the reading of thought.[36] No? Nor in hypnotism—"

"Yes," I said. "Charcot[37] has proved that pretty well." He smiled as he went on: "Then you are satisfied as to it. Yes? And of course then you understand how it act, and can follow the mind of the great Charcot—alas that he is no more![38]— into the very soul of the patient that he influence. No? Then, friend John, am I to take it that you simply accept fact, and are satisfied to let from premise to conclusion be a blank? No? Then tell me—for I am student of the brain—how you accept the hypnotism and reject the thought reading. Let me tell you, my friend, that there are things done to-day in electrical science which would have been deemed unholy by the very man who discovered electricity—who would themselves not so long before have been burned as wizards. There are always mysteries in life. Why was it that Methuselah lived nine hundred years, and 'Old Parr'[39] one hundred and sixty-nine, and yet that poor Lucy, with four men's blood in her poor veins, could not live even one day? For, had she live one more day, we could have save her. Do you know all the mystery of life and death? Do you know the altogether of comparative anatomy and can say wherefore the qualities of brutes are in some men, and not in others? Can you tell me why, when other spiders die small and soon, that one great spider lived for centuries in the tower of the old Spanish church and grew and grew, till, on descending, he could drink the oil of all the church lamps?[40] Can you tell me why in the Pampas, ay and elsewhere, there are bats that come at night and open the veins of cattle and horses and suck dry their veins; how in some islands of the Western seas there are bats which hang on the trees all day, that those who have seen describe as like giant nuts or pods,[41] and that when the sailors sleep on the deck, because that it is hot, flit down on them, and then—and then in the morning are found dead men, white as even Miss Lucy was?"[42]

"Good God, Professor!" I said, starting up. "Do you mean

33 "Corporeal transference" is the idea that the "self" can be transferred from one body to another. This sentence, and the material following—until the sentence beginning "There are always mysteries . . ."—does not appear in the Abridged Text. Perhaps "Van Helsing" was concerned about appearing gullible.

34 The phenomenal appearance of seemingly solid objects or spirit forms out of thin air. In Western culture, materialisation was a popular demonstration of the "reality" of Spiritualism. Objects ("apports," as they were termed) commonly "materialised" during séances included vases, coins, flowers, and musical instruments, as well as luminous objects and manisfestations of animal and human spirits.

35 The "astral body," a concept embraced by Theosophists and clairvoyants, among others, can be thought of as a vessel for the spirit and emotions, desires and passions. Said to be not entirely invisible or abstract but rather composed of shapes and colours discernible by others whose understanding extends to such

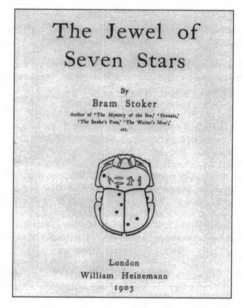

The Jewel of Seven Stars by Bram Stoker.
(London: William Heineman, 1903)

concepts, and to be attached to the physical body, usually at the navel, by a cord that has been described as resembling a string of silver, the astral body can migrate—accompanied by the mind, believers contend—while a person sleeps. The term "astral projection" describes these travels. The astral body is thought to have precisely the same psychic energy as the physical body, and in that sense to be its twin. In Bram Stoker's novel *The Jewel of Seven Stars* (1903), Mr. Trelawney explains: "The astral body, which is a part of Buddhist belief, long subsequent to the time I speak of, and which is an accepted fact of modern mysticism, had its rise in Ancient Egypt; at least, so far as we know. It is that the gifted individual can at will, quick as thought itself, transfer his body whithersoever he chooses, by the dissolution and reincarnation of particles."

36 Direct communication between minds, conveying thoughts, ideas, feelings, sensations, and mental images. The idea of telepathy, or thought transference, pervades virtually all cultures throughout history. In spiritual and primitive cultures, its reality is accepted as a common human faculty, whereas in cultures focussed on material gain and acquisition, telepathy is more often ascribed only to specially talented individuals. Although much investigation has been devoted to reported incidents, telepathy cannot yet be classed as a repeatable phenomenon, the touchstone of scientific acceptance.

37 Jean-Martin Charcot (1825–1893), French scientist, often called the father of modern neurology. Charcot studied the disorder termed "hysteria," which appeared to be the result of a combination of mental and physical causes. To conduct his studies, he mastered the techniques of hypnosis, discovered by Franz Anton Mesmer (1734–1815) and others who preached the doctrine of animal magnetism.

Mesmer, whom some viewed as a charlatan, was probably also a man ahead of his time. He used magnets, a magnetised wand, a wooden

Jean-Martin Charcot.

tub called a *baquet*, and hoses to move blocked energy in people. Up to twenty patients could sit around each of the four baquets Mesmer kept at his treatment centre, in a Paris hotel. His idea was that sickness occurred when there was not a free flow of psychic fluid in the body, and when this fluid was not in tune with the cosmic ether. Mesmer laid his hands on his patients, stared into their eyes, put them in a trance, and induced convulsions and other extreme reactions. Those most deeply affected by contact with Mesmer's animal magnetism were carried by his valet to a padded crisis room to work through their gyrations and recover.

Hypnosis was intended by Charcot, however, to serve only as a diagnostic tool. He recognised a great similarity between hysteria and the hypnotic state, though, concluding that only hysterics could be hypnotized. Charcot studied other aspects of neurology as well; for example, he researched the parts of the brain responsible for specific nerve functions. Among other discoveries, he found that cerebral haemorrhages were often the result of the rupture of small arteries in the brain.

Charcot's studies influenced future work

to tell me that Lucy was bitten by such a bat; and that such a thing is here in London in the nineteenth century?" He waved his hand for silence, and went on:—

"Can you tell me why the tortoise lives more long than generations of men, why the elephant goes on and on till he have seen dynasties;[43] and why the parrot never die only of bite of cat or dog or other complaint?[44] Can you tell me why men believe in all ages and places that there are some few men that live on always if they be permit; that there are men and women who cannot die? We all know—because science has vouched for the fact—that there have been toads shut up in rocks for thousands of years, shut in one so small hole that only hold him since the youth of the world.[45] Can you tell me how the Indian fakir can make himself to die and have been buried, and his grave sealed and corn sowed on it, and the corn reaped and be cut and sown and reaped and cut again, and then men come and take the unbroken seal and that there lie the Indian fakir, not dead, but that rise up and walk amongst them as before?"[46] Here I interrupted him. I was getting bewildered; he so crowded on my mind his list of nature's eccentricities and possible possibilities that my imagination was getting fired.[47] I had a dim idea that he was teaching me some lesson, as long ago he used to do in his study at Amsterdam; but he used then to tell me the thing, so that I could have the object of thought in mind all the time. But now I was without this help, yet I wanted to follow him, so I said:—

"Professor, let me be your pet student again. Tell me the thesis, so that I may apply your knowledge as you go on. At present I am going in my mind from point to point as a madman, and not a sane one, follows an idea. I feel like a novice lumbering through a bog in a mist, jumping from one tussock to another in the mere blind effort to move on without knowing where I am going."

"That is a good image," he said. "Well, I shall tell you. My thesis is this: I want you to believe."

"To believe what?"

"To believe in things that you cannot. Let me illustrate. I heard once of an American who so defined faith: 'that faculty which enables us to believe things which we know to be

in the field, and among his most prominent students were the pioneers Alfred Binet, Pierre Janet, and Sigmund Freud.

38 Charcot died in 1893. In light of the other serious problems with 1893, we can only take this as an interpolation by Stoker into the Harker Papers.

39 "Old Parr" refers to Thomas Parr, born 1483, who reportedly lived for 152 years and 9 months and was buried in Westminster Abbey by order of King Charles I. A 1635 pamphlet (John Taylor's *The Old, Old, Very Old Man or the Age and Long Life of Thomas Parr*) is the only written source of information about Parr. Taylor reports that Parr did not marry until he was about eighty years old. His wife bore two children, neither of whom survived infancy. At the age of a hundred he did penance by standing draped in a white sheet in the parish church for being unfaithful to his wife and having an illegitimate child by another woman. Like many another who achieved longevity, Parr attributed his long life to temperance, exercise, and regular habits, as well as a simple diet—in Parr's case, green cheese, onions, coarse bread, buttermilk

Old Parr.

or mild ale (cider on special occasions), and no smoking. At the age of 152, he was presented at Court, but the celebrity proved his undoing: he died within a few weeks, and when he was autopsied, the eminent physician Dr. William Harvey blamed the change in diet—Parr had shocked his system by partaking of rich Court food—as the principal cause of death.

It is impossible to determine today whether the tale of Parr is fact or fable. Some doubt that the old man described in 1635 was the same Thomas Parr who was born in 1484. Others admit Parr's longevity as statistically possible but "actuarially unimportant," in one writer's words.

40 The anecdote that Van Helsing has in mind is impossible to trace. The oldest known spiders are tarantulas that have been kept in captivity for twenty to thirty years.

41 Perhaps further information about the size of vampire bats caused Stoker to delete this mistaken reference to "giant nuts or pods" in preparing the Abridged Text.

42 See chapter 12, note 20, for a discussion of vampire bats. Their known habitats do not include the islands of the "Western seas."

43 The life span of elephants is 60 to 70 years. The average life span of the Galapagos tortoise is 100 years; a specimen found there by Charles Darwin and later moved to an Australian zoo remains alive today, at age 175.

44 Van Helsing's source of information about parrots is unknown.

45 Toads can live as long as thirty to forty years, although for most species the average life span is fifteen years. Again, Van Helsing refers to some unknown phenomenon.

Bat Boy.
Weekly World News, June 1992

46 Legends of Indian fakirs or holy street beggars abound in literature. From which source Van Helsing derives his information is unknown.

47 Van Helsing manages to come across here like a subscriber to the *Weekly World News,* in the pages of which he might find material such as the June 1992 revelation of "Bat Boy," half-bat and half-human (whose vampiric tendencies have not yet been studied). What are we to make of the farrago of nonsense he rattles off to Seward, in an attempt to impress him to keep an open mind? If any of these unsubstantiated anecdotes is meant to convince Seward that his education has been inadequate, then Van Helsing's own training as a scientist must be questioned.

untrue.'[48] For one, I follow that man. He meant that we shall have an open mind, and not let a little bit of truth check the rush of a big truth, like a small rock does a railway truck. We get the small truth first. Good! We keep him, and we value him; but all the same we must not let him think himself all the truth in the universe."

"Then you want me not to let some previous conviction injure the receptivity of my mind with regard to some strange matter. Do I read your lesson aright?"

"Ah, you are my favourite pupil still. It is worth to teach you. Now that you are willing to understand, you have taken the first step to understand. You think then that those so small holes in the children's throats were made by the same that made the hole in Miss Lucy?"

"I suppose so." He stood up and said solemnly:—

"Then you are wrong. Oh, would it were so! but alas! no. It is worse, far, far worse."

"In God's name, Professor Van Helsing, what do you mean?" I cried.

He threw himself with a despairing gesture into a chair, and placed his elbows on the table, covering his face with his hands as he spoke:—

"They were made by Miss Lucy!"

48 Compare "Faith does not consist, as the Sunday School pupil said, 'in the power of believing that which we know to be untrue'" (Samuel Butler, "How to Make the Best of Life," 1895) with "It was the schoolboy who said, 'Faith is believin' what you know ain't so'" (Mark Twain, "Pudd'nhead Wilson's New Calendar," 1897). In light of the publication dates, neither of these sources is likely to be Van Helsing's inspiration, but the repetition suggests it was a common anecdote used by numerous authors.

Chapter 15

DR. SEWARD'S DIARY

—continued.

1 The rationalisations of this and the following sentence do not appear in the Abridged Text.

2 Seward slightly misquotes Lord Byron's *Don Juan* (canto 1, published in 1819): "I can't tell how, or why, or what suspicion / Could enter into Don Alfonso's head; / But for a cavalier of his condition / It surely was exceedingly ill-bred, / Without a word of previous admonition, / To hold a levee round his lady's bed, / And summon lackeys, arm'd with fire and sword, / To prove himself the thing he most abhorr'd." (canto 1, stanza 138). Of course, the "thing" in the case of Don Alfonso was adultery.

The Abridged Text does not include the sentence referring to Byron or the quotation.

FOR A WHILE sheer anger mastered me; it was as if he had during her life struck Lucy on the face. I smote the table hard and rose up as I said to him:—

"Dr. Van Helsing, are you mad?" He raised his head and looked at me, and somehow the tenderness of his face calmed me at once. "Would I were!" he said. "Madness were easy to bear compared with truth like this. Oh, my friend, why, think you, did I go so far round, why take so long to tell you so simple a thing? Was it because I hate you and have hated you all my life? Was it because I wished to give you pain? Was it that I wanted, now so late, revenge for that time when you saved my life, and from a fearful death? Ah no!"

"Forgive me," said I. He went on:—

"My friend, it was because I wished to be gentle in the breaking to you, for I know you have loved that so sweet lady. But even yet I do not expect you to believe. It is so hard to accept at once any abstract truth, that we may doubt such to be possible when we have always believed the 'no' of it;[1] it is more hard still to accept so sad a concrete truth, and of such a one as Miss Lucy. To-night I go to prove it. Dare you come with me?"

This staggered me. A man does not like to prove such a truth; Byron excepted from the category, jealousy.

"And prove the very truth he most abhorred."[2]

"In an instant his hand clasped her waist with the power of an iron vice; she felt his hot breath flushing on her cheek."
Varney, the Vampyre; or, The Feast of Blood (1847)

He saw my hesitation and spoke:—

"The logic is simple, no madman's logic this time, jumping from tussock to tussock in a misty bog. If it not be true, then proof will be relief; at worst it will not harm. If it be true! Ah, there is the dread; yet very dread should help my cause, for in it is some need of belief. Come, I tell you what I propose: first, that we go off now and see that child in the hospital. Dr. Vincent, of the North Hospital,[3] where the papers say the child is, is friend of mine, and I think of yours since you were in class at Amsterdam. He will let two scientists see his case, if he will not let two friends. We shall tell him nothing, but only that we wish to learn. And then—"

"And then?" He took a key from his pocket and held it up. "And then we spend the night, you and I, in the churchyard where Lucy lies. This is the key that lock the tomb. I had it from the coffin-man to give to Arthur." My heart sank within

[3] North London Consumption Hospital was located quite near the heath. On its staff was Dr. Lyttleton Forbes Winslow, who involved himself in the hunt for Jack the Ripper and was likely known to Seward as the author of the 1877 *Handbook for Attendants on the Insane.* However, this specialty hospital would be unlikely to provide care for the child. Farther from the heath, but still within a plausible distance for removal of the injured child, is the North West London Hospital, located on Kentish Town Road; much farther still is the North London, or University College, Hospital on Gower Street, near the British Museum. McNally and Florescu (*The Essential Dracula*) first identify the "North Hospital" with this latter hospital but later seem to indicate that it is the Holborn Union Infirmary, which adjoined Highgate Cemetery. For that matter, the St. Pancras Infirmary, also known as the Central London Sick Asylum, was also adjacent to the cemetery. In short, once the name "North" is abandoned, there are many possible candidates in this area. Note that the newspaper reports do not name the hospital.

Children's ward, Westminster Hospital, London, ca. 1905.

The identification of the hospital and "Dr. Vincent" here and following do not appear in the Abridged Text.

me, for I felt that there was some fearful ordeal before us. I could do nothing, however, so I plucked up what heart I could and said that we had better hasten, as the afternoon was passing. . . .

We found the child awake. It had had a sleep and taken some food, and altogether was going on well. Dr. Vincent took the bandage from its throat, and showed us the punctures. There was no mistaking the similarity to those which had been on Lucy's throat. They were smaller, and the edges looked fresher; that was all. We asked Vincent to what he attributed them, and he replied that it must have been a bite of some animal, perhaps a rat; but, for his own part, he was inclined to think that it was one of the bats which are so numerous on the northern heights of London. "Out of so many harmless ones," he said, "there may be some wild specimen from the South of a more malignant species. Some sailor may have brought one home, and it managed to escape; or even from the Zoölogical Gardens a young one may have got loose, or one be bred there from a vampire. These things do occur, you know. Only ten days ago a wolf got out, and was, I believe, traced up in this direction.[4] For a week after, the children were playing nothing but Red Riding Hood on the Heath and in every alley in the place until this 'bloofer lady' scare came along, since when it has been quite a gala-time with them. Even this poor little mite, when he woke up to-day, asked the nurse if he might go away. When she asked him why he wanted to go, he said he wanted to play with the 'bloofer lady.' "

"I hope," said Van Helsing, "that when you are sending the child home you will caution its parents to keep strict watch over it. These fancies to stray are most dangerous; and if the child were to remain out another night, it would probably be fatal. But in any case I suppose you will not let it away for some days?"

"Certainly not, not for a week at least; longer if the wound is not healed."

Our visit to the hospital took more time than we had reckoned on,[5] and the sun had dipped before we came out. When Van Helsing saw how dark it was, he said:—

"There is no hurry. It is more late than I thought. Come, let us seek somewhere that we may eat, and then we shall go on our way."

We dined at "Jack Straw's Castle"[6] along with a little crowd of bicyclists[7] and others who were genially noisy. About ten o'clock we started from the inn. It was then very dark, and the scattered lamps made the darkness greater when we were once outside their individual radius.[8] The Professor had evidently noted the road we were to go, for he went on unhesitatingly; but, as for me, I was in quite a mix-up as to locality.[9] As we went further, we met fewer and fewer people, till at last we were somewhat surprised when we met even the patrol of horse police going their usual suburban round. At last we reached the wall of the churchyard, which we climbed over. With some little difficulty—for it was very dark, and the whole place seemed so strange to us—we found the Westenra tomb. The Professor took the key, opened the creaky door, and standing back, politely, but quite unconsciously, motioned me to precede him. There was a delicious irony in the offer, in the

4 Leatherdale (*Dracula Unearthed*) points out that the "tracing" is not reported in the narrative.

5 Perhaps the hospital or Vincent disliked appearing in so sensational a work; perhaps Seward or Van Helsing's casual treatment of their "friend" was offensive when viewed in print; perhaps, on consideration, Vincent felt that his prescription of a week's hospitalisation was an overreaction for so slight an injury. In any event, virtually all details of the hospital visit and the conversation with Dr. Vincent are eliminated in the Abridged Text.

6 Jack Straw's Castle was a well-known pub in North London, situated at the northwestern corner of Hampstead Heath at the junction of Heath Street and Spaniards Road. The pub itself was believed to be the highest above sea level in London, with extensive views across the heath. The building was originally a coaching inn (stabling horses for stagecoaches and mail coaches) built in 1721 and derived its name from a reputed comrade of Wat Tyler, leader of the peasants revolt in 1381 against King Richard II. Legend tells that Jack Straw harangued crowds of peasants on the heath from his hay wagon at this spot. During World War II, the pub was extensively damaged; it was rebuilt in 1962. In the twenty-first century, it has undergone the inevitable transformation into a collection of luxury apartments.

Jack Straw's Castle.
Photograph by Leslie S. Klinger, February 2006

7 In 1817–1818, the first two-wheeled vehicle was invented by Baron Karl Drais von Sauerbronn—a wooden contraption without pedals known variously as a *Laufmaschine* ("running machine"), *draisienne* (or drasine, in England), or hobby horse, which the rider moved by pushing his feet along the ground and which had two wheels of the same size, the first one steerable. In the century that followed, the bicycle went through numerous incarnations on its way to its current form. There was the first self-propelled two-wheeler, invented by Scottish blacksmith Kirkpatrick Macmillan in 1839; the first two-wheeler for which there was steady demand, introduced in 1861 by the French father-and-son team of Pierre and Ernest Michaux (the *vélocipède*); and the ordinary or "penny-farthing" model invented in 1870 by Englishman James Starley of the Coventry Sewing Machine Company. Incorporating a very large front wheel and smaller back wheel (the penny and the farthing were England's largest and smallest coins) and weighing far less than previous versions of the vehicle, Starley's bicycle remained fashionable for twenty years until the arrival of the chain-driven "safety" bicycle, which boasted two wheels of equal size and was far less likely to tip over. First manufactured in 1885 by Starley's nephew John, the safety bicycle had supplanted the ordinary bicycle by the early 1890s.

Cycling's popularity spread rapidly in the 1880s; clubs were founded, and men and women enjoyed taking leisurely bicycle rides in the country. But the bicycle's importance extended beyond mere novelty and sport. As a means of transportation, this new vehicle vastly expanded employment opportunities for working people who, unable to afford carriages or train fare, had previously been forced to work only as far away as they could walk within a reasonable amount of time. Millions of bicycles were in use between 1870 and 1890. Brand-new bicycles were expensive, naturally (the least expensive model listed in the 1898 Army & Navy Stores catalogue was £13 10s, equal to over £1,000 today), but cheaper second- and third-hand

Cycling in Battersea Park.
Queen's London (1897)

models were always available for rent or sale as newer, more innovative models were continually being introduced and snapped up by enthusiasts. Victorians, once sedentary, became gloriously mobile.

Some, by contrast, viewed the phenomenon with alarm, fearing the implications of this newfound emancipation, particularly in regard to young women. In 1897, Mrs. F. Harcourt Williamson, in "The Cycle in Society," moralised: "The beginning of cycling was the end of the chaperon in England, and now women, even young girls, ride alone or attended only by some casual man friend for miles together through deserted country roads. The danger of this is apparent; but parents and guardians will probably only become wise after the event. Given a lonely road, and a tramp desperate with hunger or naturally vicious, and it stands to reason that a girl, or indeed any woman riding alone must be in some considerable peril."

8 The darkness of the location and the absence of pedestrians and the police encounter are not mentioned in the Abridged Text. Near "Jack Straw's Castle" is the beginning of an unlighted path across Hampstead Heath, leading to the vicinity of the Highgate Cemetery. Stoker undoubtedly felt it was important to conceal the exact route to the Westenra tomb, to avoid publicity and vandalisation.

courtliness of giving preference on such a ghastly occasion.[10] My companion followed me quickly, and cautiously drew the door to, after carefully ascertaining that the lock was a falling, and not a spring, one. In the latter case we should have been in a bad plight. Then he fumbled in his bag, and taking out a match-box and a piece of candle, proceeded to make a light. The tomb in the day-time, and when wreathed with fresh flowers, had looked grim and gruesome enough; but now, some days afterwards, when the flowers hung lank and dead, their whites turning to rust and their greens to browns; when the spider and the beetle had resumed their accustomed dominance; when time-discoloured stone, and dust-encrusted mortar, and rusty, dank iron and tarnished brass, and clouded silver-plating gave back the feeble glimmer of a candle, the effect was more miserable and sordid than could have been imagined. It conveyed irresistibly the idea that life—animal life—was not the only thing which could pass away.

Van Helsing went about his work systematically. Holding his candle so that he could read the coffin plates, and so holding it that the sperm[11] dropped in white patches which congealed as they touched the metal, he made assurance of Lucy's coffin. Another search in his bag, and he took out a turnscrew.[12]

"What are you going to do?" I asked.

"To open the coffin. You shall yet be convinced." Straightway he began taking out the screws, and finally lifted off the lid, showing the casing of lead beneath. The sight was almost too much for me. It seemed to be as much an affront to the dead as it would have been to have stripped off her clothing in her sleep whilst living;[13] I actually took hold of his hand to stop him. He only said: "You shall see," and again fumbling in his bag, took out a tiny fret-saw. Striking the turnscrew through the lead with a swift downward stab, which made me wince, he made a small hole, which was, however, big enough to admit the point of the saw. I had expected a rush of gas from the week-old corpse. We doctors, who have had to study our dangers, have to become accustomed to such things, and I drew back towards the door. But the Professor never stopped for a moment; he sawed down a couple of feet

9 There are several candidates for the site of the Westenra tomb (see map on p. 289). Wolf (*The Essential Dracula*) describes travelling from Jack Straw's Castle to the graveyard at St. John's Church, in Church Row, just south of the West Heath. However, he admits that the location is not as isolated as described ("As we went further, we met fewer and fewer people . . ."). St John's is the parish church, its tower built in 1745. Beside the church lectern is a bust of the poet John Keats, who lived in Hampstead for a few years before his early death in 1821. The painter John Constable and his wife are buried in the churchyard, and other notable residents of Hampstead are interred in the adjoining graveyard.

Hampstead Cemetery, off Fortune Green Lane, is certainly more secluded, at least when approached from the north. It covers 37 acres and was opened in 1876. The chapels were designed by Charles Bell in 1876 in Kentish Rag and Bath Stone. The southern chapel was for those to be buried in consecrated ground south of the main avenue; the other was for burials in the unconsecrated ground to the north. Among those buried there are music-hall entertainer Marie Lloyd, scientist Joseph Lister, and children's-book illustrator Kate Greenaway.

Highgate (or North London) Cemetery, located east of the heath and certainly fitting the description of isolation, was opened in 1839 and by its closure in 1975 housed over 61,000 graves. It fits Seward's description in abutting a church, St. Michael's. In its heyday, due to its setting and beautifully landscaped grounds, the cemetery was a tourist attraction and earned distinction for the fine Romantic-Gothic architecture and Egyptian-style catacombs. The 1896 London "Baedeker" termed it "very picturesque and tastefully laid out." Among its famous nineteenth-century residents are chemist Michael Faraday, novelist George Eliot, and poet Samuel Taylor Coleridge. McNally and Florescu (*The Essential Dracula*) argue for Highgate Cemetery as the site of the Westenra tomb, partly on the basis of the proximity of St. Michael's Churchyard, often confused with

Highgate Cemetery, 1897.
Queen's London (1897)

the cemetery grounds. They also argue that Van Helsing and Seward walked across the heath to the "Spaniards" from Lucy's tomb.

Philip Temple, in the *Times Literary Supplement* (4 November 1983), contends that St. Mary's Churchyard in Hendon fits the description in the narrative far better than the cemeteries mentioned above, a contention seconded by Peter Haining and

St. Michael's Church.
Photograph by Leslie S. Klinger, February 2006

Peter Tremayne (*The Un-Dead*). Leatherdale (*Dracula Unearthed*) observes that the narrative repeatedly uses the word "churchyard" and never calls Lucy's resting place a "cemetery." The churchyard is noted as "lonely." These important locational clues are largely ignored by other scholars.

Highgate Cemetery.
Photograph by Leslie S. Klinger, February 2006

Bernard Davies visiting the tomb of the family of General Sir Loftus Otway, identified by Davies as the "Westenra" family.
Photograph by Leslie S. Klinger, February 2006

Map of Hampstead Heath area.
G. W. Bacon, *New Large-Scale Ordnance Atlas of London & Suburbs* (London: George W. Bacon, 1888)

Bernard Davies, in private correspondence with this editor, argues strenuously for Highgate Cemetery as Lucy's final resting place, tracing the path from Jack Straw's Castle and pointing out the location of a suitable low fence (at the back of the kitchen garden of Holly Lodge Estate, the lavish country home of Stoker's close friend Baroness Angela Burdett-Coutts—see chapter 3, note 53).

10 The description of Van Helsing's courtly behaviour does not appear in the Abridged Text.

11 No sexual connotation here—sperm candles were made from spermaceti, a white, odourless, waxy substance obtained from the sperm whale and other marine mammals. Although more expensive than wax candles, sperm candles were advertised by Harrods as "expressly manufactured for hot climates, ball rooms & c.," presumably because they did not soften or melt as readily as wax candles.

12 A screwdriver, that is. Van Helsing's "bag" is not described by Seward on this occasion, leading to the conclusion that it was not notable (as contrasted with the bag Van Helsing will carry on the night of 29 September).

13 Seward, the former lover, now fantasises about Lucy. Stoker politely removed the fantasy element in preparing the Abridged Text, leaving only the characterisation of the act as an affront.

14 Leatherdale (*Dracula Unearthed*) points out that this plan—for the two of them to watch the entire churchyard—is further evidence that the churchyard is small, far smaller than the cemeteries described in note 9 above.

along one side of the lead coffin, and then across, and down the other side. Taking the edge of the loose flange, he bent it back towards the foot of the coffin, and holding up the candle into the aperture, motioned to me to look.

I drew near and looked. The coffin was empty.

It was certainly a surprise to me, and gave me a considerable shock, but Van Helsing was unmoved. He was now more sure than ever of his ground, and so emboldened to proceed in his task. "Are you satisfied now, friend John?" he asked.

I felt all the dogged argumentativeness of my nature awake within me as I answered him:—

"I am satisfied that Lucy's body is not in that coffin; but that only proves one thing."

"And what is that, friend John?"

"That it is not there."

"That is good logic," he said, "so far as it goes. But how do you—how can you—account for it not being there?"

"Perhaps a body-snatcher," I suggested. "Some of the undertaker's people may have stolen it." I felt that I was speaking folly, and yet it was the only real cause which I could suggest. The Professor sighed. "Ah well!" he said, "we must have more proof. Come with me."

He put on the coffin-lid again, gathered up all his things and placed them in the bag, blew out the light, and placed the candle also in the bag. We opened the door, and went out. Behind us he closed the door and locked it. He handed me the key, saying: "Will you keep it? You had better be assured." I laughed—it was not a very cheerful laugh, I am bound to say—as I motioned him to keep it. "A key is nothing," I said; "there may be duplicates, and anyhow it is not difficult to pick a lock of that kind." He said nothing, but put the key in his pocket. Then he told me to watch at one side of the churchyard whilst he would watch at the other.[14] I took up my place behind a yew-tree, and I saw his dark figure move until the intervening headstones and trees hid it from my sight.

It was a lonely vigil. Just after I had taken my place I heard a distant clock strike twelve, and in time came one and two. I was chilled and unnerved, and angry with the Professor for taking me on such an errand and with myself for coming. I was too cold and too sleepy to be keenly observant, and not sleepy enough to betray my trust; so altogether I had a dreary, miserable time.

Suddenly, as I turned round, I thought I saw something like a white streak, moving between two dark yew-trees at the side of the churchyard farthest from the tomb; at the same time a dark mass moved from the Professor's side of the ground, and hurriedly went towards it. Then I too moved; but I had to go round headstones and railed-off tombs, and I stumbled over graves. The sky was overcast, and somewhere far off an early cock crew. A little way off, beyond a line of scattered juniper-trees, which marked the pathway to the church, a white, dim figure flitted in the direction of the tomb. The tomb itself was hidden by trees, and I could not see where the figure disappeared. I heard the rustle of actual movement where I had first seen the white figure, and coming over, found the Professor holding in his arms a tiny child. When he saw me he held it out to me, and said:—

"Are you satisfied now?"

"No," I said, in a way that I felt was aggressive.

"Do you not see the child?"

"Yes, it is a child, but who brought it here? And is it wounded?" I asked.

"We shall see," said the Professor, and with one impulse we took our way out of the churchyard, he carrying the sleeping child.

When we had got some little distance away, we went into a clump of trees, and struck a match, and looked at the child's throat. It was without a scratch or scar of any kind.

"Was I right?" I asked triumphantly.

"We were just in time," said the Professor thankfully.

We had now to decide what we were to do with the child, and so consulted about it. If we were to take it to a police-station we should have to give some account of our movements during the night; at least, we should have had to make some statement as to how we had come to find the child. So finally we decided that we would take it to the Heath, and when we heard a policeman coming, would leave it where he could not fail to find it; we would then seek our way home as quickly as

The Spaniards, still in operation as a pub.
Photograph by Leslie S. Klinger, February 2006

15 Although reportedly built in 1585 as a country house for the Spanish ambassador and converted in the mid-eighteenth century by two Spanish brothers to an inn and public house, the source of the name is obscure. Claiming visits over the centuries by highwayman Dick Turpin, poets Lord Byron and John Keats, and author Charles Dickens, the pub is located on Spaniard Road and continues in operation today. Dickens's 1888 *Dictionary of London* recommended it, the Bull and Bush, and Jack Straw's Castle as "the three best places in Hampstead for the refreshment of the inner holiday-maker."

16 Is Van Helsing staying at Purfleet? If so, this phrase is quite odd; if not, why would he travel out to Purfleet to pick up Seward, only to return to London? Perhaps Van Helsing originally intended to do something at Carfax first before returning to the Westenra tomb. The following term "expedition" seems inappropriate if Van Helsing simply intends to return to the burial site.

17 Leatherdale (*Dracula Unearthed*) notes here another clue regarding the location:

we could. All fell out well. At the edge of Hampstead Heath we heard a policeman's heavy tramp, and laying the child on the pathway, we waited and watched until he saw it as he flashed his lantern to and fro. We heard his exclamation of astonishment, and then we went away silently. By good chance we got a cab near the "Spaniards,"**15** and drove to town.

I cannot sleep, so I make this entry. But I must try to get a few hours' sleep, as Van Helsing is to call for me at noon.**16** He insists that I shall go with him on another expedition.

27 September.—It was two o'clock before we found a suitable opportunity for our attempt. The funeral held at noon was all completed, and the last stragglers of the mourners had taken themselves lazily away, when, looking carefully from behind a clump of alder-trees, we saw the sexton lock the gate after him.**17** We knew then that we were safe till morning did we desire it;**18** but the Professor told me that we should not want more than an hour at most. Again I felt that horrid sense of the reality of things, in which any effort of imagination seemed out of place; and I realised distinctly the perils of the law which we were incurring in our unhallowed work. Besides, I felt it was all so useless. Outrageous as it was to open a leaden coffin, to see if a woman dead nearly a week were really dead, it now seemed the height of folly to open the tomb again, when we knew, from the evidence of our own eyesight, that the coffin was empty. I shrugged my shoulders, however, and rested silent, for Van Helsing had a way of going on his own road, no matter who remonstrated. He took the key, opened the vault, and again courteously motioned me to precede. The place was not so gruesome as last night, but oh, how unutterably mean-looking when the sunshine streamed in. Van Helsing walked over to Lucy's coffin, and I followed. He bent over and again forced back the leaden flange; and then a shock of surprise and dismay shot through me.

There lay Lucy, seemingly just as we had seen her the night before her funeral. She was, if possible, more radiantly beautiful than ever; and I could not believe that she was dead. The lips were red, nay redder than before; and on the cheeks was a delicate bloom.

"Is this a juggle?"[19] I said to him.

"Are you convinced now?" said the Professor in response, and as he spoke he put over his hand, and in a way that made me shudder, pulled back the dead lips and showed the white teeth.

"See," he went on, "see, they are even sharper than before. With this and this"—and he touched one of the canine teeth and that below it—"the little children can be bitten. Are you of belief now, friend John?" Once more, argumentative hostility woke within me. I *could* not accept such an overwhelming idea as he suggested; so, with an attempt to argue of which I was even at the moment ashamed, I said:—

"She may have been placed here since last night."

"Indeed? That is so, and by whom?"

"I do not know. Some one has done it."

"And yet she has been dead one week. Most peoples in that time would not look so." I had no answer for this, so was silent. Van Helsing did not seem to notice my silence; at any rate, he showed neither chagrin nor triumph. He was looking intently at the face of the dead woman, raising the eyelids and looking at the eyes, and once more opening the lips and examining the teeth. Then he turned to me and said:—

"Here, there is one thing which is different from all recorded: here is some dual life that is not as the common. She was bitten by the vampire when she was in a trance, sleep-walking—oh, you start; you do not know that, friend John, but you shall know it all later—and in trance could he best come to take more blood. In trance she died, and in trance she is Un-Dead, too.[20] So it is that she differ from all other. Usually when the Un-Dead sleep at home"—as he spoke he made a comprehensive sweep of his arm to designate what to a vampire was "home"—"their face show what they are, but this so sweet that was when she not Un-Dead she go back to the nothings of the common dead.[21] There is no malign there, see, and so it make hard that I must kill her in her sleep." This turned my blood cold, and it began to dawn upon me that I was accepting Van Helsing's theories; but if she were really dead, what was there of terror in the idea of killing her? He looked up at me, and evidently saw the change in my face, for he said almost joyously:—

Highgate Cemetery was open from 9:00 A.M. to sunset daily.

18 Seward, who still knows nothing of vampires, means "safe" from intrusion by other people, but even though the funeral party has departed, there may well be a sexton, gravediggers, or gardeners about.

19 In this context, an act of deception or fraud.

20 Wolf (*The Essential Dracula*) suggests that Van Helsing is somehow exculpating Lucy here—she is a "lesser" vampire because she was "turned" in a trance state and did not act with volition.

21 Harker made no comment about Dracula's face appearing to be different in the coffin than when he was "animated." Perhaps Van Helsing's "records" are inaccurate. This idea does not appear in any other vampire literature. See "Dracula's Family Tree," in Part II.

22 Nina Auerbach and David J. Skal, in the Norton Critical Edition of *Dracula*, point out: "The function of the stake in folklore is merely to immobilize the living dead, not to destroy them."

23 The fear of premature burial was prevalent in the nineteenth century, especially in Germany and France. Horrifying stories (many, but not all of them, apocryphal) of presumed corpses having destroyed coffin lids, torn their garments, and even eaten their own fingers in panic and terror had been circulating for centuries, proliferating in the wake of plague and cholera epidemics and reaching particular intensity during the eighteenth century. Some became the basis for vampire legends, others fuelled justifiable fears of physicians and the "science" of medicine.

Pivotal to the movement was physician Jean-Jacques Bruhier d'Ablaincourt's translation of a 1740 thesis written by Danish-born anatomist Jacques-Bénigne Winslow, who claimed to have twice been mistaken for dead himself. Winslow stated that traditional methods of determining death were frequently inadequate (which they were) and, maintaining that only putrefaction constituted definitive proof, insisted that numerous attempts be made to resuscitate a corpse—including sticking a sharp object up the nose, cutting the feet with razors, and pouring vinegar or urine into the mouth—before preparing it for burial.

Bruhier not only translated Winslow's thesis into French but also added his own treatise, listing further stories and proposing

Premature burial.

"Ah, you believe now?"

I answered: "Do not press me too hard all at once. I am willing to accept. How will you do this bloody work?"

"I shall cut off her head and fill her mouth with garlic, and I shall drive a stake through her body."[22] It made me shudder to think of so mutilating the body of the woman whom I had loved. And yet the feeling was not so strong as I had expected. I was, in fact, beginning to shudder at the presence of this being, this Un-Dead, as Van Helsing called it, and to loathe it. Is it possible that love is all subjective, or all objective?

I waited a considerable time for Van Helsing to begin, but he stood as if wrapped in thought. Presently he closed the catch of his bag with a snap, and said:—

"I have been thinking, and have made up my mind as to what is best. If I did simply follow my inclining I would do now, at this moment, what is to be done; but there are other things to follow, and things that are thousand times more difficult in that them we do not know. This is simple. She have yet no life taken, though that is of time; and to act now would be to take danger from her for ever. But then we may have to want Arthur, and how shall we tell him of this? If you, who saw the wounds on Lucy's throat, and saw the wounds so similar on the child's at the hospital; if you, who saw the coffin empty last night and full to-day with a woman who have not change only to be more rose and more beautiful in a whole week after she die—if you know of this and know of the white figure last night that brought the child to the churchyard, and yet of your own senses you did not believe, how, then, can I expect Arthur, who know none of those things, to believe? He doubted me when I took him from her kiss when she was dying. I know he has forgiven me because in some mistaken idea I have done things that prevent him say good-bye as he ought; and he may think that in some more mistaken idea this woman was buried alive;[23] and that in most mistake of all we have killed her. He will then argue back that it is we, mistaken ones, that have killed her by our ideas; and so he will be much unhappy always. Yet he never can be sure; and that is the worst of all. And he will sometimes think that she he loved was buried alive, and that will paint his dreams with that corpses rest in mortuaries, supervised by physicians, for seventy-two hours before being buried. Bruhier's book became a publishing sensation and eventually turned into the two-volume *Dissertation sur l'incertitude des signes de la mort*, published as a complete work (and dropping Winslow as coauthor) in 1749. Translated into several languages, Bruhier's book swept through Europe, making its greatest impact in Germany. There, a number of "waiting mortuaries" (known as *Leichenhäuser*) were constructed in the 1790s (see chapter 1, note 4), although these were exclusively for the wealthy. Corpses were watched by an attendant or had their lifeless fingers attached by string to a bell. Germany was also the pioneer in inventing security coffins, similarly rigged with bells. The fixation spread to France, where in the first half of the nineteenth century doctors published pamphlets suggesting new methods of testing for signs of death. These ranged from holding a corpse's finger above a flame to see if a blister formed, to systemically pulling a corpse's tongue for three hours to aid in artificial respiration.

Britain managed to remain apart from the fray for some time. As late as 1852, Dr. John Simon, in the "City of London Medical Reports," decried the custom of delayed burials among the poor, writing, "Fears of premature interment, which had much to do with it, are now seldom spoken of but with a smile." Jan Bondeson, author of the absorbing *Buried Alive*, writes that when French interest began to pick up in

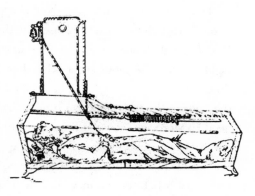

A "security" coffin, ca. 1897.

the 1830s, "the [English] medical establishment was wholly complacent, viewing the Continental preoccupation with premature burial with a mixture of amusement and disgust." Some of the French pamphlets made their way to Britain and led to various alarmist articles and books being published throughout the early 1800s, although none particularly caught fire with the general public.

Yet in 1895, just as French and German fascination with premature burial was waning, an American, Franz Hartmann, published *Buried Alive: An Examination into the Occult Causes of Apparent Death, Trance, and Catalepsy*, and the British experienced a late surge, stimulated in large part by the 1896 appearance of *Premature Burial and How It May Be Prevented*, written by political activist William Tebb and the American military surgeon Edward Perry Vollum. The book attracted its share of exasperated critics, notably among the clergy and the medical establishment—who pointed out the extreme unreliability of newspaper and verbal accounts—but it was generally well received and sold so well that a second edition appeared in 1905.

The same year that *Premature Burial* was published, Tebb, ever the savvy promoter, helped form the London Society for the Prevention of Premature Burial, primarily to help publicise the book. The society became the leading agitator in the anti-premature-burial movement, holding regular meetings, organising occasional lectures, and launching a journal, the *Burial Reformer*, in 1905. In addition to reporting on the society's meetings, the journal published articles on premature burial and stories from the world's newspapers. In "The Accrington Sensation" (1905), for example, Mrs. Elizabeth Holden escaped burial only when an undertaker saw her eyelid twitch. According to the *Burial Reformer*, her trauma did not preclude her from talking to the press: "pale, wan, extremely weak, she feebly lisped out to a representative of the *Manchester Courier* her recollections of her terrible experience." The journal also published poetry, exposing the public to such gems as Mark Melford's "Living with the Dead," printed in 1913 and containing the immortal lines: "Alive! Within the jaws of death, / No fate was ever worse! / No enemy invoked on me / So terrible a curse! / Conveyed still living to my grave! / Within a funeral hearse." By this time, the journal, now renamed *Perils of Premature Burial*. Taking an increasingly sensationalist tone, the journal ran stories—such as that of a baby found in its coffin, sucking placidly from a bottle—that were frankly preposterous. Its audience dwindling, it ceased publication in 1914, although the society itself continued to exist into the 1930s.

Edgar Allan Poe and Wilkie Collins were among those literary figures sufficiently spooked by the prospect of being buried alive, or at least intrigued by it, to pen fiction in which premature burial played a central role, and there are echoes of the phobia in the Sherlock Holmes tale "The Disappearance of Lady Frances Carfax." Poe, of course, qualifies as the "writer with the most premature burials per page," according to Jan Bondeson, who writes that Poe's "unwholesome fascination with this subject is apparent to every devotee of his horror stories." Chief among which is "The Premature Burial" (1844), in which the protagonist so fears being buried alive that he takes elaborate precautions to avoid the scenario—preparations that come to naught when he suffers a cataleptic fit while travelling. Poe's creepy tale was made into a macabre 1962 film by Roger Corman, starring Ray Milland as the death-obsessed protagonist. Wilkie Collins and Mark Twain both set works of fiction in waiting mortuaries, and countless authors wrote stories featuring characters, presumed dead, who saved themselves from a horrible fate by belatedly awakening and extracting themselves from their coffins.

The Silesian poet Friederike Kempner's "Denkschrift," a pamphlet about premature burial, appeared in 1853 and became a best seller. Kempner, whose stylistic quirks made her a target of parody but whose literary renown at the time of her death gained her admittance to Wroclaw's famed Jewish Cemetery (also

horrors of what she must have suffered; and again, he will think that we may be right, and that his so beloved was, after all, an Un-Dead. No! I told him once, and since then I learn much. Now, since I know it is all true, a hundred thousand times more do I know that he must pass through the bitter waters to reach the sweet.[24] He, poor fellow, must have one hour that will make the very face of heaven grow black to him; then we can act for good all round and send him peace. My mind is made up. Let us go. You return home for to-night to your asylum, and see that all be well. As for me, I shall spend the night here in this churchyard in my own way. To-morrow night you will come to me to the Berkeley Hotel at ten of the clock. I shall send for Arthur to come too, and also that so fine young man of America that gave his blood.[25] Later we shall have work to do. I come with you so far as Piccadilly and there dine, for I must be back here before the sun set."

So we locked the tomb and came away, and got over the wall of the churchyard, which was not much of a task, and drove back to Piccadilly.

NOTE LEFT BY VAN HELSING IN HIS PORTMANTEAU, BERKELEY HOTEL, DIRECTED TO JOHN SEWARD, M.D.
(Not delivered.)[26]

"27 September.

Friend John.—

"I write this in case anything should happen. I go alone to watch in that churchyard. It pleases me that the Un-Dead, Miss Lucy, shall not leave to-night, that so on the morrow night she may be more eager. Therefore I shall fix some things she like not—garlic and a crucifix—and so seal up the door of the tomb. She is young as Un-Dead, and will heed.[27] Moreover, these are only to prevent her coming out; they may not prevail on her wanting to get in; for then the Un-Dead is desperate, and must find the line of least resistance, whatsoever it may be. I shall be at hand all the night from sunset till after sunrise, and if there be aught that may be learned I shall learn it. For Miss Lucy or from her, I have no fear; but that other to whom is there that she is Un-Dead, he have now the power to seek her tomb and find shelter.[28] He is cunning, as I know from Mr. Jonathan and from the way that all along he have fooled us when he played with us for Miss Lucy's life, and we lost; and in many ways the Un-Dead are strong. He have always the strength in his hand of twenty men; even we four who gave our strength to Miss Lucy it also is all to him.[29] Besides, he can summon his wolf and I know not what.[30] So if it be that he come thither on this night he shall find me; but none other shall[31]—until it be too late. But it may be that he will not attempt the place. There is no reason why he should;[32] his hunting ground is more full of game than the churchyard where the Un-Dead woman sleep, and the one old man watch.

"Therefore I write this in case. . . . Take the papers that are with this, the diaries of Harker[33] and the rest, and read them, and then find this great Un-Dead, and cut off his head and burn his heart or drive a stake through it, so that the world may rest from him.[34]

"If it be so, farewell.
"Van Helsing."

DR. SEWARD'S DIARY.

28 September.—It is wonderful what a good night's sleep will do for one. Yesterday I was almost willing to accept Van Helsing's monstrous ideas; but now they seem to start out lurid before me as outrages on common sense. I have no doubt that he believes it all. I wonder if his mind can have become in any way unhinged. Surely there must be some rational explanation of all these mysterious things. Is it possible that the Professor can have done it himself? He is so abnormally clever that if he went off his head he would carry out his intent with regard to some fixed idea in a wonderful way. I am loathe to think it, and indeed it would be almost as great a marvel as the other to find that Van Helsing was mad; but anyhow I shall watch him carefully.[35] I may get some light on the mystery.

the final resting place of German Social Democratic Party founder Ferdinand Lassalle, historian Heinrich Graetz, and anatomist and neuropathologist Leopold Auerbach), wrote at least a half-dozen novellas and dramas and self-published eight editions of her poetry anthology. She conducted her career as a writer while toiling as a civil servant, campaigning tirelessly and ultimately successfully for *Leichenhäuse* for the poor. The poem for which she was perhaps best known in her lifetime was the lachrymose "Prematurely Buried Child," which describes a "coffin'd child" crying out, "Mummy, where are you!?" and continues: "His bloody hands they knock / Unyielding coffin walls / Half dead with fright and shock / 'Hear, I am not dead!' / But no one heeds his call."

24 At the direction of the Lord, Moses cast a tree into the bitter waters of Marah and made them sweet (Exod. 15:23–25).

25 Why Quincey Morris? There is no ostensible reason to convince *him*, unless it is to avoid a charge of murder of Lucy.

26 Professor Salli J. Kline (*The Degeneration of Women: Bram Stoker's Dracula as Allegorical Criticism of the Fin de Siècle*) finds it very unlikely that this note—along with the correspondence of Messrs. Billingham and Carter, Paterson—would have been preserved by the Harkers or have even reached them. Kline reasons that these were perhaps invented by Stoker to supplement the narrative.

27 Does Van Helsing have any reason to believe that these methods will not work on an "old" vampire? We saw earlier that garlic effectively prevented Dracula from entering Lucy's room.

28 Obscure—why would Dracula want to "shelter" in Lucy's tomb? First, as we have seen, any burial ground will work (for example, the suicide's grave in Whitby); second, Dracula has his own boxes of earth. Is Van Helsing suggesting that Lucy and Dracula might have some sort of tryst (or perhaps a hunting party)? The psychic link between a vampire and his or her sire is explained in the Anne Rice Vampire Chronicles; see "Dracula's Family Tree" in Part II.

29 What does this sentence mean? Roger Johnson, in private correspondence with this editor, suggests that Van Helsing means that Dracula has added the strength of Holmwood, Seward, Morris, and Van Helsing to his own by reason of imbibing Lucy's blood, which now incorporates theirs. This notion fits early-nineteenth-century ideas about transfusions but seems highly unscientific.

30 Van Helsing apparently missed the newspaper item reporting the return of the wolf to the Zoo. Wolves are not found roaming the countryside of Hampstead Heath or anywhere else in London. Although Dracula may be able to "shape-shift" into the form of a large dog, there are no wolves for him to summon.

31 What "other" is Van Helsing speaking of? The sexton? Other vampires?

32 Right—the entire discussion of Dracula and his strength and wolves is seemingly pointless.

33 Van Helsing forgets that Seward has not met Jonathan Harker and has no knowledge of his involvement in the matter.

34 This is excellent advice, which, as will be seen, the hunters utterly fail to follow.

35 The chief of the asylum seems unduly ready to proclaim Van Helsing as mad. His madness would be truly extraordinary if it enabled him to remove Lucy's body without disturbing the inner lead casing *which had to be sawn open.*

36 Alas, we can only imagine the contents of this letter, one of the few communications among the party not reproduced here. From Arthur's puzzlement, it must have been a letter only requesting his attendance on an expedition to a

29 September, morning. . . . Last night, at a little before ten o'clock, Arthur and Quincey came into Van Helsing's room; he told us all that he wanted us to do, but especially addressing himself to Arthur, as if all our wills were centred in his. He began by saying that he hoped we would all come with him too, "for," he said, "there is a grave duty to be done there. You were doubtless surprised at my letter?"**36** This query was directly addressed to Lord Godalming.

"I was. It rather upset me for a bit. There has been so much trouble around my house of late that I could do without any more. I have been curious, too, as to what you mean. Quincey and I talked it over; but the more we talked, the more puzzled we got, till now I can say for myself that I'm about up a tree as to any meaning about anything."

"Me too," said Quincey Morris laconically.

"Oh," said the Professor, "then you are nearer the beginning, both of you, than friend John here, who has to go a long way back before he can even get so far as to begin."

It was evident that he recognised my return to my old doubting frame of mind without my saying a word. Then, turning to the other two, he said with intense gravity:—

"I want your permission to do what I think good this night. It is, I know, much to ask; and when you know what it is I propose to do you will know, and only then, how much. Therefore may I ask that you promise me in the dark, so that afterwards, though you may be angry with me for a time—I must not disguise from myself the possibility that such may be—you shall not blame yourselves for anything."

"That's frank anyhow," broke in Quincey. "I'll answer for the Professor. I don't quite see his drift, but I swear he's honest; and that's good enough for me."

"I thank you, sir," said Van Helsing proudly. "I have done myself the honour of counting you one trusting friend, and such endorsement is dear to me." He held out a hand, which Quincey took.

Then Arthur spoke out:—

"Dr. Van Helsing, I don't quite like to 'buy a pig in a poke,'**37** as they say in Scotland, and if it be anything in which my honour as a gentleman or my faith as a Christian is concerned,

I cannot make such a promise. If you can assure me that what you intend does not violate either of these two, then I give my consent at once; though for the life of me, I cannot understand what you are driving at."

"I accept your limitation," said Van Helsing, "and all I ask of you is that if you feel it necessary to condemn any act of mine, you will first consider it well and be satisfied that it does not violate your reservations."

"Agreed!" said Arthur; "that is only fair. And now that the *pourparlers*[38] are over, may I ask what it is we are to do?"

"I want you to come with me, and to come in secret, to the churchyard at Kingstead."[39]

Arthur's face fell as he said in an amazed sort of way:—

"Where poor Lucy is buried?" The Professor bowed. Arthur went on: "And when there?"

"To enter the tomb!" Arthur stood up.

"Professor, are you in earnest; or is it some monstrous joke? Pardon me, I see that you are in earnest." He sat down again, but I could see that he sat firmly and proudly, as one who is on his dignity. There was silence until he asked again:—

"And when in the tomb?"

"To open the coffin."

"This is too much!" he said, angrily rising again. "I am willing to be patient in all things that are reasonable; but in this—this desecration of the grave—of one who—" He fairly choked with indignation. The Professor looked pityingly at him.

"If I could spare you one pang, my poor friend," he said, "God knows I would. But this night our feet must tread in thorny paths; or later, and for ever, the feet you love must walk in paths of flame!"

Arthur looked up with set, white face and said:—

"Take care, sir, take care!"

"Would it not be well to hear what I have to say?" said Van Helsing. "And then you will at least know the limit of my purpose. Shall I go on?"

"That's fair enough," broke in Morris.

After a pause Van Helsing went on, evidently with an effort:—

place unmentioned. What Van Helsing should have written is a letter detailing his ghoulish plan to decapitate Lucy, but perhaps he realised that his chances of obtaining Arthur's consent were slim.

37 To buy something unexamined. The expression was first recorded in 1530, but its Scottish origins are not documented.

38 French: preliminary conversation, "small talk."

39 This is a fictional location. In the Manuscript, there is a blank, filled in first in Stoker's hand with "Kings Sted," which is deleted and replaced with "Kingsted."

40 Wolf (*The Essential Dracula*) comments that Van Helsing's phraseology here sounds like acceptance of a challenge to a duel.

"Miss Lucy is dead; is it not so? Yes! Then there can be no wrong to her. But if she be not dead—"

Arthur jumped to his feet.

"Good God!" he cried. "What do you mean? Has there been any mistake; has she been buried alive?" He groaned in anguish that not even hope could soften.

"I did not say she was alive, my child; I did not think it. I go no further than to say that she might be Un-Dead."

"Un-Dead! Not alive! What do you mean? Is this all a nightmare, or what is it?"

"There are mysteries which men can only guess at, which age by age they may solve only in part. Believe me, we are now on the verge of one. But I have not done. May I cut off the head of dead Miss Lucy?"

"Heavens and earth, no!" cried Arthur in a storm of passion. "Not for the wide world will I consent to any mutilation of her dead body. Dr. Van Helsing, you try me too far. What have I done to you that you should torture me so? What did that poor, sweet girl do that you should want to cast such dishonour on her grave? Are you mad that speak such things, or am I mad to listen to them? Don't dare to think more of such a desecration; I shall not give my consent to anything you do. I have a duty to do in protecting her grave from outrage; and, by God, I shall do it!"

Van Helsing rose up from where he had all the time been seated, and said, gravely and sternly:—

"My Lord Godalming, I, too, have a duty to do, a duty to others, a duty to you, a duty to the dead; and, by God, I shall do it! All I ask you now is that you come with me, that you look and listen; and if when later I make the same request you do not be more eager for its fulfilment even than I am, then— then I shall do my duty, whatever it may seem to me. And then, to follow your Lordship's wishes, I shall hold myself at your disposal to render an account to you, when and where you will."[40] His voice broke a little, and he went on with a voice full of pity:—

"But, I beseech you, do not go forth in anger with me. In a long life of acts which were often not pleasant to do, and which sometimes did wring my heart, I have never had so heavy a task as now. Believe me that if the time comes for you to change your mind towards me, one look from you will wipe away all this so sad hour, for I would do what a man can to save you from sorrow. Just think. For why should I give myself so much of labour and so much of sorrow? I have come here from my own land to do what I can of good; at the first to please my friend John, and then to help a sweet young lady, whom, too, I came to love. For her—I am ashamed to say so much, but I say it in kindness—I gave what you gave: the blood of my veins; I gave it, I, who was not, like you, her lover, but only her physician and her friend. I gave to her my nights and days—before death, after death; and if my death can do her good even now, when she is the dead Un-Dead, she shall have it freely." He said this with a very grave, sweet pride, and Arthur was much affected by it. He took the old man's hand and said in a broken voice:—

"Oh, it is hard to think of it, and I cannot understand; but at least I shall go with you and wait."

Chapter 16

DR. SEWARD'S DIARY

—continued.

1 Thus 1886, when the moon was new on 28 September, and 1889, when the moon was about a quarter full, are unlikely years for this description; a full moon in 1890 and near full in 1885 and 1887 are more likely.

2 Van Helsing's reasons for entering first do not appear in the Abridged Text.

3 The "dark lantern" was a modification of an ordinary gas or kerosene hand lantern that could be darkened while lit, by a sliding shield that covered the light without extinguishing the flame. We may think of it as the predecessor of the electric hand torch or flashlight.

A dark lantern.

IT WAS JUST A QUARTER before twelve o'clock when we got into the churchyard over the low wall. The night was dark with occasional gleams of moonlight[1] between the rents of the heavy clouds that scudded across the sky. We all kept somehow close together, with Van Helsing slightly in front as he led the way. When we had come close to the tomb I looked well at Arthur, for I feared that the proximity to a place laden with so sorrowful a memory would upset him; but he bore himself well. I took it that the very mystery of the proceeding was in some way a counteractant to his grief. The Professor unlocked the door, and seeing a natural hesitation amongst us for various reasons, solved the difficulty by entering first himself.[2] The rest of us followed, and he closed the door. He then lit a dark lantern[3] and pointed to the coffin. Arthur stepped forward hesitatingly; Van Helsing said to me:—

"You were with me here yesterday. Was the body of Miss Lucy in that coffin?"

"It was." The Professor turned to the rest, saying:—

"You hear; and yet there is one who does not believe with me." He took his screwdriver and again took off the lid of the coffin. Arthur looked on, very pale but silent; when the lid was removed he stepped forward. He evidently did not know that there was a leaden coffin, or, at any rate, had not thought of it. When he saw the rent in the lead, the blood rushed to

"Oh, God! That thing from the grave has been sucking
my blood from my veins!"
Varney, the Vampyre; or, The Feast of Blood (1847)

his face for an instant, but as quickly fell away again, so that
he remained of a ghastly whiteness; he was still silent. Van
Helsing forced back the leaden flange, and we all looked in
and recoiled.

The coffin was empty!

For several minutes no one spoke a word. The silence was
broken by Quincey Morris:—

"Professor, I answered for you. Your word is all I want. I
wouldn't ask such a thing ordinarily—I wouldn't so dishonour
you as to imply a doubt;**4** but this is a mystery that goes beyond
any honour or dishonour. Is this your doing?"

"I swear to you by all that I hold sacred that I have not
removed nor touched her. What happened was this: Two nights
ago my friend Seward and I came here—with good purpose,

4 The balance of the paragraph in the
Manuscript reads: "But this racket goes a pile
better than an honour or dishonour or fancy
frills of any kind. Is this your doing? Honest
Injun?" Perhaps Stoker thought better of
portraying Morris as a near buffoon, and the
material does not appear in the published
text.

5 Leatherdale (*Dracula Unearthed*) points out that Holmwood must be mystified by this remark, for he knows nothing about child vampire victims, or that Lucy is the perpetrator.

6 Actually, as we (and Van Helsing, who read Harker's journal) have seen, some undead (at least, Dracula) can move before sundown. Perhaps this immobility is another trait of "young" vampires, in Van Helsing's view.

7 The philosophical reflection on the "crossing and passing" is not included in the Abridged Text. Perhaps it was too sentimental for "Seward's" self-image.

8 The lights of London are in the wrong direction for this to be Highgate Cemetery.

9 Leatherdale (*Dracula Unearthed*) explains that a lighted cigarette would be seen by anyone approaching. However, Van Helsing knows well that Lucy truly cannot choose another destination, and shortly the party boldly announces its presence to Lucy and shines a lantern in her face, calling the presence of the party to others' notice as well. Perhaps Seward simply meant that Quincey had left his other smoking apparatus—presumably, American cigarettes—behind.

believe me. I opened that coffin, which was then sealed up, and we found it, as now, empty. We then waited, and saw something white come through the trees. The next day we came here in day-time, and she lay there. Did she not, friend John?"

"Yes."

"That night we were just in time. One more so small child was missing, and we find it, thank God, unharmed amongst the graves.[5] Yesterday I came here before sundown, for at sundown the Un-Dead can move.[6] I waited here all the night till the sun rose, but I saw nothing. It was most probable that it was because I had laid over the clamps of those doors garlic, which the Un-Dead cannot bear, and other things which they shun. Last night there was no exodus, so to-night before the sundown I took away my garlic and other things. And so it is we find this coffin empty. But bear with me. So far there is much that is strange. Wait you with me outside, unseen and unheard, and things much stranger are yet to be. So"—here he shut the dark slide of his lantern—"now to the outside." He opened the door, and we filed out, he coming last and locking the door behind him.

Oh! but it seemed fresh and pure in the night air after the terror of that vault. How sweet it was to see the clouds race by, and the passing gleams of the moonlight between the scudding clouds crossing and passing—like the gladness and sorrow of a man's life;[7] how sweet it was to breathe the fresh air, that had no taint of death and decay; how humanising to see the red lighting of the sky beyond the hill, and to hear far away the muffled roar that marks the life of a great city.[8] Each in his own way was solemn and overcome. Arthur was silent, and was, I could see, striving to grasp the purpose and the inner meaning of the mystery. I was myself tolerably patient, and half inclined again to throw aside doubt and to accept Van Helsing's conclusions. Quincey Morris was phlegmatic in the way of a man who accepts all things, and accepts them in the spirit of cool bravery, with hazard of all he has at stake. Not being able to smoke,[9] he cut himself a good-sized plug of tobacco and began to chew. As to Van Helsing, he was employed in a definite way. First he took from his bag a mass of what looked like thin, wafer-like biscuit,[10] which was carefully rolled up in a white napkin; next he took out a double-handful of some whitish stuff, like dough or putty. He crumbled the wafer up fine and worked it into the mass between his hands. This he then took, and rolling it into thin strips, began to lay them into the crevices between the door and its setting in the tomb. I was somewhat puzzled at this, and being close, asked him what it was that he was doing. Arthur and Quincey drew near also, as they too were curious. He answered:—

"I am closing the tomb, so that the Un-Dead may not enter."

"And is that stuff you have put there going to do it?" asked Quincey. "Great Scott! Is this a game?"

"It is."

"What is that which you are using?" This time the question was by Arthur. Van Helsing reverently lifted his hat as he answered:

"The Host.[11] I brought it[12] from Amsterdam. I have an Indulgence."[13] It was an answer that appalled the most sceptical of us and we felt individually that in the presence of such earnest purpose as the Professor's, a purpose which could thus use the to him most sacred of things, it was impossible to distrust. In respectful silence we took the places assigned to us close round the tomb, but hidden from the sight of any one approaching. I pitied the others, especially Arthur. I had myself been apprenticed by my former visits to this watching horror; and yet I, who had up to an hour ago repudiated the proofs, felt my heart sink within me. Never did tombs look so ghastly white; never did cypress, or yew, or juniper so seem the embodiment of funereal gloom; never did tree or grass wave or rustle so ominously; never did bough creak so mysteriously; and never did the far-away howling of dogs send such a woeful presage through the night.

There was a long spell of silence, a big, aching void, and then from the Professor a keen "S-s-s-s!" He pointed; and far down the avenue of yews we saw a white figure advance—a dim white figure, which held something dark at its breast. The figure stopped, and at the moment a ray of moonlight fell between the masses of driving clouds and showed in startling

10 Described in the Manuscript as "a mass of bread cut up in small squares and rolled up in a white napkin and then opening the mouth of a wide necked phial spread some red liquid over it. Then he began to work up the mass with his hands till he had a big double handful of a kind of dough." Assuming that what Van Helsing actually had was the dough from which the sacred wafer is made, the identity of the "red liquid" is still in doubt. Perhaps sacramental wine? Or an elixir of wild rose?

11 Part of the Eucharist, the "host" is the sacramental wafer of consecrated bread used in the Catholic mass. Wolf (*The Essential Dracula*) protests that it would be impermissible under church law to use the sanctified wafer in this manner.

12 The Manuscript reads "Took some," which is more likely how Van Helsing obtained it, but the more polite version appears in the published narrative.

13 An "indulgence" is a remission of temporal punishment for a sin, not a "get-out-of-jail-free" card entitling the holder to commit sin. Wolf again asserts that the granting of an indulgence for the intended use of the host would violate church law.

Does Van Helsing have a blanket indulgence for use of the holy wafer against vampires in general, or did he have to demonstrate (as in the case of a search warrant) a specific intended use and probable cause to suspect the need for its use? And from whom did Van Helsing obtain the indulgence? He surely did not have time to seek out a high church official and plead his case during his most recent visit to Amsterdam; his entire journey to and from Amsterdam lasted only one day, and almost all of that would have been consumed by travel. He must have arranged for the indulgence in anticipation of dealing with *some* vampire *sometime*, not for this particular intended use.

McNally and Florescu (*The Essential Dracula*) make the interesting suggestion that in

Van Helsing's fractured English, he means "permission" rather than a formal indulgence, although who granted the Professor permission is unclear. This sentence does not appear in the Manuscript, and so its authenticity must be doubted.

14 This is clearly identified as Lucy; however, she is described earlier as having "sunny" hair (see text accompanying chapter 12, note 54). Wolf (*The Essential Dracula*) makes much of this discrepancy, suggesting that the dark hair symbolises Lucy's loss of innocence, but it may simply be a trick of the moonlight.

15 Strangely, this suggests that Lucy brought the children back to her tomb to feed on them. If so, how did they manage to find their way back to the heath? Surely Lucy did not return them.

16 Lucy has either gotten more voracious or more careless in her drinking, for if her corpse, when viewed by Van Helsing and Seward two nights before, had worn a robe stained by the blood of previous victims, Seward would have mentioned it.

prominence a dark-haired woman, dressed in the cerements of the grave.[14] We could not see the face, for it was bent down over what we saw to be a fair-haired child. There was a pause and a sharp little cry such as a child gives in sleep, or a dog as it lies before the fire and dreams.[15] We were starting forward, but the Professor's warning hand, seen by us as he stood behind a yew-tree, kept us back; and then as we looked the white figure moved forwards again. It was now near enough for us to see clearly, and the moonlight still held. My own heart grew cold as ice, and I could hear the gasp of Arthur as we recognised the features of Lucy Westenra. Lucy Westenra, but yet how changed. The sweetness was turned to adamantine, heartless cruelty, and the purity to voluptuous wantonness. Van Helsing stepped out, and, obedient to his gesture, we all advanced too; the four of us ranged in a line before the door of the tomb. Van Helsing raised his lantern and drew the slide; by the concentrated light that fell on Lucy's face we could see that the lips were crimson with fresh blood, and that the stream had trickled over her chin and stained the purity of her lawn death-robe.[16]

We shuddered with horror. I could see by the tremulous light that even Van Helsing's iron nerve had failed. Arthur was next to me, and if I had not seized his arm and held him up, he would have fallen.

When Lucy—I call the thing that was before us Lucy because it bore her shape—saw us she drew back with an angry snarl, such as a cat gives when taken unawares; then her eyes ranged over us. Lucy's eyes in form and colour; but Lucy's eyes unclean and full of hell-fire, instead of the pure, gentle orbs we knew. At that moment the remnant of my love passed into hate and loathing; had she then to be killed, I could have done it with savage delight. As she looked, her eyes blazed with unholy light, and the face became wreathed with a voluptuous smile. Oh, God, how it made me shudder to see it! With a careless motion, she flung to the ground, callous as a devil, the child that up to now she had clutched strenuously to her breast, growling over it as a dog growls over a bone. The child gave a sharp cry, and lay there moaning. There was a cold-bloodedness in the act which wrung a groan from Arthur; when she advanced to him with outstretched arms and a wanton smile, he fell back and hid his face in his hands.

She still advanced, however, and with a languorous, voluptuous grace, said:—

"Come to me, Arthur. Leave these others and come to me. My arms are hungry for you. Come, and we can rest together. Come, my husband, come!"

There was something diabolically sweet in her tones—something of the tinkling of glass when struck[17]—which rang through the brains even of us who heard the words addressed to another. As for Arthur, he seemed under a spell; moving his hands from his face, he opened wide his arms. She was leaping for them, when Van Helsing sprang forward and held between them his little golden crucifix.[18] She recoiled from it, and, with a suddenly distorted face, full of rage, dashed past him as if to enter the tomb.

When within a foot or two of the door, however, she stopped as if arrested by some irresistible force. Then she turned, and her face was shown in the clear burst of moonlight and by the lamp, which had now no quiver from Van Helsing's iron nerves. Never did I see such baffled malice on a face; and never, I trust, shall such ever be seen again by mortal eyes. The beautiful colour became livid, the eyes seemed to throw out sparks of hell-fire, the brows were wrinkled as though the folds of the flesh were the coils of Medusa's snakes,[19] and the lovely, blood-stained mouth grew to an open square, as in the passion masks of the Greeks and Japanese. If ever a face meant death—if looks could kill—we saw it at that moment.

And so for full half a minute, which seemed an eternity, she remained between the lifted crucifix and the sacred closing of her means of entry. Van Helsing broke the silence by asking Arthur:—

Greek masks of drama.

17 Note that Lucy's voice is more brittle than the earlier-noted "tingling sweetness" of the women vampire voices. Seward refers here to the "striking" of glasses, which produces a sound quite different from the glass armonica. (See chapter 3, note 72, and accompanying text.)

18 There is a similar scene, albeit on the verandah of Dr. Seward's home, between the almost-undead Mina Seward and her lover Jonathan Harker in the 1931 *Dracula* film.

19 Legend recounts that the goddess Athena, in a fit of anger when Medusa lay with Poseidon in Athena's temple, transformed the beautiful young woman into a serpent-haired, boar-tusked, scaly-skinned creature.

20 This is the first expression of Van Helsing's belief that the vampire can only be killed in its coffin during the daylight hours. There is nothing in the Stoker narrative to belie this notion, but other literature suggests that a wooden stake through the heart may be efficacious at any time. There is also some doubt about whether the stake must be of hardwood or if an iron stake (especially if heated) is also fatal. See "Dracula's Family Tree" in Part II.

"Answer me, oh my friend! Am I to proceed in my work?"

Arthur threw himself on his knees, and hid his face in his hands, as he answered:—

"Do as you will, friend; do as you will. There can be no horror like this ever any more!" and he groaned in spirit. Quincey and I simultaneously moved towards him, and took his arms. We could hear the click of the closing lantern as Van Helsing held it down; coming close to the tomb, he began to remove from the chinks some of the sacred emblem which he had placed there. We all looked on in horrified amazement as we saw, when he stood back, the woman, with a corporeal body as real at that moment as our own, pass in through the interstice where scarce a knife-blade could have gone. We all felt a glad sense of relief when we saw the Professor calmly restoring the strings of putty to the edges of the door.

When this was done, he lifted the child and said:—

"Come now my friends; we can do no more till to-morrow.[20] There is a funeral at noon, so here we shall all come before long after that. The friends of the dead will all be gone by two, and when the sexton lock the gate we shall remain. Then there is more to do; but not like this of to-night. As for this little one, he is not much harm, and by to-morrow night he shall be well. We shall leave him where the police will find him, as on the other night; and then to home." Coming close to Arthur, he said:—

"My friend Arthur, you have had a sore trial; but after, when you look back, you will see how it was necessary. You are now in the bitter waters, my child. By this time to-morrow you will, please God, have passed them, and have drunk of the sweet waters; so do not mourn overmuch. Till then I shall not ask you to forgive me."

Arthur and Quincey came home with me, and we tried to cheer each other on the way. We had left the child in safety, and were tired; so we all slept with more or less reality of sleep.

29 September, night.—A little before twelve o'clock we three—Arthur, Quincey Morris, and myself—called for the Professor. It was odd to notice that by common consent we had all put on black clothes. Of course, Arthur wore black, for he was in deep mourning, but the rest of us wore it by instinct. We got to the churchyard by half-past one, and strolled about, keeping out of official observation, so that when the gravediggers had completed their task and the sexton, under the belief that every one had gone, had locked the gate, we had the place all to ourselves. Van Helsing, instead of his little black bag, had with him a long leather one, something like a cricketing bag;[21] it was manifestly of fair weight.

When we were alone and had heard the last of the footsteps die out up the road, we silently, and as if by ordered intention, followed the Professor to the tomb. He unlocked the door, and we entered, closing it behind us. Then he took from his bag the lantern, which he lit, and also two wax candles, which, when lighted, he stuck, by melting their own ends, on other coffins, so that they might give light sufficient to work by. When he again lifted the lid off Lucy's coffin we all looked—Arthur trembling like an aspen—and saw that the body lay there in all its death-beauty. But there was no love in my own heart, nothing but loathing for the foul Thing which had taken Lucy's shape without her soul. I could see even Arthur's face

21 Why did Van Helsing not bring this with him on his trip with Seward on 26 September? Indeed, how did Van Helsing propose to destroy Lucy on that occasion?

"[W]e . . . saw that the body lay there in all its death-beauty."
Jack Taylor as Quincey Morris, Herbert Lom as Van Helsing, Soledad Miranda as Lucy, and Frederick Williams as Jonathan Harker.
El Conde Dracula (Corona Filmproduktion, 1970)

22 Seward is surely jesting here.

23 But see discussion in chapter 27, note 32, and in "Dracula's Family Tree" in Part II.

24 This seems to contradict the previous sentence. First, Van Helsing states that those killed by a vampire become vampires themselves. He further tells Holmwood that if he had been bitten by Lucy, then "in time" (presumably upon his death) he too would become a vampire. If this were so, the world would be overrun with vampires, until the vampires themselves died out from the lack of food supplies, leaving no humans and no vampires. The Anne Rice lore proposes that new vampires are created only intentionally by a sire sharing his blood with a victim. *Buffy* lore, however, is consistent with Van Helsing's initial statement and assumes that anyone killed by a vampire becomes a vampire. See "Dracula's Family Tree" in Part II for further discussion.

The term "nosferatu" is borrowed from Emily Gerard's 1885 "Transylvanian Superstitions," although subsequent scholars believe she misunderstood the actual Transylvanian word. For example, J. Gordon Melton (*The Vampire Book*) states that the word is a derivative of the Greek word *nosophoros*, meaning "plague carrier," whereas David Skal (*V Is for Vampire*) contends that Gerard "must have recorded a corrupted or misunderstood version of the Roumanian adjective 'nesuferit' from the Latin 'not to suffer.' "

In Mel Brooks's delicious *Dracula: Dead and Loving It* (1995), Van Helsing (played by Brooks) advises the disturbed Jonathan Harker (Steven Weber) about the recently turned Lucy. "She's alive?" Harker asks. Van Helsing replies, "She's Nosferatu." Harker blurts out: "She's Italian?"

grow hard as he looked. Presently he said to Van Helsing:—

"Is this really Lucy's body, or only a demon in her shape?"

"It is her body, and yet not it. But wait a while, and you shall see her as she was, and is."

She seemed like a nightmare of Lucy as she lay there; the pointed teeth, the bloodstained, voluptuous mouth—which it made one shudder to see—the whole carnal and unspiritual appearance, seeming like a devilish mockery of Lucy's sweet purity. Van Helsing, with his usual methodicalness, began taking the various contents from his bag and placing them ready for use. First he took out a soldering iron and some plumbing solder, and then a small oil-lamp, which gave out, when lit in a corner of the tomb, gas which burned at fierce heat with a blue flame; then his operating knives, which he placed to hand; and last a round wooden stake, some two and a half or three inches thick and about three feet long. One end of it was hardened by charring in the fire, and was sharpened to a fine point. With this stake came a heavy hammer, such as in households is used in the coal-cellar for breaking the lumps. To me, a doctor's preparations for work of any kind[22] are stimulating and bracing, but the effect of these things on both Arthur and Quincey was to cause them a sort of consternation. They both, however, kept their courage, and remained silent and quiet.

When all was ready, Van Helsing said:—

"Before we do anything, let me tell you this; it is out of the lore and experience of the ancients and of all those who have studied the powers of the Un-Dead. When they become such, there comes with the change the curse of immortality; they cannot die, but must go on age after age adding new victims and multiplying the evils of the world; for all that die from the preying of the Un-Dead become themselves Un-Dead, and prey on their kind. And so the circle goes on ever widening, like as the ripples from a stone thrown in the water.[23] Friend Arthur, if you had met that kiss which you know of before poor Lucy die; or again, last night when you open your arms to her, you would in time, when you had died, have become *nosferatu*, as they call it in Eastern Europe, and would all time make more of those Un-Deads that so have fill us with horror.[24] The career of this so unhappy dear lady is but just begun.

Those children whose blood she suck are not as yet so much the worse; but if she live on, Un-Dead, more and more they lose their blood,[25] and by her power over them they come to her; and so she draw their blood with that so wicked mouth. But if she die in truth, then all cease; the tiny wounds of the throats disappear, and they go back to their plays unknowing ever of what has been.[26] But of the most blessed of all, when this now Un-Dead be made to rest as true dead, then the soul of the poor lady whom we love shall again be free.[27] Instead of working wickedness by night and growing more debased in the assimilating of it by day, she shall take her place with the other Angels. So that, my friend, it will be a blessed hand for her that shall strike the blow that sets her free. To this I am willing; but is there none amongst us who has a better right? Will it be no joy to think of hereafter in the silence of the night when sleep is not: 'It was my hand that sent her to the stars; it was the hand of him that loved her best; the hand that of all she would herself have chosen, had it been to her to choose? Tell me if there be such a one amongst us?"

We all looked at Arthur. He saw, too, what we all did, the infinite kindness which suggested that his should be the hand which would restore Lucy to us as a holy, and not an unholy, memory; he stepped forward and said bravely, though his hand trembled, and his face was as pale as snow:—

"My true friend, from the bottom of my broken heart I thank you. Tell me what I am to do, and I shall not falter!" Van Helsing laid a hand on his shoulder, and said:—

"Brave lad! A moment's courage, and it is done. This stake must be driven through her. It will be a fearful ordeal—be not deceived in that—but it will be only a short time, and you will then rejoice more than your pain was great; from this grim tomb you will emerge as though you tread on air. But you must not falter when once you have begun. Only think that we, your true friends, are round you, and that we pray for you all the time."

"Go on," said Arthur hoarsely. "Tell me what I am to do."

"Take this stake in your left hand, ready to place the point over the heart, and the hammer in your right. Then when we begin our prayer for the dead—I shall read him, I have here

25 Presumably Van Helsing means in his use of the word "they" the general public—that Lucy will continue to seek out new victims, not that there is some continuing predation of the children.

26 This is an interesting thesis: if the vampire who is preying on a particular victim dies the true death before the victim has turned, the victim is released. We will see later the critical use of this "rule" in the case of Mina Harker. Presumably Lucy herself could have been saved by this means before her turning was completed.

27 Again, a novel thesis: most historians believe the vampire to be soulless, the reanimation of a corpse after the soul has departed the body. Rather than the soul's animating force, the vampire requires blood to remain "alive." The *Buffy* mythology is a variation of this idea, asserting that a vampire naturally has no soul but has been reanimated by a demon inhabiting the body. The vampires Angel and Spike are distinguished from their kind by having had souls restored to them, causing them to experience remorse for their predation and to align themselves with the forces of the vampire slayer and her companions. (Although the *Buffy* lore is not explicit on this point, presumably Angel and Spike's bodies are inhabited by both souls and demons—the latter the source of their vampiric characteristics.) See "Dracula's Family Tree" in Part II for a more detailed discussion.

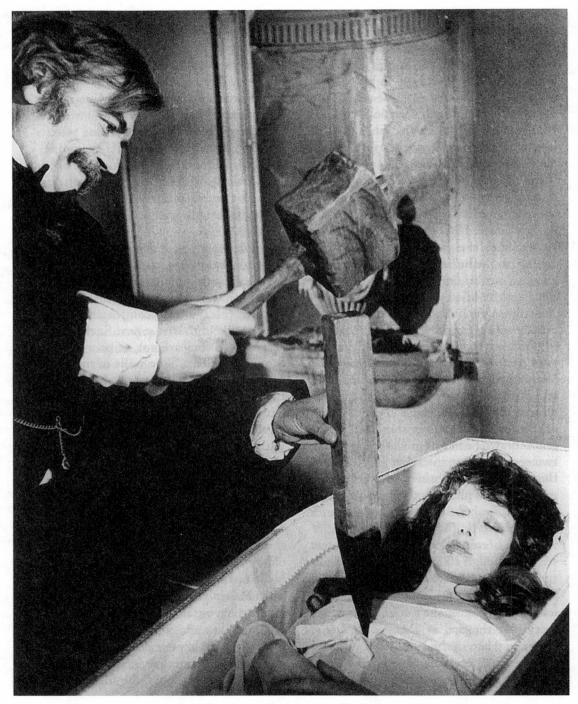

"A moment's courage, and it is done." Nigel Davenport as Van Helsing and Fiona Lewis as Lucy.
Dracula (Dan Curtis Productions, 1973)

the book, and the others shall follow—strike in God's name, that so all may be well with the dead that we love, and that the Un-Dead pass away."

Arthur took the stake and the hammer, and when once his mind was set on action his hands never trembled nor even quivered. Van Helsing opened his missal and began to read, and Quincey and I followed as well as we could. Arthur placed the point over the heart, and as I looked I could see its dint in the white flesh. Then he struck with all his might.

The Thing in the coffin writhed; and a hideous, blood-curdling screech came from the opened red lips. The body shook and quivered and twisted in wild contortions; the sharp white teeth champed together till the lips were cut, and the mouth was smeared with a crimson foam. But Arthur never faltered. He looked like a figure of Thor[28] as his untrembling arm rose and fell, driving deeper and deeper the mercy-bearing stake, whilst the blood from the pierced heart welled and spurted up around it. His face was set, and high duty seemed to shine through it; the sight of it gave us courage, so that our voices seemed to ring through the little vault.

And then the writhing and quivering of the body became less, and the teeth seemed to champ, and the face to quiver. Finally it lay still. The terrible task was over.

The hammer fell from Arthur's hand. He reeled and would have fallen had we not caught him. The great drops of sweat sprang from his forehead, and his breath came in broken gasps. It had indeed been an awful strain on him; and had he not been forced to his task by more than human considerations he could never have gone through with it. For a few minutes we were so taken up with him that we did not look towards the coffin. When we did, however, a murmur of startled surprise ran from one to the other of us. We gazed so eagerly that Arthur rose, for he had been seated on the ground, and came and looked too; and then a glad, strange light broke over his face and dispelled altogether the gloom of horror that lay upon it.

There, in the coffin lay no longer the foul Thing that we had so dreaded and grown to hate that the work of her destruction was yielded as a privilege to the one best entitled to it, but Lucy as we had seen her in her life, with her face of unequalled

28 The comparison is ironic; Arthur has been meek, irresolute, and led entirely by Van Helsing. Montague Summers (*The Vampire: His Kith and Kin*) notes that "it is highly important that the body of the Vampire should be transfixed by a single blow, for two blows or three would restore it to life. This curious idea is almost universally found in tradition and folk-lore." Apparently Van Helsing was not familiar with this tradition or else did not believe it.

29 The following appears in the Manuscript but is omitted from the published narrative: "Instinctively we all sank on our knees beside the coffin and sent forth our hearts in prayer. When we stood up . . . "

30 In the Manuscript, the phrase reads: "not a Foul Thing but a lovely woman's body."

31 Why did Van Helsing and Seward feel compelled to seal up the coffin? To preserve Lucy's body for its eventual resurrection on the Day of Judgement? Transylvanian custom (and the custom of other lands) would have dictated the cremation of the corpse.

32 Presumably as the heir to the Westenra estates.

sweetness and purity. True that there were there, as we had seen them in life, the traces of care and pain and waste; but these were all dear to us, for they marked her truth to what we knew. One and all we felt that the holy calm that lay like sunshine over the wasted face and form was only an earthly token and symbol of the calm that was to reign for ever.[29]

Van Helsing came and laid his hand on Arthur's shoulder and said to him:—

"And now, Arthur my friend, dear lad, am I not forgiven?"

The reaction of the terrible strain came as he took the old man's hand in his, and raising it to his lips, pressed it, and said:—

"Forgiven! God bless you that you have given my dear one her soul again, and me peace." He put his hands on the Professor's shoulder, and laying his head on his breast, cried for a while silently, whilst we stood unmoving. When he raised his head Van Helsing said to him:—

"And now, my child, you may kiss her. Kiss her dead lips if you will, as she would have you to, if for her to choose. For she is not a grinning devil now—not any more a foul Thing for all eternity.[30] No longer she is the devil's Un-Dead. She is God's true dead, whose soul is with Him!"

Arthur bent and kissed her, and then we sent him and Quincey out of the tomb; the Professor and I sawed the top off the stake, leaving the point of it in the body. Then we cut off the head and filled the mouth with garlic. We soldered up the leaden coffin, screwed on the coffin-lid, and gathering up our belongings, came away.[31] When the Professor locked the door he gave the key to Arthur.[32]

Outside the air was sweet, the sun shone, and the birds sang, and it seemed as if all nature were tuned to a different pitch. There was gladness and mirth and peace everywhere, for we were at rest ourselves on one account, and we were glad, though it was with a tempered joy.

Before we moved away Van Helsing said:—

"Now, my friends, one step of our work is done, one the most harrowing to ourselves. But there remains a greater task: to find out the author of all this our sorrow and to stamp him out. I have clues which we can follow; but it is a long task and a difficult, and there is danger in it, and pain. Shall you not all help me? We have learned to believe, all of us—is it not so? And since so, do we not see our duty? Yes! And do we not promise to go on to the bitter end?"

Each in turn, we took his hands, and the promise was made. Then said the Professor as we moved off:—

"Two nights hence you shall meet with me and dine together at seven of the clock with friend John. I shall entreat two others, two that you know not as yet; and I shall be ready to all our work show and our plans unfold. Friend John, you come with me home, for I have much to consult about, and you can help me. To-night I leave for Amsterdam, but shall return to-morrow night. And then begins our great quest. But first I shall have much to say, so that you may know what is to do and to dread. Then our promise shall be made to each other anew; for there is a terrible task before us, and once our feet are on the ploughshare, we must not draw back."[33]

33 Van Helsing paraphrases Luke 9:62, where Jesus admonishes a follower who wishes to return home before accompanying Jesus: "No man, having put his hand to the plough, and looking back, is fit for the kingdom of God."

Chapter 17

Sir Francis Varney.
Varney, the Vampyre; or, The Feast of Blood (1847)

Dr. Seward's Diary

—continued.

WHEN WE ARRIVED at the Berkeley Hotel, Van Helsing found a telegram waiting for him:—

"Am coming up by train. Jonathan at Whitby. Important news.—Mina Harker."

The Professor was delighted. "Ah, that wonderful Madam Mina," he said, "pearl among women! She arrive, but I cannot stay. She must go to your house, friend John. You must meet her at the station. Telegraph her *en route*, so that she may be prepared."

When the wire was dispatched he had a cup of tea; over it he told me of a diary kept by Jonathan Harker when abroad, and gave me a typewritten copy of it, as also of Mrs. Harker's diary at Whitby. "Take these," he said, "and study them well. When I have returned you will be master of all the facts, and we can then better enter on our inquisition. Keep them safe, for there is in them much of treasure. You will need all your faith, even you who have had such an experience as that of to-day. What is here told," he laid his hand heavily and gravely on the packet of papers as he spoke, "may be the beginning of the end to you and me and many another; or it may sound the knell of the Un-Dead who walk the earth. Read all, I pray you, with the open mind; and if you can add in any way to the story here told do so, for it is all-important. You have kept diary of all these so strange things; is it not so? Yes! Then we shall go through all these together when we meet." He then made ready for his departure, and shortly after drove off to Liverpool Street. I took my way to Paddington, where I arrived about fifteen minutes before the train came in.

The crowd melted away, after the bustling fashion common to arrival platforms; and I was beginning to feel uneasy, lest I might miss my guest, when a sweet-faced, dainty-looking girl stepped up to me, and, after a quick glance, said: "Dr. Seward, is it not?"

"And you are Mrs. Harker!" I answered at once; whereupon she held out her hand.

"I knew you from the description of poor dear Lucy; but—" She stopped suddenly, and a quick blush overspread her face.[1]

The blush that rose to my own cheeks somehow set us both at ease, for it was a tacit answer to her own. I got her luggage, which included a typewriter, and we took the Underground to Fenchurch Street,[2] after I had sent a wire to my housekeeper to have a sitting-room and a bedroom prepared at once for Mrs. Harker.

In due time we arrived. She knew, of course, that the place was a lunatic asylum, but I could see that she was unable to repress a slight shudder when we entered.[3]

She told me that, if she might, she would come presently to my study, as she had much to say. So here I am finishing my entry in my phonograph diary whilst I await her. As yet I have not had the chance of looking at the papers which Van Helsing left with me, though they lie open before me. I must get her interested in something, so that I may have an opportunity of reading them. She does not know how precious time is, or what a task we have in hand. I must be careful not to frighten her. Here she is!

MINA HARKER'S JOURNAL.

29 September.—After I had tidied myself, I went down to Dr. Seward's study. At the door I paused a moment, for I thought I heard him talking with some one. As, however, he had pressed me to be quick, I knocked at the door, and on his calling out, "Come in," I entered.

[1] The sentence continues in the Manuscript with the following, omitted from the published text: "as if a sudden thought." It is unclear why these two are blushing—perhaps Mina is reminded that Seward secretly proposed to Lucy, that she knows it, and that he doesn't know that she knows it.

[2] See chapter 2, note 51. From here, they would take the train to Purfleet. The Underground Railways, more properly the Metropolitan and Metropolitan District Railways, irrevocably changed the fabric of everyday life in London, carrying over 110 million passengers per year by 1896. First opened in 1863, the trains for the most part ran through tunnels or cuttings between high walls. London was the first city in the world to build underground railways.

[3] Appearing in the Manuscript but not in the published narrative is this sentence: "I wonder why, perhaps her diary will explain." Indeed, Mina's journal does not explain, and we are left wondering at her prescience.

To my intense surprise, there was no one with him. He was quite alone, and on the table opposite him was what I knew at once from the description to be a phonograph. I had never seen one, and was much interested.

"I hope I did not keep you waiting," I said; "but I stayed at the door as I heard you talking, and thought there was some one with you."

"Oh," he replied with a smile, "I was only entering my diary."

"Your diary?" I asked him in surprise.

"Yes," he answered. "I keep it in this." As he spoke he laid his hand on the phonograph. I felt quite excited over it, and blurted out:—

"Why, this beats even shorthand! May I hear it say something?"

"Certainly," he replied with alacrity, and stood up to put it in train for speaking. Then he paused, and a troubled look overspread his face.

"The fact is," he began awkwardly, "I only keep my diary in it; and as it is entirely—almost entirely—about my cases, it may be awkward—that is, I mean—" He stopped, and I tried to help him out of his embarrassment:—

"You helped to attend dear Lucy at the end. Let me hear how she died; for all that I can know of her, I shall be very grateful. She was very, very dear to me."

To my surprise, he answered, with a horrorstruck look in his face:—

"Tell you of her death? Not for the wide world!"

"Why not?" I asked, for some grave, terrible feeling was coming over me. Again he paused, and I could see that he was trying to invent an excuse. At length he stammered out:—

"You see, I do not know how to pick out any particular part of the diary." Even while he was speaking an idea dawned upon him, and he said with unconscious simplicity, in a different voice, and with the naïveté of a child: "That's quite true, upon my honour. Honest Indian!" I could not but smile, at which he grimaced. "I gave myself away that time!" he said. "But do you know that, although I have kept the diary for months past, it never once struck me how I was going to find any particular part of it in case I wanted to look it up?" By this time my mind was made up that the diary of a doctor who attended Lucy might have something to add to the sum of our knowledge of that terrible Being, and I said boldly:—

"Then, Dr. Seward, you had better let me copy it out for you on my typewriter." He grew to a positively deathly pallor as he said:—

"No! no! no! For all the world. I wouldn't let you know that terrible story!"

Then it was terrible; my intuition was right! For a moment I thought, and as my eyes ranged the room, unconsciously looking for something or some opportunity to aid me, they lit on a great batch of typewriting on the table. His eyes caught the look in mine, and, without his thinking, followed their direction. As they saw the parcel he realised my meaning.

"You do not know me," I said. "When you have read those papers—my own diary and my husband's also, which I have typed—you will know me better. I have not faltered in giving every thought of my own heart in this cause; but, of course, you do not know me—yet; and I must not expect you to trust me so far."

He is certainly a man of noble nature; poor dear Lucy was right about him. He stood up and opened a large drawer, in which were arranged in order a number of hollow cylinders of metal covered with dark wax, and said:—

"You are quite right. I did not trust you because I did not know you. But I know you now; and let me say that I should have known you long ago. I know that Lucy told you of me; she told me of you too. May I make the only atonement in my power? Take the cylinders and hear them—the first half-dozen of them are personal to me, and they will not horrify you; then you will know me better. Dinner will by then be ready. In the meantime I shall read over some of these documents, and shall be better able to understand certain things." He carried the phonograph himself up to my sitting-room and adjusted it for me. Now I shall learn something pleasant, I am sure; for it will tell me the other side of a true love episode of which I know one side already. . . .

4 The cover-up begins.

5 The day of the first transfusion.

DR. SEWARD'S DIARY.

29 September.—I was so absorbed in that wonderful diary of
Jonathan Harker and that other of his wife that I let time run
on without thinking. Mrs. Harker was not down when the maid
came running to announce dinner, so I said: "She is possibly
tired; let dinner wait an hour;" and I went on with my work. I
had just finished Mrs. Harker's diary, when she came in. She
looked sweetly pretty, but very sad, and her eyes were flushed
with crying. This somehow moved me much. Of late I have
had cause for tears, God knows! but the relief of them was
denied me; and now the sight of those sweet eyes, brightened
with recent tears, went straight to my heart. So I said as gently
as I could:—

"I greatly fear I have distressed you."

"Oh, no, not distressed me," she replied, "but I have been
more touched than I can say by your grief. That is a wonderful
machine, but it is cruelly true. It told me, in its very tones,
the anguish of your heart. It was like a soul crying out to
Almighty God. No one must hear them spoken ever again!⁴
See, I have tried to be useful. I have copied out the words on
my typewriter, and none other need now hear your heart beat,
as I did."

"No one need ever know, shall ever know," I said in a low
voice. She laid her hand on mine and said very gravely:—

"Ah, but they must!"

"Must! But why?" I asked.

"Because it is a part of the terrible story, a part of poor dear
Lucy's death and all that led to it; because in the struggle which
we have before us to rid the earth of this terrible monster we
must have all the knowledge and all the help which we can get.
I think that the cylinders which you gave me contained more
than you intended me to know; but I can see that there are in
your record many lights to this dark mystery. You will let me
help, will you not? I know all up to a certain point; and I see
already, though your diary only took me to 7 September,⁵ how
poor Lucy was beset, and how her terrible doom was being
wrought out. Jonathan and I have been working day and night
since Professor Van Helsing saw us. He is gone to Whitby to

320

get more information, and he will be here to-morrow to help us. We need have no secrets amongst us; working together and with absolute trust, we can surely be stronger than if some of us were in the dark." She looked at me so appealingly, and at the same time manifested such courage and resolution in her bearing, that I gave in at once to her wishes. "You shall," I said, "do as you like in the matter. God forgive me if I do wrong! There are terrible things yet to learn of; but if you have so far travelled on the road to poor Lucy's death, you will not be content, I know, to remain in the dark. Nay, the end—the very end—may give you a gleam of peace. Come, there is dinner. We must keep one another strong for what is before us; we have a cruel and dreadful task. When you have eaten you shall learn the rest, and I shall answer any questions you ask—if there be anything which you do not understand, though it was apparent to us who were present."

MINA HARKER'S JOURNAL.

29 September.—After dinner I came with Dr. Seward to his study. He brought back the phonograph from my room, and I took my typewriter. He placed me in a comfortable chair, and arranged the phonograph so that I could touch it without getting up and showed me how to stop it in case I should want to pause. Then he very thoughtfully took a chair, with his back to me, so that I might be as free as possible, and began to read. I put the forked metal to my ears[6] and listened.

When the terrible story of Lucy's death, and—and all that followed, was done, I lay back in my chair powerless. Fortunately I am not of a fainting disposition. When Dr. Seward saw me he jumped up with a horrified exclamation, and hurriedly taking a case-bottle from the cupboard, gave me some brandy, which in a few minutes somewhat restored me. My brain was all in a whirl, and only that there came through all the multitude of horrors, the holy ray of light that my dear dear Lucy was at last at peace, I do not think I could have borne it without making a scene. It is all so wild, and mysterious, and strange that if I had not known Jonathan's experience in Transylvania I could not have believed. As it was, I didn't know what to believe, and so

6 A primitive headset (see images following chapter 5, note 40).

Case-bottle.
Harrods catalogue, 1895

7 Manifold paper, that is: a set of thin sheets of paper interleaved with carbon paper, invented in the early nineteenth century but rising to popularity only with the advent of the typewriter.

8 This and the two preceding sentences do not appear in the Abridged Text. Perhaps Mina changed her judgement after considering Seward's treatment of Renfield.

9 This odd remark—a desire to keep herself quiet—is not included in Mina's journal as quoted in the Abridged Text.

10 Another physiognomist—see chapter 2, note 22.

got out of my difficulty by attending to something else. I took the cover off my typewriter, and said to Dr. Seward:—

"Let me write this all out now. We must be ready for Dr. Van Helsing when he comes. I have sent a telegram to Jonathan to come on here when he arrives in London from Whitby. In this matter dates are everything, and I think that if we get all of our material ready, and have every item put in chronological order, we shall have done much. You tell me that Lord Godalming and Mr. Morris are coming too. Let us be able to tell them when they come." He accordingly set the phonograph at a slow pace, and I began to typewrite from the beginning of the seventh cylinder. I used manifold,[7] and so took three copies of the diary, just as I had done with all the rest. It was late when I got through, but Dr. Seward went about his work of going his round of the patients; when he had finished he came back and sat near me, reading, so that I did not feel too lonely whilst I worked. How good and thoughtful he is; the world seems full of good men—even if there *are* monsters in it.[8] Before I left him I remembered what Jonathan put in his diary of the Professor's perturbation at reading something in an evening paper at the station at Exeter; so, seeing that Dr. Seward keeps his newspapers, I borrowed the files of "The Westminster Gazette" and "The Pall Mall Gazette," and took them to my room. I remember how much the "Dailygraph" and "The Whitby Gazette," of which I had made cuttings, helped us to understand the terrible events at Whitby when Count Dracula landed, so I shall look through the evening papers since then, and perhaps I shall get some new light. I am not sleepy, and the work will help to keep me quiet.[9]

DR. SEWARD'S DIARY.

30 September.—Mr. Harker arrived at nine o'clock. He had got his wife's wire just before starting. He is uncommonly clever, if one can judge from his face,[10] and full of energy. If his journal be true—and judging by one's own wonderful experiences, it must be—he is also a man of great nerve. That going down to the vault a second time was a remarkable piece of daring. After reading his account of it I was prepared to meet a good specimen of manhood, but hardly the quiet, business-like gentleman who came here to-day.

Later.—After lunch Harker and his wife went back to their own room, and as I passed a while ago I heard the click of the typewriter. They are hard at it. Mrs. Harker says that they are knitting together in chronological order every scrap of evidence they have. Harker has got the letters between the consignee of the boxes at Whitby and the carriers in London who took charge of them. He is now reading his wife's typescript of my diary. I wonder what they make out of it. Here he is. . . .

Strange that it never struck me that the very next house might be the Count's hiding-place![11] Goodness knows that we had enough clues from the conduct of the patient Renfield! The bundle of letters relating to the purchase of the house were with the typescript. Oh, if we had only had them earlier we might have saved poor Lucy! Stop; that way madness lies![12] Harker has gone back, and is again collating his material. He says that by dinner-time they will be able to show a whole connected narrative. He thinks that in the meantime I should see Renfield,[13] as hitherto he has been a sort of index to the coming and going of the Count. I hardly see this yet, but when I get at the dates I suppose I shall. What a good thing that Mrs. Harker put my cylinders into type! We never could have found the dates otherwise. . . .

I found Renfield sitting placidly in his room with his hands folded, smiling benignly. At the moment he seemed as sane as any one I ever saw. I sat down and talked with him on a lot of subjects, all of which he treated naturally. He then, of his own accord, spoke of going home, a subject he has never mentioned to my knowledge during his sojourn here. In fact, he spoke quite confidently of getting his discharge at once. I believe that, had I not had the chat with Harker and read the letters and the dates of his outbursts, I should have been prepared to sign for him after a brief time of observation. As it is, I am darkly suspicious. All those outbreaks were in some way linked with the proximity of the Count. What then does this absolute content mean? Can it be that his instinct is satisfied as to the vampire's ultimate triumph? Stay; he is himself zoöphagous,

11 The coincidence of Carfax being next door to Seward's asylum is impossible to credit. With thousands of suitable residences for Dracula in the vicinity of London, is it credible that mere chance causes Peter Hawkins and Harker to select a property next door to the physician-friend of Lucy Westenra? In fact, it seems much more likely that as a result of the selection of Carfax, Harker unwittingly doomed Lucy and imperiled Mina. The only logical explanation is that after selecting Carfax, Dracula telepathically explored the neighbourhood, discovered Seward and through Seward the very suitable victim Lucy Westenra (after all, Seward was obsessed with Lucy), made telepathic connection with Lucy, determining that she would be in Whitby, and based on this investigation, determined to land at Whitby—an otherwise unlikely port—where he could meet up with Lucy. Why Van Helsing never comes to this inescapable conclusion is mystifying, unless, of course, he did so conclude but the extent of Dracula's powers was intentionally deemphasised in the narrative.

12 Seward uses the popular phrase from Shakespeare's *King Lear* (act 3, scene 4). These sentences of self-remonstration do not appear in the Abridged Text.

13 Here, and in numerous other places in the Manuscript, Renfield is referred to derogatively by Seward (and others) as "the Flyman." However, it appears incorrect to say that the name Renfield was an afterthought as an alias for the patient, for there are also many places where the name appears typed without correction or change in the Manuscript.

14 Again, the name is inserted in Stoker's hand in the Mansucript, along with the number of cases of earth.

15 Another lawyer casual with his client's confidential information.

16 The preceding references to the Billingtons' hospitality do not appear in the Abridged Text. Perhaps the Billingtons were belatedly embarrassed by their breach of ethics in disclosing their client's affairs.

17 The Abridged Text omits this sentence.

18 The Abridged Text adds the following information: "They had all something to say of the strange entry of the ship, which is already taking its place in local tradition; but no one could add to the simple description, 'Fifty cases of common earth.' I then saw the station-master . . . "

and in his wild ravings outside the chapel door of the deserted house he always spoke of "master." This all seems confirmation of our idea. However, after a while I came away; my friend is just a little too sane at present to make it safe to probe him too deep with questions. He might begin to think, and then—! So I came away. I mistrust these quiet moods of his; so I have given the attendant a hint to look closely after him, and to have a strait-waistcoat ready in case of need.

JONATHAN HARKER'S JOURNAL.

29 September, in train to London.—When I received Mr. Billington's[14] courteous message that he would give me any information in his power, I thought it best to go down to Whitby and make, on the spot, such inquiries as I wanted.[15] It was now my object to trace that horrid cargo of the Count's to its place in London. Later, we may be able to deal with it. Billington Junior, a nice lad, met me at the station, and brought me to his father's house, where they had decided that I must stay the night. They are hospitable, with true Yorkshire hospitality: give a guest everything, and leave him free to do as he likes. They all knew that I was busy, and that my stay was short, and[16] Mr. Billington had ready in his office all the papers concerning the consignment of boxes. It gave me almost a turn to see again one of the letters which I had seen on the Count's table before I knew of his diabolical plans. Everything had been carefully thought out, and done systematically and with precision. He seemed to have been prepared for every obstacle which might be placed by accident in the way of his intentions being carried out. To use an Americanism, he had "taken no chances," and the absolute accuracy with which his instructions were fulfilled, was simply the logical result of his care.[17] I saw the invoice, and took note of it: "Fifty cases of common earth, to be used for experimental purposes." Also the copy of letter to Carter, Paterson, and their reply; of both of these I got copies. This was all the information Mr. Billington could give me, so I went down to the port and saw the coastguards, the Customs officers and the harbour-master.[18] They had all something to say of the strange entry of the ship, which is already taking its place in local tradition; but no one could add to the simple description "Fifty cases of common earth." I then saw the station-master, who kindly put me in communication with the men who had actually received the boxes. Their tally was exact with the list, and they had nothing to add except that the boxes were "main and mortal heavy," and that shifting them was dry work.[19] One of them added that it was hard lines that there wasn't any gentleman "such-like as like yourself, squire," to show some sort of appreciation of their efforts in a liquid form; another put in a rider that the thirst then generated was such that even the time which had elapsed had not completely allayed it. Needless to add, I took care before leaving to lift, for ever and adequately, this source of reproach.

30 September.—The station-master was good enough to give me a line to his old companion the station-master at King's Cross, so that when I arrived there in the morning I was able to ask him about the arrival of the boxes. He, too, put me at once in communication with the proper officials, and I saw that their tally was correct with the original invoice. The opportunities of acquiring an abnormal thirst had been here limited; a noble use of them had, however, been made, and again I was compelled to deal with the result in an *ex post facto* manner.

From thence I went on to Carter, Paterson's central office, where I met with the utmost courtesy. They looked up the transaction in their day-book and letter-book, and at once telephoned to their King's Cross office for more details.[20] By good fortune, the men who did the teaming[21] were waiting for work, and the official at once sent them over, sending also by one of them the way-bill and all the papers connected with the delivery of the boxes at Carfax. Here again I found the tally agreeing exactly; the carriers' men were able to supplement the paucity of the written words with a few details. These were, I shortly found, connected almost solely with the dusty nature of the job, and of the consequent thirst engendered in the operators. On my affording an opportunity, through the medium of the currency of the realm, of the allaying, at a late period, this beneficial evil, one of the men remarked:—

19 Harker may have been later embarrassed by his heavy-handed bribery, for the balance of the paragraph does not appear in the Abridged Text. Similarly, the references to further bribery in the following two paragraphs are absent.

20 Alexander Graham Bell first demonstrated the telephone in 1876 with his famous statement "Watson—come here—I want you," and in 1889 Almon Strowger patented the direct-dial telephone. London's communications were handled mainly by the National Telephone Co., which maintained numerous call-rooms throughout London and its districts that were open to the public at the rate of 3d. for each three minutes' conversation. Numerous businesses relied on the telephone, and the 1885 United Telephone Company's Professional and Trades Classified Directory listed thousands of subscribers (Carter, Paterson's telephone number was 6660). Kathryn Marocchino, in her essay "Structural Complexity in Bram Stoker's *Dracula*," erroneously sees the use of the telephone as confirmation of the 1893 date often asserted for the events described in the Harker Papers (see appendix 2, "The Dating of *Dracula*"), but the telephone's earlier acceptance is evident.

The Abridged Text does not refer to the King's Cross office.

21 The teamsters, that is.

22 The entire first paragraph of this journal entry does not appear in the Abridged Text. Perhaps Mina later worried that in light of subsequent events, Jonathan might misconstrue her honest expression of pity.

23 Wolf (*The Essential Dracula*) finds Mina's "pity" surprising, given what she already knows about Dracula's predation, but suggests that she is already coming under Dracula's influence.

"That 'ere 'ouse, guv'nor, is the rummiest I ever was in. Blyme! but it ain't been touched sence a hundred years. There was dust that thick in the place that you might have slep' on it without 'urtin' of yer bones; an' the place was that neglected that yer might 'ave smelled ole Jerusalem in it. But the ole chapel—that took the cike, that did! Me and my mate, we thort we wouldn't never git out quick enough. Lor', I wouldn't take less nor a quid a moment to stay there arter dark."

Having been in the house, I could well believe him; but if he knew what I know, he would, I think, have raised his terms.

Of one thing I am now satisfied: that *all* the boxes which arrived at Whitby from Varna in the *Demeter* were safely deposited in the old chapel at Carfax. There should be fifty of them there, unless any have since been removed—as from Dr. Seward's diary I fear.

I shall try to see the carter who took away the boxes from Carfax when Renfield attacked them. By following up this clue we may learn a good deal.

Later.—Mina and I have worked all day, and we have put all the papers into order.

MINA HARKER'S JOURNAL.

30 September.[22]—I am so glad that I hardly know how to contain myself. It is, I suppose, the reaction from the haunting fear which I have had: that this terrible affair and the reopening of his old wound might act detrimentally on Jonathan. I saw him leave for Whitby with as brave a face as I could, but I was sick with apprehension. The effort has, however, done him good. He was never so resolute, never so strong, never so full of volcanic energy, as at present. It is just as that dear, good Professor Van Helsing said: he is true grit, and he improves under strain that would kill a weaker nature. He came back full of life and hope and determination; we have got everything in order for to-night. I feel myself quite wild with excitement. I suppose one ought to pity any thing so hunted as is the Count. That is just it: this Thing is not human—not even beast. To read Dr. Seward's account of poor Lucy's death, and what followed, is enough to dry up the springs of pity in one's heart.[23]

Later.—Lord Godalming and Mr. Morris arrived earlier than we expected. Dr. Seward was out on business, and had taken Jonathan with him, so I had to see them. It was to me a painful meeting, for it brought back all poor dear Lucy's hopes of only a few months ago. Of course they had heard Lucy speak of me, and it seemed that Dr. Van Helsing, too, has been quite "blowing my trumpet," as Mr. Morris expressed it. Poor fellows, neither of them is aware that I know all about the proposals they made to Lucy. They did not quite know what to say or do, as they were ignorant of the amount of my knowledge; so they had to keep on neutral subjects. However, I thought the matter over, and came to the conclusion that the best thing I could do would be to post them in affairs right up to date. I knew from Dr. Seward's diary that they had been at Lucy's death—her real death—and that I need not fear to betray any secret before the time. So I told them, as well as I could, that I had read all the papers and diaries, and that my husband and I, having typewritten them,[24] had just finished putting them in order. I gave them each a copy to read in the library. When Lord Godalming got his and turned it over—it does make a pretty good pile—he said:—

"Did you write all this, Mrs. Harker?"

I nodded, and he went on:—

"I don't quite see the drift of it; but you people are all so good and kind, and have been working so earnestly and so energetically, that all I can do is to accept your ideas blindfold and try to help you. I have had one lesson already in accepting facts that should make a man humble to the last hour of his life. Besides, I know you loved my poor Lucy—" Here he turned away and covered his face with his hands. I could hear the tears in his voice. Mr. Morris, with instinctive delicacy, just laid a hand for a moment on his shoulder, and then walked quietly out of the room. I suppose there is something in woman's nature that makes a man free to break down before her and express his feelings on the tender or emotional side without feeling it derogatory to his manhood; for when Lord Godalming found himself alone with me he sat down on the sofa and gave way utterly and openly. I sat down beside him and took his hand. I hope he didn't think it forward of me, and that if he ever thinks

24 Does Mina really mean that Harker types too? This would be an unusual skill in a Victorian male, especially for a former solicitor's clerk, who would have taken pride in his copperplate hand. Certainly many men were capable typewritists; Mark Twain, for example, was an early adopter, and a typewritten letter from Twain dated 1874 has been preserved. In the United States in 1880, only 40 percent of the stenographer-typists were women; by 1890, this had risen to over 60 percent. Perhaps this is just a carelessly phrased remark.

25 The Abridged Text does not include this musing or the following two sentences.

26 The balance of this paragraph and the next do not appear in the Abridged Text.

27 This and the following sentence do not appear in the Abridged Text.

of it afterwards he never will have such a thought.[25] There I wrong him; I *know* he never will—he is too true a gentleman. I said to him, for I could see that his heart was breaking:—

"I loved dear Lucy, and I know what she was to you, and what you were to her. She and I were like sisters; and now she is gone, will you not let me be like a sister to you in your trouble? I know what sorrows you have had, though I cannot measure the depth of them. If sympathy and pity can help in your affliction, won't you let me be of some little service—for Lucy's sake?"

In an instant the poor dear fellow was overwhelmed with grief. It seemed to me that all he had of late been suffering in silence found a vent at once.[26] He grew quite hysterical, and raising his open hands, beat his palms together in a perfect agony of grief. He stood up and then sat down again, and the tears rained down his cheeks. I felt an infinite pity for him, and opened my arms unthinkingly. With a sob he laid his head on my shoulder, and cried like a wearied child, whilst he shook with emotion.

We women have something of the mother in us that makes us rise above smaller matters when the mother-spirit is invoked; I felt this big sorrowing man's head resting on me, as though it were that of the baby that some day may lie on my bosom, and I stroked his hair as though he were my own child. I never thought at the time how strange it all was.

After a little bit his sobs ceased, and he raised himself with an apology, though he made no disguise of his emotion. He told me that for days and nights past—weary days and sleepless nights—he had been unable to speak with any one, as a man must speak in his time of sorrow. There was no woman whose sympathy could be given to him, or with whom, owing to the terrible circumstances with which his sorrow was surrounded, he could speak freely. "I know now how I suffered," he said, as he dried his eyes, "but I do not know even yet—and none other can ever know—how much your sweet sympathy has been to me to-day.[27] I shall know better in time; and believe me that, though I am not ungrateful now, my gratitude will grow with my understanding. You will let me be like a brother, will you not, for all our lives—for dear Lucy's sake?"

"For dear Lucy's sake," I said as we clasped hands. "Ay, and for your own sake," he added, "for if a man's esteem and gratitude are ever worth the winning, you have won mine to-day. If ever the future should bring to you a time when you need a man's help, believe me, you will not call in vain. God grant that no such time may ever come to you to break the sunshine of your life; but if it should ever come, promise me that you will let me know." He was so earnest, and his sorrow was so fresh, that I felt it would comfort him, so I said:—

"I promise."[28]

As I came along the corridor I saw Mr. Morris looking out of a window. He turned as he heard my footsteps. "How is Art?" he said. Then noticing my red eyes, he went on: "Ah, I see you have been comforting him. Poor old fellow! he needs it. No one but a woman can help a man when he is in trouble of the heart; and he had no one to comfort him."

He bore his own trouble so bravely that my heart bled for him. I saw the manuscript[29] in his hand, and I knew that when he read it he would realise how much I knew; so I said to him:—

"I wish I could comfort all who suffer from the heart. Will you let me be your friend, and will you come to me for comfort if you need it? You will know, later on, why I speak." He saw that I was in earnest, and stooping, took my hand, and raising it to his lips, kissed it. It seemed but poor comfort to so brave and unselfish a soul, and impulsively I bent over and kissed him. The tears rose in his eyes, and there was a momentary choking in his throat; he said quite calmly:—

"Little girl, you will never regret that true-hearted kindness, so long as ever you live!" Then he went into the study to his friend.

"Little girl!"—the very words he had used to Lucy, and oh, but he proved himself a friend!

28 The Manuscript continues with the following, which does not appear in the published narrative: "So I came to my own room to copy out on the typewriter the papers that Lord Godalming gave me." The published narrative makes no mention of any papers from Holmwood, and they may have contained information that Stoker was unable or unwilling to disguise.

29 Capitalized in the Manuscript. This is the only hint that the parties contemporaneously understood the significance of the Harker Papers.

Chapter 18

DR. SEWARD'S DIARY.

1 "Carters men" not "carriers' men" in the Manuscript. This was evidently an editorial correction. Of course, "Carter's men" or "carters' men" would be perfectly correct to refer to the employees of Carter, Paterson.

2 A remarkable comment considering that Seward lives in an insane asylum! McNally and Florescu (*The Essential Dracula*) inexplicably identify this as a house on the Chatham Road (not Chatham Street, although plainly identified earlier by Seward—see chapter 5, note 11), near the London County Insane Asylum, where they theorise that Seward was employed. Chatham Street and Chatham Road are not far apart in Battersea; however, the nearby asylum was then the Middlesex County Lunatic Asylum (formerly the Hansell Asylum), not yet known as the London County Insane Asylum. In making this identification, McNally and Florescu somehow ignore the fact that Seward's asylum was located in Purfleet, miles from Battersea.

The sentiment does not appear in the Abridged Text.

3 The published narrative differs from the Manuscript, which reads: "the man you call the Flyman." This is evidence of how publicly Seward used the term, although Mina had read Seward's journals.

30 September.—I got home at five o'clock, and found that Godalming and Morris had not only arrived, but had already studied the transcript of the various diaries and letters which Harker and his wonderful wife had made and arranged. Harker had not yet returned from his visit to the carriers' men,[1] of whom Dr. Hennessey had written to me. Mrs. Harker gave us a cup of tea, and I can honestly say that, for the first time since I have lived in it, this old house seemed like *home*.[2] When we had finished, Mrs. Harker said:—

"Dr. Seward, may I ask a favour? I want to see your patient, Mr. Renfield.[3] Do let me see him. What you have said of him in your diary interests me so much!" She looked so appealing and so pretty that I could not refuse her, and there was no possible reason why I should; so I took her with me.[4] When I went into the room, I told the man that a lady would like to see him; to which he simply answered: "Why?"

"She is going through the house, and wants to see every one in it," I answered. "Oh, very well," he said; "let her come in, by all means; but just wait a minute till I tidy up the place." His method of tidying was peculiar: he simply swallowed all the flies and spiders in the boxes before I could stop him. It was quite evident that he feared, or was jealous of, some interference. When he had got through his disgusting task, he said cheerfully: "Let the lady come in," and sat down

The vampyre disturbed in his coffin.
Varney, the Vampyre; or, The Feast of Blood (1847)

4 The Notes indicate that it is Lucy who visits Renfield, not Mina. However, if Lucy in fact died on the date recorded in the narrative, this is impossible. It is possible that Lucy's meeting with Renfield was excised from the narrative.

on the edge of his bed with his head down, but with his eyelids raised so that he could see her as she entered. For a moment I thought that he might have some homicidal intent; I remembered how quiet he had been just before he attacked me in my own study, and I took care to stand where I could seize him at once if he attempted to make a spring at her. She came into the room with an easy gracefulness which would at once command the respect of any lunatic—for easiness is one of the qualities mad people most respect. She walked over to him, smiling pleasantly, and held out her hand.

"Good-evening, Mr. Renfield," said she. "You see, I know you, for Dr. Seward has told me of you." He made no immediate reply, but eyed her all over intently with a set frown on his face.

5 How *did* Renfield know? He never answers.

6 A Latin legal phrase, meaning "there is no reason."

7 Another Latin legal phrase: "ignorance of the charge."

8 This observation does not appear in the Abridged Text.

This look gave way to one of wonder, which merged in doubt; then, to my intense astonishment, he said:—

"You're not the girl the doctor wanted to marry, are you? You can't be, you know, for she's dead." Mrs. Harker smiled sweetly as she replied:—

"Oh no! I have a husband of my own, to whom I was married before I ever saw Dr. Seward, or he me. I am Mrs. Harker."

"Then what are you doing here?"

"My husband and I are staying on a visit with Dr. Seward."

"Then don't stay."

"But why not?" I thought that this style of conversation might not be pleasant to Mrs. Harker, any more than it was to me, so I joined in:—

"How did you know I wanted to marry any one?" His reply was simply contemptuous, given in a pause in which he turned his eyes from Mrs. Harker to me, instantly turning them back again:—

"What an asinine question!"**5**

"I don't see that at all, Mr. Renfield," said Mrs. Harker, at once championing me. He replied to her with as much courtesy and respect as he had shown contempt to me:—

"You will, of course, understand, Mrs. Harker, that when a man is so loved and honoured as our host is, everything regarding him is of interest in our little community. Dr. Seward is loved not only by his household and his friends, but even by his patients, who, being some of them hardly in mental equilibrium, are apt to distort causes and effects. Since I myself have been an inmate of a lunatic asylum, I cannot but notice that the sophistic tendencies of some of its inmates lean towards the errors of *non causæ***6** and *ignoratio elenchi*."**7** I positively opened my eyes at this new development. Here was my own pet lunatic—the most pronounced of his type that I had ever met with—talking elemental philosophy, and with the manner of a polished gentleman. I wonder if it was Mrs. Harker's presence which had touched some chord in his memory. If this new phase was spontaneous, or in any way due to her unconscious influence, she must have some rare gift or power.**8**

We continued to talk for some time; and, seeing that he

was seemingly quite reasonable, she ventured, looking at me questioningly as she began, to lead him to his favourite topic. I was again astonished, for he addressed himself to the question with the impartiality of the completest sanity; he even took himself as an example when he mentioned certain things.

"Why, I myself am an instance of a man who had a strange belief. Indeed, it was no wonder that my friends were alarmed, and insisted on my being put under control.[9] I used to fancy that life was a positive and perpetual entity, and that by consuming a multitude of live things, no matter how low in the scale of creation, one might indefinitely prolong life. At times I held the belief so strongly that I actually tried to take human life. The doctor here will bear me out that on one occasion I tried to kill him for the purpose of strengthening my vital powers by the assimilation with my own body of life[10] through the medium of his blood—relying, of course, upon the Scriptural phrase, 'For the blood is the life.' Though, indeed, the vendor of a certain nostrum has vulgarised the truism to the very point of contempt.[11] Isn't that true, doctor?" I nodded assent, for I was so amazed that I hardly knew what to either think or say; it was hard to imagine that I had seen him eat up his spiders and flies not five minutes before. Looking at my watch, I saw that I should go to the station to meet Van Helsing, so I told Mrs. Harker that it was time to leave. She came at once, after saying pleasantly to Mr. Renfield: "Good-bye, and I hope I may see you often, under auspices pleasanter to yourself," to which, to my astonishment, he replied:—

"Good-bye, my dear. I pray God I may never see your sweet face again.[12] May He bless and keep you!"

When I went to the station to meet Van Helsing I left the boys behind me. Poor Art seemed more cheerful than he has been since Lucy first took ill, and Quincey is more like his own bright self than he has been for many a long day.[13]

Van Helsing stepped from the carriage with the eager nimbleness of a boy. He saw me at once, and rushed up to me, saying:—

"Ah, friend John, how goes all? Well? So! I have been busy,

9 Renfield here reveals that he is a voluntary patient. However, a voluntary patient should be able to discharge himself at any time, not need to beg for release.

10 Curiously, the balance of this sentence and the next do not appear in the Abridged Text. Perhaps "Seward" wished to deemphasise Renfield's intelligence.

11 Leatherdale (*Dracula Unearthed*) points out that "Clarke's World-Famed Blood Mixture," a Victorian nostrum, used the slogan "For the BLOOD is the LIFE."

12 In the 1931 *Dracula* films (see p. 559), Mina is the daughter of Dr. Seward. Renfield apparently has been smitten by her and begs Dr. Seward to remove her from the asylum.

13 The Abridged Text omits these signs of recovery.

Advertisement.
Illustrated Sporting and Dramatic News,
8 November 1890

14 Presumably Van Helsing means that Mina will wish to bear children. In light of the outcome of this adventure, perhaps Van Helsing's antiquated policy of protectionism may have been justified. However, the caution does not appear in the Abridged Text.

15 Seward is either duplicitous or weak-willed; only the day before, he agreed with Mina that she should share in all information obtained.

16 The previous two sentences of "philoso-phising" are absent from the Abridged Text.

for I come here to stay if need be. All affairs are settled with me, and I have much to tell. Madam Mina is with you? Yes. And her so fine husband? And Arthur and my friend Quincey, they are with you, too? Good!"

As I drove to the house I told him of what had passed, and of how my own diary had come to be of some use through Mrs. Harker's suggestion; at which the Professor interrupted me:—

"Ah, that wonderful Madam Mina! She has man's brain—a brain that a man should have were he much gifted—and woman's heart. The good God fashioned her for a purpose, believe me, when He made that so good combination. Friend John, up to now fortune has made that woman of help to us; after to-night she must not have to do with this so terrible affair. It is not good that she run a risk so great. We men are determined—nay, are we not pledged?—to destroy this monster; but it is no part for a woman. Even if she be not harmed, her heart may fail her in so much and so many horrors; and hereafter she may suffer—both in waking, from her nerves, and in sleep, from her dreams. And, besides, she is young woman and not so long married; there may be other things to think of some time, if not now.[14] You tell me she has wrote all, then she must consult with us; but to-morrow she say good-bye to this work, and we go alone." I agreed heartily with him,[15] and then I told him what we had found in his absence: that the house which Dracula had bought was the very next one to my own. He was amazed, and a great concern seemed to come on him. "Oh that we had known it before!" he said, "for then we might have reached him in time to save poor Lucy. However, 'the milk that is spilt cries not out afterwards,' as you say. We shall not think of that, but go on our way to the end."[16] Then he fell into a silence that lasted till we entered my own gateway. Before we went to prepare for dinner he said to Mrs. Harker:—

"I am told, Madam Mina, by my friend John that you and your husband have put up in exact order all things that have been, up to this moment."

"Not up to this moment, Professor," she said impulsively, "but up to this morning."

"But why not up to now? We have seen hitherto how good light all the little things have made. We have told our secrets, and yet no one who has told is the worse for it."

Mrs. Harker began to blush, and taking a paper from her pocket, she said:—

"Dr. Van Helsing, will you read this, and tell me if it must go in. It is my record of to-day. I too have seen the need of putting down at present everything, however trivial; but there is little in this except what is personal. Must it go in?" The Professor read it over gravely and handed it back, saying—

"It need not go in if you do not wish it; but I pray that it may. It can but make your husband love you the more, and all us, your friends, more honour you—as well as more esteem and love." She took it back with another blush and a bright smile.

And so now, up to this very hour, all the records we have are complete and in order. The Professor took away one copy to study after dinner, and before our meeting, which is fixed for nine o'clock. The rest of us have already read everything; so when we meet in the study we shall all be informed as to facts, and can arrange our plan of battle with this terrible and mysterious enemy.

MINA HARKER'S JOURNAL.[17]

30 September.—When we met in Dr. Seward's study two hours after dinner, which had been at six o'clock,[18] we unconsciously formed a sort of board or committee. Professor Van Helsing took the head of the table, to which Dr. Seward motioned him as he came into the room. He made me sit next to him on his right, and asked me to act as secretary; Jonathan sat next to me. Opposite us were Lord Godalming, Dr. Seward, and Mr. Morris—Lord Godalming being next the Professor, and Dr. Seward in the centre. The Professor said:—

"I may, I suppose, take it that we are all acquainted with the facts that are in these papers." We all expressed assent, and he went on:—

"Then it were, I think good that I tell you something of the kind of enemy with which we have to deal. I shall then make known to you something of the history of this man, which has

17 Headed in the Manuscript as "Campaign Diary kept by Mina Harker," a title used subsequently as well.

18 Note that the meeting started an hour earlier than originally intended; in the previous journal entry, Seward advises that the meeting is set for "nine o'clock."

19 Leatherdale (*Dracula Unearthed*) suggests that Van Helsing is being disingenuous here. In fact, he was never sceptical, always acting within the conviction that vampirism was underway. However, he made several grievous errors with respect to safeguarding Lucy, which ultimately proved fatal to her, and he seeks here to excuse them. Apparently Stoker also saw this comment as incriminating, for the Abridged Text omits this sentence.

20 This and the two preceding sentences also do not appear in the Abridged Text.

21 Well documented in the Harker Papers and in Anne Rice's Vampire Chronicles, but unrecorded elsewhere.

22 This portion of the sentence originally read in the Manuscript: "He is of cunning more than mortal for he have big brain which perish not but which at the first was greatest of his time. His cunning thus great always have grow with centuries."

23 We see no evidence of Dracula's "command" of the dead.

24 His command of the elements is never explicitly seen but may be inferred from certain odd weather.

25 We have seen that Dracula commanded Berserker, an inhabitant of the London Zoo.

26 Van Helsing offers as his proof of this phenomenon Lucy's ability to pass through the crack of her vault. However, this seems to have been an example of transformation of the vampire into a mist, not shrinkage.

27 The ability to make himself "unknown"—to become invisible, or perhaps to dematerialise—is recorded several times in Dracula's meetings with Lucy. It will be critical in the final confrontation of the hunters and the prey. See text accompanying chapter 27, note 51.

been ascertained for me. So we then can discuss how we shall act, and can take our measure according.

"There are such beings as vampires; some of us have evidence that they exist. Even had we not the proof of our own unhappy experience, the teachings and the records of the past give proof enough for sane peoples. I admit that at the first I was sceptic.[19] Were it not that through long years I have train myself to keep an open mind, I could not have believe until such time as that fact thunder on my ear. 'See! see! I prove; I prove.' Alas! Had I known at the first what now I know—nay, had I even guess at him—one so precious life had been spared to many of us who did love her. But that is gone; and we must so work, that other poor souls perish not, whilst we can save.[20] The *nosferatu* do not die like the bee when he sting once. He is only stronger; and being stronger, have yet more power to work evil. This vampire which is amongst us is of himself so strong in person as twenty men;[21] he is of cunning more than mortal, for his cunning be the growth of ages;[22] he have still the aids of necromancy, which is, as his etymology imply, the divination by the dead, and all the dead that he can come nigh to are for him at command;[23] he is brute, and more than brute: he is devil in callous, and the heart of him is not; he can, within limitations, appear at will when, and where, and in any of the forms that are to him; he can, within his range, direct the elements: the storm, the fog, the thunder;[24] he can command all the meaner things: the rat, and the owl, and the bat—the moth, and the fox, and the wolf;[25] he can grow and become small;[26] and he can at times vanish and come unknown.[27] How then are we to begin our strife to destroy him? How shall we find his where; and having found it, how can we destroy? My friends, this is much; it is a terrible task that we undertake, and there may be consequence to make the brave shudder. For if we fail in this our fight he must surely win: and then where end we? Life is nothings; I heed him not. But to fail here, is not mere life or death. It is that we become as him; that we henceforward become foul things of the night like him—without heart or conscience, preying on the bodies and the souls of those we love best.[28] To us for ever are the gates of heaven shut; for who shall open them to us again? We go on for all time abhorred by all; a blot on the face of God's sunshine; an arrow in the side of Him who died for man. But we are face to face with duty; and in such case must we shrink? For me, I say, no; but then I am old, and life, with his sunshine, his fair places, his song of birds, his music and his love, lie far behind. You others are young. Some have seen sorrow; but there are fair days yet in store. What say you?"

Whilst he was speaking Jonathan had taken my hand. I feared, oh so much, that the appalling nature of our danger was overcoming him when I saw his hand stretch out; but it was life to me to feel its touch—so strong, so self-reliant, so resolute. A brave man's hand can speak for itself; it does not even need a woman's love to hear its music.

When the Professor had done speaking my husband looked in my eyes, and I in his; there was no need for speaking between us.

"I answer for Mina and myself," he said.[29]

"Count me in, Professor," said Mr. Quincey Morris, laconically as usual.

"I am with you," said Lord Godalming, "for Lucy's sake, if for no other reason."

Dr. Seward simply nodded. The Professor stood up and, after laying his golden crucifix on the table, held out his hand on either side. I took his right hand, and Lord Godalming his left; Jonathan held my right with his left and stretched across to Mr. Morris. So as we all took hands our solemn compact was made. I felt my heart icy cold, but it did not even occur to me to draw back. We resumed our places, and Dr. Van Helsing went on with a sort of cheerfulness which showed that the serious work had begun. It was to be taken as gravely, and in as businesslike a way, as any other transaction of life:—

"Well, you know what we have to contend against; but we, too, are not without strength. We have on our side power of combination—a power denied to the vampire kind; we have sources of science; we are free to act and think; and the hours of the day and the night are ours equally.[30] In fact, so far as

28 It is a common folkloric belief that vampires are drawn to attack first their intimate family. In contrast, in the Anne Rice universe, many of the vampires choose to prey only on the evildoers of the world. See "Dracula's Family Tree" in Part II for further discussion.

29 Jonathan—who, despite his assurances to Mina, repeatedly demonstrates himself to be a typical Victorian male with respect to the proper rôle of women—quickly succumbs to Van Helsing's commands that Mina be excluded from the councils of war.

30 A misconception of Van Helsing's. As has been seen repeatedly, Dracula is active during the daylight hours. Perhaps lesser vampires are affected differently by daylight. The powerful vampire Lestat, in Anne Rice's chronicles, is able to withstand a flight directly towards the sun (in the 1992 *Tale of the Body Thief*). See "Dracula's Family Tree" in Part II for a general discussion of the effect of sunlight on vampires.

31 In the Abridged Text, these two sentences are shortened into one: "These do not the first appear much, when the matter is one of life and death, yet we must be satisfied."

32 "Chersonese" (correct in the Manuscript and corrected in later editions) is Greek for a peninsula. While the name is usually applied to the peninsula of Greece west of the Hellespont, "Golden Chersonese" is the name applied to the Malay Peninsula. The British travel writer Isabella Bird's *The Golden Chersonese* (1883; likely consulted by Harker, according to the Notes) records her journey from Japan to Hong Kong, Canton, Saigon, and the Malay Peninsula. Bird includes accounts of several items of Malay lore that might have caught Harker's attention, including reports of "a bottle-imp, the *polong*, which will take no other sustenance than the blood of its owner" and a "vile fiend called the *penangalan* [which] takes possession of the forms of women, turns them into witches, and compels them to quit the greater part of their bodies, and fly away by night to gratify a vampire craving for human blood." Van Helsing may also have known these legends and meant the Golden Chersonese, not the Greek peninsula.

33 The following appears in the Manuscript but not in the published text: "You friend John saw that when he meet you on this road here. Alas! That you did not know of him then!" There is no record elsewhere of Seward meeting Dracula (or anyone else) on the road in Purfleet.

our powers extend, they are unfettered, and we are free to use them. We have self-devotion in a cause, and an end to achieve which is not a selfish one. These things are much.

"Now let us see how far the general powers arrayed against us are restrict, and how the individual cannot. In fine, let us consider the limitations of the vampire in general, and of this one in particular.

"All we have to go upon are traditions and superstitions. These do not at the first appear much, when the matter is one of life and death—nay of more than either life or death. Yet must we be satisfied; in the first place because we have to be—no other means is at our control—and secondly, because, after all, these things—tradition and superstition—are everything.[31] Does not the belief in vampires rest for others—though not, alas! for us—on them? A year ago which of us would have received such a possibility, in the midst of our scientific, sceptical, matter-of-fact nineteenth century? We even scouted a belief that we saw justified under our very eyes. Take it, then, that the vampire, and the belief in his limitations and his cure, rest for the moment on the same base. For, let me tell you, he is known everywhere that men have been. In old Greece, in old Rome; he flourish in Germany all over, in France, in India, even in the Chersosese;[32] and in China, so far from us in all ways, there even he is, and the peoples fear him at this day. He have follow the wake of the berserker Icelander, the devil-begotten Hun, the Slav, the Saxon, the Magyar. So far, then, we have all we may act upon; and let me tell you that very much of the beliefs are justified by what we have seen in our own so unhappy experience. The vampire live on, and cannot die by mere passing of the time; he can flourish when that he can fatten on the blood of the living. Even more, we have seen amongst us that he can even grow younger; that his vital faculties grow strenuous, and seem as though they refresh themselves when his special pabulum is plenty. But he cannot flourish without this diet; he eat not as others. Even friend Jonathan, who lived with him for weeks, did never see him to eat, never! He throws no shadow;[33] he make in the mirror no reflect, as again Jonathan observe. He has the strength of many of his hand—witness again Jonathan when he shut the door against the wolfs, and when he help him from the diligence too.[34] He can transform himself to wolf, as we gather from the ship arrival in Whitby, when he tear open the dog; he can be as bat, as Madam Mina saw him on the window at Whitby, and as friend John saw him fly from this so near house, and as my friend Quincey saw him at the window of Miss Lucy. He can come in mist which he create—that noble ship's captain proved him of this; but, from what we know, the distance he can make this mist is limited, and it can only be round himself. He come on moonlight rays as elemental dust—as again Jonathan saw those sisters in the castle of Dracula. He become so small—we ourselves saw Miss Lucy, ere she was at peace, slip through a hairbreadth space at the tomb door. He can, when once he find his way, come out from anything or into anything, no matter how close it be bound or even fused up with fire—solder you call it.[35] He can see in the dark—no small power this, in a world which is one half shut from the light. Ah, but hear me through. He can do all these things, yet he is not free. Nay; he is even more prisoner than the slave of the galley, than the madman in his cell. He cannot go where he lists; he who is not of nature has yet to obey some of nature's laws—why we know not. He may not enter anywhere at the first, unless there be some one of the household who bid him to come; though afterwards he can come as he please.[36] His power ceases, as does that of all evil things, at the coming of the day.[37] Only at certain times can he have limited freedom. If he be not at the place whither he is bound, he can only change himself at noon or at exact sunrise or sunset.[38] These things are we told, and in this record of ours we have proof by inference. Thus, whereas he can do as he will within his limit, when he have his earth-home, his coffin-home, his hell-home, the place unhallowed, as we saw when he went to the grave of the suicide at Whitby; still at other time he can only change when the time come. It is said, too, that he can only pass running water at the slack or the flood of the tide.[39] Then there are things which so afflict him that he has no power, as the garlic that we know of;[40] and as for things sacred, as this symbol, my crucifix,

34 The Manuscript continues: "when he threw down that so old corpse in Munich." This refers to the excised "Dead House" episode (see chapter 1, note 1) and is omitted from the published version.

35 And so why use solder in sealing Lucy's coffin?

36 This sentence is added to the Manuscript in Stoker's hand. There is no folkloric support for Van Helsing's assertion. See chapter 2, note 9. However, vampires in the *Buffy* universe are strictly bound by this law, even vampires with souls such as Angel and Spike.

37 Again, Van Helsing overestimates the effects of daylight.

38 The words "sunrise or" are added to the Manuscript in Stoker's hand. What Van Helsing means by "change himself" is unclear. Certainly the example of Lucy's passage through the "hairbreadth space" did not occur at one of these times. Wolf (*The Essential Dracula*) points out the coincidence of Renfield's behavioural cycles with these times, which strikes Dr. Seward only much later.

39 This is well documented later in the narrative.

40 The Manuscript contains the following phrase, which does not appear in the published narrative: "the rye which Jonathan experience." This episode is unidentifiable, although it is tantalising to note that "rye" is a term in the Romany (Gypsy) tongue meaning a "young gentleman." See *The Romany Rye* by George Borrow (1857).

"His power ceases . . . at the coming of the day."
Max Schreck as Graf Orlok.
Nosferatu (Jofa-Atelier Berlin-Johannisthal, 1922)

41 Scholars generally identify this as a reference to Arminius or Armin Vambéry, born Hermann Vamberger or Bamberger (1832–1913), a Hungarian professor of Oriental languages at the University of Buda-Pesth and a renowned wine collector. In his twenties he travelled throughout Armenia and Persia for several months, disguised in native dress, writing about his experiences in such books as *Sketches of Central Asia* (1868), *The Life and Adventures of Arminius Vámbéry* (1884), and *The Story of My Struggles* (1904). Vambéry is reported to have travelled to London in 1885, where he spent three weeks lecturing to the public on the Russian threat in central Asia. There is some evidence that Vambéry and Sherlock Holmes, actively engaged in practise in London at the time, may have met then (see "The Musgrave Ritual," written by Arthur Conan

that was amongst us even now when we resolve, to them he is nothing, but in their presence he take his place far off and silent with respect. There are others, too, which I shall tell you of, lest in our seeking we may need them. The branch of wild rose on his coffin keep him that he move not from it; a sacred bullet fired into the coffin kill him so that he be true dead; and as for the stake through him, we know already of its peace; or the cut-off head that giveth rest. We have seen it with our eyes.

"Thus when we find the habitation of this man-that-was, we can confine him to his coffin and destroy him, if we obey what we know. But he is clever. I have asked my friend Arminius, of Buda-Pesth University,[41] to make his record; and, from all the means that are, he tell me of what he has been. He must, indeed, have been that Voivode Dracula who won his name

Doyle and published in 1893, in which Holmes refers to a case involving "Vamberry, the wine merchant"). Recent disclosures by the British government confirm that Vambéry routinely supplied intelligence to the Foreign Office about the Ottoman Empire, where he was said to have the ear of the sultan. His penchant for espionage, Orientalism, and disguise suggest to professor Friedrich Kittler ("Dracula's Legacy") that Vambéry was "some sort of vampire."

There is no correspondence extant between Vambéry and "Van Helsing," although biographer Harry Ludlam (*A Biography of Bram Stoker, Creator of Dracula*) reports that in 1890 Vambéry came to dine in the Beefsteak Room of the Lyceum Theatre, set aside for guests of its proprietor, Henry Irving. Ludlam assumes that Stoker would have attended as well. In his *Personal Reminiscences of Henry Irving*, Stoker recounts two different meetings with Vambéry, one at a dinner in April 1890 and another about two years later, on the occasion of Vambéry receiving an honorary degree. On neither occasion did Stoker recall any discussions of Dracula, Vlad Ţepeş, or vampires.

Amazingly, however, there is evidence that Vambéry was an acquaintance of Friedrich Max Müller, who may well be the real "Van Helsing." Clemens Ruthner (see note 14 on p. 8) discovered that Vambéry and Müller met in Dublin in 1892 at the Tercentenary Celebration of Trinity College, and again in the summer of 1893 when Müller visited the University of Buda-Pesth. It is possible that the 1892 meeting was not their first.

Stoker seems to have been known to Van Helsing (see note 14 on p. 8) and may well have introduced him to Vambéry. However, McNally and Florescu (*In Search of Dracula*, 1994) note that "a search through all of [Vambéry's]

Arminius Vambéry.

published writings fails to reveal any comments on Vlad, Dracula, or vampires." Therefore the identification of "Arminius" as Vambéry can only be speculative.

In fact, other identifications are possible. For example, Jacobus Arminius (ca.1559–1609) was a prominent and controversial Dutch Remonstrant Reformer, born Jacob Harmenszoon in Oudewater, near Utrecht. Orphaned at the age of sixteen when the Spanish slaughtered his family in the Oudewater massacre, Arminius served as a pastor in Amsterdam and Leiden for twenty-one years. At the age of thirty-one, he married an aristocrat, Lijsbet Reael, who helped him circulate in Amsterdam society. Van Helsing may well have known descendants of this well-educated family.

42 Van Helsing here claims that Dracula is the same person as Vlad Țepeș (see chapter 2, note 47). Dracula himself makes no such assertion (see his remarks at the text accompanying chapter 3, note 26), and despite the efforts of numerous scholars to prove the identity of Dracula and Vlad, there is no convincing evidence that Vlad Țepeș ever exhibited any behaviour of a vampire, either during his human lifetime or after. The idea has been novelized in the popular 2005 work *The Historian* by Elizabeth Kostova.

43 That is, Transylvania.

44 Emily Gerard's 1885 "Transylvanian Superstitions," possibly read by Harker before his journey to Castle Dracula, describes the Scholomance as a "school supposed to exist somewhere in the heart of the mountains, and where all the secrets of nature, the language of animals, and all imaginable magic spells and charms are taught by the devil in person. Only ten scholars are admitted at a time, and when the course of learning has expired and nine of them are released to return to their homes, the tenth scholar is detained by the devil as payment, and mounted upon an *Ismeju* (dragon) he becomes henceforward the devil's aide-de-camp, and assists him in 'making the weather,' that is to say, preparing the thunderbolts." The name "Scholomance" may also be used to refer to the students themselves. More commonly, these legendary wandering alchemists are called "solomonari," or sons of Solomon.

45 Gerard (1885) places the Scholomance here. McNally and Florescu (*The Essential Dracula*) suggest that this is a garbled reference to a spot near Hermannstadt, close to the town of Paltinis. Nicolae Paduraru, noted Roumanian *Dracula* scholar, in private correspondence with this editor, identifies it as "the rocks of Solomon," where the scholars took oaths to uphold their way of life, located at Bâlea Lac (Lake Balea), high in the Carpathians between Sibiu (Hermannstadt) and Brasov, on a line

against the Turk, over the great river on the very frontier of Turkey-land.[42] If it be so, then was he no common man; for in that time, and for centuries after, he was spoken of as the cleverest and the most cunning, as well as the bravest of the sons of the 'land beyond the forest.'[43] That mighty brain and that iron resolution went with him to his grave, and are even now arrayed against us. The Draculas were, says Arminius, a great and noble race, though now and again were scions who were held by their coevals to have had dealings with the Evil One. They learned his secrets in the Scholomance,[44] amongst the mountains over Lake Hermanstadt,[45] where the devil claims the tenth scholar as his due. In the records are such words as 'stregoica'—witch, 'ordog,' and 'pokol'—Satan and hell;[46] and in one manuscript this very Dracula is spoken of as 'wampyr,' which we all understand too well.[47] There have been from the loins of this very one great men and good women, and their graves make sacred the earth where alone this foulness can dwell. For it is not the least of its terrors that this evil thing is rooted deep in all good; in soil barren of holy memories it cannot rest."[48]

Whilst they were talking Mr. Morris was looking steadily at the window, and he now got up quietly, and went out of the room. There was a little pause, and then the Professor went on:—

"And now we must settle what we do. We have here much data, and we must proceed to lay out our campaign. We know from the inquiry of Jonathan that from the castle to Whitby came fifty boxes of earth, all of which were delivered at Carfax; we also know that at least some of these boxes have been removed. It seems to me, that our first step should be to ascertain whether all the rest remain in the house beyond that wall where we look to-day; or whether any more have been removed. If the latter, we must trace—"

Here we were interrupted in a very startling way. Outside the house came the sound of a pistol-shot; the glass of the window was shattered with a bullet, which, ricocheting from the top of the embrasure, struck the far wall of the room. I am afraid I am at heart a coward, for I shrieked out. The men all jumped to their feet; Lord Godalming flew over to the window and threw up the sash. As he did so we heard Mr. Morris's voice without:—

"Sorry! I fear I have alarmed you. I shall come in and tell you about it." A minute later he came in and said:—

"It was an idiotic thing of me to do, and I ask your pardon, Mrs. Harker, most sincerely; I fear I must have frightened you terribly. But the fact is that whilst the Professor was talking there came a big bat and sat on the window-sill. I have got such a horror of the damned brutes from recent events that I cannot stand them, and I went out to have a shot, as I have been doing of late of evenings, whenever I have seen one. You used to laugh at me for it then, Art."

"Did you hit it?" asked Dr. Van Helsing.

"I don't know; I fancy not, for it flew away into the wood." Without saying any more he took his seat,[49] and the Professor began to resume his statement:—[50]

"We must trace each of these boxes; and when we are ready, we must either capture or kill this monster in his lair; or we must, so to speak, sterilise the earth, so that no more he can seek safety in it. Thus in the end we may find him in his form of man between the hours of noon and sunset, and so engage with him when he is at his most weak.

"And now for you, Madam Mina, this night is the end until all be well. You are too precious to us to have such risk. When we part to-night, you no more must question. We shall tell you all in good time. We are men and are able to bear; but you must be our star and our hope, and we shall act all the more free that you are not in the danger, such as we are."

All the men, even Jonathan, seemed relieved; but it did not seem to me good that they should brave danger and, perhaps, lessen their safety—strength being the best safety—through care of me; but their minds were made up, and, though it was a bitter pill for me to swallow, I could say nothing, save to accept their chivalrous care of me.[51]

Mr. Morris resumed the discussion:—

"As there is no time to lose, I vote we have a look at his house right now. Time is everything with him; and swift action on our part may save another victim."[52]

I own[53] that my heart began to fail me when the time for

Bâlea Lac, site of "the rocks of Solomon."
Photograph courtesy Cristian Golea

between Victoria and Poeinari. (The reference is inserted into a blank in the Manuscript in Stoker's hand, evidently the result of subsequent research.)

46 These are common words—Harker found them in his "polyglot dictionary" (see chapter 1, note 61, and accompanying text).

47 Interestingly, in the Notes, Dracula is first identified as "Count Wampyr," though this name is later deleted. The word "wampyr" may be original, although cognates of the term—vampir, upir, vampyre, upyr, vampyr, vampire—appear in a variety of sources. Katharina M. Wilson, in her essay "The History of the Word *Vampire*," traces possible Turkish, Greek, Slavic, and Hungarian roots for the term. "However, . . . linguistic studies concerning the etymology of the word in major European languages indicate that the word is neither Hungarian nor Roumanian," she concludes. Like the origins of the creatures themselves, "the origin of the word *vampire* is clouded in mystery."

48 Van Helsing's notion that the vampire cannot rest in "soil barren of holy memories" but must lie down in earth that is "sacred" derives from the folkloric belief that vampires are created by burials in unconsecrated soil. These origins, however, do not explain why vampires must

rest in consecrated soil, and it is impossible to reconcile this statement with Van Helsing's later admonitions to "sterilise" the boxes of soil brought by Dracula with holy wafers.

49 Leatherdale (*Dracula Unearthed*) wonders if Morris was shooting at someone in the room—Van Helsing, Mina Harker, and Arthur Holmwood were all seated with their backs to the window—and is puzzled by the seasoned hunter missing a sitting target. Morris was "looking steadily at the window" during the entire explanation by the Professor, yet was not chastised for inattention; therefore, it is logical to conclude that the Professor was seated at the head of the table with his back to the window, so that Morris could look over his shoulder at the window.

Why would Morris shoot at the Professor? In fact, this is only one of many puzzling aspects of Morris's alliances. Why is Morris the killer of Dracula? Why is he the only one of the hunters to die in the final raid? How can he have had all the adventures that he claims? Where did his money come from? Why does no one raise a suspicion when Lucy dies immediately following a transfusion from Morris? Why, when Morris later guards the window, is the window the means of Dracula's escape from close quarters? Semioticist Franco Moretti, in "Dialectic of Fear" (1988), has an explanation: Morris is in league with Dracula. Leatherdale (*Dracula Unearthed*) adds his own suspicions: this alliance explains Morris's nightly visits to the woods—he reports to his colleague. When it is clear that Van Helsing knows too much, Morris tries to kill him. It is Morris who shortly "discovers" the rats in the chapel—does he lead them to the party? It is Morris who delays the party from interfering with Dracula's visit to the Harkers' room. Morris is the last to see Renfield alive. Most importantly, it is Morris who delivers the coup de grâce to Dracula—or does he? And then Morris conveniently "dies," departing the scene.

This startling conjecture has some support in the Notes as well. First, the "Texan" (whose

action came so close, but I did not say anything, for I had a greater fear that if I appeared as a drag or a hindrance to their work, they might even leave me out of their counsels altogether. They have now gone off to Carfax, with means to get into the house.

Manlike, they had told me to go to bed and sleep; as if a woman can sleep when those she loves are in danger! I shall lie down and pretend to sleep, lest Jonathan have added anxiety about me when he returns.

DR. SEWARD'S DIARY.

1 October, 4 a.m.—Just as we were about to leave the house, an urgent message was brought to me from Renfield to know if I would see him at once, as he had something of the utmost importance to say to me. I told the messenger to say that I would attend to his wishes in the morning; I was busy just at the moment. The attendant added:—

"He seems very importunate, sir. I have never seen him so eager. I don't know but what, if you don't see him soon, he will have one of his violent fits." I knew the man would not have said this without some cause, so I said: "All right; I'll go now;" and I asked the others to wait a few minutes for me, as I had to go and see my "patient."

"Take me with you, friend John," said the Professor. "His case in your diary interest me much, and it had bearing, too, now and again on *our* case. I should much like to see him, and especial when his mind is disturbed."

"May I come also?" asked Lord Godalming.

"Me too?" said Quincey Morris.[54] I nodded, and we all went down the passage together.

We found him in a state of considerable excitement, but far more rational in his speech and manner than I had ever seen him. There was an unusual understanding of himself, which was unlike anything I had ever met with a lunatic; and he took it for granted that his reasons would prevail with others entirely sane. We all four went into the room, but none of the others at first said anything. His request was that I would at once release him from the asylum and send him home. This he backed up with arguments regarding his complete recovery, and adduced his own existing sanity. "I appeal to your friends;" he said, "they will, perhaps, not mind sitting in judgment on my case. By the way, you have not introduced me." I was so much astonished, that the oddness of introducing a madman in an asylum did not strike me at the moment; and, besides, there was a certain dignity in the man's manner, so much of the habit of equality, that I at once made the introduction: "Lord Godalming; Professor Van Helsing; Mr. Quincey Morris, of Texas; Mr. Renfield." He shook hands with each of them, saying in turn:—

"Lord Godalming, I had the honour of seconding your father at the Windham;[55] I grieve to know, by your holding the title, that he is no more. He was a man loved and honoured by all who knew him; and in his youth was, I have heard, the inventor of a burnt rum punch, much patronised on Derby night.[56] Mr. Morris, you should be proud of your great state. Its reception into the Union[57] was a precedent which may have far-reaching effects hereafter, when the Pole and the Tropics may hold alliance to the Stars and Stripes.[58] The power of Treaty may yet prove a vast engine of enlargement, when the Monroe doctrine takes its true place as a political fable.[59] What shall any man say of his pleasure at meeting Van Helsing? Sir, I make no apology for dropping all forms of conventional prefix. When an individual has revolutionised therapeutics by his discovery of the continuous evolution of brain-matter,[60] conventional forms are unfitting, since they would seem to limit him to one of a class. You, gentlemen, who by nationality, by heredity, or by the possession of natural gifts, are fitted to hold your respective places in the moving world, I take to witness that I am as sane as at least the majority of men who are in full possession of their liberties. And I am sure that you, Dr. Seward, humanitarian and medico-jurist[61] as well as scientist, will deem it a moral duty to deal with me as one to be considered as under exceptional circumstances." He made this last appeal with a courtly air of conviction which was not without its own charm.

I think we were all staggered. For my own part, I was under the conviction, despite my knowledge of the man's character

alias underwent frequent changes—among the names were Brutus M. Maris or Marix and Quincey P. Adams) is alternately in and out of the narrative. At one point, the Notes indicate that the Count and the Texan arrive together to visit Dr. Seward. In an early outline of the narrative, the Notes indicate that the Texan is consulted by Mina and Jonathan, who offers to visit Transylvania alone, does so, and reports at length by letter.

Was Morris a vampire? Or merely an opportunist—a fellow traveller?

50 Why no comment from the Professor? In light of his remarks only a few paragraphs earlier, Van Helsing must identify the bat as Dracula himself. One might expect a remark along the lines of "your bullets won't harm him" or "good work—we can't have him spying on us."

51 Why does Mina meekly accept exclusion from the men's councils? Does she already secretly desire to help Dracula? If so, her exclusion might help her justify her feelings.

52 Of course, Van Helsing should have vetoed this foolhardy notion—attacking Dracula during the night—on the basis of the principles he just enunciated.

53 This paragraph is headed "From Mina Harker's Private Diary" and dated 10 October (plainly a mistake) in the Manuscript.

54 In later editions (but not the Abridged Text), Harker also visits Renfield.

55 A social club named for William Windham, scholar, mathematician, and friend of Dr. Samuel Johnson. Originally, the club's full name was the Windham House Club, after Widnham's residence, which stood at 106 Pall Mall, and which may briefly have been the site of the group's first few meetings, at its founding in 1828. However, by 1892 the club had struck the word "House" from its name and had moved to St. James's Square. It then moved to 11 or 13 St. James's Square (both addresses are given), where it remained until it merged out of existence in the 1940s. Ralph Nevill, in his excellent *London Clubs: Their History & Treasures* (1911), describes it as "founded by Lord Nugent for those connected with each other by a common bond of literary or personal acquaintance."

56 The Derby (now known as the Vodafone Derby), the most important horse race in England, comparable to the Kentucky Derby in the United States, was established in 1780 and is run annually at Epsom Downs, in Surrey. "Derby Day" is described by journalist George Augustus Sala in his 1894 *London Up to Date* as "the one great London holiday, which in variety, in cheerfulness, and in cordial good fellowship of all classes of the community, beats hollow, in my opinion, even the merriest of our Bank holidays; of which very many of our superfine classes do not at all approve, and shut themselves up in elegant, but sulky seclusion on the festivals of St. Lubbock, highly indignant in their own superfine manner because their tradespeople have shut up their shops, and they, the superior ones, have some difficulty in procuring new-laid eggs and hot rolls at breakfast. No such feelings of acerbity mar the enjoyment of the Derby Day; and pure democracy, while it makes itself manifest in its scores and scores of thousands, has no kind of envy or dislike of its oligarchical or plutocratic neighbours. The races are for everybody; and the poorest creature on the Course can see the sight, with a little pushing and squeezing, as well as the princes and princesses, the grandees and the millionaires."

57 On 29 December 1845.

58 Renfield presciently refers to the admission of Alaska and Hawaii into the Union. The word "alliance" is changed to "allegiance" in the Abridged Text.

59 Renfield seems to be scoffing at the pronouncement of James Monroe that European

and history, that his reason had been restored; and I felt under a strong impulse to tell him that I was satisfied as to his sanity, and would see about the necessary formalities for his release in the morning. I thought it better to wait, however, before making so grave a statement, for of old I knew the sudden changes to which this particular patient was liable. So I contented myself with making a general statement that he appeared to be improving very rapidly; that I would have a longer chat with him in the morning, and would then see what I could do in the direction of meeting his wishes. This did not at all satisfy him, for he said quickly:—

"But I fear, Dr. Seward, that you hardly apprehend my wish. I desire to go at once here—now—this very hour—this very moment, if I may. Time presses, and in our implied agreement with the old scytheman[62] it is of the essence of the contract. I am sure it is only necessary to put before so admirable a practitioner as Dr. Seward so simple, yet so momentous a wish, to ensure its fulfilment." He looked at me keenly, and seeing the negative in my face, turned to the others, and scrutinised them closely. Not meeting any sufficient response, he went on:—

"Is it possible that I have erred in my supposition?"

"You have," I said frankly, but at the same time, as I felt, brutally. There was a considerable pause, and then he said slowly:—

"Then I suppose I must only shift my ground of request. Let me ask for this concession—boon, privilege, what you will. I am content to implore in such a case, not on personal grounds, but for the sake of others. I am not at liberty to give you the whole of my reasons; but you may, I assure you, take it from me that they are good ones, sound and unselfish, and spring from the highest sense of duty. Could you look, sir, into my heart, you would approve to the full the sentiments which animate me. Nay, more, you would count me amongst the best and truest of your friends." Again he looked at us all keenly. I had a growing conviction that this sudden change of his entire intellectual method was but yet another form or phase of his madness, and so determined to let him go on a little longer, knowing from experience that he would, like all lunatics, give himself away in the end. Van Helsing was gazing at him with a look of utmost intensity, his bushy eyebrows almost meeting with the fixed concentration of his look. He said to Renfield in a tone which did not surprise me at the time, but only when I thought of it afterwards—for it was as of one addressing an equal:—

"Can you not tell frankly your real reason for wishing to be free to-night? I will undertake that if you will satisfy even me—a stranger, without prejudice, and with the habit of keeping an open mind—Dr. Seward will give you, at his own risk and on his own responsibility, the privilege you seek." He shook his head sadly, and with a look of poignant regret on his face. The Professor went on:—

"Come, sir, bethink yourself. You claim the privilege of reason in the highest degree, since you seek to impress us with your complete reasonableness. You do this, whose sanity we have reason to doubt, since you are not yet released from medical treatment for this very defect. If you will not help us in our effort to choose the wisest course, how can we perform the duty which you yourself put upon us?[63] Be wise, and help us; and if we can we shall aid you to achieve your wish." He still shook his head as he said:—

"Dr. Van Helsing, I have nothing to say. Your argument is complete, and if I were free to speak I should not hesitate a moment; but I am not my own master in the matter. I can only ask you to trust me. If I am refused, the responsibility does not rest with me." I thought it was now time to end the scene, which was becoming too comically grave, so I went towards the door, simply saying:—

"Come, my friends, we have work to do. Good-night."

As, however, I got near the door, a new change came over the patient. He moved towards me so quickly that for the moment I feared that he was about to make another homicidal attack. My fears, however, were groundless, for he held up his two hands imploringly, and made his petition in a moving manner. As he saw that the very excess of his emotion was militating against him, by restoring us more to our old relations, he became still more demonstrative. I glanced at Van Helsing, and saw my conviction reflected in his eyes; so I became a little more fixed

powers should not meddle in the affairs of the Western Hemisphere, an opinion prevalent because the Americans lacked the naval power to enforce the Doctrine.

60 This reference to the "continuous evolution of brain-matter" may refer to studies of mutations of the human brain or of the developmental stages of the brain. The latter was famously studied by Sigmund Freud and later Charles Piaget; Van Helsing's name has scandalously been omitted from the lists of pioneers in this field.

61 There is no other evidence of either of these labels with respect to Seward. The first may well be sarcastic commentary on Seward's treatment of his patients; the latter, however, suggests that Seward testified on psychological or mental matters in the courts, an application of his talents not otherwise referred to in the narrative.

62 Saturn, personified in mythology as the son of Uranus (the Sky Father) and Gaea (the Earth Mother), was the youngest of the twelve Titans. Gaea, knowing that Uranus could never admit to the cycles of life—his hatred of his own children was proof—urged Saturn to castrate his father, separating Heaven from Earth. To accomplish this, Gaea created out of her own body—that is, minerals, chief among them flint—a sickle or scythe. The scythe thus symbolised the harvesting of life. Its crescent shape stood for the moon and its cyclic rise and fall. Saturn, called Chronos or Kronos by the Greeks, is identified as both the incarnation of time and the god of agriculture and vegetation. The comment does not appear in the Abridged Text.

63 An ironic remark in light of the way Van Helsing has expected Seward to act blindly!

in my manner, if not more stern, and motioned to him that his efforts were unavailing. I had previously seen something of the same constantly growing excitement in him when he had to make some request of which at the time he had thought much, such, for instance, as when he wanted a cat; and I was prepared to see the collapse into the same sullen acquiescence on this occasion. My expectation was not realised, for, when he found that his appeal would not be successful, he got into quite a frantic condition. He threw himself on his knees, and held up his hands, wringing them in plaintive supplication, and poured forth a torrent of entreaty, with the tears rolling down his cheeks, and his whole face and form expressive of the deepest emotion:—

"Let me entreat you, Dr. Seward, oh, let me implore you, to let me out of this house at once. Send me away how you will and where you will; send keepers with me with whips and chains; let them take me in a strait-waistcoat, manacled and leg-ironed, even to a gaol; but let me go out of this. You don't know what you do by keeping me here. I am speaking from the depths of my heart—of my very soul. You don't know whom you wrong, or how; and I may not tell. Woe is me! I may not tell. By all you hold sacred—by all you hold dear—by your love that is lost—by your hope that lives—for the sake of the Almighty, take me out of this and save my soul from guilt! Can't you hear me, man? Can't you understand? Will you never learn? Don't you know that I am sane and earnest now; that I am no lunatic in a mad fit, but a sane man fighting for his soul? Oh, hear me! hear me! Let me go! let me go! let me go!"

I thought that the longer this went on the wilder he would get, and so would bring on a fit; so I took him by the hand and raised him up.

"Come," I said sternly, "no more of this; we have had quite enough already. Get to your bed and try to behave more discreetly."

He suddenly stopped and looked at me intently for several moments. Then, without a word, he rose and moving over, sat down on the side of the bed. The collapse had come, as on the former occasion, just as I had expected.

When I was leaving the room, last of our party, he said to me in a quiet, well-bred voice:[64]—

"You will, I trust, Dr. Seward, do me the justice to bear in mind, later on, that I did what I could to convince you to-night."[65]

64 Wolf (*The Essential Dracula*) wonders why Renfield has become so rational, suggesting that his sudden infatuation with Mina and concern for her may have sobered him. Alternatively, Wolf suggests, the proximity of Dracula may have so filled Renfield's mind that the "more trivial miasmas of insanity" (as Wolf characterises them) have been dispersed. In either case, Renfield's purpose becomes clear only later: Dracula requires him to invite the vampire onto the asylum premises, to prey on Mina. If Renfield departs, then Dracula will be unable to approach Mina. Roger Johnson, in private correspondence with this editor, wonders at the comment—there is no suggestion anywhere that Renfield spoke at any time in an "ill-bred" voice.

65 Leatherdale (*Dracula Unearthed*) points out that this entry is recorded at 4:00 A.M., four hours after the exchange with Renfield. The missing hours make clear that portions of the Harker Papers have been suppressed.

Chapter 19

JONATHAN HARKER'S JOURNAL.

1 Jonathan here seems to be attempting to excuse their exclusion of Mina, certainly not her own choice. The Abridged Text omits this rationalisation.

2 This sentence does not appear in the Abridged Text, consistent with what must have been Harker's revision, correcting the previous entry to delete him from the list of Renfield's visitors. In the Manuscript, the sentence is succeeded by: "I must always think of him now in Dr. Seward's phrase 'the Flyman' "—another indication of Seward's common use of the phrase.

3 In the Manuscript the sentence reads: "Say, Jack, if that duck wasn't attempting a bluff he is about the sanest lunatic I ever struck, and if he isn't he's about fit to call Irving for the jack-pot." Roger Johnson, in private correspondence with this editor, suggests that this refers to Stoker's employer Sir Henry Irving and means that if Renfield is not sane, then he must be a greater actor than Sir Henry.

4 Van Helsing later must have regretted this admission of a shortcoming, for the previous portion of this sentence does not appear in the Abridged Text.

1 October, 5 a.m.—I went with the party to the search with an easy mind, for I think I never saw Mina so absolutely strong and well. I am so glad that she consented to hold back and let us men do the work. Somehow, it was a dread to me that she was in this fearful business at all; but now that her work is done, and that it is due to her energy and brains and foresight that the whole story is put together in such a way that every point tells, she may well feel that her part is finished, and that she can henceforth leave the rest to us.[1] We were, I think, all a little upset by the scene with Mr. Renfield.[2] When we came away from his room we were silent till we got back to the study. Then Mr. Morris said to Dr. Seward:—

"Say, Jack, if that man wasn't attempting a bluff, he is about the sanest lunatic I ever saw.[3] I'm not sure, but I believe that he had some serious purpose, and if he had, it was pretty rough on him not to get a chance." Lord Godalming and I were silent, but Dr. Van Helsing added:—

"Friend John, you know more of lunatics than I do, and I'm glad of it, for[4] I fear that if it had been to me to decide I would before that last hysterical outburst have given him free. But we live and learn, and in our present task we must take no chance, as my friend Quincey would say. All is best as they are." Dr. Seward seemed to answer them both in a dreamy kind of way:—

Lupita Tovar as Eva Seward and Carlos Villarias as Dracula.
Dracula (Spanish-language version, Universal Pictures, 1931)

5 Seward still has not made the connection between Renfield's cyclical behaviour and Van Helsing's rule of "change points." See chapter 18, note 38. However, Stoker glosses over this lack of insight in the Abridged Text, cutting the phrase "in an indexy kind of way."

6 Perhaps this and the previous sentence humanize Seward more than he wished, for they do not appear in the Abridged Text.

"I don't know but that I agree with you. If that man had been an ordinary lunatic I would have taken my chance of trusting him; but he seems so mixed up with the Count in an indexy kind of way that I am afraid of doing anything wrong by helping his fads.[5] I can't forget how he prayed with almost equal fervour for a cat, and then tried to tear my throat out with his teeth. Besides, he called the Count 'lord and master,' and he may want to get out to help him in some diabolical way. That horrid thing has the wolves and the rats and his own kind to help him, so I suppose he isn't above trying to use a respectable lunatic. He certainly did seem earnest, though. I only hope we have done what is best.[6] These things, in conjunction with the wild work we have in hand, help to unnerve a man." The Professor stepped over,

7 Holmwood does not mention his preparedness in the Abridged Text.

8 The Abridged Text does not include this otherwise inexplicable behaviour.

9 The Manuscript contains the phrase "remember the wolf and the rat"; this phrase is replaced in the published text with "more mundane."

10 Professor Jean Lorrah, in "Dracula Meets the New Woman," points out that he does not offer a crucifix or any other protective equipment to Mina, and suggests that he may be subconsciously jealous of Mina's growing dominance of the hunters. "If she had been given a crucifix . . . either it would have protected her from further attack, or it certainly would have tipped the men off to what had happened!"

and laying his hand on his shoulder, said in his grave, kindly way:—

"Friend John, have no fear. We are trying to do our duty in a very sad and terrible case; we can only do as we deem best. What else have we to hope for, except the pity of the good God?" Lord Godalming had slipped away for a few minutes, but now he returned. He held up a little silver whistle, as he remarked:—

"That old place may be full of rats, and if so, I've got an antidote on call."**7** Having passed the wall, we took our way to the house, taking care to keep in the shadows of the trees on the lawn when the moonlight shone out.**8** When we got to the porch the Professor opened his bag and took out a lot of things, which he laid on the step, sorting them into four little groups, evidently one for each. Then he spoke:—

"My friends, we are going into a terrible danger, and we need arms of many kinds. Our enemy is not merely spiritual. Remember that he has the strength of twenty men, and that, though our necks or our windpipes are of the common kind—and therefore breakable or crushable—his are not amenable to mere strength. A stronger man, or a body of men more strong in all than him, can at certain times hold him; but they cannot hurt him as we can be hurt by him. We must, therefore, guard ourselves from his touch. Keep this near your heart"—as he spoke he lifted a little silver crucifix and held it out to me, I being nearest to him—"put these flowers round your neck"—here he handed to me a wreath of withered garlic blossoms—"for other enemies more mundane,**9** this revolver and this knife; and for aid in all, these so small electric lamps, which you can fasten to your breast; and for all, and above all at the last, this, which we must not desecrate needless."**10** This was a portion of Sacred Wafer, which he put in an envelope and handed to me. Each of the others was similarly equipped. "Now," he said, "friend John, where are the skeleton keys? If so that we can open the door, we need not break house by the window, as before at Miss Lucy's."

Dr. Seward tried one or two skeleton keys, his mechanical dexterity as a surgeon standing him in good stead. Presently he got one to suit; after a little play back and forward the bolt yielded and with a rusty clang shot back. We pressed on the door, the rusty hinges creaked, and it slowly opened. It was startlingly like the image conveyed to me in Dr. Seward's diary of the opening of Miss Westenra's tomb; I fancy that the same idea seemed to strike the others, for with one accord they shrank back. The Professor was the first to move forward,[11] and stepped into the open door.

"In manus tuas, Domine!"[12] he said, crossing himself as he passed over the threshold. We closed the door behind us, lest when we should have lit our lamps we should possibly attract attention from the road. The Professor carefully tried the lock, lest we might not be able to open it from within should we be in a hurry making our exit. Then we all lit our lamps and proceeded on our search.

The light from the tiny lamps fell in all sorts of odd forms, as the rays crossed each other, or the opacity of our bodies threw great shadows. I could not for my life get away from the feeling that there was some one else amongst us.[13] I suppose it was the recollection, so powerfully brought home to me by the grim surroundings, of that terrible experience in Transylvania. I think the feeling was common to us all, for I noticed that the others kept looking over their shoulders at every sound and every new shadow, just as I felt myself doing.

The whole place was thick with dust. The floor was seemingly inches deep, except where there were recent footsteps, in which on holding down my lamp I could see marks of hobnails where the dust was caked. The walls were fluffy and heavy with dust, and in the corners were masses of spiders' webs, whereon the dust had gathered till they looked like old tattered rags as the weight had torn them partly down.[14] On a table in the hall was a great bunch of keys, with a time-yellowed label on each. They had been used several times, for on the table were several similar rents in the blanket of dust, similar to that exposed when the Professor lifted them. He turned to me and said:—

"You know this place, Jonathan. You have copied maps of it, and you know it at least more than we do. Which is the way to the chapel?" I had an idea of its direction, though on my former visit I had not been able to get admission to it; so I led the way, and after a few wrong turnings found myself opposite a low,

11 The group's fear is not mentioned in the Abridged Text.

12 Latin: "Into thy hands, Lord." A portion of the traditional Catholic prayer: *"In manus tuas, Domine, commendo spiritum meum"* ("Into Thy hands, O Lord, I commend my spirit").

13 Leatherdale (*Dracula Unearthed*) suggests that Dracula is in fact present, in some invisible form. However, his presence remains undetected in the Abridged Text: this and the following sentence do not appear there.

14 Leatherdale (*Dracula Unearthed*) expresses surprise at Harker's initial responses to the scene, which seem utterly to fail to take into account that he has visited Carfax previously.

15 This makes it all the more puzzling why Harker was unable to "get admission to it" previously. The map is not mentioned in the Abridged Text. In the Notes, the hunters discover a "blood red room." There is no indication whether this is different from the chapel where the boxes are kept.

16 "Glutted" or "bloated" in other early editions; "gorged" in the Abridged Text. In the Manuscript, the word is plainly "bloated."

17 Vampiric bad breath is a trait noted by others as well. Montague Summers in *The Vampire: His Kith and Kin* asserts that a vampire's breath is "unbearably fetid and rank with corruption, the stench of the charnel."

18 This entire paragraph does not appear in the Abridged Text.

19 The Manuscript reads: "There should be now _____ boxes." "Fifty" has been handwritten into the blank in an unidentified hand. The sentence is omitted from the published narrative. It is apparent from the handwritten change (and other similar changes) that the number of boxes tallied in the narrative is fictional.

20 In the Manuscript, this reads: "There were only Thirteen left! As we had as yet only accounted for six there were still two missing to which we had as yet no clue of any kind." The balance of the account of the visit to Carfax has been substantially shortened in the Abridged Text. There is no appearance of Dracula's visage, and the rats and dogs are omitted. There appears to be no reason for these omissions other than space considerations.

arched oaken door, ribbed with iron bands. "This is the spot," said the Professor as he turned his lamp on a small map of the house, copied from the file of my original correspondence regarding the purchase. With a little trouble we found the key on the bunch and opened the door.[15] We were prepared for some unpleasantness, for as we were opening the door a faint, malodorous air seemed to exhale through the gaps, but none of us ever expected such an odour as we encountered. None of the others had met the Count at all at close quarters, and when I had seen him he was either in the fasting stage of his existence in his rooms or, when he was gloated[16] with fresh blood, in a ruined building open to the air; but here the place was small and close, and the long disuse had made the air stagnant and foul. There was an earthy smell, as of some dry miasma, which came through the fouler air. But as to the odour itself, how shall I describe it? It was not alone that it was composed of all the ills of mortality and with the pungent, acrid smell of blood, but it seemed as though corruption had become itself corrupt. Faugh! it sickens me to think of it. Every breath exhaled by that monster seemed to have clung to the place and intensified its loathsomeness.[17]

Under ordinary circumstances such a stench would have brought our enterprise to an end; but this was no ordinary case, and the high and terrible purpose in which we were involved gave us a strength which rose above merely physical considerations. After the involuntary shrinking consequent on the first nauseous whiff, we one and all went about our work as though that loathsome place were a garden of roses.[18]

We made an accurate examination of the place, the Professor saying as we began:—

"The first thing is to see how many of the boxes are left; we must then examine every hole and corner and cranny, and see if we cannot get some clue as to what has become of the rest."[19] A glance was sufficient to show how many remained, for the great earth chests were bulky, and there was no mistaking them.

There were only twenty-nine left out of the fifty![20] Once I got a fright, for, seeing Lord Godalming suddenly turn and look out of the vaulted door into the dark passage beyond, I looked too, and for an instant my heart stood still. Somewhere, looking out from the shadow, I seemed to see the high lights of the Count's evil face, the ridge of the nose, the red eyes, the red lips, the awful pallor. It was only for a moment, for, as Lord Godalming said, "I thought I saw a face, but it was only the shadows," and resumed his inquiry, I turned my lamp in the direction, and stepped into the passage. There was no sign of any one; and as there were no corners, no doors, no aperture of any kind, but only the solid walls of the passage, there could be no hiding-place even for *him*.[21] I took it that fear had helped imagination, and said nothing.

A few minutes later I saw Morris step suddenly back from a corner, which he was examining. We all followed his movements with our eyes, for undoubtedly some nervousness was growing on us, and we saw a whole mass of phosphorescence which twinkled like stars. We all instinctively drew back. The whole place was becoming alive with rats.

For a moment or two we stood appalled, all save Lord Godalming, who was seemingly prepared for such an emergency. Rushing over to the great iron-bound oaken door, which Dr. Seward had described from the outside, and which I had seen myself, he turned the key in the lock, drew the huge bolts, and swung the door open. Then, taking his little silver whistle from his pocket, he blew a low, shrill call. It was answered from behind Dr. Seward's house by the yelping of dogs, and after about a minute three terriers came dashing round the corner of the house.[22] Unconsciously we had all moved towards the door, and as we moved I noticed that the dust had been much disturbed: the boxes which had been taken out had been brought this way. But even in the minute that had elapsed the number of the rats had vastly increased. They seemed to swarm over the place all at once, till the lamplight, shining on their moving dark bodies and glittering, baleful eyes, made the place look like a bank of earth set with fireflies. The dogs dashed on, but at the threshold suddenly stopped and snarled, and then, simultaneously lifting their noses, began to howl in most lugubrious fashion. The rats were multiplying in thousands, and we moved out.

Lord Godalming lifted one of the dogs, and carrying him

21 Wolf (*The Essential Dracula*) points out that Harker has forgotten how the vampire women "simply seemed to fade into the rays of the moonlight and pass out through the window" (see text accompanying chapter 3, note 80). If the Transylvania section of the Harker Papers is perceived as fiction, however, this forgetfulness is more easily understood. Harker also seems to have ignored Van Helsing's description of the vampire's ability to "come out from anything or into anything, no matter how close it be bound."

22 These were likely Manchester terriers, also known as "rat terriers" or "black-and-tan terriers." The last name refers to Manchester terriers having been bred by crossing whippets and black-and-tan terriers. The breed was developed as a rat hunter in nineteenth-century Manchester, England, by John Hulme and was considered the best vermin-hunting breed of the day. Manchester terriers also hunt squirrels, chipmunks, raccoons, rabbits, and opossum and will tree game birds and jump and chase deer. Stories abound of British contests in which prize Manchester terriers (in particular, one named Billy) killed dozens and dozens of rats in phenomenally short periods of time. Billy's best record was a hundred rats in 6 minutes, 13 seconds. At least Arthur was listening to Van Helsing and came prepared to

Manchester terrier.

Rat catching at the Blue Anchor Tavern,
Finsbury, in the 1850s.

deal with Dracula's "command" of rats. (See text
accompanying chapter 18, note 25.)

23 Wolf (*The Essential Dracula*) credits this
relief to Dracula's absence—in other words, he
asserts that all of the party receive Dracula's
"psychic" emanations.

24 This is not possible if Harker's diary entry
is accurately logged at 5:00 A.M. and Seward's
prior entry at 4:00 A.M. Sunrise on 1 October
does not occur until almost 6:00 A.M.

25 The following appears in the Manuscript but
is omitted from the published narrative: "and
we have for ever prevented his return to any of
those that lie there. Henceforth he must find his
unholy refuge in some other of the earth that
he has brought or exist in one form by daylight
save at noon or the turning of the tide." In other
words, if a vampire doesn't rest in native soil, he
will be trapped in the form (bat, wolf, human)
taken at the time of rest. Apparently, however,
the vampire will be able to "shape-shift" exactly
at noon or when the tide turns.

This "no-shape-shifting" is not discussed
further but clearly is a very different penalty
from (and much less severe than) the dire
consequences Van Helsing suggests will attend
the destruction of the boxes. In fact, it suggests

in, placed him on the floor. The instant his feet touched the
ground he seemed to recover his courage, and rushed at his
natural enemies. They fled before him so fast that before he
had shaken the life out of a score, the other dogs, who had by
now been lifted in the same manner, had but small prey ere
the whole mass had vanished.

With their going it seemed as if some evil presence had
departed, for the dogs frisked about and barked merrily as
they made sudden darts at their prostrate foes, and turned
them over and over and tossed them in the air with vicious
shakes. We all seemed to find our spirits rise. Whether it was
the purifying of the deadly atmosphere by the opening of the
chapel door, or the relief which we experienced by finding
ourselves in the open I know not; but most certainly the shadow
of dread seemed to slip from us like a robe, and the occasion of
our coming lost something of its grim significance, though we
did not slacken a whit in our resolution.[23] We closed the outer
door and barred and locked it, and bringing the dogs with us,
began our search of the house. We found nothing throughout
except dust in extraordinary proportions, and all untouched
save for my own footsteps when I had made my first visit.
Never once did the dogs exhibit any symptom of uneasiness,
and even when we returned to the chapel they frisked about
as though they had been rabbit-hunting in a summer wood.

The morning was quickening in the east when we emerged
from the front.[24] Dr. Van Helsing had taken the key of the hall-
door from the bunch, and locked the door in orthodox fashion,
putting the key into his pocket when he had done.

"So far," he said, "our night has been eminently successful.
No harm has come to us such as I feared might be, and yet we
have ascertained how many boxes are missing.[25] More than all
do I rejoice that this, our first—and perhaps our most difficult
and dangerous—step has been accomplished without the
bringing thereinto our most sweet Madam Mina or troubling
her waking or sleeping thoughts with sights and sounds and
smells of horror which she might never forget. One lesson, too,
we have learned, if it be allowable to argue *a particulari*:[26]
that the brute beasts which are to the Count's command are
yet themselves not amenable to his spiritual power; for look,

these rats that would come to his call, just as from his castle top he summon the wolves to your going and to that poor mother's cry, though they come to him, they run pell-mell from the so little dogs of my friend Arthur. We have other matters before us, other dangers, other fears; and that monster—he has not used his power over the brute world for the only or the last time to-night. So be it that he has gone elsewhere. Good! It has given us opportunity to cry 'check' in some ways in this chess game, which we play for the stake of human souls. And now let us go home. The dawn is close at hand, and we have reason to be content with our first night's work. It may be ordained that we have many nights and days to follow, if full of peril; but we must go on, and from no danger shall we shrink."

The house was silent when we got back, save for some poor creature who was screaming away in one of the distant wards, and a low, moaning sound from Renfield's room.[27] The poor wretch was doubtless torturing himself, after the manner of the insane, with needless thoughts of pain.

I came tiptoe into our own room, and found Mina asleep, breathing so softly that I had to put my ear down to hear it. She looks paler than usual. I hope the meeting to-night has not upset her. I am truly thankful that she is to be left out of our future work, and even of our deliberations. It is too great a strain for a woman to bear. I did not think so at first, but know better now. Therefore I am glad that it is settled. There may be things which would frighten her to hear; and yet to conceal them from her might be worse than to tell her if once she suspected that there was any concealment. Henceforth our work is to be a sealed book to her, till at least such time as we can tell her that all is finished, and the earth free from a monster of the nether world. I daresay it will be difficult to begin to keep silence after such confidence as ours; but I must be resolute, and to-morrow I shall keep dark over to-night's doings, and shall refuse to speak of anything that has happened. I rest on the sofa, so as not to disturb her.[28]

1 October, later.—I suppose it was natural that we should have all overslept ourselves, for the day was a busy one, and the night had no rest at all. Even Mina must have felt its exhaustion, for

that the refuge of native soil avoids only certain inconveniences and explains why, for example, Dracula is just as comfortable under the "suicide seat" in Whitby as in soil from his native land.

26 Generalising; that is, reasoning from the particular to the general.

27 If, as is strongly indicated in the Abridged Text, Harker did not visit Renfield's room with the others, it is strange that Harker is able to recognise the sound as coming from that room. Perhaps one of the others remarked, "Ah, Renfield!"

28 Harker's consideration, which may have been invention, is not mentioned in the Abridged Text.

29 The Manuscript reads: "Before she is up I am going out to follow up the clues that Lord Godalming's letters from the agents afforded." The letter had not yet arrived, and Stoker apparently realised this, and the sentence does not appear in the published version. See text accompanying chapter 20, note 36.

30 Inserted in Stoker's hand in the Manuscript —further proof of the falsification of the number of boxes.

31 This entire entry has been removed in the Abridged Text. In truth, it adds little or nothing to the narrative.

though I slept till the sun was high, I was awake before her, and had to call two or three times before she awoke. Indeed, she was so sound asleep that for a few seconds she did not recognise me, but looked at me with a sort of blank terror, as one looks who has been waked out of a bad dream. She complained a little of being tired, and I let her rest till later in the day.[29] We now know of twenty-one[30] boxes having been removed, and if it be that several were taken in any of these removals we may be able to trace them all. Such will, of course, immensely simplify our labour, and the sooner the matter is attended to the better. I shall look up Thomas Snelling to-day.

DR. SEWARD'S DIARY.[31]

1 October.—It was towards noon when I was awakened by the Professor walking into my room. He was more jolly and cheerful than usual, and it is quite evident that last night's work has helped to take some of the brooding weight off his mind. After going over the adventure of the night he suddenly said:—

"Your patient interests me much. May it be that with you I visit him this morning? Or if that you are too occupy, I can go alone if it may be. It is a new experience to me to find a lunatic who talk philosophy, and reason so sound." I had some work to do which pressed, so I told him that if he would go alone I would be glad, as then I should not have to keep him waiting; so I called an attendant and gave him the necessary instructions. Before the Professor left the room I cautioned him against getting any false impression from my patient. "But," he answered, "I want him to talk of himself and of his delusion as to consuming live things. He said to Madam Mina, as I see in your diary of yesterday, that he had once had such a belief. Why do you smile, friend John?"

"Excuse me," I said, "but the answer is here." I laid my hand on the type-written matter. "When our sane and learned lunatic made that very statement of how he *used* to consume life, his mouth was actually nauseous with the flies and spiders which he had eaten just before Mrs. Harker entered the room." Van Helsing smiled in turn. "Good!" he said. "Your memory is true, friend John. I should have remembered. And yet it is this very obliquity of thought and memory which makes mental disease such a fascinating study. Perhaps I may gain more knowledge out of the folly of this madman than I shall from the teaching of the most wise. Who knows?" I went on with my work, and before long was through that in hand. It seemed that the time had been very short indeed, but there was Van Helsing back in the study. "Do I interrupt?" he asked politely as he stood at the door.

"Not at all," I answered. "Come in. My work is finished, and I am free. I can go with you now, if you like."

"It is needless; I have seen him!"

"Well?"

"I fear that he does not appraise me at much. Our interview was short. When I entered his room he was sitting on a stool in the centre, with his elbows on his knees, and his face was the picture of sullen discontent. I spoke to him as cheerfully as I could, and with such a measure of respect as I could assume. He made no reply whatever. 'Don't you know me?' I asked. His answer was not reassuring: 'I know you well enough; you are the old fool Van Helsing. I wish you would take yourself and your idiotic brain theories somewhere else. Damn all thick-headed Dutchmen!' Not a word more would he say, but sat in his implacable sullenness as indifferent to me as though I had not been in the room at all. Thus departed for this time my chance of much learning from this so clever lunatic; so I shall go, if I may, and cheer myself with a few happy words with that sweet soul Madam Mina. Friend John, it does rejoice me unspeakable that she is no more to be pained, no more to be worried, with our terrible things. Though we shall much miss her help, it is better so."

"I agree with you with all my heart," I answered earnestly, for I did not want him to weaken in this matter. "Mrs. Harker is better out of it. Things are quite bad enough for us, all men of the world, and who have been in many tight places in our time; but it is no place for a woman, and if she had remained in touch with the affair, it would time[32] infallibly have wrecked her."

So Van Helsing has gone to confer with Mrs. Harker and

32 Presumably a typographical error for "in time."

33 What fatigues?

34 As we will learn, during the night Mina has suffered her first attack by Dracula. Wolf (*The Essential Dracula*) points out that unlike Lucy, whose response to the visitation by Dracula was to sleep soundly and to look "better . . . than she has done for weeks" (see text accompanying chapter 8, note 20), Mina suffers guilt and remorse—"[s]urely this is because Mina is a married woman," writes Wolf. That is, the women's reactions strike Wolf as being equivalent to postcoital behaviours one might expect of women in each of their circumstances—Lucy single and satisfied, Mina married and guilt-ridden. As will be seen in later visits, there is some confusion in the reports of what exactly occurs during Dracula's "attacks."

35 Another element of confusion in this entry: to what visit from Jonathan is Mina referring? Portions of this entry smack of being written by Stoker to pad out the narrative, and the paragraph does not appear in the Abridged Text.

Harker; Quincey and Art are all out following up the clues as to the earth-boxes. I shall finish my round of work, and we shall meet to-night.

MINA HARKER'S JOURNAL.

1 October.—It is strange to me to be kept in the dark as I am to-day; after Jonathan's full confidence for so many years, to see him manifestly avoid certain matters, and those the most vital of all. This morning I slept late after the fatigues of yesterday,[33] and though Jonathan was late too, he was the earlier. He spoke to me before he went out, never more sweetly or tenderly, but he never mentioned a word of what had happened in the visit to the Count's house. And yet he must have known how terribly anxious I was. Poor dear fellow! I suppose it must have distressed him even more than it did me. They all agreed that it was best that I should not be drawn further into this awful work, and I acquiesced. But to think that he keeps anything from me! And now I am crying like a silly fool, when I *know* it comes from my husband's great love and from the good, good wishes of those other strong men. . . . .

That has done me good. Well, some day Jonathan will tell me all; and lest it should ever be that he should think for a moment that I kept anything from him, I still keep my journal as usual. Then if he has feared of my trust I shall show it to him, with every thought of my heart put down for his dear eyes to read. I feel strangely sad and low-spirited to-day.[34] I suppose it is the reaction from the terrible excitement.

Last night I went to bed when the men had gone, simply because they told me to. I didn't feel sleepy and I did feel full of devouring anxiety. I kept thinking over everything that has been ever since Jonathan came to see me in London,[35] and it all seems like a horrible tragedy, with fate pressing on relentlessly to some destined end. Everything that one does seems, no matter how right it may be, to bring on the very thing which is most to be deplored. If I hadn't gone to Whitby, perhaps poor dear Lucy would be with us now. She hadn't taken to visiting the churchyard till I came, and if she hadn't come there in the day-time with me she wouldn't have walked there in her sleep;

and if she hadn't gone there at night and asleep, that monster couldn't have destroyed her as he did. Oh, why did I ever go to Whitby? There now, crying again! I wonder what has come over me to-day. I must hide it from Jonathan, for if he knew that I had been crying twice in one morning—I, who never cried on my own account, and whom he has never caused to shed a tear—the dear fellow would fret his heart out. I shall put a bold face on, and if I do feel weepy, he shall never see it. I suppose it is one of the lessons that we poor women have to learn. . . .

I can't quite remember how I fell asleep last night. I remember hearing the sudden barking of the dogs and a lot of queer sounds, like praying on a very tumultuous scale, from Mr. Renfield's room, which is somewhere under this. And then there was silence over everything, silence so profound that it startled me, and I got up and looked out of the window. All was dark and silent, the black shadows thrown by the moonlight seeming full of a silent mystery of their own. Not a thing seemed to be stirring, but all to be grim and fixed as death or fate; so that a thin streak of white mist, that crept with almost imperceptible slowness across the grass towards the house, seemed to have a sentience and a vitality of its own. I think that the digression of my thoughts must have done me good, for when I got back to bed I found a lethargy creeping over me. I lay a while, but could not quite sleep, so I got out and looked out of the window again. The mist was spreading, and was now close up to the house, so that I could see it lying thick against the wall, as though it were stealing up to the windows. The poor man was more loud than ever, and though I could not distinguish a word he said, I could in some way recognise in his tones some passionate entreaty on his part. Then there was the sound of a struggle, and I knew that the attendants were dealing with him. I was so frightened that I crept into bed, and pulled the clothes over my head, putting my fingers in my ears. I was not then a bit sleepy, at least so I thought; but I must have fallen asleep, for, except dreams, I do not remember anything until the morning, when Jonathan woke me. I think that it took me an effort and little time to realise where I was, and that it was Jonathan who was

36 Mina recalls the episode described in Exod. 13:21: "And the LORD went before them by day in a pillar of cloud, to lead them the way; and by night in a pillar of fire, to give them the light; to go by day and night."

bending over me. My dream was very peculiar, and was almost typical of the way that waking thoughts become merged in, or continued in, dreams.

I thought that I was asleep, and waiting for Jonathan to come back. I was very anxious about him, and I was powerless to act; my feet, and my mind and my brain were weighted, so that nothing could proceed at the usual pace. And so I slept uneasily and thought. Then it began to dawn upon me that the air was heavy, and dank, and cold. I put back the clothes from my face, and found, to my surprise, that all was dim around. The gaslight which I had left lit for Jonathan, but turned down, came only like a tiny red spark through the fog, which had evidently grown thicker and poured into the room. Then it occurred to me that I had shut the window before I had come to bed. I would have got out to make certain on the point, but some leaden lethargy seemed to chain my limbs and even my will. I lay still and endured; that was all. I closed my eyes, but could still see through my eyelids. (It is wonderful what tricks our dreams play us, and how conveniently we can imagine.) The mist grew thicker and thicker, and I could see now how it came in, for I could see it like smoke—or with the white energy of boiling water—pouring in, not through the window, but through the joinings of the door. It got thicker and thicker, till it seemed as if it became concentrated into a sort of pillar of cloud in the room, through the top of which I could see the light of the gas shining like a red eye. Things began to whirl through my brain just as the cloudy column was now whirling in the room, and through it all came the scriptural words "a pillar of cloud by day and fire by night."**36** Was it indeed such spiritual guidance that was coming to me in my sleep? But the pillar was composed of both the day- and the night-guiding, for the fire was in the red eye, which at the thought got a new fascination for me; till, as I looked, the fire divided, and seemed to shine on me through the fog like two red eyes, such as Lucy told me of in her momentary mental wandering when, on the cliff, the dying sunlight struck the windows of St. Mary's Church. Suddenly the horror burst upon me that it was thus that Jonathan had seen those awful women growing into reality through the whirling mist in the moonlight, and in my dream I must have fainted, for all became black darkness. The last conscious effort which imagination made was to show me a livid white face bending over me out of the mist. I must be careful of such dreams, for they would unseat one's reason if there were too much of them. I would get Dr. Van Helsing or Dr. Seward to prescribe something for me which would make me sleep, only that I fear to alarm them. Such a dream at the present time would become woven into their fears for me. To-night I shall strive hard to sleep naturally. If I do not, I shall to-morrow night get them to give me a dose of chloral;[37] that cannot hurt me for once, and it will give me a good night's sleep. Last night tired me more than if I had not slept at all.

2 October, 10 p.m.—Last night I slept, but did not dream. I must have slept soundly, for I was not waked by Jonathan coming to bed; but the sleep has not refreshed me, for to-day I feel terribly weak and spiritless. I spent all yesterday trying to read, or lying down dozing. In the afternoon Mr. Renfield asked if he might see me. Poor man, he was very gentle, and when I came away he kissed my hand and bade God bless me. Some way it affected me much; I am crying when I think of him. This is a new weakness, of which I must be careful. Jonathan would be miserable if he knew I had been crying. He and the others were out till dinner-time, and they all came in tired. I did what I could to brighten them up, and I suppose that the effort did me good, for I forgot how tired I was. After dinner they sent me to bed, and all went off to smoke together, as they said, but I knew that they wanted to tell each other of what had occurred to each during the day; I could see from Jonathan's manner that he had something important to communicate. I was not so sleepy as I should have been; so before they went I asked Dr. Seward to give me a little opiate of some kind, as I had not slept well the night before. He very kindly made me up a sleeping draught, which he gave to me, telling me that it would do me no harm, as it was very mild. . . . I have taken it, and am waiting for sleep, which still keeps aloof. I hope I have not done wrong, for as sleep begins to flirt with me, a new fear comes: that I may have been foolish in thus depriving myself of the power of waking. I might want it. Here comes sleep. Good-night.

37 Another example of the casual attitude of the Victorians towards opiates. See chapter 8, note 45.

Chapter 20

1 Harker may have decided to soften his characterisation of Snelling; no debauch is mentioned in the Abridged Text.

2 Harker means a mind or brain of his own, an independent thinker. This appreciative appraisal does not appear in the Abridged Text.

3 A small street off Brick Lane, a few blocks from the Aldgate East station serving the District and Metropolitan Lines and near Liverpool Street station, north of the Thames. This is Jack-the-Ripper territory—Chicksand Street is the very centre of the network of prostitute murders ascribed to "Jack the Harlot Killer" in 1888, points out Robert Eighteen-Bisang ("Dracula, Jack the Ripper, and A Thirst for Blood"). The address of 197 is fictional but cannot be more than half a mile from the five locations where the victims' bodies were found.

4 The name of this hamlet is corrected in the Abridged Text to "Mile End New Town." New Town was originally a section of Mile End, but at the end of the seventeenth century it became a separate village. It grew in the nineteenth century to nearly 113,000 people as housing was developed there, primarily for families with workers in the nearby city (including, in 1846, the model project built by the Metropolitan Association for Improving the Dwellings of the

1 October, evening.—I found Thomas Snelling in his house at Bethnal Green, but unhappily he was not in a condition to remember anything. The very prospect of beer which my expected coming had opened to him had proved too much, and he had begun too early on his expected debauch.[1] I learned, however, from his wife, who seemed a decent, poor soul, that he was only the assistant to Smollet, who of the two mates was the responsible person. So off I drove to Walworth, and found Mr. Joseph Smollet at home and in his shirtsleeves, taking a late tea out of a saucer. He is a decent, intelligent fellow, distinctly a good, reliable type of workman, and with a headpiece of his own.[2] He remembered all about the incident of the boxes, and from a wonderful dog's-eared notebook, which he produced from some mysterious receptacle about the seat of his trousers, and which had hieroglyphical entries in thick, half-obliterated pencil, he gave me the destinations of the boxes. There were, he said, six in the cartload which he took from Carfax and left at 197, Chicksand Street,[3] Mile End, New Town,[4] and another six which he deposited at Jamaica Lane, Bermondsey.[5] If then the Count meant to scatter these ghastly refuges of his over London, these places were chosen as the first of delivery, so that later he might distribute more fully. The systematic manner in which this was done made me think that he could not mean to confine himself to two sides of London. He was

"The sight was one of perfect horror, and . . . these soldiers . . . actually sickened at the sight which the mutilated corpse presented."
Varney, the Vampyre; or, The Feast of Blood (1847)

Industrious Classes). Although it had very few poor (at least in comparison with other parts of East London), William Booth began the work of the Salvation Army in Mile End New Town in 1868, and in 1870 the first Dr. Barnardo's Home for orphans was founded there, near Ben Jonson Road. In 1900, Mile End New Town was made part of the borough of Stepney.

5 The Manuscript reads as follows: "There were he said, seven in the cartload which he took from _____ of these, one was left at _____ close to the Junction. Three at Chicksand Street, Mile End New Town and three at _____ tinations mark the strategetical heart of the East End and of the South End of London." Although this is tantalising, it is impossible to decipher any additional information about the true locations of Dracula's hiding holes from the omitted material.

Jamaica Road (not Lane), Bermondsey, is directly south of the London Docks, a block from the south shore of the Thames. This was a heavily industrialised area, filled with warehouses, lodgings for sailors, disreputable public houses, and opium dens. Gustave Doré and Blanchard Jerrold, in their magnificent *London: A Pilgrimage* (1890), describe the neighborhood of the Thames dockyards as "shabby, slatternly places, . . . low and poor houses, amid shiftless riverside loungers" and note "the intensity of the squalid recklessness" of the area. The residents of Bermondsey had little use for "swells" or "West-enders," and few would venture there unescorted at night. Charles Dickens depicted the area and its squalor in *Oliver Twist* (1838).

6 The original City of London, with its own government. Charles Dickens Jr. wrote in 1888: "The Municipality of the City originally exercised jurisdiction over London proper, but the town has so outgrown its original limits that the Corporation is now entirely surrounded by rival powers" (*Dickens's Dictionary of London*). The City remains the financial centre of London.

now fixed on the far east of the northern shore, on the east of the southern shore, and on the south. The north and west were surely never meant to be left out of his diabolical scheme—let alone the City itself[6] and the very heart of fashionable London in the south-west and west. I went back to Smollet, and asked him if he could tell us if any other boxes had been taken from Carfax.

He replied:—

"Well, guv'nor, you've treated me wery 'an'some"—I had given him half a sovereign—"an' I'll tell yer all I know. I heard a man by the name of Bloxam say four nights ago in the 'Are an' 'Ounds, in Pincher's Alley,[7] as 'ow he an' his mate 'ad 'ad a rare dusty job in a old 'ouse at Purfleet. There ain't a-many such

7 This is a disguised name. Pinchin Street is in the heart of Whitechapel, less than a mile from Chicksand Street.

8 That is, in the same neighbourhood as Joseph (Jack) Smollet. See chapter 12, note 39. The street is fictional.

jobs as this 'ere, an' I'm thinkin' that maybe Sam Bloxam could tell ye summut." I asked if he could tell me where to find him. I told him that if he could get me the address it would be worth another half-sovereign to him. So he gulped down the rest of his tea and stood up, saying that he was going to begin the search then and there. At the door he stopped, and said:—

"Look 'ere, guv'nor, there ain't no sense in me a-keepin' you 'ere. I may find Sam soon, or I mayn't; but anyhow he ain't like to be in a way to tell ye much to-night. Sam is a rare one when he starts on the booze. If you can give me a envelope with a stamp on it, and put yer address on it, I'll find out where Sam is to be found and post it ye to-night. But ye'd better be up arter 'im soon in the mornin', or maybe ye won't ketch 'im; for Sam gets off main early, never mind the booze the night afore."

This was all practical, so one of the children went off with a penny to buy an envelope and a sheet of paper, and to keep the change. When she came back, I addressed the envelope and stamped it, and when Smollet had again faithfully promised to post the address when found, I took my way to home. We're on the track anyhow. I am tired to-night, and want sleep. Mina is fast asleep, and looks a little too pale; her eyes look as though she had been crying. Poor dear, I've no doubt it frets her to be kept in the dark, and it may make her doubly anxious about me and the others. But it is best as it is. It is better to be disappointed and worried in such a way now than to have her nerve broken. The doctors were quite right to insist on her being kept out of this dreadful business. I must be firm, for on me this particular burden of silence must rest. I shall not ever enter on the subject with her under any circumstances. Indeed, it may not be a hard task, after all, for she herself has become reticent on the subject, and has not spoken of the Count or his doings ever since we told her of our decision.

2 October, evening.—A long and trying and exciting day. By the first post I got my directed envelope with a dirty scrap of paper enclosed, on which was written with a carpenter's pencil in a sprawling hand:—

"Sam Bloxam, Korkrans, 4, Poters Cort, Bartel Street, Walworth.**8** Arsk for the depite."

I got the letter in bed, and rose without waking Mina. She looked heavy and sleepy and pale, and far from well. I determined not to wake her, but that, when I should return from this new search, I would arrange for her going back to Exeter.[9] I think she would be happier in our own home, with her daily tasks to interest her, than in being here amongst us and in ignorance. I only saw Dr. Seward for a moment, and told him where I was off to, promising to come back and tell the rest so soon as I should have found out anything. I drove to Walworth and found, with some difficulty, Potter's Court. Mr. Smollet's spelling misled me, as I asked for Poter's Court instead of Potter's Court. However, when I had found the court, I had no difficulty in discovering Corcoran's lodging-house. When I asked the man who came to the door for the "depite," he shook his head, and said: "I dunno 'im. There ain't no such a person 'ere; I never 'eard of 'im in all my bloomin' days. Don't believe there ain't nobody of that kind livin' 'ere or anywheres." I took out Smollet's letter, and as I read it it seemed to me that the lesson of the spelling of the name of the court might guide me. "What are you?" I asked.

"I'm the depity," he answered. I saw at once that I was on the right track; phonetic spelling had again misled me. A half-crown tip[10] put the deputy's knowledge at my disposal, and I learned that Mr. Bloxam, who had slept off the remains of his beer on the previous night at Corcoran's, had left for his work at Poplar[11] at five o'clock that morning. He could not tell me where the place of work was situated, but he had a vague idea that it was some kind of a "new-fangled ware'us;" and with this slender clue I had to start for Poplar. It was twelve o'clock before I got any satisfactory hint of such a building, and this I got at a coffee-shop, where some workmen were having their dinner. One of these suggested that there was being erected at Cross Angel Street a new "cold storage" building;[12] and as this suited the condition of a "new-fangled ware'us," I at once drove to it. An interview with a surly gatekeeper and a surlier foreman, both of whom were appeased with the coin of the realm, put me on the track of Bloxam; he was sent for on my suggesting that I was willing to pay his day's wages to his foreman for the privilege of asking him a few questions on

9 The Abridged Text omits the following details of Harker's search for Bloxam.

10 A half-crown was a silver coin worth two shillings sixpence, the modern equivalent of over £8 or about US$13.

11 An area in the East End of London, just east and south of the Whitechapel area, on the north side of the Thames, around the West India and East India Docks. Dracula has now distributed the boxes on both sides of the Thames, a prudent plan.

12 The "depity" was not far wrong in terming a cold-storage facility a "new-fangled ware'us," for it had only come on to the London scene in the decade before the latest date that may be assigned to the narrative. The long-standing problem of preserving food in transit began to be solved by 1875, when ice was first used on a large scale for the preservation of meat in transit from the United States to European markets. In 1879, the Bell-Coleman mechanical dry-air refrigerator, which used a steam engine to compress air and required no chemicals for its operation, was introduced, and soon refrigerators, freezers, and cold-storage chambers were introduced on vessels and on land at ports of lading and delivery. The *Encylopædia Britannica* (9th ed.) estimated in 1888 that "[t]he machinery at present in use is capable of freezing upwards of 300,000 tons of meat per annum, and it is rapidly being added to; and it may be said that these machines have accomplished a perfect solution of the great problem of fresh-meat preservation and distribution."

13 Dracula's choice of Piccadilly for one of his residences may have been motivated in part by the presence of a plentiful supply of nourishment: Salli J. Kline notes that Piccadilly was familiar to Londoners as the part of the metropolis in which "fallen servant girls and adulterous wives turned away from home eventually landed—and . . . the place where lechers from the West End came in hopes of picking them up" (*The Degeneration of Women*).

14 Leatherdale (*Dracula Unearthed*) and Haining and Tremayne (*The Un-Dead*) suggest that this is Christ Church in Down Street, just off Piccadilly and a short walk across Green Park to Buckingham Palace. Bernard Davies, in private correspondence with this editor, points out that the Rose and Crown Pub in Old Park Lane immediately around the corner from Christ Church on the corner of Down Street and Brick Street and only a few doors from No.

Christ Church in Down Street.
Photograph by Leslie S. Klinger, February 2006

Rose and Crown Pub.
Photograph by Leslie S. Klinger, February 2006

a private matter. He was a smart enough fellow, though rough of speech and bearing. When I had promised to pay for his information and given him an earnest, he told me that he had made two journeys between Carfax and a house in Piccadilly,[13] and had taken from this house to the latter nine great boxes—"main heavy ones"—with a horse and cart hired by him for this purpose. I asked him if he could tell me the number of the house in Piccadilly, to which he replied:—

"Well, guv'nor, I forgits the number, but it was only a few doors from a big white church, or somethink of the kind, not long built.[14] It was a dusty old 'ouse, too, though nothin' to the dustiness of the 'ouse we tooked the bloomin' boxes from."

"How did you get into the houses if they were both empty?"

"There was the old party what engaged me a-waitin' in the 'ouse at Purfleet. He 'elped me to lift the boxes and put them in the dray. Curse me, but he was the strongest chap I ever struck, an' him a old feller, with a white moustache,[15] one that thin you would think he couldn't throw a shadder."

How this phrase thrilled through me!

"Why, 'e took up 'is end o' the boxes like they was pounds of tea, and me a-puffin' an' a-blowin' afore I could up-end mine anyhow—an' I'm no chicken, neither."

"How did you get into the house in Piccadilly?" I asked.

"He was there too. He must 'a'started off and got there afore me, for when I rung of the bell he kem an' opened the door 'isself an' 'elped me to carry the boxes into the 'all."

"The whole nine?" I asked.

"Yus; there was five in the first load an' four in the second. It was main dry work, an' I don't so well remember 'ow I got 'ome." I interrupted him:—

"Were the boxes left in the hall?"

"Yus; it was a big 'all, an' there was nothin' else in it." I made one more attempt to further matters:—

"You didn't have any key?"

"Never used no key nor nothink. The old gent, he opened the door 'isself an' shut it again when I druv off. I don't remember the last time—but that was the beer."

"And you can't remember the number of the house?"

"No, sir. But ye needn't have no difficulty about that. It's a 'igh 'un with a stone front with a bow[16] on it, an' 'igh steps up to the door. I know them steps, 'avin' 'ad to carry the boxes up with three loafers what come round to earn a copper. The old gent give them shillin's, an' they seein' they got so much they wanted more; but 'e took one of them by the shoulder and was like to throw 'im down the steps, till the lot of them went away cussin'."[17] I thought that with this description I could find the house, so, having paid my friend for his information, I started off for Piccadilly. I had gained a new painful experience: the Count could, it was evident, handle the earth-boxes himself. If so, time was precious; for, now that he had achieved a certain amount of distribution, he could, by choosing his own time, complete the task unobserved. At Piccadilly Circus[18] I discharged my cab, and walked westward; beyond the Junior Constitutional[19] I came across the house described, and was satisfied that this was the next of the lairs arranged by Dracula. The house looked as though it had been long untenanted. The windows were encrusted with dust, and the shutters were up. All the framework was black with time, and from the iron the paint had mostly scaled away. It was evident that up to lately there had been a large notice-board in front of the balcony; it had, however, been roughly torn away, the uprights which had supported it still remaining.[20] Behind the rails of the balcony I saw there were some loose boards, whose raw edges looked white. I would have given a good deal to have been able to see the notice-board intact, as it would, perhaps, have given some clue to the ownership of the house. I remembered my experience of the investigation and purchase of Carfax, and I could not but feel that if I could find the former owner there might be some means discovered of gaining access to the house.

There was at present nothing to be learned from the Piccadilly side, and nothing could be done; so I went round to the back to see if anything could be gathered from this quarter. The mews[21] were active, the Piccadilly houses being mostly in occupation. I asked one or two of the grooms and helpers whom I saw around if they could tell me anything about the empty house. One of them said that he heard it had lately been

138 Piccadilly (see note 38 below) was a likely stopping place for the thirsty Bloxam. (See map on p. 370.)

15 Note the contrast with Mina's earlier (on 21 or 22 September) description of Dracula as a "thin man, with a beaky nose and black moustache and pointed beard." Bloxom saw Dracula on or about 27 September, before his visit to Mina on 30 September (see appendix 3, "The Chronology of *Dracula*"). Either Dracula is feeling the ill effects of lack of feeding (Lucy's death occurred on 20 September), or he is again deliberately altering his appearance.

16 The word "bow" is added in Stoker's hand to a blank in the Manuscript. Stoker apparently needed to revisit the house (or the Harker Papers) to verify its appearance.

17 Leatherdale (*Dracula Unearthed*) points out that Dracula has acted foolishly, calling attention to himself by overpaying the workers, displaying preternatural strength, and causing a row among the workers. The coworkers do not appear in the Abridged Text.

18 Piccadilly Circus and Oxford Circus were both originally named Regent Circus. The southern portion had been renamed Piccadilly Circus by the time of the events of *Dracula*, although references to it as "Regent Circus" persisted. The Criterion Theatre and the London Pavilion were both on the circus. The triangle in the centre of the circus is occupied by a memorial fountain to the philanthropist and member of Parliament Lord Shaftesbury (Anthony Ashley Cooper), unveiled in 1893 and commonly referred to as *Eros*. Lord Shaftesbury's anti-child-labour crusades led to the passage of the 1833 Factory Law, which restricted the workday of children between the ages of nine and thirteen to eight hours, and the 1842 Coal Mines Act, which prohibited women and children from working in the pit. He lobbied for the education of the working classes and was responsible for the creation of one hundred schools for poor children across England.

The details of Harker's walk to the house are tellingly absent from the Abridged Text.

19 The Junior Constitutional Club was established at 101–104 Piccadilly in 1887 by provincial political leaders professing Conservative principles and by 1896 had over 5,500 members. A. G. Gardiner, in his 1914 memoir *Pillars of Society*, wrote: "The Junior Constitutionalists are men of the bulldog breed, and they demand strong meat at their luncheons."

taken, but he couldn't say from whom. He told me however, that up to very lately there had been a notice-board of "For Sale" up, and that perhaps Mitchell, Sons & Candy, the house agents, could tell me something, as he thought he remembered seeing the name of that firm on the board. I did not wish to seem too eager, or to let my informant know or guess too much, so, thanking him in the usual manner, I strolled away. It was now growing dusk, and the autumn night was closing in, so I did not lose any time. Having learned the address of Mitchell, Sons & Candy from a directory at the Berkeley, I was soon at their office in Sackville Street.[22]

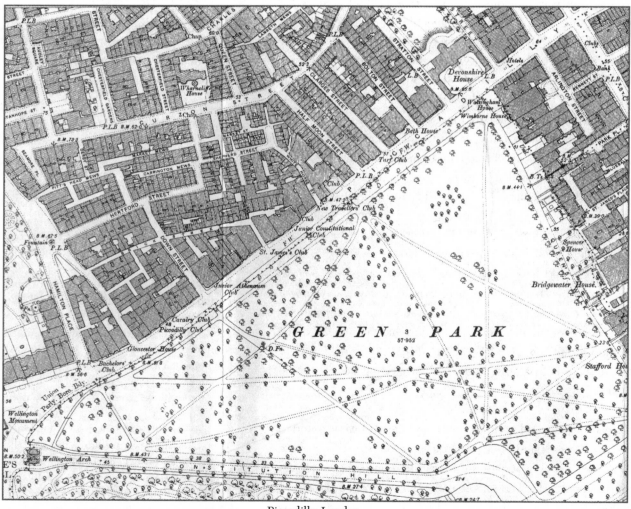

Piccadilly, London.
Ordnance survey map, 1894

The gentleman who saw me was particularly suave in manner, but uncommunicative in equal proportion. Having once told me that the Piccadilly house—which throughout our interview he called a "mansion"—was sold, he considered my business as concluded. When I asked who had purchased it, he opened his eyes a thought wider, and paused a few seconds before replying:—

"It is sold, sir."

"Pardon me," I said, with equal politeness, "but I have special reason for wishing to know who purchased it."

Again he paused longer, and raised his eyebrows still more. "It is sold, sir," was again his laconic reply.

"Surely," I said, "you do not mind letting me know so much."

"But I do mind," he answered. "The affairs of their clients are absolutely safe in the hands of Mitchell, Sons & Candy." This was manifestly a prig of the first water, and there was no use arguing with him. I thought I had best meet him on his own ground, so I said:—

"Your clients, sir, are happy in having so resolute a guardian of their confidence. I am myself a professional man." Here I handed him my card. "In this instance I am not prompted by curiosity; I act on the part of Lord Godalming, who wishes to know something of the property which was, he understood, lately for sale." These words put a different complexion on affairs. He said:—

"I would like to oblige you if I could, Mr. Harker, and especially would I like to oblige his lordship. We once carried out a small matter of renting some chambers for him when he was the Honourable Arthur Holmwood.[23] If you will let me have his lordship's address I will consult the House on the subject, and will, in any case, communicate with his lordship by to-night's post. It will be a pleasure if we can so far deviate from our rules as to give the required information to his lordship."

I wanted to secure a friend, and not to make an enemy, so I thanked him, gave the address at Dr. Seward's, and came away. It was now dark, and I was tired and hungry. I got a cup of tea at the Aërated Bread Company[24] and came down to Purfleet by the next train.[25]

20 Leatherdale (*Dracula Unearthed*) wonders at the appearance of the notice board. It is unlikely that a professional house agent would leave the property looking so shabby. Perhaps the agent was interrupted at his work by the Count's unwelcome attentions.

21 Short streets or alleys behind London's main thoroughfares. Originally intended for the stabling of horses, the mews now house mostly garages.

22 A street a few blocks west of Piccadilly Circus. No estate agents are listed in trade directories on Sackville Street for the relevant time period. However, in private correspondence with this editor, Bernard Davies points out that H. Graham & Co., Estate Agents, are listed in the 1891 Commercial Directory as having offices at 21 Piccadilly, quite near the A.B.C. (see note 24 below) at which Harker rested.

23 Leatherdale (*Dracula Unearthed*) wonders if this might be the mysterious 17 Chatham Street. See chapter 5, note 11.

24 In 1856 Dr. John Dauglish obtained a patent for his method of aerating dough by inflating it with carbonic acid gas generated by sulphuric acid reacting with chalk. This caused the dough to rise faster, reducing its preparation time from eight or ten hours to thirty minutes, and permitted the mass production of machine-made, yeastless bread. The process was not dissimilar to that used in the carbonation of lemonade or other beverages. Using Dauglish's mixers, four hundred 2-pound loaves could be produced within forty minutes.

To exploit his technique, Dauglish founded the Aërated Bread Company, or A.B.C., providing inexpensive bread around London. The first location was Islington, and other bakeries soon sprang up. According to the company's history, in 1864 the manager of the London Bridge branch persuaded the directors to allow her to effectively turn her location into a tea shop. Besides baking and selling bread, she served food and beverages. The popularity of the service led to the widespread growth of tea shops throughout England, beginning the demise of the ubiquitous "coffeehouses" of London.

The coffeehouse was a holdover from the days when coffee, which was imported into England long before tea, was the beverage of choice. The activities carried out at coffeehouses ranged from gambling to debate, with each establishment serving a regular and rather homogeneous clientele—members of a particular trade, business, or profession. For example, the St. James and the Cocoa-Tree were frequented by politicians; Will's, the Bedford, and Button's attracted literati; Garraway's, in Exchange Alley, was for those who did business around the Royal Exchange; and Sir Isaac Newton frequented the Graecian. Precursors of men's clubs and an outgrowth of taverns, coffeehouses were the exclusive province of men.

It is for this reason, among others, that some social historians credit the tea shop as an important factor in the ultimate emancipation of women, because it provided the first suitable public venue for an unchaperoned woman to meet her friends. In 1955, Allied Bakeries, the predecessor to Associated British Foods, purchased the Aërated Bread Company, which then operated a chain of 164 low-budget self-service tea rooms.

The A.B.C. shop was located at 27 Piccadilly. Harker's visit is not mentioned in the Abridged Text.

25 Sunset on 1 October was around 6:00 P.M., so it is now early evening. Harker could have caught a 7:36 P.M. train from Liverpool Street, bringing him to Purfleet at 8:34 P.M. The next train to Purfleet was not until 9:31 P.M.

26 The preceding remarks—erroneously claiming no ill effects from the group's secrecy—do not appear in the Abridged Text, perhaps as a result of Stoker's conscience.

I found all the others at home. Mina was looking tired and pale, but she made a gallant effort to be bright and cheerful; it wrung my heart to think that I had had to keep anything from her and so caused her inquietude. Thank God, this will be the last night of her looking on at our conferences, and feeling the sting of our not showing our confidence. It took all my courage to hold to the wise resolution of keeping her out of our grim task. She seemed somehow more reconciled; or else the very subject seems to have become repugnant to her, for when any accidental allusion is made she actually shudders. I am glad we made our resolution in time, as with such a feeling as this, our growing knowledge would be torture to her.

I could not tell the others of the day's discovery till we were alone; so after dinner—followed by a little music to save appearances even amongst ourselves—I took Mina to her room and left her to go to bed. The dear girl was more affectionate with me than ever, and clung to me as though she would detain me; but there was much to be talked of and I came away. Thank God, the ceasing of telling things has made no difference between us.[26]

When I came down again I found the others all gathered round the fire in the study. In the train I had written my diary so far, and simply read it off to them as the best means of letting them get abreast of my own information; when I had finished Van Helsing said:—

"This has been a great day's work, friend Jonathan. Doubtless we are on the track of the missing boxes. If we find them all in that house, then our work is near the end. But if there be some missing, we must search until we find them. Then shall we make our final *coup*, and hunt the wretch to his real death." We all sat silent awhile and all at once Mr. Morris spoke:—[27]

"Say! how are we going to get into that house?"

"We got into the other," answered Lord Godalming quickly.

"But, Art, this is different. We broke house at Carfax, but we had night and a walled park to protect us. It will be a mighty different thing to commit burglary in Piccadilly, either by day or night. I confess I don't see how we are going to get in unless that agency duck can find us a key of some sort; perhaps we shall know when you get his letter in the morning." Lord

Godalming's brows contracted, and he stood up and walked about the room. By-and-by he stopped and said, turning from one to another of us:—

"Quincey's head is level. This burglary business is getting serious; we got off once all right; but we have now a rare job on hand—unless we can find the Count's key basket."

As nothing could well be done before morning, and as it would be at least advisable to wait till Lord Godalming should hear from Mitchell's, we decided not to take any active step before breakfast time. For a good while we sat and smoked, discussing the matter in its various lights and bearings; I took the opportunity of bringing this diary right up to the moment. I am very sleepy and shall go to bed. . . .

Just a line. Mina sleeps soundly and her breathing is regular. Her forehead is puckered up into little wrinkles, as though she thinks even in her sleep. She is still too pale, but does not took[28] so haggard as she did this morning. To-morrow will, I hope, mend all this; she will be herself at home in Exeter. Oh, but I am sleepy!

DR. SEWARD'S DIARY.

1 October.—I am puzzled afresh about Renfield.[29] His moods change so rapidly that I find it difficult to keep touch of them, and as they always mean something more than his own well-being, they form a more than interesting study. This morning, when I went to see him after his repulse of Van Helsing, his manner was that of a man commanding destiny. He was, in fact, commanding destiny—subjectively. He did not really care for any of the things of mere earth; he was in the clouds and looked down on all the weaknesses and wants of us poor mortals. I thought I would improve the occasion and learn something, so I asked him:—

"What about the flies these times?" He smiled on me in quite a superior sort of way—such a smile as would have become the face of Malvolio[30]—as he answered me:—

"The fly, my dear sir, has one striking feature: its wings are typical of the aërial powers of the psychic faculties. The ancients did well when they typified the soul as a butterfly!"[31]

27 The Abridged Text omits the entire discussion of the proposed means of entry.

28 Evidently a typographical error for "look."

29 The interview with Renfield is shortened in the Abridged Text in ways that do not appear to be meaningful.

30 Malvolio is the straitlaced, self-loving, arrogant, much derided, but ultimately also somewhat sympathetic steward employed by Lady Olivia, the heroine of Shakespeare's *Twelfth Night.* Sir Toby Belch, the foolish and unfortunate Sir Andrew Aguecheek, and Maria, Olivia's maid, despise Malvolio's priggish attitude and, as a jest, lead him to believe that his mistress is in love with him. In act 2, scene 5, the jokers send him a letter purporting to be from Olivia which instructs him that "if thou entertainest my love, let it appear in thy smiling." They also convince him to wear yellow stockings cross-gartered, because Olivia detests cross-gartered fashion, and to be rude to everyone in sight. In act 3, scene 4, Malvolio responds to a summons from Lady Olivia. Attired exactly as instructed in the bogus letter, grinning like a fool and insulting the entire household, he endures the ultimate humiliation when Olivia concludes that he is mad.

31 In many cultures and time periods, including those of the ancient Greeks and Romans as well as North American indigenous peoples, the butterfly is identified with the human soul, and the life cycle of the butterfly equated with the resurrection or karmic cycles of humans. Indeed, the word *psyche* in modern Greek means "soul" as well as "butterfly."

32 The father of Methuselah. Gen. 5:21–24: "And Enoch lived sixty and five years, and begat Methuselah: And Enoch walked with God after he begat Methuselah three hundred years, and begat sons and daughters: And all the days of Enoch were three hundred sixty and five years: And Enoch walked with God: and he was not; for God took him."

I thought I would push his analogy to its utmost logically, so I said quickly:—

"Oh, it is a soul you are after now, is it?" His madness foiled his reason, and a puzzled look spread over his face as, shaking his head with a decision which I had but seldom seen in him, he said:—

"Oh no, oh no! I want no souls. Life is all I want." Here he brightened up; "I am pretty indifferent about it at present. Life is all right; I have all I want. You must get a new patient, doctor, if you wish to study zoöphagy!"

This puzzled me a little, so I drew him on:—

"Then you command life; you are a god, I suppose?" He smiled with an ineffably benign superiority.

"Oh no! Far be it from me to arrogate to myself the attributes of the Deity. I am not even concerned in His especially spiritual doings. If I may state my intellectual position I am, so far as concerns things purely terrestrial, somewhat in the position which Enoch[32] occupied spiritually!" This was a poser to me. I could not at the moment recall Enoch's appositeness; so I had to ask a simple question, though I felt that by so doing I was lowering myself in the eyes of the lunatic:—

"And why with Enoch?"

"Because he walked with God." I could not see the analogy, but did not like to admit it; so I harked back to what he had denied:—

"So you don't care about life and you don't want souls. Why not?" I put my question quickly and somewhat sternly, on purpose to disconcert him. The effort succeeded; for an instant he unconsciously relapsed into his old servile manner, bent low before me, and actually fawned upon me as he replied:—

"I don't want any souls, indeed, indeed! I don't. I couldn't use them if I had them; they would be no manner of use to me. I couldn't eat them or—" he suddenly stopped and the old cunning look spread over his face, like a wind-sweep on the surface of the water. "And doctor, as to life, what is it after all? When you've got all you require, and you know that you will never want, that is all. I have friends—good friends—like you, Dr. Seward;" this was said with a leer of inexpressible cunning, "I know that I shall never lack the means of life!"

I think that through the cloudiness of his insanity he saw some antagonism in me, for he at once fell back on the last refuge of such as he—a dogged silence. After a short time I saw that for the present it was useless to speak to him. He was sulky, and so I came away.

Later in the day he sent for me. Ordinarily I would not have come without special reason, but just at present I am so interested in him that I would gladly make an effort. Besides, I am glad to have anything to help pass the time. Harker is out, following up clues; and so are Lord Godalming and Quincey. Van Helsing sits in my study poring over the record prepared by the Harkers; he seems to think that by accurate knowledge of all details he will light upon some clue. He does not wish to be disturbed in the work, without cause. I would have taken him with me to see the patient, only I thought that after his last repulse he might not care to go again. There was also another reason: Renfield might not speak so freely before a third person as when he and I were alone.

I found him sitting out in the middle of the floor on his stool, a pose which is generally indicative of some mental energy on his part. When I came in, he said at once, as though the question had been waiting on his lips:—

"What about souls?" It was evident then that my surmise had been correct. Unconscious cerebration was doing its work, even with the lunatic. I determined to have the matter out. "What about them yourself?" I asked. He did not reply for a moment but looked all around him, and up and down, as though he expected to find some inspiration for an answer.

"I don't want any souls!" he said in a feeble, apologetic way. The matter seemed preying on his mind, and so I determined to use it—to "be cruel only to be kind."[33] So I said:—

"You like life, and you want life?"

"Oh yes! but that is all right; you needn't worry about that!"

"But," I asked, "how are we to get the life without getting the soul also?" This seemed to puzzle him, so I followed it up:—

"A nice time you'll have some time when you're flying out there, with the souls of thousands of flies and spiders and birds

33 Seward, the most introspective of the principals, who may see himself as Hamlet-like, quotes Shakespeare's Hamlet, to his mother: "I must be cruel, only to be kind: / Thus bad begins, and worse remains behind" (*Hamlet*, act 3, scene 4).

34 Renfield, who is well aware of his own madness, slightly misquotes Edgar, who in Shakespeare's *King Lear* (act 3, scene 4) has disguised himself as a mad beggar, Tom: "Poor Tom, that eats the swimming frog, the toad, the tadpole, the wall-newt and the water; that in the fury of his heart, when the foul fiend rages, eats cow-dung for sallets; swallows the old rat and the ditch-dog; drinks the green mantle of the standing pool . . . ; / But mice and rats, and such small deer / Have been Tom's food for seven long year."

35 Although the reference may seem anachronistic and Chinese restaurants did not proliferate in London until after World War II, the use of chopsticks was well known and even merited an entry in the 1910 *Encyclopædia Britannica* (11th ed.). In *David Copperfield* (1849–1850) Mrs. Heep is described as working away with "Chinese chopsticks of knitting-needles." The Chinese Collection, an exhibition of all things Chinese, flourished near Hyde Park Corner in the 1840s, and the streets of working London were filled with Chinese seamen, dock workers, and labourers.

and cats buzzing and twittering and miauing all around you. You've got their lives, you know, and you must put up with their souls!" Something seemed to affect his imagination, for he put his fingers to his ears and shut his eyes, screwing them up tightly just as a small boy does when his face is being soaped. There was something pathetic in it that touched me; it also gave me a lesson, for it seemed that before me was a child—only a child, though the features were worn, and the stubble on the jaws was white. It was evident that he was undergoing some process of mental disturbance, and, knowing how his past moods had interpreted things seemingly foreign to himself, I thought I would enter into his mind as well as I could and go with him. The first step was to restore confidence, so I asked him, speaking pretty loud so that he would hear me through his closed ears:—

"Would you like some sugar to get your flies round again!" He seemed to wake up all at once, and shook his head. With a laugh he replied:—

"Not much! flies are poor things, after all!" After a pause he added, "But I don't want their souls buzzing round me, all the same."

"Or spiders?" I went on.

"Blow spiders! What's the use of spiders? There isn't anything in them to eat or"—he stopped suddenly, as though reminded of a forbidden topic.

"So, so!" I thought to myself, "this is the second time he has suddenly stopped at the word 'drink;' what does it mean?" Renfield seemed himself aware of having made a lapse, for he hurried on, as though to distract my attention from it:—

"I don't take any stock at all in such matters. 'Rats and mice and such small deer,' as Shakespeare has it,[34] 'chicken-feed of the larder' they might be called. I'm past all that sort of nonsense. You might as well ask a man to eat molecules with a pair of chop-sticks,[35] as to try to interest me about the lesser carnivora, when I know of what is before me."

"I see," I said. "You want big things that you can make your teeth meet in? How would you like to breakfast on an elephant?"

"What ridiculous nonsense you are talking!" He was getting

too wide awake, so I thought I would press him hard. "I wonder," I said reflectively, "what an elephant's soul is like!"

The effect I desired was obtained, for he at once fell from his high-horse and became a child again.

"I don't want an elephant's soul, or any soul at all!" he said. For a few moments he sat despondently. Suddenly he jumped to his feet, with his eyes blazing and all the signs of intense cerebral excitement. "To hell with you and your souls!" he shouted. "Why do you plague me about souls. Haven't I got enough to worry, and pain, and distract me already, without thinking of souls!" He looked so hostile that I thought he was in for another homicidal fit, so I blew my whistle. The instant, however, that I did so he became calm, and said apologetically:—

"Forgive me, Doctor; I forgot myself. You do not need any help. I am so worried in my mind that I am apt to be irritable. If you only knew the problem I have to face, and that I am working out, you would pity, and tolerate, and pardon me. Pray do not put me in a strait-waistcoat. I want to think and I cannot think freely when my body is confined. I am sure you will understand!" He had evidently self-control; so when the attendants came I told them not to mind, and they withdrew. Renfield watched them go; when the door was closed he said, with considerable dignity and sweetness:—

"Dr. Seward, you have been very considerate towards me. Believe me that I am very very grateful to you!" I thought it well to leave him in this mood, and so I came away. There is certainly something to ponder over in this man's state. Several points seem to make what the American interviewer calls "a story," if one could only get them in proper order. Here they are:—

Will not mention "drinking."

Fears the thought of being burdened with the "soul" of anything.

Has no dread of wanting "life" in the future.

Despises the meaner forms of life altogether, though he dreads being haunted by their souls.

Logically all these things point one way! he has assurance of some kind that he will acquire some higher life. He dreads the

36 The letter does not appear in the Abridged Text. The letter that appears in the Manuscript is completely different from that which appears in the published version. It reads:

"My Lord,

"We have no objection whatever to give you the information concerning which you have written to us and are only too pleased to be able to meet your Lordship's wishes. It is true that we effected the sale of 347, Piccadilly. The vendor Mr. Archibald Suffield placed this property with some other real estate in our hands for disposal. We had on the 4.September about two o'clock a call from a gentleman who said he was Mr. Mandeville and that he had called to make a purchase of the house in Piccadilly. As such purchases are not generally effect over the Counter so to speak if your Lordship will pardon the trade familiarity of the phrase our Mr Leitch who was attending to him suggested a reference or the name of his solicitor at the same time explaining since the gentleman was evidently a stranger and in spite of the purity of his accent evidently a foreigner the usual process of the purchase of real estate. The gentleman simply asked how much was the price and on our Mr Leitch naming the sum £2,000 he took from his pocket a cheque book and wrote out a cheque for the amount drawn in our favour on Coutts & Co. He handed over the cheque and said 'When you have received the money from the bank please to have the deed of sale made out in my favour. I shall call for it in two days.' and walked out. He has evidently been accustomed to an offhand method of business. The cheque was duly honoured by Messrs. Coutts & Co and the deed of sale was made out to him. The christian name had to be left blank but at our request he filled it up himself when he called with the name '~~Dracula~~ de Ville. We handed him the keys and we have not since heard of or from him.

We are my Lord,
Your Lordship's humble servts.
Mitchell Sons & Candy"

consequence—the burden of a soul. Then it is a human life he looks to!

And the assurance—?

Merciful God! the Count has been to him, and there is some new scheme of terror afoot!

Later.—I went after my round to Van Helsing and told him my suspicion. He grew very grave; and, after thinking the matter over for a while asked me to take him to Renfield. I did so. As we came to the door we heard the lunatic within singing gaily, as he used to do in the time which now seems so long ago. When we entered we saw with amazement that he had spread out his sugar as of old; the flies, lethargic with the autumn, were beginning to buzz into the room. We tried to make him talk of the subject of our previous conversation, but he would not attend. He went on with his singing, just as though we had not been present. He had got a scrap of paper and was folding it into a note-book. We had to come away as ignorant as we went in.

His is a curious case indeed; we must watch him to-night.

LETTER FROM MITCHELL, SONS & CANDY TO LORD GODALMING. [36]

"1 October.[37]

"My Lord,

"We are at all times only too happy to meet your wishes. We beg, with regard to the desire of your Lordship, expressed by Mr. Harker on your behalf, to supply the following information concerning the sale and purchase of No. 347, Piccadilly.[38] The original vendors are the executors of the late Mr. Archibald Winter-Suffield. The purchaser is a foreign nobleman, Count de Ville,[39] who effected the purchase himself paying the purchase money in notes 'over the counter,' if your Lordship will pardon us using so vulgar an expression. Beyond this we know nothing whatever of him.

"We are, my Lord,
"Your Lordship's humble servants,
"Mitchell, Sons & Candy."

No. 138, Piccadilly.
Photograph by Leslie S. Klinger, February 2006

DR. SEWARD'S DIARY.

2 October.—I placed a man in the corridor last night, and told him to make an accurate note of any sound he might hear from Renfield's room, and gave him instructions that if there should be anything strange he was to call me. After dinner, when we had all gathered round the fire in the study—Mrs. Harker having gone to bed—we discussed the attempts and discoveries of the day. Harker was the only one who had any result, and we are in great hopes that his clue may be an important one.

Before going to bed I went round to the patient's room and looked in through the observation trap. He was sleeping soundly, and his heart rose and fell with regular respiration.

37 Either Harker's previous diary entry, in which he records visiting the agents on 2 October, or this letter is misdated. The confirmation of the other journals for Harker's date suggests that the copyist employed by Messrs. Mitchell, Sons & Candy was in error.

38 A fictional street number. Several scholars point out that Nos. 138 and 139 Piccadilly both had the requisite bow window, iron balcony, and mews. Haining and Tremayne (*The Un-Dead*) assert that No. 137, refurbished in the mid-1990s, formerly possessed a balcony and iron railings along the front and is therefore the likely building. *Dracula* scholar Art Roney, in an article in the *Los Angeles Herald-Examiner*, argues strenuously for No. 138. However, Bernard Davies, in private correspondence with this editor, notes that No. 138 lacked the requisite yard mentioned in the text, whereas No. 139 had such a yard.

39 Enthusiast Patrick Wynne, in his online review of Wolf's *The Essential Dracula*, points out that "Count de Ville = Count Devil = Count Dracula, since Dracul means 'the Devil' in Roumanian. Which just goes to show that even a blood-sucking fiend can't resist a good pun!" Wynne suggests that this is a variant of the rule discovered in Sheridan Le Fanu's "Carmilla" that a vampire assuming a pseudonym must choose a name that is an anagram of his or her real name: the vampire Millarca used the aliases Carmilla and Mircalla. Subsequent historians have recorded numerous adventures of Count Alucard. McNally and Florescu (*The Essential Dracula*) note that a Baron De Ville (1840–1885) is buried at Highgate Cemetery.

40 If the information was available at the British Museum, Leatherdale (*Dracula Unearthed*) wonders, why did Van Helsing make so many trips to Amsterdam? Although his friend Arminius provided valuable information, it would have been far quicker to proceed to the museum.

41 Actually the previous day.

This morning the man on duty reported to me that a little after midnight he was restless and kept saying his prayers somewhat loudly. I asked him if that was all; he replied that it was all he heard. There was something about his manner so suspicious that I asked him point blank if he had been asleep. He denied sleep, but admitted to having "dozed" for a while. It is too bad that men cannot be trusted unless they are watched.

To-day Harker is out following up his clue, and Art and Quincey are looking after horses. Godalming thinks that it will be well to have horses always in readiness, for when we get the information which we seek there will be no time to lose. We must sterilise all the imported earth between sunrise and sunset; we shall thus catch the Count at his weakest, and without a refuge to fly to. Van Helsing is off to the British Museum looking up some authors on ancient medicine.[40] The old physicians took account of things which their followers do not accept, and the Professor is searching for witch and demon cures which may be useful to us later.

I sometimes think we must be all mad and that we shall wake to sanity in strait-waistcoats.

Later.—We have met again. We seem at last to be on the track, and our work of to-morrow may be the beginning of the end. I wonder if Renfield's quiet has anything to do with this. His moods have so followed the doings of the Count, that the coming destruction of the monster may be carried to him in some subtle way. If we could only get some hint as to what passed in his mind, between the time of my argument with him to-day[41] and his resumption of fly-catching, it might afford us a valuable clue. He is now seeming quiet for a spell. . . . Is he?— that wild yell seemed to come from his room. . . .

The attendant came bursting into my room and told me that Renfield had somehow met with some accident. He had heard him yell; and when he went to him found him lying on his face on the floor, all covered with blood. I must go at once. . . .

Chapter 21

DR. SEWARD'S DIARY.

3 October.—Let me put down with exactness all that happened, as well as I can remember it, since last I made an entry. Not a detail that I can recall must be forgotten; in all calmness I must proceed.

When I came to Renfield's room I found him lying on the floor on his left side in a glittering pool of blood. When I went to move him, it became at once apparent that he had received some terrible injuries; there seemed none of that unity of purpose between the parts of the body which marks even lethargic sanity. As the face was exposed I could see that it was horribly bruised, as though it had been beaten against the floor— indeed it was from the face wounds that the pool of blood originated. The attendant who was kneeling beside the body said to me as we turned him over:—

"I think, sir, his back is broken. See, both his right arm and leg and the whole side of his

"'Villain, monster, vampyre!' he shrieks, 'I have thee now;' and locked in a deadly embrace, they roll upon the damp earth, struggling for life together."
Varney, the Vampyre; or, The Feast of Blood (1847)

1 Shockingly poor medical treatment, in the opinion of Wolf (*The Essential Dracula*), of a man with a suspected broken back. Perhaps to protect Seward's reputation, the following sentence, which appears in the Manuscript, is omitted from the published version: " 'I fear so myself' I said and a very slight examination satisfied me on the point." There is no mention of this treatment in the Abridged Text.

2 A fictional asylum.

3 This diagnosis is not noted in the Abridged Text.

face are paralysed."[1] How such a thing could have happened puzzled the attendant beyond measure. He seemed quite bewildered, and his brows were gathered in as he said:—

"I can't understand the two things. He could mark his face like that by beating his own head on the floor. I saw a young woman do it once at the Eversfield Asylum[2] before anyone could lay hands on her. And I suppose he might have broken his back by falling out of bed, if he got in an awkward kink. But for the life of me I can't imagine how the two things occurred. If his back was broke, he couldn't beat his head; and if his face was like that before the fall out of bed, there would be marks of it." I said to him:—

"Go to Dr. Van Helsing, and ask him to kindly come here at once. I want him without an instant's delay." The man ran off, and within a few minutes the Professor, in his dressing gown and slippers, appeared. When he saw Renfield on the ground, he looked keenly at him a moment and then turned to me. I think he recognised my thought in my eyes, for he said very quietly, manifestly for the ears of the attendant:—

"Ah, a sad accident! He will need very careful watching, and much attention. I shall stay with you myself; but I shall first dress myself. If you will remain I shall in a few minutes join you."

The patient was now breathing stertorously, and it was easy to see that he had suffered some terrible injury.[3] Van Helsing returned with extraordinary celerity, bearing with him a surgical case. He had evidently been thinking and had his mind made up; for, almost before he looked at the patient, he whispered to me:—

"Send the attendant away. We must be alone with him when he becomes conscious, after the operation." So I said:—

"I think that will do now, Simmons. We have done all that we can at present. You had better go your round, and Dr. Van Helsing will operate. Let me know instantly if there be anything unusual anywhere."

The man withdrew, and we went into a strict examination of the patient. The wounds of the face were superficial; the real injury was a depressed fracture of the skull, extending right up through the motor area. The Professor thought a moment and said:—

"We must reduce the pressure and get back to normal conditions, as far as can be; the rapidity of the suffusion shows the terrible nature of his injury. The whole motor area seems affected.[4] The suffusion of the brain will increase quickly, so we must trephine[5] at once or it may be too late." As he was speaking there was a soft tapping at the door. I went over and opened it and found in the corridor without, Arthur and Quincey in pajamas and slippers: the former spoke:—

"I heard your man call up Dr. Van Helsing and tell him of an accident. So I woke Quincey, or rather called for him as he was not asleep. Things are moving too quickly and too strangely for sound sleep for any of us these times.[6] I've been thinking that to-morrow night will not see things as they have been. We'll have to look back—and forward a little more than we have done. May we come in?" I nodded, and held the door open till they had entered; then I closed it again. When Quincey saw the attitude and state of the patient, and noted the horrible pool on the floor, he said softly:—

"My God! what has happened to him? Poor, poor devil!" I told him briefly, and added that we expected he would recover consciousness after the operation—for a short time, at all events. He went at once and sat down on the edge of the bed, with Godalming beside him; we all watched in patience.

"We shall wait," said Van Helsing, "just long enough to fix the best spot for trephining, so that we may most quickly and perfectly remove the blood clot; for it is evident that the hæmorrhage is increasing."[7]

The minutes during which we waited passed with fearful slowness. I had a horrible sinking in my heart, and from Van Helsing's face I gathered that he felt some fear or apprehension as to what was to come. I dreaded the words that Renfield might speak. I was positively afraid to think; but the conviction of what was coming was on me, as I have read of men who have heard the death-watch.[8] The poor man's breathing came in uncertain gasps. Each instant he seemed as though he would open his eyes and speak; but then would follow a prolonged stertorous breath, and he would relapse into a more fixed insensibility. Inured as I was to sick beds and death, this suspense grew, and grew upon me. I could almost hear the beating of my own

4 Wolf (*The Essential Dracula*) suggests a cortical edema, a swelling of the brain that results from accumulation of fluid. The swelling applies pressure to the cranial nerves and brain cells. The "motor area" referred to by Seward is the motor strip, or motor cortex, of the frontal lobe of the cerebral cortex (the frontal lobe being located just behind the forehead). Damage to the motor cortex may cause loss of control of motor function. Of course, damage to the frontal lobe generally may cause a far greater range of problems, including change in personality, cognitive dysfunction, lack of impulse control, inability to carry out a sequence of actions, aphasia, impaired spontaneity, and facial expressions unrelated to felt emotions, but it would seem that Seward is here speaking strictly of damage to the motor cortex.

5 A trephine is an instrument with circular toothed edges for sawing out cylindrical pieces of bone and hard tissue, usually from either the skull or the cornea; trephining is the cutting of such holes. Anthropologists have found evidence that trephining, or trepanning, is the

Pre-Incaic trephined skulls from Lake Titicaca.
Discovered and photographed by
Adolph F. Bandelier, ca. 1894

oldest form of neurosurgery; it was well known to Hippocrates (460–377 BC), Paul of Aegina (AD 625–690), and other ancient surgeons. Trephining was also performed in some of the earliest efforts to treat mental illness. According to Anton Sebastion's *Dictionary of the History of Medicine* (1999), nineteenth-century studies

Trephination tools.
Photograph courtesy Alex Peck Medical Antiques

of Melanesians and Algerians document its use as a treatment for epilepsy and head injuries as well as demonic possession.

6 However, no one seems to have thought to call Harker. The following two sentences—among the few remaining contributions of Holmwood to the planning—do not appear in the Abridged Text.

7 Wolf (*The Essential Dracula*) points out that it is virtually impossible to tell from visual observation where a bore hole should be made, and substantial brain damage could result from delay. "Localized paralysis, coming on immediately after an injury to the skull, calls for trephining at once. It is always better to operate early than to defer interference until inflammatory symptoms are present," opines John A. Wyeth, M.D., in his classic 1888 *Text-Book on Surgery*. "The danger is enhanced by delay. The disrepute which this operation has fallen into has been chiefly due to too great procrastination in surgical interference."

However, this viewpoint was already falling into disfavour. The state of the art of neurosurgery had been greatly advanced, by necessity, during the Napoleonic and Crimean wars and reached a state in which it would remain until the twentieth century. George H. B. Macleod, whose highly influential *Notes on the Surgery of the War in the Crimea, with Remarks on the Treatment of Gunshot Wounds* (1862) was widely used during the American Civil War, wrote of the trephine: "[L]ess difference of opinion, I believe, exists among the experienced army surgeons than among civilians; and I think the decided tendency among them is to endorse the modern 'treatment by expectancy,' and to avoid operation, except in rare cases. In this, I believe, they judge wisely; for, when we examine the question carefully, we find that there is not one single indication for having recourse to operation, which cannot, by the adduction of pertinent cases, be shown often fallacious; while, if we turn to authorities for advice, we find that not a great name can be ranged on one side, which cannot be balanced by as illustrious on the other."

After consideration of various cases of simple contusion, wounding caused by firearms, and symptoms of compression, Macleod concludes: "There are, I believe, very few surgeons of experience in the army now-a-days who approve of 'preventive trephining.' It may be said in our time to be a practice of the past—a practice to be pointed at as a milestone which we have left behind. . . . It is too much the custom, I think, to deny or overlook the danger which arises from the operation itself."

T. Forcht Dagi, summarising the state of the art in "The Management of Head Trauma" (1997), writes: "Toward the close of the premodern era, the preponderance of opinion favored surgical reticence, although the controversy was by no means resolved. This attitude certainly prevailed with respect to closed head injury and in most instances of open injuries. The two major arguments advanced against trephination were, first, the perceived inability to distinguish between the sizable number of cases that would heart; and the blood surging through my temples sounded like blows from a hammer. The silence finally became agonising. I looked at my companions, one after another, and saw from their flushed faces and damp brows that they were enduring equal torture. There was a nervous suspense over us all, as though overhead some dread bell would peal out powerfully when we should least expect it.

At last there came a time when it was evident that the patient was sinking fast; he might die at any moment. I looked up at the Professor and caught his eyes fixed on mine. His face was sternly set as he spoke:—

"There is no time to lose. His words may be worth many lives;[9] I have been thinking so, as I stood here. It may be there is a soul at stake! We shall operate just above the ear."

Without another word he made the operation.[10] For a few moments the breathing continued to be stertorous. Then there came a breath so prolonged that it seemed as though it would tear open his chest. Suddenly his eyes opened, and became fixed in a wild, helpless stare.[11] This was continued for a few moments; then it was softened into a glad surprise, and from the lips came a sigh of relief. He moved convulsively, and as he did so, said:—

"I'll be quiet, Doctor. Tell them to take off the strait-waistcoat. I have had a terrible dream, and it has left me so weak that I cannot move. What's wrong with my face? it feels all swollen, and it smarts dreadfully." He tried to turn his head; but even with the effort his eyes seemed to grow glassy again, so I gently put it back. Then Van Helsing said in a quiet grave tone:—

"Tell us your dream, Mr. Renfield." As he heard the voice his face brightened through its mutilation, and he said:—

"That is Dr. Van Helsing. How good it is of you to be here. Give me some water, my lips are dry; and I shall try to tell you. I dreamed"—he stopped and seemed fainting. I called quietly to Quincey—"The brandy—it is in my study—quick!" He flew and returned with a glass, the decanter of brandy and a carafe of water. We moistened the parched lips, and the patient quickly revived. It seemed, however, that his poor injured brain had been working in the interval, for, when he was quite conscious,

recover spontaneously and those that would be improved by trephination; and second, an increased appreciation of the dangers of trephination."

Van Helsing's eagerness to operate is out of step with this more modern medical thinking and may be seen as another example of the generally shabby quality of medical practise ascribed to him and Seward throughout the narrative. Again, it is quite possible they were not physicians at all but that, instead, the medical material was added by Stoker to the narrative to aid in concealing of their identities.

8 The "death-watch beetle" (*Xestobium rufovillosum*), a pest that feeds on wood, makes a noise like a ticking clock when its head bangs against the wood, a sound that attracts its mates; its clicking at night is said to foretell death. However, Wolf (*The Essential Dracula*) interprets this as a reference to the residents of London during the plague who listened day after day to the calls of those manning the "dead-carts," retrieving the corpses and removing them, in many cases, to mass burials. The narrator of Daniel Defoe's fictional *Journal of the Plague Year* (1722) tells of being reviled by tavern-goers: "They immediately fell upon me with ill language and oaths, asked me what I did out of my grave at such a time when so many honester men were carried into the churchyard, and why I was not at home saying my prayers against the dead-cart came for me, and the like." Bram Stoker's mother, Charlotte, recounts similar incidents in Sligo during a cholera epidemic. Seward may well have thought of the deaths following Dracula's arrival in London (Mrs. Westenra, Lucy, Renfield) as the onslaught of a plague.

This and the preceding three sentences do not appear in the Abridged Text.

9 This and the following two sentences justifying Van Helsing's surgery do not appear in the Abridged Text. Perhaps "Van Helsing" felt no further justifications were required after the revelations of the narrative.

10 Note that there is no precise description of the operation, as one might expect from an observing or assisting surgeon. Also, how convenient that Van Helsing just happens to have his trephination kit—a very specialised set of equipment—with him.

11 This kind of instantaneous relief from trephination—when it did not kill the patient—is borne out by Sir William Thornley Stoker, M.D., brother of Bram Stoker, who wrote in a letter preserved among the Notes: "Trephining to remove the depressed bone, or to give the surgeon opportunity to remove the blood clot might give instant relief. I have seen a patient in profound coma, begin to move his limbs and curse and swear during the operation. The more recent the injury, the more rapid the relief." Thornley, born in 1845, was from the same generation of physicians as Van Helsing and so seems to share his readiness to trephine the patient. See note 7 above for a discussion of the more contemporary view.

12 Is Renfield implying that he may become undead? There is no other indication that he has been turned, nor is there any apparent basis for his belief that he has been turned. Wolf (*The Essential Dracula*) suggests that Renfield may simply anticipate suffering in a hell of his own deserving.

13 The Abridged Text omits Renfield's description of the insect enticements offered by Dracula that follows.

he looked at me piercingly with an agonised confusion which I shall never forget, and said:—

"I must not deceive myself; it was no dream, but all a grim reality." Then his eyes roved round the room; as they caught sight of the two figures sitting patiently on the edge of the bed he went on:—

"If I were not sure already, I would know from them." For an instant his eyes closed—not with pain or sleep but voluntarily, as though he were bringing all his faculties to bear; when he opened them he said, hurriedly, and with more energy than he had yet displayed:—

"Quick, Doctor, quick. I am dying! I feel that I have but a few minutes; and then I must go back to death—or worse![12] Wet my lips with brandy again. I have something that I must say before I die; or before my poor crushed brain dies anyhow. Thank you! It was that night after you left me, when I implored you to let me go away. I couldn't speak then, for I felt my tongue was tied; but I was as sane then, except in that way, as I am now. I was in an agony of despair for a long time after you left me; it seemed hours. Then there came a sudden peace to me. My brain seemed to become cool again, and I realised where I was. I heard the dogs bark behind our house, but not where He was!" As he spoke, Van Helsing's eyes never blinked, but his hand came out and met mine and gripped it hard. He did not, however, betray himself; he nodded slightly, and said: "Go on," in a low voice. Renfield proceeded:—

"He came up to the window in the mist, as I had seen him often before; but he was solid then—not a ghost, and his eyes were fierce like a man's when angry. He was laughing with his red mouth; the sharp white teeth glinted in the moonlight when he turned to look back over the belt of trees, to where the dogs were barking. I wouldn't ask him to come in at first, though I knew he wanted to—just as he had wanted all along.[13] Then he began promising me things—not in words but by doing them." He was interrupted by a word from the Professor:—

"How?"

"By making them happen; just as he used to send in the flies when the sun was shining. Great big fat ones with steel and sapphire on their wings; and big moths, in the night, with skull and cross-bones on their backs." Van Helsing nodded to him as he whispered to me unconsciously:—

"The *Acherontia Atropos of the Sphinges*—what you call the 'Death's-head Moth!'"[14] The patient went on without stopping.

"Then he began to whisper: 'Rats, rats, rats! Hundreds, thousands, millions of them, and every one a life; and dogs to eat them, and cats too. All lives! all red blood, with years of life in it; and not merely buzzing flies!' I laughed at him, for I wanted to see what he could do. Then the dogs howled, away beyond the dark trees in His house. He beckoned me to the window. I got up and looked out, and He raised his hands, and seemed to call out without using any words. A dark mass spread over the grass, coming on like the shape of a flame of fire; and then He moved the mist to the right and left, and I could see that there were thousands of rats with their eyes blazing red—like His, only smaller. He held up his hand, and they all stopped; and I thought He seemed to be saying: 'All these lives will I give you, ay, and many more and greater, through countless ages, if you will fall down and worship me!'[15] And then a red cloud, like the colour of blood, seemed to close over my eyes; and before I knew what I was doing, I found myself opening the sash and saying to Him: 'Come in, Lord and Master!' The rats were all gone, but He slid into the room through the sash, though it was only open an inch wide—just as the Moon herself has often come in through the tiniest crack, and has stood before me in all her size and splendour."

His voice was weaker, so I moistened his lips with the brandy again, and he continued; but it seemed as though his memory had gone on working in the interval for his story was further advanced. I was about to call him back to the point, but Van Helsing whispered to me: "Let him go on. Do not interrupt him; he cannot go back, and may-be could not proceed at all if once he lost the thread of his thought." He proceeded:—

"All day I waited to hear from him, but he did not send me anything, not even a blow-fly, and when the moon got up I was pretty angry with him. When he slid in through the window, though it was shut, and did not even knock, I got mad with him. He sneered at me, and his white face looked out of the

14 Death's-head hawk moths (e.g., *Acherontia atropos*) are known for the colouration on their thorax, suggestive of a skull, and for their squeaking sound, not unlike that made by a queen bee—a similarity that allows them to feast undisturbed at beehives. European cultures regarded the moths as a harbinger of war, pestilence, and death, and Agnes Murgoçi, in "The Vampire in Roumania," reports that in Valcea souls of vampires are thought to be incarnated in death's-head hawk moths "which, when caught, should be impaled on a pin and stuck to a wall to prevent their flying further." A death's-head hawk moth features prominently in Thomas Harris's 1988 *The Silence of the Lambs* and the 1991 Oscar-winning film of the same name, in which the serial killer places a pupa of the moth in the mouths of his victims. The artwork for both the film and some editions of the book depicts a moth prominently emblazoned with what appears to be a skull—an image that itself references several sources: a

A death's-head hawk moth.
The Silence of the Lambs
(Orion Pictures Corporation, 1991)

Salvador Dalí charcoal-and-gouache drawing of seven nude female figures, arranged carefully to form the image of a skull, a 1951 collaboration by Dalí and photographer Philippe Halsman titled *In Voluptate Mors*, in which the aforementioned Dalí drawing appears, and the 1928 Luis Buñuel and Dalí short film *Un Chien Andalou*. So does the truly terrible film *The Blood Beast Terror* (1968), also released as *Blood Beast from Hell*, *The Vampire-Beast Craves Blood*, and *The Deathshead Vampire* and starring the venerable Peter Cushing as a Victorian police inspector, in which a scientist breeds a creature of horror that is a human/moth hybrid.

15 Many critics see biblical references here and liken this scene to Jesus's temptation in the wilderness by the devil (Matthew, chapter 4). Renfield, who earlier displayed his familiarity with the Bible (see chapter 11, note 36), interprets Dracula's attempt at seduction in his own (self-aggrandising) terms.

16 Apparently Renfield's madness-enhanced senses detect the odour of Dracula's infusions of the blood of Mina Harker, although for a moment he fails to identify the source of the changed odour. How acute his senses must have been to note a change in the "loathsomeness" of the odour (see chapter 19, note 17).

17 Again, Renfield senses that Mina's blood supply has been diminished. This perceptive remark does not appear in the Abridged Text.

18 Still no one makes a move to go up to the Harkers' room.

19 Dracula has bungled badly in his dealings with Renfield. If Dracula had merely lived up to his promises of hosts of pests, Renfield would never have ratted on him. Then when Dracula unnecessarily confronts Renfield, he fails to kill him, leaving him sufficiently conscious to reveal the Dracula-Mina connection.

20 The two doctors now abandon Renfield to die.

mist with his red eyes gleaming, and he went on as though he owned the whole place, and I was no one. He didn't even smell the same as he went by me.[16] I couldn't hold him. I thought that, somehow, Mrs. Harker had come into the room."

The two men sitting on the bed stood up and came over, standing behind him so that he could not see them, but where they could hear better. They were both silent, but the Professor started and quivered; his face, however, grew grimmer and sterner still. Renfield went on without noticing:—

"When Mrs. Harker came in to see me this afternoon she wasn't the same; it was like tea after the teapot has been watered."[17] Here we all moved, but no one said a word;[18] he went on:—

"I didn't know that she was here till she spoke; and she didn't look the same. I don't care for the pale people; I like them with lots of blood in them, and hers had all seemed to have run out. I didn't think of it at the time; but when she went away I began to think, and it made me mad to know that He had been taking the life out of her." I could feel that the rest quivered, as I did, but we remained otherwise still. "So when He came to-night I was ready for Him. I saw the mist stealing in, and I grabbed it tight. I had heard that madmen have unnatural strength; and as I knew I was a madman—at times anyhow—I resolved to use my power. Ay, and He felt it too, for He had come out of the mist to struggle with me. I held tight; and I thought I was going to win, for I didn't mean Him to take any more of her life, till I saw His eyes. They burned into me, and my strength became like water. He slipped through it, and when I tried to cling to Him, He raised me up and flung me down. There was a red cloud before me, and a noise like thunder, and the mist seemed to steal away under the door."[19] His voice was becoming fainter and his breath more stertorous. Van Helsing stood up instinctively.[20]

"We know the worst now," he said. "He is here, and we know his purpose. It may not be too late. Let us be armed—the same as we were the other night, but lose no time; there is not an instant to spare." There was no need to put our fear, nay our conviction, into words—we shared them in common. We all hurried and took from our rooms the same things that we had when we entered the Count's house. The Professor had his ready, and as we met in the corridor he pointed to them significantly as he said:—

"They never leave me; and they shall not till this unhappy business is over. Be wise also, my friends. It is no common enemy that we deal with. Alas! alas! that that dear Madam Mina should suffer!" He stopped; his voice was breaking, and I do not know if rage or terror predominated in my own heart.

Outside the Harkers' door we paused. Art and Quincey held back, and the latter said:—

"Should we disturb her?"

"We must," said Van Helsing grimly. "If the door be locked, I shall break it in."

"May it not frighten her terribly? It is unusual to break into a lady's room!" Van Helsing said solemnly.[21]

"You are always right; but this is life and death. All chambers are alike to the doctor; and even were they not they are all as one to me to-night. Friend John, when I turn the handle, if the door does not open, do you put your shoulder down and shove; and you too, my friends. Now!"

He turned the handle as he spoke, but the door did not yield. We threw ourselves against it; with a crash it burst open, and we almost fell headlong into the room. The Professor did actually fall, and I saw across him as he gathered himself up from hands and knees. What I saw appalled me. I felt my hair rise like bristles on the back of my neck, and my heart seemed to stand still.

The moonlight was so bright that through the thick yellow blind the room was light enough to see. On the bed beside the window lay Jonathan Harker, his face flushed and breathing heavily as though in a stupor. Kneeling on the near edge of the bed facing outwards was the white-clad figure of his wife. By her side stood a tall, thin man, clad in black. His face was turned from us, but the instant we saw we all recognised the Count—in every way, even to the scar on his forehead.[22] With his left hand he held both Mrs. Harker's hands, keeping them away with her arms at full tension; his right hand gripped her by the back of the neck, forcing her face down on his bosom. Her white nightdress was smeared with blood, and a thin

21 The punctuation in the first edition is incorrect here; this should be a colon and em-dash, introducing the remarks that follow, which are Van Helsing's.

22 The scar could not have been visible if "[h]is face was turned from us." This suggests that the scene is a constructed one, a fictionalised version of the true events, which may in fact have been sexual. See the next note.

23 What is going on here? Wolf (*The Essential Dracula*), not alone in his leering response, calls this an "extraordinary scene . . . crammed with implications, nearly all of them sexual." Although Seward's narrative mentions no sex acts, the picture of Harker, "his face flushed and breathing heavily," Mina's dishevelled nightdress, the Count's "torn-open dress" (torn open by him or by Mina?), the Count forcing her head down, all bear resemblance to rape of one or both victims. Wolf suggests as possibilities "a vengeful cuckoldry . . . a ménage à trois . . . mutual oral sexuality . . . [and] the impregnation of Mina." Leatherdale (*Dracula Unearthed*) is bolder, contending that the references to milk and the smearing of blood on Mina (rather than dripping, as Dracula is described) make clear what fluids have been exchanged.

24 The Manuscript continues: "Even then at that awful moment with such a tragedy before my eyes, the figure of Mephistopheles in the Opera [Charles Gounod's 1859 *Faust*] cowering before Margaret's [Marguerite's] lifted cross swam up before me and for an instant I wondered if I were mad." The scene as described does not exist in the libretto and was undoubtedly added by a zealous director to a production seen by Seward. The sentence does not appear in the published narrative.

stream trickled down the man's bare chest which was shown by his torn-open dress. The attitude of the two had a terrible resemblance to a child forcing a kitten's nose into a saucer of milk to compel it to drink.[23] As we burst into the room, the Count turned his face, and the hellish look that I had heard described seemed to leap into it. His eyes flamed red with devilish passion; the great nostrils of the white aquiline nose opened wide and quivered at the edge; and the white sharp teeth, behind the full lips of the blood-dripping mouth, clamped together like those of a wild beast. With a wrench, which threw his victim back upon the bed as though hurled from a height, he turned and sprang at us. But by this time the Professor had gained his feet, and was holding towards him the envelope which contained the Sacred Wafer. The Count suddenly stopped, just as poor Lucy had done outside the tomb, and cowered back.[24] Further and further back he cowered, as we, lifting our crucifixes, advanced. The moonlight suddenly failed, as a great black cloud sailed across the sky; and when the gaslight sprang up under Quincey's match, we saw nothing

Van Helsing (Eduardo Arozamena) brandishes
his crucifix at Dracula (Carlos Villarias).
Dracula (Spanish-language version, Universal Pictures, 1931)

but a faint vapour.[25] This, as we looked, trailed under the door, which with the recoil from its bursting open, had swung back to its old position. Van Helsing, Art, and I moved forward to Mrs. Harker, who by this time had drawn her breath and with it had given a scream so wild, so ear-piercing, so despairing that it seems to me now that it will ring in my ears till my dying day. For a few seconds she lay in her helpless attitude and disarray. Her face was ghastly, with a pallor which was accentuated by the blood which smeared her lips and cheeks and chin; from her throat trickled a thin stream of blood. Her eyes were mad with terror. Then she put before her face her poor crushed hands, which bore on their whiteness the red mark of the Count's terrible grip, and from behind them came a low desolate wail which made the terrible scream seem only the quick expression of an endless grief. Van Helsing stepped forward and drew the coverlet gently over her body,[26] whilst Art, after looking at her face for an instant despairingly, ran out of the room. Van Helsing whispered to me:—

"Jonathan is in a stupor such as we know the Vampire can produce.[27] We can do nothing with poor Madam Mina for a few moments till she recovers herself; I must wake him!" He dipped the end of a towel in cold water and with it began to flick him on the face, his wife all the while holding her face between her hands and sobbing in a way that was heartbreaking to hear. I raised the blind, and looked out of the window. There was much moonshine; and as I looked I could see Quincey Morris run across the lawn and hide himself in the shadow of a great yew-tree. It puzzled me to think why he was doing this;[28] but at the instant I heard Harker's quick exclamation as he woke to partial consciousness, and turned to the bed. On his face, as there might well be, was a look of wild amazement. He seemed dazed for a few seconds, and then full consciousness seemed to burst upon him all at once, and he started up. His wife was aroused by the quick movement, and turned to him with her arms stretched out, as though to embrace him; instantly, however, she drew them in again, and putting her elbows together,[29] held her hands before her face, and shuddered till the bed beneath her shook.

"In God's name what does this mean?" Harker cried out.

25 This is a new phenomenon—a vapour trail, which surprisingly went unnoticed by Harker in Castle Dracula. Perhaps this was not vapour but rather a milky substance expressed from Dracula's body.

26 Apparently exposed, for her clothing was in "disarray."

27 This is a new symptom, notwithstanding Van Helsing's comment, and the Manuscript describes it merely as "a stupor of some sort." Certainly Lucy was in no stupor on the evening she was fatally attacked by Dracula; she retained the ability to compose a detailed memorandum of the events. The Notes indicate that the vampire has the power of creating evil thoughts or destroying good thoughts or the will. However, there is no other demonstration of any "stupefying" ability. Leatherdale (*Dracula Unearthed*) speculates that this may be postcoital stupor, if Jonathan has been forced into a three-way coupling, or shock from having to watch Dracula exact his revenge for Harker's attack.

28 Indeed, it seems pointless to hide in shadows when your target can see in the dark. Morris has an explanation for his quick exit from the building, but is it not more likely that he wished to consult with his "colleague" Dracula? See chapter 18, note 49.

29 To cover her breasts, Leatherdale (*Dracula Unearthed*) points out.

30 Some see this as meaning that Harker has become sexually aroused.

31 The highly religious Mina accuses herself of moral leprosy—compare Lev. 13:45–46: "And the leper in whom the plague is, his clothes shall be rent, and his head bare, and he shall put a covering upon his upper lip, and shall cry, Unclean, unclean. All the days wherein the plague shall be in him he shall be defiled; he is unclean: he shall dwell alone; without the camp shall his habitation be."

Mina's insight, that vampirism is an infectious disease, is certainly consistent with much of the folklore. See "Dracula's Family Tree" in Part II.

"Dr. Seward, Dr. Van Helsing, what is it? What has happened? What is wrong? Mina, dear, what is it? What does that blood mean? My God, my God! has it come to this!" and, raising himself to his knees, he beat his hands wildly together. "Good God help us! help her! oh, help her!" With a quick movement he jumped from bed, and began to pull on his clothes,—all the man in him awake at the need for instant exertion.[30] "What has happened? Tell me all about it!" he cried without pausing. "Dr. Van Helsing, you love Mina, I know. Oh, do something to save her. It cannot have gone too far yet. Guard her while I look for *him*!" His wife, through her terror and horror and distress, saw some sure danger to him: instantly forgetting her own grief, she seized hold of him and cried out:—

"No! no! Jonathan, you must not leave me. I have suffered enough to-night, God knows, without the dread of his harming you. You must stay with me. Stay with these friends who will watch over you!" Her expression became frantic as she spoke; and, he yielding to her, she pulled him down sitting on the bed side, and clung to him fiercely.

Van Helsing and I tried to calm them both. The Professor held up his little golden crucifix, and said with wonderful calmness:—

"Do not fear, my dear. We are here; and whilst this is close to you no foul thing can approach. You are safe for to-night; and we must be calm and take counsel together." She shuddered and was silent, holding down her head on her husband's breast. When she raised it, his white night-robe was stained with blood where her lips had touched, and where the thin open wound in her neck had sent forth drops. The instant she saw it she drew back, with a low wail, and whispered, amidst choking sobs:—

"Unclean, unclean! I must touch him or kiss him no more.[31] Oh, that it should be that it is I who am now his worst enemy, and whom he may have most cause to fear." To this he spoke out resolutely:—

"Nonsense, Mina. It is a shame to me to hear such a word. I would not hear it of you; and I shall not hear it from you. May God judge me by my deserts, and punish me with more bitter suffering than even this hour, if by any act or will of mine anything ever come between us!" He put out his arms and folded her to his breast; and for a while she lay there sobbing. He looked at us over her bowed head, with eyes that blinked damply above his quivering nostrils; his mouth was set as steel. After a while her sobs became less frequent and more faint, and then he said to me, speaking with a studied calmness which I felt tried his nervous power to the utmost:—

"And now, Dr. Seward, tell me all about it. Too well I know the broad fact; tell me all that has been." I told him exactly what had happened, and he listened with seeming impassiveness; but his nostrils twitched and his eyes blazed as I told how the ruthless hands of the Count had held his wife in that terrible and horrid position, with her mouth to the open wound in his breast. It interested me, even at that moment, to see, that, whilst the face of white set passion worked convulsively over the bowed head, the hands tenderly and lovingly stroked the ruffled hair.[32] Just as I had finished, Quincey and Godalming knocked at the door. They entered in obedience to our summons. Van Helsing looked at me questioningly. I understood him to mean if we were to take advantage of their coming to divert if possible the thoughts of the unhappy husband and wife from each other and from themselves; so on nodding acquiescence to him he asked them what they had seen or done. To which Lord Godalming answered:—

"I could not see him anywhere in the passage, or in any of our rooms. I looked in the study but, though he had been there, he had gone. He had, however—" He stopped suddenly, looking at the poor drooping figure on the bed. Van Helsing said gravely:—

"Go on, friend Arthur. We want here no more concealments. Our hope now is in knowing all. Tell freely!" So Art went on:—

"He had been there, and though it could only have been for a few seconds, he made rare hay of the place.[33] All the manuscript had been burned, and the blue flames were flickering amongst the white ashes; the cylinders of your phonograph too were thrown on the fire, and the wax had helped the flames."[34] Here I interrupted. "Thank God there is the other copy in the safe!" His face lit for a moment, but fell again as he went on: "I ran downstairs then, but could see no sign of him. I looked into

32 A deliberate, jealous echo of the Count's act of holding Mina's head to his breast?

33 To "make hay" of a thing is to create confusion, a mess; hence, a "rare hay" is very confused or messy.

34 Leatherdale (*Dracula Unearthed*) points out that Renfield knew nothing about the Harker Papers, and Dracula could only have learned about them from Mina.

Renfield's room; but there was no trace there except—!" Again he paused. "Go on," said Harker hoarsely; so he bowed his head and moistening his lips with his tongue, added: "except that the poor fellow is dead." Mrs. Harker raised her head, looking from one to the other of us she said solemnly:—

"God's will be done!" I could not but feel that Art was keeping back something; but, as I took it that it was with a purpose, I said nothing. Van Helsing turned to Morris and asked:—

"And you, friend Quincey, have you any to tell?"

"A little," he answered. "It may be much eventually, but at present I can't say. I thought it well to know if possible where the Count would go when he left the house. I did not see him; but I saw a bat rise from Renfield's window, and flap westward. I expected to see him in some shape go back to Carfax; but he evidently sought some other lair. He will not be back to-night; for the sky is reddening in the east, and the dawn is close. We must work to-morrow!"

He said the latter words through his shut teeth. For a space of perhaps a couple of minutes there was silence, and I could fancy that I could hear the sound of our hearts beating; then Van Helsing said, placing his hand tenderly on Mina Harker's head:—

"And now, Madam Mina—poor, dear, dear Madam Mina— tell us exactly what happened. God knows that I do not want that you be pained; but it is need that we know all. For now more than ever has all work to be done quick and sharp, and in deadly earnest. The day is close to us that must end all, if it may be so; and now is the chance that we may live and learn."

The poor, dear lady shivered, and I could see the tension of her nerves as she clasped her husband closer to her and bent her head lower and lower still on his breast. Then she raised her head proudly, and held out one hand to Van Helsing who took it in his, and, after stooping and kissing it reverently, held it fast. The other hand was locked in that of her husband, who held his other arm thrown round her protectingly. After a pause in which she was evidently ordering her thoughts, she began:—

"I took the sleeping draught which you had so kindly given me, but for a long time it did not act. I seemed to become more wakeful, and myriads of horrible fancies began to crowd in upon my mind—all of them connected with death, and vampires; with blood, and pain, and trouble." Her husband involuntarily groaned as she turned to him and said lovingly: "Do not fret, dear. You must be brave and strong, and help me through the horrible task. If you only knew what an effort it is to me to tell of this fearful thing at all, you would understand how much I need your help. Well, I saw I must try to help the medicine to its work with my will, if it was to do me any good, so I resolutely set myself to sleep. Sure enough sleep must soon have come to me, for I remember no more. Jonathan coming in had not waked me, for he lay by my side when next I remember. There was in the room the same thin white mist that I had before noticed. But I forget now if you know of this; you will find it in my diary which I shall show you later. I felt the same vague terror which had come to me before and the same sense of some presence. I turned to wake Jonathan, but found that he slept so soundly that it seemed as if it was he who had taken the sleeping draught, and not I. I tried, but I could not wake him. This caused me a great fear, and I looked around terrified. Then indeed, my heart sank within me: beside the bed, as if he had stepped out of the mist—or rather as if the mist had turned into this figure, for it had entirely disappeared—stood a tall, thin man, all in black. I knew him at once from the description of the others. The waxen face; the high aquiline nose, on which the light fell in a thin white line; the parted red lips, with the sharp white teeth showing between; and the red eyes that I had seemed to see in the sunset on the windows of St. Mary's Church at Whitby. I knew, too, the red scar on his forehead where Jonathan had struck him. For an instant my heart stood still, and I would have screamed out, only that I was paralysed. In the pause he spoke in a sort of keen, cutting whisper, pointing as he spoke to Jonathan:—

"'Silence! If you make a sound I shall take him and dash his brains out before your very eyes.'[35] I was appalled and was too bewildered to do or say anything. With a mocking smile, he placed one hand upon my shoulder and, holding me tight, bared my throat with the other, saying as he did so: 'First, a little refreshment to reward my exertions. You may as well be

35 This seems to be Mina's rationalisation. Surely Dracula had no need to bargain with her and had every reason to kill Harker.

36 As we have seen, these "appeasements" occurred on the evenings of 30 September and 1 October—that is, the two prior evenings.

37 Dracula here ironically paraphrases Adam, who says upon discovering Eve: "And Adam said, This is now bone of my bones, and flesh of my flesh: she shall be called Woman, because she was taken out of Man" (Gen. 2:23).

38 Presumably, Dracula means in the same way as the vampire women, who do not feed him but are his companions.

39 The Manuscript continues with the phrase "you shall have the Vampire's baptism of blood!" In other words, in the Manuscript, this is Dracula's expression, not Van Helsing's. This strengthens the theory that drinking the vampire's blood is a critical step in turning a victim. Whether Lucy was similarly baptised cannot be determined from the narrative, but it cannot be ruled out.

quiet; it is not the first time, or the second, that your veins have appeased my thirst!'[36] I was bewildered, and, strangely enough, I did not want to hinder him. I suppose it is a part of the horrible curse that such is, when his touch is on his victim. And oh, my God, my God, pity me! He placed his reeking lips upon my throat!" Her husband groaned again. She clasped his hand harder, and looked at him pityingly, as if he were the injured one, and went on:—

"I felt my strength fading away, and I was in a half swoon. How long this horrible thing lasted I know not; but it seemed that a long time must have passed before he took his foul, awful, sneering mouth away. I saw it drip with the fresh blood!" The remembrance seemed for a while to overpower her, and she drooped and would have sunk down but for her husband's sustaining arm. With a great effort she recovered herself and went on:—

"Then he spoke to me mockingly, 'And so you, like the others, would play your brains against mine. You would help these men to hunt me and frustrate me in my designs! You know now, and they know in part already, and will know in full before long, what it is to cross my path. They should have kept their energies for use closer to home. Whilst they played wits against me—against me who commanded nations, and intrigued for them, and fought for them, hundreds of years before they were born—I was countermining them. And you, their best beloved one, are now to me, flesh of my flesh; blood of my blood;[37] kin of my kin; my bountiful wine-press for a while; and shall be later on my companion and my helper.[38] You shall be avenged in turn; for not one of them but shall minister to your needs. But as yet you are to be punished for what you have done. You have aided in thwarting me; now you shall come to my call. When my brain says "Come!" to you, you shall cross land or sea to do my bidding; and to that end this!'[39] With that he pulled open his shirt, and with his long sharp nails opened a vein in his breast. When the blood began to spurt out, he took my hands in one of his, holding them tight, and with the other seized my neck and pressed my mouth to the wound, so that I must either suffocate or swallow some of the—Oh my God! my God! what have I done? What

"[H]e pulled open his shirt, and with his long sharp nails opened a vein in his breast." Christopher Lee as Dracula and Suzan Farmer as Diana Kent.
Dracula, Prince of Darkness (Hammer Film Productions, 1965)

40 There may be other techniques for turning a victim, but Dracula applies this method because he wants to use Mina as his "winepress" for a while. There is no evidence that Dracula forced Lucy to drink his blood, but he may well have done so. Van Helsing seems to believe that dying from the vampire's bite during sleep is sufficient to cause the victim to become a vampire, although this makes no difference with Lucy. See chapter 12, note 53, and "Dracula's Family Tree" in Part II for other theories.

41 Contrary to myth, Harker's hair cannot have turned white in an instant of fright. Legends abound that, for example, the hair of Thomas More became entirely white the evening before his execution in 1535; the hair of Henry of Navarre, later Henry IV of France, changed following his escape from the Saint Bartholomew's Day Massacre in 1572; and Marie Antoinette's hair turned white the night before she was beheaded. The phenomenon is described as a proven medical fact in Thomas Pettigrew's *On Superstitions Connected with the History and Practice of Medicine and Surgery* (1844), referenced in the Notes.

In fact, whitening is caused by a progressive decline in the absolute number of melanocytes (pigment-producing cells in the skin, hair, and eye), which normally decrease over time. However, it is possible that patchy loss of nonwhite hairs—possibly the sudden result of a condition known as diffuse alopecia areata, thought to be an autoimmune disease or to be stress induced—might cause a partly grey-haired individual to appear to have turned white-haired almost overnight.

have I done to deserve such a fate, I who have tried to walk in meekness and righteousness all my days. God pity me! Look down on a poor soul in worse than mortal peril; and in mercy pity those to whom she is dear!" Then she began to rub her lips as though to cleanse them from pollution.[40]

As she was telling her terrible story, the eastern sky began to quicken, and everything became more and more clear. Harker was still and quiet; but over his face, as the awful narrative went on, came a grey look which deepened and deepened in the morning light, till when the first red streak of the coming dawn shot up, the flesh stood darkly out against the whitening hair.[41]

We have arranged that one of us is to stay within call of the unhappy pair till we can meet together and arrange about taking action.

Of this I am sure: the sun rises to-day on no more miserable house in all the great round of its daily course.

Chapter 22

JONATHAN HARKER'S JOURNAL.

1 The Abridged Text omits the following two paragraphs, discussing the demise of Renfield and the need for a cover-up of his death.

3 October.—As I must do something or go mad, I write this diary. It is now six o'clock, and we are to meet in the study in half an hour and take something to eat; for Dr. Van Helsing and Dr. Seward are agreed that if we do not eat we cannot work our best. Our best will be, God knows, required to-day. I must keep writing at every chance, for I dare not stop to think. All, big and little, must go down; perhaps at the end the little things may teach us most. The teaching, big or little, could not have landed Mina or me anywhere worse than we are to-day. However, we must trust and hope. Poor Mina told me just now, with the tears running down her dear cheeks, that it is in trouble and trial that our faith is tested—that we must keep on trusting; and that God will aid us up to the end. The end! oh my God! what end? . . . To work! To work![1]

When Dr. Van Helsing and Dr. Seward had come back from seeing poor Renfield, we went gravely into what was to be done. First, Dr. Seward told us that when he and Dr. Van Helsing had gone down to the room below they had found Renfield lying on the floor, all in a heap. His face was all bruised and crushed in, and the bones of the neck were broken.

Dr. Seward asked the attendant who was on duty in the passage if he had heard anything. He said that he had been sitting down—he confessed to half dozing—when he heard loud voices in the room, and then Renfield had called out

"Now—now's the time—death to the monster."
Varney, the Vampyre; or, The Feast of Blood (1847)

loudly several times, "God! God! God!" After that there was a sound of falling, and when he entered the room he found him lying on the floor, face down, just as the doctors had seen him. Van Helsing asked if he had heard "voices" or "a voice," and he said he could not say; that at first it had seemed to him as if there were two, but as there was no one in the room it could have been only one. He could swear to it, if required, that the word "God" was spoken by the patient. Dr. Seward said to us, when we were alone, that he did not wish to go into the matter; the question of an inquest had to be considered, and it would never do to put forward the truth, as no one would believe it. As it was, he thought that on the attendant's evidence he could give a certificate of death by misadventure in falling from bed.[2] In case the coroner should demand it, there would be a formal inquest, necessarily to the same result.

2 Seward again gives a false death certificate.

3 A little late, what? Of course, now not only is it too late—it is actually detrimental to the cause.

4 That is, "Aren't you afraid that you've become a vampire?"

5 Interestingly, Mina's symptoms of turning do not correspond to Lucy's. At roughly this interval in Lucy's service as a source of nourishment for Dracula, she was markedly weak and had little sense of the danger she faced or what had happened to her. Mina, however, shows only a tendency to become nocturnal and is lucid about her peril. Can this be attributed to Mina's drinking Dracula's blood? Of course, the possibility that Lucy did the same cannot be dismissed, and there are those who believe that notwithstanding Van Helsing's expostulations, vampires are created only by the sharing of blood, not merely by a one-way transfer. See "Dracula's Family Tree" in Part II for a further discussion.

6 As noted previously, folklore ascribed vampirism to all suicides; yet Mina sees self-murder as a way to end her infection. See "Dracula's Family Tree" in Part II. Does Van Helsing know this, or is he only giving voice to his Catholic faith?

When the question began to be discussed as to what should be our next step, the very first thing we decided was that Mina should be in full confidence;[3] that nothing of any sort—no matter how painful—should be kept from her. She herself agreed as to its wisdom, and it was pitiful to see her so brave and yet so sorrowful, and in such a depth of despair. "There must be no concealment," she said, "Alas! we have had too much already. And besides there is nothing in all the world that can give me more pain than I have already endured—than I suffer now! Whatever may happen, it must be of new hope or of new courage to me!" Van Helsing was looking at her fixedly as she spoke, and said, suddenly but quietly:—

"But dear Madam Mina, are you not afraid; not for yourself, but for others from yourself, after what has happened?"[4] Her face grew set in its lines, but her eyes shone with the devotion of a martyr as she answered:—

"Ah no! for my mind is made up!"

"To what?" he asked gently, whilst we were all very still; for each in our own way we had a sort of vague idea of what she meant. Her answer came with direct simplicity, as though she were simply stating a fact:—

"Because if I find in myself—and I shall watch keenly for it—a sign of harm to any that I love, I shall die!"[5]

"You would not kill yourself?" he asked, hoarsely.

"I would; if there were no friend who loved me, who would save me such a pain, and so desperate an effort!" She looked at him meaningly as she spoke. He was sitting down; but now he rose and came close to her and put his hand on her head as he said solemnly:—

"My child, there is such an one if it were for your good. For myself I could hold it in my account with God to find such an euthanasia for you, even at this moment if it were best. Nay, were it safe! But my child—" for a moment he seemed choked, and a great sob rose in his throat; he gulped it down and went on:—

"There are here some who would stand between you and death. You must not die. You must not die by any hand; but least of all by your own.[6] Until the other, who has fouled your sweet life, is true dead you must not die; for if he is still with the quick Un-Dead, your death would make you even as he is. No, you must live! You must struggle and strive to live, though death would seem a boon unspeakable. You must fight Death himself, though he come to you in pain or in joy; by the day, or the night; in safety or in peril! On your living soul I charge you that you do not die—nay, nor think of death—till this great evil be past." The poor dear grew white as death, and shook and shivered, as I have seen a quicksand shake and shiver at the incoming of the tide. We were all silent; we could do nothing. At length she grew more calm and turning to him said, sweetly, but oh! so sorrowfully, as she held out her hand:—

"I promise you, my dear friend, that if God will let me live, I shall strive to do so; till, if it may be in His good time, this horror may have passed away from me." She was so good and brave that we all felt that our hearts were strengthened to work and endure for her, and we began to discuss what we were to do. I told her that she was to have all the papers in the safe, and all the papers or diaries and phonographs we might hereafter use; and was to keep the record as she had done before. She was pleased with the prospect of anything to do—if "pleased" could be used in connection with so grim an interest.

As usual Van Helsing had thought ahead of everyone else, and was prepared with an exact ordering of our work.

"It is perhaps well," he said, "that at our meeting after our visit to Carfax we decided not to do anything with the earth-boxes that lay there. Had we done so, the Count must have guessed our purpose, and would doubtless have taken measures in advance to frustrate such an effort with regard to the others; but now he does not know our intentions. Nay, more, in all probability, he does not know that such a power exists to us as can sterilise his lairs, so that he cannot use them as of old.[7] We are now so much further advanced in our knowledge as to their disposition, that, when we have examined the house in Piccadilly, we may track the very last of them. To-day, then, is ours; and in it rests our hope. The sun that rose on our sorrow this morning guards us in its course. Until it sets to-night, that monster must retain whatever form he now has. He is confined within the limitations of his earthly envelope. He cannot melt into thin air nor disappear through

[7] Leatherdale (*Dracula Unearthed*) wonders why Dracula did not then return to Carfax to rest rather than fly all the way to London.

8 A phrase still in use in the much-diminished pursuit of foxhunting, meaning to fill up the fox's burrows to prevent it from running to ground. The alternative is referred to as "terrier work," in which the "hounds" dig the fox out of the burrow.

cracks or chinks or crannies. If he go through a door-way, he must open the door like a mortal. And so we have this day to hunt out all his lairs and sterilise them. So we shall, if we have not yet catch him and destroy him, drive him to bay in some place where the catching and the destroying shall be, in time, sure." Here I started up for I could not contain myself at the thought that the minutes and seconds so preciously laden with Mina's life and happiness were flying from us, since whilst we talked action was impossible. But Van Helsing held up his hand warningly. "Nay, friend Jonathan," he said, "in this, the quickest way home is the longest way, so your proverb say. We shall all act, and act with desperate quick, when the time has come. But think, in all probable the key of the situation is in that house in Piccadilly. The Count may have many houses which he has bought. Of them he will have deeds of purchase, keys and other things. He will have paper that he write on; he will have his book of cheques. There are many belongings that he must have somewhere; why not in this place so central, so quiet, where he come and go by the front or the back at all hour, when in the very vast of the traffic there is none to notice. We shall go there and search that house; and when we learn what it holds, then we do what our friend Arthur call, in his phrases of hunt, 'stop the earths'[8] and so we run down our old fox—so? is it not?"

"Then let us come at once," I cried, "we are wasting the precious, precious time!" The Professor did not move, but simply said:—

"And how are we to get into that house in Piccadilly?"

"Any way!" I cried. "We shall break in if need be."

"And your police; where will they be, and what will they say?"

I was staggered; but I knew that if he wished to delay he had a good reason for it. So I said, as quietly as I could:—

"Don't wait more than need be; you know, I am sure, what torture I am in."

"Ah, my child, that I do; and indeed there is no wish of me to add to your anguish. But just think, what can we do, until all the world be at movement. Then will come our time. I have thought and thought, and it seems to me that the simplest way is the best of all. Now we wish to get into the house, but we have no key; is it not so?" I nodded.

"Now suppose that you were, in truth, the owner of that house, and could not still get it;[9] and think there was to you no conscience of the housebreaker, what would you do?"

"I should get a respectable locksmith, and set him to work to pick the lock for me."

"And your police, they would interfere, would they not?"

"Oh, no! not if they knew the man was properly employed."

"Then," he looked at me as keenly as he spoke, "all that is in doubt is the conscience of the employer, and the belief of your policemen as to whether or no that employer has a good conscience or a bad one. Your police must indeed be zealous men and clever—oh, so clever!—in reading the heart, that they trouble themselves in such matter. No, no, my friend Jonathan, you go take the lock off a hundred empty house in this your London, or of any city in the world; and if you do it as such things are rightly done, and at the time such things are rightly done, no one will interfere. I have read of a gentleman who owned a so fine house in London,[10] and when he went for months of summer to Switzerland and lock up his house, some burglar came and broke window at back and got in. Then he went and made open the shutters in front and walk out and in through the door, before the very eyes of the police. Then he have an auction in that house, and advertise it, and put up big notice: and when the day come he sell off by a great auctioneer all the goods of that other man who own them. Then he go to a builder, and he sell him that house, making an agreement that he pull it down and take all away within a certain time. And your police and other authority help him all they can. And when that owner come back from his holiday in Switzerland he find only an empty hole where his house had been. This was all done *en règle;*[11] and in our work we shall be *en règle* too. We shall not go so early that the policemen, who have then little to think of, shall deem it strange; but we shall go after ten o'clock when there are many about, and such things would be done were we indeed owners of the house."

I could not but see how right he was, and the terrible despair

9 Evidently a typographical error for "get in."

10 The anecdote of the absent tourist does not appear in the Abridged Text.

11 French: in the proper order.

12 Leatherdale (*Dracula Unearthed*) makes the logical deduction from this that Ring is not far from central London. The suggestion of a carriage and the rejection of it that follows do not appear in the Abridged Text.

13 The Manuscript contains the following, omitted from the published narrative: "So it was arranged that Lord Godalming was to have three horses ready at Piccadilly close to the Junior Constitutional Club where they would not attract attention. He also arranged for a groom to"—

14 The description of Mina's symptoms is not included in the Abridged Text. Perhaps Harker wanted to excuse his failure to see the impending problem.

15 The reasonable suggestions of this and the preceding sentence do not appear in the Abridged Text, perhaps because they turned out to be impractical.

of Mina's face became relaxed in thought; there was hope in such good counsel. Van Helsing went on:—

"When once within that house we may find more clues; at any rate some of us can remain there whilst the rest find the other places where there be more earth-boxes—at Bermondsey and Mile End."

Lord Godalming stood up. "I can be of some use here," he said. "I shall wire to my people to have horses and carriages where they will be most convenient."[12]

"Look here, old fellow," said Morris, "it is a capital idea to have all ready in case we want to go horsebacking; but don't you think that one of your snappy carriages with its heraldic adornments in a byeway of Walworth or Mile End would attract too much attention for our purposes? It seems to me that we ought to take cabs when we go south or east; and even leave them somewhere near the neighbourhood we are going to."

"Friend Quincey is right!" said the Professor. "His head is what you call in plane with the horizon. It is a difficult thing that we go to do, and we do not want no peoples to watch us if so it may."[13]

Mina took a growing interest in everything and I was rejoiced to see that the exigency of affairs was helping her to forget for a time the terrible experience of the night. She was very, very pale—almost ghastly, and so thin that her lips were drawn away, showing her teeth in somewhat of prominence. I did not mention this last, lest it should give her needless pain; but it made my blood run cold in my veins to think of what had occurred with poor Lucy when the Count had sucked her blood. As yet there was no sign of the teeth growing sharper; but the time as yet was short, and there was time for fear.[14]

When we came to the discussion of the sequence of our efforts and of the disposition of our forces, there were new sources of doubt. It was finally agreed that before starting for Piccadilly we should destroy the Count's lair close at hand. In case he should find it out too soon, we should thus be still ahead of him in our work of destruction; and his presence in his purely material shape, and at his weakest, might give us some new clue.[15]

As to the disposal of forces, it was suggested by the Professor that, after our visit to Carfax, we should all enter the house in Piccadilly; that the two doctors and I should remain there, whilst Lord Godalming and Quincey found the lairs at Walworth and Mile End and destroyed them. It was possible, if not likely, the Professor urged, that the Count might appear in Piccadilly during the day, and that if so we might be able to cope with him then and there. At any rate, we might be able to follow him in force. To this plan I strenuously objected, in so far as my going was concerned, for I said that I intended to stay and protect Mina. I thought that my mind was made up on the subject; but Mina would not listen to my objection. She said that there might be some law matter in which I could be useful; that amongst the Count's papers might be some clue which I could understand out of my experience in Transylvania; and that, as it was, all the strength we could muster was required to cope with the Count's extraordinary power. I had to give in, for Mina's resolution was fixed; she said that it was the last hope for *her* that we should all work together. "As for me," she said, "I have no fear. Things have been as bad as they can be; and whatever may happen must have in it some element of hope or comfort. Go, my husband! God can, if He wishes it, guard me as well alone as with any one present." So I started up crying out: "Then in God's name let us come at once, for we are losing time. The Count may come to Piccadilly earlier than we think."

"Not so!" said Van Helsing, holding up his hand.

"But why?" I asked.

"Do you forget," he said, with actually a smile, "that last night he banqueted heavily, and will sleep late?"[16]

Did I forget! Shall I ever—can I ever! Can any of us ever forget that terrible scene! Mina struggled hard to keep her brave countenance; but the pain overmastered her and she put her hands before her face, and shuddered whilst she moaned. Van Helsing had not intended to recall her frightful experience. He had simply lost sight of her and her part in the affair in his intellectual effort. When it struck him what he said, he was horrified at his thoughtlessness and tried to comfort her. "Oh, Madam Mina," he said, "dear, dear Madam Mina, alas! that

16 Not only is this an unbelievably thoughtless remark, it is pure supposition. There is no evidence that Dracula rests longer after he has supped. In addition, he was interrupted in the middle of his interaction with Mina on the previous night, and his "little refreshment" may have been intended only as an "appetiser" preliminary to a longer draught.

The Abridged Text omits this terrible faux pas and Van Helsing's apology, in an obvious effort at rehabilitation of his cold character.

405

I of all who so reverence you should have said anything so forgetful. These stupid old lips of mine and this stupid old head do not deserve so; but you will forget it, will you not?" He bent low beside her as he spoke; she took his hand, and looking at him through her tears, said hoarsely:—

"No, I shall not forget, for it is well that I remember; and with it I have so much in memory of you that is sweet, that I take it all together. Now, you must all be going soon. Breakfast is ready, and we must all eat that we may be strong."

Breakfast was a strange meal to us all. We tried to be cheerful and encourage each other, and Mina was the brightest and most cheerful of us. When it was over, Van Helsing stood up and said:—

"Now, my dear friends, we go forth to our terrible enterprise. Are we all armed, as we were on that night when first we visited our enemy's lair; armed against ghostly as well as carnal attack?" We all assured him. "Then it is well. Now, Madam Mina, you are in any case *quite* safe here until the sunset; and before then we shall return—if— We shall return! But before we go let me see you armed against personal attack. I have myself, since you came down, prepared your chamber by the placing of things of which we know, so that He may not enter. Now let me guard yourself. On your forehead I touch this piece of Sacred Wafer in the name of the Father, the Son, and—"

There was a fearful scream which almost froze our hearts to hear. As he had placed the Wafer on Mina's forehead, it had seared it—had burned into the flesh as though it had been a piece of white-hot metal. My poor darling's brain had told her the significance of the fact as quickly as her nerves received the pain of it; and the two so overwhelmed her that her overwrought nature had its voice in that dreadful scream. But the words to her thought came quickly; the echo of the scream had not ceased to ring on the air when there came the reaction, and she sank on her knees on the floor in an agony of abasement. Pulling her beautiful hair over her face, as the leper of old his mantle, she wailed out:—

"Unclean! Unclean! Even the Almighty shuns my polluted flesh! I must bear this mark of shame upon my forehead until the Judgment Day." They all paused. I had thrown myself beside her in an agony of helpless grief, and putting my arms around held her tight. For a few minutes our sorrowful hearts beat together, whilst the friends around us turned away their eyes that ran tears silently. Then Van Helsing turned and said gravely; so gravely that I could not help feeling that he was in some way inspired, and was stating things outside himself:—

"It may be that you may have to bear that mark till God Himself see fit, as He most surely shall, on the Judgment Day, to redress all wrongs of the earth and of His children that He has placed thereon. And oh, Madam Mina, my dear, my dear, may we who love you be there to see, when that red scar, the sign of God's knowledge of what has been, shall pass away and leave your forehead as pure as the heart we know. For so surely as we live, that scar shall pass away when God sees right to lift the burden that is hard upon us. Till then we bear our Cross, as His Son did in obedience to His Will. It may be that we are chosen instruments of His good pleasure, and that we ascend to His bidding as that other[17] through stripes[18] and shame; through tears and blood; through doubts and fears, and all that makes the difference between God and man."[19]

There was hope in his words, and comfort; and they made for resignation. Mina and I both felt so, and simultaneously we each took one of the old man's hands and bent over and kissed it. Then without a word we all knelt down together, and, all holding hands, swore to be true to each other.[20] We men pledged ourselves to raise the veil of sorrow from the head of her whom, each in his own way, we loved; and we prayed for help and guidance in the terrible task which lay before us.

It was then time to start. So I said farewell to Mina, a parting which neither of us shall forget to our dying day; and we set out.

To one thing I have made up my mind: if we find out that Mina must be a vampire in the end, then she shall not go into that unknown and terrible land alone. I suppose it is thus that in old times one vampire meant many; just as their hideous bodies could only rest in sacred earth, so the holiest love was the recruiting sergeant for their ghastly ranks.[21]

17 Meaning Jesus.

18 That is, the marks of whipping.

19 Van Helsing must be puzzled by Mina's reaction to the wafer, for Lucy, clearly much deeper in Dracula's toils as her death approached, showed no antipathy to garlic, the vampire's bane. Mina's painful scarring is likely to have been an hysterical reaction to the wafer arising out of her deep conviction of uncleanness, rather than a true physical burning—much like stigmata.

20 By this point the hunters see Dracula as the incarnation of the Antichrist and their mission a holy one. As discussed in "Dracula's Family Tree" in Part II, the church aligned itself against vampires in the fifteenth century, but this opposition based on religious principles was not always the case; for centuries before, vampirism was regarded as a natural phenomenon without demonic aspects, to be studied and prevented.

21 As discussed in chapter 18, note 48, this is a dubious idea about vampires. Harker's comment about love's recruiting power sounds much like one of the tragedies of the plague years, in which terrified Londoners often confined a family when one member developed the plague, effectively condemning the entire family. However, tradition has it that the vampire always attacks his or her own family first.

We entered Carfax without trouble and found all things the same as on the first occasion. It was hard to believe that amongst so prosaic surroundings of neglect and dust and decay there was any ground for such fear as already we knew. Had not our minds been made up, and had there not been terrible memories to spur us on, we could hardly have proceeded with our task. We found no papers, or any sign of use in the house; and in the old chapel the great boxes looked just as we had seen them last. Dr. Van Helsing said to us solemnly as we stood before them:—

"And now, my friends, we have a duty here to do. We must sterilise this earth, so sacred of holy memories, that he has brought from a far distant land for such fell use. He has chosen this earth because it has been holy. Thus we defeat him with his own weapon, for we make it more holy still. It was sanctified to such use of man, now we sanctify it to God." As he spoke he took from his bag a screw-driver and a wrench, and very soon the top of one of the cases was thrown open. The earth smelled musty and close; but we did not somehow seem to mind, for our attention was concentrated on the Professor. Taking from his box a piece of the Sacred Wafer he laid it reverently on the earth, and then shutting down the lid began to screw it home, we aiding him as he worked.

One by one we treated in the same way each of the great boxes, and left them as we had found them to all appearance; but in each was a portion of the Host.

When we closed the door behind us, the Professor said solemnly:—

"So much is already done. If it may be that with all the others we can be so successful, then the sunset of this evening may shine on Madam Mina's forehead all white as ivory and with no stain!"

As we passed across the lawn on our way to the station to catch our train we could see the front of the asylum. I looked eagerly, and in the window of my own room saw Mina. I waved my hand to her, and nodded to tell that our work there was successfully accomplished. She nodded in reply to show that she understood. The last I saw, she was waving her hand in farewell. It was with a heavy heart that we sought the station and just caught the train, which was steaming in as we reached the platform.

I have written this in the train.

Piccadilly 12:30 o'clock.[22]—Just before we reached Fenchurch Street Lord Godalming said to me:—

"Quincey and I will find a locksmith. You had better not come with us in case there should be any difficulty; for under the circumstances it wouldn't seem so bad for us to break into an empty house. But you are a solicitor and the Incorporated Law Society might tell you that you should have known better."[23] I demurred as to my not sharing any danger even of odium, but he went on: "Besides, it will attract less attention if there are not too many of us. My title will make it all right with the locksmith,[24] and with any policeman that may come along. You had better go with Jack and the Professor and stay in the Green Park, somewhere in sight of the house; and when you see the door opened and the smith has gone away, do you all come across. We shall be on the lookout for you, and shall let you in."

"The advice is good!" said Van Helsing, so we said no more. Godalming and Morris hurried off in a cab, we following in another. At the corner of Arlington Street our contingent got out and strolled into the Green Park.[25] My heart beat as I saw the house on which so much of our hope was centred, looming up grim and silent in its deserted condition amongst its more lively and spruce-looking neighbours.[26] We sat down on a bench within good view, and began to smoke cigars so as to attract as little attention as possible. The minutes seemed to pass with leaden feet as we waited for the coming of the others.

At length we saw a four-wheeler drive up. Out of it, in leisurely fashion, got Lord Godalming and Morris; and down from the box descended a thick-set working man with his rush-woven basket of tools. Morris paid the cabman, who touched his hat and drove away. Together the two ascended the steps, and Lord Godalming pointed out what he wanted done. The workman took off his coat leisurely and hung it on one of the spikes of the rail, saying something to a policeman who just

22 The time intervals here make little sense. To arrive at Piccadilly after 10:00 A.M., the hunters could have caught the 8:35 A.M. train from Purfleet to Fenchurch Street (the next was not until 9:55 A.M.), which would have brought them there at 9:17 A.M. By the time they travelled to Piccadilly (by cab or Underground), it would have been around 10:00 A.M. However, this would have required them to work at fever pitch at Carfax, to unscrew, sterilise, and screw up twenty-nine boxes. Even arriving at 10:00 A.M. would require swift work to find a locksmith, enter, and cleanse the Piccadilly residence. If they took the later train, permitting more time at Carfax, they could not have arrived at Piccadilly before 11:00 A.M., making it virtually impossible to be done with their tasks at Piccadilly (including the leisure for Harker to write up his entry) by 12:30 P.M.

23 Indeed, the society might have much to say about a great deal of Harker's conduct—why worry now? Again, Stoker attempts to cover up the unsavoury aspects of the characters of the principals. These telling comments, demonstrating Harker's full knowledge of his unethical and illegal behaviour, do not appear in the Abridged Text.

24 Of course—everyone knows that a lord couldn't possibly be engaged in wrongdoing!

25 See map on page 370.

26 In fact, this was likely Harker's imagination. As will be seen from the photograph on page 379, the proximity of the house to its neighbours makes it unlikely to stand out.

27 The odorous aspects of the house are not mentioned in the Abridged Text.

28 Evidently a typographical error for "painted."

then sauntered along. The policeman nodded acquiescence, and the man kneeling down placed his bag beside him. After searching through it, he took out a selection of tools which he proceeded to lay beside him in orderly fashion. Then he stood up, looked into the keyhole, blew into it, and turning to his employers, made some remark. Lord Godalming smiled, and the man lifted a good-sized bunch of keys; selecting one of them, he began to probe the lock, as if feeling his way with it. After fumbling about for a bit he tried a second, and then a third. All at once the door opened under a slight push from him, and he and the two others entered the hall. We sat still; my own cigar burnt furiously, but Van Helsing's went cold altogether. We waited patiently as we saw the workman come out and bring in his bag. Then he held the door partly open, steadying it with his knees, whilst he fitted a key to the lock. This he finally handed to Lord Godalming, who took out his purse and gave him something. The man touched his hat, took his bag, put on his coat and departed; not a soul took the slightest notice of the whole transaction.

When the man had fairly gone, we three crossed the street and knocked at the door. It was immediately opened by Quincey Morris, beside whom stood Lord Godalming lighting a cigar.

"The place smells so vilely," said the latter as we came in. It did indeed smell vilely—like the old chapel at Carfax—and with our previous experience it was plain to us that the Count had been using the place pretty freely.[27] We moved to explore the house, all keeping together in case of attack; for we knew we had a strong and wily enemy to deal with, and as yet we did not know whether the Count might not be in the house. In the dining-room, which lay at the back of the hall, we found eight boxes of earth. Eight boxes only out of the nine which we sought! Our work was not over, and would never be until we should have found the missing box. First we opened the shutters of the window which looked out across a narrow stone-flagged yard at the blank face of a stable, pointed[28] to look like the front of a miniature house. There were no windows in it, so we were not afraid of being overlooked. We did not lose any time in examining the chests. With the tools which we had brought with us we opened them, one by one, and treated them as we had treated those others in the old chapel. It was evident to us that the Count was not at present in the house, and we proceeded to search for any of his effects.

After a cursory glance at the rest of the rooms, from basement to attic, we came to the conclusion that the dining-room contained any effects which might belong to the Count; and so we proceeded to minutely examine them. They lay in a sort of orderly disorder on the great dining-room table. There were title deeds of the Piccadilly house in a great bundle; deeds of the purchase of the houses at Mile End and Bermondsey; notepaper, envelopes, and pens and ink. All were covered up in thin wrapping paper to keep them from the dust. There were also a clothes brush, a brush and comb, and a jug and basin—the latter containing dirty water which was reddened as if with blood. Last of all was a little heap of keys of all sorts and sizes, probably those belonging to the other houses. When we had examined this last find, Lord Godalming and Quincey Morris, taking accurate notes of the various addresses of the houses in the East and the South, took with them the keys in a great bunch, and set out to destroy the boxes in these places.[29] The rest of us are, with what patience we can, waiting their return—or the coming of the Count.

29 There is no apparent reason for the hunters to have put off this destruction, for the addresses have been known for several days. This is one more unaccountable delay in a series of delays seemingly incurred to help Dracula succeed in his plans.

Chapter 23

Dr. Seward's Diary.

1 The scene of the action is confused here. This entry is written on the morning of 3 October, the same time period covered in Harker's journal entry for the same date. The group has breakfasted together, presumably at Seward's asylum, and then proceeded together to the Piccadilly house, which, as we have seen, they cleansed. Did Seward, Harker, and Van Helsing then proceed to Van Helsing's hotel? From the description of the confrontation with Dracula following, it appears that they must have remained at the house. But how did Mina obtain the address to send them a telegram there?

2 Is Seward referring to the death of "his" Lucy? This seems to be posturing.

The Abridged Text omits Van Helsing's entire explanation to Harker of the characteristics of the vampire, which follows here in the next paragraph.

3 October.—The time seemed terribly long whilst we were waiting for the coming of Godalming and Quincey Morris.[1] The Professor tried to keep our minds active by using them all the time. I could see his beneficent purpose, by the side glances which he threw from time to time at Harker. The poor fellow is overwhelmed in a misery that is appalling to see. Last night he was a frank, happy-looking man, with strong, youthful face, full of energy, and with dark brown hair. To-day he is a drawn, haggard old man, whose white hair matches well with the hollow burning eyes and grief-written lines of his face. His energy is still intact; in fact, he is like a living flame. This may yet be his salvation, for, if all go well, it will tide him over the despairing period; he will then, in a kind of way, wake again to the realities of life. Poor fellow, I thought my own trouble was bad enough,[2] but his—! The Professor knows this well enough, and is doing his best to keep his mind active. What he has been saying was, under the circumstances, of absorbing interest. So well as I can remember, here it is:—

"I have studied, over and over again since they came into my hands, all the papers relating to this monster; and the more I have studied, the greater seems the necessity to utterly stamp him out. All through there are signs of his advance; not only of his power, but of his knowledge of it. As I learned from the researches of my friend Arminius of Buda-Pesth,

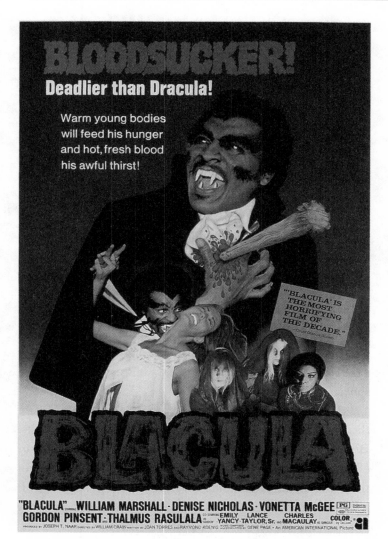

Blacula, starring William Marshall as Mamuwalde/Blacula.
(American International Pictures, 1972)

he was in life a most wonderful man. Soldier, statesman, and alchemist—which latter was the highest development of the science-knowledge of his time. He had a mighty brain, a learning beyond compare, and a heart that knew no fear and no remorse. He dared even to attend the Scholomance, and there was no branch of knowledge of his time that he did not essay. Well, in him the brain powers survived the physical death; though it would seem that memory was not all complete. In some faculties of mind he has been, and is, only a child; but he

3 The Victorians viewed the "child-brain" as highly suggestible, because of its relatively small store of knowledge and low degree of organisation, or in the words of the *Enyclopædia Britannica* (11th ed.), because "it does not form a logically coherent system whose parts reciprocally support one another."

Van Helsing's "child-brain" thesis makes little sense. Earlier, Van Helsing describes Dracula as having a "mighty brain." Is he now suggesting that the process of vampirisation has deprived Dracula of his original brainpower? Admittedly, Van Helsing is the discoverer "of the continuous evolution of brain-matter" and so beyond mere mortals in his understanding of neurology, but there is no evidence (at least in the narrative) that Dracula's reasoning abilities are in any way less keen than those of mortal man. Indeed the impression given by Harker's journal is that of a highly intelligent man, studiously pursuing his course of invasion of England. Of course, Harker's comment there that Dracula would have made a wonderful solicitor may be viewed by some as a validation of Van Helsing's observations!

4 That is, "make haste slowly."

5 See text accompanying chapter 18, note 36.

6 Van Helsing attributes this to the growth of Dracula's child-brain. Is it not instead simply a matter of volume? For Dracula to move all fifty boxes himself would have been a nearly insurmountable challenge; to move a few boxes at a time, however, was well within his power and would not draw undue attention.

is growing, and some things that were childish at the first are now of man's stature. He is experimenting, and doing it well; and if it had not been that we have crossed his path he would be yet—he may be yet if we fail—the father or furtherer of a new order of beings, whose road must lead through Death, not Life."

Harker groaned and said, "And this is all arrayed against my darling! But how is he experimenting? The knowledge may help us to defeat him!"

"He has all along, since his coming, been trying his power, slowly but surely; that big child-brain of his is working.[3] Well for us, it is, as yet, a child-brain; for had he dared, at the first, to attempt certain things he would long ago have been beyond our power. However, he means to succeed, and a man who has centuries before him can afford to wait and go slow. *Festina lente*[4] may well be his motto."

"I fail to understand," said Harker wearily. "Oh, do be more plain to me! Perhaps grief and trouble are dulling my brain." The Professor laid his hand tenderly on his shoulder as he spoke:—

"Ah, my child, I will be plain. Do you not see how, of late, this monster has been creeping into knowledge experimentally. How he has been making use of the zoöphagous patient to effect his entry into friend John's home; for your Vampire, though in all afterwards he can come when and how he will, must at the first make entry only when asked thereto by an inmate.[5] But these are not his most important experiments. Do we not see how at the first all these so great boxes were moved by others. He knew not then but that must be so. But all the time that so great child brain of his was growing, and he began to consider whether he might not himself move the box. So he began to help; and then, when he found that this be all right, he try to move them all alone.[6] And so he progress, and he scatter these graves of him; and none but he know where they are hidden. He may have intend to bury them deep in the ground. So that only he use them in the night, or at such time as he can change his form, they do him equal well; and none may know these are his hiding-place! But, my child, do not despair: this knowledge come to him just too late! Already all of his lairs but one be sterilise as for him; and before the sunset this shall be so. Then he have no place where he can move and hide. I delayed this morning that so we might be sure.[7] Is there not more at stake for us than for him? Then why we not be even more careful than him? By my clock it is one hour, and already, if all be well, friend Arthur and Quincey are on their way to us. To-day is our day, and we must go sure, if slow, and lose no chance. See! there are five of us when those absent ones return."

Whilst he was speaking we were startled by a knock at the hall door, the double postman's knock[8] of the telegraph boy. We all moved out to the hall with one impulse, and Van Helsing, holding up his hand to us to keep silence, stepped to the door and opened it. The boy handed in a despatch.[9] The Professor closed the door again and, after looking at the direction,[10] opened it and read aloud.

"Look out for D. He has just now, 12:45, come from Carfax hurriedly and hastened towards the South. He seems to be going the round and may want to see you: Mina."[11]

There was a pause, broken by Jonathan Harker's voice:—

"Now, God be thanked, we shall soon meet!" Van Helsing turned to him quickly and said:—

"God will act in His own way and time. Do not fear, and do not rejoice as yet; for what we wish for at the moment may be our undoings."

"I care for nothing now," he answered hotly, "except to wipe out this brute from the face of creation. I would sell my soul to do it!"

"Oh, hush, hush, my child!" said Van Helsing. "God does not purchase souls in this wise; and the Devil, though he may purchase, does not keep faith. But God is merciful and just, and knows your pain and your devotion to that dear Madam Mina. Think you, how her pain would be doubled, did she but hear your wild words. Do not fear any of us, we are all devoted to this cause, and to-day shall see the end. The time is coming for action; to-day this Vampire is limit to the powers of man, and till sunset he may not change. It will take him time to arrive here—see, it is twenty minutes past one—and there are yet some times before he can hither come, be he never so

7 Actually, Van Helsing's delay fosters Dracula's plans; with one box undiscovered, Dracula is able to escape from London.

8 The postman's double knock is heard in *The Pickwick Papers* (1836–1837) and elsewhere in the works of Charles Dickens. Christopher Morley (*Sherlock Holmes and Dr. Watson: A Textbook of Friendship*) observes that this traditional knock was replaced later by the double ring of the bell—the basis of the title for James M. Cain's hard-boiled first novel, *The Postman Always Rings Twice* (1934). The novel was made in 1946 into the brilliant film noir of the same name, starring John Garfield and Lana Turner, and in 1981 remade into a vehicle for Jack Nicholson and Jessica Lange.

9 Note that the message is delivered within thirty-five minutes of its sending. Many in the late nineteenth century remained addicted to the telegram, even after the invention of the telephone in 1876. For example, in "The Adventure of the Devil's Foot" (1910), Dr. Watson said of Sherlock Holmes: "[H]e has never been known to write where a telegram would serve." England's first electromagnetic telegraph was patented in 1837 by William Cooke, a former army officer and aspiring entrepreneur, and Charles Wheatstone, an academic physicist and the inventor of the concertina. That year, the first practical telegraph was introduced in London with the purpose of enabling railway stations to relay simple emergency signals to each other. The lines were laid underground along the train tracks. Meanwhile, in the United States, Samuel Morse had invented his own telegraph and alphabetic code (his first message, sent in 1844 on a wire between Washington and Baltimore, was "What hath God wrought!"). The Morse telegraph would eventually become the most commonly used telegraph in the world.

An important factor in the public's acceptance of the telegram as a powerful means of communication was the sensational 1845 Tawell murder case. Tawell was hunted for the murder by poisoning of a woman near Windsor. When he was spotted at the Slough railway station boarding a train to London's Paddington station, a telegram was dispatched to London officials with his description, and he was apprehended on his arrival. After his conviction and execution, the telegraph was dubbed "the wires that hanged Tawell." By 1869, some 80,000 miles of telegraph wire had been erected on raised posts throughout the United Kingdom. Designed along the low-cost lines of the postal system, an ordinary telegram from 1885 to 1915 cost 6d. for twelve words or less, plus ½ d. more for every excess word.

10 The addressee.

11 Wolf (*The Essential Dracula*) wonders appropriately how Mina happened to spot Dracula. Perhaps he paid a quick visit to his "winepress"? There is no other reason for his return to Carfax; recall that he was seen flying off to London. The Notes indicate that he was heading east, not south, which makes little sense, for Purfleet is east of the various lairs noted. If Dracula is headed south, he must cross the river. See text accompanying note 15 below.

What exactly did Mina see? Dracula in a carriage or cab? Dracula on foot? Certainly, this being daytime, it was not Dracula in bat form, flying south.

12 This is the only time when Lord Godalming is so termed, and unlike the form of address of a knight, a viscount would never be referred to by his title and Christian name; "Lord Godalming" is the correct manner of speech (as is "my lord" or, more familiarly, "Godalming"). See, for example, Patrick Montague-Smith's *Debrett's Correct Form* (1992). However, Van Helsing is a foreigner and cannot be expected to know these niceties.

13 As noted earlier, sunset occurred a little before 6:00 P.M. It would be impossible to leave Piccadilly after 5:00 P.M. and arrive back at the asylum by sunset.

quick. What we must hope for is that my Lord Arthur[12] and Quincey arrive first."

About half an hour after we had received Mrs. Harker's telegram, there came a quiet, resolute knock at the hall door. It was just an ordinary knock, such as is given hourly by thousands of gentlemen, but it made the Professor's heart and mine beat loudly. We looked at each other, and together moved out into the hall; we each held ready to use our various armaments—the spiritual in the left hand, the mortal in the right. Van Helsing pulled back the latch, and holding the door half open, stood back, having both hands ready for action. The gladness of our hearts must have shown upon our faces when on the step, close to the door, we saw Lord Godalming and Quincey Morris. They came quickly in and closed the door behind them, the former saying, as they moved along the hall:—

"It is all right. We found both places; six boxes in each and we destroyed them all!"

"Destroyed?" asked the Professor.

"For him!" We were silent for a minute, and then Quincey said:—

"There's nothing to do but to wait here. If, however, he doesn't turn up by five o'clock, we must start off; for it won't do to leave Mrs. Harker alone after sunset."[13]

"He will be here before long now," said Van Helsing, who had been consulting his pocket-book. "*Nota bene*[14] in Madam's telegram he went south from Carfax, that means he went to cross the river, and he could only do so at slack of tide, which should be something before one o'clock.[15] That he went south has a meaning for us. He is as yet only suspicious; and he went from Carfax first to the place where he would suspect interference least. You must have been at Bermondsey only a short time before him. That he is not here already shows that he went to Mile End next. This took him some time; for he would then have to be carried over the river in some way. Believe me, my friends, we shall not have long to wait now. We should have ready some plan of attack, so that we may throw away no chance. Hush, there is no time now. Have all your arms! Be ready!" He held up a warning hand as he spoke, for we all could hear a key softly inserted in the lock of the hall door.

I could not but admire, even at such a moment, the way in which a dominant spirit asserted itself. In all our hunting parties and adventures in different parts of the world, Quincey Morris had always been the one to arrange the plan of action, and Arthur and I had been accustomed to obey him implicitly. Now, the old habit seemed to be renewed instinctively. With a swift glance around the room, he at once laid out our plan of attack, and, without speaking a word, with a gesture, placed us each in position. Van Helsing, Harker, and I were just behind the door, so that when it was opened the Professor could guard it whilst we two stepped between the incomer and the door. Godalming behind and Quincey in front stood just out of sight ready to move in front of the window. We waited in a suspense that made the seconds pass with nightmare slowness. The slow, careful steps came along the hall; the Count was evidently prepared for some surprise—at least he feared it.

Suddenly with a single bound he leaped into the room, winning a way past us before any of us could raise a hand to stay him. There was something so panther-like in the movement—something so unhuman, that it seemed to sober us all from the shock of his coming. The first to act was Harker, who, with a quick movement, threw himself before the door leading into the room in the front of the house. As the Count saw us, a horrible sort of snarl passed over his face, showing the eye-teeth long and pointed; but the evil smile as quickly passed into a cold stare of lion-like disdain. His expression again changed as, with a single impulse, we all advanced upon him. It was a pity that we had not some better organised plan of attack, for even at the moment I wondered what we were to do. I did not myself know whether our lethal weapons would avail us anything.[16] Harker evidently meant to try the matter, for he had ready his great Kukri knife,[17] and made a fierce and sudden cut at him. The blow was a powerful one; only the diabolical quickness of the Count's leap back saved him. A second less and the trenchant blade had shorn through his heart. As it was, the point just cut the cloth of his coat, making a wide gap whence a bundle of bank-notes and a stream of gold fell out. The expression of the Count's face was so hellish, that for a moment I feared for Harker, though I saw him throw

14 Latin: note well.

15 High and low tides occurred as follows on 3 October. Thus, with the exception of 1893, none of the dates appear to match Van Helsing's assertion respecting low tide. However, in 1885 and 1889 Dracula would not have had long to wait.

Year	Low Tide		High Tide	
1885	2:21	P.M.	8:59	P.M.
1886	11:18	A.M.	5:28	P.M.
1887	8:42	A.M.	2:33	P.M.
1888	5:51	A.M.	11:46	A.M.
1889	1:25	P.M.	8:13	P.M.
1890	10:52	A.M.	4:51	P.M.
1893	12:45	P.M.	7:19	P.M.

Computed using Tide Prediction Program 2.42 by Hans Pieper.

16 Van Helsing has specifically advised the hunters that these weapons will not harm Dracula. Later all seem to change their view; see text accompanying chapter 27, note 51.

Kukri knife.

17 Spelled "Cucherry" in the Manuscript, in which appears the phrase "which I had seen him use with such effect on the jaguar in Brazil." The information in this deleted phrase is the only indication that Seward knew Harker before the events of the narrative, and Stoker must have misattributed the identification—Seward surely meant Morris's bowie knife, for it is plain elsewhere that Morris has been in South America, and Seward and he have travelled extensively together.

The kukri is a broad heavy blade, associated with the Gurkhas of Nepal serving in the British and Indian Armies. In 1768 Prithwi Naraayan Shah, King of Gorkha, conquered the Nepal valley and became the first king of Nepal. Some historians credit his troops' victory to their unusual weapon, the kukri. The oldest known kukri may be the weapon on display in the arsenal museum in Kathmandu, which belonged to Rajah Drabya Shah, King of Gorkha, in 1627. However, the origins of the kukri may be far older. Weapons resembling the kukri are the machaira, the cavalry sword of the ancient Macedonians, carried by Alexander's troops in the fourth century BC on his invasion of northwest India; the *kopis* ("chopper"), a sword/knife with a blade that curves inward, used by the ancient Greeks along with its straight-bladed relative the *xiphos*; the Greek *harpé*, which has a spur at the end of the blade; and the Iberian *falcata*.

That Jonathan Harker owned a kukri knife should not be taken as an indication of military service—the weapon was a popular souvenir of the Indian Mutiny and other wars in which the British Empire took part, frequently noted in military memoirs. Many a knife must have been brought home by returning troops, just as German bayonets were in the twentieth century.

Harry McEvoy, founder of the American Knife Throwers Association, in his *Knife Throwing: A Practical Guide* (1973), points out although the kukri is renowned for its use as a chopping or machete-like weapon, it is ideally suited to throwing and that the only other common knife as well suited to throwing is the bowie knife.

18 Astonishingly, Dracula is uninjured by the jagged glass. That he can bleed is made evident by his earlier self-inflicted chest wound.

19 The rôle of the earthen boxes is far from clear, for Dracula has already demonstrated his ability to rest without one—recall that in Whitby, he rested in the grave of a suicide without benefit of his native soil.

20 Leatherdale (*Dracula Unearthed*) finds this speech enlightening. Dracula is not seeking

the terrible knife aloft again for another stroke. Instinctively I moved forward with a protective impulse, holding the Crucifix and Wafer in my left hand. I felt a mighty power fly along my arm; and it was without surprise I saw the monster cower back before a similar movement made spontaneously by each one of us. It would be impossible to describe the expression of hate and baffled malignity—of anger and hellish rage—which came over the Count's face. His waxen hue became greenish-yellow by the contrast of his burning eyes, and the red scar on the forehead showed on the pallid skin like a palpitating wound. The next instant, with a sinuous dive he swept under Harker's arm, ere his blow could fall, and, grasping a handful of the money from the floor, dashed across the room, threw himself at the window. Amid the crash and glitter of the falling glass, he tumbled into the flagged area below.[18] Through the sound of the shivering glass I could hear the "ting" of the gold, as some of the sovereigns fell on the flagging.

We ran over and saw him spring unhurt from the ground. He, rushing up the steps, crossed the flagged yard, and pushed open the stable door. There he turned and spoke to us:—

"You think to baffle me, you—with your pale faces all in a row, like sheep in a butcher's. You shall be sorry yet, each one of you! You think you have left me without a place to rest;[19] but I have more. My revenge is just begun! I spread it over centuries, and time is on my side.[20] Your girls that you all love are mine already;[21] and through them you and others shall yet be mine—my creatures, to do my bidding and to be my jackals when I want to feed.[22] Bah!" With a contemptuous sneer, he passed quickly through the door, and we heard the rusty bolt creak as he fastened it behind him. A door beyond opened and shut. The first of us to speak was the Professor, as, realising the difficulty of following him through the stable, we moved toward the hall.

"We have learnt something—much! Notwithstanding his brave words, he fears us; he fear time, he fear want! For if not, why he hurry so? His very tone betray him, or my ears deceive. Why take that money? You follow quick. You are hunters of wild beast, and understand it so. For me, I make sure that nothing here may be of use to him, if so that he return." As he spoke he put the money remaining into his pocket; took the title-deeds in the bundle as Harker had left them; and swept the remaining things into the open fireplace, where he set fire to them with a match.[23]

Godalming and Morris had rushed out into the yard, and Harker had lowered himself from the window to follow the Count. He had, however, bolted the stable door; and by the time they had forced it open there was no sign of him. Van Helsing and I tried to make inquiry at the back of the house; but the mews was deserted and no one had seen him depart.

It was now late in the afternoon,[24] and sunset was not far off. We had to recognise that our game was up; with heavy hearts we agreed with the Professor when he said:—

"Let us go back to Madam Mina—poor, poor, dear Madam Mina. All we can do just now is done; and we can there, at least, protect her. But we need not despair. There is but one more earth-box, and we must try to find it; when that is done all may yet be well." I could see that he spoke as bravely as he could to comfort Harker. The poor fellow was quite broken down; now and again he gave a low groan which he could not suppress—he was thinking of his wife.

With sad hearts we came back to my house, where we found Mrs. Harker waiting us, with an appearance of cheerfulness which did honour to her bravery and unselfishness. When she saw our faces, her own became as pale as death; for a second or two her eyes were closed as if she were in secret prayer; and then she said cheerfully:—

"I can never thank you all enough. Oh, my poor darling!" As she spoke, she took her husband's grey head in her hands and kissed it—"Lay your poor head here and rest it. All will yet be well, dear! God will protect us if He so will it in His good intent." The poor fellow groaned. There was no place for words in his sublime misery.

We had a sort of perfunctory supper together, and I think it cheered us all up somewhat. It was, perhaps, the mere animal heat of food to hungry people—for none of us had eaten anything since breakfast—or the sense of companionship may have helped us; but anyhow we were all less miserable,

revenge against the hunters; rather, he is seeking revenge for some act that occurred earlier in his life. In *The Tomb of Dracula* and *Dracula Lives!*, a highly successful series of comic books published between 1972 and 1979, Marv Wolfman imagines that it is the murder of Dracula's mortal wife, before Dracula turned.

21 The use of the plural "girls" is curious. Does Dracula not know that Lucy has been destroyed? Or are there other unmentioned victims?

22 Jackals are nocturnal animals that occasionally prey on carrion as well as smaller mammals. They hunt in packs, however—a trait not shared by the vampires of the narrative. Dracula may be suggesting that, like a lion, if he brings down prey, his "leftovers" may then feed his "jackals."

23 What "remaining things"—the brush and washbasin? The envelopes and notepaper?

24 Dracula must have arrived at Piccadilly around 2:00 or 2:30 P.M. The telegram arrived at 1:20 P.M., and Morris and Lord Godalming arrived about a half hour later. Therefore, Dracula must have fled the house at around 3:00 P.M. Sunset occurred at around 5:30 P.M.

25 Wolf (*The Essential Dracula*) makes the interesting suggestion that Mina's urging of mercy is dictated by Dracula himself, using his telepathic connection with Mina.

and saw the morrow as not altogether without hope. True to our promise, we told Mrs. Harker everything which had passed; and although she grew snowy white at times when danger had seemed to threaten her husband, and red at others when his devotion to her was manifested, she listened bravely and with calmness. When we came to the part where Harker had rushed at the Count so recklessly, she clung to her husband's arm, and held it tight as though her clinging could protect him from any harm that might come. She said nothing, however, till the narration was all done, and matters had been brought right up to the present time. Then without letting go her husband's hand she stood up amongst us and spoke. Oh, that I could give any idea of the scene; of that sweet, sweet, good, good woman in all the radiant beauty of her youth and animation, with the red scar on her forehead, of which she was conscious, and which we saw with grinding of our teeth—remembering whence and how it came; her loving kindness against our grim hate; her tender faith against all our fears and doubting; and we, knowing that so far as symbols went, she with all her goodness and purity and faith, was outcast from God.

"Jonathan" she said, and the word sounded like music on her lips it was so full of love and tenderness. "Jonathan dear, and you all my true, true friends, I want you to bear something in mind through all this dreadful time. I know that you must fight—that you must destroy even as you destroyed the false Lucy so that the true Lucy might live hereafter; but it is not a work of hate. That poor soul who has wrought all this misery is the saddest case of all. Just think what will be his joy when he, too, is destroyed in his worser part that his better part may have spiritual immortality. You must be pitiful to him, too, though it may not hold your hands from his destruction."[25]

As she spoke I could see her husband's face darken and draw together, as though the passion in him were shrivelling his being to its core. Instinctively the clasp on his wife's hand grew closer, till his knuckles looked white. She did not flinch from the pain which I knew she must have suffered, but looked at him with eyes that were more appealing than ever.

As she stopped speaking he leaped to his feet, almost tearing his hand from hers as he spoke:—

"May God give him into my hand just for long enough to destroy that earthly life of him which we are aiming at. If beyond it I could send his soul for ever and ever to burning hell I would do it!"

"Oh, hush! oh, hush! in the name of the good God. Don't say such things, Jonathan, my husband; or you will crush me with fear and horror. Just think, my dear—I have been thinking all this long, long day of it—that . . . perhaps . . . some day . . . I too may need such pity; and that some other like you—and with equal cause for anger—may deny it to me! Oh my husband! my husband, indeed I would have spared you such a thought had there been another way; but I pray that God may not have treasured your wild words, except as the heart-broken wail of a very loving and sorely stricken man. Oh God, let these poor white hairs go in evidence of what he has suffered, who all his life has done no wrong, and on whom so many sorrows have come."

We men were all in tears now. There was no resisting them, and we wept openly. She wept too, to see that her sweeter counsels had prevailed. Her husband flung himself on his knees beside her, and putting his arms round her, hid his face in the folds of her dress. Van Helsing beckoned to us and we stole out of the room, leaving the two loving hearts alone with their God.

Before they retired the Professor fixed up the room against any coming of the Vampire,[26] and assured Mrs. Harker that she might rest in peace. She tried to school herself to the belief, and, manifestly for her husband's sake, tried to seem content. It was a brave struggle; and was, I think and believe, not without its reward. Van Helsing had placed at hand a bell which either of them was to sound in case of any emergency. When they had retired, Quincey, Godalming, and I arranged that we should sit up, dividing the night between us, and watch over the safety of the poor stricken lady. The first watch falls to Quincey, so the rest of us shall be off to bed as soon as we can. Godalming has already turned in, for his is the second watch. Now that my work is done I, too, shall go to bed.

26 Seward seems not to have noticed that Van Helsing did this in the morning, not now. He may have just noticed the wards and assumed that Van Helsing placed them at this time.

JONATHAN HARKER'S JOURNAL.

3-4 October, close to midnight.—I thought yesterday would never end. There was over me a yearning for sleep, in some sort of blind belief that to wake would be to find things changed, and that any change must now be for the better. Before we parted, we discussed what our next step was to be, but we could arrive at no result. All we knew was that one earth-box remained, and that the Count alone knew where it was. If he chooses to lie hidden, he may baffle us for years; and in the meantime!—the thought is too horrible, I dare not think of it even now. This I know: that if ever there was a woman who was all perfection, that one is my poor wronged darling. I love her a thousand times more for her sweet pity of last night, a pity that made my own hate of the monster seem despicable. Surely God will not permit the world to be the poorer by the loss of such a creature. This is hope to me. We are all drifting reefwards now, and faith is our only anchor. Thank God! Mina is sleeping, and sleeping without dreams. I fear what her dreams might be like, with such terrible memories to ground them in. She has not been so calm, within my seeing, since the sunset. Then, for a while, there came over her face a repose which was like spring after the blasts of March. I thought at the time that it was the softness of the red sunset on her face, but somehow now I think it has a deeper meaning. I am not sleepy myself, though I am weary—weary to death. However, I must try to sleep; for there is to-morrow to think of, and there is no rest for me until. . . .

Later.—I must have fallen asleep, for I was awaked by Mina, who was sitting up in bed, with a startled look on her face. I could see easily, for we did not leave the room in darkness; she had placed a warning hand over my mouth, and now she whispered in my ear:—

"Hush! there is someone in the corridor!" I got up softly, and crossing the room, gently opened the door.

Just outside, stretched on a mattress, lay Mr. Morris, wide awake. He raised a warning hand for silence as he whispered to me:—

"Hush! go back to bed; it is all right. One of us will be here all night. We don't mean to take any chances!"

His look and gesture forbade discussion, so I came back and told Mina. She sighed, and positively a shadow of a smile stole over her poor, pale face as she put her arms round me and said softly:—

"Oh, thank God for good brave men!" With a sigh she sank back again to sleep. I write this now as I am not sleepy, though I must try again.

4 October, morning.—Once again during the night I was wakened by Mina. This time we had all had a good sleep, for the grey of the coming dawn was making the windows into sharp oblongs, and the gas flame was like a speck rather than a disc of light. She said to me hurriedly:—

"Go, call the Professor. I want to see him at once."

"Why?" I asked.

"I have an idea. I suppose it must have come in the night, and matured without my knowing it. He must hypnotise me before the dawn, and then I shall be able to speak. Go quick, dearest; the time is getting close." I went to the door. Dr. Seward was resting on the mattress, and, seeing me, he sprang to his feet.

"Is anything wrong?" he asked, in alarm.

"No," I replied; "but Mina wants to see Dr. Van Helsing at once."

"I will go," he said, and hurried into the Professor's room.

In two or three minutes later Van Helsing was in the room in his dressing-gown, and Mr. Morris and Lord Godalming were with Dr. Seward at the door asking questions. When the Professor saw Mina a smile—a positive smile ousted the anxiety of his face; he rubbed his hands as he said:—

"Oh, my dear Madam Mina, this is indeed a change. See! friend Jonathan, we have got our dear Madam Mina, as of old, back to us to-day!" Then turning to her, he said, cheerfully: "And what am I to do for you? For at this hour you do not want me for nothings."

"I want you to hypnotise me!" she said. "Do it before the dawn, for I feel that then I can speak, and speak freely. Be quick, for the time is short!" Without a word he motioned her to sit up in bed.

27 Hypnosis was of course well known in the late nineteenth century (see chapter 14, note 37). The "passes" employed by Van Helsing refer to the early technique used by Franz Anton Mesmer of passing the operator's hands slowly and regularly over the subject's face, with or without contact. Note that the theory of mesmerism credited the operator with the power of inducing the trance state by will, with little credit to the subject.

The terms "hypnotism" and "hypnotist" were coined by British surgeon James Braid (1795–1860) in his 1843 book *Neurypnology; or, the Rationale of Nervous Sleep, Considered in Relation with Animal Magnetism*. Braid, who practised in Manchester, England, challenged Mesmer's theories, proposing that hypnotism was a form of sleep, brought on by the fatigue that intense concentration on an object could induce. With this technique he claimed to have cured patients of rheumatism and paralysis. Over time, more physicians, among them Sigmund Freud, began using hypnosis to treat psychological disorders such as hysteria. True hypnosis, of course, is largely a matter of the subject's cooperation and mental state, and self-hypnosis is readily accomplished; no "passes" or willpower of the operator are required. We must wonder again at Van Helsing's scientific credentials, for he is clearly revealed in the narrative as a mesmerist and not a true hypnotist.

28 McNally and Florescu (*The Essential Dracula*) calculate that Dracula has entered the English Channel, a distance of about 50 miles from the embarkation point, and that the journey would have taken at least six or seven hours. Dawn on 4 October in London occurred at about 6:00 A.M. Therefore, the ship likely left around 10:00 or 11:00 P.M. on 3 October. The times of high tide for 1885 and 1889 fit this hypothesis.

Looking fixedly at her, he commenced to make passes in front of her, from over the top of her head downward, with each hand in turn.[27] Mina gazed at him fixedly for a few minutes, during which my own heart beat like a trip hammer, for I felt that some crisis was at hand. Gradually her eyes closed, and she sat, stock still; only by the gentle heaving of her bosom could one know that she was alive. The Professor made a few more passes and then stopped, and I could see that his forehead was covered with great beads of perspiration. Mina opened her eyes; but she did not seem the same woman. There was a far-away look in her eyes, and her voice had a sad dreaminess which was new to me. Raising his hand to impose silence, the Professor motioned to me to bring the others in. They came on tip-toe, closing the door behind them, and stood at the foot of the bed, looking on. Mina appeared not to see them. The stillness was broken by Van Helsing's voice speaking in a low level tone which would not break the current of her thoughts:—

"Where are you?" The answer came in a neutral way:—

"I do not know. Sleep has no place it can call its own." For several minutes there was silence. Mina sat rigid, and the Professor stood staring at her fixedly; the rest of us hardly dared to breathe. The room was growing lighter; without taking his eyes from Mina's face, Dr. Van Helsing motioned me to pull up the blind. I did so, and the day seemed just upon us. A red streak shot up, and a rosy light seemed to diffuse itself through the room. On the instant the Professor spoke again:—

"Where are you now?" The answer came dreamily, but with intention; it were as though she were interpreting something. I have heard her use the same tone when reading her shorthand notes.

"I do not know. It is all strange to me!"

"What do you see?"

"I can see nothing; it is all dark."

"What do you hear?" I could detect the strain in the Professor's patient voice.

"The lapping of water. It is gurgling by, and little waves leap. I can hear them on the outside."[28]

"Then you are on a ship?" We all looked at each other,

trying to glean something each from the other. We were afraid to think. The answer came quick:—

"Oh, yes!"

"What else do you hear?"

"The sound of men stamping overhead as they run about. There is the creaking of a chain, and the loud tinkle as the check of the capstan falls into the rachet."[29]

"What are you doing?"

"I'm still—oh, so still. It is like death!" The voice faded away into a deep breath as of one sleeping, and the open eyes closed again.[30]

By this time the sun had risen, and we were all in the full light of day. Dr. Van Helsing placed his hands on Mina's shoulders, and laid her head down softly on her pillow. She lay like a sleeping child for a few moments, and then, with a long sigh, awoke and stared in wonder to see all around her. "Have I been talking in my sleep?" was all she said. She seemed, however, to know the situation without telling; though she was eager to know what she had told. The Professor repeated the conversation, and she said:—

"Then there is not a moment to lose; it may not be yet too late!" Mr. Morris and Lord Godalming started for the door but the Professor's calm voice called them back:—

"Stay, my friends. That ship, wherever it was, was weighing anchor whilst she spoke. There are many ships weighing anchor at the moment in your so great Port of London. Which of them is it that you seek? God be thanked that we have once again a clue, though whither it may lead us we know not. We have been blind somewhat; blind after the manner of men, since when we can look back we see what we might have seen looking forward if we had been able to see what we might have seen! Alas! but that sentence is a puddle;[31] is it not? We can know now what was in the Count's mind, when he seize that money, though Jonathan's so fierce knife put him in the danger that even he dread.[32] He meant escape. Hear me, ESCAPE! He saw that with but one earth-box left, and a pack of men following like dogs after a fox, this London was no place for him. He have take his last earth-box on board a ship, and he leave the land. He think to escape, but no! we follow him. Tally Ho! as friend

29 Evidently a typographical error for "ratchet." One wonders whether these are Mina's words or Dracula's. In either case, the speaker reveals a degree of technical knowledge about the mechanism of ship operations beyond that of most casual passengers.

30 The scene of Mina's hypnotic trance is reminiscent of a séance. Spiritualism was a widespread movement in England and the United States by the time of the events of *Dracula*. Its principal tenet was that communication between the living and spirits of the dead was possible, through the channel of a medium. Spiritualism was no mere fringe phenomenon, and among its prominent supporters were British scientists Alfred Russel Wallace and Sir William Crookes as well as Sir Arthur Conan Doyle. The Society for Psychical Research, which was formed to investigate the claims of Spiritualism, included in its membership many persons known to and admired by Bram Stoker, such as William Gladstone and Alfred, Lord Tennyson. Stephanie Moss, in "Bram Stoker and the Society for Psychical Research" (1998), argues that Stoker knew the Spiritualists and their methodologies well, and surely the eerie similarities of Mina's communications with those regularly reported by purported mediums would not have been lost on the observers. Many mediums and most trance lecturers—who explained the workings of Spiritualism to the public and sometimes summoned the dead onstage, before groups of observers—were young women.

Interestingly, the Notes suggest that the vampire hunters may have used even more occult techniques to track down Dracula. There are several tantalising references to "sortes Virgilianae" (singular, sors Virgiliana), a medieval method of divination by bibliomancy, in which Virgil—then considered to be a magician and a prophet—was a conduit to ascertaining one's fortune. A question was posed, the pages of the *Aeneid* were opened at random, and the seeker put his or her finger on a passage, which answered the question or foretold the sought-after fate. Other texts used in bibliomancy (or stichomancy or libromancy, as the method of receiving these auguries was sometimes called) included the Old and New Testaments, the Koran, the works of Shakespeare, and classical poetry. However, there is no indication of who sought these prognostications or when they were used.

31 This is a wonderful portmanteau of "puzzle" and "muddle." The sentence is so much of a puddle, indeed, that it does not appear in the Abridged Text.

32 What "danger" could Dracula dread, with no wooden stakes on display? Van Helsing suggests that Dracula panicked, seized some of the money, and fled England. However, it is evident that Dracula acted deliberately and carefully (and may well have put into motion plans made earlier) to effect his evacuation: in the few hours between Dracula's confrontation with the hunters at Piccadilly and 5:00 P.M., when he coolly approached the captain of the *Czarina Catherine*, he managed to locate the only ship bound for Varna, negotiate passage, arrange for carters to pick up his remaining box, devise a secret destination (Galatz), and direct a letter to an agent there.

33 The foxhunting metaphor—and Van Helsing's admission that he thinks like Dracula—do not appear in the Abridged Text.

34 The Manuscript continues with the following phrase, omitted from the published narrative: "save at dawn or sunset." The balance is added to the Manuscript in Stoker's hand. Stoker seems to be inventing some of these "rules" for vampire behaviour, rather than obtaining them from the Harkers or Van Helsing's sources. See "Dracula's Family Tree" in Part II for a discussion of other rules.

Arthur would say when he put on his red frock! Our old fox is wily; oh! so wily, and we must follow with wile. I too am wily and I think his mind in a little while.[33] In meantime we may rest and in peace, for there are waters between us which he do not want to pass, and which he could not if he would[34]— unless the ship were to touch the land, and then only at full or slack tide. See, and the sun is just rose, and all day to sunset is to us. Let us take bath, and dress, and have breakfast which we all need, and which we can eat comfortable since he be not in the same land with us." Mina looked at him appealingly as she asked:—

"But why need we seek him further, when he is gone away from us?" He took her hand and patted it as he replied:—

"Ask me nothings as yet. When we have breakfast, then I answer all questions." He would say no more, and we separated to dress.

After breakfast Mina repeated her question. He looked at her gravely for a minute and then said sorrowfully:—

"Because my dear, dear Madam Mina, now more than ever must we find him even if we have to follow him to the jaws of Hell!" She grew paler as she asked faintly:—

"Why?"

"Because," he answered solemnly, "he can live for centuries, and you are but mortal woman. Time is now to be dreaded— since once he put that mark upon your throat."

I was just in time to catch her as she fell forward in a faint.

Chapter 24

DR. SEWARD'S PHONOGRAPH DIARY, SPOKEN BY VAN HELSING.

THIS TO JONATHAN HARKER.

You are to stay with your dear Madam Mina. We shall go to make our search—if I can call it so, for it is not search but knowing, and we seek confirmation only. But do you stay and take care of her to-day. This is your best and most holiest office. This day nothing can find him here. Let me tell you that so you will know what we four know already, for I have tell them. He, our enemy, have gone away; he have gone back to his Castle in Transylvania. I know it so well, as if a great hand of fire wrote it on the wall.[1] He have prepare for this in some way, and that last earth-box was ready to ship somewheres. For this he took the money; for this he hurry at the last, lest we catch him before the sun go down. It was his last hope, save that he might hide in the tomb that he think poor Miss Lucy, being as he thought like him, keep open to him. But there was not of time. When that fail he make straight for his last resource—his last earthwork I might say did I wish *double entente*.[2] He is clever, oh so clever! he know that his game here was finish; and so he decide he go back home. He find ship going[3] by the route he came, and he go in it. We go off now to find what ship, and whither bound; when we have discover that, we come back and tell you all. Then we will comfort you and poor Madam Mina with new hope. For it will be hope when you think it over: that all is not lost. This very creature that we pursue, he take hundreds of years to get so far as London; and

"'You may depend he's a vampyre,' said one, 'or it wouldn't be so difficult to get him out of the grave.'"
Varney, the Vampyre; or, The Feast of Blood (1847)

1 The "writing on the wall" was done by the Lord in Dan. 5:5, but not by a hand of fire.

2 The correct French, usually incorrectly rendered as "double entendre," for a double meaning or pun.

3 In the Manuscript, "to the Danube mouth" is replaced by the phrase "how he came." The Danube is not part of the route described in the narrative. However, Varna is also on the Black Sea, into which the Danube empties, and this may be the true route of the hunters.

4 Did someone transcribe the message? Evidently not Mina.

5 Mina's date is wrong; this is the afternoon of the same day as the hypnotic trance. According to Jonathan's journal entry on the morning of 4 October, Mina envisioned Dracula already onboard the ship. Here she records Van Helsing as stating that "last afternoon at about five o'clock" Dracula came to the wharf to secure passage on the *Czarina Catherine*, and by morning (of this day) the ship was on the tide. Therefore, if Jonathan's journal date is accurate, the morning must have been 4, not 5, October.

yet in one day, when we know of the disposal of him we drive him out. He is finite, though he is powerful to do much harm and suffers not as we do. But we are strong, each in our purpose; and we are all more strong together. Take heart afresh, dear husband of Madam Mina. This battle is but begun, and in the end we shall win—so sure as that God sits on high to watch over His children. Therefore be of much comfort till we return.

Van Helsing.

JONATHAN HARKER'S JOURNAL.

4 October.—When I read to Mina, Van Helsing's message in the phonograph,[4] the poor girl brightened up considerably. Already the certainty that the Count is out of the country has given her comfort; and comfort is strength to her. For my own part, now that his horrible danger is not face to face with us, it seems almost impossible to believe in it. Even my own terrible experiences in Castle Dracula seem like a long-forgotten dream. Here in the crisp autumn air in the bright sunlight—

Alas! how can I disbelieve! In the midst of my thought my eye fell on the red scar on my poor darling's white forehead. Whilst that lasts, there can be no disbelief. And afterwards the very memory of it will keep faith crystal clear. Mina and I fear to be idle, so we have been over all the diaries again and again. Somehow, although the reality seems greater each time, the pain and the fear seem less. There is something of a guiding purpose manifest throughout, which is comforting. Mina says that perhaps we are the instruments of ultimate good. It may be! I shall try to think as she does. We have never spoken to each other yet of the future. It is better to wait till we see the Professor and the others after their investigations.

The day is running by more quickly than I ever thought a day could run for me again. It is now three o'clock.

MINA HARKER'S JOURNAL.

5 October 5 p.m.[5]—Our meeting for report. Present: Professor Van Helsing, Lord Godalming, Dr. Seward, Mr. Quincey Morris, Jonathan Harker, Mina Harker.

Dr. Van Helsing described what steps were taken during the day to discover on what boat and whither bound Count Dracula made his escape:—

"As I knew that he wanted to get back to Transylvania, I felt sure that he must go by the Danube mouth; or by somewhere in the Black Sea, since by that way he come.[6] It was a dreary blank that was before us. *Omne ignotum pro magnifico*;[7] and so with heavy hearts we start to find what ships leave for the Black Sea last night. He was in sailing ship, since Madam Mina tell of sails being set. These not so important as to go in your list of the shipping in the *Times*, and so we go, by suggestion of Lord Godalming, to your Lloyd's,[8] where are note of all ships that sail, however so small. There we find that only one Black-Sea-bound ship go out with the tide.[9] She is the *Czarina Catherine*,[10] and she sail from Doolittle's Wharf[11] for Varna,[12] and thence on to other parts and up the Danube. 'Soh!' said I, 'this is the ship whereon is the Count.' So off we go to Doolittle's Wharf, and there we find a man in an office of wood so small that the man look bigger than the office. From him we inquire of the goings of the *Czarina Catherine*. He swear much, and he red face and loud of voice, but he good fellow all the same; and when Quincey give him something from his pocket which crackle as he roll it up, and put it in a so small bag which he have hid deep in his clothing, he still better fellow and humble servant to us. He come with us, and ask many men who are rough and hot; these be better fellows too when they have been no more thirsty. They say much of blood and bloom,[13] and of others which I comprehend not, though I guess what they mean; but nevertheless they tell us all things which we want to know.

"They make known to us among them, how last afternoon at about five o'clock comes a man so hurry. A tall man, thin and pale, with high nose and teeth so white, and eyes that seem to be burning. That he be all in black, except that he have a hat of straw which suit not him or the time.[14] That he scatter his money in making quick inquiry as to what ship sails for the Black Sea and for where. Some took him to the office and then to the ship, where he will not go aboard but halt at shore end of gang-plank, and ask that the captain come to him. The captain

6 The Manuscript continues: "He had been only so far north and east as Munich and this in experiment and so he know not at first quite how he get from London to there." This refers to the excised Munich "Dead House" episode (see chapter 1, note 1) and does not appear in the published text.

7 Latin, from Tacitus's *Agricola*: "That which is not known is wonderful." The quotation seems inapt here.

8 The world's first and largest ship-classification society began in 1760 as a register of ships likely to be insured by marine insurance underwriters meeting at Lloyd's coffeehouse in London. Though it remains headquartered in London, Lloyd's Register is now an international nonprofit organisation focussed on maritime management and safety. Its register book, issued annually, lists all merchant ships of 100 or more tons gross. The register is accessible on the Internet and in CD-ROM format, a development that would have speeded up Van Helsing's researches.

9 For the times of high tide, see chapter 23, note 15.

10 There is no record of a ship with this name. Wolf (*The Essential Dracula*) finds the ship's name suggestive, noting that the *Encyclopædia Britannica* (11th ed.) describes Catherine as "perfectly immoral in her sexual relations to men. The scandalous chronicle of her life was the commonplace of all Europe." However, this is Catherine II (1729–1796), empress of Russia, usually referred to as Catherine the Great. Is not a more likely candidate Catherine I (1683–1727), also empress of Russia (and second wife of Peter the Great), described in the same *Britannica* as "an uncommonly shrewd and sensible woman, [whose] imperturbable good nature under exceptionally difficult circumstances . . . testifies equally to the soundness of her head and the goodness of her heart"?

11 Wharfs were plentiful along the Thames, and they generally bore the name of a proprietor, past or present. The Doolittle's Wharf visit does not appear in the Abridged Text.

12 It will be recalled that Dracula had long before established a beachhead in Varna, through "Herr Leutner," apparently a local solicitor.

13 Although many theories have been expressed for its origin, including oaths such as "Christ's blood" or "by God's blood," the word "bloody" most likely arose from hostility towards the "bloods," or nobles. The *Oxford English Dictionary* (1971) describes the word "bloody" in foul language as a "vague epithet expressing anger, resentment, detestation." In 1880, John Ruskin (*Fiction, Fair and Foul*) opined that "[t]he use of the word 'bloody' in modern low English is a deeper corruption, not altering the form of the word, but defiling the thought of the word." In the 1887 edition of the *OED*, editor James Murray noted that it was "now constantly in the mouths of the lowest classes, but by respectable people considered 'a horrid word,' on a par with obscene or profane language." Michael Quinion, the doyen of *World Wide Words*, a popular Internet site, and author of numerous books on language, points out that Victorian police reports often abbreviated the word as "b——y," a practise that continued into the twentieth century, when George Bernard Shaw shocked playgoing London with the line "Walk! Not bloody likely! I am going in a taxi!" (uttered by flower girl Eliza Doolittle) in *Pygmalion* (1916). The controversy still lingers; in 2006, an advertising campaign created by Tourism Australia featuring the word drew worldwide criticism.

"Blooming" is a euphemism for "bloody." Although the phrase is ironic in the context of Dracula's presence, presumably Van Helsing overheard foul language that he cautiously translates in this manner.

14 Van Helsing is making fun of Dracula's attire, which is somewhat out of season; while come, when told that he will be pay well; and though he swear much at the first he agree to term. Then the thin man go and some one tell him where horse and cart can be hired. He go there, and soon he come again, himself driving cart on which is a great box; this he himself lift down, though it take several to put it on truck for the ship. He give much talk to captain as to how and where his box to be place; but the captain like it not and swear at him in many tongues, and tell him that if he like he can come and see where it shall be.[15] But he say 'no;' that he come not yet, for that he have much to do. Whereupon the captain tell him that he had better be quick—with blood—for that his ship will leave the place—of blood—before the turn of the tide—with blood. Then the thin man smile, and say that of course he must go when he think fit; but he will be surprise if he go quite so soon. The captain swear again, polyglot, and the thin man make him bow, and thank him, and say that he will so far intrude on his kindness as to come aboard before the sailing. Final the captain, more red than ever, and in more tongues, tell him that he doesn't want no Frenchmen—with bloom upon them and also with blood—in his ship—with blood on her also. And so, after asking where there might be close at hand a shop where he might purchase ship forms, he departed.

"No one knew where he went 'or bloomin' well cared,' as they said, for they had something else to think of—well with blood again; for it soon became apparent to all that the *Czarina Catherine* would not sail as was expected. A thin mist began to creep up from the river, and it grew, and grew; till soon a dense fog enveloped the ship and all around her. The captain swore polyglot—very polyglot—polyglot with bloom and blood; but he could do nothing. The water rose and rose; and he began to fear that he would lose the tide altogether. He was in no friendly mood, when just at full tide, the thin man came up the gang-plank again and asked to see where his box had been stowed. Then the captain replied that he wished that he and his box—old and with much bloom and blood—were in hell. But the thin man did not be offend, and went down with the mate and saw where it was place, and came up and stood awhile on deck in fog. He must have come off by himself, for none notice him. Indeed they thought not of him; for soon the fog begin to melt away, and all was clear again. My friends of the thirst and the language that was of bloom and blood laughed, as they told how the captain's swears exceeded even his usual polyglot, and was more than ever full of picturesque, when on questioning other mariners who were on movement up and down the river that hour, he found that few of them had seen any of fog at all, except where it lay round the wharf. However, the ship went out on the ebb tide; and was doubtless by morning far down the river mouth. She was by then, when they told us, well out to sea.

"And so, my dear Madam Mina, it is that we have to rest for a time, for our enemy is on the sea, with the fog at his command,[16] on his way to the Danube mouth. To sail a ship takes time, go she never so quick; and when we start we go on land more quick,[17] and we meet him there. Our best hope is to come on him when in the box between sunrise and sunset; for then he can make no struggle, and we may deal with him as we should.[18] There are days for us, in which we can make ready our plan. We know all about where he go; for we have seen the owner of the ship, who have shown us invoices and all papers that can be. The box we seek is to be landed in Varna, and to be given to an agent, one Ristics who will there present his credentials;[19] and so our merchant friend will have done his part. When he ask if there be any wrong, for that so, he can telegraph and have inquiry made at Varna, we say 'no;' for what is to be done is not for police or of the customs. It must be done by us alone and in our own way."

When Dr. Van Helsing had done speaking, I asked him if he were certain that the Count had remained on board the ship. He replied: "We have the best proof of that: your own evidence, when in the hypnotic trance this morning." I asked him again if it were really necessary that they should pursue the Count, for oh! I dread Jonathan leaving me, and I know that he would surely go if the others went. He answered in growing passion, at first quietly. As he went on, however, he grew more angry and more forceful, till in the end we could not but see wherein was at least some of that personal dominance which made him so long a master amongst men:[20]—

the straw boater was extremely popular, it was worn primarily in the summer. Dracula evidently viewed the hat as quintessentially English and hence part of his effort to blend in. The description of "straw" and the judgement that the hat is out of season do not appear in the Abridged Text. Was Dracula self-conscious about his appearance?

15 The tale of the captain is considerably shortened in the Abridged Text.

16 There is no mention of the command of the fog in the Abridged Text, although it is obvious from the events that Dracula does command it.

17 Why did Dracula travel by ship and not by the quicker land route? Wolf (*The Essential Dracula*) speculates that Dracula believed the dangers of discovery to be less onboard ship, with fewer customs inspectors, or that his powers over the weather would be more useful at sea. Perhaps a better question is why didn't Dracula simply fly to or from Transylvania, at least in stages? (Van Helsing believed that vampires could not cross running water except at high or low tide, it will be recalled; this would present severe problems to a flight across the Channel.) Bats have been known to travel as far as 1,240 miles, from summer to winter roosts, and Transylvania is not much farther from London. It would have been prudent to deposit boxes of soil in depots along various routes and permit such a flight. Marv Wolfman's *The Tomb of Dracula* and *Dracula Lives!* record Dracula's use of this device. See "Dracula's Family Tree" in Part II.

18 Van Helsing has either forgotten about the female vampires, whose destruction will require a trip to Transylvania, or he sees them as minor threats, to be ignored. After all, they are not invading England—and they are only women.

19 These details do not appear in the Abridged Text, perhaps to make the hunters look less foolish for being taken in by Dracula.

20 The Abridged Text also makes no mention of this anger—"Van Helsing" apparently being uncomfortable with that aspect of his portrait.

21 Van Helsing doesn't seem to be able to make up his mind whether vampires are a natural occurrence or the work of the Devil. In this extended speech he seems to suggest some form of mutant origin. The balance of this paragraph to the cold "He have infect you—" does not appear in the Abridged Text.

"Yes, it is necessary—necessary—necessary! For your sake in the first, and then for the sake of humanity. This monster has done much harm already, in the narrow scope where he find himself, and in the short time when as yet he was only as a body groping his so small measure in darkness and not knowing.[21] All this have I told these others; you, my dear Madam Mina, will learn it in the phonograph of my friend John, or in that of your husband. I have told them how the measure of leaving his own barren land—barren of peoples—and coming to a new land where life of man teems till they are like the multitude of standing corn, was the work of centuries. Were another of the Un-Dead, like him, to try to do what he has done, perhaps not all the centuries of the world that have been, or that will be, could aid him. With this one, all the forces of nature that are occult and deep and strong must have worked together in some wondrous way. The very place, where he have been alive, Un-Dead for all these centuries, is full of strangeness of the geologic and chemical world. There are deep caverns and fissures that reach none know whither. There have been volcanoes, some of whose openings still send out waters of strange properties, and gases that kill or make to vivify. Doubtless, there is something magnetic or electric in some of these combinations of occult forces which work for physical life in strange way; and in himself were from the first some great qualities. In a hard and warlike time he was celebrate that he have more iron nerve, more subtle brain, more braver heart, than any man. In him some vital principle have in strange way found their utmost; and as his body keep strong and grow and thrive, so his brain grow too. All this without that diabolic aid which is surely to him; for it have to yield to the powers that come from, and are, symbolic of good. And now this is what he is to us. He have infect you—oh forgive me, my dear, that I must say such; but it is for good of you that I speak. He infect you in such wise, that even if he do no more, you have only to live—to live in your own old, sweet way; and so in time, death, which is of man's common lot, and with God's sanction, shall make you like to him. This must not be! We have sworn together that it must not. Thus are we ministers of God's own wish: that the world, and men for whom His Son die, will not be given over to monsters, whose very existence would defame Him. He have allowed us to redeem one soul already, and we go out as the old knights of the Cross to redeem more. Like them we shall travel towards the sunrise; and like them, if we fall, we fall in good cause." He paused and I said:—

"But will not the Count take his rebuff wisely? Since he has been driven from England, will he not avoid it, as a tiger does the village from which he has been hunted?"[22]

"Aha!" he said, "your simile of the tiger good, for me, and I shall adopt him. Your man-eater, as they of India call the tiger who has once tasted blood of the human, care no more for the other prey, but prowl unceasing till he get him. This that we hunt from our village is a tiger, too, a man-eater, and he never cease to prowl. Nay, in himself he is not one to retire and stay afar. In his life, his living life, he go over the Turkey frontier and attack his enemy on his own ground; he be beaten back, but did he stay?[23] No! He come again, and again, and again. Look at his persistence and endurance. With the child-brain that was to him he have long since conceive the idea of coming to a great city. What does he do? He find out the place of all the world most of promise for him. Then he deliberately set himself down to prepare for the task. He find in patience just how is his strength, and what are his powers. He study new tongues. He learn new social life; new environment of old ways, the politic, the law, the finance, the science, the habit of a new land and a new people who have come to be since he was. His glimpse that he have had, whet his appetite only and enkeen his desire. Nay, it help him to grow as to his brain; for it all prove to him how right he was at the first in his surmises. He have done this alone; all alone! from a ruin tomb in a forgotten land. What more may he not do when the greater world of thought is open to him. He that can smile at death, as we know him; who can flourish in the midst of diseases that kill off whole peoples. Oh, if such an one was to come from God, and not the Devil, what a force for good might he not be in this old world of ours. But we are pledged to set the world free. Our toil must be in silence, and our efforts all in secret; for in this enlightened age, when men believe not even what they see, the doubting of wise men would be his greatest strength. It would be at once his sheath

22 The Abridged Text omits the tiger metaphor and much of Van Helsing's following analysis of why Dracula would return to England. This suppression may have sinister purposes, as explored below.

23 Did Van Helsing learn this from Harker's journal or from his friend Arminius?

24 This paragraph does not appear in the Abridged Text.

25 Note that Mina still has a reflection. Perhaps mirror-invisibility occurs only when the soul departs the body. See chapter 2, note 68.

26 Seward's entry seems to be the day after the hypnotic trance and tracing of the *Czarina Catherine*—that is, the day after the preceding entry. Its reference to a general meeting of the hunters is to a second meeting. This confirms that Mina's entry is misdated.

27 Seward's philosophising in this paragraph is not included in the Abridged Text.

and his armour, and his weapons to destroy us, his enemies, who are willing to peril even our own souls for the safety of one we love—for the good of mankind, and for the honour and glory of God."

After a general discussion it was determined that for to-night nothing be definitely settled; that we should all sleep on the facts, and try to think out the proper conclusions. To-morrow at breakfast we are to meet again, and, after making our conclusions known to one another, we shall decide on some definite course of action.[24]

I feel a wonderful peace and rest to-night. It is as if some haunting presence were removed from me. Perhaps. . . .

My surmise was not finished, could not be; for I caught sight in the mirror of the red mark upon my forehead; and I knew that I was still unclean.[25]

DR. SEWARD'S DIARY.

5 October.[26]—We all arose early, and I think that sleep did much for each and all of us. When we met at early breakfast there was more general cheerfulness than any of us had ever expected to experience again.

It is really wonderful how much resilience there is in human nature.[27] Let any obstructing cause, no matter what, be removed in any way—even by death—and we fly back to first principles of hope and enjoyment. More than once as we sat around the table, my eyes opened in wonder whether the whole of the past days had not been a dream. It was only when I caught sight of the red blotch on Mrs. Harker's forehead that I was brought back to reality. Even now, when I am gravely revolving the matter, it is almost impossible to realise that the cause of all our trouble is still existent. Even Mrs. Harker seems to lose sight of her trouble for whole spells; it is only now and again, when something recalls it to her mind, that she thinks of her terrible scar. We are to meet here in my study in half an hour and decide on our course of action. I see only one immediate difficulty, I know it by instinct rather than reason: we shall all have to speak frankly; and yet I fear that in some mysterious way poor Mrs. Harker's tongue is tied. I *know* that she forms conclusions of her own, and from all that has been I can guess how brilliant and how true they must be; but she will not, or cannot, give them utterance. I have mentioned this to Van Helsing, and he and I are to talk it over when we are alone. I suppose it is some of that horrid poison which has got into her veins beginning to work. The Count had his own purposes when he gave her what Van Helsing[28] called "the Vampire's baptism of blood." Well, there may be a poison that distills itself out of good things; in an age when the existence of ptomaines is a mystery we should not wonder at anything![29] One thing I know: that if my instinct be true regarding poor Mrs. Harker's silences, then there is a terrible difficulty—an unknown danger—in the work before us.[30] The same power that compels her silence may compel her speech. I dare not think further; for so I should in my thoughts dishonour a noble woman!

Van Helsing is coming to my study a little before the others. I shall try to open the subject with him.

Later.—When the Professor came in, we talked over the state of things. I could see that he had something on his mind which he wanted to say, but felt some hesitancy about broaching the subject. After beating about the bush a little, he said suddenly:—

"Friend John, there is something that you and I must talk of alone, just at the first at any rate. Later, we may have to take the others into our confidence;" then he stopped, so I waited; he went on:—

"Madam Mina, our poor, dear Madam Mina is changing." A cold shiver ran through me to find my worst fears thus endorsed. Van Helsing continued:—

"With the sad experience of Miss Lucy, we must this time be warned before things go too far. Our task is now in reality more difficult than ever, and this new trouble makes every hour of the direst importance. I can see the characteristics of the vampire coming in her face. It is now but very, very slight; but it is to be seen if we have eyes to notice without to prejudge. Her teeth are some sharper, and at times her eyes are more

28 Changed in the Manuscript from "he." See chapter 21, note 39.

29 A ptomaine (from Greek *ptoma*, "corpse") is a toxic nitrogenous organic substance formed by the putrefaction of proteins and amino acids, usually in meat but sometimes in vegetable matter. First noted in decaying fish in 1814, the putrefactive alkaloids were named by the toxicologist and founder of colloid chemistry Francesco Selmi in 1872, two years after Selmi coined the term "ptomaine poisoning," and were isolated in 1876. By the time of Stoker's narrative, the "mystery" had been effectively dispelled by science.

30 This astute observation, and the three sentences following, do not appear in the Abridged Text. In the narrative, Mina does not appear to betray the hunters. If in fact she did so and, as discussed below, Dracula actually survived and worked to "cover up" this fact, the suggestion of her betrayal would need to be excised from the text.

31 Leatherdale (*Dracula Unearthed*) notes that these symptoms, too, have developed in Mina much more quickly than in Lucy. Perhaps this is the result of sharing Dracula's blood, although, as discussed earlier, Lucy may have done so as well. See chapter 22, note 5.

32 This paragraph does not appear in the Abridged Text. Perhaps "Van Helsing" wished to deemphasise his religiosity.

33 The Abridged Text does not contain this or the next two sentences; they was likely removed to avoid further discussion of Mina's possible betrayal.

hard.[31] But these are not all, there is to her the silence now often; as so it was with Miss Lucy. She did not speak, even when she wrote that which she wished to be known later. Now my fear is this. If it be that she can, by our hypnotic trance, tell what the Count see and hear, is it not more true that he who have hypnotise her first, and who have drink of her very blood and make her drink of his, should, if he will, compel her mind to disclose to him that which she know?" I nodded acquiescence; he went on:—

"Then, what we must do is to prevent this; we must keep her ignorant of our intent, and so she cannot tell what she know not. This is a painful task! Oh! so painful that it heart-break me to think of; but it must be. When to-day we meet, I must tell her that for reason which we will not to speak she must not more be of our council, but be simply guarded by us." He wiped his forehead, which had broken out in profuse perspiration at the thought of the pain which he might have to inflict upon the poor soul already so tortured. I knew that it would be some sort of comfort to him if I told him that I also had come to the same conclusion; for at any rate it would take away the pain of doubt. I told him, and the effect was as I expected.

It is now close to the time of our general gathering. Van Helsing has gone away to prepare for the meeting, and his painful part of it. I really believe his purpose is to be able to pray alone.[32]

Later.—At the very outset of our meeting a great personal relief was experienced by both Van Helsing and myself. Mrs. Harker had sent a message by her husband to say that she would not join us at present, as she thought it better that we should be free to discuss our movements without her presence to embarrass us. The Professor and I looked at each other for an instant, and somehow we both seemed relieved.[33] For my own part, I thought that if Mrs. Harker realised the danger herself, it was much pain as well as much danger averted. Under the circumstances we agreed, by a questioning look and answer, with finger on lip, to preserve silence in our suspicions, until we should have been able to confer alone again. We went at once into our Plan of Campaign. Van Helsing roughly put the facts before us first:—

"The *Czarina Catherine* left the Thames yesterday morning.[34] It will take her at the quickest speed she has ever made at least three weeks to reach Varna; but we can travel overland to the same place in three days.[35] Now, if we allow for two days less for the ship's voyage, owing to such weather influence as we know that the Count can bring to bear; and if we allow a whole day and night for any delays which may occur to us, then we have a margin of nearly two weeks.[36] Thus, in order to be quite safe, we must leave here on 17th at latest. Then we shall at any rate be in Varna a day before the ship arrives, and able to make such preparations as may be necessary. Of course we shall all go armed—armed against evil things, spiritual as well as physical." Here Quincey Morris added:—

"I understand that the Count comes from a wolf country,[37] and it may be that he shall get there before us. I propose that we add Winchesters[38] to our armament. I have a kind of belief in a Winchester when there is any trouble of that sort around. Do you remember Art, when we had the pack after us at Tobolsk?[39] What wouldn't we have given then for a repeater apiece!"

"Good!" said Van Helsing, "Winchesters it shall be. Quincey's head is level at all times, but most so when there is to hunt, though my metaphor be more dishonour to science than wolves be of danger to man. In the meantime we can do nothing here; and as I think that Varna is not familiar to any of us, why not go there more soon? It is as long to wait here as there. To-night and to-morrow we can get ready, and then, if all be well, we four can set out on our journey."

"We four?" said Harker interrogatively, looking from one to another of us.

"Of course!" answered the Professor quickly, "You must remain to take care of your so sweet wife!" Harker was silent for awhile and then said in a hollow voice:—

"Let us talk of that part of it in the morning.[40] I want to consult with Mina." I thought that now was the time for Van Helsing to warn him not to disclose our plans to her; but he

34 That is, early on the morning of the hypnotic trance. Dracula boarded the ship the evening before the trance.

35 McNally and Florescu (*The Essential Dracula*) calculate that the trip would take at least six days, if all connections were made. See chapter 25, note 12, below, for a discussion of the connections.

36 The words "two weeks" and, in the next sentence, "17th" are inserted in Stoker's hand in the Manuscript, illustrating that the calendar aspects were added later.

37 Wolves were largely exterminated in England by the 1500s and the balance of Europe by the mid-1700s. However, they still abounded in the remote countryside. Emily Gerard, in "Transylvanian Superstitions" (1885), remarks: "Every winter here brings fresh proof of the boldness and cunning of these terrible animals, whose attacks on flocks and farms are often conducted with a skill which would do honour to a human intellect. Sometimes a whole village is kept in trepidation for weeks together by some particularly audacious leader of a flock of wolves, to whom the peasants not unnaturally attribute a more than animal nature, and one may safely prophesy that so long as the real wolf continues to haunt the Transylvanian forests, so long will his spectre brother survive in the minds of the inhabitants."

Wolves have long been enmeshed in myth, from the suckling of Romulus and Remus, the founders of Rome, by a she-wolf to the devouring of Odin by the wolf Fenris (or Fenrir in some sources). European culture associates wolves with evil, as is most evident in the tale of "Little Red Riding Hood." The plague of lycanthropy that swept Europe between 1520 and 1630, when over thirty thousand people in France alone were tried on charges of werewolfism, may be seen as emblematic of the deep-rooted fear of wolves, although the annals of medicine also provide clues to the phenomenon. One later presumed cause of the concentration of cases

Winchester rifle, 1873 model.

was ergot poisoning, caused by the consumption of rye (used in bread and cereals) infected with a parasite; severe symptoms of this disease, which is also known as St. Anthony's Fire, include hallucinations, convulsions, extreme thirst, and visions of being attacked by a beast or of turning into one. See "Dracula's Family Tree" in Part II for a discussion of the relationship between werewolves and vampires.

38 In 1848, Oliver Fisher Winchester set up a dress-shirt factory in New Haven, Connecticut, and with the windfall from this business was able to purchase the Volcanic Repeating Arms Company in 1857. Reorganised as the Winchester Repeating Arms Company in 1867, the gun manufacturer made a policy of aggressively acquiring others' designs, including a lever-action repeating rifle designed by B. T. Henry, the Winchester plant manager and chief mechanic. Patented in 1860, it was widely used in the Civil War. Also tremendously popular among American settlers was the Model 73 (short for The New Model of 1873), favoured by such lawmakers, ruffians, and Wild West legends as Billy the Kid, Wyatt Earp, and Buffalo Bill Cody. It remained in production for fifty-two years, and 720,610 were manufactured in all. It is likely the Model 73 of which Quincey Morris speaks so fondly.

39 An historic capital of Western Siberia. Defoe's Robinson Crusoe stayed there from 1703 to 1704.

40 There is a transcription error here: it is morning.

41 Jonathan confirms Seward's date and Mina's misdating.

took no notice. I looked at him significantly and coughed. For answer he put his finger on his lip and turned away.

JONATHAN HARKER'S JOURNAL.

5 October, afternoon.[41]—For some time after one[42] meeting this morning I could not think. The new phases of things leave my mind in a state of wonder which allows no room for active thought. Mina's determination not to take any part in the discussion set me thinking; and as I could not argue the matter with her, I could only guess. I am as far as ever from a solution now. The way the others received it, too, puzzled me; the last time we talked of the subject we agreed that there was to be no more concealment of anything amongst us. Mina is sleeping now, calmly and sweetly like a little child. Her lips are curved and her face beams with happiness. Thank God there are such moments still for her.

Later.—How strange it all is. I sat watching Mina's happy sleep, and came as near to being happy myself as I suppose I shall ever be. As the evening drew on, and the earth took its shadows from the sun sinking lower, the silence of the room grew more and more solemn to me. All at once Mina opened her eyes, and looking at me tenderly, said:—

"Jonathan, I want you to promise me something on your word of honour. A promise made to me, but made holily in God's hearing, and not to be broken though I should go down on my knees and implore you with bitter tears. Quick, you must make it to me at once."

"Mina," I said, "a promise like that, I cannot make at once. I may have no right to make it."

"But, dear one," she said, with such spiritual intensity that her eyes were like pole stars,[43] "it is I who wish it; and it is not for myself. You can ask Dr. Van Helsing if I am not right; if he disagrees you may do as you will. Nay, more, if you all agree, later, you are absolved from the promise."

"I promise!" I said, and for a moment she looked supremely happy; though to me all happiness for her was denied by the red scar on her forehead. She said:—

"Promise me that you will not tell me anything of the plans formed for the campaign against the Count. Not by word, or inference, or implication; not at any time whilst this remains to me!" and she solemnly pointed to the scar. I saw that she was in earnest, and said solemnly:—

"I promise!" and as I said it I felt that from that instant a door had been shut between us.

Later, midnight.—Mina had been bright and cheerful all the evening. So much so that all the rest seemed to take courage, as if infected somewhat with her gaiety; as a result even I myself felt as if the pall of gloom which weighs us down were somewhat lifted. We all retired early. Mina is now sleeping like a little child; it is wonderful thing that her faculty of sleep remains to her in the midst of her terrible trouble. Thank God for it, for then at least she can forget her care. Perhaps her example may affect me as her gaiety did to-night. I shall try it. Oh! for a dreamless sleep.

6 October, morning.—Another surprise. Mina woke me early, about the same time as yesterday,[44] and asked me to bring Dr. Van Helsing. I thought that it was another occasion for hypnotism, and without question went for the Professor. He had evidently expected some such call, for I found him dressed in his room. His door was ajar, so that he could hear the opening of the door of our room. He came at once; as he passed into the room, he asked Mina if the others might come too.

"No," she said quite simply, "it will not be necessary. You can tell them just as well. I must go with you on your journey."

Dr. Van Helsing was as startled as I was. After a moment's pause he asked:—

"But why?"

"You must take me with you. I am safer with you, and you shall be safer too."

"But why, dear Madam Mina? You know that your safety is our solemnest duty. We go into danger, to which you are, or may be, more liable than any of us from—from circumstances— things that have been."[45] He paused embarrassed.

42 Probably "our," not "one"; changed to "our" in the Abridged Text.

43 Polaris, the pole star marking north, is a magnitude 2 star, about one-fifteenth as bright as the brightest star. Of course there is only one "pole star."

44 Jonathan's "yesterday" is incorrect if he is referring to Mina awakening on the morning of 4 October, but he may simply mean that she woke him early on 5 October to convey her decision that she would not attend the morning meeting.

45 Van Helsing's reasoning is not clear. Earlier he explains that the risk to Mina is death. Surely there is nothing more that Dracula can do to her, short of slaying her, and his intentions to keep her alive have been made explicit. That is, there is no evident enhanced risk to Mina from accompanying the hunting party, and if the hunters were to fail to slay Dracula, there is no reason to believe that he would not return to London to regain his "winepress."

46 Or, under Dracula's influence, she is an excellent actress. It surely would occur to Dracula, who may well have felt her telepathic contact, that Mina's presence in the hunting party would be an excellent tracking device. Did this obvious risk escape Van Helsing? Or did he recognise that Mina could be useful, as the proverbial two-edged sword?

As she replied, she raised her finger and pointed to her forehead:—

"I know. That is why I must go. I can tell you now, whilst the sun is coming up; I may not be able again. I know that when the Count wills me I must go. I know that if he tells me to come in secret, I must come by wile; by any device to hoodwink—even Jonathan." God saw the look that she turned on me as she spoke, and if there be indeed a Recording Angel that look is noted to her everlasting honour. I could only clasp her hand. I could not speak; my emotion was too great for even the relief of tears. She went on:—

"You men are brave and strong. You are strong in your numbers, for you can defy that which would break down the human endurance of one who had to guard alone. Besides, I may be of service, since you can hypnotise me and so learn that which even I myself do not know." Dr. Van Helsing said very gravely:—

"Madam Mina, you are, as always, most wise. You shall with us come; and together we shall do that which we go forth to achieve." When he had spoken, Mina's long spell of silence made me look at her. She had fallen back on her pillow asleep; she did not even wake when I had pulled up the blind and let in the sunlight which flooded the room. Van Helsing motioned to me to come with him quietly. We went to his room, and within a minute Lord Godalming, Dr. Seward, and Mr. Morris were with us also. He told them what Mina had said, and went on:—

"In the morning we shall leave for Varna. We have now to deal with a new factor: Madam Mina. Oh, but her soul is true. It is to her an agony to tell us so much as she has done;[46] but it is most right, and we are warned in time. There must be no chance lost, and in Varna we must be ready to act the instant when that ship arrives."

"What shall we do exactly?" asked Mr. Morris laconically.

The Professor paused before replying:—

"We shall at the first board that ship; then, when we have identified the box, we shall place a branch of the wild rose on it. This we shall fasten, for when it is there none can emerge;

so at least says the superstition. And to superstition must we trust at the first; it was man's faith in the early, and it have its root in faith still. Then, when we get the opportunity that we seek, when none are near to see, we shall open the box, and—and all will be well."

"I shall not wait for any opportunity," said Morris. "When I see the box I shall open it and destroy the monster, though there were a thousand men looking on, and if I am to be wiped out for it the next moment!"[47] I grasped his hand instinctively and found it as firm as a piece of steel. I think he understood my look; I hope he did.[48]

"Good boy," said Dr. Van Helsing. "Brave boy. Quincey is all man. God bless him for it. My child, believe me none of us shall lag behind or pause from any fear. I do but say what we may do—what we must do. But, indeed, indeed we cannot say what we shall do. There are so many things which may happen, and their ways and their ends are so various that until the moment we may not say. We shall all be armed, in all ways; and when the time for the end has come, our effort shall not be lack. Now let us to-day put all our affairs in order. Let all things which touch on others dear to us, and who on us depend, be complete; for none of us can tell what, or when, or how, the end may be. As for me, my own affairs are regulate; and as I have nothing else to do, I shall go make arrangements for the travel. I shall have all tickets and so forth for our journey."

There was nothing further to be said, and we parted. I shall now settle up all my affairs of earth, and be ready for whatever may come. . . .

Later.—It is done; my will is made, and all complete. Mina if she survive is my sole heir. If it should not be so, then the others who have been so good to us shall have remainder.

It is now drawing towards the sunset; Mina's uneasiness calls my attention to it. I am sure that there is something on her mind which the time of exact sunset will reveal. These occasions are becoming harrowing times for us all, for each sunrise and sunset opens up some new danger—some new

47 Did Morris plan to fake his own death? See chapter 18, note 49, for a discussion of his suspicious activities.

48 The reader certainly hopes Quincey did not interpret this hand-grasping as flirtatious.

pain, which, however, may in God's will be means to a good end. I write all these things in the diary since my darling must not hear them now; but if it may be that she can see them again, they shall be ready.

She is calling to me.

Bram Stoker's Dracula, starring Gary Oldman as Dracula and Anthony Hopkins as Van Helsing.
(American Zoetrope, 1992)

Chapter 25

DR. SEWARD'S DIARY.

11 October, Evening.[1]—Jonathan Harker has asked me to note this, as he says he is hardly equal to the task, and he wants an exact record kept.[2]

I think that none of us were surprised when we were asked to see Mrs. Harker a little before the time of sunset. We have of late come to understand that sunrise and sunset are to her times of peculiar freedom; when her old self can be manifest without any controlling force subduing or restraining her, or inciting her to action. This mood or condition begins some half hour or more before actual sunrise or sunset, and lasts till either the sun is high, or whilst the clouds are still aglow with the rays streaming above the horizon. At first there is a sort of negative condition, as if some tie were loosened, and then the absolute freedom quickly follows; when, however, the freedom ceases the change-back or relapse comes quickly, preceded only by a spell of warning silence.

To-night, when we met she was somewhat constrained, and bore all the signs of an internal struggle.[3] I put it down myself to her making a violent effort at the earliest instant she could do so. A very few minutes, however, gave her complete control of herself; then, motioning her husband to sit beside her on the sofa where she was half reclining, she made the rest of us bring chairs up close. Taking her husband's hand in hers began:—

"We are all here together in freedom, for perhaps the last

1 Another delay—Van Helsing said on 6 October that they would leave "in the morning."

2 This reference to Harker's weakness does not appear in the Abridged Text.

3 It is unclear with what Mina struggles. Is she shaking off Dracula's mind control? Is she submerging her own vampiric nature? Is she struggling to hear Dracula more clearly?

4 Although Mina may have meant the phrase in its colloquial cookery sense, like many another lawyer's spouse, she drops this legal jargon into conversation. It means "the blending or gathering together of properties for the purpose of securing equality of division, especially as practised in certain cases in the distribution of the property of an intestate parent" (*Oxford English Dictionary*, 1971). It does not appear in the Abridged Text.

time! I know, dear; I know that you will always be with me to the end." This was to her husband whose hand had, as we could see, tightened upon hers. "In the morning we go out upon our task, and God alone knows what may be in store for any of us. You are going to be so good to me as to take me with you. I know that all that brave earnest men can do for a poor weak woman, whose soul perhaps is lost—no, no, not yet, but is at any rate at stake—you will do. But you must remember that I am not as you are. There is a poison in my blood, in my soul, which may destroy me; which must destroy me, unless some relief comes to us. Oh, my friends, you know as well as I do, that my soul is at stake; and though I know there is one way out for me, you must not and I must not take it!" She looked appealingly to us all in turn, beginning and ending with her husband.

"What is that way?" asked Van Helsing in a hoarse voice. "What is that way, which we must not—may not—take?"

"That I may die now, either by my own hand or that of another, before the greater evil is entirely wrought. I know, and you know, that were I once dead you could and would set free my immortal spirit, even as you did my poor Lucy's. Were death, or the fear of death, the only thing that stood in the way I would not shrink to die here, now, amidst the friends who love me. But death is not all. I cannot believe that to die in such a case, when there is hope before us and a bitter task to be done, is God's will. Therefore, I, on my part, give up here the certainty of eternal rest, and go out into the dark where may be the blackest things that the world or the nether world holds!" We were all silent, for we knew instinctively that this was only a prelude. The faces of the others were set, and Harker's grew ashen grey; perhaps he guessed better than any of us what was coming. She continued:—

"This is what I can give into the hotch-pot."**4** I could not but note the quaint legal phrase which she used in such a place, and with all seriousness. "What will each of you give? Your lives I know," she went on quickly, "that is easy for brave men. Your lives are God's, and you can give them back to Him; but what will you give to me?" She looked again questioningly, but this time avoided her husband's face. Quincey seemed to understand; he nodded, and her face lit up. "Then I shall tell you plainly what I want, for there must be no doubtful matter in this connection between us now. You must promise me, one and all—even you my beloved husband—that, should the time come, you will kill me."

"What is that time?" The voice was Quincey's, but it was low and strained.

"When you shall be convinced that I am so changed that it is better that I die that I may live. When I am thus dead in the flesh, then you will, without a moment's delay, drive a stake through me and cut off my head; or do whatever else may be wanting to give me rest!"

Quincey was the first to rise after the pause. He knelt down before her and taking her hand in his said solemnly:—

"I'm only a rough fellow, who hasn't, perhaps, lived as a man should to win such a distinction, but I swear to you by all that I hold sacred and dear that, should the time ever come, I shall not flinch from the duty that you have set us. And I promise you, too, that I shall make all certain, for if I am only doubtful I shall take it that the time has come!"

"My true friend!" was all she could say amid her fast-falling tears, as, bending over, she kissed his hand.

"I swear the same, my dear Madam Mina!" said Van Helsing.

"And I!" said Lord Godalming, each of them in turn kneeling to her to take the oath. I followed, myself. Then her husband turned to her, wan-eyed and with a greenish pallor which subdued the snowy whiteness of his hair, and asked:—

"And must I, too, make such a promise, oh, my wife?"[5]

"You too, my dearest," she said, with infinite yearning of pity in her voice and eyes. "You must not shrink. You are nearest and dearest and all the world to me; our souls are knit into one, for all life and all time. Think, dear, that there have been times when brave men have killed their wives and their womenkind, to keep them from falling into the hands of the enemy. Their hands did not falter any the more because those that they loved implored them to slay them. It is men's duty towards those whom they love, in such times of sore trial! And oh, my dear,

5 And, it should be noted, he does not.

6 Mina, who transcribed Seward's record of Lucy's death, obviously knows the import of this phrase to Van Helsing and Lord Godalming.

7 The change of phrase does not appear in the Abridged Text. Did Mina recall that four men had "loved" Lucy by exchanging bodily fluids with her?

if it is to be that I must meet death at any hand, let it be at the hand of him that loves me best.**6** Dr. Van Helsing, I have not forgotten your mercy in poor Lucy's case to him who loved"— she stopped with a flying blush, and changed her phrase—"to him who had best right to give her peace.**7** If that time shall come again, I look to you to make it a happy memory of my husband's life that it was his loving hand which set me free from the awful thrall upon me."

"Again I swear!" came the Professor's resonant voice. Mrs. Harker smiled, positively smiled, as with a sigh of relief she leaned back and said:—

"And now one word of warning, a warning which you must never forget: this time, if it ever come, may come quickly and unexpectedly, and in such case you must lose no time in using your opportunity. At such a time I myself might be—nay! if the time ever comes, *shall* be—leagued with your enemy against you."

"One more request;" she became very solemn as she said this, "it is not vital and necessary like the other, but I want you to do one thing for me, if you will." We all acquiesced, but no one spoke; there was no need to speak:—

"I want you to read the Burial Service." She was interrupted by a deep groan from her husband; taking his hand in hers, she held it over her heart, and continued. "You must read it over me some day. Whatever may be the issue of all this fearful state of things, it will be a sweet thought to all or some of us. You, my dearest, will I hope read it, for then it will be in your voice in my memory for ever—come what may!"

"But oh, my dear one," he pleaded, "death is afar off from you."

"Nay," she said, holding up a warning hand. "I am deeper in death at this moment than if the weight of an earthly grave lay heavy upon me!"

"Oh, my wife, must I read it?" he said, before he began.

"It would comfort me, my husband!" was all she said; and he began to read when she had got the book ready.

How can I—how could any one—tell of that strange scene, its solemnity, its gloom, its sadness, its horror; and, withal, its sweetness. Even a sceptic, who can see nothing but a travesty of bitter truth in anything holy or emotional, would have been melted to the heart had he seen that little group of loving and devoted friends kneeling round that stricken and sorrowing lady; or heard the tender passion of her husband's voice, as in tones so broken with emotion that often he had to pause, he read the simple and beautiful service from the Burial of the Dead.[8] I—I cannot go on—words—and v-voice—f-fail m-me![9]

She was right in her instinct. Strange as it all was, bizarre as it may hereafter seem even to us who felt its potent influence at the time, it comforted us much; and the silence, which showed Mrs. Harker's coming relapse from her freedom of soul, did not seem so full of despair to any of us as we had dreaded.

JONATHAN HARKER'S JOURNAL.

15 October. Varna.—We left Charing Cross[10] on the morning of the 12th,[11] got to Paris the same night, and took the places secured for us in the Orient Express.[12] We travelled night and day, arriving here at about five o'clock. Lord Godalming went to the Consulate to see if any telegram had arrived for him, whilst the rest of us came on to this hotel—the Odessus.[13] The journey may have had incidents; I was, however, too eager to get on, to care for them. Until the *Czarina Catherine* comes into port there will be no interest for me in anything in the wide world. Thank God! Mina is well, and looks to be getting stronger; her colour is coming back. She sleeps a great deal; throughout the journey she slept nearly all the time. Before sunrise and sunset, however, she is very wakeful and alert; and it has become a habit for Van Helsing to hypnotise her at such times. At first, some effort was needed, and he had to make many passes;[14] but now, she seems to yield at once, as if by habit, and scarcely any action is needed. He seems to have power at these particular moments to simply will, and her thoughts obey him. He always asks her what she can see and hear. She answers to the first:—

"Nothing; all is dark." And to the second:—

"I can hear the waves lapping against the ship, and the water rushing by. Canvas and cordage strain and masts and yards

8 The Book of Common Prayer, the liturgy of the Church of England, was not revised between 1662 and 1928, when the events of the narrative occurred. The service Mina wishes to hear— The Order for the Burial of the Dead—begins with the recital of the following by the clergy: "I am the resurrection and the life, saith the Lord: he that believeth in me, though he were dead, yet shall he live: and whosoever liveth and believeth in me shall never die. I know that my Redeemer liveth, and that he shalt stand at the latter day upon the earth. And though after my skin worms destroy this body, yet in my flesh shall I see God: whom I shall see for myself, and mine eyes shall behold, and not another. We brought nothing into this world, and it is certain we can carry nothing out. The Lord gave, and the Lord hath taken away; blessed be the Name of the Lord."

9 Mina's transcription must be incredibly accurate.

10 Charing Cross station is closer than any other terminus to the true centre of London. It opened in 1864 and quickly became the terminus for the boat trains to and from Dover and Folkestone. A large clock on the inner wall of the hotel became a favourite meeting place for young women and their partners (both amateur and professional), inspiring A. H. Binstead's 1903 quatrain: "The terminus of Charing Cross / Is haunted when it rains / By Nymphs, who there a shelter seek / And wait for mythic trains" (*Pitcher in Paradise*).

11 The Notes indicate that the hunters first planned to leave on 5 October.

12 Harker compresses the complexity of the journey; the train did not run directly to Varna in three days. It took at least one day to travel to Paris and, if one arrived on a day that the train departed for Giurgiu, another four days to travel to that town. Another day's journey by steamer and train would deliver the passenger to Varna.

The legendary Orient Express was the

The Orient Express.

train service between Paris and Vienna, later extended to Constantinople. In 1876, Georges Nagelmackers emulated the success of George Pullman in America and founded La Compagnie Internationale des Wagons-Lits, to operate luxury sleeping cars and dining cars in Europe. The Wagons-Lits company provided and staffed sleeping and dining cars on regular trains and charged passengers a supplement to a first-class ticket. By 1883, Nagelmackers's flagship, the Express d'Orient (it was not renamed the Orient Express until 1891) began its regular run, twice a week, from Paris (Gare de l'Est) to Vienna, continuing on through Budapest, Bucharest, and Giurgiu. There, a ferry crossed the Danube to Ruse in Bulgaria, where a second train was waiting for the seven-hour journey to Varna. This is the likely route taken by the hunters.

13 Odessus was an ancient Thracian town, flourishing in the second and third centuries, eventually incorporated into Varna. A sign of its prosperity was the issuance of Thracian coins bearing the source "Odessus" or "Odessos."

14 No mention is made in the Abridged Text of any increasing difficulties in hypnotizing Mina.

15 Why would Dracula care about avoiding suspicion in Varna any more than he did in Whitby? He certainly did not restrict himself to his box onboard the *Demeter*, and one wonders why the crew of the *Czarina Catherine* survived the voyage.

creak. The wind is high—I can hear it in the shrouds, and the bow throws back the foam." It is evident that the *Czarina Catherine* is still at sea, hastening on her way to Varna. Lord Godalming has just returned. He had four telegrams, one each day since we started, and all to the same effect: that the *Czarina Catherine* had not been reported to Lloyd's from anywhere. He had arranged before leaving London that his agent should send him every day a telegram saying if the ship had been reported. He was to have a message even if she were not reported, so that he might be sure that there was a watch being kept at the other end of the wire.

We had dinner and went to bed early. To-morrow we are to see the Vice-Consul, and to arrange, if we can, about getting on board the ship as soon as she arrives. Van Helsing says that our chance will be to get on the boat between sunrise and sunset. The Count, even if he takes the form of a bat, cannot cross the running water of his own volition, and so cannot leave the ship. As he dare not change to man's form without suspicion—which he evidently wishes to avoid—he must remain in the box.[15] If, then, we can come on board after sunrise, he is at our mercy; for we can open the box and make sure of him, as we did of poor Lucy,[16] before he wakes. What mercy he shall get from us will not count for much.[17] We think that we shall not have much trouble with officials or the seamen. Thank God! this is the country where bribery can do anything, and we are well supplied with money. We have only to make sure that the ship cannot come into port between sunset and sunrise without our being warned, and we shall be safe. Judge Moneybag will settle this case, I think![18]

16 October.—Mina's report still the same: lapping waves and rushing water, darkness and favouring winds. We are evidently in good time, and when we hear of the *Czarina Catherine* we shall be ready. As she must pass the Dardanelles we are sure to have some report.

17 October.—Everything is pretty well fixed now, I think, to welcome the Count on his return from his tour.[19] Godalming told the shippers[20] that he fancied that the box sent aboard might contain something stolen from a friend of his, and got a half consent that he might open it at his own risk. The owner gave him a paper telling the Captain to give him every facility in doing whatever he chose on board the ship, and also a similar authorisation to his agent at Varna. We have seen the agent, who was much impressed with Godalming's kindly manner to him, and we are all satisfied that whatever he can do to aid our wishes will be done. We have already arranged what to do in case we get the box open. If the Count is there, Van Helsing and Seward will cut off his head at once and drive a stake through his heart. Morris and Godalming and I shall prevent interference, even if we have to use the arms which we shall have ready. The Professor says that if we can so treat the Count's body, it will soon after fall into dust.[21] In such case there would be no evidence against us, in case any suspicion of murder were aroused. But even if it were not, we should stand or fall by our act, and perhaps some day this very script may be evidence to come between some of us and a rope.[22] For myself, I should take the chance only too thankfully if it were to come. We mean to leave no stone unturned to carry out our intent. We have arranged with certain officials that the instant the *Czarina Catherine* is seen, we are to be informed by a special messenger.

24 October.—A whole week of waiting. Daily telegrams to Godalming, but only the same story: "Not yet reported." Mina's morning and evening hypnotic answer is unvaried: lapping waves, rushing water, and creaking masts.

TELEGRAM, OCTOBER 24TH.
RUFUS[23] SMITH, LLOYD'S, LONDON, TO LORD GODALMING, CARE OF H.B.M.[24]10 VICE-CONSUL, VARNA.

"*CZARINA CATHERINE* REPORTED THIS

MORNING FROM DARDANELLES."

16 The "we" is a collective figure of speech; Harker of course had no part in the staking of Lucy.

17 This grim purpose and the following cynical observations about bribery do not appear in the Abridged Text.

18 Harker seems to think nothing of Dracula's money bag, which we know was well filled, and the presence of his prearranged agent.

19 The details of the hunters' machinations are omitted from this paragraph in the Abridged Text.

20 The Manuscript reads "the ship owner Mr. Hopgood," the only indication of his identity. Roger Johnson, in private correspondence with this editor, points out that "the London firm of Hapgood" is somehow connected with the ship—see text accompanying chapter 26, note 7.

21 This is the first indication that Van Helsing believes Dracula's demise will be different from Lucy's. Note that the "dust" is predicted to appear "soon after" decapitation and staking.

22 This illogical remark—coming from a lawyer, no less—and the following clear expression of murderous intent do not appear in the Abridged Text.

23 "Victor" in the Manuscript, replaced by "Rufus." Both are clearly pseudonyms.

24 "Her Britannic Majesty."

25 Probably 24 October, not 25, for Seward's following comment about the distance of the Dardenelles and the intended plan of action to make sense. The first paragraph does not appear in the Abridged Text.

26 This is a very subtle dental examination, for on 5 October Seward reported that Mina's teeth were "sharper." See text accompanying chapter 24, note 31.

27 What a cold statement! The Greek *euthanasia*, from *eu* ("good") and *thanatos* ("death"), means painless death, or the methodology of intentionally causing a gentle and easy death. Mina's would be what is characterised as voluntary euthanasia, because she requested death. However, human euthanasia remains illegal and highly controversial almost everywhere.

The ethical and legal issue involved is by no means new. In 1881, journalist Richard Rowe, in *Life in the London Streets*, considered the "homeless" of London: "But are such lives, lives that ought to be, must be, led? I cannot believe it. We shoot old horses when they have become a weariness to themselves. If we cannot help our pariahs, it would be a kindness, I think, to kill them off—to hand them over, in that way, to the tender mercies of the all-seeing One in whom we are so fond of bidding them to trust. But the pariah first selected for this euthanasia might probably object, otherwise he would have previously 'his own quietus ta'en,' and the benevolent murderer would be strung up between the gloomy walls of a gaol, with a black flag flapping over him."

DR. SEWARD'S DIARY.

25 October.[25]—How I miss my phonograph! To write diary with a pen is irksome to me; but Van Helsing says I must. We were all wild with excitement yesterday when Godalming got his telegram from Lloyd's. I know now what men feel in battle when the call to action is heard. Mrs. Harker, alone of our party, did not show any signs of emotion. After all, it is not strange that she did not; for we took special care not to let her know anything about it, and we all tried not to show any excitement when we were in her presence. In old days she would, I am sure, have noticed, no matter how we might have tried to conceal it; but in this way she is greatly changed during the past three weeks. The lethargy grows upon her, and though she seems strong and well, and is getting back some of her colour, Van Helsing and I are not satisfied. We talk of her often; we have not, however, said a word to the others. It would break poor Harker's heart—certainly his nerve—if he knew that we had even a suspicion on the subject. Van Helsing examines, he tells me, her teeth carefully, whilst she is in the hypnotic condition, for he says that so long as they do not begin to sharpen there is no active danger of a change in her.[26] If this change should come, it would be necessary to take steps! . . . We both know what those steps would have to be, though we do not mention our thoughts to each other. We should neither of us shrink from the task—awful though it be to contemplate. "Euthanasia" is an excellent and a comforting word! I am grateful to whoever invented it.[27]

It is only about 24 hours' sail from the Dardanelles to here, at the rate the *Czarina Catherine* has come from London. She should therefore arrive some time in the morning; but as she cannot possibly get in before then, we are all about to retire early. We shall get up at one o'clock, so as to be ready.

25 October, Noon.—No news yet of the ship's arrival. Mrs. Harker's hypnotic report this morning was the same as usual, so it is possible that we may get news at any moment. We men are all in a fever of excitement, except Harker, who is calm; his hands are cold as ice, and an hour ago I found him whetting the edge of the great Ghoorkha knife[28] which he now always carries with him. It will be a bad lookout for the Count if the edge of that "Kukri" ever touches his throat, driven by that stern, ice-cold hand!

Van Helsing and I were a little alarmed about Mrs. Harker to-day. About noon she got into a sort of lethargy which we did not like; although we kept silence to the others, we were neither of us happy about it. She had been restless all the morning, so that we were at first glad to know that she was sleeping. When, however, her husband mentioned casually that she was sleeping so soundly that he could not wake her, we went to her room to see for ourselves. She was breathing naturally and looked so well and peaceful that we agreed that the sleep was better for her than anything else. Poor girl, she has so much to forget that it is no wonder that sleep, if it brings oblivion to her, does her good.

Later.—Our opinion was justified, for when after a refreshing sleep of some hours she woke up, she seemed brighter and better than she had been for days. At sunset she made the usual hypnotic report. Wherever he may be in the Black Sea, the Count is hurrying to his destination. To his doom, I trust!

26 October.—Another day and no tidings of the *Czarina Catherine.* She ought to be here by now. That she is still journeying *somewhere* is apparent, for Mrs. Harker's hypnotic report at sunrise was still the same. It is possible that the vessel may be lying by, at times, for fog; some of the steamers which came in last evening reported patches of fog both to north and south of the port. We must continue our watching, as the ship may now be signalled any moment.

27 October, Noon.—Most strange; no news yet of the ship we wait for. Mrs. Harker reported last night and this morning as usual: "lapping waves and rushing water," though she added that "the waves were very faint." The telegrams from London have been the same: "no further report." Van Helsing is terribly anxious, and told me just now that he fears the Count is escaping us. He added significantly:—

28 See chapter 23, note 17.

29 The Notes contain an erased entry indicating that the telegram arrived on 27 October, followed by an entry for 28 October confirming the arrival of the telegram on that date.

30 The chief Moldavian port of entry, approached by the Danube, the Sereth, and the Pruth, and the largest exporter of Roumanian timber, Galatz is about 150 miles north of Varna and 130 miles northeast of Bucharest.

31 The balance of this paragraph—up to the phrase "When does the next train . . ."—does not appear in the Abridged Text, and the sentence remaining seems to be missing words. The effect of the amendment is to make the hunters appear to be more confident and able to adjust their plans.

32 Is this the same John Seward who quoted Disraeli, saying "The unexpected always happens"? See chapter 9, note 25.

33 Transcendentalism was a nineteenth-movement of American writers and philosophers who generally believed in the essential unity of all creation, the innate goodness of man, and the supremacy of insight over logic and experience for the revelation of the deepest truths. However, that is not likely Seward's meaning: rather, he probably refers to the philosophy of Immanuel Kant (1724–1804), who considered "transcendental idealism"—"transcendental" in this case as differentiated from "empirical." The chief precept of transcendental idealism is that knowledge is based on "subjective existence" rather than on experience—that is, that the self, or ego, uses sense perceptions to build stores of knowledge.

"I did not like that lethargy of Madam Mina's. Souls and memories can do strange things during trance." I was about to ask him more, but Harker just then came in, and he held up a warning hand. We must try to-night at sunset to make her speak more fully when in her hypnotic state.

28 October.—Telegram, Rufus Smith, Lloyd's, London, to Lord Godalming, care of H.B.M. Vice-Consul, Varna.[29]

"*Czarina Catherine* reported entering Galatz[30] at one o'clock to-day."

Dr. Seward's Diary.

28 October.—When the telegram came announcing the arrival in Galatz[31] I do not think it was such a shock to any of us as might have been expected. True, we did not know whence, or how, or when, the bolt would come; but I think we all expected that something strange would happen. The day of arrival at Varna made us individually satisfied that things would not be just as we had expected; we only waited to learn where the change would occur. None the less, however, it was a surprise. I suppose that nature works on such a hopeful basis that we believe against ourselves that things will be as they ought to be, not as we should know that they will be.[32] Transcendentalism[33] is a beacon to the angels, even if it be a will-o'-the-wisp to man. It was an odd experience, and we all took it differently. Van Helsing raised his hands over his head for a moment, as though in remonstrance with the Almighty; but he said not a word, and in a few seconds stood up with his face sternly set. Lord Godalming grew very pale, and sat breathing heavily. I was myself half stunned and looked in wonder at one after another. Quincey Morris tightened his belt with that quick movement which I knew so well; in our old wandering days it meant "action." Mrs. Harker grew ghastly white, so that the scar on her forehead seemed to burn, but she folded her hands meekly and looked up in prayer. Harker smiled—actually smiled—the dark, bitter smile of one who is without hope; but at the same time his action belied his words, for his hands instinctively sought the hilt of the great Kukri knife and rested there. "When does the next train start for Galatz?" said Van Helsing to us generally.

"At 6:30 to-morrow morning!" We all started, for the answer came from Mrs. Harker.

"How on earth do you know?" said Art.

"You forget—or perhaps you do not know, though Jonathan does and so does Dr. Van Helsing—that I am the train fiend. At home in Exeter I always used to make up the time-tables, so as to be helpful to my husband. I found it so useful sometimes, that I always make a study of the time-tables now. I knew that if anything were to take us to Castle Dracula we should go by Galatz, or at any rate through Bucharest, so I learned the times very carefully.[34] Unhappily there are not many to learn, as the only train to-morrow leaves as I say."

"Wonderful woman!" murmured the Professor.

"Can't we get a special?" asked Lord Godalming.[35] Van Helsing shook his head: "I fear not. This land is very different from yours or mine; even if we did have a special, it would probably not arrive as soon as our regular train. Moreover, we have something to prepare. We must think. Now let us organize. You, friend Arthur, go to the train and get the tickets and arrange that all be ready for us to go in the morning. Do you, friend Jonathan, go to the agent of the ship and get from him letters to the agent in Galatz, with authority to make search the ship just as it was here. Morris Quincey,[36] you see the Vice-Consul, and get his aid with his fellow in Galatz and all he can do to make our way smooth, so that no times be lost when over the Danube. John will stay with Madam Mina and me, and we shall consult. For so if time be long you may be delayed; and it will not matter when the sun set, since I am here with Madam to make report."

"And I," said Mrs. Harker brightly, and more like her old self than she had been for many a long day, "shall try to be of use in all ways, and shall think and write for you as I used to do. Something is shifting from me in some strange way, and I feel freer than I have been of late!" The three younger men

34 Mina, at least, perceives the wisdom of seeking Dracula at his castle rather than en route. However, with her divided loyalties, Mina's plan should be suspected and is not.

35 Lord Godalming means hiring a smaller, dedicated train to take them to their intended destination. In England, this could generally be done for 5s. a mile. This sum allowed one to hire a first-class carriage and a light engine, and it also granted the privilege of a line cleared of slower traffic.

36 Van Helsing talks like Dracula!

37 Van Helsing does not admit his deception in the Abridged Text.

38 Interestingly, the last phrase—about the "rise and set of sun"—does not appear in the Abridged Text. In light of the critical event that occurs at the setting of the sun at the conclusion of the narrative, this omission is telling.

39 The Abridged Text does not include this patronising remark.

looked happier at the moment as they seemed to realise the significance of her words; but Van Helsing and I, turning to each other, met each a grave and troubled glance. We said nothing at the time, however.

When the three men had gone out to their tasks Van Helsing asked Mrs. Harker to look up the copy of the diaries and find him the part of Harker's journal at the Castle. She went away to get it; when the door was shut upon her he said to me:—

"We mean the same! speak out!"

"There is some change. It is a hope that makes me sick, for it may deceive us."

"Quite so. Do you know why I asked her to get the manuscript?"**37**

"No!" said I, "unless it was to get an opportunity of seeing me alone."

"You are in part right, friend John, but only in part. I want to tell you something. And oh, my friend, I am taking a great—a terrible—risk; but I believe it is right. In the moment when Madam Mina said those words that arrest both our understanding, an inspiration come to me. In the trance of three days ago the Count sent her his spirit to read her mind; or more like he took her to see him in his earth-box in the ship with water rushing, just as it go free at rise and set of sun.**38** He learn then that we are here; for she have more to tell in her open life with eyes to see and ears to hear than he, shut, as he is, in his coffin-box. Now he make his most effort to escape us. At present he want her not. He is sure with his so great knowledge that she will come at his call; but he cut her off—take her, as he can do, out of his own power, that so she come not to him. Ah! there I have hope that our man-brains, that have been of man so long and that have not lost the grace of God, will come higher than his child-brain that lie in his tomb for centuries, that grow not yet to our stature, and that do only work selfish and therefore small.**39** Here comes Madam Mina; not a word to her of her trance! She know it not; and it would overwhelm her and make despair just when we want all her hope, all her courage; when most we want all her great brain which is trained like man's brain, but is of sweet woman and have a special power which the Count give her, and which he may not take away altogether—though he think not so. Hush! let me speak, and you shall learn. Oh John, my friend, we are in awful straits. I fear, as I never feared before. We can only trust the good God. Silence! here she comes!"

I thought that the Professor was going to break down and have hysterics,[40] just as he had when Lucy died, but with a great effort he controlled himself and was at perfect nervous poise when Mrs. Harker tripped into the room, bright and happy-looking, and, in the doing of work, seemingly forgetful of her misery. As she came in, she handed a number of sheets of typewriting to Van Helsing. He looked over them gravely, his face brightening up as he read. Then holding the pages between his finger and thumb he said:—

"Friend John, to you with so much of experience already—and you too, dear Madam Mina, that are young—here is a lesson: do not fear ever to think. A half-thought has been buzzing often in my brain, but I fear to let him loose his wings. Here now, with more knowledge, I go back to where that half-thought come from and I find that he be no half-thought at all; that be a whole thought, though so young that he is not yet strong to use his little wings. Nay, like the 'Ugly Duck' of my friend Hans Andersen,[41] he be no duck-thought at all, but a big swan-thought that sail nobly on big wings, when the time come for him to try them. See I read here what Jonathan have written:—

" 'That other of his race who, in a later age, again and again, brought his forces over The Great River into Turkey-land; who, when he was beaten back, came again, and again, and again, though he had to come alone from the bloody field where his troops were being slaughtered, since he knew that he alone could ultimately triumph.'[42]

"What does this tell us? Not much? no![43] The Count's child-thought see nothing; therefore he speak so free. Your man-thought see nothing; my man-thought see nothing, till just now. No! But there comes another word from some one who speak without thought because she too know not what it mean—what it *might* mean. Just as there are elements which rest, yet when in nature's course they move on their way and they touch—then pouf! and there comes a flash of light, heaven's

40 The "hysterics" are not mentioned in the Abridged Text.

41 Can Van Helsing really mean that he was a friend of Hans Christian Andersen (1805–1875), the great writer and retailer of fairy tales? Andersen was the most widely travelled Danish writer of his day, making twenty-nine trips abroad, and spent over nine years outside Denmark. Van Helsing, a collector of fairy tales of a different sort, and Andersen shared an interest in folktales, and it is certainly possible that they met. However, the Abridged Text drops the entire "Ugly Duck" metaphor and reference to Andersen.

42 See text accompanying chapter 3, note 30.

43 Van Helsing's praise of Mina's insight and comparison with the lack of insight of Dracula, Van Helsing, and Seward do not appear in the Abridged Text. Nor do the discussions of the philosophy of crime and Archimedes' fulcrum that follow.

44 Latin: from the particular to the universal. Note that in fact Mina *has* evidently studied the philosophy of crime, for she is familiar with Lombroso and Nordau (see note 46 below).

45 What he actually said in *Geometra* was "Dos moi pou sto Kai ten gen kineso," which Van Helsing translates loosely.

46 Italian criminologist and physician Cesare Lombroso (1835–1909), who held that individuals engaged in criminal acts not by choice but because they were "atavistic" and had never evolved past the uncivilised nature of our primitive forebears. The 1888 *Encyclopædia Britannica* (9th ed.) refers to such individuals as men "who live in the midst of our civilization as mere savages. . . . the existing system of law can scarcely be brought to distinguish them from criminals. Moralists attribute to atavism a large number of offences which lawyers attribute to guilty dispositions." But the *Britannica* editor appears sceptical of this view: "It is not, however, owing to atavism, but to the mere continuance of an old order of things, that so many of our ill-educated

Cesare Lombroso.

wide, that blind and kill and destroy some; but that show up all earth below for leagues and leagues. Is it not so? Well, I shall explain. To begin, have you ever study the philosophy of crime? 'Yes' and 'No.' You, John, yes; for it is a study of insanity. You, no, Madam Mina; for crime touch you not—not but once. Still, your mind works true, and argues not *a particulari ad universale*.[44] There is this peculiarity in criminals. It is so constant, in all countries and at all times, that even police, who know not much from philosophy, come to know it empirically, that *it is*. That is to be empiric. The criminal always work at one crime—that is the true criminal who seems predestinate to crime, and who will of none other. This criminal has not full man-brain. He is clever and cunning and resourceful; but he be not of man-stature as to brain. He be of child-brain in much. Now this criminal of ours is predestinate to crime also; he too have child-brain, and it is of the child to do what he have done. The little bird, the little fish, the little animal learn not by principle, but empirically; and when he learn to do, then there is to him the ground to start from to do more. '*Dos pou sto*,' said Archimedes.[45] 'Give me a fulcrum, and I shall move the world!' To do once, is the fulcrum whereby child-brain become man-brain; and until he have the purpose to do more, he continue to do the same again every time, just as he have done before! Oh, my dear, I see that your eyes are opened, and that to you the lightning flash show all the leagues," for Mrs. Harker began to clap her hands, and her eyes sparkled. He went on:—

"Now you shall speak. Tell us two dry men of science what you see with those so bright eyes." He took her hand and held it whilst she spoke. His finger and thumb closed on her pulse, as I thought instinctively and unconsciously, as she spoke:—

"The Count is a criminal and of criminal type. Nordau and Lombroso[46] would so classify him, and *quâ* criminal he is of imperfectly formed mind. Thus, in a difficulty he has to seek resource in habit. His past is a clue, and the one page of it that we know—and that from his own lips—tells that once before, when in what Mr. Morris would call a 'tight place,' he went back to his own country from the land he had tried to invade, and thence, without losing purpose, prepared himself

Max Nordau.

views of inherited degeneracy in his 1892 book *Degeneration*. Nordau concluded that various artists of the nineteenth century were victims of decaying brains and labeled their art as "degenerate." He characterised Baudelaire as showing "all the mental stigmata of degeneration during the whole of his life" and termed Rossetti and Verlaine "imbeciles," Swinburne "a criminal," and Wagner a "crazed graphomaniac." Although, ironically, Nordau was an early Zionist leader, his thinking was readily adopted by the Nazi regime, which began in 1937 to purge German museums of "degenerate art." With the demise of Lombroso's scientific theories, Nordau's pseudoscientific criticism of art suffered the same fate.

classes, shepherds, agricultural labourers, and even factory hands, are as little developed, and live a life as little intellectual as savages. Latent in our small hamlets and large cities there is more savagery than many reformers are aware of, and it needs but little experience to discover something of the old barbarity lurking still in minds and hearts under a thin veil of civilisation."

In his *L'uomo delinquente* (1876, partially translated in 1911 as *Criminal Man*), Lombroso pointed to certain physical and mental abnormalities of these "born criminals," such as skull size and asymmetry of the face and other body parts. His views have since been discredited, but Lombroso's role in bringing science to the study of criminal behavior is regarded as pivotal. Wolf (*The Essential Dracula*) points out many resemblances between the description of Dracula and Lombroso's archetypal criminal.

Max Nordau (1849–1923), Hungarian physician, author, and critic, adapted Lombroso's

47 See text accompanying chapter 3, note 30, for Dracula's own remarks on this topic.

48 This is a truly amazing talent—to take Mina's pulse in a few seconds while kissing her hand! In short, it's another display of Van Helsing's medical quackery.

49 Van Helsing's and Mina's comments are a naive view of Dracula's tactics. First, his ancestor (or Dracula, if we identify him with the ancestor) did not act selfishly or to preserve his own skin; rather, he made the sound tactical decision that his initial attack had been rash, and when he found himself outnumbered, he returned to recruit new forces to return to the battle. If anything, Dracula's (or his ancestor's) history should frighten the hunters, rather than encourage them, for Dracula's remorselessness is his great advantage over lesser foes who lack his longevity. Second, to describe Dracula's actions as the product of a child-brain, compared with the wise actions of the hunters (who totally failed to consider that their prey might not arrive where they expected), is the height of foolishness. Third, to describe Dracula's evident return to Transylvania in the case of a man who has left the Continent exactly once in five hundred years as the product of "habit" seems further foolishness. One expects this kind of pompous reasoning from Van Helsing, but Mina's parroted confirmations may well be seen as the product of Dracula's mind control. That is, Dracula can only benefit from his enemies seeing his behaviour as predictable and irrational, instilling in them a false sense of confidence.

50 There are many similar phrases in the Psalms, though none quite like the words of Van Helsing, who is ever vague about the Scriptures.

for a new effort. He came again better equipped for his work; and won. So he came to London to invade a new land. He was beaten, and when all hope of success was lost, and his existence in danger, he fled back over the sea to his home; just as formerly he had fled back over the Danube from Turkey-land."[47]

"Good, good! oh, you so clever lady!" said Van Helsing, enthusiastically, as he stooped and kissed her hand. A moment later he said to me, as calmly as though we had been having a sick-room consultation:—

"Seventy-two only; and in all this excitement.[48] I have hope." Turning to her again, he said with keen expectation:—

"But go on. Go on! there is more to tell if you will. Be not afraid; John and I know. I do in any case, and shall tell you if you are right. Speak, without fear!"

"I will try to; but you will forgive me if I seem egotistical."

"Nay! fear not, you must be egotist, for it is of you that we think."

"Then, as he is criminal he is selfish; and as his intellect is small and his action is based on selfishness, he confines himself to one purpose. That purpose is remorseless. As he fled back over the Danube, leaving his forces to be cut to pieces, so now he is intent on being safe, careless of all.[49] So his own selfishness frees my soul somewhat from the terrible power which he acquired over me on that dreadful night. I felt it, Oh! I felt it. Thank God, for His great mercy! My soul is freer than it has been since that awful hour; and all that haunts me is a fear lest in some trance or dream he may have used my knowledge for his ends." The Professor stood up:—

"He has so used your mind; and by it he has left us here in Varna, whilst the ship that carried him rushed through enveloping fog up to Galatz, where, doubtless, he had made preparation for escaping from us. But his child-mind only saw so far; and it may be that, as ever is in God's Providence, the very thing that the evil doer most reckoned on for his selfish good, turns out to be his chiefest harm. The hunter is taken in his own snare, as the great Psalmist says.[50] For now that he think he is free from every trace of us all, and that he has escaped us with so many hours to him, then his selfish child-brain will whisper him to sleep. He think, too, that as he cut himself off from knowing your mind, there can be no knowledge of him to you; there is where he fail! That terrible baptism of blood which he give you[51] makes you free to go to him in spirit, as you have as yet done in your times of freedom, when the sun rise and set. At such times you go by my volition and not by his;[52] and this power to good of you and others, you have won from your suffering at his hands. This is now all more precious that he know it not, and to guard himself have even cut himself off from his knowledge of our where. We, however, are not selfish, and we believe that God is with us through all this blackness, and these many dark hours. We shall follow him; and we shall not flinch; even if we peril ourselves that we become like him. Friend John, this has been a great hour; and it have done much to advance us on our way. You must be scribe and write him all down, so that when the others return from their work you can give it to them; then they shall know as we do."

And so I have written it whilst we wait their return, and Mrs. Harker has written with her typewriter all since she brought the MS. to us.

51 Van Helsing continues to mangle his religious metaphors. Mina was not "baptised"; according to her, she was forced to drink Dracula's blood, in a parallel to the Communion.

52 What ego! How can Van Helsing possibly know about the mental link between Mina and Dracula? If Van Helsing is correct that Mina's intrusions into Dracula's mind, producing the sensory impressions recorded, are unnoticed by Dracula, then how can he possibly believe that Dracula is not capable of doing the same, gathering Mina's sensory impressions without her noticing? In fact, is it not more likely that Dracula—with five hundred years of practise—is able to probe Mina's mind at will, without leaving any traces?

Chapter 26

DR. SEWARD'S DIARY.

1 It is unclear why it should become more difficult to hypnotize Mina. If she is drawing closer to Dracula, one would expect that the mental link between them would strengthen. Perhaps this is meant to indicate that Mina is closer to completion of her turning and therefore is unconsciously resisting the hypnotic sessions that she believes are antithetical to her master. Of course, resistance is also a sound tactic if her purpose is to deceive Van Helsing into believing he is obtaining high-grade intelligence from her trances. Consistent with earlier edits suppressing thoughts of Mina's betrayal, the difficulties of hypnotizing Mina (including the passage relating her dramatic movements) are not mentioned in the Abridged Text.

29 October.—This is written in the train from Varna to Galatz. Last night we all assembled a little before the time of sunset. Each of us had done his work as well as he could; so far as thought, and endeavour, and opportunity go, we are prepared for the whole of our journey, and for our work when we get to Galatz. When the usual time came round Mina Harker prepared herself for her hypnotic effort; and after a longer and more strenuous effort on the part of Van Helsing than has been usually necessary,[1] she sank into the trance. Usually she speaks on a hint; but this time the Professor had to ask her questions, and to ask them pretty resolutely, before we could learn anything; at last her answer came:—

"I can see nothing; we are still; there are no waves lapping, but only a steady swirl of water softly running against the hawser. I can hear men's voices calling, near and far, and the roll and creak of oars in the rowlock. A gun is fired somewhere; the echo of it seems far away. There is tramping of feet overhead, and ropes and chains are dragged along. What is this? There is a gleam of light; I can feel the air blowing upon me."

Here she stopped. She had risen, as if impulsively, from where she lay on the sofa, and raised both her hands, palms upwards, as if lifting a weight. Van Helsing and I looked at each other with understanding. Quincey raised his eyebrows slightly and looked at her intently, whilst Harker's hand

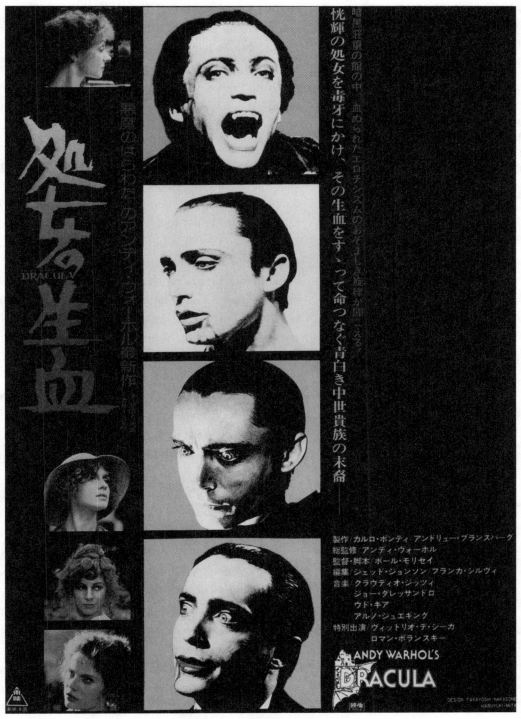

Andy Warhol's Dracula, *starring Udo Kier as Count Dracula.*
(C. F. S. Kosutnjak, 1974)

2 The trip from Varna to Bucharest was about 130 miles, but there was no regular train connection. The train from Bucharest to Galatz, also about 130 miles, took about seven hours, testimony to the irregular route. The entire trip, a straight-line distance of 150 miles, took the hunters almost twenty-four hours, although McNally and Florescu (*The Essential Dracula*) calculate that it should have taken them at least two days. The paragraph does not appear in the Abridged Text. The Notes actually indicate that the hunters arrived in Galatz at 1:20 A.M.

instinctively closed round the hilt of his kukri. There was a long pause. We all knew that the time when she could speak was passing; but we felt that it was useless to say anything. Suddenly she sat up, and, as she opened her eyes, said sweetly:—

"Would none of you like a cup of tea? You must all be so tired!" We could only make her happy, and so acquiesced. She bustled off to get tea; when she had gone Van Helsing said:—

"You see, my friends. *He* is close to land: he has left his earth-chest. But he has yet to get on shore. In the night he may lie hidden somewhere; but if he be not carried on shore, or if the ship do not touch it, he cannot achieve the land. In such case he can, if it be in the night, change his form and can jump or fly on shore, as he did at Whitby. But if the day come before he get on shore, then, unless he be carried he cannot escape. And if he be carried, then the customs men may discover what the box contains. Thus, in fine, if he escape not on shore to-night, or before dawn, there will be the whole day lost to him. We may then arrive in time; for if he escape not at night we shall come on him in daytime, boxed up and at our mercy; for he dare not be his true self, awake and visible, lest he be discovered."

There was no more to be said, so we waited in patience until the dawn; at which time we might learn more from Mrs. Harker.

Early this morning we listened, with breathless anxiety, for her response in her trance. The hypnotic stage was even longer in coming than before; and when it came the time remaining until full sunrise was so short that we began to despair. Van Helsing seemed to throw his whole soul into the effort; at last, in obedience to his will she made reply:—

"All is dark. I hear lapping water, level with me, and some creaking as of wood on wood." She paused, and the red sun shot up. We must wait till to-night.

And so it is that we are travelling towards Galatz in an agony of expectation. We are due to arrive between two and three in the morning; but already, at Bucharest,**2** we are three hours late, so we cannot possibly get in till well after sun-up. Thus we shall have two more hypnotic messages from Mrs.

Harker; either or both may possibly throw more light on what is happening.

Later.—Sunset has come and gone. Fortunately it came at a time when there was no distraction; for had it occurred whilst we were at a station, we might not have secured the necessary calm and isolation. Mrs. Harker yielded to the hypnotic influence even less readily than this morning. I am in fear that her power of reading the Count's sensations may die away, just when we want it most. It seems to me that her imagination is beginning to work. Whilst she has been in the trance hitherto she has confined herself to the simplest of facts. If this goes on it may ultimately mislead us. If I thought that the Count's power over her would die away equally with her power of knowledge it would be a happy thought; but I am afraid that it may not be so.[3] When she did speak, her words were enigmatical:—

"Something is going out; I can feel it pass me like a cold wind. I can hear, far off, confused sounds—as of men talking in strange tongues, fierce-falling water, and the howling of wolves." She stopped and a shudder ran through her, increasing in intensity for a few seconds, till, at the end, she shook as though in a palsy. She said no more, even in answer to the Professor's imperative questioning. When she woke from the trance, she was cold, and exhausted, and languid; but her mind was all alert. She could not remember anything, but asked what she had said; when she was told, she pondered over it deeply for a long time and in silence.

30 October, 7 a.m.—We are near Galatz now, and I may not have time to write later. Sunrise this morning was anxiously looked for by us all. Knowing of the increasing difficulty of procuring the hypnotic trance, Van Helsing began his passes earlier than usual. They produced no effect, however, until the regular time, when she yielded with a still greater difficulty, only a minute before the sun rose. The Professor lost no time in his questioning; her answer came with equal quickness:—

"All is dark. I hear water swirling by, level with my ears, and the creaking of wood on wood. Cattle low far off. There

3 Again, consistent with the removal of hints of Mina's betrayal, this paragraph and portions of the following paragraph—including Van Helsing's embarrassing efforts to command her—are not recorded in the Abridged Text.

4 Or as if Van Helsing actually had anything to do with the linkage.

5 None of this entry appears in the Abridged Text.

6 McNally and Florescu (*The Essential Dracula*) suggest that this was likely the Metropole Hotel, on Domneasca Street, or possibly the Regal Hotel.

is another sound, a queer one like—" she stopped and grew white, and whiter still.

"Go on; Go on! Speak, I command you!" said Van Helsing in an agonized voice. At the same time there was despair in his eyes, for the risen sun was reddening even Mrs. Harker's pale face. She opened her eyes, and we all started as she said, sweetly and seemingly with the utmost unconcern:—

"Oh, Professor, why ask me to do what you know I can't? I don't remember anything." Then, seeing the look of amazement on our faces, she said, turning from one to the other with a troubled look:—

"What have I said? What have I done? I know nothing, only that I was lying here, half asleep, and heard you say 'go on! speak, I command you!' It seemed so funny to hear you order me about, as if I were a bad child!"[4]

"Oh, Madam Mina," he said, sadly, "it is proof, if proof be needed, of how I love and honour you, when a word for your good, spoken more earnest than ever, can seem so strange because it is to order her whom I am proud to obey!"

The whistles are sounding; we are nearing Galatz. We are on fire with anxiety and eagerness.

MINA HARKER'S JOURNAL.[5]

30 October.—Mr. Morris took me to the hotel[6] where our rooms had been ordered by telegraph, he being the one who could best be spared, since he does not speak any foreign language. The forces were distributed much as they had been at Varna, except that Lord Godalming went to the Vice-Consul, as his rank might serve as an immediate guarantee of some sort to the official, we being in extreme hurry. Jonathan and the two doctors went to the shipping agent to learn particulars of the arrival of the *Czarina Catherine*.

Later.—Lord Godalming has returned. The Consul is away, and the Vice-Consul sick; so the routine work has been attended to by a clerk. He was very obliging, and offered to do anything in his power.

JONATHAN HARKER'S JOURNAL.[7]

30 October.—At nine o'clock Dr. Van Helsing, Dr. Seward, and I called on Messrs. Mackenzie & Steinkoff, the agents of the London firm of Hapgood. They had received a wire from London, in answer to Lord Godalming's telegraphed request, asking them to show us any civility in their power. They were more than kind and courteous, and took us at once on board the *Czarina Catherine*, which lay at anchor out in the river harbor. There we saw the Captain, Donelson by name, who told us of his voyage.[8] He said that in all his life he had never had so favourable a run.

"Man!" he said, "but it made us afeard, for we expeckit that she should have to pay for it wi' some rare piece o' ill luck, so as to keep up the average. It's no canny[9] to run frae London to the Black Sea wi' a wind ahint[10] ye, as though the Deil himself were blawin' on yer sail for his ain purpose. An' a' the time we could no speer[11] a thing. Gin[12] we were nigh a ship, or a port, or a headland, a fog fell on us and travelled wi' us, till when after it had lifted and we looked out, the deil a thing could we see. We ran by Gibraltar wi'oot bein' able to signal; an' till we came to the Dardanelles and had to wait to get our permit to pass, we never were within hail o' aught. At first I inclined to slack off sail and beat about till the fog was lifted; but whiles, I thocht that if the Deil was minded to get us into the Black Sea quick, he was like to do it whether we would or no. If we had a quick voyage it would be no to our miscredit wi' the owners, or no hurt to our traffic; an' the Old Mon[13] who had served his ain purpose wad be decently grateful to us for no hinderin' him." This mixture of simplicity and cunning, of superstition and commercial reasoning, aroused Van Helsing, who said:—

"Mine friend, that Devil is more clever than he is thought by some; and he know when he meet his match!" The skipper was not displeased with the compliment, and went on:—

"When we got past the Bosphorus the men began to grumble; some o' them, the Roumanians, came and asked me to heave overboard a big box which had been put on board by a queer lookin' old man[14] just before we had started frae London. I had seen them speer at the fellow, and put out their twa fingers

7 Headed in the Manuscript: "SHORTHAND REPORT BY JONATHAN HARKER TYPED BY HIS WIFE."

8 The captain's story is somewhat shorter in the Abridged Text but without apparent purpose other than brevity.

9 That is, uncanny.

10 Behind.

11 See.

12 When.

13 The Devil.

14 Apparently a disguise, for Dracula has just "banqueted heavily" on Mina and should be rejuvenated, if this is truly a consequence of his nourishment.

15 See chapter 1, note 68.

16 About.

17 That is, a caricature. The venerable Theatre Royal, Adelphi, was on the north side of the Strand, at No. 411, near Bedford Street. Originally the Sans Pareil Theatre when it opened in 1806, it became the Adelphi, then the Theatre Royal, Adelphi (under which name it was substantially rebuilt in 1858), later renamed the Royal Adelphi, and briefly the Century

A nineteenth-century American advertisement.

"Der Rosenbaum und sein Ableger." This is a pun. A "rosenbaum" (a common Jewish name) is a rose tree, and an "ableger" is a scion or branch.
Nineteenth-century German postcard

when they saw him, to guard them against the evil eye.[15] Man! but the supersteetion of foreigners is pairfectly rideeculous! I sent them aboot their business pretty quick; but as just after a fog closed in on us I felt a wee bit as they did anent[16] something, though I wouldn't say it was agin the big box. Well, on we went, and as the fog didn't let up for five days I joost let the wind carry us; for if the Deil wanted to get somewheres—well, he would fetch it up a'reet. An' if he didn't, well, we'd keep a sharp lookout anyhow. Sure enuch, we had a fair way and deep water all the time; and two days ago, when the mornin' sun came through the fog, we found ourselves just in the river opposite Galatz. The Roumanians were wild, and wanted me right or wrong to take out the box and fling it in the river. I had to argy wi' them aboot it wi' a handspike; an' when the last o' them rose off the deck wi' his head in his hand, I had convinced them that, evil eye or no evil eye, the property and the trust of my owners were better in my hands than in the river Danube. They had, mind ye, taken the box on the deck ready to fling in, and as it was marked Galatz *via* Varna, I thocht I'd let it lie till we discharged in the port an' get rid o't althegither. We didn't do much clearin' that day, an' had to remain the nicht at anchor; but in the mornin', braw an' airly, an hour before sun-up, a man came aboard wi' an order, written to him from England, to receive a box marked for one Count Dracula. Sure enuch the matter was one ready to his hand. He had his papers a' reet, an' glad I was to be rid o' the dam' thing, for I was beginnin' masel' to feel uneasy at it. If the Deil did have any luggage aboard the ship, I'm thinkin' it was nane ither than that same!"

"What was the name of the man who took it?" asked Dr. Van Helsing with restrained eagerness.

"I'll be tellin' ye quick!" he answered, and, stepping down to his cabin, produced a receipt signed "Immanuel Hildesheim." Burgen-strasse 16 was the address. We found out that this was all the Captain knew; so with thanks we came away.

We found Hildesheim in his office, a Hebrew of rather the Adelphi Theatre type,[17] with a nose like a sheep, and a fez. His arguments were pointed with specie—we doing the punctuation—and with a little bargaining he told us what he knew. This turned out to be simple but important. He had received a letter from Mr. de Ville[18] of London, telling him to receive, if possible before sunrise so as to avoid customs, a box which would arrive at Galatz in the *Czarina Catherine*.[19] This he was to give in charge to a certain Petrof Skinsky, who dealt with the Slovaks who traded down the river to the port. He had been paid for his work by an English bank note, which had been duly cashed for gold at the Danube International Bank.[20] When Skinsky had come to him, he had taken him to the ship and handed over the box, so as to save porterage. That was all he knew.

We then sought for Skinsky, but were unable to find him. One of his neighbours, who did not seem to bear him any affection, said that he had gone away two days before, no one knew whither. This was corroborated by his landlord, who had received by messenger the key of the house together with the rent due, in English money. This had been between ten and eleven o'clock last night. We were at a standstill again.

Whilst we were talking one came running and breathlessly gasped out that the body of Skinsky had been found inside the wall of the churchyard of St. Peter, and that the throat had been torn open as if by some wild animal. Those we had been speaking with ran off to see the horror, the women crying out, "This is the work of a Slovak!"[21] We hurried away lest we should have been in some way drawn into the affair, and so detained.

As we came home we could arrive at no definite conclusion. We were all convinced that the box was on its way, by water, to somewhere; but where that might be we would have to discover. With heavy hearts we came home to the hotel to Mina.

When we met together, the first thing was to consult as to taking Mina again into our confidence. Things are getting desperate, and it is at least a chance, though a hazardous one. As a preliminary step, I was released from my promise to her.[22]

MINA HARKER'S JOURNAL.

30 October, evening.—They were so tired and worn out and dispirited that there was nothing to be done till they had some rest; so I asked them all to lie down for half an hour whilst I should enter everything up to the moment. I feel so grateful

The Adelphi, 1858.

Theatre in 1901. However, it quickly reverted to the Royal Adelphi. It was rebuilt again in 1930, and in 1940 the "Royal" was dropped. The second great success of the 1872–1873 season was Leopold Lewis's *The Wandering Jew*, which played 151 times between 22 March and 1 October. This unpleasant bit of anti-Semitism does not appear in the Abridged Text.

18 In the Manuscript, the letter is from "D. Mandevill." The published text substitutes this name. See also chapter 20, note 36.

19 This is further evidence of Dracula's meticulous planning: he had time to dispatch a letter to Galatz, having planned this escape route carefully.

20 This detail and the details of payment of the landlord do not appear in the Abridged Text.

21 Whom, it will be recalled, Harker characterised on his first visit as "more barbarian than the rest." In the Abridged Text, the accusation is made by the "one" reporting the crime.

22 The hand-wringing over taking Mina into the hunters' "confidence" does not appear in the Abridged Text.

23 Mina is quite up-to-date in her technology, indeed suspiciously so. George C. Blickensderfer invented and produced the first small portable typewriter. He commenced manufacturing at Stamford, Connecticut, in 1889, but it was not until 1893 that Blickensderfer's lightweight typewriter was sold in any material amounts. (The model pictured here is a No. 7, which was produced in 1897.) Although it is possible that the American Quincey Morris has an early pre-1893 production model, there is no indication that he is a typewritist who would have carried his own machine, and it would have been virtually impossible to obtain one for Mina before their hurried departure from London. Several commentators suggest (without any evidence) that the typewriter in question is a machine of the Columbia Company. In the mid-1880s, the Columbia Bar-Lock was produced in the United States, but it was not introduced into Europe until 1888. However, the Bar-Lock was a standard desktop machine, not particularly portable, and used vertical type-

Blickensderfer typewriter, 1897.

Columbia Bar-Lock typewriter.

to the man who invented the "Traveller's" typewriter,[23] and to Mr. Morris for getting this one for me. I should have felt quite astray doing the work if I had to write with a pen. . . .

It is all done; poor dear, dear Jonathan, what he must have suffered, what must he be suffering now. He lies on the sofa hardly seeming to breathe, and his whole body appears in collapse. His brows are knit; his face is drawn with pain. Poor fellow, maybe he is thinking, and I can see his face all wrinkled up with the concentration of his thoughts. Oh! if I could only help at all. . . . I shall do what I can. . . .

I have asked Dr. Van Helsing, and he has got me all the papers that I have not yet seen. . . . Whilst they are resting, I shall go over all carefully, and perhaps I may arrive at some conclusion. I shall try to follow the Professor's example, and think without prejudice on the facts before me. . . .

I do believe that under God's providence I have made a discovery. I shall get the maps and look over them. . . .

I am more than ever sure that I am right. My new conclusion is ready, so I shall get our party together and read it. They can judge it; it is well to be accurate, and every minute is precious.

MINA HARKER'S MEMORANDUM.— (*ENTERED IN HER JOURNAL.*)

Ground of inquiry.—Count Dracula's problem is to get back to his own place.[24]

(a) He must be *brought back* by some one.[25] This is evident; for had he power to move himself as he wished he could go either as man, or wolf, or bat, or in some other way. He evidently fears discovery or interference, in the state of helplessness in which he must be—confined as he is between dawn and sunset in his wooden box.[26]

(b) *How is he to be taken?*—Here a process of exclusions may help us. By road, by rail, by water?

1. *By Road.*—There are endless difficulties, especially in leaving the city.

(x) There are people; and people are curious, and investigate. A hint, a surmise, a doubt as to what might be in the box, would destroy him.

(y) There are, or there may be, customs and octroi[27] officers to pass.

(z) His pursuers might follow. This is his greatest fear; and in order to prevent his being betrayed he has repelled, so far as he can, even his victim—me![28]

2. *By Rail.*—There is no one in charge of the box. It would have to take its chance of being delayed; and delay would be fatal, with enemies on the track. True, he might escape at night; but what would he be, if left in a strange place with no refuge that he could fly to? This is not what he intends; and he does not mean to risk it.

3. *By Water.*—Here is the safest way, in one respect, but with most danger in another. On the water he is powerless except at night; even then he can only summon fog and storm and snow[29] and his wolves. But were he wrecked, the living water would engulf him, helpless; and he would indeed be lost. He could have the vessel drive to land; but if it were unfriendly land, wherein he was not free to move, his position would still be desperate.

We know from the record that he was on the water; so what we have to do is to ascertain *what* water.

The first thing is to realise exactly what he has done as yet; we may, then, get a light on what his task is to be.

Firstly.—we must differentiate between what he did in London as part of his general plan of action, when he was pressed for moments and had to arrange as best he could.

Secondly We must see, as well as we can surmise it from the facts we know of, what he has done here.

As to the first, he evidently intended to arrive at Galatz, and sent invoice to Varna to deceive us lest we should ascertain his means of exit from England; his immediate and sole purpose then was to escape. The proof of this, is the letter of instructions sent to Immanuel Hildesheim to clear and take away the box *before sunrise.* There is also the instruction to Petrof Skinsky. These we must only guess at; but there must have been some letter or message, since Skinsky came to Hildesheim.

That, so far, his plans were successful we know. The *Czarina Catherine* made a phenomenally quick journey—so much so that Captain Donelson's suspicions were aroused; but his

bars (see accompanying picture). In light of the dating issues of the narrative (see appendix 2, "The Dating of *Dracula*"), this is likely an anachronism inadvertently inserted by Stoker. It does not appear in the Abridged Text.

24 Mina evidently reached this conclusion earlier, for she researched the means of travel to the castle. See chapter 25, note 34.

25 This seems to be a highly dubious conclusion. Dracula certainly had no problem travelling from Whitby to London; why is there any reason to believe he will have any greater difficulty travelling from Galatz to the Borgo Pass, in familiar territory? He could fly by night or travel as a wolf, and he can travel by day—he must have taken the train from Carfax to Piccadilly.

26 And, of course, as we have seen repeatedly, Dracula is far from "confined" in his coffin and has frequently been noted as active during the day, even in the limited record of the Harker Papers. He could travel separately from the box, repairing to its comforts only when needed.

27 Tax collectors.

28 It is unclear what constitutes this "repulsion" in which Mina believes. It appears that Dracula has not called Mina to him, but here she is following him.

29 This is news, perhaps something Mina learned in her telepathic connection. See chapter 27, note 10.

30 This is evidence that the narrative does not coincide with the Harker Papers, for there is no mention of Skinsky in the portions of Harker's journal reproduced in the narrative.

31 Actually, it was a woman. See text accompanying note 21 above.

32 That is, his plan was under way.

33 Leatherdale (*Dracula Unearthed*) wonders why, if Dracula was intent on covering his tracks, he did not murder Hildesheim.

34 The Prut, or Pruth, River was almost entirely within the borders of Roumania, running for 591 miles. It originates in the C arpathian Mountains and flows southeast to join the Danube just east of Galatz.

35 The Siretul, Seret, or Sereth River also originates in the Carpathians and flows southeast to the Danube. Its chief tributaries are the Bistrita and Moldava rivers.

36 A village located on a dirt road, a few miles southeast of Bacau, at 47° E, 25.5° N, also known as Fundu lui Bogdan or Fundul Valei ("the bottom of the marsh" or "the bottom of the valley").

superstition united with his canniness played the Count's game for him, and he ran with his favouring wind through fogs and all till he brought up blindfold at Galatz. That the Count's arrangements were well made, has been proved. Hildesheim cleared the box, took it off, and gave it to Skinsky. Skinsky took it—and here we lose the trail. We only know that the box is somewhere on the water, moving along. The customs and the octroi, if there be any, have been avoided.

Now we come to what the Count must have done after his arrival—*on land*, at Galatz.

The box was given to Skinsky before sunrise. At sunrise the Count could appear in his own form. Here, we ask why Skinsky was chosen at all to aid in the work? In my husband's diary, Skinsky is mentioned as dealing with the Slovaks who trade down the river to the port;[30] and the man's remark,[31] that the murder was the work of a Slovak, showed the general feeling against his class. The Count wanted isolation.

My surmise is this: that in London the Count decided to get back to his Castle by water, as the most safe and secret way. He was brought from the Castle by Szgany, and probably they delivered their cargo to Slovaks who took the boxes to Varna, for there they were shipped for London. Thus the Count had knowledge of the persons who could arrange this service. When the box was on land, before sunrise or after sunset, he came out from his box, met Skinsky and instructed him what to do as to arranging the carriage of the box up some river. When this was done, and he knew that all was in train,[32] he blotted out his traces, as he thought, by murdering his agent.[33]

I have examined the map and find that the river most suitable for the Slovaks to have ascended is either the Pruth[34] or the Sereth.[35] I read in the typescript that in my trance I heard cows low and water swirling level with my ears and the creaking of wood. The Count in his box, then, was on a river in an open boat—propelled probably either by oars or poles, for the banks are near and it is working against stream. There would be no such sound if floating down stream.

Of course it may not be either the Sereth or the Pruth, but we may possibly investigate further. Now of these two, the Pruth is the more easy navigated, but the Sereth is, at Fundu,[36]

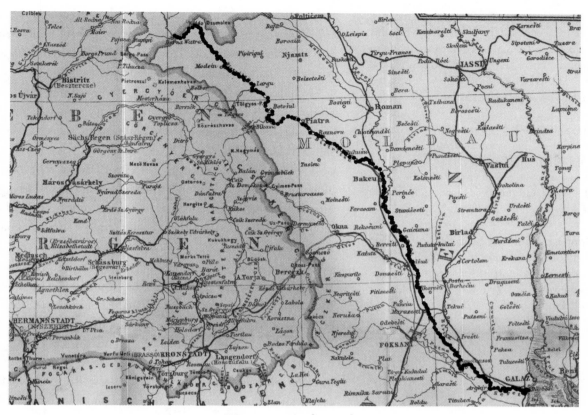

Water route to the castle.
Karl Baedeker, *Austria, Including Hungary, Transylvania, Dalmatia, and Bosnia; Handbook for Travellers* (1896)

joined by the Bistritza[37] which runs up round the Borgo Pass. The loop it makes is manifestly as close to Dracula's Castle as can be got by water.[38]

MINA HARKER'S JOURNAL—*continued*.

When I had done reading, Jonathan took me in his arms and kissed me.[39] The others kept shaking me by both hands, and Dr. Van Helsing said:—

"Our dear Madam Mina is once more our teacher. Her eyes have seen where we were blinded. Now we are on the track once again, and this time we may succeed. Our enemy is at his most helpless; and if we can come on him by day, on the water, our task will be over. He has a start, but he is powerless to hasten, as he may not leave his box lest those who carry him

37 The Bistritza, or Bistrita, River, also known as the Golden Bistritz (as distinguished from the Bistritz, a small river flowing into the town of Bistritz) flows into the Seret at Bakeu or Bacau, approximately at the location of the village of Fundu.

38 Leatherdale (*Dracula Unearthed*) notes that if the terrain surrounding Castle Dracula were as mountainous as described in the narrative, no navigable river could pass anywhere near the castle.

39 This bit of affection is not reported in the Abridged Text.

40 Again, the hunters ignore their own records: Did Dracula onboard the *Demeter* cower in his coffin because the sailors could "throw him in the [ocean] where he perish"? And why was he confined to his box when the Szgany transported him from the water to his castle?

41 McNally and Florescu (*The Essential Dracula*) call this "wishful thinking." There was no commercial steam service on either the Bistrita or the Streth rivers, and the rapids on the rivers and numerous low bridges make passage by steam launch difficult.

42 And apparently were eager to use it, even against human associates of the vampire.

43 Note well that Dr. Seward, at least, has not forgotten the only effective means of destroying Dracula.

may suspect; for them to suspect would be to prompt them to throw him in the stream where he perish.[40] This he knows, and will not. Now men, to our Council of War; for, here and now, we must plan what each and all shall do."

"I shall get a steam launch and follow him," said Lord Godalming.[41]

"And I, horses to follow on the bank lest by chance he land," said Mr. Morris.

"Good!" said the Professor, "both good. But neither must go alone. There must be force to overcome force if need be; the Slovak is strong and rough, and he carries rude arms." All the men smiled, for amongst them they carried a small arsenal.[42] Said Mr. Morris:—

"I have brought some Winchesters; they are pretty handy in a crowd, and there may be wolves. The Count, if you remember, took some other precautions; he made some requisitions on others that Mrs. Harker could not quite hear or understand. We must be ready at all points." Dr. Seward said:—

"I think I had better go with Quincey. We have been accustomed to hunt together, and we two, well armed, will be a match for whatever may come along. You must not be alone Art. It may be necessary to fight the Slovaks, and a chance thrust—for I don't suppose these fellows carry guns—would undo all our plans. There must be no chances, this time; we shall not rest until the Count's head and body have been separated, and we are sure that he cannot re-incarnate."[43] He looked at Jonathan as he spoke, and Jonathan looked at me. I could see that the poor dear was torn about in his mind. Of course he wanted to be with me; but then the boat service would, most likely, be the one which would destroy the . . . the . . . the . . . Vampire. (Why did I hesitate to write the word?) He was silent awhile, and during his silence Dr. Van Helsing spoke:—

"Friend Jonathan, this is to you for twice reasons. First, because you are young and brave and can fight, and all energies may be needed at the last; and again that it is your right to destroy him—that—which has wrought such woe to you and yours. Be not afraid for Madam Mina; she will be my care, if I may. I am old. My legs are not so quick to run as once; and I am not used to ride so long or to pursue as need be, or to fight with lethal weapons. But I can be of other service; I can fight in other way. And I can die, if need be, as well as younger men. Now let me say that what I would is this: while you, my Lord Godalming, and friend Jonathan go in your so swift little steamboat up the river, and whilst John and Quincey guard the bank where perchance he might be landed, I will take Madam Mina right into the heart of the enemy's country. Whilst the old fox is tied in his box, floating on the running stream whence he cannot escape to land—where he dares not raise the lid of his coffin-box lest his Slovak carriers should in fear leave him to perish[44]—we shall go in the track where Jonathan went—from Bistritz over the Borgo, and find our way to the Castle of Dracula. Here, Madam Mina's hypnotic power will surely help, and we shall find our way—all dark and unknown otherwise—after the first sunrise when we are near that fateful place. There is much to be done, and other places to be made sanctify, so that that nest of vipers be obliterated." Here Jonathan interrupted him hotly:—

"Do you mean to say, Professor Van Helsing, that you would bring Mina, in her sad case and tainted as she is with that devil's illness, right into the jaws of his death-trap? Not for the world! Not for Heaven or Hell!" He became almost speechless for a minute, and then went on:—

"Do you know what the place is? Have you seen that awful den of hellish infamy—with the very moonlight alive with grisly shapes, and every speck of dust that whirls in the wind a devouring monster in embryo? Have you felt the Vampire's lips upon your throat?" Here he turned to me, and as his eyes lit on my forehead, he threw up his arms with a cry: "Oh, my God, what have we done to have this terror upon us!" and he sank down on the sofa in a collapse of misery. The Professor's voice, as he spoke in clear, sweet tones, which seemed to vibrate in the air, calmed us all:—

"Oh my friend, it is because I would save Madam Mina from that awful place that I would go. God forbid that I should take her into that place. There is work—wild work—to be done there, that her eyes may not see. We men here, all save Jonathan, have seen with their own eyes what is to be done before that place can be purify. Remember that we are in terrible straits.

44 Leatherdale (*Dracula Unearthed*) points out that this indicates that the Slovaks have no notion of Dracula's presence in the box; only the Gypsies are entrusted with this confidence.

45 The Manuscript replaces the phrase "nursing boy" with "moving bag." There is no evidence that the bag contained a baby, although this change suggests that the Harker Papers made that clear. See chapter 3, note 79.

46 Van Helsing has at least part of a sensible plan in hand here. Dracula's destination is evident—why not hurry en masse to await him there? There is no real risk that the solitary coffin will depart from its course to the castle, and if there is "wild work" to be done there, would it not be better for all the men to participate?

47 This makes no sense: Veresti, Verestie, or Bereztie, as shown on the enlarged portion of the map from the 1896 Austria "Baedeker," is a station near Suczawa (Suceava), almost triple the distance (nearly 105 miles) to the Borgo Pass (and the castle) from Bistritz (about 35 miles). According to *Bradshaw's* continental railway guide, it was possible in 1896 to catch the 10:00 P.M. train from Galatz to Bucharest, arriving at 6:00 A.M., in time for the 8:30 A.M. train for Veresti, arriving there at 4:46 P.M., a journey of about eighteen hours. It was about the same length trip to take the train to Bucharest and Kronstadt and from there to Bistritz. The travellers certainly know that there is a diligence to the Borgo Pass, but they may expect that the locals would decline to take them to the castle itself. Nonetheless, with Jonathan's journal in hand, one would have expected them to trace the same route. Another problem: Jonathan's journal is vague about directions to the castle, the result of his being deliberately misled by Dracula. Unless he took careful notes on his departure from the castle, not included in the narrative, how do Van Helsing and Mina expect to find it without a local guide?

48 We must suppose that this means Mina cannot carry a cross.

If the Count escape us this time—and he is strong and subtle and cunning—he may choose to sleep him for a century, and then in time our dear one"—he took my hand—"would come to him to keep him company, and would be as those others that you, Jonathan, saw. You have told us of their gloating lips; you heard their ribald laugh as they clutched the moving bag**45** that the Count threw to them. You shudder; and well may it be. Forgive me that I make you so much pain, but it is necessary. My friend, is it not a dire need for the which I am giving, if need me, my life? If it were that any one went into that place to stay, it is I who have to go, to keep them company."

"Do as you will;" said Jonathan, with a sob that shook him all over, "We are in the hands of God!"**46**

Later.—Oh, it did me good to see the way that these brave men worked. How can women help loving men when they are so earnest, and so true, and so brave! And, too, it made me think of the wonderful power of money! What can it not do when it is properly applied; and what might it do when basely used. I felt so thankful that Lord Godalming is rich, and both he and Mr. Morris, who also has plenty of money, are willing to spend it so freely. For if they did not, our little expedition could not start, either so promptly or so well equipped, as it will within another hour. It is not three hours since it was arranged what part each of us was to do; and now Lord Godalming and Jonathan have a lovely steam launch, with steam up ready to start at a moment's notice. Dr. Seward and Mr. Morris have half a dozen beautiful horses, well appointed. We have all the maps and appliances of various kinds that can be had. Professor Van Helsing and I are to leave by the 11:40 train to-night for Veresti,**47** where we are to get a carriage to drive to the Borgo Pass. We are bringing a good deal of ready money, as we are to buy a carriage and horses. We shall drive ourselves, for we have no one whom we can trust in the matter. The Professor knows something of a great many languages, so we shall get on all right. We have all got arms, even for me a large-bore revolver; Jonathan would not be happy unless I was armed like the rest. Alas! I cannot carry one arm that the rest do; the scar on my forehead forbids that.**48** Dear Dr. Van Helsing comforts me by telling me that I

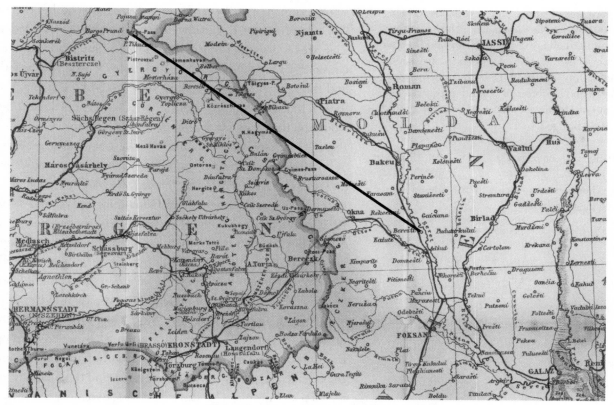

Land route to the castle (roads unknown).
Karl Baedeker, *Austria, Including Hungary, Transylvania, Dalmatia, and Bosnia; Handbook for Travellers* (1896)

am fully armed as there may be wolves; the weather is getting colder every hour, and there are snow-flurries which come and go as warnings.

Later.—It took all my courage to say good-bye to my darling. We may never meet again. Courage, Mina! the Professor is looking at you keenly; his look is a warning. There must be no tears now—unless it may be that God will let them fall in gladness.

JONATHAN HARKER'S JOURNAL.

October 30. Night.—I am writing this in the light from the furnace door of the steam launch; Lord Godalming is firing up. He is an experienced hand at the work, as he has had for

49 An area of large, marshy wetlands covering 5,000 acres. In the Victorian era, the Broads was a popular holiday destination for middle- and upper-class vacationers interested in fishing and sailing; today, it is both a recreational centre and a protected wildlife preserve. The detail of Holmwood's launches do not appear in the Abridged Text.

50 See map on page 471.

51 Thus permitting Mina to ride sidesaddle in acceptable fashion.

years a launch of his own on the Thames, and another on the Norfolk Broads.[49] Regarding our plans, we finally decided that Mina's guess was correct, and that if any waterway was chosen for the Count's escape back to his Castle, the Sereth and then the Bistritza at its junction, would be the one. We took it, that somewhere about the 47th degree, north latitude, would be the place chosen for crossing the country between the river and the Carpathians.[50] We have no fear in running at good speed up the river at night; there is plenty of water, and the banks are wide enough apart to make steaming, even in the dark, easy enough. Lord Godalming tells me to sleep for a while, as it is enough for the present for one to be on watch. But I cannot sleep—how can I with the terrible danger hanging over my darling, and her going out into that awful place. . . . My only comfort is that we are in the hands of God. Only for that faith it would be easier to die than to live, and so be quit of all the trouble. Mr. Morris and Dr. Seward were off on their long ride before we started; they are to keep up the right bank, far enough off to get on higher lands where they can see a good stretch of river and avoid the following of its curves. They have, for the first stages, two men to ride and lead their spare horses—four in all, so as not to excite curiosity. When they dismiss the men, which shall be shortly, they shall themselves look after the horses. It may be necessary for us to join forces; if so they can mount our whole party. One of the saddles has a moveable horn,[51] and can be easily adapted for Mina, if required.

It is a wild adventure we are on. Here, as we are rushing along through the darkness, with the cold from the river seeming to rise up and strike us; with all the mysterious voices of the night around us, it all comes home. We seem to be drifting into unknown places and unknown ways; into a whole world of dark and dreadful things. Godalming is shutting the furnace door. . . .

31 October.—Still hurrying along. The day has come, and Godalming is sleeping. I am on watch. The morning is bitterly cold; the furnace heat is grateful, though we have heavy fur coats. As yet we have passed only a few open boats, but none of them had on board any box or package of anything like the size of the one we seek. The men were scared every time we turned our electric lamp on them, and fell on their knees and prayed.

1 November, evening.—No news all day; we have found nothing of the kind we seek. We have now passed into the Bistritza; and if we are wrong in our surmise our chance is gone. We have overhauled every boat, big and little. Early this morning, one crew took us for a Government boat, and treated us accordingly. We saw in this a way of smoothing matters, so at Fundu, where the Bistritza runs into the Sereth, we got a Roumanian flag which we now fly conspicuously.[52] With every boat which we have overhauled since then this trick has succeeded; we have had every deference shown to us, and not once any objection to whatever we chose to ask or do. Some of the Slovaks tell us that a big boat passed them, going at more than usual speed as she had a double crew on board. This was before they came to Fundu, so they could not tell us whether the boat turned into the Bistritza or continued on up the Sereth. At Fundu we could not hear of any such boat, so she must have passed there in the night. I am feeling very sleepy; the cold is perhaps beginning to tell upon me, and nature must have rest some time. Godalming insists that he shall keep the first watch. God bless him for all his goodness to poor dear Mina and me.

2 November, morning.—It is broad daylight. That good fellow would not wake me.[53] He says it would have been a sin to, for I slept peacefully and was forgetting my trouble. It seems brutally selfish to me to have slept so long, and let him watch all night; but he was quite right. I am a new man this morning; and, as I sit here and watch him sleeping, I can do all that is necessary both as to minding the engine, steering, and keeping watch. I can feel that my strength and energy are coming back to me. I wonder where Mina is now, and Van Helsing. They should have got to Veresti about noon on Wednesday.[54] It would take them some time to get the carriage and horses; so if they had started and travelled hard, they would be about

52 The Roumanian flag was adopted in 1872, with blue, yellow, and red vertical stripes (left to right) and the royal coat of arms in the middle. Although the geographical detail is correct, it does not appear in the Abridged Text.

53 This criticism of Harker does not appear in the Abridged Text, which does not mention his sleeping through his watch.

54 Mina and Van Helsing arrived at Veresti on 31 October, a Wednesday in 1883 and not again until 1894.

55 This sentence and the following pondering do not appear in the Abridged Text.

56 Wolf (*The Essential Dracula*) and McNally and Florescu (*The Essential Dracula*) both correct this to "Straja," a village opposite the village of Isvorul, near Bacau, where the Streth and Bistrita join.

57 Perhaps because of the preposterous nature of these details, the Abridged Text omits them.

58 A steam-pipe fitter, a sort of plumber. Holmwood has a decidedly odd set of hobbies—not many combine tennis, hunting, and plumbing.

now at the Borgo Pass. God guide and help them! I am afraid to think what may happen. If we could only go faster! but we cannot; the engines are throbbing and doing their utmost. I wonder how Dr. Seward and Mr. Morris are getting on.[55] There seem to be endless streams running down the mountains into this river, but as none of them are very large—at present, at all events, though they are terrible doubtless in winter and when the snow melts—the horsemen may not have met much obstruction. I hope that before we get to Strasba[56] we may see them; for if by that time we have not overtaken the Count, it may be necessary to take counsel together what to do next.

DR. SEWARD'S DIARY.

2 November.—Three days on the road. No news, and no time to write it if there had been, for every moment is precious. We have had only the rest needful for the horses; but we are both bearing it wonderfully. Those adventurous days of ours are turning up useful. We must push on; we shall never feel happy till we get the launch in sight again.

3 November.—We heard at Fundu that the launch had gone up the Bistritza. I wish it wasn't so cold. There are signs of snow coming; and if it falls heavy it will stop us. In such case we must get a sledge and go on, Russian fashion.

4 November.—To-day we heard of the launch having been detained by an accident when trying to force a way up the rapids.[57] The Slovak boats get up all right, by aid of a rope, and steering with knowledge. Some went up only a few hours before. Godalming is an amateur fitter[58] himself, and evidently it was he who put the launch in trim again. Finally, they got up the Rapids all right, with local help, and are off on the chase afresh. I fear that the boat is not any better for the accident; the peasantry tell us that after she got upon smooth water again, she kept stopping every now and again so long as she was in sight. We must push on harder than ever; our help may be wanted soon.

MINA HARKER'S JOURNAL.

31 October.—Arrived at Veresti at noon.[59] The Professor tells me that this morning at dawn he could hardly hypnotise me at all, and that all I could say was: "dark and quiet." He is off now buying a carriage and horses. He says that he will later on try to buy additional horses, so that we may be able to change them on the way. We have something more than 70 miles before us.[60] The country is lovely, and most interesting; if only we were under different conditions, how delightful it would be to see it all. If Jonathan and I were driving through it alone what a pleasure it would be. To stop and see people, and learn something of their life, and to fill our minds and memories with all the colour and picturesqueness of the whole wild, beautiful country and the quaint people! But, alas!—

Later.—Dr. Van Helsing has returned. He has got the carriage and horses; we are to have some dinner, and to start in an hour. The landlady is putting us up a huge basket of provisions; it seems enough for a company of soldiers. The Professor encourages her, and whispers to me that it may be a week before we can get any good food again. He has been shopping too, and has sent home[61] such a wonderful lot of fur coats and wraps, and all sorts of warm things. There will not be any chance of our being cold.

We shall soon be off. I am afraid to think what may happen to us. We are truly in the hands of God. He alone knows what may be, and I pray Him, with all the strength of my sad and humble soul, that He will watch over my beloved husband; that whatever may happen, Jonathan may know that I loved him and honoured him more than I can say, and that my latest and truest thought will be always for him.

59 That is, in only thirteen hours—incredibly fast by later time schedules. Virtually the entire first paragraph is absent from the Abridged Text.

60 This is wrong, unless Mina means "70 miles until we stop and buy new horses" or something similar. The Borgo Pass is over 100 miles from Veresti. See note 47 above, and map on page 475.

61 Meaning, presumably, sent them to where Mina and Van Helsing are staying in Veresti.

Chapter 27

1 Wolf (*The Essential Dracula*) complains, "But there is never any mention of getting there." Of course not: Bistritz is on the other side of the Borgo Pass, west of the Pass and the castle. Interestingly, Mina makes no mention of the large villages that do lie along their road.

2 Mina self-consciously attributes this to her scar, but of course Jonathan received the same treatment on his trip. Although scars were often viewed by physiognomists as "nature's danger signals," in the words of John H. Watson, M.D. (in "The Adventure of the Empty House"), there is no folkloric connection between disfigurement and the evil eye, perhaps because the former was so common among the peasantry.

3 Mina fails to see this as a kindly gesture, presumably intended to keep the travellers from evil. However, there is no suggestion in folklore that garlic taken internally has any prophylactic properties; only the raw bulbs and flowers seem to repel vampires.

4 Does Mina mean that if they had a driver, the driver would gossip with the locals about Mina and Van Helsing? But what is there to tell? The following sentence does not appear in the Abridged Text.

MINA HARKER'S JOURNAL.

1 November.—All day long we have travelled, and at a good speed. The horses seem to know that they are being kindly treated, for they go willingly their full stage at best speed. We have now had so many changes and find the same thing so constantly that we are encouraged to think that the journey will be an easy one. Dr. Van Helsing is laconic; he tells the farmers that he is hurrying to Bistritz,[1] and pays them well to make the exchange of horses. We get hot soup, or coffee, or tea; and off we go. It is a lovely country; full of beauties of all imaginable kinds, and the people are brave, and strong, and simple, and seem full of nice qualities. They are *very, very* superstitious. In the first house where we stopped, when the woman who served us saw the scar on my forehead, she crossed herself and put out two fingers towards me, to keep off the evil eye.[2] I believe they went to the trouble of putting an extra amount of garlic into our food; and I can't abide garlic.[3] Ever since then I have taken care not to take off my hat or veil, and so have escaped their suspicions. We are traveling fast, and as we have no driver with us to carry tales, we go ahead of scandal;[4] but I daresay that fear of the evil eye will follow hard behind us all the way. The Professor seems tireless; all day he would not take any rest, though he made me sleep for a long spell. At sunset time he hypnotized me, and he says that I answered as usual "darkness, lapping water and creaking wood;" so our

Cover of first American edition of *Dracula*.
(New York: Doubleday & McClure, 1899)

5 The Manuscript continues with the following phrase, omitted from the published text: "though the oppressiveness of the air at times concerns us." This is the first of numerous references to the volcanic aspects of the air around the castle, which may have been intended to provide support for the "big bang" deleted ending. See note 53 below.

6 If Mina and Van Helsing are on the dirt road leading through the Borgo Pass (and there is no other road suitable for a carriage), they must have been passed at least daily by the Bistritz-Bukovina diligence. Mina probably means that there are no independent horsemen. The sentence is not included in the Abridged Text.

enemy is still on the river. I am afraid to think of Jonathan, but somehow I have now no fear for him, or for myself. I write this whilst we wait in a farmhouse for the horses to be got ready. Dr. Van Helsing is sleeping. Poor dear, he looks very tired and old and grey, but his mouth is set as firmly as a conqueror's; even in his sleep he is instinct with resolution. When we have well started I must make him rest whilst I drive. I shall tell him that we have days before us, and we must not break down when most of all his strength will be needed. . . . All is ready, we are off shortly.

2 November, morning.—I was successful, and we took turns driving all night; now the day is on us, bright though cold. There is a strange heaviness in the air—I say heaviness for want of a better word; I mean that it oppresses us both. It is very cold, and only our warm furs keep us comfortable. At dawn Van Helsing hypnotised me; he says I answered "darkness, creaking wood and roaring water," so the river is changing as they ascend. I do hope that my darling will not run any chance of danger—more than need be; but we are in God's hands.

2 November, night.—All day long driving. The country gets wilder as we go, and the great spurs of the Carpathians, which at Veresti seemed so far from us and so low on the horizon, now seem to gather round us and tower in front. We both seem in good spirits;[5] I think we make an effort each to cheer the other; in the doing so we cheer ourselves. Dr. Van Helsing says that by morning we shall reach the Borgo Pass. The houses are very few here now, and the Professor says that the last horse we got will have to go on with us, as we may not be able to change. He got two in addition to the two we changed, so that now we have a rude four-in-hand. The dear horses are patient and good, and they give us no trouble. We are not worried with other travelers, and so even I can drive.[6] We shall get to the Pass in daylight; we do not want to arrive before. So we take it easy, and have each a long rest in turn. Oh, what will tomorrow bring to us? We go to seek the place where my poor darling suffered so much. God grant that we may be guided aright, and that He will deign to watch over my husband and those dear to us both, and who are in such deadly peril. As for me, I am not worthy in His sight. Alas! I am unclean to His eyes, and shall be until He may deign to let me stand forth in His sight as one of those who have not incurred His wrath.[7]

MEMORANDUM BY ABRAHAM VAN HELSING.

4 November.—This to my old and true friend John Seward, M.D. of Purfleet,[8] London, in case I may not see him. It may explain. It is morning, and I write by a fire which all the night I have kept alive—Madam Mina aiding me.[9] It is cold, cold; so cold that the grey heavy sky is full of snow, which when it falls will settle for all winter as the ground is hardening to receive it.[10] It seems to have affected Madam Mina; she has been so heavy of head all day that she was not like herself. She sleeps, and sleeps, and sleeps! She, who is usual so alert, have done literally nothing all the day; she even have lost her appetite. She make no entry into her little diary, she who write so faithful at every pause. Something whisper to me that all is not well. However, to-night she is more *vif*.[11] Her long sleep all day have refresh and restore her, for now she is all sweet and bright as ever. At sunset I try to hypnotise her, but alas! with no effect; the power has grown less and less with each day, and to-night it fail me altogether. Well, God's will be done— whatever it may be, and whithersoever it may lead!

Now to the historical, for as Madam Mina write not in her stenography, I must, in my cumbrous old fashion, that so each day of us may not go unrecorded.

We got to the Borgo Pass just after sunrise yesterday morning. When I saw the signs of the dawn I got ready for the hypnotism. We stopped our carriage, and got down so that there might be no disturbance. I made a couch with furs, and Madam Mina, lying down, yield herself as usual, but more slow and more short time than ever, to the hypnotic sleep.[12] As before, came the answer: "darkness and the swirling of water." Then she woke, bright and radiant, and we go on our way and soon reach the Pass. At this time and place, she become all on

7 Wolf (*The Essential Dracula*) speculates that Mina's self-abasement is grounded in her confession that when Dracula first drank her blood "strangely enough, I did not want to hinder him." (See text accompanying chapter 21, note 36.) The statement does not appear in the Abridged Text.

8 The Manuscript replaces the word "Plaistow" with "Purfleet." This is an important locational clue: Plaistow is a residential district in the London borough of Newham, encompassing the East London Cemetery, much closer to central London than Purfleet, and may well be the true location of Carfax and Seward's asylum, inadvertently left in by Stoker. Roger Johnson, in private correspondence with this editor, points out that Purfleet has never been considered to be part of London—the postal address would have been "Purfleet, Essex."

9 The Manuscript continues with the following sentence, which is omitted from the published narrative: "There are atmospheric disturbances which I know not and which much concern me."

10 This poetic sentence does not appear in the Abridged Text. The Manuscript adds the following that does not appear in the published narrative: "and yet the thermometer go up and up and up. I would that my old friend Palmieri of Naples were here and with him his wonderful seismograph for he could give me some clue to what is happening—or about to happen. Whatever it is,"

This is startling information, for unlike the identification of "Van Helsing's" other friends "Vanderpool" and "Arminius," there is no ambiguity about "Palmieri of Naples": Luigi Palmieri was a prominent physicist and meteorologist, born at Faicchio, Benevento, Italy, 22 April 1807, who died in Naples on 9 September 1896. Palmieri's work is chiefly connected with the observation of the eruptions on Mount Vesuvius and with the study of earthquakes and meteorological phenomena in general. Palmieri was also an inventor of many delicate apparatuses; in particular, his seismometer for the detection and measurement of ground vibration was said to be so sensitive that he was able to detect very slight movements and to predict the eruption of the volcano. Where he and "Van Helsing" met is unknown.

It is likely that Dracula has summoned the snow, for, as will be seen, it hinders the pursuers.

11 French: lively, vivacious.

12 Again, the Abridged Text makes no comment about Mina's slowness to "go under."

13 If this is true, it is certainly lucky for the travellers: notwithstanding Mina's assertion, Jonathan's journal sheds no light on when or where to turn off the main road. Is it not more likely that Mina's certainty is the result of directions provided to her by Dracula? He surely must have anticipated that the hunters would follow him (and in any event the psychic connection between Dracula and Mina must have been two-way, so that Dracula would be aware of her location, just as she was of his), and if so, he would desire to face them at the castle, where he would have allies. For reasons discussed in note 30 on page xlix, the Abridged Text does not include even the following vague description of the road.

14 Van Helsing must be imagining this. Jonathan's diary records virtually nothing of specific places other than Isten szek.

15 From the shadow, we can deduce that Van Helsing and Mina are travelling east towards the mountains. This means that they have gone through the Borgo Pass (a long stretch of road) to the westward end of the Pass and now have curved back facing eastwards. This is consistent with their arrival at the eastwards end of the Pass two days earlier, for they did not travel all the way to the Pass only to turn back eastwards from it. But Jonathan describes a ride to "the

fire with zeal; some new guiding power be in her manifested, for she point to a road and say:—

"This is the way."

"How know you it?" I ask.

"Of course I know it," she answer, and with a pause, add: "Have not my Jonathan travel it and wrote of his travel?"

At first I think somewhat strange, but soon I see that there be only one such by-road.[13] It is used but little, and very different from the coach road from the Bukovina to Bistritz, which is more wide and hard, and more of use.

So we came down this road; when we meet other ways—not always were we sure that they were roads at all, for they be neglect and light snow have fallen—the horses know and they only. I give rein to them, and they go on so patient. By-and-by we find all the things which Jonathan have note in that wonderful diary of him.[14] Then we go on for long, long hours and hours. At the first, I tell Madam Mina to sleep; she try, and she succeed. She sleep all the time; till at the last, I feel myself to suspicious grow, and attempt to wake her. But she sleep on, and I may not wake her though I try. I do not wish to try too hard lest I harm her; for I know that she have suffer much, and sleep at times be all-in-all to her. I think I drowse myself, for all of sudden I feel guilt, as though I have done something; I find myself bolt up, with the reins in my hand, and the good horses go along jog, jog, just as ever. I look down and find Madam Mina still sleep. It is now not far off sunset time, and over the snow the light of the sun flow in big yellow flood, so that we throw great long shadow on where the mountain rise so steep. For we are going up, and up; and all is oh! so wild and rocky, as though it were the end of the world.[15]

Then I arouse Madam Mina. This time she wake with not much trouble, and then I try to put her to hypnotic sleep. But she sleep not, being as though I were not. Still I try and try, till all at once I find her and myself in dark; so I look round, and find that the sun have gone down. Madam Mina laugh, and I turn and look at her. She is now quite awake, and look so well as I never saw her since that night at Carfax when we first enter the Count's house. I am amaze, and not at ease then; but she is so bright and tender and thoughtful for me that I forget all fear. I light a fire, for we have brought supply of wood with us, and she prepare food while I undo the horses and set them, tethered in shelter, to feed. Then when I return to the fire she have my supper ready. I go to help her; but she smile, and tell me that she have eat already—that she was so hungry that she would not wait. I like it not, and I have grave doubts; but I fear to affright her, and so I am silent of it. She help me and I eat alone; and then we wrap in fur and lie beside the fire, and I tell her to sleep while I watch. But presently I forget all of watching; and when I sudden remember that I watch, I find her lying quiet, but awake, and looking at me with so bright eyes. Once, twice more the same occur, and I get much sleep till before morning. When I wake I try to hypnotise her; but alas! though she shut her eyes obedient, she may not sleep. The sun rise up, and up, and up; and then sleep come to her too late, but so heavy that she will not wake. I have to lift her up, and place her sleeping in the carriage when I have harnessed the horses and made all ready. Madam still sleep, and sleep, and she look in her sleep more healthy and more redder than before. And I like it not.[16] And I am afraid, afraid, afraid!—I am afraid of all things—even to think; but I must go on my way. The stake we play for is life and death, or more than these, and we must not flinch.[17]

5 November, morning.—Let me be accurate in everything, for though you and I have seen some strange things together, you may at the first think that I, Van Helsing, am mad—that the many horrors and the so long strain on nerves has at the last turn my brain.

All yesterday we travel, ever getting closer to the mountains, and moving into a more and more wild and desert land.[18] There are great, frowning precipices and much falling water, and Nature seem to have held sometime her carnival.[19] Madam Mina still sleep and sleep; and though I did have hunger and appeased it, I could not waken her—even for food. I began to fear that the fatal spell of the place was upon her, tainted as she is with that Vampire baptism. "Well," said I to myself, "if it be that she sleep all the day, it shall also be that I do not sleep at night." As we travel on the rough road, for a road of an

far side of the Pass" and a sharp turn to the right. When Jonathan reaches the castle, he describes unbroken vistas to the east (see text accompanying chapter 3, note 64). That is, the castle must be on the eastern slopes of this branch of the Carpathians, not the western slopes as seemingly described by Van Helsing. There is something seriously inconsistent in the two descriptions. See also note 38 below.

16 The Manuscript continues: "the air is till more upsetting and I wish more and more that Palmieri were here to tell me what is going to happen." The material does not appear in the published text.

17 The foregoing makes clear that Mina is behaving more and more like a vampire, sleeping during the day and active after dark, with little or no appetite for human comestibles.

18 Where are they? Van Helsing and Mina arrived at the Borgo Pass "yesterday morning." Why did they then proceed across a "wild and desert land" *towards* the mountains?

19 This inaccurate geographical detail does not appear in the Abridged Text.

20 Astonishingly, Van Helsing and Mina seem to take almost two full days to reach Castle Dracula from the Borgo Pass, a trip that took Jonathan only a few hours. Apparently, despite Mina's confidence, they have been hopelessly lost, wandering around on various back roads. A more sinister interpretation, however, is that they have been deliberately led in circles by Dracula's mental commands to Mina, and they arrive at the castle at precisely the time intended by Dracula.

21 Although Wolf (*The Essential Dracula*) tries to make out Van Helsing as a practitioner of "white magic," drawing a magic circle, in fact he is only behaving in a tested military manner, "circling the wagons" around the campfire and, using his knowledge of geometry, creating the smallest possible perimeter.

Leatherdale (*Dracula Unearthed*) wonders why Van Helsing did not use this prophylaxis with Lucy. Perhaps he learned the tactic only after her death.

ancient and imperfect kind there was, I held down my head and slept. Again I waked with a sense of guilt and of time passed, and found Madam Mina still sleeping, and the sun low down. But all was indeed changed; the frowning mountains seemed further away, and we were near the top of a steep-rising hill, on summit of which was such a castle as Jonathan tell of in his diary. At once I exulted and feared; for now, for good or ill, the end was near.[20] I woke Madam Mina, and again tried to hypnotise her; but alas! unavailing till too late. Then, ere the great dark came upon us—for even after down-sun the heavens reflected the gone sun on the snow, and all was for a time in a great twilight—I took out the horses and fed them in what shelter I could. Then I make a fire; and near it I make Madam Mina, now awake and more charming than ever, sit comfortable amid her rugs. I got ready food: but she would not eat, simply saying that she had not hunger. I did not press her, knowing her unavailingness. But I myself eat, for I must needs now be strong for all. Then, with the fear on me of what might be, I drew a ring so big for her comfort, round where Madam Mina sat; and over the ring I passed some of the Wafer, and I broke it fine so that all was well guarded.[21] She sat still all the time—so still as one dead; and she grew whiter and ever whiter till the snow was not more pale; and no word she said. But when I drew near, she clung to me, and I could know that the poor soul shook her from head to feet with a tremor that was pain to feel. I said to her presently, when she had grown more quiet:—

"Will you not come over to the fire?" for I wished to make a test of what she could. She rose obedient, but when she have made a step she stopped, and stood as one stricken.

"Why not go on?" I asked. She shook her head, and, coming back, sat down in her place. Then, looking at me with open eyes, as of one waked from sleep, she said simply:—

"I cannot!" and remained silent. I rejoiced, for I knew that what she could not, none of those that we dreaded could. Though there might be danger to her body, yet her soul was safe!

Presently the horses began to scream, and tore at their tethers till I came to them and quieted them. When they did feel my hands on them, they whinnied low as in joy, and licked at my hands and were quiet for a time. Many times through the night did I come to them, till it arrive to the cold hour when all nature is at lowest; and every time my coming was with quiet of them. In the cold hour the fire began to die, and I was about stepping forth to replenish it, for now the snow came in flying sweeps and with it a chill mist. Even in the dark there was a light of some kind, as there ever is over snow; and it seemed as though the snow-flurries and the wreaths of mist took shape as of women with trailing garments. All was in dead, grim silence only that the horses whinnied and cowered, as if in terror of the worst. I began to fear—horrible fears; but then came to me the sense of safety in that ring wherein I stood. I began, too, to think that my imaginings were of the night, and the gloom, and the unrest that I have gone through, and all the terrible anxiety. It was as though my memories of Jonathan's horrid experience were befooling me; for the snow flakes and the mist began to wheel and circle round, till I could get as though a shadowy glimpse of those women that would have kissed him. And then the horses cowered lower and lower, and moaned in terror as men do in pain. Even the madness of fright was not to them, so that they could break away. I feared for my dear Madam Mina when these weird figures drew near and circled round. I looked at her, but she sat calm, and smiled at me; when I would have stepped to the fire to replenish it, she caught me and held me back, and whispered, like a voice that one hears in a dream, so low it was:—

"No! No! Do not go without. Here you are safe!" I turned to her, and looking in her eyes, said:—

"But you? It is for you that I fear!" whereat she laughed—a laugh, low and unreal, and said:—

"Fear for *me!* Why fear for me? None safer in all the world from them than I am," and as I wondered at the meaning of her words, a puff of wind made the flame leap up, and I see the red scar on her forehead. Then, alas! I knew. Did I not, I would soon have learned, for the wheeling figures of mist and snow came closer, but keeping ever without the Holy circle. Then they began to materialise, till—if God have not taken away my reason, for I saw it through my eyes—there were before me in actual flesh the same three women that Jonathan

22 See chapter 3, note 72.

23 It is curious that the vampire women do not seek to tempt Van Helsing. Without him, Mina would quickly succumb and find a way to join them.

24 Appearing in the Manuscript but not in the published text is: "The oppression in the air grows more, and more I know not what is to happen."

saw in the room, when they would have kissed his throat. I knew the swaying round forms, the bright hard eyes, the white teeth, the ruddy colour, the voluptuous lips. They smiled ever at poor dear Madam Mina; and as their laugh came through the silence of the night, they twined their arms and pointed to her, and said in those so sweet tingling tones that Jonathan said were of the intolerable sweetness of the water-glasses:[22]—

"Come, sister. Come to us. Come! Come!"[23] In fear I turned to my poor Madam Mina, and my heart with gladness leapt like flame; for oh! the terror in her sweet eyes, the repulsion, the horror, told a story to my heart that was all of hope. God be thanked she was not, yet, of them. I seized some of the firewood which was by me, and holding out some of the Wafer, advanced on them towards the fire. They drew back before me, and laughed their low horrid laugh. I fed the fire, and feared them not; for I knew that we were safe within our protections. They could not approach me, whilst so armed, nor Madam Mina whilst she remained within the ring, which she could not leave no more than they could enter. The horses had ceased to moan, and lay still on the ground; the snow fell on them softly, and they grew whiter. I knew that there was for the poor beasts no more of terror.

And so we remained till the red of the dawn began to fall through the snow-gloom. I was desolate and afraid, and full of woe and terror; but when that beautiful sun began to climb the horizon life was to me again. At the first coming of the dawn the horrid figures melted in the whirling mist and snow; the wreaths of transparent gloom moved away towards the castle, and were lost.

Instinctively, with the dawn coming, I turned to Madam Mina, intending to hypnotise her; but she lay in a deep and sudden sleep, from which I could not wake her. I tried to hypnotise through her sleep, but she made no response, none at all; and the day broke. I fear yet to stir. I have made my fire and have seen the horses, they are all dead. To-day I have much to do here, and I keep waiting till the sun is up high; for there may be places where I must go, where that sunlight, though snow and mist obscure it, will be to me a safety.[24]

I will strengthen me with breakfast, and then I will to my

terrible work. Madam Mina still sleeps; and, God be thanked! she is calm in her sleep. . . .

JONATHAN HARKER'S JOURNAL.

4 November,[25] *evening.*—The accident to the launch has been a terrible thing for us. Only for it we should have overtaken the boat long ago; and by now my dear Mina would have been free. I fear to think of her, off on the wolds near that horrid place. We have got horses, and we follow on the track. I note this whilst Godalming is getting ready. We have our arms. The Szgany must look out if they mean fight.[26] Oh, if only Morris and Seward were with us. We must only hope! If I write no more Good-bye, Mina! God bless and keep you.

DR. SEWARD'S DIARY.

5 November.—With the dawn we saw the body of Szgany before us dashing away from the river with their leiter-waggon. They surrounded it in a cluster, and hurried along as though beset. The snow is falling lightly and there is a strange excitement in the air. It may be our own excited feelings, but the depression is strange. Far off I hear the howling of wolves; the snow brings them down from the mountains, and there are dangers to all of us, and from all sides. The horses are nearly ready, and we are soon off. We ride to death of some one. God alone knows who, or where, or what, or when, or how it may be. . . .

DR. VAN HELSING'S MEMORANDUM.

5 November, afternoon.—I am at least sane. Thank God for that mercy at all events, though the proving it has been dreadful. When I left Madam Mina sleeping within the Holy circle, I took my way to the castle. The blacksmith hammer which I took in the carriage from Veresti was useful; though the doors were all open I broke them off the rusty hinges, lest some ill-intent or ill-chance should close them, so that being entered I might not get out. Jonathan's bitter experience served me here.

25 The Manuscript reads "(?)," suggesting that Jonathan is uncertain about the date.

26 Jonathan has no reason at this point to suspect the further involvement of Szgany, although Mina posited it as likely, and this interjection may have been added to the Harker Papers with hindsight. As will be seen momentarily, the Slovaks—who have unknowingly carried Dracula up the river—turn Dracula over to the Szgany, who quickly resume their rôle as palace guards. The turnover itself is not recorded in the narrative but must have been observed by Harker or Seward.

27 Does this mean that Van Helsing is finally prepared to acknowledge that daylight is not a complete safeguard against the vampire?

28 There are of course four graves to be found, Van Helsing knows; he means that there are three currently occupied graves to find.

29 Why is the she-vampire inert? Vampires can move around during the day, and Dracula himself opened his eyes to look at Harker in the castle. Again, this seems to be evidence of the stupefying effect of the coffin.

By memory of his diary I found my way to the old chapel, for I knew that here my work lay. The air was oppressive; it seemed as if there was some sulphurous fume, which at times made me dizzy. Either there was a roaring in my ears or I heard afar off the howl of wolves. Then I be-thought me of my dear Madam Mina, and I was in terrible plight. The dilemma had me between his horns. Her, I had not dare to take into this place, but left safe from the Vampire in that Holy circle;[27] and yet even there would be the wolf! I resolve me that my work lay here, and that as to the wolves we must submit, if it were God's will. At any rate it was only death and freedom beyond. So did I choose for her. Had it but been for myself the choice had been easy; the maw of the wolf were better to rest in than the grave of the Vampire! So I make my choice to go on with my work.

I knew that there were at least three graves to find—graves that are inhabit;[28] so I search, and search, and I find one of them. She lay in her Vampire sleep, so full of life and voluptuous beauty that I shudder as though I have come to do murder.[29] Ah, I doubt not that in old time, when such things were, many a man who set forth to do such a task as mine, found at the last his heart fail him, and then his nerve. So he delay, and delay, and delay, till the mere beauty and the fascination of the wanton Un-Dead have hypnotise him; and he remain on and on, till sunset come, and the Vampire sleep be over. Then the beautiful eyes of the fair woman open and look love, and the voluptuous mouth present to a kiss—and man is weak. And there remain one more victim in the Vampire fold; one more to swell the grim and grisly ranks of the Un-Dead! . . .

There is some fascination, surely, when I am moved by the mere presence of such an one, even lying as she lay in a tomb fretted with age and heavy with the dust of centuries, though there be that horrid odour such as the lairs of the Count have had. Yes, I was moved—I, Van Helsing, with all my purpose and with my motive for hate—I was moved to a yearning for delay which seemed to paralyse my faculties and to clog my very soul. It may have been that the need of natural sleep, and the strange oppression of the air were beginning to overcome me. Certain it was that I was lapsing into sleep, the open-eyed sleep of one who yields to a sweet fascination, when there came through the snow-stilled air a long, low wail, so full of woe and pity that it woke me like the sound of a clarion. For it was the voice of my dear Madam Mina that I heard.

Then I braced myself again to my horrid task, and found by wrenching away tomb-tops one other of the sisters, the other dark one. I dared not pause to look on her as I had on her sister, lest once more I should begin to be enthrall; but I go on searching until, presently, I find in a high great tomb as if made to one much beloved that other fair sister which, like Jonathan, I had seen to gather herself out of the atoms of the mist.[30] She was so fair to look on, so radiantly beautiful, so exquisitely voluptuous, that the very instinct of man in me, which calls some of my sex to love and to protect one of hers, made my head whirl with new emotion. But God be thanked, that soul-wail of my dear Madam Mina had not died out of my ears;[31] and, before the spell could be wrought further upon me, I had nerved myself to my wild work. By this time I had searched all the tombs in the chapel, so far as I could tell; and as there had been only three of these Un-Dead phantoms around us in the night, I took it that there were no more of active Un-Dead existent.[32] There was one great tomb more lordly than all the rest; huge it was, and nobly proportioned. On it was but one word

DRACULA.[33]

This then was the Un-Dead home of the King-Vampire, to whom so many more were due. Its emptiness spoke eloquent to make certain what I knew. Before I began to restore these women to their dead selves through my awful work, I laid in Dracula's tomb some of the Wafer, and so banished him from it, Un-Dead, for ever.[34]

Then began my terrible task, and I dreaded it. Had it been but one, it had been easy, comparative. But three! To begin twice more after I had been through a deed of horror; for it was terrible with the sweet Miss Lucy, what would it not be with these strange ones who had survived through centuries, and who had been strengthened by the passing of the years; who would, if they could, have fought for their foul lives. . . .

30 For further evidence of her primacy, see text accompanying chapter 3, note 73.

31 How convenient for Van Helsing—but what caused Mina to wail? When Van Helsing returns to her, nothing has disturbed her repose. Was this wailing a figment of Van Helsing's imagination? Or a convenient fiction to explain his "success" in resisting the female vampires where others had failed? Roger Johnson, in private correspondence with this editor, suggests that Van Helsing here is remembering Mina's reaction to the holy wafer.

32 But this is inconsistent with Van Helsing's theory of circles of vampires arising from their victims (see text accompanying chapter 16, note 23). Clearly Dracula and the women vampires have been active in the neighbourhood for centuries. If the small number of vampires is in fact accurate, this is strong evidence that turning a victim is required before vampire progeny arise. See "Dracula's Family Tree" in Part II for a further discussion.

33 Ah, but as Harker and Van Helsing were informed earlier, there were many Draculas. Which one is this? And why is there no epitaph beyond the word "Dracula"? Perhaps by "tomb" Van Helsing means a large mausoleum, housing many graves of the family.

34 Jonathan's journal makes no mention of this or any of the other tombs, and of course Jonathan saw Dracula sleeping in an entirely different location, a "vault" with no tombs in sight, and in a "great box," not a coffin. Dracula and the others may have had many sleeping places in the castle. Leatherdale (*Dracula Unearthed*) makes the important observation that very little about this castle resembles the castle described by Harker in the earlier part of the narrative.

35 This is evidence of Van Helsing's thesis about the bodies of older vampires turning to dust. However, here this occurs only after the stake has been driven home and the body has been decapitated—and the body does not instantly disintegrate. Instantaneous disintegration is the common death of all vampires in the *Buffy* universe. Importantly, this sentence does not appear in the Abridged Text. It is likely that Dracula—who, as is argued below, wishes to emphasise his death at the conclusion of the narrative—concluded that this description, showing a lapse of time between decapitation and disintegration, raised unwanted questions about his own "death."

36 This is of course impossible in the case of the castle described by Harker. Did Van Helsing crawl up the outside wall of the castle and place wafers around each of the windows?

37 If the passage is "steeply downhill," it is curious that the Szgany were so readily able to bring the boxes to the castle. Again, this reinforces the doubt as to whether this is the same castle described by Harker.

Oh, my friend John, but it was butcher work; had I not been nerved by thoughts of other dead, and of the living over whom hung such a pall of fear, I could not have gone on. I tremble and tremble even yet, though till all was over, God be thanked, my nerve did stand. Had I not seen the repose in the first face, and the gladness that stole over it just ere the final dissolution came, as realisation that the soul had been won, I could not have gone further with my butchery. I could not have endured the horrid screeching as the stake drove home; the plunging of writhing form, and lips of bloody foam. I should have fled in terror and left my work undone. But it is over! And the poor souls, I can pity them now and weep, as I think of them placid each in her full sleep of death, for a short moment ere fading. For, friend John, hardly had my knife severed the head of each, before the whole body began to melt away and crumble into its native dust, as though the death that should have come centuries agone had at last assert himself and say at once and loud "I am here!"[35]

Before I left the castle I so fixed its entrances that never more can the Count enter there Un-dead.[36]

When I stepped into the circle where Madam Mina slept, she woke from her sleep, and, seeing me, cried out in pain that I had endured too much.

"Come!" she said, "Come away from this awful place! Let us go to meet my husband who is, I know, coming towards us." She was looking thin and pale and weak; but her eyes were pure and glowed with fervour. I was glad to see her paleness and her illness, for my mind was full of the fresh horror of that ruddy vampire sleep.

And so with trust and hope, and yet full of fear, we go eastward to meet our friends—and *him*—whom Madam Mina tell me that she *know* are coming to meet us.

MINA HARKER'S JOURNAL.

6 November.—It was late in the afternoon when the Professor and I took our way towards the east whence I knew Jonathan was coming. We did not go fast, though the way was steeply downhill,[37] for we had to take heavy rugs and wraps with us;

we dared not face the possibility of being left without warmth in the cold and the snow. We had to take some of our provisions too, for we were in a perfect desolation, and, so far as we could see through the snow-fall, there was not even the sign of a habitation. When we had gone about a mile, I was tired with the heavy walking and sat down to rest. Then we looked back and saw where the clear line of Dracula's castle cut the sky;[38] for we were so deep under the hill whereon it was set that the angle of perspective of the Carpathian mountains was far below it. We saw it in all its grandeur, perched a thousand feet on the summit of a sheer precipice, and with seemingly a great gap between it and the steep of the adjacent mountain on any side. There was something wild and uncanny about the place. We could hear the distant howling of wolves. They were far off, but the sound, even though coming muffled through the deadening snowfall, was full of terror. I knew from the way Dr. Van Helsing was searching about that he was trying to seek some strategic point, where we would be less exposed in case of attack. The rough roadway still led downwards; we could trace it through the drifted snow.

In a little while the Professor signalled to me, so I got up and joined him. He had found a wonderful spot, a sort of natural hollow in a rock, with an entrance like a doorway between two boulders.[39] He took me by the hand and drew me in: "See!" he said, "here you will be in shelter; and if the wolves do come I can meet them one by one." He brought in our furs, and made a snug nest for me, and got out some provisions and forced them upon me. But I could not eat; to even try to do so was repulsive to me, and, much as I would have liked to please him, I could not bring myself to the attempt. He looked very sad, but did not reproach me. Taking his field-glasses from the case, he stood on the top of the rock, and began to search the horizon. Suddenly he called out:—

"Look! Madam Mina, look! look!" I sprang up and stood beside him on the rock; he handed me his glasses and pointed. The snow was now falling more heavily, and swirled about fiercely, for a high wind was beginning to blow. However, there were times when there were pauses between the snow flurries and I could see a long way round. From the height where we

38 Mina and Van Helsing found the castle on the western side of the mountains; downhill would have been to travel west and then go east through the Pass. Therefore, her remark about travelling east is only in a goal-oriented sense— for the first mile, they must have travelled west. They must travel eastwards now to join up with those following the Bistrita River, in the neighbourhood of its source near Dorna Watra (now Vatra Dornei, a ski resort). However, Castle Dracula seems to be in a different location for Mina and Van Helsing than it was for Jonathan. See note 15 above.

39 Of course, for the vistas afforded, this can only be on the eastern side of the Carpathians, through the Pass.

40 Mina fails to note the "jagged" horizon recorded by Harker as the vista from the castle. Again, there is little resemblance between the two descriptions, and no one would describe the area east of the Borgo Pass—in the midst of the "ring" of the Carpathians—as a "plain."

41 Mina and Van Helsing have gone about a mile from the castle and now see the Szgany "not far off"—another mile or two at best. Why, then, does it take an hour for the group to reach them, if the horses are "galloping as hard as they can," as Van Helsing will shortly remark? The entire climax in fact takes place in dreamlike slowness.

42 Why are the Szgany "racing for the sunset"? Nothing they can do will bring it any faster, and Dracula did not need to be at his castle by sunset. All the Szgany really need to do is evade the riders who are following them by heading for any cave or hideaway they know of and then, after sunset, leisurely proceed to the castle. Their pace is truly inexplicable. They left the banks of the Bistrita the preceding morning at sunrise and yet have only gotten this far! Although the exact point of their departure from the river is not stated, it would most likely be as far along the river as possible—that is, as close to the Pass and the castle as possible. Dorna Watra, the last village along the river before the Pass, is only about 15 miles from the Pass. How could it have taken them two days to traverse this distance?

43 There is no explanation of how half the party ended up south of the Gypsies and the other half north.

were it was possible to see a great distance; and far off, beyond the white waste of snow, I could see the river lying like a black ribbon in kinks and curls as it wound its way.[40] Straight in front of us and not far off[41]—in fact so near that I wondered we had not noticed before—came a group of mounted men hurrying along. In the midst of them was a cart, a long leiter-waggon which swept from side to side, like a dog's tail wagging, with each stern inequality of the road. Outlined against the snow as they were, I could see from the men's clothes that they were peasants or gypsies of some kind.

On the cart was a great square chest. My heart leaped as I saw it, for I felt that the end was coming. The evening was now drawing close, and well I knew that at sunset the Thing, which was till then imprisoned there, would take new freedom and could in any of many forms elude pursuit. In fear I turned to the Professor; to my consternation, however, he was not there. An instant later, I saw him below me. Round the rock he had drawn a circle, such as we had found shelter in last night. When he had completed it he stood beside me again, saying:—

"At least you shall be safe here from *him!*" He took the glasses from me, and at the next lull of the snow swept the whole space below us. "See," he said, "they come quickly; They are flogging the horses, and galloping as hard as they can." He paused and went on in a hollow voice:—

"They are racing for the sunset.[42] We may be too late. God's will be done!" Down came another blinding rush of driving snow, and the whole landscape was blotted out. It soon passed, however, and once more his glasses were fixed on the plain. Then came a sudden cry:—

"Look! Look! Look! See, two horsemen follow fast, coming up from the south. It must be Quincey and John. Take the glass. Look, before the snow blots it all out!" I took it and looked. The two men might be Dr. Seward and Mr. Morris. I knew at all events that neither of them was Jonathan. At the same time I *knew* that Jonathan was not far off; looking around I saw on the north side of the coming party two other men, riding at break-neck speed.[43] One of them I knew was Jonathan, and the other I took, of course, to be Lord Godalming. They, too, were pursuing the party with the cart. When I told the Professor he shouted in glee like a schoolboy, and, after looking intently till a snowfall made sight impossible, he laid his Winchester rifle ready for use against the boulder at the opening of our shelter. "They are all converging," he said. "When the time comes we shall have the gypsies on all sides." I got out my revolver ready to hand, for whilst we were speaking the howling of wolves came louder and closer. When the snowstorm abated a moment we looked again. It was strange to see the snow falling in such heavy flakes close to us, and beyond, the sun shining more and more brightly as it sank down towards the far mountain tops.[44] Sweeping the glass all around us I could see here and there dots moving singly and in twos and threes and larger numbers—the wolves were gathering for their prey.[45]

Every instant seemed an age whilst we waited. The wind came now in fierce bursts, and the snow was driven with fury as it swept upon us in circling eddies. At times we could not see an arm's length before us; but at others, as the hollow-sounding wind swept by us, it seemed to clear the air-space around us so that we could see afar off. We had of late been so accustomed to watch for sunrise and sunset, that we knew with fair accuracy when it would be; and we knew that before long the sun would set.

It was hard to believe that by our watches it was less than an hour that we waited in that rocky shelter before the various bodies began to converge close upon us. The wind came now with fiercer and more bitter sweeps, and more steadily from the north. It seemingly had driven the snow clouds from us, for, with only occasional bursts, the snow fell. We could distinguish clearly the individuals of each party, the pursued and the pursuers. Strangely enough those pursued did not seem to realize, or at least to care, that they were pursued; they seemed, however, to hasten with redoubled speed as the sun dropped lower and lower on the mountain tops.

Closer and closer they drew. The Professor and I crouched down behind our rock, and held our weapons ready; I could see that he was determined that they should not pass. One and all were quite unaware of our presence.

All at once two voices shouted out to: "Halt!" One was my Jonathan's, raised in a high key of passion; the other Mr. Morris'

44 With the sun sinking in the west, this must be back the way they came. Why is Van Helsing looking in that direction? Indeed, it is curious that in the midst of the snowstorm the sun is so clearly visible.

45 If true, why did Dracula wait until this stage of the pursuit to summon a wolf escort? Surely he could have had a pack of wolves meet him at the riverside.

46 Why did the hunters not use their rifles earlier? If they had moral scruples about shooting the Szgany, they could have shot the horses and brought the wagon to an immediate halt.

strong resolute tone of quiet command. The gypsies may not have known the language, but there was no mistaking the tone, in whatever tongue the words were spoken. Instinctively they reined in, and at the instant Lord Godalming and Jonathan dashed up at one side and Dr. Seward and Mr. Morris on the other. The leader of the gypsies, a splendid-looking fellow who sat his horse like a centaur, waved them back, and in a fierce voice gave to his companions some word to proceed. They lashed the horses which sprang forward; but the four men raised their Winchester rifles, and in an unmistakable way commanded them to stop.**46** At the same moment Dr. Van Helsing and I rose behind the rock and pointed our weapons at them. Seeing that they were surrounded the men tightened their reins and drew up. The leader turned to them and gave a word at which every man of the gipsy party drew what weapon he carried, knife or pistol, and held himself in readiness to attack. Issue was joined in an instant.

The leader, with a quick movement of his rein, threw his horse out in front, and pointing first to the sun—now close down on the hill tops—and then to the castle, said something which I did not understand. For answer, all four men of our party threw themselves from their horses and dashed towards the cart. I should have felt terrible fear at seeing Jonathan in such danger, but that the ardour of battle must have been upon me as well as the rest of them; I felt no fear, but only a wild, surging desire to do something. Seeing the quick movement of our parties, the leader of the gypsies gave a command; his men instantly formed round the cart in a sort of undisciplined endeavour, each one shouldering and pushing the other in his eagerness to carry out the order.

In the midst of this I could see that Jonathan on one side of the ring of men, and Quincey on the other, were forcing a way to the cart; it was evident that they were bent on finishing their task before the sun should set. Nothing seemed to stop or even to hinder them. Neither the levelled weapons nor the flashing knives of the gypsies in front, or the howling of the wolves behind, appeared to even attract their attention. Jonathan's impetuosity, and the manifest singleness of his purpose, seemed to overawe those in front of him; instinctively they cowered aside and let him pass. In an instant he had jumped upon the cart, and with a strength which seemed incredible, raised the great box, and flung it over the wheel to the ground.[47] In the meantime, Mr. Morris had had to use force to pass through his side of the ring of Szgany. All the time I had been breathlessly watching Jonathan I had, with the tail of my eye, seen him pressing desperately forward, and had seen the knives of the gypsies flash as he won a way through them, and they cut at him. He had parried with his great bowie knife,[48] and at first I thought that he too had come through in safety; but as he sprang beside Jonathan, who had by now jumped from the cart, I could see that with his left hand he was clutching at his side, and that the blood was spurting through his fingers. He did not delay notwithstanding this, for as Jonathan, with desperate energy, attacked one end of the chest, attempting to prize off the lid with his great Kukri knife, he attacked the other frantically with his bowie. Under the efforts of both men the lid began to yield; the nails drew with a quick screeching sound, and the top of the box was thrown back.

By this time the gypsies, seeing themselves covered by the Winchesters, and at the mercy of Lord Godalming and Dr. Seward, had given in and made no further resistance. The sun was almost down on the mountain tops, and the shadows of the whole group fell long upon the snow. I saw the Count lying within the box upon the earth, some of which the rude falling from the cart had scattered over him. He was deathly pale,[49] just like a waxen image, and the red eyes glared with the horrible vindictive look which I knew too well.[50]

As I looked, the eyes saw the sinking sun, and the look of hate in them turned to triumph.

But, on the instant, came the sweep and flash of Jonathan's great knife. I shrieked as I saw it shear through the throat; whilst at the same moment Mr. Morris's bowie knife plunged into the heart.

It was like a miracle; but before our very eyes, and almost in the drawing of a breath, the whole body crumbled into dust and passed from our sight.[51]

I shall be glad as long as I live that even in that moment of

47 This is astonishing. All previous indications are that only Dracula, with the strength of twenty men, could accomplish such a feat. Is this attributable to a surge of adrenaline, or are we to suspect that Jonathan himself may be turning? Luckily for Jonathan, the box lands right-side-up; otherwise, he would never have been able to get at Dracula.

Bowie knife.

48 It is fitting that American Quincey Morris carries the bowie knife. Legend has it that American frontiersman Jim Bowie carried one at the famous battle of the Alamo. Bowie had ordered the knife from blacksmith James Black, of Washington, Arkansas, to be made from a whittled wooden design Bowie himself fabricated. In addition to filling the order, Black made a modified version, which Bowie preferred. It was double-edged (that is, sharpened) along the length of the curve, which permitted one to use the back of the blade to parry and back slash. Bowie is reported to have killed three hired assassins with the modified knife shortly after purchase, securing its fame. Customers began seeking out Black to manufacture "Bowie's knife" for them. However, even proponents of the Black/Bowie source admit that Bowie, as a famous knife fighter, used many weapons during his career, all of which may have been appropriately labelled "bowie" knives, and it is only tradition that fixes on this particular model.

49 "Still," not "pale" in the Manuscript. It is not clear whether this is a significant difference.

50 At Castle Dracula, no physical action was needed to deter Harker from taking any effective steps—a look was sufficient. Scholars wonder why Dracula failed, in this instance, to simply leap "panther-like" from the coffin and do battle. Again, the suggestion is that the coffin itself somehow creates a stuporous condition in the vampire, preventing it from physical action in a way that daylight never does.

51 Not a wooden stake in sight. Of course, some scholars question whether Dracula was in fact destroyed, or whether, as seems more likely, he chose the occasion of the setting of the sun to disincorporate and turn to a mist. In any case, it has been suggested that to dissuade future generations of hunters from pursuing him, Dracula himself coerced the Harkers—or Stoker—to author a fiction, telling the tale of

final dissolution, there was in the face a look of peace, such as I never could have imagined might have rested there.[52]

The Castle of Dracula now stood out against the red sky, and every stone of its broken battlements was articulated against the light of the setting sun.[53]

The gypsies, taking us as in some way the cause of the extraordinary disappearance of the dead man, turned, without a word, and rode away as if for their lives. Those who were unmounted jumped upon their leiter-wagon and shouted to the horsemen not to desert them.[54] The wolves, which had withdrawn to a safe distance, followed in their wake, leaving us alone.

What they should have done. Christopher Lee as Dracula.
Dracula Has Risen from the Grave (Hammer Film Productions, 1968)

Mr. Morris, who had sunk to the ground, leaned on his elbow, holding his hand pressed to his side; the blood still gushed through his fingers. I flew to him, for the Holy circle did not now keep me back; so did the two doctors. Jonathan knelt behind him and the wounded man laid back his head on his shoulder. With a sigh he took, with a feeble effort, my hand in that of his own which was unstained. He must have seen the anguish of my heart in my face, for he smiled at me and said:—

"I am only too happy to have been of service! Oh, God!" he cried suddenly, struggling to a sitting posture and pointing to me, "It was worth for this to die! Look! look!"

The sun was now right down upon the mountain top, and the red gleams[55] fell upon my face, so that it was bathed in rosy light. With one impulse the men sank on their knees and a deep and earnest "Amen" broke from all as their eyes followed the pointing of his finger as the dying man spoke:—

"Now God be thanked that all has not been in vain! See! the snow is not more stainless than her forehead! The curse has passed away!"

And, to our bitter grief, with a smile and in silence, he died, a gallant gentleman.

Note

Seven years ago we all went through the flames;[56] and the happiness of some of us since then is, we think, well worth the pain we endured.[57] It is an added joy to Mina and to me that our boy's birthday is the same day as that on which Quincey Morris died. His mother holds, I know, the secret belief that some of our brave friend's spirit has passed into him.[58] His bundle of names links all our little band of men together; but we call him Quincey.[59]

In the summer of this year we made a journey to Transylvania, and went over the old ground which was, and is, to us so full of vivid and terrible memories.[60] It was almost impossible to believe that the things which we had seen with our own eyes and heard with our own ears were living truths. Every trace of all that had been was blotted out.[61] The castle stood as before, reared high above a waste of desolation.

the utter destruction of the vampire-king. In reviewing the changes appearing in the Abridged Text, it is impossible to fail to see the hand of the Count working to strengthen the illusion of his death.

52 This sentence does not appear in the Abridged Text, nor do the two following paragraphs. The effect is to make the hunters appear relentless, hardened, remorseless—strengthening the impression that good British (and American) men triumphed over the evil vampire.

53 The following material appears in the Manuscript: "As we looked there came a terrible convulsion of the earth so that we seemed to rock to and fro and fell to our knees. At the same moment with a roar which seemed to shake the very heavens the whole castle and the rock and even the hill on which it stood seemed to rise into the air and scatter ~~skywards~~ in fragments while a mighty cloud of black and yellow smoke volume on volume in rolling grandeur was shot upwards with inconceivable rapidity. Then there was a stillness in nature as the echoes of that thunderous report seemed to come as with the hollow boom of a thunder clap—the long reverberating roll which seems as though the floors of heaven shook. Then down in a mighty ruin falling whence they rose came the fragments that had been tossed skywards in the cataclysm.

"From where we stood it seemed as though the one fierce volcano burst had satisfied the need of nature and that the castle and the structure of the hill had sunk again into the void. We were so appalled with the suddenness and the grandeur that we forgot to think of ourselves. The first to recover were the gypsies, and these probably taking us as in some way the cause of the earthquake as well as of . . ."

One may examine the Notes in vain for verification of the destruction of the castle. Was it in fact destroyed? If, as is suggested, Dracula wished to perpetuate the myth that he perished and so forestall future hunters, a record of the destruction of the castle would surely dissuade future generations from seeking Dracula's lair. It appears that originally the falsehood of the destruction was to be included in the narrative. However, in a subversive act, someone—perhaps one of the Harkers—induced Stoker at the last minute to print the truth—that the castle remained. Once done, it was not practical to "cover up" the existence of the castle by restoring the "destruction" scene to the Abridged Text.

54 As Wolf (*The Essential Dracula*) notes, suddenly Mina understands the speech of the Gypsies. Roger Johnson, in private correspondence with this editor, suggests that Mina may be interpreting gestures.

55 The published text does not contain the following phrase, which appears in the Manuscript: "came through the thin smoke of the earthquake and"

56 Startlingly, the Manuscript reads: "Eleven years ago . . ." This "Note" is Jonathan Harker's addendum. When, one may ask, was it added? The Stoker narrative was published in 1897. Therefore, "[s]even years ago" can be no later than 1890, if Stoker allowed Harker to tack on this note immediately before publication. If the "[e]leven years ago" text is the correct one, then the events must have occurred even earlier, no later than 1886. See appendix 2, "The Dating of *Dracula*."

57 And who is it who has not found happiness? Presumably Jonathan does not mean Seward or Holmwood, who he notes have married. The only possibilities are Van Helsing—who is shown in a seemingly happy pose, dandling Quincey on his knee, but who may have secret sorrows—or Mina. The latter idea is most tantalising. Curiously, the Manuscript reads, "the happiness of all of us"—did a sudden sad event, just preceding publication, cause this to be changed at the last minute?

When we got home we were talking of the old time—which we could all look back on without despair, for Godalming and Seward are both happily married. I took the papers from the safe where they had been ever since our return so long ago. We were struck with the fact, that in all the mass of material of which the record is composed, there is hardly one authentic document;[62] nothing but a mass of type-writing, except the later note-books of Mina and Seward and myself, and Van Helsing's memorandum. We could hardly ask any one, even did we wish to, to accept these as proofs of so wild a story. Van Helsing summed it all up as he said, with our boy on his knee:[63]—

"We want no proofs; we ask none to believe us! This boy will some day know what a brave and gallant woman his mother is. Already he knows her sweetness and loving care; later on he will understand how some men so loved her, that they did dare much for her sake."

—Jonathan Harker.

58 This sentence does not appear in the Manuscript. Who added it? And on whose authority?

59 Quincey Harker (presumably, Quincey John Abraham Harker) is the leader of a team of vampire hunters in the late twentieth century, including Anthony Drake, the grandson of Count Dracula, and Nina Van Helsing, the granddaughter of the Professor, whose exploits are chronicled in Marv Wolfman's *The Tomb of Dracula* and *Dracula Lives!*

60 Why did the Harkers return to Transylvania? To begin the training of Quincey Harker, vampire hunter? Or because Mina was "called" by Dracula? Mina's continuing troubles may also explain why Harker chose to include Van Helsing's final encomium respecting this "brave and gallant woman."

61 This sentence was evidently intended to be part of the "destruction of the castle" myth (see note 53 above) and was inadvertently retained even though the fraud was eliminated. The Manuscript continues: "the site of the castle was a desert waste where as yet no seed could flourish and whence came no bird or insect or even a crawling thing. In its cold sulphurous silent loneliness it was a very abomination of desolation." The material does not appear in the published narrative.

62 Truer words may never have been spoken, at least insofar as the reproduction of the Harker Papers in the Stoker narrative.

63 If the boy was on Van Helsing's knee, he was evidently born at least four or five years after the events of the narrative if the "[e]leven years ago" reference is to be believed; one cannot credit Van Helsing seating a boy of much above five on his lap! Even if the "[s]even years ago" reference is accepted, Quincey Harker is unlikely to have been born sooner than two years after the climax of the narrative.

"'I sprung upon her. There was a shriek, but not before I had secured
a draught of life blood from her neck.'"
Varney, the Vampyre; or, The Feast of Blood (1847)

Appendix 1

"Dracula's Guest" [1]

WHEN WE STARTED for our drive the sun was shining brightly on Munich, [2] and the air was full of the joyousness of early summer. Just as we were about to depart, Herr Delbrück (the maître d'hôtel of the Quatre Saisons, [3] where I was staying) came down, bareheaded, to the carriage and, after wishing me a pleasant drive, said to the coachman, still holding his hand on the handle of the carriage door:—

"Remember you are back by nightfall. The sky looks bright but there is a shiver in the north wind that says there may be a sudden storm. But I am sure you will not be late." Here he smiled, and added, "for you know what night it is."

Johann answered with an emphatic, "Ja, mein Herr," and, touching his hat, drove off quickly. When we had cleared the town, I said, after signalling to him to stop:

"Tell me, Johann, what is tonight?"

He crossed himself, as he answered laconically: "Walpurgis Nacht." [4] Then he took out his watch, a great, old-fashioned German silver thing as big as a turnip, and looked at it, with his eyebrows gathered together and a little impatient shrug of his shoulders. I realized that this was his way of respectfully protesting against the unnecessary delay, and sank back in the carriage, merely motioning him to proceed. He started off rapidly, as if to make up for lost time. Every now and then the horses seemed to throw up their heads and sniff the air

1 First published, after Stoker's death, as a short story in *Dracula's Guest and Other Weird Stories* (1914). See chapter 1, note 1.

2 See chapter 1, note 4. Note that the narrator is not named. It is tempting to identify the narrator as Jonathan Harker, but discrepancies between this account and the Stoker narrative prevent a definite identification. Leatherdale (*Dracula Unearthed*) argues that the material may have been included as the first chapter of the narrative in an earlier draft. Substantial evidence in the Manuscript (unknown to Leatherdale), including numerous references to the events of "Dracula's Guest," makes it plain that it was written contemporaneously with the narrative and was originally to be included. It is impossible to determine why the material was suppressed and later edited by Stoker into its more generic form.

If this is Harker's narrative, then the action took place shortly before Harker left Munich at 8:35 P.M. on 1 May.

3 The Quatre Saisons, or Vier Jahreszeiten, as it is known locally, opened on Maximilianstrasse on 25 July 1858 and remains in operation today. It often hosted royalty and built its reputation on catering to its clients' every desire. By 1884, the hotel boasted telephone service, and by 1889 it had been completely "electrified."

Vier Jahreszeiten Hotel, Munich.

4 The night before 1 May, Walpurgis-Nacht, the antipode of Halloween, is said to mark the final victory of spring over winter. Traditionally, before the evil spirits occupying winter depart, they have one last gathering, on the Brocken, the highest peak in the Harz Mountains. Goethe records the scene in his play *Faust* (published in parts, 1790–1833), when Mephistopheles takes Faust to the Brocken to revel with the witches.

Walpurgis-Nacht is named after Walpurga or Walburga, Abbess of Heidenheim near Eichstätt, a Catholic saint whose protection was often invoked against witchcraft and sorcery. As the festival became Christianised, the eve became marked with tolling bells and prayers, blessings with holy water, and displays of blessed sprigs in homes and barns. The most widespread precaution adopted during Walpurgis-Nacht is noise making, produced by diverse means, including the beating of boards on the ground and the firing of weapons.

5 Leatherdale (*Dracula Unearthed*) points out that this therefore cannot be Harker, who has a "smattering" of German (see text accompanying chapter 1, note 14). The narrator does mysteriously manage to read the epitaph on the Doric tomb unaided. Perhaps he memorised it, and someone translated it for him later.

6 See chapter 2, note 56.

suspiciously. On such occasions I often looked round in alarm. The road was pretty bleak, for we were traversing a sort of high, wind-swept plateau. As we drove, I saw a road that looked but little used, and which seemed to dip through a little, winding valley. It looked so inviting that, even at the risk of offending him, I called Johann to stop—and when he had pulled up, I told him I would like to drive down that road. He made all sorts of excuses, and frequently crossed himself as he spoke. This somewhat piqued my curiosity, so I asked him various questions. He answered fencingly, and repeatedly looked at his watch in protest. Finally I said:

"Well, Johann, I want to go down this road. I shall not ask you to come unless you like; but tell me why you do not like to go, that is all I ask." For answer he seemed to throw himself off the box, so quickly did he reach the ground. Then he stretched out his hands appealingly to me, and implored me not to go. There was just enough of English mixed with the German for me to understand the drift of his talk. He seemed always just about to tell me something—the very idea of which evidently frightened him; but each time he pulled himself up saying, as he crossed himself: "Walpurgis Nacht!"

I tried to argue with him, but it was difficult to argue with a man when I did not know his language.[5] The advantage certainly rested with him, for although he began to speak in English, of a very crude and broken kind, he always got excited and broke into his native tongue—and every time he did so, he looked at his watch. Then the horses became restless and sniffed the air. At this he grew very pale, and, looking around in a frightened way, he suddenly jumped forward, took them by the bridles and led them on some twenty feet. I followed, and asked why he had done this. For an answer he crossed himself, pointed to the spot we had left and drew his carriage in the direction of the other road, indicating a cross, and said, first in German, then in English: "Buried him—him what killed themselves."

I remembered the old custom of burying suicides at crossroads:[6] "Ah! I see, a suicide. How interesting!" But for the life of me I could not make out why the horses were frightened.

Whilst we were talking, we heard a sort of sound between a

yelp and a bark. It was far away; but the horses got very restless, and it took Johann all his time to quiet them. He was pale, and said, "It sounds like a wolf—but yet there are no wolves here now."[7]

"No?" I said, questioning him; "isn't it long since the wolves were so near the city?"

"Long, long," he answered, "in the spring and summer; but with the snow the wolves have been here not so long."

Whilst he was petting the horses and trying to quiet them, dark clouds drifted rapidly across the sky. The sunshine passed away, and a breath of cold wind seemed to drift past us. It was only a breath, however, and more in the nature of a warning than a fact, for the sun came out brightly again. Johann looked under his lifted hand at the horizon and said:

"The storm of snow, he comes before long time." Then he looked at his watch again, and, straightway holding his reins firmly—for the horses were still pawing the ground restlessly and shaking their heads—he climbed to his box as though the time had come for proceeding on our journey.

I felt a little obstinate and did not at once get into the carriage.

"Tell me," I said, "about this place where the road leads," and I pointed down.

Again he crossed himself and mumbled a prayer, before he answered, "It is unholy."

"What is unholy?" I enquired.

"The village."

"Then there is a village?"

"No, no. No one lives there hundreds of years." My curiosity was piqued. "But you said there was a village."

"There was."

"Where is it now?"

Whereupon he burst out into a long story in German and English, so mixed up that I could not quite understand exactly what he said, but roughly I gathered that long ago, hundreds of years, men had died there and been buried in their graves; and sounds were heard under the clay, and when the graves were opened, men and women were found rosy with life, and their mouths red with blood. And so, in haste to save their

[7] See chapter 24, note 37.

8 Compare these tales to those collected by Calmet and discussed in "Dracula's Family Tree," note 2, in Part II.

9 The arrogance of the narrator seems quite different from the attitude displayed by Harker, who graciously accepts the crucifix offered by a Bistritz woman who warns him about St. George's Eve. If this in fact is Harker, it is possible that his experience in Munich led him to be more accepting of the cultural differences.

10 The tall and thin description matches that of Dracula, and possibly the reader is being asked to assume that this is he, coming to deliver his message to Herr Delbrück. However, why would Dracula come in person, when he has already sent a telegram to the hotel? McNally and Florescu (*The Essential Dracula*) conclude that the "gigantic wolf" that appears later is Dracula in changed form; if that is so, Dracula had no faith in the efficacy of his warning, and it seems pointless to have sent it. And how did Dracula know that the narrator would be in danger here and not elsewhere on his journey?

lives (aye, and their souls!—and here he crossed himself) those who were left fled away to other places, where the living lived, and the dead were dead and not—not something.[8] He was evidently afraid to speak the last words. As he proceeded with his narration, he grew more and more excited. It seemed as if his imagination had got hold of him, and he ended in a perfect paroxysm of fear—white-faced, perspiring, trembling and looking round him, as if expecting that some dreadful presence would manifest itself there in the bright sunshine on the open plain. Finally, in an agony of desperation, he cried:

"Walpurgis Nacht!" and pointed to the carriage for me to get in. All my English blood rose at this, and, standing back, I said:

"You are afraid, Johann—you are afraid. Go home; I shall return alone; the walk will do me good." The carriage door was open. I took from the seat my oak walking stick—which I always carry on my holiday excursions—and closed the door, pointing back to Munich, and said, "Go home, Johann—Walpurgis Nacht doesn't concern Englishmen."[9]

The horses were now more restive than ever, and Johann was trying to hold them in, while excitedly imploring me not to do anything so foolish. I pitied the poor fellow, he was so deeply in earnest; but all the same I could not help laughing. His English was quite gone now. In his anxiety he had forgotten that his only means of making me understand was to talk my language, so he jabbered away in his native German. It began to be a little tedious. After giving the direction, "Home!" I turned to go down the cross-road into the valley.

With a despairing gesture, Johann turned his horses towards Munich. I leaned on my stick and looked after him. He went slowly along the road for a while: then there came over the crest of the hill a man tall and thin. I could see so much in the distance. When he drew near the horses, they began to jump and kick about, then to scream with terror. Johann could not hold them in; they bolted down the road, running away madly. I watched them out of sight, then looked for the stranger, but I found that he, too, was gone.[10]

With a light heart I turned down the side road through the deepening valley to which Johann had objected. There was not the slightest reason, that I could see, for his objection; and I daresay I tramped for a couple of hours without thinking of time or distance, and certainly without seeing a person or a house. So far as the place was concerned, it was desolation itself. But I did not notice this particularly till, on turning a bend in the road, I came upon a scattered fringe of wood; then I recognized that I had been impressed unconsciously by the desolation of the region through which I had passed.

I sat down to rest myself, and began to look around. It struck me that it was considerably colder than it had been at the commencement of my walk—a sort of sighing sound seemed to be around me, with, now and then, high overhead, a sort of muffled roar. Looking upwards I noticed that great thick clouds were drifting rapidly across the sky from north to south at a great height. There were signs of coming storm in some lofty stratum of the air. I was a little chilly, and, thinking that it was the sitting still after the exercise of walking, I resumed my journey.

The ground I passed over was now much more picturesque. There were no striking objects that the eye might single out; but in all there was a charm of beauty. I took little heed of time and it was only when the deepening twilight forced itself upon me that I began to think of how I should find my way home. The brightness of the day had gone. The air was cold, and the drifting of clouds high overhead was more marked. They were accompanied by a sort of far-away rushing sound, through which seemed to come at intervals that mysterious cry which the driver had said came from a wolf. For a while I hesitated. I had said I would see the deserted village, so on I went, and presently came on a wide stretch of open country, shut in by hills all around. Their sides were covered with trees which spread down to the plain, dotting, in clumps, the gentler slopes and hollows which showed here and there. I followed with my eye the winding of the road, and saw that it curved close to one of the densest of these clumps and was lost behind it.

As I looked there came a cold shiver in the air, and the snow began to fall. I thought of the miles and miles of bleak country I had passed, and then hurried on to seek shelter of the wood in front. Darker and darker grew the sky, and faster and heavier fell the snow, till the earth before and around me was a glistening white carpet the further edge of which was lost in misty vagueness. The road was here but crude, and when on the level its boundaries were not so marked, as when it passed through the cuttings; and in a little while I found that I must have strayed from it, for I missed underfoot the hard surface, and my feet sank deeper in the grass and moss. Then the wind grew stronger and blew with ever-increasing force, till I was fain to run before it. The air became icy-cold, and in spite of my exercise I began to suffer. The snow was now falling so thickly and whirling around me in such rapid eddies that I could hardly keep my eyes open. Every now and then the heavens were torn asunder by vivid lightning, and in the flashes I could see ahead of me a great mass of trees, chiefly yew and cypress all heavily coated with snow.

I was soon amongst the shelter of the trees, and there, in comparative silence, I could hear the rush of the wind high overhead. Presently the blackness of the storm had become merged in the darkness of the night. By-and-by the storm seemed to be passing away: it now only came in fierce puffs or blasts. At such moments the weird sound of the wolf appeared to be echoed by many similar sounds around me.

Now and again, through the black mass of drifting cloud, came a straggling ray of moonlight, which lit up the expanse, and showed me that I was at the edge of a dense mass of cypress and yew trees. As the snow had ceased to fall, I walked out from the shelter and began to investigate more closely. It appeared to me that, amongst so many old foundations as I had passed, there might be still standing a house in which, though in ruins, I could find some sort of shelter for a while. As I skirted the edge of the copse, I found that a low wall encircled it, and following this I presently found an opening. Here the cypresses formed an alley leading up to a square mass of some kind of building. Just as I caught sight of this, however, the drifting clouds obscured the moon, and I passed up the path in darkness. The wind must have grown colder, for I felt myself shiver as I walked; but there was hope of shelter, and I groped my way blindly on.

I stopped, for there was a sudden stillness. The storm had passed; and, perhaps in sympathy with nature's silence, my heart seemed to cease to beat. But this was only momentarily; for suddenly the moonlight broke through the clouds, showing me that I was in a graveyard, and that the square object before me was a great massive tomb of marble, as white as the snow that lay on and all around it. With the moonlight there came a fierce sigh of the storm, which appeared to resume its course with a long, low howl, as of many dogs or wolves. I was awed and shocked, and I felt the cold perceptibly grow upon me till it seemed to grip me by the heart. Then while the flood of moonlight still fell on the marble tomb, the storm gave further evidence of renewing, as though it was returning on its track. Impelled by some sort of fascination, I approached the sepulchre to see what it was, and why such a thing stood alone in such a place. I walked around it, and read, over the Doric door, in German:

COUNTESS DOLINGEN OF GRATZ[11]
IN STYRIA SOUGHT
AND FOUND DEATH
1801

On the top of the tomb, seemingly driven through the solid marble—for the structure was composed of a few vast blocks of stone—was a great iron spike or stake. On going to the back I saw, graven in great Russian letters:[12]

The dead travel fast.[13]

There was something so weird and uncanny about the whole thing that it gave me a turn and made me feel quite faint. I began to wish, for the first time, that I had taken Johann's advice. Here a thought struck me, which came under almost mysterious circumstances and with a terrible shock. This was Walpurgis Night!

Walpurgis Night, when, according to the belief of millions of people, the devil was abroad—when the graves were opened and the dead came forth and walked. When all evil things of

11 Gratz (also spelled Graz) was the capital of Styria, a province of Austria. Interestingly, the Notes make clear that Stoker originally planned to recount a trip to Styria rather than Transylvania. See chapter 1, note 17, above, for a discussion of another Styrian vampire.

12 Amazingly, the narrator now can read Russian as well. Again, he must have memorised the inscription and asked someone else to translate it.

13 See chapter 1, note 90, and accompanying text. Why is the quotation in Russian? McNally and Florescu (*The Essential Dracula*) surmise that the countess was an Orthodox Christian (hence the Russian inscription), but if this were so, why is the entire epitaph not in Russian? Furthermore, if the narrator is Harker, would he not comment on the coincidence when he hears the remark again only a few days later?

14 The Notes identify the woman as the fair vampire who appears to Harker in Dracula's castle. See text accompanying chapter 3, note 70. However, if the fair vampire died in 1801, she is hardly an ancient vampire (whose body turns to dust upon destruction), and the tomb underneath Castle Dracula is not hers. Furthermore, at the castle, Dracula warned off the fair vampire from attacking Jonathan Harker by a mere gesture—why would he need to travel all the way to Munich (an arduous trip, as is evident by Jonathan's subsequent journey) or send a wolf to protect the narrator, instead of again simply warning off the attacker? In short, although the Manuscript definitely corroborates the Notes about the woman's identity, Harker may well have been mistaken.

earth and air and water held revel. This very place the driver had specially shunned. This was the depopulated village of centuries ago. This was where the suicide lay; and this was the place where I was alone—unmanned, shivering with cold in a shroud of snow with a wild storm gathering again upon me! It took all my philosophy, all the religion I had been taught, all my courage, not to collapse in a paroxysm of fright.

And now a perfect tornado burst upon me. The ground shook as though thousands of horses thundered across it; and this time the storm bore on its icy wings, not snow, but great hailstones which drove with such violence that they might have come from the thongs of Balearic slingers—hailstones that beat down leaf and branch and made the shelter of the cypresses of no more avail than though their stems were standing-corn. At the first I had rushed to the nearest tree; but I was soon fain to leave it and seek the only spot that seemed to afford refuge, the deep Doric doorway of the marble tomb. There, crouching against the massive bronze door, I gained a certain amount of protection from the beating of the hailstones, for now they only drove against me as they ricocheted from the ground and the side of the marble.

As I leaned against the door, it moved slightly and opened inwards. The shelter of even a tomb was welcome in that pitiless tempest, and I was about to enter it when there came a flash of forked-lightning that lit up the whole expanse of the heavens. In the instant, as I am a living man, I saw, as my eyes were turned into the darkness of the tomb, a beautiful woman, with rounded cheeks and red lips, seemingly sleeping on a bier.[14] As the thunder broke overhead, I was grasped as by the hand of a giant and hurled out into the storm. The whole thing was so sudden that, before I could realize the shock, moral as well as physical, I found the hailstones beating me down. At the same time I had a strange, dominating feeling that I was not alone. I looked towards the tomb. Just then there came another blinding flash, which seemed to strike the iron stake that surmounted the tomb and to pour through to the earth, blasting and crumbling the marble, as in a burst of flame. The dead woman rose for a moment of agony, while she was lapped in the flame, and her bitter scream of pain was drowned in the thunder-crash.[15] The last thing I heard was this mingling of dreadful sound, as again I was seized in the giant-grasp and dragged away, while the hailstones beat on me, and the air around seemed reverberant with the howling of wolves. The last sight that I remembered was a vague, white, moving mass, as if all the graves around me had sent out the phantoms of their sheeted dead, and that they were closing in on me through the white cloudiness of the driving hail.

Gradually there came a sort of vague beginning of consciousness; then a sense of weariness that was dreadful. For a time I remembered nothing; but slowly my senses returned. My feet seemed positively racked with pain, yet I could not move them. They seemed to be numbed. There was an icy feeling at the back of my neck and all down my spine, and my ears, like my feet, were dead, yet in torment; but there was in my breast a sense of warmth which was, by comparison, delicious.[16] It was as a nightmare—a physical nightmare, if one may use such an expression; for some heavy weight on my chest made it difficult for me to breathe.

This period of semi-lethargy seemed to remain a long time, and as it faded away I must have slept or swooned. Then came a sort of loathing, like the first stage of seasickness, and a wild desire to be free from something—I knew not what. A vast stillness enveloped me, as though all the world were asleep or dead—only broken by the low panting as of some animal close to me. I felt a warm rasping at my throat, then came a consciousness of the awful truth, which chilled me to the heart and sent the blood surging up through my brain. Some great animal was lying on me and now licking my throat.[17] I feared to stir, for some instinct of prudence bade me lie still; but the brute seemed to realize that there was now some change in me, for it raised its head. Through my eyelashes I saw above me the two great flaming eyes of a gigantic wolf.[18] Its sharp white teeth gleamed in the gaping red mouth, and I could feel its hot breath fierce and acrid upon me.

For another spell of time I remembered no more. Then I became conscious of a low growl, followed by a yelp, renewed again and again. Then, seemingly very far away, I

15 McNally and Florescu (*The Essential Dracula*) credit the lightning bolt to Dracula's mastery of storms.

16 McNally and Florescu (*The Essential Dracula*) term this "in keeping with the initial reaction to the vampire in folklore; at first the victim finds the experience pleasant, erotic, and attractive." However, they overlook the true source of the reaction: there is a large wolf lying on the narrator's chest!

17 Why is the animal licking the narrator's throat? Could there have been blood on it? The narrator later feels pain in his throat, but the skin has not been broken. The pain is evidently from the creature's rough tongue. This is confirmed by the Manuscript (see chapter 3, note 75).

18 McNally and Florescu (*The Essential Dracula*) identify the wolf as Dracula himself. Van Helsing advises that Dracula has the power to change his shape to that of a wolf (although witnesses to such a change describe him as an "immense dog" or "great dog"—see text accompanying chapter 7, notes 24 and 58). However, if it were Dracula himself, why would he be "excited" to hear about Harker's adventures in Munich, as revealed in the Manuscript (see chapter 2, note 21)? More likely, the wolf was commanded by Dracula.

19 Roger Johnson, in private correspondence with this editor, points out that conveniently, the narrator now understands German (unless the soldiers were speaking in English for his benefit).

heard a "Holloa! holloa!" as of many voices calling in unison. Cautiously I raised my head and looked in the direction whence the sound came; but the cemetery blocked my view. The wolf still continued to yelp in a strange way, and a red glare began to move round the grove of cypresses, as though following the sound. As the voices drew closer, the wolf yelped faster and louder. I feared to make either sound or motion. Nearer came the red glow, over the white pall which stretched into the darkness around me. Then all at once from beyond the trees there came at a trot a troop of horsemen bearing torches. The wolf rose from my breast and made for the cemetery. I saw one of the horsemen (soldiers by their caps and their long military cloaks) raise his carbine and take aim. A companion knocked up his arm, and I heard the ball whiz over my head. He had evidently taken my body for that of the wolf. Another sighted the animal as it slunk away, and a shot followed. Then, at a gallop, the troop rode forward—some towards me, others following the wolf as it disappeared amongst the snow-clad cypresses.

As they drew nearer I tried to move, but was powerless, although I could see and hear all that went on around me. Two or three of the soldiers jumped from their horses and knelt beside me. One of them raised my head, and placed his hand over my heart.

"Good news, comrades!" he cried. "His heart still beats!"[19]

Then some brandy was poured down my throat; it put vigour into me, and I was able to open my eyes fully and look around. Lights and shadows were moving among the trees, and I heard men call to one another. They drew together, uttering frightened exclamations; and the lights flashed as the others came pouring out of the cemetery pell-mell, like men possessed. When the further ones came close to us, those who were around me asked them eagerly:

"Well, have you found him?"

The reply rang out hurriedly:

"No! No! Come away quick—quick! This is no place to stay, and on this of all nights!"

"What was it?" was the question, asked in all manner of keys. The answer came variously and all indefinitely as though the men were moved by some common impulse to speak, yet were restrained by some common fear from giving their thoughts.

"It—it—indeed!" gibbered one, whose wits had plainly given out for the moment.

"A wolf—and yet not a wolf!" another put in shudderingly.

"No use trying for him without the sacred bullet," a third remarked in a more ordinary manner.[20]

"Serve us right for coming out on this night! Truly we have earned our thousand marks!" were the ejaculations of a fourth.

"There was blood on the broken marble," another said after a pause—"the lightning never brought that there. And for him—is he safe? Look at his throat! See, comrades, the wolf has been lying on him and keeping his blood warm."

The officer looked at my throat and replied:

"He is all right; the skin is not pierced. What does it all mean? We should never have found him but for the yelping of the wolf."

"What became of it?" asked the man who was holding up my head, and who seemed the least panic-stricken of the party, for his hands were steady and without tremor. On his sleeve was the chevron of a petty officer.

"It went to its home," answered the man, whose long face was pallid, and who actually shook with terror as he glanced around him fearfully. "There are graves enough there in which it may lie. Come, comrades—come quickly! Let us leave this cursed spot."

The officer raised me to a sitting posture, as he uttered a word of command; then several men placed me upon a horse. He sprang to the saddle behind me, took me in his arms, gave the word to advance; and, turning our faces away from the cypresses, we rode away in swift, military order.

As yet my tongue refused its office, and I was perforce silent. I must have fallen asleep; for the next thing I remembered was finding myself standing up, supported by a soldier on each side of me. It was almost broad daylight, and to the north a red streak of sunlight was reflected, like a path of blood, over the waste of snow. The officer was telling the men

20 What causes the soldiers to conclude that this is not a wolf but rather a werewolf or vampire? The folklore is quite confused on the topic of silver, with older Slavic tales reporting that it sickened vampires but did not kill them. Other cultures apply the remedy of silver weapons to virtually all night creatures, vampires as well as were-animals. See, for example, Montague Summers, *The Werewolf in Lore and Legend*.

21 It is not clear what has happened here: the man has not been "vampirised," for his skin has not been pierced. Are we to understand that his throat has been abraded by the animal's licking (to keep him warm somehow)? Wolves use their tongues as means of communication, to show respect, submissiveness, or community. Could the wolf have been attempting to convey a message to the man? And what difference is there between the abrasions caused by a wolf's tongue and those made by a large dog that causes the soldier to so positively identify the abrasions as the "work" of a wolf?

22 There were numerous reports of vampires and werewolves filed by soldiers. See "Dracula's Family Tree" in Part II.

to say nothing of what they had seen, except that they found an English stranger, guarded by a large dog.

"Dog! That was no dog," cut in the man who had exhibited such fear. "I think I know a wolf when I see one."

The young officer answered calmly: "I said a dog."

"Dog!" reiterated the other ironically. It was evident that his courage was rising with the sun; and, pointing to me, he said, "Look at his throat. Is that the work of a dog, master?"

Instinctively I raised my hand to my throat, and as I touched it I cried out in pain.[21] The men crowded round to look, some stooping down from their saddles; and again there came the calm voice of the young officer:

"A dog, as I said. If aught else were said we should only be laughed at."[22]

I was then mounted behind a trooper, and we rode on into the suburbs of Munich. Here we came across a stray carriage, into which I was lifted, and it was driven off to the Quatre Saisons—the young officer accompanying me, whilst a trooper followed with his horse, and the others rode off to their barracks.

When we arrived, Herr Delbrück rushed so quickly down the steps to meet me, that it was apparent he had been watching within. Taking me by both hands he solicitously led me in. The officer saluted me and was turning to withdraw, when I recognized his purpose, and insisted that he should come to my rooms. Over a glass of wine I warmly thanked him and his brave comrades for saving me. He replied simply that he was more than glad, and that Herr Delbrück had at the first taken steps to make all the searching party pleased; at which ambiguous utterance the maître d'hôtel smiled, while the officer pleaded duty and withdrew.

"But Herr Delbrück," I enquired, "how and why was it that the soldiers searched for me?"

He shrugged his shoulders, as if in depreciation of his own deed, as he replied:

"I was so fortunate as to obtain leave from the commander of the regiment in which I served, to ask for volunteers."

"But how did you know I was lost?" I asked.

"The driver came hither with the remains of his carriage, which had been upset when the horses ran away."

"But surely you would not send a search party of soldiers merely on this account?"

"Oh, no!" he answered; "but even before the coachman arrived, I had this telegram from the Boyar[23] whose guest you are," and he took from his pocket a telegram which he handed to me, and I read:

Bistritz.[24]

BE CAREFUL OF MY GUEST—HIS SAFETY IS MOST PRECIOUS TO ME. SHOULD AUGHT HAPPEN TO HIM, OR IF HE BE MISSED, SPARE NOTHING TO FIND HIM AND ENSURE HIS SAFETY. HE IS ENGLISH AND THEREFORE ADVENTUROUS.[25] THERE ARE OFTEN DANGERS FROM SNOW AND WOLVES AND NIGHT. LOSE NOT A MOMENT IF YOU SUSPECT HARM TO HIM. I ANSWER YOUR ZEAL WITH MY FORTUNE.—*Dracula.*"

As I held the telegram in my hand, the room seemed to whirl around me; and, if the attentive maître d'hôtel had not caught me, I think I should have fallen. There was something so strange in all this, something so weird and impossible to imagine, that there grew on me a sense of my being in some way the sport of opposite forces—the mere vague idea of which seemed in a way to paralyse me.[26] I was certainly under some form of mysterious protection. From a distant country had come, in the very nick of time, a message that took me out of the danger of the snow-sleep and the jaws of the wolf.[27]

23 See chapter 2, note 42.

24 Presumably the nearest telegraph office to Dracula's castle.

25 No one would describe Harker's later behaviour as particularly "adventurous"— timorous might be more apt. Perhaps this incident cooled his normal recklessness. Furthermore, Dracula (at least according to the Stoker narrative) expected Peter Hawkins to arrive, an older man, hardly likely to be "adventurous." This suggests that for dramatic reasons, Stoker suppressed the truth: that Hawkins notified Dracula in an earlier letter that he could not travel to Dracula and would be sending Harker instead.

26 What "opposite forces"? The countess and Dracula? The countess appears to be such an ineffectual vampire, who never even touches her intended victim, that the narrator's reaction appears vastly overblown. He has been threatened by a creature of the night and saved by a fortunate lightning bolt. When he could have been frozen to death, he is succoured by a gigantic wolf. Mysterious protection, yes, but only from somewhat minor hazards, it appears. Indeed, the narrator does not even conceive the risk, for he states in the final sentence of his narrative that his danger was "the jaws of the wolf."

27 And so what may we make of the narrative? Without the name "Dracula" appearing in the title and message, there would be very little to connect this traveller's tale with the narrative produced from the Harker Papers. The style is completely different; the narrator shares few characteristics with Jonathan Harker; and the action somehow fails to connect to the story set forth in the Stoker narrative. However, there are numerous references in the Manuscript to some version of the tale eventually published as "Dracula's Guest." Most likely, a different draft—one that identified the narrator as Harker—was included in the Harker Papers and in an early version of Stoker's narrative. It may be that Stoker's publisher requested that the book be shortened, or the publisher (or Stoker) may have felt that the "stylistic" aspects of the narrative were more important than its veracity. For whatever reason, the material was excised, and only later did Stoker return to the material and work it into its published form.

Nosferatu: Phantom der Nacht (*Nosferatu the Vampyre*), starring Klaus Kinski as Graf Orlok.
(Werner Herzog Filmproduktion, 1979)

Appendix 2

THE DATING OF DRACULA

In this matter dates are everything . . .

—MINA HARKER'S JOURNAL

WHEN DID THE events described in the Harker Papers occur? The Notes contain a calendar (with the printed date "189_") upon which dates have been entered by hand against printed days of the week. (See p. 519 for a facsimile of a page of the calendar.) The days and dates appearing on the calendar correspond with the years 1882 and 1893. Rejecting 1882 as too early, many scholars unquestioningly accept 1893 as the only possible year. The only corroboration of this year in the Stoker narrative is a reference that implies the recent death of the eminent physician Jean-Martin Charcot, which occurred in 1893.[1]

However, the "Note" appended by Jonathan Harker at the end of chapter 27 should immediately dispel the notion that the events described in the main body of the narrative occurred in 1893, for Harker's "Note" describes events seven years after the year of the narrative[2] and was published in 1897. Bernard Davies, dean of English *Dracula* scholars, admonished this editor in private correspondence that "there is no perfect solution," but this seems to be a large and definite anachronism simply to ignore. In addition, there are numerous inconsistencies in the Stoker narrative that undercut the 1893 premise, noted variously above.

Students of the Sherlock Holmes canon have spent over seventy years studying the dates of the events described in the chronicles of Dr. John H. Watson, and fifteen chronologies have been published to date attempting to place the sixty stories in their correct order and assign defencible dates to the events described in

---

[1] See chapter 14, note 38.

[2] Or eleven years after, if the Manuscript is viewed as the accurate source.

them.[3] Sherlockian chronologists lean upon cross-references in the stories, partial dates supplied by Dr. Watson, references to the weather and the appearance of the moon, deliveries of the post, historical events, and the like. Likewise, some students of *Dracula* have attempted to apply the same approaches—most notably Leonard Wolf, in *The Annotated Dracula*, who argues for 1887 and largely accepts the calendar dates placed on the events in the narrative. Wolf even suggests, without careful analysis, that the phases of the moon mentioned in the narrative match the year 1887, and he includes in his book a calendar for the year 1887 complete with moon phases. However, as is demonstrated repeatedly above, the narrative's descriptions of the appearance of the moon are in many cases at odds with the astronomical data, and one must conclude that Stoker has added or subtracted moonlight as it suited him to enhance the artistic aspects of the narrative.

Rickey Shanklin reaches an equally unsupported conclusion (quoted in Carol Margaret Davison's "Blood Brothers") that the moon phases support 1890. Peter Haining, in *The Dracula Centenary Book*, supports Wolf's choice of 1887, finding loosely parallel occurrences reported in the press for the year 1887. Kim Newman, in a note at the conclusion of *Anno Dracula*, proposes, without evidence, that the year was 1885.

Elizabeth Miller, perhaps the most sensible of *Dracula* scholars writing today, calls the moon-phase chronologizing "lunacy" and Haining's parallel newspaper articles "reasoning . . . beyond belief," and dismisses Newman's assertion as relying on the use of an "alternate time track" to avoid anachronisms such as references to the "New Woman" (a phrase not in vogue until 1893, according to Miller). "In fact," Miller writes in *Dracula: Sense & Nonsense*, "there is no longer any doubt that the novel is set in 1893."[4] She points to the following evidence:

- The calendar appearing in the Notes;
- Mr. Swales's observation that he has sat on the "suicide seat" for "nigh twenty years past," noting that the suicide died in 1873 (see chapter 6, note 37);
- The establishment of the *Westminster Gazette* in 1893 (see chapter 13, note 54);
- The death of Charcot (see chapter 14, note 38); and
- The day and date of Mr. Hawkins's funeral (see chapter 13, note 42).

---

[3] See, for example, *"The Date Being?"—A Compendium of Chronological Data* by Andrew Jay Peck and Leslie S. Klinger (New York: Magico Magazine, 1996).

[4] Elizabeth Miller, *Dracula: Sense & Nonsense* (Southend-on-Sea, England: Desert Island Books, 2006), 86–88.

However, this "evidence" is not truly conclusive. Swales's comment of "nigh twenty years" leaves leeway. At least one fictional newspaper account is included in the narrative of *Dracula*, and therefore mention of a real newspaper is hardly definitive proof of the events, especially because there is no evidence of publication of the actual article in question. Van Helsing's reference to the death of Charcot may well have been inserted by Stoker, as well as Mina's use of the "New Woman" phrase (for the sentiments respecting New Women were certainly not new in 1893), and as noted above, the day of the week of Hawkins's funeral is not certain. In short, notwithstanding Miller's assertion of the definiteness of 1893, there remains much doubt. This doubt is heightened by an examination of the Manuscript, which makes evident that many of the dates were added late in the process of publication of the narrative and may well be fictional.

A "calendar" page from Bram Stoker's notes for *Dracula*,
ca. 1890–1897.
Reprinted with the permission of Rosenbach Museum and
Library, Phildelphia, PA

It must be admitted that if the "Note" added by Jonathan Harker is accepted as genuine, there are near-fatal problems with the acceptance of a date much earlier than 1889 or 1890. For example, Kodaks were not introduced in Britain until 1888; portable typewriters did not become readily available until after 1890. However, there is also a fatal problem with any date after 1889: it is evident that Stoker could not have seen the Harker Papers before the events described in them occurred. If it is accepted that the Notes are based on Stoker's examination of the Harker Papers, the inescapable conclusion is that the events of the narrative occurred before 8 March 1890, the first date recorded in the Notes.

What can the intelligent reader conclude? Only that large segments of the narrative have been fictionalised, in a careless manner, by Stoker, who inadvertently introduced anachronisms. Any other conclusion can rest only on the contrived theory that the events underlying the narrative never occurred, which must be rejected out of hand. In sum, it is most likely that the events narrated in the Harker Papers and partially recounted in the narrative took place during late 1888 or 1889.

Blood of the Vampire, starring Donald Wolfit as Dr. Callistratus.

(Artistes Alliance Ltd., 1958)

Appendix 3

THE CHRONOLOGY OF DRACULA

[I]f we . . . have every item put in chronological order,

we shall have done much.

—MINA HARKER

Date	Principal Action	Date	Principal Action
24 Apr.	D[1] telegraphs Peter Hawkins.[2]	*12 May*	JH observes D crawling down castle wall.
25 Apr.	JH leaves Exeter, arrives in London.	*15 May*	JH again observes D crawl like "lizard." Encounters three young women in castle, D interferes.
26 Apr.	JH arrives in Paris, departs for Munich.		
1 May	JH leaves Munich.		
2 May	JH arrives in Vienna.	*16 May*	D returns JH to his bed after encounter with three women.
3 May	JH arrives in Bistritz.		
4 May	St. George's Day Eve. JH travels to Borgo Pass, met by D, arrives at Castle Dracula.	*18 May*	JH explores castle. D asks JH to write three letters.
		24 May	LW receives three proposals, from JS, QM, and AH.
6 May	JH examines D's library, converses with D about history of Transylvania.		
		25 May	JS makes first notes about RR, who exhibits no zoöphagy at this time. QM invites AH and JS to gathering on following evening.
8 May	JH observes D is not reflected in mirror, discovers he is a prisoner.		
9 May	JH receives another history lesson from D. MH (at school?) reports to LW that she has just heard from JH in Transylvania.	*26 May*	AH accepts invitation.
		28 May	Szgany come to castle. JH attempts to bribe them to post his letters. D returns letters.
10 or 11 May (approx.)			
	LW (in "Chatham Street") tells MH about AH, JS. Reveals that she loves AH, who "often comes to see" LW and her mother.	*31 May*	JH discovers all writing materials gone, as well as his suit.
		5 Jun.	JS observes RR collecting flies.

[1] The following abbreviations are used in this table: D=Dracula, JH=Jonathan Harker, MH=Mina Murray Harker, AH=Arthur Holmwood, QM=Quincey Morris, RR=R. M. Renfield, JS=John Seward, VH=Abraham Van Helsing, LW=Lucy Westenra. There are numerous date conflicts between the Notes and the published narrative; the dates reflected here, unless otherwise indicated, follow the published text.

[2] The first three entries here are detailed only in the Notes.

Date	Principal Action	Date	Principal Action
17 Jun.	JH observes Szgany bringing boxes to castle.	*26 Jul.*	MH receives letter from JH, forwarded by Peter Hawkins and dated from castle, stating JH is starting for home. Records that LW has "lately" taken to sleepwalking.
18 Jun.	JS observes RR collecting spiders.		
23 Jun.	JH observes D in JH's suit, sees women materialise. Peasant woman accuses JH of taking her child.	*27 Jul.*	More sleepwalking previous night. AH called home, to see his ill father.
25 Jun.	JH resolves action. Climbs from room and discovers D in great box of earth.	*28 Jul.*	*Demeter* concludes four days of storm.
		29 Jul.	Second mate of *Demeter* disappears.
29 Jun.	D tells JH that JH will leave on following day; D will not be there.	*30 Jul.*	More crew of *Demeter* disappear; only two hands, mate, and captain remain.
30 Jun.	JH again climbs from room, finds D in box of earth. JH attacks D in box, gashing D's forehead. JH resolves to flee.	*1 Aug.*	*Demeter* running in fog, mate demoralised.
		2 Aug.	*Demeter* through Straits of Dover and into North Sea; another crew-member disappears.
1 Jul.	JS observes RR eat fly.		
6 Jul.	*Demeter* sails from Varna with cargo of boxes of earth.	*3 Aug.*	LW sleepwalking less, but MH observes "odd concentration." No news from JH. Another crew-member of *Demeter* disappears; mate goes mad, claiming "*He* is there," and jumps overboard, leaving only captain.
8 Jul.	JS observes RR has captured sparrow.		
11 Jul.	*Demeter* enters Bosphorus.		
12 Jul.	*Demeter* through Dardanelles and into Aegean.		
13 Jul.	*Demeter* crew "dissatisfied" and "scared."	*4 Aug.*	*Demeter* in fog. Last logbook entry: captain sees "Him," ties himself to wheel.
14 Jul.	*Demeter* crew badly disturbed.		
16 Jul.	One *Demeter* crew-member missing; report that "*something*" is aboard.	*6 Aug.*	No news from JH. Mr. Swales appears morbid. *Demeter* spotted off Whitby shore.
17 Jul.	Report of "strange man" aboard *Demeter*. Search of ship conducted.	*7 Aug.*	Tempest in Whitby; *Demeter* wrecked early on following morning. LW "restless all night," gets up twice (in her sleep) and dresses herself.
19 Jul.	RR requests kitten; JS concludes he is an "undeveloped homicidal maniac."		
20 Jul.	JS concludes RR has eaten sparrow colony and classifies him as a "zoöphagus . . . maniac."	*8 Aug.*	*Demeter* wrecked in Whitby, large dog (D) disembarks. LW and MH visit Whitby harbour.
22 Jul.	*Demeter* passes Gibraltar; no disturbances since search.	*9 Aug.*	Whitby solicitor S. F. Billington takes possession of boxes onboard *Demeter*. Local Whitby dog found dead. Reporter inspects logbook of *Demeter*.
23 Jul.	Another *Demeter* crew-member disappears.		
24 Jul.	LW meets MH in Whitby; they meet local man, Mr. Swales. *Demeter* enters Bay of Biscay; crew panicked.	*10 Aug.*	Funeral of *Demeter*'s captain. Mr. Swales found dead. Local dog terrorised near "suicide seat" in Whitby cemetery. LW and MH walk to Robin Hood's Bay.
25 Jul.[3]	MH and LW converse with Mr. Swales. MH has not heard from JH.		

[3] The narrative erroneously dates Mina's journal entry "1 August."

Date	Principal Action	Date	Principal Action
11 Aug.	LW "sleepwalks" to Whitby cemetery. MH observes "long and black" figure bent over LW, "pin-pricks" on LW's throat. LW sleeps late.	*24 Aug.*	AH observes LW looking ill. LW has "another bad night." JH and MH marry in Buda-Pesth.
12 Aug.	At night, MH locks room; LW wakes MH trying to get out. Sister Agatha writes to MH that JH is in her care in Buda-Pesth and has been for "nearly six weeks."	*31 Aug.*	AH requests that JS come to Hillingham.
		1 Sep.	AH summoned to see worsening father. JS examines LW at Hillingham, writes to VH in Amsterdam.
13 Aug.	LW, in her sleep, points to window; MH observes "great bat."	*2 Sep.*	JS informs AH of his diagnosis. VH leaves for London.
14 Aug.	At sunset, LW and MH observe figure seated on "suicide seat." MH goes out for late-night walk; on her return sees LW at window with a "good-sized bird." LW is looking pale and haggard.	*3 Sep.*	JS and VH travel to Hillingham, examine LW. RR has outburst just before noon.
		4 Sep.	LW better. At 5 P.M., RR claims "he has deserted me." At sunset RR has another outburst. VH returns to Amsterdam.
15 Aug.	LW languid, tired. AH's father better. Mrs. Westenra tells MH she has not long to live.	*5 Sep.*	LW better.
		6 Sep.	LW relapses (D presumably visited her on night of 5 Sep.).
17 Aug.	MH observes LW has grown weaker and that MH often has found her at night sitting by open window. MH notices "pin-pricks" have not healed. S. F. Billington ships fifty boxes to Carter, Paterson & Co., for delivery to King's Cross next day. Presumably D is in one of boxes, departing Whitby. LW sleeps well.	*7 Sep.*	VH returns to London. AH transfuses LW. VH departs London for Amsterdam.
		8 Sep.	LW expresses fear of sleeping but has restful night under JS's watch.
		9 Sep.	JS sleeps next door to LW; she is attacked again.
18 Aug.	LW recounts her "out-of-body" experience on night of 11 Aug. RR excited: "the Master is at hand."	*10 Sep.*	VH returns from Amsterdam. JS transfuses LW; she has restful night.
19 Aug.	RR escapes from asylum, runs to Carfax. MH receives letter from Buda-Pesth hospital about JH.	*12 Sep.*	Garlands of garlic arrive, and LW expects restful night although unguarded by VH or JS.
20 Aug.	RR talks to JS, tells him he doesn't need cats, he "can wait." JS notes cycles of daytime excitement, nighttime quietude.	*13 Sep.*	Mrs. Westenra removes garlic garlands. LW is attacked again. VH transfuses LW.
21 Aug.	Carter, Paterson acknowledges receipt of boxes and transfer per instructions. MH in Buda-Pesth.	*14 or 15 Sep. (approx.)* MH and JH return from Buda-Pesth; are met by Peter Hawkins, who invites them to live with him and tells them he has left them everything.	
22 Aug.	LW remains in Whitby, stops sleepwalking, feels recovered, congratulates MH. Announces wedding to be held 28 Sep.	*17 Sep.*	All well at Hillingham. D visits London Zoo; wolf breaks out of cage before midnight. RR attacks JS with dinner knife. VH telegrams JS to be on watch, delivery delayed; VH leaves London for Amsterdam. Wolf breaks through window at Hillingham, attacks LW and Mrs. Westenra. Mrs. Westenra dies.
23 Aug.	RR escapes again, again runs to Carfax. LW at Hillingham, has dreams as at Whitby.		

Date	Principal Action	Date	Principal Action
18 Sep.	Wolf returns to Zoo. JS meets VH in street, break into Hillingham, discover servants drugged, Mrs. Westenra dead, LW near death. QM transfuses LW. Peter Hawkins dies.	*30 Sep.*	JH interviews station-master at King's Cross and personnel at Carter, Paterson, then travels to Purfleet. JS realises D is at Carfax. RR calm. AH and QM read MH's transcripts; MH comforts them. MH meets RR. VH arrives at Purfleet; council held, and JH, VH, QM, AH, and JS go off to search Carfax. Before they leave, JS, VH, QM, and AH meet with RR, who requests release. MH attacked by D.
19 Sep.	JS, VH, and QM sit with LW. AH is summoned to Hillingham by telegram.		
20 Sep.	Carriers call on Carfax, are verbally attacked by RR. RR escapes, physically attacks carriers. LW dies.		
21–22 Sep.		*1 Oct.*	JH interviews Thomas Snelling, Joseph Smollet.
	Funerals of LW and Mrs. Westenra. Funeral of Mr. Hawkins. JH sees D outside Guiliano's. JH and MH return to Exeter. AH returns to Ring with QM. VH leaves for Amsterdam. Likely first appearance of "bloofer lady."	*2 Oct.*	JH interviews Sam Bloxam, house agents. In evening, RR attacked by D, dies. JS, VH, AH, and QM rush to Harkers' room, find D, JH, and MH together.
23 Sep.	VH returns from Amsterdam. MH reads JH's journal. Bloofer lady preys on children on Hampstead Heath.	*3 Oct.*	MH, JH, JS, VH, QM, and AH meet to plan. MH remains at asylum; the men travel to Carfax and Piccadilly house, "destroying" boxes. QM and AH go to other lairs to destroy them. JS, VH, and JH receive telegram from MH alerting them to D's impending visit. QM and AH return from Piccadilly. D confronts men, escapes, goes to dock to arrange passage.
24 Sep.	Further attacks by bloofer lady. MH begins transcribing JH's journal. VH requests MH's help.		
25 Sep.	VH visits MH in Exeter; MH gives VH transcription of JH's journal.		
26 Sep.	VH returns to Exeter to visit JH and MH. VH reads newspaper accounts of bloofer lady. RR acting sane. VH shows newspaper accounts to JS. VH and JS visit child victim, Westenra tomb. Coffin empty.	*4 Oct.*	MH suggests hypnosis, discovers D onboard ship, which has sailed. Men determine which ship, return for general meeting. Decide to pursue D.
27 Sep.	In early morning, JS and VH see white figure near Westenra tomb, find child. Return to tomb in afternoon, find LW in coffin. VH decides not to stake LW without AH, keeps watch in cemetery.	*5 Oct.*	VH expresses concern about MH "turning," suggests excluding MH. Another meeting, from which MH excludes herself. VH proposes leaving MH behind.
		6 Oct.	MH convinces VH she must accompany group.
28 Sep.	AH, QM, VH, and JS meet, proceed to cemetery at midnight.	*11 Oct.*	MH swears men to slay her if she turns.
29 Sep.	In early morning, LW returns to tomb, confronts AH, QM, VH, and JS, who rescue another child. AH, QM, VH, and JS return to tomb at noon. AH stakes LW. JS meets MH at train station. MH begins transcribing JS's phonographic diary. JH meets with solicitor Billington in Whitby, travels to London.	*12 Oct.*	Party departs for Paris, where they board Orient Express.
		15 Oct.	Party arrives in Varna.
		16 Oct.	*Czarina Catherine* en route.
		17 Oct.	Party arranges to meet D in Varna.
		24 Oct.	Ship reported in Dardanelles.

Date	Principal Action
25 Oct.	Party expects arrival of ship in Varna. MH begins to display signs of proximity of D.
27 Oct.	No sign of ship.
28 Oct.	Ship enters port of Galatz. Party plans to travel to Galatz.
29 Oct.	Travel by train to Galatz.
30 Oct.	Party arrives in Galatz. JH, VH, and JS interview Capt. Donelson. Body of Skinsky discovered. MH deduces D's plan. Party splits up and hurriedly departs from Galatz. JH and AH travel on steam launch, QM and JS by horseback. MH and VH leave by rail for Veresti.
31 Oct.	MH and VH arrive in Veresti and depart by carriage.
1 Nov.	JH and AH pass into the Bistritza at Fundu. MH and VH continue by carriage towards Borgo Pass.
2 Nov.	JH and AH expect to arrive in Strasba. QM and JS continue on road, having lost sight of steam launch. MH convinces VH to let her drive, continue on towards Pass.
3 Nov.	QM and JS arrive at Fundu. MH and VH arrive at Borgo Pass just after sunrise.
4 Nov.	Launch detained by accident at rapids. MH and VH apparently lost, looking for castle.
5 Nov.	VH and MH, apparently near castle, terrorised by vampire women. At dawn, JS and QM see Szgany leave river with a leiter-waggon. VH destroys vampire women, "cleanses" castle.
6 Nov.	VH and MH leave castle vicinity, travel eastward to vantage point, watch convergence of JS, QM, JH, AH, and Szgany. D destroyed at sunset.

The Return of Dracula, starring Francis Lederer as Dracula.
(Gramercy Pictures, 1958)

Appendix 4

A WHITBY GLOSSARY

I did not quite understand his dialect . . .

—MINA HARKER

Whitby Dialect	English
aboon	up
acant	leaning to one side
acrewk'd	one side twisted
addle	to earn money, to settle down
ageeanwards	towards
air-blebs	bubbles
airt	quarter or direction
anent	concerning
antherums	doubts or hesitations
aught	anything
bairns	children
balm-bowl	chamber pot
bans	curses
bar-guests	terrifying apparitions, taking human or animal shape
belderin'	blubbering
belly-timber	food
beuk-bodies	learned persons
bogles	hobgoblins
boh-ghosts	terrifying apparitions, taking human or animal shape
caffin'	jeering
chafts	jaws
clegs	horseflies

527

Whitby Dialect	English
comers	visitors
consate	imagine
crammle	hobble (with corns on one's feet)
creed	believe
daffled	weak-minded with age
deeath-sark	shroud
dooal	grieve
dowps	carrion birds
dozzened	shriveled
fash	trouble
feet-folks	tourists
gang	go
gawm	understand
grees	stairs
greet	weep
grims	ghosts
hafflin's	half-wits
haped	buried
hoast	mist
illsome	disposed to evil
jouped	jumbled together
keckle	chuckle
kirk-garth	churchyard
krok-hooal	grave
lamiter	deformed person
laybeds	graves
masel'	myself
quare scowderment	a confused jumble
sairly	sorely, severely
skeer an' scunner	frighten
snod an' snog	smooth and compact
thruff-stean	table tomb covering the entire body
tombsteans	tombstones
toom	empty
trimmlin'	trembling
wafts	ghosts
yabblins	possibly

Part II

CONDISERING THE COUNT

He certainly is a wonderfully
interesting study.

—DR. JOHN SEWARD

Blood of Dracula (*Blood of the Demon*, also *Blood Is My Heritage*),
starring Sandra Harrison as Nancy Perkins.
(American International Pictures, 1957)

DRACULA AFTER STOKER
Fictional Accounts of the Count

Do you know all the mystery of life and death?

—PROFESSOR ABRAHAM VAN HELSING

AFTER *DRACULA*, STORIES and books about vampires multiplied in ever-widening circles, "as the ripples from a stone thrown in the water," in Van Helsing's words. Although scholar Margaret L. Carter considers *Dracula* to be a work of fiction, she is accurate in her assessment that "[m]ore quickly and thoroughly than any work of fiction in any other field . . . Bram Stoker's *Dracula* became the definitive model for subsequent vampire fiction."[1] Subsequent writing can be divided into two broad categories: vampire tales with no direct reference to *Dracula* and serious works considering the events described in *Dracula* and later events. The first category is enormous, and its detailed consideration

Raymond Rudorff, *The Dracula Archives* (1971).

---

[1] Margaret L. Carter, "Share Alike: *Dracula* and the Sympathetic Vampire in Mid-Twentieth Century Pulp Fiction," in *Bram Stoker's Dracula: Sucking Through the Century, 1897–1997*, ed. Carol Margaret Davison (Toronto: Dundurn Press, 1997), 175.

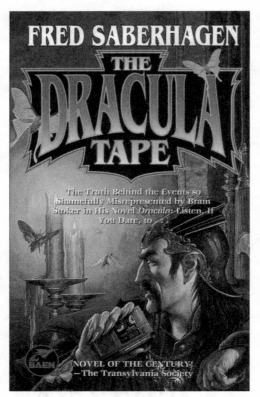

Fred Saberhagen, *The Dracula Tape* (1975).

is well beyond the scope of this material.[2] A few of the more important works—the books of Anne Rice and Chelsea Quinn Yarbro, and the chronicles of Buffy the vampire slayer—are considered in "Dracula's Family Tree" below.

The earliest reinterpretation of the Stoker narrative is Raymond Rudorff's *The Dracula Archives* (1971). Recounting events leading up to Jonathan Harker's meeting with the Count (and explicitly dated from 1876 to 1890), the work exposes the vampire lord's preparations for conquest and suggests that Van Helsing's destruction of the Dracula line was not as complete as he had hoped. Dracula is depicted as unalterably evil, however, having lost all aspects of his humanity when he was transformed into an undead being.

Fred Saberhagen's *The Dracula Tape* (1975) is an amusing, fresh look at the events described in Stoker's narrative. Saberhagen posits that Dracula is innocent of any crimes, his activities misunderstood; all he sought was to be accepted as "normal." Van Helsing is the bigoted villain of the piece, who kills Lucy with his mistyped blood transfusions and leads the superstitious lot of hunters to pursue Dracula ruthlessly. Dracula ends up faking his death to gain relief from his tormentors and happily pursues a casual relationship with Mina Harker for many years.

Saberhagen's book was a success, and not surprisingly, he turned to more tales of the "good" Count Dracula. One of the more interesting of the series[3] is *The Holmes-Dracula File* (1978), in which Dracula and Sherlock Holmes work together to defeat a dastardly plot by John Seward (!). The series goes back

---

[2] For a bibliography of the genre, see Sharon A. Russell, James Craig Holte, and Mary Pharr, "Vampire Fiction and Criticism: A Core Collection," in *The Blood Is the Life: Vampires in Literature*, ed. Leonard G. Heldreth and Mary Pharr (Bowling Green, OH: Bowling Green State Univ. Popular Press, 1999), 261–66; and for a fine collection of examples of the genre, David J. Skal, ed., *Vampires: Encounters with the Undead* (New York: Black Dog & Leventhal, 2001) is recommended.

[3] The series includes *The Holmes-Dracula File* (1978), *An Old Friend of the Family* (1979), *Thorn* (1980), *Dominion* (1982), *A Matter of Taste* (1990), *A Question of Time* (1992), *Seance for a Vampire* (1994), in which Dr. Watson seeks Dracula's help in tracing a missing Holmes, *A Sharpness in the Neck* (1996), and *A Coldness in the Blood* (2002). Dracula seems to be less and less vampiric and more of a superhero as the series progresses.

and forth in time, from Chicago in the 1990s to Dracula's origins, and often finds Dracula combatting vampiric enemies—vampires who don't share his taste for doing good.

The interconnection between Dracula and Sherlock Holmes has been explored in other books as well. Mystery writer Loren Estleman began his career with *Sherlock Holmes vs. Dracula: or, The Adventure of the Sanguinary Count* (1978), a "corrective" to the Stoker narrative, revealing Holmes's critical rôle in the defeat of the Count. *Scarlet in Gaslight* (1987–1988), a series of four comic books by Martin Powell and Seppo Makinen, traces a complex tale of Holmes versus Moriarty, involving Van Helsing, Lucy Westenra, actress Sarah Bernhardt, and Dracula (who allies with Holmes to defeat the undead Moriarty). In David Stuart Davies's *A Tangled Skein* (1995), Holmes must solve a series of mysterious murders on Hampstead Heath, leading to Dracula.[4]

Tangentially involving the Holmes brothers (Sherlock and Mycroft) but exploring the future of Dracula in a serious but highly entertaining manner is Kim Newman's *Anno Dracula* (1992) and its sequels.[5] Newman assumes that Van Helsing and

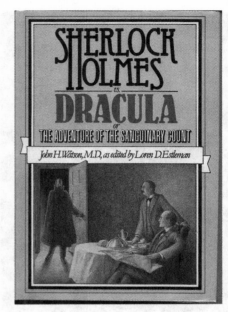

Loren Estleman, *Sherlock Holmes vs. Dracula: or, The Adventure of the Sanguinary Count* (1978).

Martin Powell and Seppo Makinen, *Scarlet in Gaslight* (1987–1988).

---

[4] There are considerably more: In *The Incredible Umbrella* by Marvin Kaye (1979), J. Adrian Phillimore encounters Holmes, Moriarty, and Count Dracula; in *Dracula's Diary* by Michael Geare and Michael Corby (1982), a not overly funny tale of Dracula's youth, Dracula pays a short visit to Baker Street; *The Dracula Caper* by Simon Hawke (no. 8 in the "Time Wars" series; 1988) pits Arthur Conan Doyle, H. G. Wells, and Bram Stoker against Dracula; and *A Night in the Lonesome October* by Roger Zelazny (1993), brilliantly illustrated by Gahan Wilson, recounts a gathering of living and undead villains in London—one is "the Count who sleeps by day," who must confront the "Great Detective." There are also several short stories and comic books featuring this inevitable encounter.

[5] Newman's "Anno Dracula" universe now includes *Anno Dracula* (set in 1888), *The Bloody Red Baron* (set in 1914–1918), *Dracula Cha Cha Cha* (also published as

Kim Newman, *Anno Dracula* (1992).

his colleagues failed in their attempt to destroy Dracula, who has gone on to establish himself firmly in London. He becomes prince consort to Victoria and by royal decree makes England safe for vampires, establishing them in nearly every position of authority and prestige. *Anno Dracula* traces Dracula's conflict with the Diogenes Club, a secret fraternity organised by Mycroft Holmes. Many figures from Stoker's narrative appear, and some from the Harker Papers as well: Mina Harker's friend Kate Reed, for example, becomes a vampire and appears in many of Newman's tales. Involving much more of fin-de-siècle London than is mentioned here, including the shocking identity of Jack the Ripper, the book explores how mortals are seduced by the attractions of vampirism and how the need for vampiric sustenance is only an extension of the social order.

In Newman's *The Bloody Red Baron* (1995), Dracula has been expelled from England and finds new status and power as the chancellor of Kaiser Wilhelm, helping to creating an air force of vampires under the vampirised Baron von Richthofen. Not until 1959 does Dracula die, on the eve of his wedding to a Transylvanian princess, destroyed by a mysterious assailant in Fellini's Rome, surrounded by la dolce vita. Scholar David L. Hammer concurs with Newman's view of the potential "civilization" of the traditional monster, writing, "Vampirism stands a fair chance of being regarded as essentially an eccentricity in England, provided of course the vampire observes good form, adheres to what is proper, eschews excessive public displays, and doesn't harm birds or animals."[6]

Judgment of Tears; set in 1959 and including the death of Dracula), the novella "Red Reign" (expanded into *Anno Dracula*), and the post-Dracula tales of his descendants: "Coppola's Dracula" (set in 1976), "Castle in the Desert" (in 1977), "Andy Warhol's Dracula" (in 1978), "Who Dares Wins" (in 1980), "The Other Side of Midnight" (in 1981), and "You Are the Wind Beneath My Wings" (in 1984). Some of these tales have been published in Newman's books (the three novels); others have appeared in collections or on the Internet. Newman's works incorporate numerous figures from other allegedly fictional sources; for a near-exhaustive compilation by Win Scott Eckert and others of the sources (books, films, television) in which many of these persons first appear, see www.pjfarmer.com/woldnewton/AnnoDracula.htm.

[6] David L. Hammer, *For the Sake of the Game* (Dubuque, IA: Gasogene Press, 1986), 240.

Marv Wolfman's highly successful series of comic books, published under the titles *The Tomb of Dracula* and *Dracula Lives!* (1972–1979), also imagine the adventures of Dracula after his encounter with Van Helsing. Spanning the fifteenth century to the present, these tales present Dracula as neither good nor evil. Many are drawn to him who seek immortality or power, but he goes his own way, simply surviving. In modern times, he is pursued by a team of hunters led by Quincey Harker, son of Mina and Jonathan, and including a descendant of Van Helsing and a mortal descendant of Dracula. In the final issue, Dracula spurns an offer of immortal love, observing to the female vampire that all vampires must remain apart from and above the human "cattle," and returns—alone—to his tomb.

Elizabeth Kostova's best seller *The Historian* (2005) also embraces the Stoker narrative. Paul, the historian of the title, was drawn as a student into an historical search for Vlad the Impaler. Paul's daughter narrates the story,

Marv Wolfman,
The Essential Tomb of Dracula.
(vol. 1. New York: Marvel Comics, 2003)

telling of her exploration of her parents' mysterious past. Through the study of ancient texts and the unearthing of clues scattered across Europe, she discovers that Vlad (or Dracula) remains sufficiently powerful to block those seeking to find him. Dracula himself appears in only a few scenes in the book, but the story he reveals of his origin and subsequent activities is well grounded in history and connected tightly to Stoker's narrative.

The powerful story conveyed in Stoker's narrative, with its ambiguities and uncertainties, is likely to continue to challenge writers for many years. While some criticise writings such as Saberhagen's or Newman's as "pastiche"—a word coined from the Italian *pasticcio*, a pastry, to describe imitative works and connoting a dessertlike quality to such fare—there can be sustenance in such writings. Author/filmmaker Nicholas Meyer, himself a "pastichist," points out that just as the limited text of the Catholic Mass has inspired practitioners from Vivaldi to Leonard Bernstein to create highly rewarding musical variations on the text, so too may great narratives inspire other authors to create important "variations."[7] The Harker Papers and Stoker's interpretation will continue to induce future generations to ponder in art the truth of Dracula's history.

[7] Nicholas Meyer, "Sherlock Holmes, Wine Bottles, and the Catholic Mass," *Baker Street Journal* 48, 1 (March 1998): 12–25. Meyer (author of the highly acclaimed *Seven Per-Cent Solution* [1974], a novel reimagining a period of the life of Sherlock Holmes) explained that pouring his "new wine" into the bottle that was Arthur Conan Doyle's Sherlock Holmes was an invigorating restriction and that his writing was motivated by the dual love of the original tales and detestation of the quality of the copies produced by others.

SEX, LIES, AND BLOOD
Dracula in Academia

. . . we have sources of science; we are free to act and think . . .

—PROFESSOR ABRAHAM VAN HELSING

PERHAPS BECAUSE OF its popularity (until recently, "popularity" seemed to brand a work as being of little interest to academia), perhaps because of its subject matter, *Dracula* was not a subject for academic or critical scrutiny for almost sixty years after its publication. One of the earliest "serious" considerations of Stoker's narrative was part of a larger study by Maurice Richardson in 1959, titled "The Psychoanalysis of Ghost Stories."[1] Richardson urged a Freudian interpretation, calling Dracula a "huge father-figure" and the narrative "a quite blatant demonstration of the Oedipal complex."[2] He also casually suggested that a Marxist interpretation of *Dracula* was plausible.[3] Others made similar suggestions of psychological complexity in passing—for

[1] Maurice Richardson, "The Psychoanalysis of Ghost Stories," *Twentieth Century* 166 (1959): 419–31, extracted as "The Psychoanalysis of Count Dracula" in *Vampyres: Lord Byron to Count Dracula*, ed. Christopher Frayling (London: Faber and Faber, 1991), 418–22. Richardson (1907–1978) was a well-known British writer and critic who wrote numerous short pieces for such publications as *Lilliput*, the *Times Literary Supplement*, and the *Daily Telegraph*, and several books, including his best known, *Exploits of Engelbrecht* (1950), a collection of fantasies about a dwarf sportsman. Richardson was fascinated by cults and wrote an important reminiscence of Aleister Crowley, the self-styled "Beast 666," titled "Luncheon with Beast 666," reprinted posthumously in Richardson's collection of essays *Fits and Starts* (1979).

[2] Richardson was well aware of the seminal "On the Vampire" by Ernest Jones, the famous protegé and biographer of Sigmund Freud, first published in 1931 in *On the Nightmare* (New York: Liveright Publishing). As early as 22 December 1957, Richardson hinted at Freudian themes to be explored in *Dracula*, writing in the *Observer* that the work "deploys a powerful psychological situation."

[3] Karl Marx wrote in *Das Kapital* (1867, thirty years before *Dracula*): "Capital is dead labour which, vampire-like, lives only by sucking living labour, and lives the more, the more labour it sucks." (New York: Modern Library, 1906.) Another early study of the narrative is Richard Wasson, "The Politics of *Dracula*," *English Literature in Transition* 9 (1966): 24–7.

La Noche de Walpurgis (The Werewolf vs. Vampire Woman),
starring Patty Shepard as Countess Wandessa d'Arville de Nadasdy.
(HIFI Stereo, 1972)

example, Anthony Boucher, mystery writer, critic, and eminent Sherlockian, in his introduction to the 1965 Limited Editions Club *Dracula*.

Eventually, the trickle of studies became a steady stream. Certainly the most influential was Raymond McNally and Radu Florescu's 1972 *In Search of Dracula* (updated in 1994). Although published before the authors' discovery of the Notes, it marked the earliest significant study of the historical background of the narrative. Gabriel Ronay's *The Truth about Dracula*, also published in 1972, traces the folkloric and historical backgrounds for Stoker's narrative. Ronay includes a history of Vlad the Impaler and Countess Elizabeth Bathory (a Magyar who, in the late sixteenth and early seventeenth centuries, murdered young women to bathe in their blood and so, she believed, preserve her beauty and youth), whose histories he calls sources for Stoker's narrative. Ronay also points out the chilling use of the vampire legends in Nazi myths.[4]

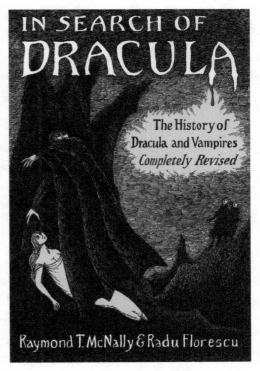

Raymond T. McNally and Radu Florescu,
In Search of Dracula (1994).

Ignoring the historical material, Joseph S. Bierman's "Dracula: Prolonged Childhood Illness, and the Oral Triad" also appeared in 1972, to some extent following in the trail of Richardson's psychoanalysis but going far beyond Richardson in exploring Stoker's psychological history in studying the narrative.[5] At about the same time, Christopher F. Bentley's "The Monster in the Bedroom: Sexual Symbolism in Bram Stoker's *Dracula*"[6] appeared, with analyses of what Bentley terms the "perverse" sexual imagery of the narrative. Bentley's paper draws heavily on the works of Freud and

---

[4] Gabriel Ronay, *The Truth about Dracula* (New York: Stein and Day, 1972), 157–63. Other early important studies of historical and folkloric sources are Bacil F. Kirtley, "*Dracula*, The Monastic Chronicles and Slavic Folklore," *Midwest Folklore* 6 (1956): 133–39, reprinted in *Dracula: The Vampire and the Critics*, ed. Margaret L. Carter (Ann Arbor, MI: UMI Research Press, 1988), 11–17, and Grigore Nandris, "The Historical Dracula: The Theme of His Legend in the Western and in the Eastern Literatures of Europe," *Comparative Literature Studies* 3 (1966): 367–96.

[5] Joseph S. Bierman, "Dracula: Prolonged Childhood Illness, and the Oral Triad," *American Imago* 29 (1972): 186–98. Of course, the study of Stoker's psychology is important only in understanding how he may have twisted the Harker Papers to dispel his own personal demons.

[6] Christopher F. Bentley, "The Monster in the Bedroom: Sexual Symbolism in Bram Stoker's *Dracula*," *Literature and Psychology* 22 (1972): 27–34.

Ernest Jones, especially the latter's 1931 essay "On the Vampire."

The stream became a river by the late 1970s and early 1980s, as critical studies of vampire histories and literature in general and *Dracula* in particular proliferated. Elizabeth Miller's *Bram Stoker's Dracula: A Documentary Volume* (2005) lists in its "Checklist for Reference and Further Reading" over 250 works of *Dracula* criticism and dozens of bibliographical references and annotated editions.

The Stoker narrative obviously provides ample material for weaving complex theories. As Ken Gelder observes in *Reading the Vampire*, it is dense, with shifting points of view, and "brings together a multiplicity of discursive fields—ethnography, imperialist ideologies, medicine, criminality, discourses of degeneration (and, conversely, evolution), physiognomy, . . . feminism, . . . 'masculinism,' occultism, and so on."[7] A sampling of critical themes and critical approaches follows.

Regarding Stoker's narrative techniques, early critics complain that the style of the narrative was derived from Wilkie Collins but was not as well executed. Later studies point out how the different voices ("polyphony," as one writer describes it) encourage questioning the views of the vampire hunters—see, for example, Carol Senf's 1979 "*Dracula:* The Unseen Face in the Mirror."[8] Others have studied in detail the Notes and the process of creating the narrative. David Seed, in "The Narrative Method of *Dracula*," and Alan P. Johnson, in "Bent and Broken Necks: Signs of Design in Stoker's *Dracula*,"[9] observe the "doubling" of characters. Seed points out that narration in itself is a significant theme of the work: "Since understanding Dracula is a necessary precondition to defeating him, the exchange and accumulation of information literally is resistance to him."[10]

The sexual aspects of the work have been scrutinised with almost prurient interest. Christopher Bentley, mentioned earlier, calls Stoker's narrative "quasi-pornography." Maurice Richardson, also noted above, observes that *Dracula* engages "in a kind of incestuous, necrophilious, oral-anal-sadistic, all-in wrestling match."[11] "James Twitchell, in "The Vampire Myth," describes

---

[7] Ken Gelder, *Reading the Vampire* (London: Routledge, 1994), 65.

[8] Carol Senf, "*Dracula:* The Unseen Face in the Mirror," *Journal of Narrative Technique* 9 (1979): 160–70.

[9] David Seed, "The Narrative Method of *Dracula*," *Nineteenth Century Fiction* 40 (1985): 61–75, and Alan P. Johnson, "Bent and Broken Necks: Signs of Design in Stoker's *Dracula*," *Victorian Newsletter* 72 (1987): 17–24.

[10] Seed, "The Narrative Method."

[11] Richardson, 418.

the events of the narrative as "sex without genitalia, sex without confusion, sex without responsibility, sex without guilt, sex without love—better yet, sex without mention."[12] No contemporary critic raised the subject. Clive Leatherdale concludes: "The sexuality with which *Dracula* seethes was able to titillate Victorian readers by being symbolic and hidden. It could therefore be enjoyed without admitting the nature of the pleasure."[13]

The critics have not ignored the homoerotic aspects of the narrative. For example, Christopher Craft, in "'Kiss Me with Those Red Lips': Gender and Inversion in Bram Stoker's *Dracula*," claims that the anxiety caused by the journals of Jonathan Harker which form the opening chapters of the narrative is largely the result of the sexual threat that they evoke: "that Dracula will seduce, penetrate, drain another male. . . . Always postponed and never directly enacted, this desire finds evasive fulfillment in . . . heterosexual displacements."[14] Similarly, Marjorie Howes, in "The Mediation of the Feminine: Bisexuality, Homoerotic Desire, and Self-Expression in Bram Stoker's *Dracula*," calls the fears and fantasies evoked by the narrative "exclusively male." "Because the fundamental ambivalences . . . revolve around an issue which few fin de siècle texts could discuss explicitly, male homosexuality," suggests Howes, "*Dracula* uses the feminine to displace and mediate the anxiety-causing elements of masculine character, representing the forbidden desires that men fear in themselves as monstrous femininity."[15]

Several seminal works that use psychoanalysis as a tool for dissection and interpretation have been mentioned previously. Of course, the narrative is filled with material ripe for the analyst. Teeth, long knives, stakes—phallic symbols—as well as numerous families with one or more missing parents, plus the dreamlike nature of several sequences and the constant presence of the insane asylum all lend weight to the theme. In "Good Men and Monsters: The Defenses of *Dracula*," Thomas Byers sees the narrative as expressing a fear of male dependence, overcome by destruction of the vampire and preservation of

[12] James Twitchell, "The Vampire Myth," *American Imago* 37 (1980): 88. See also Judith Weissman, "Women and Vampires: *Dracula* as a Victorian Novel," *Midwest Quarterly* 18 (1977): 392–405.

[13] Clive Leatherdale, *Dracula: The Novel & The Legend: A Study of Bram Stoker's Gothic Masterpiece* (Westcliff-on-Sea, England: Desert Island Books, 2001), 172.

[14] Christopher Craft, " 'Kiss Me with Those Red Lips': Gender and Inversion in Bram Stoker's *Dracula*," *Representations* 8 (1984): 107–33.

[15] Marjorie Howes, "The Mediation of the Feminine: Bisexuality, Homoerotic Desire, and Self-Expression in Bram Stoker's *Dracula*," *Texas Studies in Literature and Language* 30 (1988): 104–19. See also Talia Schaffer, " 'Wilde Desire Took Me': The Homoerotic History of *Dracula*," *ELH* 61 (1994): 381–425.

the male hierarchy, and Laurence A. Rickels's *The Vampire Lectures* revisits the Oedipal theme.[16]

The narrative is viewed as Christian allegory. As the anti-Christ, Dracula reverses virtually every aspect of the depictions of Christ. Perhaps most strikingly, Dracula drinks the blood of the "faithful," rather than the opposite. Although both offer resurrection and immortality, one promotes the path of good and the other evil. As Clive Leatherdale points out,[17] folkloric precautions such as garlic ultimately fail to deter Dracula; only Christian symbols—the crucifix and the holy wafer— are effective against him. However, the narrative offers more than mere Christian allegory: it also presents a confrontation between Christian ethics and Darwinian evolution, a topic of great interest to the Victorian audience. Charles S. Blinderman, in "Vampurella: Darwin and Count Dracula," explores this theme. *Dracula*, he writes, "presents a contest between two evolutionary options: the ameliorative, progressive, Christian congregation, or the Social Darwinian superman in the form of the ultimate parasitic degenerate, Count Dracula."[18] Of course, the narrative is also viewed as a repository of arcana, myth, and folklore, including the symbols of the Tarot and the Grail and "Fisher-King" of Arthurian romance.[19]

The sociological aspects of the narrative are explored, including the sharp, clear distinctions drawn between the working class, who are constantly bribed; the professional class (Harker, Seward, Van Helsing), who scoff at the law, and the upper class (Holmwood), who seem oblivious of the law; Of course, the politics of the age are reflected in the book, as are the views of its sociological thinkers, such as Cesar Lombroso,[20] who is studied in Ernest Fontana's "Lombroso's Criminal Man and Stoker's Dracula."[21] The text has also been subjected to Marxist analysis,

[16] Thomas Byers, "Good Men and Monsters: The Defenses of *Dracula*," *Literature and Psychology* 31 (1981): 24–31, and Lawrence A. Rickels, *The Vampire Lectures* (Minneapolis: Univ. of Minnesota Press, 1999).

[17] Clive Leatherdale, "Stoker's Banana Skins: Errors, Illogicalities and Misconceptions in *Dracula*," in *Dracula: The Shade and the Shadow*, ed. Elizabeth Miller (Westcliff-on-Sea, England: Desert Island Books, 1998), 138–54.

[18] Charles S. Blinderman, "Vampurella: Darwin and Count Dracula," *Massachussetts Review* 21 (1980): 411, 428.

[19] See, for example, Thomas Ray Thornburg, "The Quester and the Castle: The Gothic Novel as Myth, with Special Reference to Bram Stoker's *Dracula*," PhD thesis, Ball State Univ., Muncie, IN, 1970; Thomas P. Walsh, "*Dracula*: Logos and Myth," *Research Studies* 47 (1979): 229–37; and Mark M. Hennelly Jr., "*Dracula*: The Gnostic Quest and the Victorian Wasteland," *English Literature in Transition* 20 (1977): 13–26. The theme is also considered in detail, Tarot card by card, in Leatherdale, *Dracula: The Novel & The Legend*, 210–23.

[20] See chapter 25, note 46.

[21] Ernest Fontana, "Lombroso's Criminal Man and Stoker's Dracula," *Victorian Newsletter* 66 (1984): 25–27.

as noted earlier, and judged to be capitalist[22] and anti-monopolistic.[23] John Allen Stevenson's "The Vampire in the Mirror: The Sexuality of *Dracula*"[24] examines the anthropological aspects of the incestuous and miscegenistic relationships suggested in the narrative and the reaction of the British Empire to cultures with different values.

Stoker's Irishness leads some critics to see the narrative as more about the Irish revolution and Irish sensibilities than vampires. For example, Raymond T. McNally writes that "Transylvania is at a minimum a metaphor for Ireland as both Transylvania and Ireland are frontier territories on the fringe of the empire, fought over often by foreigners."[25] A famous political cartoon of the age illustrates the popular linkage.

With the advent of feminist studies, the narrative has been studied as a portrait of contemporary views of the proper rôle of women, including reaction to the "New Woman."[26] The true theme of the book, some scholars argue, is

THE IRISH "VAMPIRE."

"The Irish 'Vampire.'"
John Tenniel, *Punch*, 24 October 1885

[22] See Franco Moretti's important "Dialectic of Fear" in *Signs Taken for Wonders: Essays in the Sociology of Literary Forms*, trans. Susan Fischer, David Forgacs, and David Miller (London: Verso, 1988), 83–108.

[23] Robert Smart, "Blood and Money in Bram Stoker's *Dracula*: The Struggle Against Monopoly," in *Money: Lure, Lore, and Literature*, ed. John Louis DiGaetani (Wesport, CT: Greenwood Press, 1994), 253–60.

[24] John Allen Stevenson, "The Vampire in the Mirror: The Sexuality of *Dracula*," *PMLA* 103 (1988): 139–49.

[25] Raymond T. McNally, "Bram Stoker and Irish Gothic," in *The Fantastic Vampire: Studies in the Children of the Night*, ed. James Craig Holte (Westport, CT: Greenwood Press, 2002), 11–21, p. 16 quoted. See also Alison Milbank, " 'Powers Old and New': Stoker's Alliances with Anglo-Irish Gothic," in *Bram Stoker: History, Psychoanalysis and the Gothic*, ed. William Hughes (London: Palgrave Macmillan, 1998), 12–28; Michael Valdez Moses, "The Irish Vampire: *Dracula*, Parnell, and the Troubled Dreams of Nationhood," *Journal x* [Univ. of Mississippi] 2 (1997): 67–111; Cannon Schmitt, "Mother Dracula: Orientalism, Degeneration, and Anglo-Irish National Subjectivity at the Fin de Siècle," in *Irishness and (Post) Modernism*, ed. John S. Rickard (London: Associated Univ. Press, 1994), 25–43; and Kellie Donovan Wixson, "*Dracula*: An Anglo-Irish Gothic Novel," in *Dracula: The Shade and the Shadow*, ed. Elizabeth Miller (Westcliff-on-Sea, England: Desert Island Books, 1998), 247–56. Most recently, see especially the extended commentary *Dracula's Crypt: Bram Stoker, Irishness and the Question of Blood* by Joseph Valente (Urbana: Univ. of Illinois Press, 2002).

[26] See chapter 8, note 2, for a discussion of the "New Woman."

that the real horror is "the released, transforming sexuality of the Good Woman," in the words of Gail B. Griffin.[27] Judith Weissman calls the hunters' fight with Dracula "a fight to keep women from knowing what the men and women of the Middle Ages, the Renaissance, the seventeenth and eighteenth centuries knew, and what people of the nineteenth century must also have known, even if they did not want to—that women's sexual appetites are greater than men's."[28]

For many Victorians, the New Woman, whom Mina characterises as offering her own marriage proposals, represented the epitome of their fears about cultural disintegration and the collapse of the moral values of the Empire. The New Woman was viewed as the antithesis of the Victorian ideal woman / wife, the "angel in the house" (from the 1854 poem by Coventry Patmore). Carol Senf, in her influential "*Dracula*: Stoker's Response to the New Woman,"[29] argues that Stoker, while hardly a feminist, did not utterly reject the benefits of a changing model for womanhood, making Mina represent the attractive elements of those changes. Similarly, Sos Eltis, in "Corruption of the Blood and Degeneration of the Race: *Dracula* and Policing the Borders of Gender,"[30] sees Mina as combining the best masculine and feminine elements.

The fin de siècle brought many doomsayers decrying the demise of the culture, and critics see the narrative as an allegory of the battle for the future of the Empire. Historian H. L. Malchow argues that Dracula symbolises one of the most potent perceived threats to England, the influx of eastern European Jews. "That Dracula is in some sense coded as racial threat is obvious," concludes Malchow. "We may note his strong, if ambivalent, sexuality; his offensive odor; his corruption of the blood of his victims. . . . Dracula immigrates to England and becomes the invisible threat within."[31] The anti-Semitic overtones of the

[27] Gail B. Griffin, " 'Your Girls That You Love Are Mine': *Dracula* and the Victorian Male Sexual Imagination," *International Journal of Women's Studies* 3 (1980): 454–65.

[28] Weissman, "Women and Vampires," 403. Phyllis Roth, in "Suddenly Sexual Women in Bram Stoker's *Dracula*," *Literature and Psychology* 27 (1977): 113–21, describes her view of the psychoanalytic basis for the vampire horror: "The threatening Oedipal fantasy, the regression to a primary oral obsession, the atttraction, and destruction of the vampires of *Dracula* are . . . interrelated and interdependent. What they spell out is a fusion of the memory of nursing at the mother's breast with a primal scene fantasy which results in the conviction that the sexually desirable woman will annihilate if she is not first destroyed." Roth is also the author of the superb literary biography *Bram Stoker*.

[29] Carol Senf, "*Dracula*: Stoker's Response to the New Woman," *Victorian Studies* 26 (1982): 33–49.

[30] Sos Eltis, "Corruption of the Blood and Degeneration of the Race: *Dracula* and Policing the Borders of Gender," in *Dracula*, ed. John Paul Riquelme (New York: Bedford/St. Martin's Press, 2002), 450–64.

[31] H. L. Malchow, *Gothic Images of Race in Nineteenth-Century Britain* (Stanford, CA: Stanford Univ. Press, 1996).

narrative, with several deplorable characterisations of Jews, are only part of a larger fear of "reverse colonisation," however. Stephen D. Arata explores the national terror in more detail in "The Occidental Tourist: *Dracula* and the Anxiety of Reverse Colonization."[32] Nor is the xenophobia of the narrative restricted to Jews: eastern Europeans generally fare poorly, and one scholar argues that the narrative encodes the prevailing Russophobia.[33]

The confrontations of science and faith, technology and folklore, and the modern and the traditional are self-evident themes in the narrative, and several critics examine the implications. John L. Greenway's "Seward's Folly: *Dracula* as a Critique of 'Normal Science' "[34] characterises John Seward's science in particular as deluded and ineffectual, suggesting that Stoker himself had some scepticism about the ambitions of Victorian science. In "Pollution and Redemption in *Dracula*,"[35] Anne McWhir observes the blurring of the lines between science and myth. "Vampiric Typewriting: *Dracula* and Its Media" by Jennifer Wicke[36] was one of the earliest studies to point out the contrasts drawn between technology, folklore, and faith. Valerie Clemens, in "Dracula: The Reptilian Brain at the Fin de Siècle,"[37] suggests that Van Helsing, known for his work on the "continuous evolution of brain-matter," would have been aware of physician Paul Broca's discovery in 1878 of the limbic node, a portion of the brain beneath the neocortical mantle popularly termed the "reptilian brain." Broca theorised that the physiological and neurological nature of this portion of the brain causes behaviour much like that attributed to Dracula. However, in normal humans, the reptilian brain is subjugated by the neocortical brain; in

---

[32] Stephen D. Arata, "The Occidental Tourist: *Dracula* and the Anxiety of Reverse Colonization," *Victorian Studies* 33 (1990): 621–45.

[33] Jimmie E. Cain, " 'With the Unspeakable': *Dracula* and Russophobia—Tourism, Racism and Imperialism," in *Dracula: The Shade and the Shadow*, ed. Elizabeth Miller (Westcliff-on-Sea, England: Desert Island Books, 1998), 104–15. See also Troy Boone, " 'He is English and therefore adventurous': Politics, Decadence and *Dracula*," *Studies in the Novel* 25 (1993): 76–91; Athena Vrettos, "Physical Immunity and Racial Destiny: Stoker and Haggard," in *Somatic Fictions: Imagining Illness in Victorian Culture* (Stanford, CA: Stanford Univ. Press, 1995), 154–76; L. S. Warren, "Buffalo Bill Meets Dracula: William F. Cody, Bram Stoker, and the Frontiers of Racial Decay," *American Historical Review* 107 (2002): 1124–57.

[34] John L. Greenway, "Seward's Folly: *Dracula* as a Critique of 'Normal Science,' " *Stanford Literature Review* 3 (1986): 213–30.

[35] Anne McWhir, "Pollution and Redemption in *Dracula*," *Modern Language Studies* 17 (1987): 31–40.

[36] Jennifer Wicke, "Vampiric Typewriting: *Dracula* and Its Media," *ELH* 59 (1992): 467–93.

[37] Valerie Clemens, "Dracula: The Reptilian Brain at the Fin de Siècle," in *Dracula: The Shade and the Shadow,* ed. Elizabeth Miller (Westcliff-on-Sea, England: Desert Island Books, 1998), 205–18.

Dracula (and other vampires), evidently, this portion of the brain is dominant. The existence of the "reptilian brain" in humans, Clemens concludes, means the vampire will never be extinct as a species.

The possibilities for critical analysis of the narrative seem endless. In its highly revealing portrait of a century (and a world) in transition, and through its exploration of conflicts arising from the depths of the human brain and heart, *Dracula* mirrors for scholars what Nina Auerbach calls "our vampires, ourselves."[38]

---

[38] See Nina Auerbach, *Our Vampires, Ourselves* (Chicago: Univ. of Chicago Press, 1995).

THE PUBLIC LIFE
OF DRACULA
Dracula on Stage and Screen[1]

*On the stage they would be set down at once as some
old Oriental band of brigands.*

—JONATHAN HARKER

BEFORE *DRACULA* WAS PUBLISHED, Bram Stoker took steps to protect his right to produce the work on the stage and mounted a reading of a playscript at the Lyceum Theatre on 18 May 1897. With the play consisting of five acts, forty-seven scenes, and lasting over five hours, it is unlikely that Stoker intended it to be performed in this form. The playscript survives[2] in the form of a cut-and-paste typescript of the book, with a handwritten prologue and other handwritten additions and changes. Because it follows the book so closely, it is ungainly theatre, with long-winded speeches, confusing changes of scene, and a stupefying number of characters. Surprisingly, Stoker seems to have had little difficulty with the censors, causing Stoker scholar Sylvia Starshine to

Opening page of *Dracula, or The Un-Dead* in Stoker's handwriting.

---

[1] The following discussion considers only stage and screen depictions of Count Dracula himself. Not discussed are countless films about vampires and vampire hunters, many of which draw heavily on the Stoker narrative—or the 1931 Tod Browning film—for their ideas of vampire traits. Also not considered are many films and television productions in which Dracula, or a thinly disguised version of him, appears as a minor or onetime character. For example, in the highly successful television series *Buffy the Vampire Slayer*, considered at length in "Dracula's Family Tree," Dracula appears in an episode ("Buffy vs. Dracula," which aired in the United States on 26 September 2000).

[2] It was submitted to the Lord Chamberlain's Office on 31 May 1897. The playscript was published in 1997 as *Dracula; or The Un-Dead*, ed. Sylvia Starshine (Nottingham, England: Pumpkin Books).

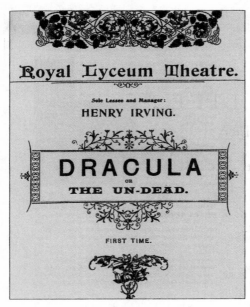

Program for a dramatic reading of *Dracula, or The Un-Dead* at the Lyceum Theatre, 1897.

Hamilton Deane.
From the private collection of
Jeanne Youngson

speculate that he promised the lord chamberlain not to offer full performances for the public.

The book was first licensed for dramatisation in the mid-1920s, to a touring actor-manager named Hamilton Deane, a family friend. Deane had a solid record of provincial success, and he conceived of his version of *Dracula* as a touring vehicle. Deane reduced the play to a standard drawing-room mystery, with limited scenery and stage effects.[3] He apparently originally intended to play the title rôle himself but quickly determined that the part of Van Helsing was better, casting himself in the part, with his wife, Dora Mary Patrick, as Mina. He cast Edmund Blake and then twenty-year-old Raymond Huntley as the Count, both presenting the suave appearance often associated with the stage magician— evening dress and opera cloak. Gone was the image of the gaunt old man with bad breath, to be replaced by a sophisticated man-about-town. The play also incorporated special effects similar to those of stage magic: flash boxes, demonstrations of hypnotism, and a coffin in which the vampire's corpse vanished.

The play began production in 1924 in the provinces, where it was a great hit. After three years on the road, Deane hesitantly opened the play on the West End, at the Little Theatre, Adelphi. True to Deane's fears, the critics savaged the play. "For us," wrote the critic of *Punch* (23 February 1927), "it only remains to sidle quietly into the Adelphi, wondering sadly why this sort of thing should be supposed to be adequate

[3] The play (in both the Deane and Deane/Balderston versions) has been published as Hamilton Deane and John L. Balderston, *Dracula: The Ultimate, Illustrated Edition of the World-Famous Vampire Play*, ed. and annot. David J. Skal (New York: St. Martin's Press, 1993). Deane cast a woman, Frieda Hearn, as Quincey Morris in the original production.

Dora Mary Patrick as Mina and Hamilton Deane as Van Helsing.
Dracula (ca. 1924)

Raymond Huntley as Dracula and Dora Mary Patrick as Mina.
Dracula (ca. 1924)

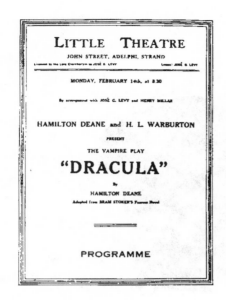

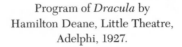

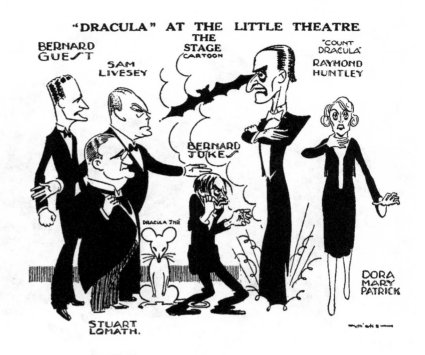

Program of *Dracula* by
Hamilton Deane, Little Theatre,
Adelphi, 1927.

Newspaper cartoon of the London cast of *Dracula*, 1927.

entertainment for adults in this year of grace in one of the world's capital cities."
Yet adequate it was—more than adequate, and audiences thronged to see the
play. The production moved to larger quarters at the Duke of York's, causing the
London *Evening News* to wonder, "while glittering productions costing thousands
of pounds have wilted and died after a week or so in the West End, 'Dracula' has
gone on drinking blood nightly."[4] Three companies continued to tour the English
provinces.

Impressed by the London success, legendary American publisher/producer
Horace Liveright[5] arranged with Deane to produce the play on Broadway. Liveright disliked the script, however, and brought in American journalist and drama-

[4] Quoted in Harry Ludlam, *A Biography of Bram Stoker, Creator of Dracula* (New York:
New English Library), 161.

[5] Liveright was notorious for his extravagant spending, great successes, and great failures.
He created the Modern Library and published the works of "radicals" such as William
Faulkner. He staffed his company with the best talent, including Bennett Cerf, Lillian
Hellman, Louis Kronenberger, and Richard Simon. In 1930, in financial ruin, Liveright sold
his publishing house to W. W. Norton & Co. "Typical of Liveright's track record," recounted
Drake McFeely, chairman of Norton, in private correspondence with this editor, "was that
while he was astute enough to produce the *Dracula* stage play in America, he failed to
secure the film rights!"

Horace Liveright.

Edward Van Sloan as Van Helsing and Bela
Lugosi as Dracula.
Dracula (1927)

tist John L. Balderston to rewrite the dialogue.[6]
The play opened for tryouts in Connecticut in
September 1927, moving to Broadway on 5 October,
where it ran for 261 performances, starring the
Austro-Hungarian actor Bela Lugosi (who had
first appeared on Broadway in 1922) as Dracula
and Edward Van Sloan as Van Helsing.[7] It then
toured America extensively, in two companies, one
starring Huntley and the other Lugosi. Although

[6] There was a third adaptation licensed by Florence Stoker,
written in 1927 by Charles Morrel. The script ran into some
difficulties with the censor's office. "This is a disgusting
play . . . and I regret that it ever was put on stage," wrote
the Lord Chamberlain's Office on 14 September 1927.
"The present object seems to make this horrible play even
more horrid and disgusting than it was before"(?). The
production died a quick death.

[7] Despite appearances, Van Sloan and Lugosi were born
only a year apart, in 1881 and 1882, respectively. Van Sloan
began his acting career in the 1910s in film and appeared
on Broadway in 1918. Lugosi's Broadway career did not
commence until 1922, with his appearance in a small part
in *The Red Poppy*.

Handbill.
Dracula (1927)

Frank Langella as Dracula.
Dracula (1977)

Jeremy Brett as Dracula.
Dracula (1978)

David Dukes as Dracula.
Dracula (ca. 1979)

critics were not impressed by Lugosi's acting (the *New York Post* likened his performance to that of an "operatically inclined but cheerless mortician," and the *New York Herald-Tribune* described him as a "rigid hobgoblin"), he was showered with romantic fan attention.[8]

The play was revived numerous times with many different players. Lugosi himself toured in 1943, performed summer stock in the late 1940s, and toured again in the late 1950s. The play was restaged in 1977 with sets and costumes by Edward Gorey and starred Frank Langella in the title rôle. Although the critics again had little good to say about the play (for example, *New York Times* theatre critic Richard Eder described the production as "elegant" but "bloodless" and Langella as "stunning" but failing to elicit terror in his audience),[9] the revival was an enormous success, eventually starring such disparate actors as soap-opera star Jean LeClerc, Jeremy Brett (pre–Sherlock Holmes), popular television actor David Dukes, and the magnetic Raúl Juliá as the romantic Count.[10] Since 1970, at least nine other theatrical versions of *Dracula* have been staged, including three

[8] John Anderson, "Dracula," *New York Post*, 6 October 1927; Percy Hammond, "The Theaters," *New York Herald-Tribune*, 6 October 1927.

[9] Richard Eder, "Theater: An Elegant but Bloodless 'Dracula,'" *New York Times*, 21 October 1977.

[10] Terence Stamp starred in the 1978 London production of the revival, which did poorly at the box office.

Filmbook, *Death of Drakula* (1921).

musical productions,[11] as well as countless revivals and summer-stock productions of the Deane and Deane/Balderston plays.

The earliest known film—although no copy survives—was made in 1921 in Hungary, probably titled *Death of Drakula* and directed by Károly Lajthay.[12] Only the filmbook remains, and while it is impossible to state the plot with

[11] These include Leon Katz's *Dracula: Sabbat* (1970), a performance piece; Ted Tiller's *Count Dracula* (1972); *The Passion of Dracula* (1977) by Bob Hall and David Richmond; *Dracula: A Musical Nightmare* (1978) by Douglas Johnson and John Aschenbrenner, the story of an English touring company's production of *Dracula*; Richard Sharpe's *Dracula: The Story You Thought You Knew* (1983); Liz Lochhead's *Dracula* (1985); *Mac Wellman's Dracula* (1994), decidedly postmodernist; Richard Ouzounian's *Dracula: A Chamber Musical* (1999); and Des McAnuff's *Dracula, the Musical* (2001), which ran on Broadway for almost six months beginning in August 2004.

[12] Although this is the earliest known film using the name "Dracula," it is not the first vampire-themed film. David J. Skal lists forty-one earlier films with the word "vampire" in the title or as part of the theme, including many about predatory women who drain their victims sexually or financially (David J. Skal, ed., *Vampires: Encounters with the Undead* [New York: Black Dog & Leventhal, 2001], 555–58).

F. W. Murnau.

certainty, it appears to be based thematically on Stoker's narrative but with no blood sucking; rather, the film develops the familiar theme of a powerful, dynamic man hypnotizing (literally or figuratively) a pure, innocent girl.[13]

In March 1922, arguably the most artistically successful film of *Dracula* ever made—certainly one of the scariest—opened in Berlin. *Nosferatu, eine Symphonie des Grauens*, directed by F. W. Murnau, has achieved the status of legend. Renowned for its depiction of Expressionist angst and modern alienation, the silent film is surprisingly modern in its uses of close-ups and point-of-view shots. It was remade virtually shot for shot in 1979 by Werner Herzog (*Nosferatu: Phantom der Nacht*, starring Klaus Kinski) and became the subject of a fanciful film (*Shadow of the Vampire*, 2000) starring John Malkovich as Murnau and Willem Dafoe as Max Schreck. *Nosferatu* made major changes to the Stoker narrative, with Count Dracula renamed Graf Orlok. Mina is Ellen; Harker, Hutter; Renfield, Knock; and Van Helsing, Bulwer. The other major characters are dropped. The action takes place in three places: in Transylvania, where Orlok first sees a photograph of Hutter's fiancée; onboard a ship bringing the Graf to Germany; and in Bremen, Hutter's home. It is Ellen who brings about the destruction of the vampire, offering herself to him only to lure him into the

---

[13] The film is considered in detail in Lokke Heiss's "Discovery of a Hungarian *Drakula*," in *Bram Stoker's Dracula: A Documentary Volume*, ed. Elizabeth Miller (Detroit: Thomson Gale, 2005), 296–300.

Nosferatu.
Albin Grau (Jofa-Atelier Berlin-Johannisthal, 1922)

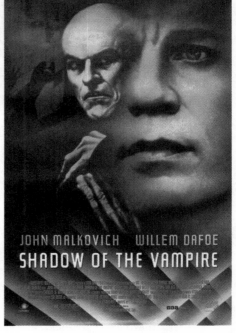

Shadow of the Vampire.
(BBC Films, 2000)

Tod Browning.

Dracula.
(Universal Pictures, 1931)

exterminating sunlight.[14] Max Schreck, who portrayed Orlok, is magnetic as the vampire, although not in a handsome or seductive style; Orlok is rat faced, ugly, emaciated, and horrible, but radiates powerful evil.

Nosferatu enjoyed commercial success in Europe upon release but did not do well in the United States. Florence Stoker, learning of the film, was incensed that the producer had not secured permission and sued for copyright infringement. In 1925, a court ordered that all copies of the film be destroyed. To Florence's dismay, however, prints continued to surface, and the film has survived as a masterpiece of German expressionism.

If *Nosferatu* is the most artistically successful film of *Dracula*, Tod Browning's 1931 "talkie" version of *Dracula*, made for Universal Studios as the cornerstone of its series of horror classics, cannot be denied the title of most successful, at least in creating indelible images that have permanently changed the general public's vision of the vampire. Based more on the Deane/Balderston play than on the Stoker narrative (and accused by many critics of being stage-bound), the film tells a different story: the trip to Transylvania is made by Renfield, and Lucy becomes a minor character. Mina is transformed into Dr. Seward's daughter, and Jonathan Harker, so vital in Stoker's narrative, is relegated to the decorative rôle of Mina's fiancé. The film has its shortcomings: scenes are left undeveloped, the subplot of Lucy is abandoned, the editing is often poor, and props are occasionally in the wrong place. Virtually all of the action takes place in Seward's asylum and Dracula's neighbouring villa, and, disappointingly, the final confrontation between

[14] This convention—that the vampire burns in the sun, to the point of destruction—has been slavishly copied in virtually every succeeding film, although as pointed out in various notes in this volume, Dracula repeatedly demonstrates his ability to move about freely in the daytime. For example, in *Blacula* (1972), the eponymous vampire deliberately exposes himself on a rooftop to obtain his release from "un-death." See "Dracula's Family Tree" for a further discussion of this vampire trait.

Dracula (Bela Lugosi) welcomes his guest (Dwight Frye).
Dracula (Universal Pictures, 1931)

Van Helsing and Dracula occurs offscreen. Although Browning's direction of the English scenes displays none of the overt symbolism and flair of Murnau's, the extravagant Transylvanian scenes brilliantly capture the atmosphere of Dracula's castle, and Browning elicits stunning performances from Bela Lugosi as the stylised but compelling vampire and Edward Van Sloan as the doctor who may share more similarities with Dracula than he admits.

Although twenty-three-year-old producer Carl Laemmle Jr.[15] made a long and public search for the lead actor, he eventually settled on Lugosi, who had made the part his own on the stage. Laemmle also chose Van Sloan to repeat his stage rôle as Van Helsing. Dwight Frye, a little-known actor who subsequently made a career in character parts (for example, Wilmer the gunsel in the first filmed version of *The Maltese Falcon*, later in 1931),

Carl Laemmle Jr.

[15] Laemmle was a prolific producer, whose first picture was made in 1926, at the age of eighteen, and whose producer credits include more than 130 films, including *Frankenstein* (1931), *Destry Rides Again* (1932), *The Wolfman* (1932), *The Bride of Frankenstein* (1935), *The Werewolf of London* (1935), and *Show Boat* (1936). Laemmle's *All Quiet on the Western Front* (1930) won the Oscar for Best Picture.

Edward Van Sloan as Van Helsing and Bela Lugosi as Dracula.
Dracula (Universal Pictures, 1931)

appeared as the lunatic Renfield, and his portrayal is described by one scholar as "the standard by which all other cinematic Renfields are measured."[16] Wide initial distribution, constant rereleases and airing on television, and an unending stream of exploitative licenses of the film's images have made the movie the only version ever seen by many. Unlike the three great actors who have portrayed Sherlock Holmes,[17] the appeal of

Publicity photo of
Bela Lugosi as Dracula.
Dracula (Universal Pictures, 1931)

[16] James Craig Holte, "Film Adaptations of *Dracula*," in *Bram Stoker's Dracula: A Documentary Volume*, ed. Elizabeth Miller (Detroit: Thomson Gale, 2005), 318–24.

[17] William Gillette, who appeared continuously in the part from 1899 to 1933; Basil Rathbone, from 1939 to 1946; and Jeremy Brett, from 1985 to 1994.

Portrait of Bela Lugosi.

Dracula.
(Spanish-language version,
Universal Pictures, 1931)

whom is generational, Bela Lugosi has been fixed in the public mind as the only "real" Dracula.

Curiously, in 1931 Universal produced another version of *Dracula*, using the same sets as Browning (and filming at night): a Spanish-language version, with entirely different actors and a somewhat different script.[18] There are actually several improvements in the script. The shipboard scenes are more developed (Dracula is viewed attacking the crew while Renfield watches), and on arrival in port, one spectator declares that the captain must have died of fright. Lucy and Mina (renamed Eva) are much more seductive, and their attraction to Dracula is clearly sexual. Van Helsing discloses that Dracula's family disappeared over five centuries ago. Also, unlike the Browning version, this film reveals Lucy's ultimate fate, when Van Helsing and Jonathan Harker are shown returning from the cemetery after staking her. The final staking of Dracula produces an audible

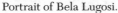

[18] The film was directed by the prolific George Melford, who reportedly spoke no Spanish. Melford directed well over a hundred films in twenty-five years, many in Spanish, and after 1937 became a character actor, with parts in more than seventy-five films. Carlos Villarias (appearing as Carlos Villar), who was seen in over eighty films throughout his career, played a less flamboyant Dracula; the popular Lupita Tovar, mother of actress Susan Kohner and wife of producer Paul Kohner for fifty-six years, smoldered as Eva (Mina).

Atif Kaptan as Dracula.
Drakula Istanbul'da (And Film, 1953)

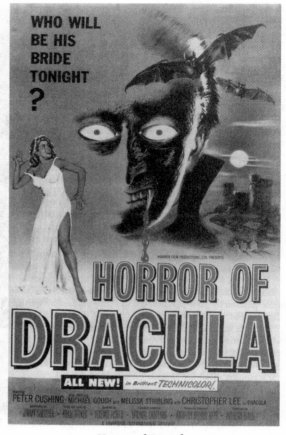

Horror of Dracula.
(Hammer Film Productions, 1958)

groan—no sudden disintegration into dust here! Eva comments that we should have seen the look on Dracula's face when he saw the sunlight. The film is a fascinating contrast to the Browning version. Universal has released both versions on a single DVD.

There were other notable attempts to produce stories drawn from the Stoker narrative. The 1953 Turkish production *Drakula Istanbul'da*, directed by Mehmet Muhtar, was the first to show Dracula climbing his castle wall facedown and suggests a connection to Vlad the Impaler. Set in contemporary Istanbul, the script is based on Ali Riza Seyfi's 1928 novel *The Impaling Voivode*, "inspired" by Stoker's work, and features a fine, bald, fang-sporting vampire.

Dracula (also known as *Horror of Dracula*), made in 1958, was the first of a series of vampire films by Britain's Hammer Films. It stars Christopher Lee as Dracula and Peter Cushing as Van Helsing—the mentor of vampire hunter Jonathan Harker in this telling. The film borrows heavily from the Deane/

Balderston play and resets the tale in a nameless village near a mysterious castle. Renfield does not appear in the story, Arthur Holmwood is married to Mina Holmwood, Lucy is Mina's sister, and Dr. Seward is a minor character, the Holmwood family physician. The essential elements of sexuality, violence, and horror are intact. Cushing's Van Helsing is a picture of rationality (the portrayal a precursor, of sorts, to his depiction of Sherlock Holmes in Hammer Films' 1959 production of *The Hound of the Baskervilles*). Christopher Lee is a fine, handsome, menacing villain. The two appeared repeatedly in these rôles over the years, until Lee balked, complaining in an interview that the original Stoker narrative had all but disappeared from the films, making them "progressively less and less interesting."[19]

Lee again appeared as Dracula in the Spanish production *El Conde Dracula* (1970), directed by Jesus Franco. Including Herbert Lom as Van Helsing and Klaus Kinski as Renfield (Kinski also played Graf Orlok in the 1979 *Nosferatu*), the picture begins well, closely following the Stoker narrative account of Harker's encounter with Dracula. The film rapidly proceeds into banality, however, and except for the characterisation of Lee as an older Dracula and the brilliant Kinski, the film is largely forgettable. In a 1993 interview, Lee complained that the film was shot on such a tight budget that he and Lom were never actually in any scenes together. "If you're going to make a picture that way . . . ," he said, "well, you can't save it."[20]

Two television productions in the 1970s, Dan Curtis's 1973 *Dracula* made for Universal, and the 1978 BBC production of *Count Dracula*, are noteworthy. The first was scripted by Richard Matheson, author of the 1954 vampire novel *I Am Legend*,[21] and used Stoker's narrative in an original manner. Curtis, creator of the

---

[19] "Christopher Lee on Dracula," interviewed by John Exshaw, 1 May 1993, *Bram Stoker Society Journal* 6 (1994): 7–10.

[20] Ibid.

[21] Itself made into three interesting films, *The Last Man on Earth* (1964), starring Vincent Price as Dr. Robert Morgan, remade as *The Omega Man* (1971), starring Charlton Heston as Dr. Robert Neville and remade again in 2007 as *I Am Legend*, starring Will Smith as Dr. Robert Neville. Each doctor survives a biological-warfare-induced plague of vampirism.

Vincent Price as Dr. Robert Morgan.
The Last Man on Earth
(Associated Producers, 1964)

The Omega Man
(Warner Bros. Pictures, 1971)

Jack Palance as Dracula.
Dracula (Dan Curtis Productions, 1973)

only vampire soap opera, *Dark Shadows*,[22] made a film that draws heavily on the scholarship of McNally and Florescu, associating Dracula with Vlad the Impaler. Dracula, played by Jack Palance, discovers a photograph of Mina in a newspaper and concludes that she is the reincarnation of his long-deceased mortal wife. Palance's Dracula is a monster when thwarted but otherwise seems an appealing, almost sympathetic victim of his vampirism.

[22] *Dark Shadows*, which aired from 1966 to 1971 as an afternoon soap opera and in 1991 in prime time, told of the coming of Barnabas Collins to the town of Collinsport, Maine. Collins was a deeply troubled vampire, seeking to regain his humanity and live in peace with his reincarnated love. The series engendered a huge fan base, with viewers drawn equally to well-buried plot riffs on such classics as *Wuthering Heights*, *The Turn of the Screw*, and *The Picture of Dorian Gray*; the unmistakable sex appeal of cast members Jonathan Frid and Joan Bennett, who turned in performances by turns expertly melodramatic and vaguely tongue-in-cheek; and the show's endearingly low-budget sets (occasionally walls could be heard falling offstage). Robert Cobert's tremulous musical score contibuted mightily to the atmosphere, as did a well-designed Gothic log, the name "Dark Shadows" in a Teutonic typeface superimposed on the brooding silhouette of the roof of a house. Two theatrical spin-offs were produced, *House of Dark Shadows* (1970) and *Night of Dark Shadows* (1971). For more information, see Kathryn Leigh Scott, ed., *The Dark Shadows Companion: 25th Anniversary Collection* (Los Angeles: Pomegranate Press, 1990), with a foreword by Jonathan Frid.

Louis Jourdan as Dracula.
Count Dracula (British Broadcasting
Corporation, 1977)

Frank Langella as Dracula.
Dracula (Universal Pictures, 1979)

The BBC production, directed by Philip Saville, also conveys a sympathetic portrait, largely as a result of Louis Jourdan's portrayal of the Count as a tragic romantic hero. The film downplays the blood and violence and emphasises the Count's loneliness and pain. Uniquely among major productions, the film is true to the Stoker narrative, including every major character and even filming the Whitby scenes on location. The film received much critical acclaim, and Jourdan's evocation of the Count set the tone for two major films that followed.

John Badham's *Dracula* (1979) is essentially a filmed version of the Deane/Balderston play, as interpreted by Frank Langella on Broadway in 1977. Badham also chose to downplay the horror. He emphasised the romantic elements and focussed on campiness and humor. Langella's vampire is a creature who falls in love but can never find happiness; not only can he not consummate his love, but he will outlive his companions and must be forever lonely.

Francis Ford Coppola's 1992 production of *Bram Stoker's Dracula* (an ill-chosen name for a film with a script so deviant from Stoker's narrative) was highly ambitious. Not only did it include a star-laden cast (Gary Oldman as Dracula, Anthony Hopkins as Van Helsing, Winona Ryder as Mina Harker, Keanu Reeves as Jonathan Harker, and songwriter-singer and occasional actor Tom Waits

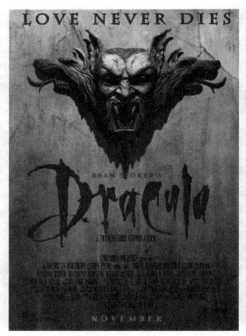

Bram Stoker's Dracula.
(American Zoetrope, 1992)

Van Helsing.
(Carpathian Pictures, 2004)

as Renfield), it had an enormous budget, lavish sets and costumes, and a lush soundtrack. Although the film won three Oscars, the script is a hodgepodge of the McNally-Florescu historical perspective, reincarnation, rampant sexuality, and the ultimate redemptive power of love. One critic compared it to *Beauty and the Beast,* in which love transforms the monster—Dracula—into a handsome prince. Here, however, the monster is ultimately destroyed for his consuming love.[23]

Illustrative of the character's power—though with little enough connection to the Stoker narrative—is the 2004 *Van Helsing,* starring Hugh Jackman in the title rôle. Here Van Helsing is the agent of a Vatican-connected agency dealing with the supernatural, and with the help of a Transylvanian princess (played by Kate Beckinsale, who has made a minicareer as a vampire/vampire hunter), he must combat not only Dracula but Dracula's brides, Frankenstein's monster, and the Universal Pictures monster known as the Wolfman, as well as the hunchback Igor, a character from the Universal Pictures *Frankenstein.* The film is silly but fun and affords an opportunity for Richard Roxburgh (who played Sherlock Holmes in a

---

[23] Kim Newman's brilliant 1997 "Coppola's Dracula" (in Skal, *Vampires: Encounters with the Undead,* 553–94) imagines if Coppola had made his Dracula film with the same cast (and the same problems) as his 1979 *Apocalypse Now.* The depiction of Martin Sheen as Harker and Marlon Brando as Dracula is breathtaking.

Bela Lugosi as Dracula and Lou Costello as himself in
Abbott and Costello Meet Frankenstein.
(Universal Pictures, 1948)

George Hamilton as Dracula and Susan Saint
James as Cindy Sondheim, his bride-to-be.
Love at First Bite
(Melvin Simon Productions, 1979)

2002, poorly received BBC production of *The Hound of the Baskervilles*) to ham it up as the übervillain.

Of course, not all screen depictions of Dracula have been serious. In the 1948 *Abbott and Costello Meet Frankenstein*, the boys meet Count Dracula (played by Lugosi) and the Wolfman (Lon Chaney Jr.) in a crass but funny exploitation of Universal's horror properties. More seriously (well, more seriously funny), *Love at First Bite* (1979), starring George Hamilton, recounts the adventures of Dracula in New York after he is evicted from his Transylvanian castle by Roumanian bureaucrats. There are

Leslie Nielsen as Dracula.
Dracula: Dead and Loving It (Brooksfilms Ltd., 1995)

numerous parodic references to the Stoker narrative, Susan Saint James is charming as Dracula's actress love-interest, and Arte Johnson channels Dwight Frye as Renfield, Dracula's loyal bug-eating manservant.

Leslie Nielsen, after reinventing himself as a comic actor in the *Naked Gun* film series, took on the rôle of Dracula in Mel Brooks's predictably and deliciously foolish *Dracula: Dead and Loving It* (1995). Surprisingly true to elements of the Deane/Balderston play, earlier films, and the Stoker narrative, the film features Mel Brooks as a Jewish version of Van Helsing, Harvey Korman the elder Dr. Seward, and Peter MacNicol a wacky Renfield. The film is sparked by dialogue such as the following, which occurs when Harker (Steven Weber) is told by Van Helsing that he must drive a stake into Lucy:

HARKER: Oh, this is horrid. Is there no other way?

VAN HELSING: Well, we could cut off her head, stuff her mouth with garlic, and tear off her ears.

HARKER: Give me the stake. No. No, I can't do it . . . you do it.

VAN HELSING: It must be done by one who loved her in life.

HARKER: But I only liked her.

VAN HELSING: Close enough.

or Dracula's comment (in a heavy Lugosi-style accent) as a bat leaves droppings on his stairs:

"The children of the night . . . what a mess they make!"

The film must be seen to be believed.[24]

Director Jan de Bont (*Speed, Twister, Lara Croft Tomb Raider: The Cradle of Life*) has reportedly obtained the rights from Stoker's estate to create a new film, with the working title *The Un-Dead*. Elizabeth Miller, in private correspondence with this editor, reports that the initial script takes place thirty years after the events of the narrative, and a book, described as a sequel to Stoker's narrative, is planned. However, the film has not commenced production. A much-touted original script of *Sherlock Holmes and the Vengeance of Dracula*, reportedly sold to Columbia Pictures in 1999, apparently died tragically with its screenwriter, Michael Valle, in 2001, and "development hell" is a special place populated by many beings besides vampires. However, Dracula will surely return to the screen soon, in one form or another. In the words of film critic James Craig Holte, "It is difficult, after all, to kill the undead."[25]

---

[24] Adult-film versions of the narrative include the 1979 *Dracula's Bride*, rereleased as *Dracula Sucks* and in 1980 as *Lust at First Bite*, starring Jaime Gillis as Dracula and borrowing heavily from Stoker's narrative; *Dracula* (1994), distinguished only by inclusion of the ubiquitous Ron Jeremy as a hunchback; *Dracula the Dirty Old Man* (1969), starring the legendary John Holmes as "Count Spatula" and Vince Kelly as Alucard; *Guess What Happened to Dracula* (1970), in which Dracula has taken the name Count Adrian; and *Dracula and the Boys* (1969; also known as *Does Dracula Really Suck?*), a gay vampire film.

[25] Holte, "Film Adaptations of *Dracula*," 324.

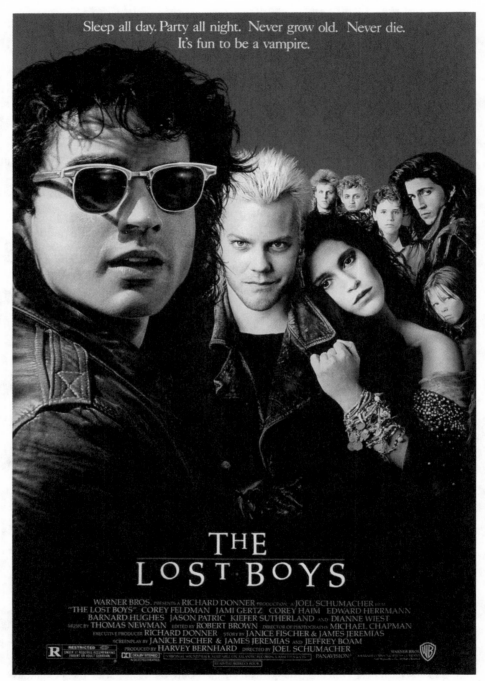

The Lost Boys, starring Kiefer Sutherland as David.
(Warner Bros. Pictures, 1987)

DRACULA'S FAMILY TREE

. . . he is known everywhere that men have been.

—Professor Abraham Van Helsing

"THROUGHOUT THE WHOLE vast shadowy world of ghosts and demons," writes Montague Summers, "there is no figure so terrible, no figure so dreaded and abhorred, yet dight with such fearful fascination, as the vampire, who is himself neither ghost nor demon, but yet who partakes the dark natures and possesses the mysterious and terrible qualities of both."[1] What is a vampire? For purposes of this history, the simplest definition may be applied: a formerly dead person returned to life.[2]

[1] Montague Summers, *The Vampire: His Kith and Kin* (New York: E. P. Dutton, 1929), 1. The Reverend Montague Summers (1880–1948) pursued stories of vampires throughout his life and gained a reputation as something more than an academic historian of the black arts. "It seems likely," wrote Father Brocard Sewell in his introduction to Summers's *The Vampire in Europe*, "that there were certain events in his younger days, known only to himself and a few others, which were best forgotten. It is quite probable that the warnings sounded in his books against the dangers of dabbling in necromancy were based on some early experiences of his own" (Montague Summers, *The Vampire in Europe* [Hyde Park, NY: University Books, 1961]).

[2] Calmet labelled as revenants those who "have been dead a considerable time, sometimes more, sometimes less; who leave their tombs, and come and disturb the living, sucking their blood, appearing to them, making a noise at their doors and in their houses, and lastly, often causing their death" (*The Phantom World: Concerning Apparitions and Vampires* [London: Wordsworth Editions, Ltd., in assocation with The Folklore Society, 2001], 211). The masterful treatise of Dom Augustine Calmet (1672–1757), titled *Dissertations sur les apparitions des anges, des démons et des espirits. Et sur les revanans et vampires de Hongrie, de Boheme, de Maravie et de Silésie*, was first published in Paris in 1746. In 1850, the English scholar-clergyman Dr. Henry Christmas translated and edited Calmet's work and published it as *The Phantom World: The Philosophy of Spirits, Apparitions, &c.* (London: Richard Bentley). Most recently the entire two-volume treatise (volume 2 covers, among other subjects, "apparitions of the souls of the dead") has been reprinted by Wordsworth Editions, Ltd., in association with The Folklore Society in a trade paperback edition (2001). Calmet's work was a response to the plague of vampirism sweeping Europe in the early 1700s and approached the subject

Here the vampire is distinguished from the zombie, an animated corpse with no intelligence.

The vampire, the revenant, the undead, is reportedly of ancient origins, with myths and legends traced back to Egyptian, Chinese, Greek, Babylonian, Assyrian, and other Eastern cultures of antiquity. Not all associate the undead with blood and blood-sucking, and some tales report the vampire as having the ability to change shape or to pass through the earth or a coffin or tomb. There is little resemblance among these early accounts, and only after 1670 did a pattern of observations of vampires begin to emerge—labelled by some as "epidemics" of vampirism.

The first widely published report (1672) related to Istria, in modern Croatia, on the Adriatic. Subsequently widespread incidents were recorded in East Prussia (1710 and 1721), Hungary (1725–1730), Austrian Serbia (1725–1732), East Prussia (1750), Silesia (1755), Wallachia (1756), and Russia (1772). Some of these early cases related to named individuals—Giure Grando (Istria), Peter Plogojowitz (Serbia), Arnold Paole (Medvegia, near Belgrade), and several villagers from Olmutz, Austria—and government reports record in detail the testimony of reputable churchmen, scientists, and military personnel who examined the bodies of the alleged vampires. The signs of vampirism were unmistakable to these witnesses: corpses bloated with blood, often with luxuriant hair and nails, evidence of movement of the corpses, and sounds of protest emitted when the corpses were impaled or punctured with wooden or iron stakes.

What caused the appearance of these vampires? That is, what made some corpses into vampires while others rested in peace? Not surprisingly, there are almost as many ascriptions of causes as there are cultures with traditions of vampirism.[3] For example, the *Nachzehrer* of Bavaria is the end result of being born with a second skin or caul; the *pijawica* of Croatia is cursed by reason of incestuous relations with the mother; the *Kuzlak* of Dalmatia has been weaned too early; the *upir* of Poland are born with teeth; the *myertovets*, *vurdalak*, and *upirzhy* of Russia are the offspring of a witch or werewolf, whereas the *strigoil* and *muronul* of Roumania were born out of wedlock to parents also born out of wedlock; and the *bruxsa* of Portugal are the product of witchcraft.[4]

---

from a religious perspective. He sought to distinguish the folklore tales of vampirism from the Catholic doctrine of miracles and to expose blasphemous doctrines and ignorance. Although later scholars (such as Voltaire) accused Calmet of being credulous and uncritical, his analysis represents a serious consideration of the problem of extensive reports of vampiric incidents.

[3] For example, the BBC website (www.bbc.co.uk/dna/h2g2/A273566) lists thirty-nine different cultures with vampire legends and myths.

[4] See, for example, Gabriel Ronay, *The Truth about Dracula* (New York: Stein and Day, 1972),

And how may the vampire be destroyed? Again, remedies are contradictory and various, although many involve decapitation, staking (with wood or iron), burning, and other means of ensuring that the corpse will not be in a physical condition to be mobile. Some of the more unusual prophylactics are burial of the corpse at a crossroads (Bohemia), chaining the corpse to the grave with wild roses (Bulgaria), piling stones on the grave (Ireland), burial facedown, which presumably confuses the revenant so that he or she cannot escape upward (Poland), placing a lemon in the corpse's mouth (Saxony), and burying poppy seeds in the grave—this for the curious reason that the undead cannot resist obsessively counting the seeds to the point of ignoring everything else and therefore will not bother the family (Prussia).[5] One of the more pleasant remedies is that prescribed in the village of Căzăneşti in Roumania: in order to be rid of a *strigoi* generated by a cat or a dog walking over or under an unburied body, bury a bottle of wine near the person's grave, wait six weeks, dig up the bottle, and share it with those you wish to protect.[6]

Of course, not all corpses become vampires, and tests have been devised to determine the true vampire from the merely bloated corpse. Agnes Murgoçi, whose 1926 article on Roumanian folklore is widely respected and reprinted,[7] explains the local tests:

1. The vampire's household, family, and livestock, and possibly even the livestock of the whole village, die off rapidly.
2. The vampire comes back in the night and speaks with the family. This intercourse may be disruptive or helpful; for example, some vampires have helped with the housework and cut wood. Female vampires are reported to return to their children.
3. If the local priest reads a service at the grave and the evil that is occurring does not cease, the occupant of the grave must be a vampire.
4. A hole about the size of a serpent may be found near the tombstone of the dead man. This is the exit of the vampire from the grave.

22–23, for a more complete table, and of course Summers's books have extensive chapters on the origins of vampires. There are also numerous country-by-country studies; see, for example, Jan Louis Perkowski's "The Romanian Folkloric Vampire" (in *The Vampire: A Casebook*, ed. Alan Dundes [Madison: Univ. of Wisconsin Press, 1998], 35–46) for a detailed listing of causes of vampirism found in Roumanian folklore, including a cat walking over or under an unburied corpse.

[5] See Ronay, Summers, and Perkowski in notes 1 and 4 above.

[6] Perkowski, "The Romanian Folkloric Vampire."

[7] Agnes Murgoçi, "The Vampire in Roumania," *Folk-Lore* 37, 4 (1926): 320–49; reprinted in *The Vampire: A Casebook*, ed. Alan Dundes (Madison: Univ. of Wisconsin Press, 1998), 12–34.

5. Neither a white horse nor a gander will walk over the grave of a vampire.
6. On exhuming the corpse, if it is a vampire it will be found to be:
   a. red in the face, even for months and years after burial,
   b. with the face turned downwards,
   c. with a foot retracted and forced into a corner of the grave or coffin.

If relations have died, the mouth will be red with blood. If the vampire has ruined things at home, the mouth will be covered with maize meal.

Murgoçi warns that if the vampire is not destroyed, it will pursue its evil ways for seven years, preying on its family, its village, its country, and eventually travelling to another country, where it may become a human again.

Many artistic records of vampires appear in the literature of Europe after the epidemics ran their courses and before *Dracula*.[8] The earliest long account is that in Johann Ludwig Tieck's "Wake Not the Dead," which tells of Brunhilda, a Burgundian noble who preyed mainly on children.[9] The English Lord Ruthven, described in John Polidori's "The Vampyre" (1819), is discussed in the introductory essay "The Context of *Dracula*." Gorcha and Sdenka are peasant vampires from Moldavia, whose fates are recounted in Aleksei Tolstoi's "The Family of the Vourdalak."[10] Another English lord, Sir Francis Varney, won widespread fame in *Varney, the Vampyre* (1847), also discussed in "The Context of *Dracula*." Alexandre Dumas's Kostaki ("The Pale Lady," also known as "The Pale-Faced Lady," 1848) was from the Carpathians, like Dracula. Another aristocrat from the Carpathians, Count Azzo von Klatka, is the central figure in "The Mysterious Stranger" (translated into English in 1860), by an unknown writer.[11] Sir Richard Francis Burton, in 1870, published *Vikram and the Vampire*, an account of a *baital* from Benares, India, set in the early Christian era. The Countess Mircalla, the focus of Joseph Sheridan Le Fanu's "Carmilla" (1872), is discussed in "The Context of *Dracula*." Guy de Maupassant's "The Horla" (1887) records the discovery of the invisible Horla, a kind of spiritual vampire. In 1894, two notable vampire accounts surfaced: the German poet and fantasy writer Count Eric Stenbock's "A True Story of a Vampire," about Count Vardalek of Hungary, and "A Kiss of Judas," by "X. L." (Julian Osgood Field), a tale of Isaac Lebedenko, who—uniquely—returns as a female vampire. Just before *Dracula* appeared, in 1896,

---

[8] A superb "Vampire Mosaic," with a much more detailed listing, appears in Christopher Frayling, ed., *Vampyres: Lord Byron to Count Dracula* (London: Faber and Faber, 1991).

[9] The exact date of publication is unknown; Frayling (*Vampyres*) suggests ca. 1800.

[10] Frayling (*Vampyres*) suggests a publication date of the early 1840s.

[11] The account is discussed in chapter 2, note 9.

Title illustration for Mary E. Braddon's "Good Lady Ducayne."
Gordon Brown, *Strand Magazine*, February 1896

Title illustration by Gordon Browne for the Strand Magazine, *February 1896.*

Mary E. Braddon, a neighbour of Stoker's, published an account of Lady Adeline Ducayne ("Good Lady Ducayne"), who sustained herself on blood procured by her physician.

Frayling divides these records into four categories: the folkloric vampire, the female vampire, the aristocratic vampire, and the "unseen force." Although there is wild disparity among the records, the consensus regarding the characteristics of the vampire seems to be that (a) the vampire drinks blood, usually that of a carefully selected victim, (b) the drinking of blood not only sustains the vampire but produces a youthful appearance, or "rejuvenates," the creature, and (c) the vampire is affected by holy artifacts and can be destroyed by decapitation, burning, or a wooden or iron stake through the heart.[12] Of course, the vampires recorded in *Dracula* exhibit further characteristics not necessarily in evidence in these earlier accounts: the lack of a shadow, unphotographability, supernatural strength, shape-shifting abilities, and telepathic command. Only shape-shifting is part of the folkloric record. In some cultures, the werewolf (or other were-beast) and vampire are linked by the common shape-shifting trait. However, the literature of the nineteenth century failed to provide a coherent description of the origin of the vampire.

Three late-twentieth-century accounts of vampires offer independent suggestions of the vampire's origins, powers, and weaknesses. The supernatural-

[12] Frayling, *Vampyres*.

themed books of Anne Rice—including the collection known as the Vampire Chronicles—began to appear in 1976 and now number seventeen volumes.[13] The popular television series *Buffy the Vampire Slayer* and its spin-off *Angel* (referred to in this work as the "*Buffy* universe") appeared from 1997 to 2003.[14] The tales of Comte de Saint-Germain, by Chelsea Quinn Yarbro, are recounted in twenty-four books to date, with more scheduled.[15]

In the mythos created by Anne Rice, vampires are descended from two Egyptian nobles, Akasha and Enkil ("Those Who Must Be Kept"), who worship the god Osiris. Akasha and Enkil are possessed by a spirit who desires to experience a corporeal existence. The spirit entered into them through wounds, and its presence causes Akasha and Enkil to create other vampires, to share the burden of obtaining blood for the spirit. Once created, the spirit then invades

[13] The Vampire Chronicles consist of *Interview with the Vampire* (1976), *The Vampire Lestat* (1985), *The Queen of the Damned* (1988), *The Tale of the Body Thief* (1992), *Memnoch The Devil* (1995), *The Vampire Armand* (1998), *Merrick* (2000), *Blood and Gold* (2001), *Blackwood Farm* (2002), and *Blood Canticle* (2003) (all published in New York by Alfred A. Knopf). Two other books, which Rice calls "New Tales of the Vampires," are not strictly part of the Chronicles: *Pandora* (1998) and *Vittorio the Vampire* (1999). Rice has written five books about the powerful Mayfair witches, *The Witching Hour* (1990), *Lasher* (1993), *Taltos* (1994), *Blackwood Farm* (in which the Mayfair family enters the Vampire Chronicles), and *Blood Canticle*; therefore, the three books prior to *Blackwood Farm* may be seen as part of the Chronicles as well. A link among many of the books is the presence of the Talamasca, a secret organisation of scholars founded in AD 758 to study the supernatural; its motto is "We watch. And we are always there." Rice has indicated in interviews that there will be no more books from her about vampires. Also see Gary Hoppenstand and Ray B. Browne, eds., *The Gothic World of Anne Rice* (Bowling Green, OH: Bowling Green State Univ. Popular Press, 1996), and Katherine Ramsland, *The Vampire Companion: The Official Guide to Anne Rice's The Vampire Chronicles* (New York: Ballantine Books, 1995).

[14] Buffy Summers, the vampire slayer of the current generation ("into each generation a slayer is born"), first appeared in the theatrical film *Buffy the Vampire Slayer* (1992), which introduced many of the elements continued in the television series but fortunately none of the actors. The film takes place in Los Angeles; after the events of the film, Buffy moves to the fictional town of Sunnydale, California, where she attended Sunnydale High School (before its destruction at her graduation by a gigantic demon) and Sunnydale Community College. See Kathleen Tracy, *The Girl's Got Bite: The Original Unauthorized Guide to Buffy's World* (New York: St. Martin's Press, 2003), and Christopher Golden, Stephen R. Bissette, and Thomas E. Sniegoski, *Buffy the Vampire Slayer: The Monster Book* (New York: Simon Spotlight, 2000).

[15] As a result of the length of Saint-Germain's undead existence, Yarbro's books include as much historical epic as horror, and each is preceded by an historical essay regarding the period. See Sharon A. Russell, "Introducing Count Saint-Germain: Chelsea Quinn Yarbro's Heroic Vampire" (in *The Blood Is the Life: Vampires in Literature*, ed. Leonard G. Heldreth and Mary Pharr [Bowling Green, OH: Bowling Green State Univ. Popular Press, 1999], 141–54), and Sondra Ford Swift, "Toward the Vampire as Savior: Chelsea Quinn Yarbro's *Saint-Germain* Series Compared with Edward Bulwer-Lytton's *Zanoni*" (in *The Blood Is the Life*, 155–64).

these others, changing their cellular makeup and connecting them via a weak telepathic link.[16] The vampires populating Rice's books are all direct descendants of Akasha and Enkil—the more direct the relationship of a vampire to them, the more powerful the vampire.

Rice's view of vampires differs in many ways from traditional folklore. Although the vampires are sustained by blood and are immortal, Christian symbols and other religious relics have no power over them (and of course there is no satanic heritage). Like Dracula, they can survive exposure to the sun, although fire will destroy them. Wooden stakes, garlic, and other folkloric preventatives are not effective against them. They are reflected in mirrors, photographable, need no invitation to enter new places, and have souls like mortals. Although some sleep in coffins, this is a matter of "traditionalism" or personal choice, not necessity, and their native soil has no power. They are often unusually attractive, magnetic personalities, and the drinking of blood is a highly erotic experience for both vampire and prey. The "Dark Trick," as the

The vampire Lestat (Tom Cruise) in the film of Anne Rice's *Interview with the Vampire*.
(Geffen Pictures, 1994)

Rice vampires call it, of turning is accomplished by drinking most of the victim's blood, then causing the victim to drink the blood of the vampire. (Recall the transfer of blood between Dracula and Mina in Stoker's narrative.) Many of Rice's vampires are concerned with the same moral issues as mortals: right and wrong, good and evil, love and hate. Louis, the narrator of Rice's *Interview with the Vampire* (1976), is deeply troubled by the need to kill in order to survive. He and others eventually develop a credo of only victimising those who deserve death—wrongdoers.

---

[16] Unlike most vampire literature that preceded them, Rice's books are accounts of vampires told by the vampires themselves. The roots of vampirism are made clear in *The Queen of the Damned* (1988) and subsequent tales.

There is little sexuality in Rice's world, and such love as occurs is more likely to be male bonding than a male-female relationship. There is a great degree of intimacy between vampires and victims, and vampires often choose their victims because of their desire for intimacy. There are families of vampires in Rice's world too, although the immortality of the family members often leads to dysfunctional relationships and long separations, and the Dark Trick itself destroys the intimacy of vampire and victim, for vampires are unable to communicate telepathically with their "sires" (not unlike mortal children who cannot understand their parents).

In Rice's view, vampires possess powers setting them apart from the mortal world. They possess great strength and speed of movement, and their voices can be pitched differently from mortals (either too low for mortal hearing or extremely loud as a weapon). Some can leap to great heights, fly, and even levitate; others are able to practise astral projection, leaving their physical bodies behind. Vampires heal quickly from wounds. Their senses are acute, and they can read the minds of mortals and can project images and thoughts. Emotionally, vampires seem to have heightened experiences as well, perhaps because of their immortality.

The rules of the *Buffy* universe are considerably different from Rice's and lean more heavily on traditional folklore. According to Joss Whedon and the other writers of the film and series, in the early days of this world "pure" demons and their offspring were a large part of the population. As humans evolved, however, demons fled this world for separate dimensions, "hell" dimensions, where they could thrive unmolested. Dozens and dozens of species of half-demons (demons interbred with humans) remained, however, and continue to make up a significant portion of our population. Many half-demons (lesser demons, although often referred to as just "demons") are functioning members of society, and not necessarily evil; there is a thriving demon underworld, complete with demon businesses, clubs, and social networks.

The vampire, in the view of these creators, is a human corpse inhabited by an otherwise bodiless demon. Vampires have no shape-shifting powers, turn to ash or dust when killed, and can be killed by decapitation, penetration of the heart with wood, or fire. They are burnt by direct sunlight but can function during the day. Vampires in the *Buffy* universe are affected by religious symbols but can cross running water, enter a church, and have no need to sleep in a coffin or bed of native earth. They cast no reflection but do cast a shadow and can be photographed. *Buffy*'s vampires do not breathe.

These vampires may not enter a private home unless invited to do so by a resident. This does not apply to public domiciles (hotel rooms) or former residences, and any person residing in the home or apartment appears able to give the requisite consent. Once the vampires have been invited into a home, they may return at any time. However, these "rules" do not apply to the residence of a vampire. In *Buffy* culture, the vampire's attentions are most commonly unwanted; although there are instances of seduction, they are far overshadowed by brutal and often indiscriminate attacks by vampires seeking sustenance. These vampires, although strong, do not possess human souls[17] and therefore share none of Anne Rice's vampires' concern for moral issues. It appears that there may be a scientific means of rendering vampires incapable of harming humans. Spike, one of the most ruthless of the *Buffy* vampires, is "tamed" by a chip implanted in his brain by a mysterious government agency.

Although vampires pervade the *Buffy* universe, many of the adventures of Buffy and her friends have little to do with vampires. Buffy herself is the Slayer, a hero who is endowed with special strength and agility but who must learn her craft from the Council of Watchers. Eventually, Buffy comes to depend more on her friends than her advisors. In the final season of the *Buffy* television series,

The vampire Angel/Angelus with Buffy (David Boreanaz as Angel, Sarah Michelle Gellar as Buffy). From the television series *Buffy the Vampire Slayer* (Mutant Enemy, 1997–2004)

Buffy must confront the First, the source of all evil in the world. The mythos is expanded in *Angel*, set in Los Angeles. Ultimately, Angel, a vampire with a soul, becomes a champion on the side of the Powers That Be, in the great battle with the Senior Partners of the law firm of Wolfram & Hart. Numerous novelisations have taken the story beyond the events described in the two series,[18] and a new series of comic books written by Joss Whedon (described by fans as "season eight of *Buffy*") has begun to appear.

There are twenty-six books about Comte de Saint-Germain and his friends. The first, *Hotel Transylvania*, appeared in 1978 and laid the groundwork for the Yarbro vampire legends: Saint-Germain himself is over four thousand years

---

[17] Of course, the vampires Angel (formerly Angelus) and Spike are the two great exceptions to this rule. Angel's soul has been restored to him by a Gypsy curse, as punishment for his terrible slaughters; his conscience is tormented by memories of his evil deeds. Spike, a vicious killer also known as William the Bloody, seeks to have his soul restored out of love for Buffy.

[18] For example, *Queen of the Slayers* by Nancy Holder (2005), which recounts the events immediately following the conclusion of season 7, the final season, of *Buffy*.

Comte de Saint-Germain.
Miran Kim, for the cover of
Chelsea Quinn Yarbro's
Hotel Transylvania (Lancaster, PA:
Stealth Press, 2001)

old and requires his native earth for his rest. He casts no reflection, finds sunlight harmful, and although he heals rapidly, is physically vulnerable. He is essentially human in appearance. He requires intimacy with mortals and only takes blood in a setting of erotic exchange and emotional release. He often offers his partners the vampire life, but once a woman becomes a vampire, he can no longer share the bond of vampire/victim relations.

Saint-Germain became a vampire when he offered himself in sacrifice to the "god" of his people (pre-Etruscan). His great wisdom, generosity, and supportive nature have led him to be likened to the figure of Jesus. He is prepared to die "the true death" to save others. He also frequently risks his life by practising medicine and offering healing in cultures that little understand and often vilify his skills. Unlike Rice's vampires, Saint-Germain seems long ago to have solved his moral issues. He does not require death to survive, only blood, and he has chosen a life of goodness, mercy, and aid to the less fortunate mortals among whom he lives. Saint-Germain is the opposite of the vampires depicted in the *Buffy* saga (with the marked exception of Angel and eventually Spike), because unlike them, he has retained his immortal soul along with an immortal body.

Modern tales of vampires continue to appear with regularity, each with its own interpretation of the consequences of vampirism. The family tree appears to have no limit to its growth, so long as immortality and the mysteries of death continue to fascinate.

Billy the Kid vs. Dracula, starring John Carradine as Dracula.
(Circle Productions, 1966)

THE FRIENDS OF DRACULA

*We have on our side power of combination—
a power denied to the vampire kind . . .*

—Professor Abraham Van Helsing

BRAM STOKER'S NARRATIVE *Dracula* has spawned legions of fans over the century since its publication, but it was not until 1965 that the first legion was organised. Dr. Jeanne Keyes Youngson, who remains active in *Dracula* circles, formed the Count Dracula Fan Club (later the International Count Dracula Fan Club), based in New York, and created a number of fan-written publications—newsletters, handbooks, and the like. Today known as the Vampire Empire, its influence is small, but Dr. Youngson maintains a reference library available to scholars, and the organisation continues to make its presence known through the Internet.[1]

The Count Dracula Society was created in Hollywood, California, in 1962 by Dr. Donald Reed. The group focussed primarily on genre films and in 1972 transformed into the Academy of Science Fiction, Fantasy & Horror Films. In 1973, the Dracula Society was formed in London by Bruce Wightman (its first chairman) and Bernard Davies (who initially was its secretary and now serves as its chairman emeritus) and other friends of the work. Its initial honorary president was Christopher Lee, and Peter Cushing and Vincent Price were made honorary life members. The society published four issues of an occasional journal (the *Dracula Journal*) from 1976 to 1982, with amateur scholarship in the finest tradition of Holmesian studies (and with a substantial common membership with the Sherlock Holmes Society of London). The organisation continues today, conducting regular meetings in London as well as trips to sites associated with *Dracula* and associated Gothic literature. Its chair is Julia Kruk, and its current publication is titled *Voices from the Vaults*. The society annually presents its

---

[1] See www.benecke.com/vampire.html.

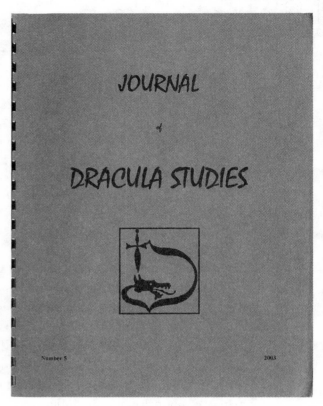

Voices from the Vaults,
official publication of
The Dracula Society.

Journal of Dracula Studies,
published by the Canadian chapter
of the Transylvanian Society of Dracula.

Children of the Night Award for literature in the field as well as its Hamilton Deane Award for noteworthy stage or screen material.[2]

The Transylvanian Society of Dracula was founded in 1991 in Bucharest and has established chapters in several countries. The Roumanian chapter has organised symposia attracting scholars from around the world, and the proceedings are among the best *Dracula*-related scholarship published. The Canadian chapter (with several American members) is particularly active as well, under the leadership of Dr. Elizabeth Miller, and publishes the excellent *Journal of Dracula Studies*.[3]

[2] The society maintains a website at www.thedraculasociety.org.uk, and Julia Kruk may be reached at juliakruk@hotmail.com.

[3] The Canadian chapter's website is www.chebucto.ns.ca/recreation/TSD/tsdhompg.html. Dr. Miller's own homepage, www.ucs.mun.ca/~emiller/, contains many useful links to *Dracula*-related material.

The Bram Stoker Society Journal, published from 1989 to 2001 by the Bram Stoker Society.

The Bram Stoker Society, formed in 1980 in Dublin by Leslie Shepherd and Dr. Albert Power, continues today under Dr. Power's stewardship. The society published a CD-ROM containing all thirteen issues of its fine *Bram Stoker Society Journal*, which ceased publication in 2001. (Shepherd's splendid collection of Stoker material is housed at the Dublin City Library, and its catalogue is accessible on the Internet.)[4] The society also works closely with the Bram Stoker Cultural Heritage Visitor Centre in Clontarf (Dublin). The centre maintains a small museum of Stoker-related material and has sponsored a summer school on Stoker and his writing.[5]

---

[4] See www.dublincity.ie/Images/LeslieShepardCollection_tcm35-38174.pdf.

[5] The centre's website is www.thebramstokerdraculaexperience.com. Visitors to the centre, both virtual and real, are encouraged.

The Fearless Vampire Killers, directed by Roman Polanski and starring Sharon Tate.
(Cadre Films, 1967)

BIBLIOGRAPHY

. . . a vast number of English books, whole shelves of them . . .

—JONATHAN HARKER

Ainsley's Nautical Almanac and Tide Tables for 1887. South Shields, England: Thomas L. Ainsley, 1887.

Allen, Vivien. *Hall Caine: Portrait of a Victorian Romancer*. Sheffield, England: Sheffield Academic Press, 1997.

Andrreescu, Stefan. *Vlad the Impaler: Dracula*. Bucaresti: Romanian Cultural Foundation Pub. House, 1999.

Anonymous. "The Mysterious Stranger." In *Odds and Ends*. 1860. Reprinted in *The Literary Gothic*, 13 June 2003; available online at www.litgothic.com/Texts/mysterious_stranger.pdf.

Anonymous. "A Thirst for Blood." *East London Advertiser*, 6 October 1888.

Anonymous. *In Highgate Cemetery*. London: Highgate Cemetery, Ltd., 2005.

Arata, Stephen D. "The Occidental Tourist: *Dracula* and the Anxiety of Reverse Colonization." *Victorian Studies* 33 (1990): 621–45.

Atkinson, John Christopher. *Forty Years in a Moorland Parish*. New York: Macmillan & Co., 1891.

Auerbach, Nina. *Woman and the Demon: The Life of a Victorian Myth*. Cambridge, MA: Harvard Univ. Press, 1982.

———. *Our Vampires, Ourselves*. Chicago: Univ. of Chicago Press, 1995.

Aylesworth, Thomas G. *The Story of Vampires*. Middletown, CT: Xerox Education Publications, 1977.

Babcock, Michael A. *The Night Attila Died: Solving the Murder of Attila the Hun*. New York: Berkley Books, 2005.

Baedeker, Karl. *Great Britain: Handbook for Travellers*. 3d rev. ed. Leipsic: Karl Baedeker, 1894.

———. *Austria, Including Hungary, Transylvania, Dalmatia, and Bosnia; Handbook for Travellers*. 8th rev. ed. Leipsic: Karl Baedeker, 1896.

———. *London and Its Environs: Handbook for Travellers*. 10th rev. ed. Leipsic: Karl Baedeker, 1896.

Bandelier, Adolph F. *The Islands of Titicaca and Koati.* New York: The Hispanic Society of America, 1910.

Barber, Paul. *Vampires, Burial, and Death: Folklore and Reality.* New Haven, CT: Yale Univ. Press, 1990.

Baring-Gould, Sabine. *A Book of Folk-Lore.* London: W. Collins Sons & Co., Ltd., 1913.

———. *The Book of Were-Wolves.* London: Smith, Elder & Co., 1865.

———. *Curious Myths of the Middle Ages.* Edinburgh: John Grant, 1896.

———. *Germany: Present and Past.* New York: Dodd, Mead & Co., n. d. [ca. 1882].

Bassett, Fletcher S. *Legends and Superstitions of the Sea and of Sailors.* Detroit, MI: Singing Tree Press, 1971.

Beeton, Isabella. *Book of Household Management.* London: S. O. Beeton, 1861.

Belford, Barbara. *Bram Stoker and the Man Who Was Dracula.* Cambridge, MA: Da Capo Press, 2002.

Bentley, Christopher F. "The Monster in the Bedroom: Sexual Symbolism in Bram Stoker's *Dracula.*" *Literature and Psychology* 22 (1972): 27–34.

Bierman, Joseph S. "Dracula: Prolonged Childhood Illness, and the Oral Triad." *American Imago* 29 (1972): 186–98.

———. "The Genesis and Dating of *Dracula* from Bram Stoker's Working Notes." *Notes and Queries* 24 (1977): 34–41.

Binstead, Arthur M. "Charing Cross." In *Pitcher in Paradise.* London: Sands & Co., 1903.

Bird, Isabella. *The Golden Chersonese.* London: John Murray, 1883.

Blinderman, Charles S. "Vampurella: Darwin and Count Dracula." *Massachusetts Review* 21 (1980): 411, 428.

Bohren, Craig F., and Alistair B. Fraser. "Fall Streaks: Parabolic Trajectories with a Twist." *American Journal of Physics* 60 (1992): 1030–33.

Bondeson, Jan. *Buried Alive: The Terrifying History of Our Most Primal Fear.* New York: W. W. Norton, 2001.

Boner, Charles. *Transylvania: Its Products and Its People.* London: Longmans, Green, Reader and Dyer, 1865.

Book of Common Prayer. Stereotype Edition. Oxford: Bensley, Cooke and Collingwood, 1815.

Boone, Troy. "'He is English and therefore adventurous': Politics, Decadence and *Dracula.*" *Studies in the Novel* 25 (1993): 76–91.

Booth, Charles. *Life and Labour of the People in London.* 17 vols. London: Macmillan & Co., 1902–1903.

Borrow, George. *The Romany Rye.* London: Nelson, 1857.

Braddon, Mary E. "Good Lady Ducayne." *Strand Magazine,* February 1896.

Bradshaw's Continental Railway, Steam Transit, and General Guide. Manchester, England: Henry Blacklock & Co., 1903.

Bradshaw's General Railway and Steam Navigation Guide for Great Britain and Ireland. Manchester, England: Henry Blacklock & Co., 1887. Reprint, Newton Abbot, England: David & Charles, 1968.

Brandes-Latea, Stefan, and Luminita Dimulescu. *Dracula's Descendants*. Bucaresti: Nemira Publishing House, 1998.

Brewer, E. Cobham. *Dictionary of Phrase and Fable*. Philadelphia: Henry Altemus, 1894.

Bryant, Joseph D. *Manual of Operative Surgery*. New York: D. Appleton and Co., 1887.

Bucknill, John Charles. *A Manual of Psychological Medicine: Containing the History, Nosology, Description, Statistics, Diagnosis, Pathology, and Treatment of Insanity, with an Appendix of Cases*. New York: Classics of Psychiatry and Behavioral Sciences Library, 1993.

Bud, Robert, Bernard Finn, and Helmuth Trischler, eds. *Manifesting Medicine: Bodies and Machines. Studies in the History of Science, Technology & Medicine*. Amsterdam: Harwood Academic Publishers, 1999.

Bunson, Matthew. *The Vampire Encyclopedia*. New York: Gramercy, 2000.

Burton, Richard F. *Vikram and the Vampire, or, Tales of Hindu Devilry*. London: Longmans, Green & Co., 1870.

Butler, Samuel. "How to Make the Best of Life." In *Essays on Life, Art, and Science*. London: Grant Richards, 1904.

Byers, Thomas. "Good Men and Monsters: The Defenses of *Dracula*." *Literature and Psychology* 31 (1981): 24–31.

Bynum, W. F., and Roy Porter, eds. *Medicine and the Five Senses*. Cambridge, England: Cambridge Univ. Press, 2005.

Byron, Lord [George Gordon]. *The Giaour, A Fragment of a Turkish Tale*. 3d ed. London: John Murray, 1813.

————. *Letters and Journals of Lord Byron: With Notices of His Life*. Edited by Thomas Moore. London: John Murray, 1830.

Cain, Jimmie E. " 'With the Unspeakable': *Dracula* and Russophobia—Tourism, Racism and Imperialism." In *Dracula: The Shade and the Shadow*, edited by Elizabeth Miller, 104–15. Westcliff-on-Sea, England: Desert Island Books, 1998.

Caine, Hall. "Bram Stoker: The Story of a Great Friendship." [London] *Daily Telegraph*, 24 April 1912.

Calmet, Dom Augustine. *The Phantom World: Concerning Apparitions and Vampires*. London: Wordsworth Editions, Ltd., in association with The Folklore Society, 2001.

Carpenter, William, M.D. *Principles of Mental Physiology*. London: Henry S. King, 1874.

Carter, Margaret L. "Share Alike: *Dracula* and the Sympathetic Vampire in Mid-Twentieth Century Pulp Fiction." In *Bram Stoker's Dracula: Sucking Through the Century, 1897–1997*, edited by Carol Margaret Davison, 175–94. Toronto: Dundurn Press, 1997.

Cassell's Household Guide: Being A Complete Encylopædia of Domestic and Social Economy and Forming a Guide to Every Department of Practical Life. 4 vols. London: Cassell, Petter, and Galpin, n. d. [ca. 1880].

Charlton. Lionel. *History of Whitby and of Whitby Abbey*. York, England: A. Ward, 1779.

Chetwynd-Hayes, R. *Dracula's Children*. London: William Kimber, 1987.

Chiretu, Marilena Hertanu. *Draula legenda si istorie*. Bucaresti: Editura Paralela 45, 2000.

Clemens, Valerie. "Dracula: The Reptilian Brain at the Fin de Siècle." In *Dracula: The Shade *and the Shadow,* edited by Elizabeth Miller, 205–18. Westcliff-on-Sea, England: Desert Island Books, 1998.

Cole, Simon. *Suspect Identities.* Cambridge, MA: Harvard Univ. Press, 2002.

Coleridge, Henry Nelson, ed. *The Poetical Works of S. T. Coleridge.* London: W. Pickering, 1834.

Collins, Charles M. *A Feast of Blood.* New York: Avon Books, 1975.

Cooley, Winnifred Harper. *The New Womanhood.* New York: Broadway Publishing Co., 1904.

Copper, Basil, ed. *The Vampire.* New York: Carol Publishing Corp., 1989.

Cowper, Katie. "The Decline of Reserve Among Women." *The Nineteenth Century* 27 (1890): 65–71.

Craft, Christopher. " 'Kiss Me with Those Red Lips': Gender and Inversion in Bram Stoker's *Dracula.*" *Representations* 8 (1984): 107–33.

Crosse, Andrew F. *Round About the Carpathians.* London: Blackwood, 1878.

Curl, James Stevens. *The Victorian Celebration of Death.* Phoenix Mill, England: Sutton Publishing, 2004.

Dagi, T. Forcht. "The Management of Head Trauma." In *A History of Neurosurgery in Its Scientific and Professional Contexts,* edited by Samuel H. Greenblatt, 289–94. Park Ridge, IL: American Association of Neurological Surgeons, 1997.

Dalby, Richard, and William Hughes, eds. *Bram Stoker: A Bibliography.* Westcliff-on-Sea, England: Desert Island Books, 2004.

Davies, Bernard. "Bram Stoker's Transylvania—A Critical Reassessment." *Bram Stoker Society Journal* 10 (1998): 3–16.

———. "Unearthing *Dracula*—Burying Stoker." *Bram Stoker Society Journal* 11 (1999): 38–45.

———. "Grinding Slowly . . . But Exceeding Small." *Bram Stoker Society Journal* 12 (2000): 33–43.

Davies, David Stuart. *A Tangled Skein.* Ashcroft, BC: Calabash Press, 1995.

Davison, Carol Margaret. "Blood Brothers: Dracula and Jack the Ripper." In *Bram Stoker's Dracula: Sucking Through the Century, 1897–1997,* edited by Carol Margaret Davison, 147–73. Toronto: Dundurn Press, 1997.

Deane, Hamilton, and John L. Balderston. *Dracula: The Ultimate, Illustrated Edition of the World-Famous Vampire Play.* Edited and annotated by David J. Skal. New York: St. Martin's Press, 1993.

de Maupassant, Guy. *The Horla, or Modern Ghosts.* Paris: Paul Ollendorf, 1887.

de Voragine, Jacobus. *The Golden Legend, or Lives of the Saints.* London: William Caxton, 1485.

Dickens, Charles, Jr. *Dickens's Dictionary of London, 1888: An Unconventional Handbook.* London: Charles Dickens & Evans, 1888.

———. *Dictionary of the Thames, from Its Source to the Nore. 1894. An Unconventional Handbook.* London: J. Smith, 1894.

Dickens, David B. "The German Matrix of Stoker's *Dracula.*" In *Dracula: The Shade and the Shadow*, edited by Elizabeth Miller, 31–40. Westcliff-on-Sea, England: Desert Island Books, 1998.

Doré, Gustave, and Blanchard Jerrold. *London: A Pilgrimage*. New York: Harper & Bros., 1890.

Dorman, Rushton M. *The origin of primitive superstitions and their development into the worship of spirits and doctrine of spirtual agency among the aborigines of America*. Philadelphia: J. B. Lippincott, 1881.

Druitt, Robert. "Report on the Cheap Wines from France, Italy, Austria, Greece, and Hungary; their quality, wholesomeness, and price, etc." London: privately printed, 1865.

Dumas, Alexandre. "The Pale Lady," with Paul Bocage, *Les Mille et Un Fantômes: Une Journeé à Fontenay-aux-Roses*. Brussels: [n. p.], 1848.

Dundes, Alan, ed. *The Vampire: A Casebook*. Madison: Univ. of Wisconsin Press, 1998.

Edmunds, Henry. "The Graphophone." Paper presented at a meeting of the British Association for the Advancement of Science, 7 September 1888. Reproduced at http://history.sandiego.edu/GEN/recording/ar312.html. (Original in Tainter Papers, Smithsonian National Museum of American History, Washington, D.C.)

Eighteen-Bisang, Robert. "Dracula, Jack the Ripper, and A Thirst for Blood." *Ripperologist* 60 (2005): 3–12.

Eling, Paul, ed. *Reader in the History of Aphasia: From Franz Gall to Norman Geschwind*. Philadelphia: J. Benjamins Pub. Co., 1994.

Ellmann, Richard. *Oscar Wilde*. New York: Vintage Books, 1988.

Ellmers, Chris, and Alex Werner. *Dockland Life: A Pictorial History of London's Docks 1860–2000*. Edinburgh: Mainstream Publishing, 2000.

Eltis, Sos. "Corruption of the Blood and Degeneration of the Race: *Dracula* and Policing the Borders of Gender." In *Dracula*, edited by John Paul Riquelme, 450–64. New York: Bedford/St. Martin's Press, 2002.

Elworthy, Frederick Thomas. *The Evil Eye*. London: John Murray, 1895.

Encyclopædia Britannica. 9th ed. 1888. Reprint, Chicago: R. S. Peale and Werner Company, 1893.

Encyclopædia Britannica. 11th ed. New York: Encyclopædia Britannica Co., 1910.

Estleman, Loren. *Sherlock Holmes vs. Dracula: or, The Adventure of the Sanguinary Count*. Garden City, NY: Doubleday, 1978.

Evans, Arthur B. "Optograms and Fiction: Photo in a Dead Man's Eye." *Science Fiction Studies* 20, 3, 61 (1993): 341–61.

Farson, Daniel. *The Man Who Wrote Dracula: A Biography of Bram Stoker*. London: Michael Joseph, 1975.

A Fellow of the Carpathian Society. [Elizabeth Sara (Nina) Mazuchelli.] *"Magyarland": Being the Narrative of Our Travels Through the Highlands and Lowlands of Hungary*. 2 vols. London: Sampson Low, Marston, Searle & Rivington, 1881.

Ferrier, James. *Institutes of Metaphysic*. Edinburgh: William Blackwood & Sons, 1854.

Flanders, Judith. *Inside the Victorian Home*. New York: W. W. Norton, 2005.

Fontana, Ernest. "Lombroso's Criminal Man and Stoker's Dracula." *Victorian Newsletter* 66 (1984): 25-27.

Frayling, Christopher, ed. *Vampyres: Lord Byron to Count Dracula.* London: Faber and Faber, 1991.

Freeman, Michael J., and Derek H. Aldcroft, eds. *Transport in Victorian Britain.* Manchester, England: Manchester Univ. Press, 1991.

Gall, Franz. Letter to Mr. Joseph F. von Retzer, 1 October 1798. In *Reader in the History of Aphasia: From Franz Gall to Norman Geschwind,* edited by Paul Eling. Philadelphia: J. Benjamins Pub. Co., 1994.

Galton, Francis, W. R. Inge, [Arthur Cecil] Pigou, and Mary Denby. *The Problem of the Feeble-Minded.* London: P. S. King & Son, 1909. [Abstract of *Report of the Royal Commission on the Control and Care of the Feeble-minded* (London: His Majesty's Stationery Office, 1908).]

Garden, Nancy. *Vampires.* Philadelphia: J. B. Lippincott, 1973.

Gardiner, A. G. *Pillars of Society.* New York: Dodd, Mead & Co., 1914.

Geare, Michael. *Dracula's Diary.* Toronto: Saunders of Toronto, Ltd., 1982.

Gelder, Ken. *Reading the Vampire.* London: Routledge, 1994.

Gerard, Emily. "Transylvanian Superstitions." *The Nineteenth Century* 18 (1885): 130–50.

———. *The Land Beyond the Forest: Facts, Figures and Fancies.* New York: Harper, 1888.

Gerard, John. *The Herbal: or, General History of Plants.* The complete 1633 ed., as rev. and enl. by Thomas Jefferson. New York: Dover Publications, 1975.

Gibbon, Edward. *The History of the Decline and Fall of the Roman Empire.* 6 vols. London: Strahan and Cadell, 1776, 1781, 1788.

Glut, Donald F. *The Dracula Book.* Metuchen, NJ: Scarecrow Press, 1975.

Golden, Christopher, Stephen R. Bissette, and Thomas E. Sniegoski. *Buffy the Vampire Slayer: The Monster Book.* New York: Simon Spotlight, 2000.

Goleman, Daniel. "Clues to a Dark Nurturing Ground for One Serial Killer." *New York Times,* 7 August 1991; available online at www.nytimes.com.

Gordon, W. J. *The Horse World of London.* London: Leisure Hour Library, 1893.

Gould, Charles. *Mythical Monsters.* New York: Crescent Books, 1989.

Greenway, John L. "Seward's Folly: *Dracula* as a Critique of 'Normal Science.' " *Stanford Literature Review* 3 (1986): 213–30.

Gregory, Constantine, and Craig Glenday. *Vampire Watcher's Handbook: A Guide for Slayers.* New York: St. Martin's Press, 2003.

Griffin, Gail B. " 'Your Girls That You Love Are Mine': *Dracula* and the Victorian Male Sexual Imagination." *International Journal of Women's Studies* 3 (1980): 454–65.

Gross, Edward, and Marc Shapiro. *The Vampire Interview Book.* New York: Image Publishing, 1991.

Gulley, Rosemary. *The Complete Vampire Companion.* New York: Macmillan, 1994.

Haining, Peter, ed. *The Dracula Centenary Book.* London: Souvenir Press, 1987.

Haining, Peter, and Peter Tremayne. *The Un-Dead: The Legend of Bram Stoker and Dracula.* London: Constable & Co., 1997.

Hammer, David L. *For the Sake of the Game.* Dubuque, IA: Gasogene Press, 1986.

Harker, Joseph. *Studio and Stage*. London: Nisbet & Co., 1924.

Hartmann, Franz. *Buried Alive: An Examination into the Occult Causes of Apparent Death, Trance, and Catalepsy*. Boston: Occult Publishing, 1895.

Hatcher, R. A. *The Pharmacopeia and the Physician*. Chicago: American Medical Association Press, 1907.

Haworth-Maden, Clare. *Dracula*. New York: Crescent, 1992.

Heath, Frederic. "The Typewriter in Wisconsin." *Wisconsin Magazine of History*, March 1944: 263–75.

Heiss, Lokke. "Discovery of a Hungarian *Drakula*." In *Bram Stoker's Dracula: A Documentary Volume*, edited by Elizabeth Miller, 296–300. Detroit, MI: Thomson Gale, 2005.

Heldreth, Leonard G., and Mary Pharr, eds. *The Blood Is the Life: Vampires in Literature*. Bowling Green, OH: Bowling Green State Univ. Popular Press, 1999.

Hennelly, Mark M., Jr. "*Dracula*: The Gnostic Quest and the Victorian Wasteland." *English Literature in Transition* 20 (1977): 13–26.

Holcombe, Lee. *Victorian Ladies at Work: Middle-Class Working Women in England and Wales 1850–1914*. Hamden, CT: Archon Books, 1973.

Holmes, Ronald M., and Stephen T. Holmes. *Suicide: Theory, Practice, and Investigation*. Thousand Oaks, CA: Sage Publications, 2006.

Holte, James Craig. *Dracula in the Dark*. Westport, CT: Greenwood Press, 1997.

———. *The Fantastic Vampire*. Westport, CT: Greenwood Press, 2002.

———. "Film Adaptations of *Dracula*." In *Bram Stoker's Dracula: A Documentary Volume*, edited by Elizabeth Miller, 318–24. Detroit, MI: Thomson Gale, 2005.

Homer. *The Odyssey*. Translated by Samuel Butler. London: Longmans, Green & Co., 1900.

Hoppen, K. Theodore. *The Mid-Victorian Generation, 1846–1886*. Oxford: Clarendon Press, 1998.

Hoppenstand, Gary, and Ray B. Browne, eds. *The Gothic World of Anne Rice*. Bowling Green, OH: Bowling Green State Univ. Popular Press, 1996.

Horne's Guide to Whitby (Profusely Illustrated). Whitby, England: Horne & Son, 1891.

Howes, Marjorie. "The Mediation of the Feminine: Bisexuality, Homoerotic Desire, and Self-Expression in Bram Stoker's *Dracula*." *Texas Studies in Literature and Language* 30 (1988): 104–19.

Hurwood, Bernhardt J. *Vampires, Werewolves, and Ghouls*. New York: Ace Books, 1968.

———. *Vampire Papers*. New York: Pinnacle Books, 1976.

Johnson, Alan P. "Bent and Broken Necks: Signs of Design in Stoker's *Dracula*." *Victorian Newsletter* 72 (1987): 17–24.

Johnson, Major E. C. *On the Track of the Crescent: Erratic Notes from the Piræus to Pesth*. London: Hurst and Blackett, 1885.

Johnson, Roger. "The Bloofer Ladies." *The Dracula Journals* 1, 4 (1982): 131–34.

Jones, John. *The Natural and Supernatural or Man Physical, Apparitional and Spiritual*. London: Bailliere, 1861. Reprint, Whitefish, MT: Kessinger Publishing, 2004.

Jones, Kathleen. *Asylums and After: A Revised History of the Mental Health Services: From the Early 18th Century to the 1990s.* London: Athlone Press, 1993.

Jones, Stephen, ed. *The Mammoth Book of Dracula: Vampire Tales for the New Millennium.* New York: Carroll & Graf Publishers, 1997.

Jones, W. Henry, and Lewis L. Kropf. *The Folk-Tales of the Magyars.* London: Elliott Stock, 1889.

Jones, William. *Credulities Past and Present.* London: Chatto & Windus, 1880. Reprint, Detroit, MI: Singing Tree Press, 1968.

———. *Precious Stones: Their History and Mystery.* London: Richard Bentley & Son, 1880. Reprint, Detroit, MI: Singing Tree Press, 1968.

Jones, William Llywelyn. *The Trade in Lunacy.* London: Routledge and Kegan Paul, 1971.

Joslin, Lydon W. *Count Dracula Goes to the Movies: Stoker's Novel Adapted, 1922–1995.* Jefferson, NC: McFarland & Co., 1999.

———. *Count Dracula Goes to the Movies: Stoker's Novel Adapted, 1922–2003.* 2d ed. Jefferson, NC: McFarland & Co., 2006.

Kipling, Rudyard. *From Sea to Sea and Other Sketches.* New York: Doubleday & McClure, 1899.

Kirtley, Bacil F. "*Dracula*, The Monastic Chronicles and Slavic Folklore." *Midwest Folklore* 6 (1956): 133–39. Reprinted in *Dracula: The Vampire and the Critics*, edited by Margaret L. Carter, 11–17. Ann Arbor, MI: UMI Research Press, 1988.

Kittler, Friedrich. "Dracula's Legacy." *Stanford Humanities Review* 1 (1989): 143–73.

Kline, Salli J. *The Degeneration of Women: Bram Stoker's Dracula as Allegorical Criticism of the Fin de Siècle.* Rheinbach-Merzbach: CMZ-Verlag, 1992.

Klinger, Leslie S., ed. *The New Annotated Sherlock Holmes.* Vols. 1 and 2. New York: W. W. Norton, 2005.

Langbridge, R. H., comp. *Edwardian Shopping: A Selection from the Army & Navy Stores Catalogues, 1898–1913.* Newton Abbot, England: David & Charles, 1975.

Lea, Henry C. *Superstition and Force: Torture, Ordeal, and Trial by Combat in Medieval Law.* Philadelphia: Henry C. Lea, 1866. Reprint, New York: Barnes & Noble Books, 1996.

Leatherdale, Clive. *The Origins of Dracula: The Background to Bram Stoker's Gothic Masterpiece.* Westcliff-on-Sea, England: Desert Island Books, 1995.

———. "Stoker's Banana Skins: Errors, Illogicalities and Misconceptions in *Dracula*." In *Dracula: The Shade and the Shadow*, edited by Elizabeth Miller, 138–54. Westcliff-on-Sea, England: Desert Island Books, 1998.

———. *Dracula: The Novel & The Legend: A Study of Bram Stoker's Gothic Masterpiece.* 1985. Rev. ed. Westcliff-on-Sea, England: Desert Island Books, 2001.

Leatherdale, Clive, ed. *Bram Stoker's Dracula Unearthed.* Westcliff-on-Sea, England: Desert Island Books, 1998.

Lee, Christopher. "Christopher Lee on Dracula." Interview by John Exshaw, 1 May 1993. *Bram Stoker Society Journal* 6 (1994): 7–10.

Lee, Frederick George. *The Other World; or, Glimpses of the Supernatural.* London: Henry S. King & Co., 1875.

Le Fanu, Joseph Sheridan. "Carmilla." In *In a Glass Darkly*. London: Richard Bentley & Son, 1872.

Lewis, Matthew Gregory. *The Monk: A Romance*. London: printed for J. Saunders, 1796.

Light, Duncan. "The People of Bram Stoker's Transylvania." *Journal of Dracula Studies* 7 (2005): 38–44.

Lomax, Montagu. *The Experiences of an Asylum Doctor*. London: Allen and Unwin, 1921.

Lorrah, Jean. "Dracula Meets the New Woman." In *The Blood Is the Life: Vampires in Literature*, edited by Leonard G. Heldreth and Mary Pharr, 31–42. Bowling Green, OH: Bowling Green State Univ. Popular Press, 1999.

Ludlam, Harry. *A Biography of Bram Stoker, Creator of Dracula*. New York: New English Library, 1977.

Macdonald, D. L., and Kathleen Scherf, eds. *The Vampyre and Ernestus Berchtold; Or, the Modern Oedipus: Collected Fiction of John William Polidori*. Toronto: Univ. of Toronto Press, 1994.

MacDougall, Shane. *The Vampire Slayers' Field Guide to the Undead*. Doylestown, PA: Strider Nolan Publishing, 2003.

Mackenzie, Andrew. *Dracula Country*. London: A. Barker, 1977.

Macleod, George H. B. *Notes on the Surgery of the War in the Crimea, with Remarks on the Treatment of Gunshot Wounds*. Philadelphia and London: J. B. Lippincott and John Churchill, 1862.

Malchow, H. L. *Gothic Images of Race in Nineteenth-Century Britain*. Stanford, CA: Stanford Univ. Press, 1996.

Maluf, N. R. S. "History of Blood Transfusion." *Journal of the History of Medicine* 9 (1954): 59–107.

Marocchino, Kathryn. "Structural Complexity in Bram Stoker's *Dracula*: Unravelling the 'Mysteries.'" *Bram Stoker Society Journal* 2 (1990): 3–21.

Martin, Paul. *Victorian Snapshots*. Literature of Photography Series. New York: Arno Press, 1959.

Mascetti, Manuela Dunn. *Chronicles of the Vampires*. New York: Doubleday, 1991.

Masters, Anthony. *Natural History of the Vampire*. Frogmore, St. Albans, England: Mayflower, 1974.

Mayhew, Henry. *The London Underworld in the Victorian Period: Authentic First-Person Accounts by Beggars, Thieves, and Prostitutes*. London: Griffin, Bohn, and Co., 1861. Reprint, Mineola, NY: Dover Publications, 2005.

Mayo, Herbert. *Letters on the Truths Contained in Popular Superstitions*. Frankfort: John David Sauerlander, 1849. Reprint, Whitefish, MT: Kessinger Publishing, 2003.

McEvoy, Harry K. *Knife Throwing: A Practical Guide*. Rutland, VT: C. E. Tuttle Co., 1973.

McLaughlin, Robert J. *The First Jack the Ripper Victim Photographs*. Edmonton, AB: Zwerghaus Books, 2005.

McNally, Raymond T. "Bram Stoker and Irish Gothic." In *The Fantastic Vampire: Studies in the Children of the Night*, edited by James Craig Holte, 11–21. Westport, CT: Greenwood Press, 2002.

McNally, Raymond T., ed. *A Clutch of Vampires*. Greenwich, CT: New York Graphic Society, 1974.

McNally, Raymond T., and Radu Florescu. *In Search of Dracula: A True History of Dracula and Vampire Legends*. Greenwich, CT: New York Graphic Society, 1972.

———. *The Essential Dracula*. New York: Mayflower Books, 1979.

———. *In Search of Dracula: The History of Dracula and Vampires*. Boston: Houghton Mifflin Co., 1994.

McWhir, Anne. "Pollution and Redemption in *Dracula*." *Modern Language Studies* 17 (1987): 31–40.

Medico-Psychological Association of Great Britain and Ireland. *Handbook for Attendants on the Insane*. 4th ed. London: Bailliere, 1906.

Melton, J. Gordon. *The Vampire Book: The Encyclopedia of the Undead*. 2d ed. Detroit, MI: Visible Ink Press, 1999.

Melton, J. Gordon, and Robert Eighteen-Bisang. "Vampire Fiction for Children and Youth, 1960–Present." *Transylvanian Journal* 2 (1996): 24–30.

Meyer, Nicholas. "Sherlock Holmes, Wine Bottles, and the Catholic Mass." *Baker Street Journal* 48, 1 (1998): 12–25.

Milbank, Alison. " 'Powers Old and New': Stoker's Alliances with Anglo-Irish Gothic." In *Bram Stoker: History, Psychoanalysis and the Gothic*, edited by William Hughes, 12–28. London: Palgrave Macmillan, 1998.

Miller, Elizabeth. "Shape-Shifting Text: Editions and Versions of Dracula." In *Reflections on Dracula: Ten Essays*, 170–98. White Rock, BC: Transylvania Press, 1997.

———. *A Dracula Handbook*. Philadelphia: Xlibris, 2005.

———. *Dracula: Sense & Nonsense*. 2d ed. Southend-on-Sea, England: Desert Island Books, 2006.

Miller, Elizabeth, ed. *Bram Stoker's Dracula: A Documentary Volume*. Detroit, MI: Thomson Gale, 2005.

Mitchell, Ann. "Dracula: A Century Undead." *Dalesman* 59, 1 (1997): 25–28.

Mogg, Edward. *Mogg's New Picture of London and Visitor's Guide to Its Sights*. London: E. Mogg, 1844.

Montague-Smith, Patrick. *Debrett's Correct Form*. London: Headline Book Publishing, 1992.

Moretti, Franco. "Dialectic of Fear." In *Signs Taken for Wonders: Essays in the Sociology of Literary Forms*, translated by Susan Fischer, David Forgacs, and David Miller, 83–108. Rev. ed. London: Verso, 1988.

Morley, Christopher, ed. *Sherlock Holmes and Dr. Watson: A Textbook of Friendship*. New York: Harcourt, Brace & Co., 1944.

Moses, Michael Valdez. "The Irish Vampire: *Dracula*, Parnell, and the Troubled Dreams of Nationhood." *Journal x* [Univ. of Mississippi] 2 (1997): 67–111.

Moss, Stephanie. "Bram Stoker and the Society for Psychical Research." In *Dracula: The Shade and the Shadow*, edited by Elizabeth Miller, 82–91. Westcliff-on-Sea, England: Desert Island Books, 1998.

Murgoçi, Agnes. "The Vampire in Roumania." *Folk-Lore* 37, 4 (1926): 320–49. Reprinted in *The Vampire: A Casebook*, edited by Alan Dundes, 12–34. Madison: Univ. of Wisconsin Press, 1998.

Nandris, Grigore. "The Historical Dracula: The Theme of His Legend in the Western and in the Eastern Literatures of Europe." *Comparative Literature Studies* 3 (1966): 367–96.

Nead, Lynda. *Victoria Babylon: People, Streets, and Images in Nineteenth-Century London*. New Haven, CT: Yale Univ. Press, 2005.

Nevill, Ralph. *London Clubs: Their History & Treasures*. London: Chatto & Windus, 1911.

Newman, Kim. *Anno Dracula*. London: Simon & Schuster, 1992.

Ouellette, Jennifer. *The Physics of the Buffyverse*. London: Penguin, 2006.

Oxford English Dictionary. Oxford: Oxford Univ. Press, 1887.

Oxford English Dictionary. Compact ed. Oxford: Oxford Univ. Press, 1971.

Paget, John. *Hungary and Transylvania; with Remarks on Their Condition, Social, Political, and Economical*. London: John Murray, 1850.

Perkowski, Jan Louis. "The Romanian Folkloric Vampire." In *The Vampire: A Casebook*, edited by Alan Dundes, 35–46. Madison: Univ. of Wisconsin Press, 1998.

Peter, Laszlo, ed. *Historians and the History of Transylvania*. Boulder, CO: East European Monographs, 1992.

Pettigrew, Thomas Joseph. *On Superstitions Connected with the History and Practice of Medicine and Surgery*. London: John Churchill, 1844. Reprint, Whitefish, MT: Kessinger Publishing, 2004.

Phillips, Charles, and Michael Kerrigan. *Forests of the Vampire: Slavic Myth*. New York: Barnes & Noble Books, 1999.

Polidori, John William. "The Vampyre." *New Monthly Magazine*, April 1819.

Polidori, John William, and Charles Nodier. *Lord Ruthven the Vampire*. Encino, CA: Hollywood Comics, 2004.

Porter, Roy. *London: A Social History*. London: Hamish Hamilton, 1994.

———. *Madness: A Brief History*. Oxford: Oxford Univ. Press, 2002.

Powell, Martin, and Seppo Makinen. *Scarlet in Gaslight*. Nos. 1–4. Newbury Park, CA: Eternity Comics, November 1987, January 1988, March 1988, June 1988.

Queen's London. London: Cassell & Co., 1897.

Ramsland, Katherine. *The Vampire Companion: The Official Guide to Anne Rice's The Vampire Chronicles*. New York: Ballantine Books, 1995.

———. *The Science of Vampires*. New York: Berkley Trade, 2002.

Rayner, J. L., and G. T. Crook. *The Complete Newgate Calendar*. London: The Navarre Society, Ltd., 1926.

Reville, Albert. *The Devil: His Origin, Greatness and Decadence*. London: Williams & Norgate, 1877. Reprint, Whitefish, MT: Kessinger Publishing, 2004.

Richardson, John. *The Sorcerer's Apprentice: Picasso, Provence, and Douglas Cooper*. New York: Alfred A. Knopf, 2005.

Richardson, Maurice. "The Psychoanalysis of Ghost Stories." *Twentieth Century* 166 (1959): 419–31. Extracted as "The Psychoanalysis of Count Dracula" in *Vampyres: Lord Byron to Count Dracula*, edited by Christopher Frayling, 418–22. London: Faber and Faber, 1991.

Rickels, Laurence A. *The Vampire Lectures.* Minneapolis: Univ. of Minnesota Press, 1999.

Riess, Jana. *What Would Buffy Do: The Vampire Slayer as Spiritual Guide.* San Francisco: Jossey-Bass, 2004.

Riley, Peter. *The Highways and Byways of Jack the Ripper.* Cheshire, England: P & D Riley, 2001.

Riquelme, John Paul. "A Critical History of *Dracula*." In *Bram Stoker's Dracula: A Documentary Volume*, edited by Elizabeth Miller, 358–75. Detroit, MI: Thomson Gale, 2005. [Revised and updated version of "A Critical History of *Dracula*" in *Dracula*, edited by John Paul Riquelme, 409–33. New York: Bedford/St. Martin's, 2002.]

Robinson, F. K. *A Glossary of Words Used in the Neighbourhood of Whitby.* London: English Dialect Society, 1876.

Rodin, Alvin E., and Jack D. Key. *Medical Casebook of Dr. Arthur Conan Doyle.* Malabar, FL: Robert E. Krieger Publishing Co., 1984.

Rolfe, W. J. *Satchel Guide to Europe.* Boston and New York: Houghton Mifflin Co., 1910.

Ronay, Gabriel. *The Truth about Dracula.* New York: Stein and Day, 1972.

Roth, Phyllis. "Suddenly Sexual Women in Bram Stoker's *Dracula*." *Literature and Psychology* 27 (1977): 113–21.

———. *Bram Stoker.* Boston: Twayne Publishers, 1982.

Rowe, Richard. *Life in the London Streets.* London: J. C. Nimmo and Bain, 1881.

Rudorff, Raymond. *The Dracula Archives.* New York: Arbor House, 1971.

Ruskin, John. *Fiction, Fair and Foul.* London: John W. Lovell Co., 1880.

Russell, Sharon A. "Introducing Count Saint-Germain: Chelsea Quinn Yarbro's Heroic Vampire." In *The Blood Is the Life: Vampires in Literature*, edited by Leonard G. Heldreth and Mary Pharr, 141–54. Bowling Green, OH: Bowling Green State Univ. Popular Press, 1999.

Russell, Sharon A., James Craig Holte, and Mary Pharr. "Vampire Fiction and Criticism: A Core Collection." In *The Blood Is the Life: Vampires in Literature*, edited by Leonard G. Heldreth and Mary Pharr, 261–66. Bowling Green, OH: Bowling Green State Univ. Popular Press, 1999.

Ruthner, Clemens. "Bloodsuckers with Teutonic Tongues: The German-Speaking World and the Origins of *Dracula*." In *Dracula: The Shade and the Shadow*, edited by Elizabeth Miller, 54–67. Westcliff-on-Sea, England: Desert Island Books, 1998.

Saberhagen, Fred. *The Dracula Tape.* New York: Warner Paperback Library, 1975.

Sala, George Augustus. *London Up to Date.* London: Adam & Charles, 1894.

Schaffer, Talia. " 'Wilde Desire Took Me': The Homoerotic History of *Dracula*." *ELH* 61 (1994): 381–425.

Schmitt, Cannon. "Mother Dracula: Orientalism, Degeneration, and Anglo-Irish National Subjectivity at the Fin de Siècle." In *Irishness and (Post) Modernism*, edited by John S. Rickard, 25–43. London: Associated Univ. Press, 1994.

Scott, Kathryn Leigh, ed. *The Dark Shadows Companion: 25th Anniversary Collection.* Foreword by Jonathan Frid. Los Angeles: Pomegranate Press, 1990.

Scull, Andrew, Charlotte MacKenzie, and Nicholas Hervey. *Masters of Bedlam.* Princeton, NJ: Princeon Univ. Press, 1998.

Sebastian, Anton. *Dictionary of the History of Medicine.* New York: Parthenon Publishing Group, 1999.

Seed, David. "The Narrative Method of *Dracula.*" *Nineteenth Century Fiction* 40 (1985): 61–75.

Seitz, Stephen. *Sherlock Holmes and the Plague of Dracula.* Shaftsbury, VT: Mountainside Press, 2007.

Senf, Carol. "*Dracula:* The Unseen Face in the Mirror." *Journal of Narrative Technique* 9 (1979): 160–70.

———. "*Dracula:* Stoker's Response to the New Woman." *Victorian Studies* 26 (1982): 33–49.

———. *The Vampire in 19th Century English Literature.* Bowling Green, OH: Bowling Green State Univ. Popular Press, 1988.

———. *Dracula: Between Tradition and Modernism.* Boston: Twayne Publishers, 1998.

Shanklin, Rickey, and Mark Wheatley. *Blood of the Innocent.* Poughkeepsie, NY: Warp Graphics, 1986.

Shaw, Donald. *London in the Sixties: with a few digressions, by one of the old school.* London: Everett, 1908.

Shorter, Edward. *A History of Psychiatry.* New York: John Wiley & Sons, 1998.

Silver, Alain, and James Ursini. *The Vampire Film: From Nosferatu to Interview with a Vampire.* 3d ed. New York: Limelight Editions, 1997.

Simon, André L., ed. *Wines of the World.* New York: McGraw-Hill, 1967.

Simon, John. "City of London Medical Report. Special Report of Intramural Interments." 1852. Available online at www.victorianlondon.org/death/awaiting.htm.

Skal, David J. *Hollywood Gothic: The Tangled Web of Dracula from Novel to Stage to Screen.* New York: W. W. Norton, 1990.

———. *V Is for Vampire: The A to Z Guide to Everything Undead.* New York: Plume/Penguin Books, 1996.

Skal, David J., ed. *Vampires: Encounters with the Undead.* New York: Black Dog & Leventhal, 2001.

Slater, Elliot. "Psychiatry in the Thirties." *Contemporary Review* 226 (1975): 70–75.

Smart, Robert. "Blood and Money in Bram Stoker's *Dracula*: The Struggle Against Monopoly." In *Money: Lure, Lore, and Literature,* edited by John Louis DiGaetani, 253–60. Westport, CT: Greenwood Press, 1994.

Smith, Andrew. *Victorian Demons.* Manchester, England: Manchester Univ. Press, 2004.

Soister, John T. *Of Gods and Monsters.* Jefferson, NC: McFarland & Co., 2005.

Sperlinger, Michael. "Cinema's Future, Film's Afterlife." *Mute* [online magazine], 23 March 2004; www.metamute.org/en/Cinemas-Future-Films-Afterlife.

Starr, Douglas. *Blood: An Epic History of Medicine and Commerce.* New York: Harper Perennial, 2000.

Stenbock, Stanislaus Eric. "A True Story of a Vampire." In *Studies of Death: Romantic Tales.* London: David Nutt, 1894.

Stevenson, John Allen. "The Vampire in the Mirror: The Sexuality of *Dracula.*" *PMLA* 103 (1988): 139–49.

Stoddard, Jane. "Mr. Bram Stoker. A Chat with the Author of *Dracula.*" *British Weekly,* 1 July 1897.

Stoker, Bram. *Dracula.* Westminster, England: Archibald Constable & Co., 1897.

———. *Dracula.* Hutchinson's Colonial Library. London: Hutchinson & Co., 1897.

———. *Dracula.* New York: Doubleday & McClure, 1899.

———. *Dracula.* Westminster, England: Archibald Constable & Co., 1901.

———. *Makt Myrkranna* [Powers of Darkness]. Translated by Valdimar Asmundsson. Reykjavik: Nokkrir Prentarar, 1901.

———. *The Jewel of Seven Stars.* London: William Heineman, 1903.

———. *Personal Reminiscences of Henry Irving.* 2 vols. New York: Macmillan & Co., 1906.

———. *Dracula.* London: W. Rider & Son, 1912.

———. *Dracula's Guest and Other Weird Stories.* London: Routledge, 1914.

———. *Dracula.* Limited Editions Club. New York: Heritage Press, 1965.

———. *A Bram Stoker Omnibus.* Introduction and preface by Richard Dalby. London: W. Foulsham Books, 1986.

———. *Dracula: The Rare Text of 1901.* Foreword by Robert Eighteen-Bisang, introduction by Raymond T. McNally. White Rock, BC: Transylvania Press, 1994.

———. *Dracula.* Norton Critical Edition. Edited by Nina Auerbach and David J. Skal. New York: W. W. Norton, 1997.

———. *Dracula; or The Un-Dead.* Edited by Sylvia Starshine. Nottingham, England: Pumpkin Books, 1997.

———. *Dracula.* Edited by John Paul Riquelme. New York: Bedford/St. Martin's, 2002.

Strachey, Lytton. *Eminent Victorians.* New York: G. P. Putnam's Sons, 1918.

The Student's Cyclopædia: A Ready Reference Library for School and Home Embracing History, Biography, Geography, Discovery, Invention, Arts, Sciences, Literature. Edited by C. B. Beach. St. Louis, MO: H. M. Dixon & Co., 1901.

Summers, Montague. *The Vampire: His Kith and Kin.* New York: E. P. Dutton, 1929. First published 1928 by K. Paul, Trench, Trubner & Co., London.

———. *The Vampire in Europe.* Introduction by Father Brocard Sewell. Hyde Park, NY: University Books, 1961. First published 1929 by E. P. Dutton, New York.

———. *The Vampire in Lore and Legend.* New York: E. P. Dutton, 1929. Reprint, Mineola, NY: Dover Publications, 2001.

———. *The Werewolf in Lore and Legend.* Mineola, NY: Dover Publications, 2003. First published 1933 as *The Werewolf* by K. Paul, Trench, Trubner & Co., London.

Sutherland, John. *The Literary Detective: 100 Puzzles in Classic Fiction*. New York: Oxford Univ. Press, 2000.

Swift, Sondra Ford. "Toward the Vampire as Savior: Chelsea Quinn Yarbro's *Saint-Germain* Series Compared with Edward Bulwer-Lytton's *Zanoni*." In *The Blood Is the Life: Vampires in Literature*, edited by Leonard G. Heldreth and Mary Pharr, 155–64. Bowling Green, OH: Bowling Green State Univ. Popular Press, 1999.

Temple, Philip. *Times Literary Supplement*, 4 November 1983.

Terry, Ellen. *The Story of My Life*. New York: McClure Company, 1908.

Thomas, Donald. *The Victorian Underworld*. London: John Murray, 1999.

Thornburg, Thomas Ray. "The Quester and the Castle: The Gothic Novel as Myth, with Special Reference to Bram Stoker's *Dracula*." PhD thesis, Ball State Univ., Muncie, IN, 1970.

Tieck, Johann Ludwig. "Wake Not the Dead." In *Popular Tales and Romances of the Northern Nations*. Vol. 1. London: Simpkin, Marshall, 1823.

Timbs, John. *Curiosities of London*. London: Virtue & Co., 1855.

Tolstoi, Aleksei. "The Family of the Vourdalak." 1884. Reprinted in *Vampyres: Lord Byron to Count Dracula*, edited by Christopher Frayling, 253–79. London: Faber and Faber, 1991.

Topping, Keith. *The Complete Slayer: An Unofficial and Unauthorized Guide to Every Episode of Buffy the Vampire Slayer*. London: Virgin Books, 2004.

Tracy, Kathleen. *The Girl's Got Bite: The Original Unauthorized Guide to Buffy's World*. New York: St. Martin's Press, 2003.

Twain, Mark. "Pudd'nhead Wilson's New Calendar." In *Following the Equator*. New York: Harper & Bros., 1897.

———. *Life on the Mississippi*. New York: Harper & Bros., 1899.

Twitchell, James. "The Vampire Myth." *American Imago* 37 (1980): 88.

Valente, Joseph. *Dracula's Crypt: Bram Stoker, Irishness and the Question of Blood*. Urbana: Univ. of Illinois Press, 2002.

Vambéry, Arminius. *The Life and Adventures of Arminius Vambéry*. Boston: Adamant Media Corp., 2005. First published 1914 by T. F. Unwin, London.

Van Doren, Carl. *Benjamin Franklin*. 1938. Reprint, New York: Penguin Books, 1991.

Varney, the Vampyre; or, The Feast of Blood, by James Malcolm Rymer or Thomas Peckett Prest. 1847. Reprint, with a new introduction by E. F. Bleiler, New York: Dover Books, 1972.

Vrettos, Athena. "Physical Immunity and Racial Destiny: Stoker and Haggard." In *Somatic Fictions: Imagining Illness in Victorian Culture*, 154–76. Stanford, CA: Stanford Univ. Press, 1995.

Volta, Ornella. *The Vampire*. 1965. Reprint, London: Tandem Books, 1970.

Walker, Gerald, and Lorraine Wright. "Locating *Dracula*: Contextualising the Geography of Transylvania." In *Bram Stoker's Dracula: Sucking Through the Century, 1897–1997*, edited by Carol Margaret Davison, 49–73. Toronto: Dundurn Press, 1997.

Walkowitz, Judith R. *City of Dreadful Delight: Narratives of Sexual Danger in Late-Victorian London*. Chicago: Univ. of Chicago Press, 1992.

Walsh, Thomas P. "*Dracula*: Logos and Myth." *Research Studies* 47 (1979): 229–37.

Warner, Charles Dudley. *Saunterings*. Boston: J. R. Osgood & Co., 1872.

Warner, William R. *Warner's Pocket Medical Dictionary: To-Day Comprising Pronunciation and Definition of 10,000 Essential Words and Terms Used in Medicine and Associated Sciences*. Philadelphia: William R. Warner & Co., 1897.

Warren, David J. *Old Medical and Dental Instruments*. London: Shire Publications, 1994.

Warren, L. S. "Buffalo Bill Meets Dracula: William F. Cody, Bram Stoker, and the Frontiers of Racial Decay." *American Historical Review* 107 (2002): 1124–57.

Wasson, Richard. "The Politics of *Dracula*." *English Literature in Transition* 9 (1966): 24–27.

Waters, Colin. *Whitby and the Dracula Connection*. Whitby, England: Whitby Press, n. d.

Webster, Richard. *Freud*. Great Philosophers Series. London: Weidenfeld & Nicolson, 2003.

Weeks, Jeffrey. "Inverts, Perverts, and Mary-Annes: Male Prostitution and the Regulation of Homosexuality in England in the Nineteenth and Early Twentieth Centuries." *Journal of Homosexuality* 6 (1980–1981): 118–19.

Weissman, Judith. "Women and Vampires: *Dracula* as a Victorian Novel." *Midwest Quarterly* 18 (1977): 392–405.

Whitaker, Joseph. *Whitaker's Almanack*. 1900. [Facsimile ed.]. Reprint, London: A&C Black Publishers, Ltd., 2002.

Wicke, Jennifer. "Vampiric Typewriting: *Dracula* and Its Media." *ELH* 59 (1992): 467–93.

Wilkins, Robert. *Death: A History of Man's Obsessions and Fears*. New York: Barnes & Noble Books, 1990.

Wilkinson, William. *An Account of the Principalities of Wallachia and Moldavia: with Various Political Observations Relating to Them*. London: Longman, Hurst, Rees, Orme and Brown, 1820.

Williamson, F. Harcourt. "The Cycle in Society." In *The Complete Cyclist*, edited by B. Fletcher Robinson, 47–62. London: A. D. Innes & Co., 1897.

Wilson, A. N. *The Victorians*. New York: W. W. Norton, 2003.

Wilson, Katharina M. "The History of the Word *Vampire*." *Journal of the History of Ideas* 46 (1985): 577–83. Reprinted in *The Vampire: A Casebook*, edited by Alan Dundes, 3–11. Madison: Univ. of Wisconsin Press, 1998.

Wixson, Kellie Donovan. "*Dracula*: An Anglo-Irish Gothic Novel." In *Dracula: The Shade and the Shadow*, edited by Elizabeth Miller, 247–56. Westcliff-on-Sea, England: Desert Island Books, 1998.

Wolf, Leonard. *A Dream of Dracula: In Search of the Living Dead*. Boston: Little, Brown and Co., 1972.

———. *Dracula: The Connoisseur's Guide*. New York: Broadway Books, 1997.

Wolf, Leonard, ed. *The Annotated Dracula*. New York: Clarkson N. Potter, 1975.

———. *The Essential Dracula*. New York: Plume, 1993.

Wolfman, Marv. With, in order of appearance, Gerry Conway, Archie Goodwin, Gardner F. Fox, Chris Claremont, and David Kraft. *Dracula Lives!* Nos.1–13. New York: Marvel Comics Group, 1972–1975.

————. With, in order of appearance, Gerry Conway, Archie Goodwin, Gardner F. Fox, Chris Claremont, and David Kraft. *The Tomb of Dracula*. Nos.1–70. New York: Marvel Comics Group, 1972–1979.

Woodall, Edwin T. *Jack the Ripper, or When London Walked in Terror*. Cheshire, England: P & D Riley, 1997.

Wright, David. *Mental Disability in Victorian England: The Earlswood Asylum 1847–1901*. Oxford: Clarendon Press, 2001.

Wright, Dudley. *Vampires and Vampirism: Legends from Around the World*. Maple Shade, NJ: Lethe Press, 2001. First published 1914 by William Rider and Son, Ltd., London.

Wyeth, John A., M.D. *Text-Book on Surgery: General, Operative and Mechanical*. New York: D. Appleton and Co., 1888.

Wynne, Deborah. *The Sensation Novel and the Victorian Family Magazine*. London: Palgrave Macmillan, 2001.

Wynne, Patrick H. "Review—*The Essential Dracula*, by Leonard Wolf." 2003. Available online at www.pa2rick.com/belfry/essential_dracula.html.

X. L. [Julian Osgood Field.] "A Kiss of Judas." *Pall Mall Magazine*, July 1893.

TEXTUAL SOURCES

I leave the manuscript unaltered ...

—BRAM STOKER

THE TEXT OF Stoker's narrative is drawn from the first edition, printed in 1897, and significant textual variations appearing in later editions are noted. In particular, the abridgement of the 1901 Constable & Co. paperback edition is contrasted.[1]

No study of the factual basis for the book published by Bram Stoker as *Dracula* could proceed without consideration of Stoker's working notes, referred to in this volume as the "Notes" and prepared circa 1890–1896. These valuable documents, a combination of notes in handwritten and typewritten entries, reside in the Rosenbach Museum and Library in Philadelphia, Pennsylvania. If we accept the Stoker narrative as based on fact, then these must be Stoker's gleanings from the Harker Papers themselves and notes on Stoker's interviews with the actual people mentioned in the papers (whom he disguised as the "Harkers," "Dr. Seward," et al.). The first section consists of forty-nine leaves of manuscript, including a list of characters, notes on vampires, outlines for the entire book and for most chapters, chronologies, and miscellaneous notes. The second section consists of thirty manuscript leaves tipped onto ten sheets, two photographs, and a clipping, which record notes on Stoker's readings on the subjects of vampires, werewolves, shipwrecks, weather, geography, and the dialect indigenous to Whitby (the English seaside village in which the second "act" of the drama occurs). The last section consists of thirty-seven leaves of typescript notes (with manuscript corrections).

---

[1] Robert Eighteen-Bisang, who in 1994 published a reprint of the abridged edition, titled *Dracula: The Rare Text of 1901* (White Rock, BC: Transylvania Press), kindly lent this editor his electronic files, permitting—apparently for the first time—a computerised comparison of the first-edition and abridged texts.

Page of Bram Stoker's notes for *Dracula*, ca. 1890–1897.
Reprinted with permission of Rosenbach Museum and Library, Philadelphia, PA

These are extracts from various works consulted by Stoker about the history and geography of the Carpathians (the mountainous area encompassing much of Transylvania and Hungary, where the first and fourth "acts" of the drama take place) and about dream theory. In addition, there is an extensive list of epitaphs Stoker apparently copied from Whitby tombstones.

The Notes were sold along with other items from Stoker's library at Sotheby's on 7 July 1913. They passed through various collectors' and dealers' hands, and in 1970 they were purchased by the Rosenbach Museum and Library. In 1973 they were examined by Raymond McNally and Radu Florescu in the course of preparing *The Essential Dracula*, but no details were published by these two writers until 1979. McNally and Florescu were the first to make extensive use of the Notes in annotating the text of *Dracula*, but they proceeded on the assumption that *Dracula* is a work of fiction. Joseph Bierman, who also had some access to the Notes, published an essay in 1977 titled "The Genesis and Dating of *Dracula* from Bram Stoker's Working Notes"[2] which first alerted other scholars to the existence of the Notes. Subsequently, the Notes have been studied by many, but no complete facsimiles have been published. The Rosenbach has kindly permitted the reproduction in this volume of a sample page of the Notes, on page 603.

Another critical tool in attempting to determine the facts underlying the narrative is the manuscript (actually, a typescript) delivered by Bram Stoker to his publisher (referred to in this volume as the "Manuscript"). No typescript or manuscript was included among Stoker's papers auctioned at Sotheby's after his death. According to Peter Haining and Peter Tremayne, it was discovered in a Pennsylvania barn among the relics of Thomas Donaldson, a mutual friend of Walt Whitman and Stoker, to whom Stoker apparently sent it.[3] Donaldson's heirs reportedly sold the manuscript to a dealer, who passed it along to a dealer/private collector in Orange County, California. In the late 1990s, the collector unsuccessfully attempted to sell the manuscript at auction, and it was eventually sold to its present owner, Mr. Paul G. Allen.

The Manuscript is 541 pages of various sizes and consists of typed material (apparently all produced on the same typewriter), some of which has been pasted over other material. Three different sets of handwritten corrections, insertions, and notes appear on the document: Stoker's; those of an editor (whether Otto Kyllmann, Constable's chief editor, or an assistant editor is unknown), in blue pencil; and those of Stoker's brother, Sir William Thornley Stoker, a well-known physician. Pages and chapters have been renumbered (in many cases twice), and blank spaces occur throughout the text, most of which have been filled in in Stoker's hand, although a few were filled in by the editor. A page of the Manuscript appears in facsimile on page 605.

It is difficult to determine how close the Manuscript lies to the end of the chain of creation of the published narrative. Though it bears many changes and corrections, it is definitely not the final version that appeared in print; there are numerous instances of differences between the published text and the Manuscript, some major, and it cannot be determined who made these changes unless galley proofs are discovered. In addition, the Manuscript appears in itself to be a work in progress. The first page is unnumbered (although it bears a handwritten

---

[2] Joseph S. Bierman, "The Genesis and Dating of *Dracula* from Bram Stoker's Working Notes," *Notes and Queries* 24 (1977): 34–41.

[3] Peter Haining and Peter Tremayne, *The Un-Dead: The Legend of Bram Stoker and Dracula* (London: Constable & Co., 1997), 22.

(1094)   9   Euot

not feeling nearly as easy in my mind as usual. If this book should ever reach Mina before I do, let it bring my good bye. Here *comes* the Coach !

Jonathan Harker's ~~Diary~~ *Journal* (continued)

The Castle. May 5.

The grey of the morning has passed and the sun is high over the distant horizon, which seems jagged whether with trees or hills I know not, for it is so far off that big things and little are mixed. I am not sleepy and as I am not to be called till I awake naturally I write till sleep comes. There are many odd things to put down and *let me put down my dinner exactly. I dined on* lest who reads them may fancy that I dined well before I left Bistritz on what they call "Robber steak" - bits of bacon, onion and beef, seasoned with red pepper and strung on sticks and roasted over the fire ~~"an brochette" as the French call it~~ *in* like the simple style of ~~the~~ London cats'-meat! The wine was *G*olden Mediasch which produces a queer sting on the tongue which is however not disagreeable I had only a couple of glasses of this and nothing else, ~~until supper with which I had two glasses of old Tokay - the nicest wine I ever tasted ; but I did not take as much as I should have liked for I feared it might be too strong and the Count might want to talk business at once. A roast chicken was my supper.~~

When I got on the coach the driver had not got into his seat and I saw him talking with the landlady. They were evi-

Page of the "manuscript" of *Dracula*, 1897.
Reprinted with permission of the owner

chapter number of "ii," changed in the editor's hand to "I"), and the second page is numbered "103," suggesting that a great deal of material was excised. The second chapter is hand-numbered "iii," changed to "II." Succeeding chapters bear similar renumbering.[4] Some pages of the Manuscript are so little changed as to suggest retyping. The word "Cucherry" has been changed by hand to "kukri" in many places; in other places, the word "kukri" is typed without correction. Similarly, "Czarina Kathrine" has been changed by hand to "Czarina Catherine" in several places; in other places, the corrected spelling is used. This suggests that the pages without corrections were prepared later. Similarly, in many places

[4] The chapter numbering in the Manuscript is as follows.

Typed number (° denotes handwritten)	First alternate number (editor's hand)	Final number (editor's hand)
ii°	na	I
iii°	na	II
vii	IV	III
viii	VI	IV
ix	VII	V
na	na	VI
na	VIII	VII
xi	IX	VIII
xii	X	IX
xiii	XI	X
xii	na	XI
xv	XIII	XII
xvi	XIV	XIII
xvii	XV	XIV
xviii	XVI	XV
xix	XVII	XVI
xviii	na	XVII
xxi	XIX	XVIII
xxii	na	XIX
xxiii	na	XX
xxiv	na	XXI
xxv	na	XXII
xxvi	na	XXIII
xxvii	na	XXIV
xxix	XXVII	XXV
xxx	XXVIII	XXVI
xxxi	na	XXVII

the name of "Renfield" has been left blank, but elsewhere the name has been typed in. Furthermore, many items that were evidently checked later (historical references, place names, and even the number of boxes of earth) have been filled in in Stoker's hand. Some of the dates are handwritten; others are typed. In short, the Manuscript appears to be at best a working draft, albeit a fairly late one.

The owner of the Manuscript graciously granted this editor permission to examine it in detail. The Manuscript, one step further removed from the Harker Papers than the Notes, is considered in the notes to this work as an additional means of reconstructing the contents of the Harker Papers, and material changes are discussed that demonstrate further concealments of people, places, events, and the true character of the personae of the narrative. Mere stylistic changes are not noted. While the notes compare the Manuscript to the published text, it is not possible in most cases to determine whether differences between them were the result of emendations by Stoker or an editor, and therefore the notes do not generally differentiate between material that appears in the Manuscript and is marked in it for deletion and material that appears in the Manuscript but fails to appear in the published text.

ACKNOWLEDGEMENTS

These . . . have been good friends to me . . .

—DRACULA,

recorded in Jonathan Harker's Journal

ALTHOUGH WRITING IS purportedly a solitary occupation, in fact all of my books are the products of a community of colleagues, friends, and family.

Professor Elizabeth Miller, friend, eminent *Dracula* scholar, and leader of the Canadian chapter of the Transylvanian Society of Dracula, was most generous with her time and advice as well as her ţuică! Edward Zinna, Clive Leatherdale, Kim Newman, Dr. Albert Power, Brian J. Showers, and Nancy Holder all supplied material and encouragement. Elizabeth E. Fuller, librarian, and Gregory M. Giuliano, library assistant at the Rosenbach Museum and Library, were most generous with their time and assistance during my visit to study the Stoker notes. Christiane Kroebel, honorary librarian and archivist, Whitby Literary and Philosophical Society, researched many points of local history for me, far beyond the call of duty. A special acknowledgement to Paul G. Allen and the Experience Music Project/Science Fiction Museum and Hall of Fame in Seattle for providing valuable access to the manuscript of *Dracula*. The curatorial staff went the extra mile in helping me on my two-day visit to examine that treasure.

Special thanks are due Robert Eighteen-Bisang for permitting me to run a computer comparison of his electronic text of the abridged *Dracula* to the first edition. Bernard Davies, a longtime friend from Holmesian circles, spent an entire day shepherding me around London, to visit the sites described in the book.

I was privileged to travel to Transylvania in 2007 with the Canadian chapter of the Transylvanian Society of Dracula. The touring members, especially Jason Nolan, Barbi McClennen, and Anita Vagovics, were tolerant of my crackpot theories and ramblings, and our late-night drinking sessions provided a valuable sounding board. Renowned Stoker scholar Carol Senf and her intrepid husband,

Jay Farlow, were good friends to me in the course of our Carpathian journey, and Carol's suggestions and corrections were very helpful. Fellow traveller and scholar Marius Crisan and our unflappable tour guide Nicolae Padraru patiently answered every question about Roumanian folklore, geography, and history.

In the United States, Sherlockians Don Hobbs and Henry Zecher shared their collections of Draculiana, and Susan Dahlinger, Jerry Margolin, Andy Peck, and Mike Whelan warmed me with their friendship. The real authors among my friends—Laura Caldwell, Michael Dirda, Neil Gaiman, and Laurie R. King—were most generous with advice and encouragement. My dear friend Barbara Roisman Cooper seemed to have an unending supply of *Dracula* materials which she kindly provided, and she endured numerous conversations about this book while working on her own writing.

Roger Johnson, a *Dracula* scholar for many years and, in his spare time, one of the deans of Holmesiana, read every word of my notes and supplied extremely valuable corrections and suggestions. My agent, Don Maass, steered me through numerous contractual and commercial issues and provided unstinting enthusiasm. My lawyer and dear friend Jonathan Kirsch also had valuable advice, but more importantly, is my rôle model as an author and gentleman.

It was very important to me that this book be published by W. W. Norton, a company that is incredibly supportive of its authors. I very much wanted to work again with the team of Bob Weil, my senior editor, and his assistants, Tom Mayer and Lucas Wittmann, in producing this volume. Their friendship and professionalism make it a matter of great pride to be a Norton author. Elizabeth Pierson did an amazing job of copyediting. Julia Druskin oversaw, with great patience and skill, the production and design of the book, and Eleen Cheung contributed the stunning jacket design. Louise Brockett of Norton and Megan Beatie, Angela Hayes, and Lynn Goldberg of Goldberg McDuffie Communications provided wise advice and logistics with respect to publicity.

Janet Byrne, who collaborated previously with me on *The New Annotated Sherlock Holmes*, graciously agreed to fit work on this book into her busy schedule, and I was most grateful. Our friendly debates about the issues raised in my notes, the topics to be covered, and the handling of the textual sources all made this book better than I had dared to hope. Her diligence in wading through the hundreds of footnotes and thousands of facts held me to a high standard of scholarship. That her ability is coupled with a winning personality, ready wit, and tireless energy makes her an ideal collaborator.

As always, my law partners Bob Kopple, Douglas Schwartz, and David Elbaz were generous with their support and tolerance of my juggling of law practice and writing. The love of my children, Matt, Wendy, Stacy, Evan, and Amanda, and my grandchildren, Maya, Devin, and Matthew, is the fuel that powers my devotion to writing.

In the place of preeminence, however, must—as always—stand my own Mina Harker, my beloved wife, Sharon. She deserves credit for the concept of this book, and she shared vicariously in my adventures in England and Roumania. Sharon listened patiently to every note that I found fascinating, every crackpot theory that I needed to try out, every "Eureka!" in the course of my research. Unlike Mina, Sharon didn't have to type this book for me; but she was there when Norton said "yes" to the project, and she was there when I wrote "finis" to the work. In between, she's been my inspiration, my muse, and my light.

Leslie S. Klinger
Los Angeles, California
September 2007

ABOUT THE AUTHOR

Abraham "Bram" Stoker (1847–1912), best remembered for *Dracula*, was a prolific writer of romances, short stories, reviews, and nonfiction books. Born in a Dublin suburb, he began his career contributing theatrical reviews and short stories to local newspapers and magazines. In the course of that writing, he met actor Henry Irving (later knighted). In 1878, Irving invited Stoker to become the business manager of Irving's Lyceum Theatre repertory company in London, a post that Stoker filled until Irving's death in 1905. In his college days at Trinity College, Dublin, Stoker became a supporter of the controversial works of Walt Whitman, and on his later travels to the United States with Irving, he arranged to visit the aged poet. Stoker's circle of friends encompassed numerous other writers and actors of the day, including Arthur Conan Doyle, Hall Caine, and Ellen Terry. In 1906, Stoker authored a well-received two-volume reminiscence of his time with Irving. By the time of his death, Stoker had published twelve novels, numerous short stories, and several collections of essays and travel books.

ABOUT THE EDITOR

Leslie S. Klinger is considered to be one of the world's foremost authorities on Sherlock Holmes and Dracula. He is the editor of the three-volume set *The New Annotated Sherlock Holmes*, published by W. W. Norton in 2005–2006. The first two volumes, comprising the complete short stories, won the Edgar, the highest award of the Mystery Writers of America, for Best Critical/Biographical work in 2005 and were short-listed for the Macavity, the Anthony, and the Agatha awards. The third volume, *The Novels*, was nominated for the Edgar, the Macavity, the Anthony, and the Agatha awards, as well as a Quill award in the Mystery/Thriller category.

Born in Chicago, Illinois, Leslie S. Klinger attended the University of California at Berkeley and received an A.B. in English in 1967, followed by a J.D. from Boalt Hall (School of Law, UC Berkeley) in 1970. He then moved to Los Angeles and began a legal career of tax, estate, and business planning for entrepreneurs, entertainers, and other high-net-worth individuals. He has lectured and written extensively on tax and estate planning. He and his wife Sharon have five children and four grandchildren and live in Malibu with their two dogs and three cats.